How to TEPS intro

독해편

How to TEPS *intro* 독해편

지은이 한정림
펴낸이 임상진
펴낸곳 (주)넥서스

초판 1쇄 발행 2007년 12월 10일
초판 25쇄 발행 2018년 1월 25일

출판신고 1992년 4월 3일 제311-2002-2호
10880 경기도 파주시 지목로 5
Tel (02)330-5500 Fax (02)330-5555

ISBN 978-89-6000-335-4 13740

www.nexusbook.com

출제 원리와 해법, 정답이 보이는

How to TEPS intro

독해편

한정림 지음

넥서스

Preface

I'm me!
I'm special!
There's no one else like me!

언어 습득의 과정은 어쩔 수 없이 항상 부족하고 틀리는 과정이 반복됩니다. 또한 이런 과정을 나만 겪는 것이 아니라 모든 언어 습득자가 겪어야 할 과정이라는 것을 처음부터 인정하면 영어 습득 과정에서 자신감을 잃어가는 일은 줄일 수 있습니다. 특히 영어습득 단계 중에서 초보자 수준일 때는 더욱 더 자신감을 갖고, 독해 기본기부터 다지는 것이 궁극적으로 보았을 때 효과적입니다. 그래서 본서를 집필하면서 다음과 같은 것에 더욱 신경을 썼습니다.

● TEPS 수험서로서 충실하자!
이제 TEPS를 시작하려고 하시는 분들이나, 오래 전부터 TEPS를 접하기는 했으나 성적이 제대로 오르지 않는 분들에게 TEPS 시험의 특징과 성격을 잘 알리고자 출제 유형 분석, 특징, 풀이 전략 등을 쉽게 이해할 수 있도록 했습니다.

● 기왕에 하는 공부 TEPS 점수도 올리고, 영어 실력도 올리자!
영어 독해를 잘 하기 위해 필요한 기본기들을 TEPS의 다양한 문제 유형을 사용하여 소개하였습니다. 특히 속독을 잘 할 수 있도록, 또한 연습할 때 도움이 되도록 한글 번역을 되도록 영문 어순과 같게 하려고 노력했습니다.

● 짧은 시간에 최대의 효과를 볼 수 있도록 하자!
주제별 필수 어휘 분류, 영어 주요 문법, 독해 기본 전략 등을 TEPS 실전 문제 유형과 함께 제시하여 기본기를 충실히 다지면서, 실전 대비를 바로 시작할 수 있도록 했습니다.

끝으로 필자의 영어교육 철학과 경험을 믿고 기회를 주신 (주)도서출판 넥서스에 감사를 드리고, 본서가 영어를 습득하는 모든 학습자들에게 의미 있는 책이 되기를 바랍니다.

Well begun is half done!
Good luck!

저자 한정림

Contents

- 이 책의 구성과 특징   8
- TEPS 정보   10

I   Introduction to TEPS Reading

| Unit 01 | 출제유형과 문제풀이 전략 | 34 |
| Unit 02 | TEPS 일반 독해 전략 | 40 |

II   Understanding the Structures in TEPS Reading

Unit 01	분사 구문(Reduced Structures)	46
Unit 02	비교 구문(Comparative Structures)	49
Unit 03	병렬 구문(Parallel Structure)	53
Unit 04	도치 구문(Inverted Structure)	56
Unit 05	강조 구문(Emphasized Structure)	59
Unit 06	가정 구문(Conditionals)	61
Unit 07	원인, 결과, 목적을 나타내는 구문(Cause / Effect / Purpose)	66
Unit 08	수동태 구문(Passive Structure)	70

III   Building Up Vocabulary for TEPS Reading

Unit 01	관련 있는 내용끼리 묶어서 익히기(Categorizing Related Words)	76
Unit 02	주제별 어휘 익히기(Topic-Based Vocabulary)	78
Unit 03	연어 익히기(Collocations)	82
Unit 04	어휘 형성 규칙 이해하기(Word Formation)	84
Unit 05	문맥 속에서 품사 이해하기(Vocabulary in Context)	87
Unit 06	합성어 익히기(Compound Words)	88
Unit 07	동사구 익히기(Phrasal Verbs)	90
Unit 08	혼동하기 쉬운 어휘(Confusing Words)	91

IV Skills for TEPS Reading

Unit 01 대의 찾기(Identifying the Main Ideas)   100

Unit 02 주요 내용을 패러프레이즈하기(Paraphrasing the Main Ideas)   103

Unit 03 세부 내용 파악하기(Locating Details in the Text)   109

Unit 04 예측하기 & 추론하기(Making Predictions & Inferences)   112

Unit 05 시각적 묘사(Visualizing the Text)   117

V Categorizing TEPS Reading Based upon Topics

Unit 01 정치(Politics)   120

Unit 02 경제(Economy)   121

Unit 03 사회(Social Studies)   122

Unit 04 문화(Culture)   123

Unit 05 예술(Art)   124

Unit 06 환경(Environment)   125

Unit 07 과학(Science)   126

VI Actual Tests

Actual Test 1   130

Actual Test 2   152

Actual Test 3   174

Actual Test 4   196

Actual Test 5   218

Plus   ■ 책속의 책   정답 및 해설

Structure

Unit 01 출제유형과 문제풀이 전략

Part I-1 빈 칸 채우기(일반유형)

문항수	1번부터 16번까지의 16문항
지시문	Read the passage. Then choose the option that best completes the
지문형식	1. 실용문: 공고문, 광고, 보고문, 편지 등 다양한 형식을 취한다.
	2. 교양 학술 지문: 경제, 사회, 인문, 과학, 의학 등의 다양한 주제를 다룬다.
	3. 빈 칸에 알맞은 표현과 연결어를 고르는 문제로 구성된다.
출제 경향	기존의 시험에서는 빈 칸 주변 문장을 집중적으로 분석하면 정답을 고를 확률이 높 에 들어서는 빈 칸 주변 뿐 아니라 전체적인 내용의 흐름을 파악하고 있는지 확 두드러지게 많아지고 있다. 빈 칸의 위치는 서두, 중간, 말미 등 다양하지만, 지문 경우가 많다.

● Introduction

문항 수, 지시문, 지문 형식, 출제 경향 등 TEPS 독해문제를 푸는데 필요한 다양한 전략에 관한 소개가 자세히 설명되어 있습니다.

Tips

Trigger Words를 이해하고 연습해야한다. 예를 들어, "He's handsome, **but** he's...."에서 but 이어지는 내용은 앞에 나온 내용과 다른 내용이 나온다. 여기서 handsome은 긍정적인 내용이므로 bu 에는 부정적인 내용이 와야 한다. 예를 들어, mean, rude, impolite 등과 같이 부정적인 내용이 담긴 로 이어지는 것이 자연스럽다.

앞 내용의 흐름이 달라지거나 반대 내용이 이어질 때 사용하는 표현:

but	however	although	even though	in spite of	desp
on the contrary	in contrast	rather		yet

위의 예문에서 한 단어만 바꾸어도, 즉 but을 and로 바꾸면 다음에 이어지는 내용이 완전히 달라져야 한 "He's handsome, **and** he's ..."에서 and는 앞에 나온 내용에 부연하거나 내용이 계속 이어질 때 므로, and 뒤에는 긍정적인 내용 즉, kind, generous, polite 등이 와야 한다.

● Tips

TEPS 독해 입문자들이 탄탄히 기초를 다질 수 있도록 핵심 내용들을 Tips에 쉽고 친절하게 실었습니다.

Sample Question

① Camels are known as the "ships of the desert" for their extraordinary ability to travel across vast expanses of barren sands while transporting heavy loads. ② They have wide, cushioned feet, which spread out as they walk and thus help them to maneuver easily across the soft sand, as well as ③ two rows of eyelashes and closeable nostrils that protect them from sandstorms. ④ In order to survive in a desert landscape, often void of water and food, camels have developed the ability to store great amounts of nutrients for long periods of time. When food and water is plentiful, they consume as much as possible, storing reserve fat in their humps and water in stomach sacs that can hold up to twenty-five gallons.

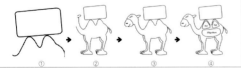

● Sample Question

본문에서 배운 내용이 실제 영어 독해에서 어떻게 적용되고 응용되는지에 대한 유형별 예문을 실었습니다.

● Practice Test

기본적인 사항을 점검한 후 실전 적용 훈련이 될 수 있도록
구문 연습 및 문법 문제를 풀어볼 수 있는 Mini Test입니다.

● Actual Tests

실제 TEPS 시험지와 같은 형식으로 구성하여 시험장에서
시험을 보는 것과 똑같은 Simulation 효과를 얻을 수 있는
단계입니다.

● 정답 및 해설

본문의 Sample Question, Practice Test, Actual Test
에 대한 해석, 해설, 어휘, 정답을 자세히 수록하였습니다.

TEPS 개요

TEPS란 Test of English Proficiency developed by Seoul National University의 약자로 서울대학교 언어교육원에서 개발하고, TEPS관리위원회에서 주관하는 국내 토종 영어 인증시험입니다.

- 서울대학교 언어교육원은 대한민국 정부가 공인하는 외국어 능력 측정 기관으로 32년간 정부기관, 각급 단체 및 기업체를 대상으로 어학능력을 측정해 왔습니다.

- TEPS는 국내외 유수한 대학에 종사하는 최고 수준의 영어 관련 전문가 100여명 가까운 인원이 출제하고 세계의 권위자로 구성된 자문위원회에서 검토하는 시험입니다.

- TEPS는 청해, 문법, 어휘, 독해에 걸쳐 총 200문항, 990점 만점의 시험입니다.

- TEPS는 언어 테스팅 분야의 세계적 권위자인 Bachman 교수(미국UCLA)와 Oller 교수(미국 뉴멕시코대)에게서 타당성을 검증받았으며, 여러 번의 시험적 평가에서 이미 그 신뢰도와 타당도가 입증된 시험입니다.

- TEPS는 우리나라 사람들의 살아 있는 영어 실력, 즉 의사소통 능력을 가장 효과적이고 정확하게 측정해 주는 시험이라고 할 수 있습니다.

- TEPS는 진정한 실력자와 비실력자를 확실히 구분할 수 있도록 구성된 시험으로서 변별력에 있어서 본인의 정확한 실력 파악에 실제적인 도움이 됩니다.

- TEPS 성적표는 수험생의 영어 능력을 영역별로 세분화한 평가를 해주기 때문에 수험자의 어느 부분이 탁월한지 잘 알 수 있을 뿐만 아니라 효과적인 영어공부 방향을 제시해 주기도 합니다.

- TEPS는 다양하고 일반적인 영어능력을 평가하는 시험으로 대학교, 기업체, 각종 기관 및 단체, 개인이 다양한 목적을 위해 응시할 수 있는 시험입니다.

TEPS의 구성

영역	파트별 내용	문항 수	총문항/시간	배점
청 해 Listening Comprehension	**Part I :** 질의응답 (문장 하나를 듣고 이어질 대화 고르기) **Part II :** 짧은 대화 (3개 문장의 대화를 듣고 이어질 대화 고르기) **Part III :** 긴 대화 (6-8개 문장의 대화를 듣고 질문에 알맞은 답 고르기) **Part IV :** 담화문 (담화문의 내용을 듣고 질문에 알맞은 답 고르기)	15 15 15 15	60문항 / 55분	400점
문 법 Grammar	**Part I :** 구어체 (대화문의 빈칸에 적절한 표현 고르기) **Part II :** 문어체 (문장의 빈칸에 적절한 표현 고르기) **Part III :** 대화문 (대화에서 어법상 틀리거나 어색한 부분 고르기) **Part IV :** 담화문 (담화문에서 문법상 틀리거나 어색한 부분 고르기)	20 20 5 5	50문항 / 25분	100점
어 휘 Vocabulary	**Part I :** 구어체 (대화문의 빈칸에 적절한 단어 고르기) **Part II :** 문어체 (문장의 빈칸에 적절한 단어 고르기)	25 25	50문항 / 15분	100점
독 해 Reading Comprehension	**Part I :** 빈칸 채우기 (지문을 읽고 질문의 빈칸에 들어갈 내용 고르기) **Part II :** 내용 이해 (지문을 읽고 질문에 가장 적절한 내용 고르기) **Part III :** 흐름 찾기 (지문을 읽고 문맥상 어색한 내용 고르기)	16 21 3	40문항 / 45분	400점
총 계	13개의 세부 영역	200	140분	990점

*IRT(Item Response Theory)에 의하여 최고점은 990점, 최하점은 10점으로 조정됨.

TEPS의 특징

한국인에게 알맞은 영어 시험

우리 국민 대다수가 초·중·고교에서 10년 동안 영어를 배우고, 대학과 직장에서 또다시 영어교육을 받지만 한국은 아시아에서도 한참 뒤떨어진 영어후진국 신세를 면치 못하고 있습니다.

미국과 영국에서 개발한 영어교육체계와 어학검정시험을 쫓아 매년 수십만 명이 동분서주하지만 눈에 띄는 성과를 거두지는 못했습니다. 사고방식과 언어 습관이 다른 외국인이 한국인의 고민을 알기는 어렵습니다. TEPS는 영어와 한국어를 다 잘하는 국내 최고의 연구진이 영어와 한국어의 언어적 특성을 대조·분석하고 한국인들이 범하기 쉬운 오류를 찾아 출제에 적극 반영합니다. 따라서 TEPS는 한국인에게 가장 필요한 영어 학습 지침을 제공하는 시험이라고 할 수 있습니다.

편법이 통하지 않는 시험

개인의 어학 능력은 결코 단기간에 급속도로 향상되지 않습니다. 그런데도 실력 배양은 아랑곳하지 않고 영어성적만을 올리기 위해 요령과 편법을 가르치는 교육기관이 많습니다.

TEPS는 있는 그대로의 영어 능력을 정확하게 진단합니다. 예를 들어 청해 시험은 인쇄된 질문지 및 선택지 없이 방송으로만 들려주기 때문에 미리 문제를 보고 답을 예측해 보는 요령이 통하지 않습니다. 또한 독해 시험에 있어서는 '1지문 1문항 원칙'을 지켜 한 문제로 다음 문제의 답을 유추할 수 있는 가능성을 원천적으로 배제하고 있습니다. 따라서 TEPS는 편법이 통하지 않는 시험입니다.

활용 능력을 중시하는 시험

외국인과 영어로 대화할 때 상대방이 질문을 던질 경우, 한참동안 문법과 어휘를 고민해서 대답할 수는 없는 노릇입니다. 암기식으로 배운 영어로는 실제 상황에서 제 실력을 발휘할 수 없습니다.

TEPS는 일상생활에서의 활용능력을 정확하게 측정해 주는 시험입니다. TEPS는 기존의 다른 시험에 비해 많은 지문을 주고 이를 짧은 시간 내에 이해하여 풀어낼 수 있는지를 측정합니다. 이는 실제 생활에서 활용할 수 없는 암기식 영어가 아니라 완전히 습득되어 자유롭게 구사할 수 있는 '살아 있는' 영어 실력을 평가하기 위한 것입니다.

경제성과 효율성을 갖춘 시험

TEPS는 서울대 언어교육원이 자체 개발한 시험으로 외국에 비싼 로열티를 지불하는 다른 시험과는 달리 응시 비용이 매우 저렴합니다.

➕ 채점방식이 다른 시험

TEPS는 첨단 어학 능력 검증 기법인 문항 반응 이론(IRT: Item Response Theory)을 도입했습니다. 문항 반응 이론은 문항을 개발할 때 문항별로 1차 난이도를 정의하고 시험 시행 후 전체 수험자들이 각각의 문항에 대해 맞고 틀린 것을 종합해 그 문항의 난이도를 재조정한 다음, 이를 근거로 다시 한 번 채점해 최종성적을 내게 됩니다. 이 과정에서 최고점은 990점, 최하점은 10점으로 조정됩니다.

문항 반응 이론은 맞은 개수의 합을 총점으로 하는 전근대적인 평가방식과는 달리, 각 문항의 난이도와 변별도에 대한 수험자의 반응 패턴을 근거로 영어 능력을 추정하는 확률 이론입니다.

문항 반응 이론을 적용할 경우, 낮은 난이도의 문제를 많이 틀린 수험자가 높은 난이도의 문제를 맞힐 경우 실력에 관계없이 추측이나 우연히 맞힐 가능성이 높다고 보고 감점 처리합니다. 이러한 문항 반응 이론은 가장 선진적인 검정 방식으로서 TEPS는 이 이론에 기초한 국내 최초의 영어 능력 평가 시험입니다.

➕ 실용영어 능력 평가

실용영어는 사소한 대화를 위주로 하는 생활영어와는 다른 범주입니다. 평균적인 교양을 갖춘 일반인이 가정, 직장, 공공장소 등 일상적인 환경과 생활에서 사용하는 영어를 뜻합니다. 일상적인 대화는 물론, 신문, 잡지, 방송, 매뉴얼, 예약, 주문, 구매, 일반적인 상담 등이 모두 실용영어의 범주에 포함됩니다.

TEPS는 누구나 쉽게 접하는 상황에서 추출된 소재를 중심으로 문제를 구성하여, 범용적인 영어 능력을 평가합니다. 따라서 성별, 직업, 나이에 관계없이 일반 대중들의 영어 능력을 객관적으로 평가할 수 있는 시험입니다.

➕ 신속한 결과 통보, 학습 방향을 제시해주는 성적 진단

TEPS는 점수만 알려주고 끝나는 시험이 아닙니다. 청취, 문법, 어휘, 독해 등 영역별로 점수를 산출하고, 다시 각 영역을 기능, 소재, 문체별로 세분하여 18개 부문에서 항목별 성취도를 알려 줍니다. 따라서 성적표를 통해 수험자의 강점, 약점은 물론 추후 학습 방향을 명확하게 제시합니다.

TEPS 출제 원칙

✛ 통합식 시험 (Integrative Test)

지엽적인 학습을 조장할 우려가 있는 분리식 시험(Discrete-Point Test) 유형을 배제하고 실제 의사소통 상황과 문맥 파악을 중시하는 통합식 시험(Integrative Test) 유형을 강조함으로써 수험자의 폭넓은 어학 능력을 평가할 수 있습니다.

✛ 국부 독립성 (Local Independence)

첨단 테스트 기술인 문항 반응 이론(IRT: Item Response Theory)을 활용하여 각 부분의 독립성을 보장합니다. 예를 들어 '1지문 1문항'의 원칙에 따라 다양한 내용의 지문을 수험생들이 접할 수 있게 하고, 동시에 어느 한 지문을 이해하지 못함으로써 몇 개의 문항을 연이어 틀리는 일이 없도록 했습니다. 국부 독립성에 따른 문항 반응 이론은 환상의 어학 능력 평가로 기대를 모으고 있는 컴퓨터 개별 적응 언어 평가(CALT: Computer Adaptive Language Test)의 핵심 요소이기도 합니다.

✛ 속도화 시험 (Speeded Test)

간접적인 의사소통 능력 평가로서 문법 및 어휘 시험에서는 속도 시험의 속성을 극대화하여 언어학적 지식 (Learning)이 아닌 잠재적인 의사소통 능력(Acquisition)을 평가합니다.

✛ 진단 평가 (Diagnostic Test)

세부 영역별로 평가 결과를 제시하여 수험자 개인의 능력을 정확하게 진단합니다. 교육과 평가가 마치 실과 바늘처럼 서로 맞물려 발전해야 한다는 원칙에 따라 최대한 자세히 검정 결과를 분석해 수험생들의 향후 학습 방향을 알려줍니다.

TEPS 출제 경향

✦ 청해 (Listening Comprehension) – 60문항

정확한 청해 능력을 측정하기 위하여 문제와 보기 문항을 문제지에 인쇄하지 않고 들려줌으로써 자연스러운 의사소통의 인지 과정을 최대한 반영하였습니다. 다양한 의사소통 기능(Communicative Functions)의 대화와 다양한 상황(공고, 방송, 일상 생활, 업무 상황, 대학 교양 수준의 강의 등)을 이해하는 데 필요한 전반적인 청해력을 측정하기 위해 대화문(dialogue)과 담화문(monologue)의 소재를 균형 있게 다루었습니다.

✦ 문법 (Grammar) – 50문항

밑줄 친 부분 중 오류를 식별하는 유형 등의 단편적이며 기계적인 문법 지식 학습을 조장할 우려가 있는 분리식 시험 유형을 배제하고, 의미 있는 문맥을 근거로 오류를 식별하는 유형을 통하여 진정한 의사소통 능력의 바탕이 되는 살아 있는 문법, 어법 능력을 문어체와 구어체를 통하여 측정합니다.

✦ 어휘 (Vocabulary) – 50문항

문맥 없이 단순한 동의어 및 반의어를 선택하는 시험 유형을 배제하고 의미 있는 문맥을 근거로 가장 적절한 어휘를 선택하는 유형을 문어체와 구어체로 나누어 측정합니다.

✦ 독해 (Reading Comprehension) – 40문항

교양 있는 수준의 글(신문, 잡지, 대학 교양과목 개론 등)과 실용적인 글(서신, 광고, 홍보, 지시문, 설명문, 도표, 양식 등)을 이해하는 데 요구되는 총체적인 독해력을 측정하기 위해서 실용문 및 비전문적 학술문과 같은 독해 지문의 소재를 균형 있게 다루었습니다.

TEPS 영역별 유형

청해 (Listening Comprehension)-60문항

🎙 PART Ⅰ (15문항)

영역 설명　Part Ⅰ은 질의 응답 문제를 다루며 한 번만 들려줍니다. 내용 자체는 단순하고 기본적인 수준의 생활 영어 표현으로 구성되어 있지만 교과서적인 지식보다는 재빠른 상황 판단 능력을 요구합니다. 따라서 Part Ⅰ에서는 속도 적응 능력뿐만 아니라 순발력 있는 상황 판단 능력이 요구됩니다.

Listen and choose the most appropriate response to the statement.

M　How shall I address you?

W　_____

(a) Just call me John.
(b) 39 Morrison Avenue.
(c) Don't send me a letter.
(d) I don't like making speeches.

정답 : (a)

🎙 PART Ⅱ (15문항)

영역 설명　Part Ⅱ는 짧은 대화 문제로서 두 사람이 A-B-A-B 순으로 보통 속도로 대화하는 형식이며, 소요 시간은 약 12초 전후로 짧게 구성되어 있습니다. Part Ⅰ과 마찬가지로 한 번만 들려줍니다.

Listen and choose the most appropriate response to complete the conversation.

M　How long were you thinking of renting a car?

W　For ten days in September.

M　When exactly do you have in mind?

W　_____

(a) I thought of it last Monday.
(b) The end of September.
(c) I'm too young to rent one yet.
(d) Nothing is further from my mind.

정답 : (b)

🎙 PART Ⅲ (15문항)

영역 설명　Part Ⅲ는 앞의 두 파트에 비해 다소 긴 대화를 들려줍니다. 대신 대화 부분과 질문을 두 번씩 들려주기 때문에 길이가 긴 데 비해 많이 어렵다고 할 수는 없습니다.

Listen and choose the option that best answers the question.

W The conference is only two months away and we still don't have a venue.

M Maybe we should reserve the same hall we used last time.

W I think it might be too small this year.

M You're probably right. The company has really grown over the past year.

W How about looking into one of the rooms at the convention center?

M Sure. I heard they have connections with a good caterer, too.

Q What is the conversation mainly about?

(a) Hiring new employees
(b) Organizing an annual event
(c) Expanding an office building
(d) Catering a party in two months

정답 : (b)

PART IV (15문항)

영역 설명 Part IV는 담화문을 다룹니다. 영어권 국가에서 영어로 뉴스를 듣거나 강의를 들을 때와 비슷한 상황을 설정하여 얼마나 잘 이해하는지를 측정합니다. 이야기의 주제, 세부 사항, 사실 여부 및 이를 근거로 한 추론 등을 다룹니다. 직청 직해 실력, 즉 들으면서 곧바로 내용을 이해할 수 있는지를 평가합니다. 담화 부분과 질문을 두 번씩 들려줍니다.

Listen and choose the option that best answers the question.

Hello, everyone. We'll continue our discussion of American newspapers today. Does anyone care to guess what the most popular section of the paper is? Well, it's not the front page, the weather report, or even - sorry to disappoint you sports fans - the sports page. It's the comics. Now, my bet is that even those of you who rarely read the paper at all can't resist glancing at the comics. True?

Q According to the talk, what is the most popular section of the paper?

(a) The front page
(b) The weather report
(c) The sports page
(d) The comics

정답 : (d)

문법 (Grammar)-50문항

PART I (20문항)

영역 설명　Part I은 A, B 두 사람의 짧은 대화를 통해 전치사 표현력, 구문 이해력, 품사 이해도, 시제, 접속사 등 문법에 대한 이해력을 묻는 형태로 되어 있습니다. 주로 후자(B)의 대화 중에 빈칸이 있고, 그곳에 들어갈 적절한 표현을 고르는 형식입니다.

Fill in the blank with the most appropriate word or phrase.

A　Have you read the book the italics, no quotes?
B　No. Who ＿＿＿＿＿＿ it?
(a) wrote
(b) writes
(c) has written
(d) had written

정답 : (a)

PART II (20문항)

영역 설명　Part II는 문어체 질문을 다룹니다. 서술문 속의 빈칸을 채우는 문제로 총 20문항으로 되어 있습니다. 이 파트에서는 문법 자체에 대한 이해도는 물론 구문에 대한 이해력도 중요합니다.

Fill in the blank with the most appropriate word or phrase.

On reaching ＿＿＿＿＿＿ four, Mozart was given harpsichord lessons by his father.
(a) age of
(b) the age
(c) an age of
(d) the age of

정답 : (d)

PART III (5문항)

영역 설명　Part III는 대화문에서 어법상 틀리거나 어색한 부분이 있는 문장을 고르는 다섯 문항으로 구성되어 있습니다. 이 영역 역시 문법뿐만 아니라 정확한 구문 파악, 회화 내용의 식별능력이 대단히 중요합니다.

Identify the grammatical error in the dialogue.

(a) A: That cold sounds pretty bad.
(b) B: Yeah, it is. Don't get too close.
(c) A: Let me make you a cup of herbal tea.
(d) B: Gee, that's nice for you!

정답 : (d)

PART IV (5문항)

영역 설명　Part IV는 한 문단을 주고 그 가운데 문법적으로 틀리거나 어색한 문장을 고르는 다섯 문항으로 되어 있습니다. 틀린 부분을 신속하게 골라야 하므로 속독 능력도 중요한 작용을 합니다.

Identify the ungrammatical sentence in the passage.

(a) Put an ice cube into a glass of water.
(b) Look through the side of the glass.
(c) You will see that most ice cube is under the surface of the water.
(d) The little ice cube in the glass acts just like a giant iceberg in the ocean.

정답 : (c)

어휘 (Vocabulary)-50문항

PART I (25문항)

영역 설명　Part I은 구어체로 되어 있는 A, B의 대화 중 빈칸에 가장 적절한 단어를 넣는 25문항으로 구성되어 있습니다. 단어의 단편적인 의미보다는 문맥에서 쓰인 상대적인 의미를 더 중요시합니다.

Choose the most appropriate word or expression for the blank in the conversation.

A　Could you tell me how to get to First National Bank?
B　Sure, make a left ＿＿＿＿＿＿＿ at the first light and go straight for two blocks.
(a) stop
(b) turn
(c) way
(d) path

정답 : (b)

PART II (25문항)

영역 설명 Part II는 하나 또는 두 개의 문장으로 구성된 글 속의 빈칸에 가장 적당한 단어를 골라 넣는 부분입니다. 어휘를 늘릴 때 한 개씩 단편적으로 암기하는 것보다는 하나의 표현으로, 즉 의미구로 알아 놓는 것이 15분이라는 제한된 시간 내에 어휘 시험을 정확히 푸는 데 많은 도움이 될 것입니다.

Choose the most appropriate word or expression for the blank in the statement.

This videotape _____ for three and a half hours.
(a) gets
(b) views
(c) runs
(d) takes

정답 : (c)

독해 (Reading Comprehension)-40문항

PART I (16문항)

영역 설명 Part I은 빈칸 넣기 유형입니다. 한 단락의 글을 주고 그 안에 빈칸을 넣어 알맞은 표현을 고르는 16문항으로 이루어져 있습니다. 글 전체의 흐름을 파악하여 문맥상 빈칸에 들어 갈 내용을 찾는 문제입니다.

Read the passage and choose the option that best fits the blank.

Athletes look good while they work out, but they may not feel so great. A report suggests that up to 70% may experience stomach distress during exercise. Competitive runners are prone to lower-bowel problems like diarrhea, probably because blood rushes from the intestines to their hardworking leg muscles. Weight lifters and cyclists, for their part, tend to _____.
(a) feel stronger
(b) exercise too much
(c) strive for weight loss
(d) suffer from heartburn

정답 : (d)

영역 설명 Part II는 글의 내용 이해를 측정하는 문제로 21문항으로 구성되어 있습니다. 주제나 대의 혹은 전반적 논조 파악, 세부내용 파악, 논리적 추론 등이 있습니다.

Choose the option that correctly answers the question.

Parents who let kids surf online without supervision may want to think again. Though most children and teens know they shouldn't give strangers personal information, a new study finds that many young people feel it's OK to reveal potentially sensitive family data in exchange for a prize. Nearly two out of every three children were willing to name their favorite stores, and about a third would tell about their parents' driving records, alcohol consumption, political discussions, work attendance and church-going habits.

Q What is the best title for the passage?

(a) Unsupervised Children Reveal Personal Information
(b) Parents Have Difficulty Controlling Their Children
(c) Prizes Given to Children on the Internet
(d) Internet Privacy: a Thing of the Past

정답 : (a)

⚕ PART III (3문항)

영역 설명   Part III는 한 문단의 글에서 내용의 흐름상 어색한 곳을 고르는 문제로 3문항으로 이루어져 있습니다. 전체 흐름을 파악하여 흐름상 필요 없는 내용을 고르는 문제입니다. 이런 유형의 문제는 응집력 있는 영작문 실력을 간접적으로 측정할 수도 있습니다.

Identify the sentence that least fits the context of the passage.

The emphasis on winning-whether a soccer game or spelling contest-is especially inappropriate for school-age children. (a) This is a time when they're mastering basic skills, both in sports and academic subjects. (b) The real challenge is when children grow up and become teenagers. (c) Children should be encouraged for doing their best, no matter what. (d) Building confidence is what's important, not just winning.

정답 : (b)

TEPS 등급표

등급	점수	영역	능력검정기준(Description)
1+급 Level 1	901-990	전반	외국인으로서 최상급 수준의 의사소통능력 : 교양 있는 원어민에 버금가는 정도로 의사소통이 가능하고 전문분야 업무에 대처할 수 있음. (Native Level of Communicative Competence)
1급 Level 1	801-900	전반	외국인으로서 거의 최상급 수준의 의사소통능력 : 단기간 집중 교육을 받으면 대부분의 의사소통이 가능하고 전문분야 업무에 별 무리 없이 대처할 수 있음. (Near-Native Level of Communicative Competence)
2+급 Level 2	701-800	전반	외국인으로서 상급 수준의 의사소통능력 : 단기간 집중 교육을 받으면 일반분야 업무를 큰 어려움 없이 수행할 수 있음. (Advanced Level of Communicative Competence)
2급 Level 2	601-700	전반	외국인으로서 중상급 수준의 의사소통능력 : 중장기간 집중 교육을 받으면 일반분야 업무를 큰 어려움 없이 수행할 수 있음. (High Intermediate Level of Communicative Competence)
3+급 Level 3	501-600	전반	외국인으로서 중급 수준의 의사소통능력 : 중장기간 집중 교육을 받으면 한정된 분야의 업무를 큰 어려움 없이 수행할 수 있음. (Mid Intermediate Level of Communicative Competence)
3급 Level 3	401-500	전반	외국인으로서 중하급 수준의 의사소통능력 : 중장기간 집중 교육을 받으면 한정된 분야의 업무를 다소 미흡하지만 큰 지장은 없이 수행할 수 있음. (Low Intermediate Level of Communicative Competence)
4+급 Level 4	201-400	전반	외국인으로서 하급수준의 의사소통능력 : 장기간의 집중 교육을 받으면 한정된 분야의 업무를 대체로 어렵게 수행할 수 있음. (Novice Level of Communicative Competence)
5+급 Level 5	101-200	전반	외국인으로서 최하급 수준의 의사소통능력 : 단편적인 지식만을 갖추고 있어 의사소통이 거의 불가능함. (Near-Zero Level of Communicative Competence)

TEPS 성적표

TEPS | Test of English Proficiency
developed by
Seoul National University

SCORE REPORT

NAME	**REGISTRATION NO.**
HONG GIL DONG	0123456
DATE OF BIRTH	**TEST DATE**
JAN. 01. 1980	MAR. 02. 2008
GENDER	**VALID UNTIL**
MALE	MAR. 01. 2010

NO : RAAAA0000BBBB

TOTAL SCORE AND LEVEL

SCORE	LEVEL
768	**2+**

SECTION	SCORE	LEVEL	%	0%	100%
Listening	307	2+	77 / 59		
Grammar	76	2+	76 / 52		
Vocabulary	65	2	65 / 56		
Reading	320	2+	80 / 61		

■ your percentage ■ average

OVERALL COMMUNICATIVE COMPETENCE

768

89.89%

A score at this level typically indicates an advanced level of communicative competence for a non-native speaker. A test taker at this level is able to execute general tasks after a short-term training.

SECTION			PERFORMANCE EVALUATION
Listening	PART I	86%	A score at this level typically indicates that the test taker has a good grasp of the given situation and its context and can make relevant responses. Can understand main ideas in conversations and lectures when they are explicitly stated, understand a good deal of specific information and make inferences given explicit information.
	PART II	66%	
	PART III	86%	
	PART IV	66%	
Grammar	PART I	84%	A score at this level typically indicates that the test taker has a fair understanding of the rules of grammar and syntax and has internalized them to a degree enabling them to carry out meaningful communication.
	PART II	75%	
	PART III	99%	
	PART IV	21%	
Vocabulary	PART I	72%	A score at this level typically indicates that the test taker has a good command of vocabulary for use in everyday speech. Able to understand vocabulary used in written contexts of a more formal nature, yet may have difficulty using it appropriately.
	PART II	56%	
Reading	PART I	68%	A score at this level typically indicates that the test taker is at an advanced level of understanding written texts. Can abstract main ideas from a text, understand a good deal of specific information and draw basic inferences when given texts with clear structure and explicit information.
	PART II	90%	
	PART III	66%	

THE TEPS COUNCIL

TEPS-TOEIC-TOEFL 비교

등급	TEPS	TOEIC	TOEFL (iBT)
시험명	Test of English Proficiency developed by Seoul National University	Test of English for International Communication	Test of English as a Foreign Language (Internet-Based Test)
개발기관	서울대학교 언어교육원	미국 ETS (Educational Testing Service)	미국 ETS (Educational Testing Service)
개발목적	한국인의 실용 영어능력 평가	비즈니스 커뮤니케이션 영어 능력 평가	미국 등 영어권 국가의 대학 또는 대학원에서 외국인의 영어능력 평가
시행기관	TEPS 관리위원회	재단법인 국제교류진흥회	ETS
시험시간	2시간 20분	2시간	약 4시간
문항수	200문항	200문항	78~129문항
만점	990점	990점	120점
구성	청해: 60문항 / 55분 / 400점 문법: 50문항 / 25분 / 100점 어휘: 50문항 / 15분 / 100점 독해: 40문항 / 45분 / 400점	L/C: 100문항 / 45분 / 495점 R/C: 100문항 / 75분 / 495점	Reading: 36~70문항 / 60~100분 / 0~30점 Listening: 34~51문항 / 60~90분 / 0~30점 Speaking: 6문항 / 20분 / 0~30점 Writing: 2문항 / 50분 / 0~30점
검정 기준	Criterion-referenced Test (절대 평가)	Norm-referenced Test (상대 평가)	Norm-referenced Test (상대 평가)
시행방법	정기시험: 연 12회 특별시험: 수시	정기시험: 연 12회 특별시험: 수시	연 30~40회
성적통보	정기시험: 2주 특별시험: 5일	정기시험: 20일 특별시험: 10일 이내	15일
성적 유효기간	2년	2년	2년
응시료	36,000원	42,000원	$170

TEPS	TOEIC	IBT	TEPS	TOEIC	IBT	TEPS	TOEIC	IBT
953~	990	120	756~763	850	100	582~587	710	83
948~952	985	120	750~755	845	100	578~571	705	83
941~947	980	119	743~749	840	98	572~577	700	82
935~940	975	118	736~742	835	98	567~571	695	82
928~934	970	118	729~735	830	96	561~566	690	80
922~927	965	117	723~728	825	96	557~560	685	80
915~921	960	116	716~722	820	95	551~556	680	78
908~914	955	114	710~715	815	95	546~550	675	78
901~907	950	114	702~709	810	94	541~545	670	76
894~900	945	114	696~701	805	94	536~540	665	75
887~893	940	113	689~695	800	94	532~535	660	75
880~886	935	113	684~688	795	93	527~531	655	75
872~879	930	111	677~683	790	93	521~526	650	73
865~871	925	110	671~676	785	91	517~520	645	71
857~864	920	110	664~670	780	91	512~516	640	71
851~856	915	109	658~663	775	91	508~511	635	70
843~850	910	109	652~657	770	89	503~507	630	70
836~842	905	107	646~651	765	89	498~502	625	70
828~835	900	107	640~645	760	89	494~497	620	68
822~827	895	105	634~639	755	89	490~493	615	65
814~821	890	105	628~633	750	87	485~489	610	64
807~813	885	103	622~627	745	87	481~484	605	57
799~806	880	103	616~621	740	87	476~480	600	57
793~798	875	103	611~615	735	87	472~475	595	57
785~792	870	101	605~610	730	85	468~471	590	57
778~784	865	101	600~604	725	85	464~467	585	56
771~777	860	100	593~599	720	83	460~463	580	51
764~770	855	100	588~592	715	83	456~459	575	50

1. **TEPS의 성적 유효 기간은 어떻게 되나요?**

    - 2년입니다.

2. **TEPS 관리위원회에서 인정하는 신분증은 무엇인가요?**

    ▶ **주민등록증 발급자 〈만 17세 이상〉** - 주민등록증, 운전면허증, 기간 만료 전의 여권, 공무원증

    기타   장교라면 → 장교신분증

               사병이라면 → TEPS 정기시험 신분확인증명서

               주민등록증을 분실했다면 → 주민등록증 발급확인서(동, 읍, 면사무소에서 발급)

               외국인이라면 → 외국인 등록증

    ▶ **주민등록증 미발급자 〈만 17세 미만〉** - 기간 만료 전의 여권, TEPS 정기시험 신분확인증명서, 청소년증

    기타   외국인이라면 → 기간 만료 전의 여권, 외국인 등록증

    ※ 시험당일 신분증 미지참자 및 규정에 맞지 않는 신분증 소지자는 시험에 절대로 응시할 수 없습니다. 중 · 고등학교, 대학교 학생증은 신분증으로 인정되지 않습니다.

3. **TEPS 문제지에 메모해도 되나요?**

    - 네. 그러나, 별도의 용지(좌석표, 수험표 등)에 메모를 하면 부정행위로 간주되어 규정에 의거하여 처리됩니다.

4. **TEPS의 고사장 변경은 어떻게 하나요?**

    ▶ **변경 기간** - 응시일 13일 전부터 7일 전까지

    ▶ **변경 방법** - www.teps.or.kr → 나의 시험 정보 → 접수 정보 관리

    ▶ **변경 조건**

    ① 1회에 한하여 변경 가능합니다.

    ② 고사장의 지역을 변경할 경우에만 가능합니다. (같은 지역 내 고사장 변경은 불가함)

    ③ 고사장의 여분에 맞춰 선착순 신청이며 조기에 마감될 수 있습니다.

    ※ 추가 접수의 경우에는, 시험일 5일 전까지 유선을 통하여 신청해야 합니다.

5. **TEPS 시험 볼 때 사용할 수 있는 필기구는 무엇인가요?**

    - 컴퓨터용 사인펜, 수정테이프 (컴퓨터용 연필, 수정액은 사용 불가)

6. **TEPS 시험을 연기할 수 있나요?**

    - 아니오. 접수 취소를 해야 합니다.

7. **TEPS는 추가 접수를 할 수 있나요?**

    - 네. 시험일자 10일 전부터 4일간 추가 접수 기간이 있습니다. 추가 접수 응시료에는 일반 응시료의 10%가 특별 수수료로 부가됩니다.

8. **TEPS는 인터넷으로 접수 취소할 수 있나요?**

  - 네. www.teps.or.kr에 회원가입을 해야 합니다.

  ▶ **접수 기간 내** - 전액 환불
  ▶ **접수 기간 1일 후 ~ 2주** - 18,000원 환불
  ▶ **접수 기간 2주 후 ~ 시험 당일** - 12,000원 환불
  ▶ **추가 접수 기간 1일 후 ~ 시험 당일** - 12,000원 환불

9. **수험표는 흑백프린터를 사용해도 되나요?**

  - 수험표는 흑백, 칼라 아무거나 사용하셔도 상관없습니다.

10. **OMR Sheet에 기재한 비밀번호가 생각나지 않을 때는 어떻게 해야 하나요?**

  - www.teps.or.kr에 로그인 하신 다음 비밀번호 입력란에 로그인 password를 다시 한 번 입력하시면 성적확
  인이 가능합니다.

11. **성적표 주소 변경은 어떻게 해야 하나요?**

  ▶ **변경 기간** - 응시일 13일 전부터 7일 전까지
  ▶ **변경 방법** - www.teps.or.kr → 나의 시험 정보 → 접수 정보 관리

12. **시험 점수는 얼마 후에 알게 되나요?**

  - 정기시험의 성적은 시험일로부터 15일 이후 ARS나 www.teps.or.kr에서 확인이 가능합니다. 정기시험 성적
  표는 시험일로부터 대략 20일 안에 우편으로 발송되고, 특별시험 성적표는 시험일로부터 7일 이내에 해당 기관이
  나 단체로 통보됩니다.

TEPS 활용 - 대학교

학교명	전형유형	전형명	TEPS 점수	기타
가톨릭대학교	수시2	특기자전형(영어)	TEPS 766점 이상	2008학년도 요강
강릉대학교	수시2	어학특기자전형(영어)	TEPS 502점 이상	2008학년도 요강
건국대학교(서울)	수시2	국제화특별전형	TEPS 739점 이상	2008학년도 요강
건양대학교	수시2	특기자전형(영어)	TEPS 500점 이상	2008학년도 요강
경동대학교	수시2-1	영어능력우수자전형	자체기준	2008학년도 요강
경북대학교	수시2-1	영어능력우수자전형	TEPS 713점 이상	2008학년도 요강
경상대학교	수시2	특기자전형(영어)	TEPS 848점 이상	2008학년도 요강
경성대학교	수시2	외국어특별전형	TEPS 720점 이상	2008학년도 요강
계명대학교	수시2	KIC외국어특기자전형	TEPS 550점 이상	2008학년도 요강
고려대학교	수시1	국제학부 특별전형	TEPS 900점 이상	2008학년도 요강
	수시2	글로벌전형, 글로벌KU	TEPS 900점 이상	2008학년도 요강
광주대학교	수시2-1	특기자전형	TEPS 500점 이상	2008학년도 요강
국민대학교	수시2	국제화특별전형	TEPS 651점(인문)/ 633점(자연) 이상	2008학년도 요강
		어학특기자전형(영어영문학과)	TEPS 850점 이상	2008학년도 요강
군산대학교	수시2	어학특기자전형	TEPS 500점 이상	2008학년도 요강
금강대학교	수시	어학특기자전형	TEPS 550점 이상	2007학년도 요강
단국대학교(서울)	수시, 2	국제화(어학)특기자전형	TEPS 850점(수시1), 700점 (수시2) 이상	2007학년도 요강
단국대학교(천안)	수시2	국제화(어학)특기자전형	TEPS 720점 이상	
덕성여자대학교	수시2	어학특기자	TEPS 623점 이상	2008학년도 요강
대진대학교	수시2	어학특기자	TEPS 601점 이상	2007학년도 요강
동덕여자대학교	수시2	영어특기자	TEPS 750점 이상	2008학년도 요강
동명대학교	수시2	어학특기자	TEPS 400점 이상	2008학년도 요강
동아대학교	수시2	국제관광인력전형	TEPS 650점 이상	2008학년도 요강
		국제무역인력전형	TEPS 650점 이상	
동의대학교	수시2	자격증·실적보유자(어학)	자체기준	2008학년도 요강
목포대학교	수시2	외국어특기자(영어)	TEPS 600점 이상	2008학년도 요강
부산대학교	수시2	표준외국어 능력시험(영어)	TEPS 685점 이상	2008학년도 요강
부산외국어대학교	수시2	외국어능력우수자	TEPS 680점 이상	2008학년도 요강
삼육대학교	수시2	영어특기자(일반학과)	TEPS 600점 이상	2008학년도 요강
상명대학교(서울)	수시2	영어특기자	TEPS 737점 이상	2008학년도 요강
상명대학교(천안)	수시2	영어특기자	TEPS 600점 이상	2008학년도 요강

서울대학교	수시2	외국어능력 우수자전형	TEPS 850점 이상	2008학년도 요강
서울시립대학교	수시2-1	어학특기자전형	자체기준	2008학년도 요강
서울여자대학교	수시2	어학특기자전형	자체기준	2008학년도 요강
선문대학교	수시2	어학우수자전형	TEPS 522점 이상	2008학년도 요강
성결대학교	수시2	외국어특기자전형	TEPS 650점 이상	2008학년도 요강
성균관대학교(서울)	수시2-1	글로벌리더전형	TEPS 800점 이상	2008학년도 요강
		글로벌경영전형	TEPS 900점 이상	2008학년도 요강
성신여자대학교	수시2	어학특기자전형(영어)	TEPS 650점 이상	2008학년도 요강
세종대학교	수시2-2	국제화추진 특별전형	TEPS 790점 이상	2008학년도 요강
순천대학교	수시2	외국어특기자전형	TEPS 700점 이상	2008학년도 요강
신라대학교	수시2	어학특기자전형	TEPS 600점 이상	2008학년도 요강
아세아연합신학대학교	수시2	어학특기자전형	TEPS 650점 이상	2008학년도 요강
아주대학교	수시2-1	영어특기자전형	자체기준	2007학년도 요강
연세대학교	수시1	일반우수자전형	자체기준	2008학년도 요강
	수시2	글로벌리더전형	자체기준	2008학년도 요강
용인대학교	수시2	외국어성적우수자전형	TEPS 550점 이상	2008학년도 요강
울산대학교	수시2	어학특기자전형	TEPS 600점 이상	2008학년도 요강
이화여자대학교	수시2	스크랜튼국제학부 1, 2	자체기준	2008학년도 요강
		이화글로벌인재전형		
인제대학교	수시2	외국어능력우수자 및 자격증소지자	자체기준	2008학년도 요강
장로회신학대학교	수시2	어학특기자전형	TEPS 560점 이상	2008학년도 요강
전북대학교	수시2	어학능력우수자전형	자체기준	2008학년도 요강
전주대학교	수시2	어학특기자전형	TEPS 625점(언어문화학부)/ TEPS 712점(영어교육과)	2008학년도 요강
청주대학교	수시2-2	국제화전형	TEPS 500점 이상	2008학년도 요강
총신대학교	정시 나	외국어특기자전형(영어)	TEPS 640점 이상	2008학년도 요강
충남대학교	수시2	전문분야 우수자(영어)	TEPS 850점 이상	2008학년도 요강
한남대학교	수시2-2	외국어공인시험우수자전형	TEPS 550점 이상	2008학년도 요강
한동대학교	수시2-3	어학특기자전형	TEPS 833점 이상	2008학년도 요강
한성대학교	수시2-1	어학특기자전형	TEPS 650점 이상	2008학년도 요강
한신대학교	수시2	어학특기자전형	TEPS 600점 이상	2008학년도 요강
홍익대학교	수시2	어학특기자전형	자체기준	2008학년도 요강

TEPS 활용 기업 및 정부 기관

✚ 국내 기업 – 신입사원 채용

(주)포스코, (주)현대오토넷, CJ그룹, GM 대우, GS건설, GS칼텍스(주), GS홀딩스, KTF, KTFT, LG CNS, LG PHILIPS, LG전자, LG텔레콤, LG화학, LS산전, LS전선, SK그룹, SPC그룹, 경남기업(주), 교원그룹, 국도화학, 국민일보, 금강고려화학, 남양유업, 농심, 대림산업, 대우건설, 대우건설, 대우인터내셔널, 대우자동차판매(주), 대우정보시스템(주), 대우조선해양, 동부그룹, 동부제강, 동양그룹, 동양시멘트(주), 동원 F&B, 삼성그룹, 새한그룹, 신세계, 쌍용건설, 오뚜기, 오리온, 유한킴벌리, 일진그룹, 제일화재, (주)벽산, (주)코오롱, (주)태평양, 코리아나화장품, 포스코건설, 풀무원, 하이닉스반도체, 하이마트, 한솔제지(주), 한진중공업, 한진해운, 현대건설, 현대기아자동차그룹, 현대모비스(주), 현대상선, 현대오일뱅크, 현대종합상사, 현대하이스코, 효성그룹

✚ 공기업 – 신입사원 채용

KOTRA, KT, KT&G, 공무원연금관리공단, 교통안전공단, 국립공원관리공단, 국민연금관리공단, 국민체육진흥공단, 근로복지공단, 농수산물유통공사, 농업기반공사, 대한광업진흥공사, 대한법률구조공단, 대한주택공사, 대한주택보증, 대한지적공사, 마사회, 서울메트로, 서울시농수산물공사, 서울시도시철도공사, 수출보험공사, 에너지관리공단, 인천관광공사, 인천국제공항공사, 인천항만공사, 자산관리공사, 중소기업진흥공단, 중소기업협동조합중앙회, 한국가스공사, 한국공항공사, 한국관광공사, 한국국제협력단, 한국남동발전(주), 한국남부발전(주), 한국농촌공사, 한국도로공사, 한국동서발전(주), 한국방송광고공사, 한국산업단지공단, 한국산업안전공단, 한국서부발전(주), 한국석유공사, 한국소방검정공사, 한국수력원자력, 한국수자원공사, 한국수출입은행, 한국원자력연료(주), 한국인삼공사, 한국전력, 한국조폐공사, 한국주택금융공사, 한국중부발전(주), 한국지역난방공사, 한국철도공사, 한국철도시설공단, 한국컨테이너부두공단, 한국토지공사, 한국환경자원공사, 한전기공(주), 행원채용, 환경관리공단

✚ 금융권 – 신입사원 채용

LG화재, SK생명, 광주은행, 교보생명보험(주), 국민은행, 기술신용보증기금, 기업은행, 농협중앙회, 대우캐피털, 동양화재, 새마을금고연합회, 수협은행, 수협중앙회, 신동아화재, 신한은행, 신한카드, 쌍용화재, 알리안츠생명, 우리은행, 제일화재, 푸르덴셜생명(주), 하나은행, 현대해상화재보험(주)

+ 언론사 – 기자, 아나운서, 직원 채용

기자, 아나운서, 직원 채용 - 경기방송, CBS, EBS, GTB(강원방송), KBS, MBC, PSB(부산방송), SBS, UBC(울산방송), YTN

기자, 직원 채용 - 경상일보, 대구매일신문, 동아일보, 매일신문, 부산일보, 서울경제신문, 연합뉴스, 영남일보, 전자신문, 조선일보, 중앙일보, 충청투데이, 파이낸셜 뉴스, 한국일보

직원 채용 - 한국방송위원회

+ 외국계 – 직원 평가, 신입사원 채용

직원 평가 - (주)스타벅스커피 코리아, AB코리아, ABB코리아, 토비스, 푸르덴셜생명보험, 한국썬마이크로 시스템즈, 한국하인즈, 한국화이자

신입사원 채용 - 마이크로소프트코리아(인턴), 소니코리아, 한국쓰리엠(주), 한국아스트라제네카

+ 정부 기관 – 직원 채용, 해외 파견, 해외 연수, 직원 평가 등

강원도 교육청, 건설공제조합, 경기도 교육청, 경기도청, 경남교육청, 광주시교육청, 교육인적자원부, 국립암센터, 국립의료원, 국방부, 국방품질관리소, 국세청, 국제교육진흥원, 국회사무처, 금융감독원, 금융결제원, 기술표준원, 농촌진흥청, 대구시교육청, 대전시교육청, 대통령경호실, 대한상공회의소, 대한적십자사, 대한체육회, 법무부, 법원행정처, 보건복지부, 부산시교육청, 부산시청, 산림청, 산재의료관리원, 서울대병원, 서울시교육청, 서울시청, 서울지방경찰청, 소방협회, 여성부, 외교통상부, 인천시교육청, 전남교육청, 전북교육청, 정보통신부, 중앙공무원교육원, 충남교육청, 충북교육청, 충북지방경찰청, 한국감정원, 한국산업은행, 한국원자력연구소, 한국은행, 한국전산원, 한국전자통신연구원, 해양경찰청, 행정자치부

Ⅰ Introduction to TEPS Reading

Unit 01   출제유형과 문제풀이 전략

Unit 02   TEPS 일반 독해 전략

Unit 01 출제유형과 문제풀이 전략

Part I-1 빈 칸 채우기(일반유형)

문항수	1번부터 16번까지의 16문항
지시문	Read the passage. Then choose the option that best completes the passage.
지문형식	1. 실용문: 공고문, 광고, 보고문, 편지 등 다양한 형식을 취한다.
	2. 교양 학술 지문: 경제, 사회, 인문, 과학, 의학 등의 다양한 주제를 다룬다.
	3. 빈 칸에 알맞은 표현과 연결어를 고르는 문제로 구성된다.
출제 경향	기존의 시험에서는 빈 칸 주변 문장을 집중적으로 분석하면 정답을 고를 확률이 높았으나 최근에 들어서는 빈 칸 주변 뿐 아니라 전체적인 내용의 흐름을 파악하고 있는지 확인하는 문제가 두드러지게 늘어나고 있다. 빈 칸의 위치는 서두, 중간, 말미 등 다양하지만, 지문 뒷부분에 오는 경우가 많다.

Tips

• 단어를 나열하는 단순 번역을 지양한다.
• 지엽적인 내용의 파악 자세를 버리고, 문장 간의 연계성과 흐름을 파악하는 연습을 한다.
• 직독 직해의 기술을 익혀, 영어 어순과 가능한 한 같은 순서로 글을 읽어 내려가는 연습을 한다. 특히 연결어 중에 but, however, and yet, though, in spite of 등 앞의 내용과 다른 내용이 연결되는 경우를 조심한다.

Sample Question

Doctors say they are seeing more sports injuries in younger children simply due to too much physical strain. More injuries such as stress fractures and tendon problems are now treated in athletes as young as four years old. Doctors say that year-round, high-impact sports overuse developing bones. Doctors also place blame on parents and coaches who put too much pressure on physical performance and often don't allow children _____.

(a) the chance to physically prove themselves

(b) adequate time to recover from injuries

(c) enough opportunities to participate in sports

(d) rewards for their improved performance

Part I-2 빈 칸 채우기(연결어)

문항수   Part I의 마지막 두 문항, 15번과 16번이 이에 해당한다.

지문형식   1번에서 14번 문제와 유사하다.

출제 경향   지문 내용에 가장 적합한 접속사, 접속 부사 등의 연결어를 고르는 문제이다.

> **Tips**
>
> Trigger Words를 이해하고 연습해야한다. 예를 들어, "He's handsome, **but** he's...."에서 but 다음에 이어지는 내용은 앞에 나온 내용과 다른 내용이 나온다. 여기서 handsome은 긍정적인 내용이므로 but 다음에는 부정적인 내용이 와야 한다. 예를 들어, mean, rude, impolite 등과 같이 부정적인 내용이 담긴 내용으로 이어지는 것이 자연스럽다.
>
> 앞 내용의 흐름이 달라지거나 반대 내용이 이어질 때 사용하는 표현:
>
> | | | | | |
> |---|---|---|---|---|
> | but | however | although | even though | in spite of   despite |
> | on the contrary | in contrast | rather | yet | |
>
> 위의 예문에서 한 단어만 바꾸어도, 즉 but을 and로 바꾸면 다음에 이어지는 내용이 완전히 달라져야 한다. "He's handsome, **and** he's ..."에서 and는 앞에 나온 내용에 부연하거나 내용이 계속 이어질 때 사용하므로, and 뒤에는 긍정적인 내용 즉, kind, generous, polite 등이 와야 한다.

■□ Sample Question

Researchers are examining whether a new computer game can help adolescents fight cancer. The game features a character that wages war on cancer and teaches facts about the disease and how to fight it. One study on the results of the game suggests that it encourages those with cancer to tackle the challenges of fighting off the disease more hopefully. _____, they noticed an increase in the desire to take medication in an effort to recover.

(a) Similarly

(b) Additionally

(c) Unfortunately

(d) Ideally

Part II-1 주제 파악

지시문   Read the passage and the question. Then choose the option that best answers the question.

주제파악 문제 질문유형

주로 17번부터 23번까지이며, 다른 영역에 비해 비교적 난이도가 높지 않다. 영어 독해 실력을 향상하기 위해서는 필수적으로 알아야 할 문제유형이므로, 관련 문제를 통해 연습을 많이 하도록 한다.

대표적 질문예시

What is the passage mainly about?

What is the purpose of the passage?

What is the main idea of the passage?

What would be the best title of the passage?

Which of the following best summarizes the passage?

Tips

• 이런 것이 오답이다!

본문에 나온 어휘, 표현들을 이용하여 선택지를 만드는 경우가 많다. 따라서 본문에 나오는 표현을 그대로 사용하는 것은 오답일 확률이 높다. 특히 선택지의 내용이 지엽적인 경우가 오답의 함정으로 많이 나온다.

• 이런 것이 정답이다!

Paraphrasing이 중요하다. 본문의 내용을 다른 단어나, 표현으로 paraphrasing한 경우 정답일 확률이 높다.

 ## Sample Question

Characters in novels can generally be categorized as one of two different kinds. A dynamic character is someone that adapts and changes. It is important to note, however, that a dynamic character does not always make positive changes; backward movement can also occur. A static character, on the other hand, is a person in a novel that remains consistent and experiences little or no change in perception, morals, or personality.

Q **What is the passage mainly about?**

(a) The two different types of fiction

(b) The changes of dynamics in a novel

(c) The static categories of characters in a novel

(d) The kinds of characters in a novel

Part Ⅱ-2 세부사항 파악하기

문항수　주로 24번부터 34번까지

세부사항 파악 문제 질문유형

Which (of the following) is correct according to the passage?

Which (of the following) is NOT correct according to the passage?

Who is Linda Sue Park?

What's the matter with the man?

출제 경향　지문 내용은 Part Ⅰ과 비슷하다.

질문, 지문, 보기를 꼼꼼히 읽어야 정답을 고를 수 있다.

다른 유형의 문제들보다 문제 푸는 시간이 더 오래 걸린다.

Tips

- 문제 푸는 순서를 정한다.
- 연습을 할 때 세부사항을 파악하는데 유독 시간이 많이 든다고 생각하면, 시간이 적게 걸리는 뒤에 있는 문제를 먼저 푸는 것도 시험을 치르는 효과적인 방법이 될 수 있다. 단, 이 때 뛰어넘고 푸는 경우 번호를 혼동하지 않는 세심함이 필요하다.
- 오답 선택지의 특성 중에는 문장 안에 일부는 맞고, 일부는 틀린 내용을 제시하는 경우가 많다.

Sample Question

The toys and games of children reflect the experience and values of the times. When I was a young boy, my friends and I played soldier games. Our fathers' experiences in fighting a world war were reenacted in our play. My sisters and other little girls played with dolls and cooking toys, mimicking the real-life activities of their mothers. But now, as a father myself, I see that the times have changed.

Q What is the next paragraph likely to be about?

(a) The effects of playing with guns or dolls

(b) The toys and games of the author's children

(c) Similarities between past and present toys

(d) Internet-based games of the future

Part II-3 추론문제

문항수   주로 35번부터 37번까지

추론 문제 질문유형

What can be inferred from the passage?

What is the tone of the passage?

What can best describe the author's attitude toward the lecture?

출제 경향   지문 뒤에 따라올 내용, 글의 어조, 저자의 태도 등 지문 전체의 이해를 묻거나 본문 내용을 바탕으로 추론하는 능력을 측정하는 문제이다. 특히 지문에 나오는 어휘나 표현으로 오답을 만드는 경우가 많다.

Tips

추론(inferring)은 문제 유형 중 가장 고난이도의 문제에 속한다. 지문의 주제와 세부사항 모두 파악해야 하기 때문이다. 초급 수험자들은 처음부터 너무 많은 시간을 투자하지 말고, 어렵더라도 꾸준히 기본 실력을 향상하면 맞힐 수 있다는 여유있는 마음을 갖고 점차 학습 시간을 늘려나가자. 추론에서는, 논리적으로 무리한 내용은 오답일 확률이 높다.

◼◻ Sample Question

The U.S. Census Bureau published a profile of the United States population at the close of the 20th Century. The report noted that 30% of the nation's foreign-born population lived in the state of California in 1999, for example. Much of the information revealed how Americans lived. Among other things, the study showed that nearly three-fifths of American men age 18-24 lived with their parents or in a college dormitory. Yet more than half of the women of that age lived independently.

Q **What can be inferred from the passage?**

(a) Less than 1/2 of 18-to-24-year-old women lived with their parents.

(b) More young men than women attended colleges in America.

(c) The U.S. Census Bureau published a book titled At the Close of the 20th Century.

(d) The percentage of foreigners living in California is increasing.

Part III 내용의 일관성 파악

문항수   38번부터 40번까지 3개 문항

지시문   Read the passage. Then identify the option that does NOT belong.

내용의 일관성 파악 출제 경향

첫 문장이 주어지고 4개의 선택 문장이 이어진다. 이 선택 문장 중 글의 흐름에 어울리지 않는 문장을 찾는 문제이다. 많은 경우, 첫 번째 문장은 주제문인 경우가 많으므로, 글에서 전달하고자 하는 대의를 먼저 잘 파악하도록 한다.

Tips

항상 다음 질문을 선택지마다 해본다.

질문1   나머지 보기들과 비교하여 내용이 상반되지는 않는가?

질문2   앞 뒤 문장과 논리적인 결함이 있지는 않은가?

질문3   전체적인 주제와 일관성이 있는가?

Sample Question

There are things that can be done to "cure" the problem of being messy. The first step is recognizing the problem. (a) Another lesson is that cleanliness makes life much easier. (b) Following this, messy individuals must refrain from adding to the clutter. (c) However, this will not eliminate the problem, only control it. (d) The final thing that must be done is to sort through the piles of needless junk and to maintain the organization.

Unit 02 TEPS 일반 독해 전략

A 객관식 문제를 풀 때 어떤 것을 유념해야 하나요?

TEPS는 요령이 통하지 않는 시험이다. 사실이기는 하지만, 객관식 시험(multiple choices)이기 때문에 객관식 시험문제를 푸는 요령이 도움이 되기는 한다. 가장 일반적인 조언 몇 가지를 소개한다.

1. Keep in mind that the answers come from the passage.

모든 문제의 답은 지문에 나와 있거나, 지문에서 고를 수 있거나 추론할 수 있다. 따라서 지문을 유의해서 읽어야 한다.

2. Remember that every word counts.

사람, 사물, 사건을 묘사하는 어휘들에 유의하라. 예를 들면, 어떤 사람을 묘사할 때 "with a beautiful smile" or "scarred"라고 한다면, 독자에게 그 인물에 대한 다른 내용을 전달하기 위해서 사용하는 표현들이니 놓치지 않도록 한다.

3. Read the questions and answers carefully.

1. 질문의 내용이 무엇인가?
2. 질문에 답을 찾기 위해 필요한 정보가 있는 부분을 다시 읽어본다.
3. 찾아낸 정보를 질문의 답을 찾는데 어떻게 이용할지 다시 생각해본다.

4. Try to eliminate incorrect choices.

선택지와 지문을 비교하면 확실하게 오답인 것들이 나온다. 이런 선택지를 먼저 제거하면, 정답을 고를 수 있는 확률이 높아진다.

5. Don't be misled by an answer that looks correct but is not supported by the actual text.

선택지 중 정답처럼 보인다 하더라도, 본문에 충실하지 않으면 오답이다.

6. Make sure that the reading passage supports your answer.

고른 답이 지문에 있는 내용과 일치하는지 확인해야 한다. 추론문제의 경우에도, 행간의 의미를 파악해야 하지만, 그것이 답이라면 지문에 그것을 뒷받침하는 내용이 반드시 있다.

7. Double-check the other choices.

답을 고른 다음, 빨리 다른 선택지들도 다시 한 번 더 읽어보면서, 더 나은 답이 있지는 않은지 확인해보도록 한다.

8. A key word in the question may be the clue you need to arrive at the best answer. Pay attention to the words that carry the meaning of the sentences.

주제를 찾거나 대의를 찾는 문제의 경우 핵심어(key word)를 찾는 것이 정답을 고르는데 도움이 된다. 핵심어 찾는 것은 독해의 기본이기도 하니 평소에 문제를 풀 때마다 연습할 것을 권한다.

9. Correct errors when you practice, even if you are asked only to identify the error.

이 조언은 문법 문제를 풀 때도 도움이 된다. 하지만 독해의 경우 역시 틀린 답이 왜 틀렸는지 확인하는 습관을 평소에 키워두는 것이 좋다. 독해 문제를 풀 때, 오답이 왜 오답인지 확인하는 것은 실전에서 문제의 함정을 찾아내는데 도움이 된다.

10. Pronouns should always clearly refer back to a word or phrase.

독해를 할 때 대명사가 나오면 항상 명확하게 그것이 받는 단어나 구 또는 문장이 무엇인지 확인하는 습관을 키운다.

11. Use your background knowledge.

배경 지식이 없는 지문을 접하고 당황할 필요가 없다. TEPS는 상식 실력을 측정하는 시험이 아니다. 하지만 평소에 다양한 형식과 내용의 글을 통해 연습을 한 경우, 주어진 지문을 이해하는데 큰 도움이 된다. 특히 TEPS에서 자주 나오는 주제들의 경우 관심을 갖고 꾸준히 읽는 것이 중요하다.

12. Mark questions in your test booklet that you've skipped so you can go back to them later.

빼 놓고 푼 문제를 표시했다가 다시 나중에 풀 수 있도록 한다. 사람마다 어렵게 여겨지고, 특히 점수가 잘 안 나오는 부분이 다르지만, Part II의 세부사항을 파악하는 문제는 전반적으로 시간을 많이 요하고, 정확성을 요하기 때문에 초급 수준에서는 문제 푸는 순서를 바꾸어서 뒤를 먼저 풀고 이 부분에 돌아오는 것도 한 가지 방법이다. 이 때 건너 뛴 부분은 잘 표시해두자.

B 시간이 절대적으로 부족해요!

TEPS 시험을 치루고 나온 대부분의 수험생들이 공통적으로 보이는 반응이다. 처음으로 시험을 치루거나, 영어가 아직 일정 수준에 도달하지 못한 경우 독해문제의 뒷부분은 읽어볼 시간이 없어서 답만 표시했다고 안타까움을 호소하는 사람들을 쉽게 접할 수 있다. TEPS의 출제 원칙 중 속도화 시험(Speeded Test)은 일반 수험자가 가장 피부로 느끼는 어려운 부분 중에 하나이다. 어떻게 하면, 절대적으로 부족한 시간에 가능한 한 정확하게 답을 고를 수 있을까? 먼저 각 Part 유형에 익숙해져야하고 유형별 특징 및 소요시간을 체크한 후, 45분 동안의 시간 계획을 수립하고 본인에게 쉽고 시간이 적게 걸리는 문제부터 푸는 것이 좋다. 이렇게 해나가면 시험 볼 때마다 풀지 못하는 문항의 수가 점점 줄어들 것이다.

C TEPS 독해에서는 무엇을 확인하나요?

모든 시험에서 고득점을 받으려면, 시험의 특성을 파악하고, 출제자의 의도를 파악하는 것이 중요하다. 수험생으로서가 아니라 출제자 입장에서 문제를 파악하고, 이해하는 습관을 초급에서부터 갖는다면, 더 빠른 시일에 고득점 고지에 오를 수 있다.

출제자들이 출제할 때 염두에 두는 몇 가지는 아래와 같다.

1. 속독을 요하는 문제이다.

총 40문제를 45분에 풀어야 하는데, 1지문 1문항으로 되어 있기 때문에 1문항 당 평균적으로 1분 이내에 풀어야 한다. 따라서 시간 조절(pacing)이 고득점의 관건이다. TEPS 출제 원칙 중 속도화 시험(Speeded Test)은 문법 및 어휘 시험에서 뿐만 아니라 독해에서도 잠재적인 의사소통능력(Acquisition)을 확인하기 위함이며 암기한 언어학적 지식(Learning)에만 의존하는 수험자는 고득점을 내지 못하도록 출제하고 있다.

2. 지문 형식과 내용이 다양하다.

공고, 광고, 보고, 편지 등 지문의 형식이 다양하다. 경제, 인문, 사회, 과학, 의학 등 다루는 분야가 다양하여 풍부한 어휘 실력을 가진 사람에게 유리하다. TEPS의 출제 원칙 중 통합식 시험(Integrative Test)을 구현하기 위하여, 실제적인 상황과 문맥 파악을 중시하는 문제를 통해 수험자의 폭넓은 어학 능력을 평가한다. 1지문 1문항의 원칙은 특정 한 지문을 이해하지 못해서 여러 개의 문항을 연이어 틀리는 일이 없도록 하기 위함이며 TEPS 출제 원칙 중 국부 독립성(Local Independence)을 구현하기 위함이다. 첨단 테스트 기술인 문항 반응 이론(IRT: Item Response Theory)을 활용하여 각 문항의 독립성을 보장하고 있다.

3. 문제 유형이 정해져 있다.

문제 유형에 따라 정답을 찾는 방법도 달라질 수 있으므로 먼저 유형을 숙지한다.

Part I

1- 14번 빈 칸 채우기 (일반유형)
문맥에 맞는 내용을 선택지 중 골라서 빈 칸을 채우는 형식이다.
지문의 대의 뿐 아니라 빈 칸 앞뒤의 문맥의 흐름을 이해하고 있는지 확인하는 문제이다.

15 - 16번 빈 칸 채우기 (연결어 찾기)
빈 칸 앞뒤 문장을 가장 잘 연결하는 연결어, 즉 접속사 또는 접속 부사의 올바른 활용을 확인하는 문제이다. 연결어의 용법도 중요하지만, 빈 칸을 중심으로 문장의 흐름을 파악하는 것이 중요한 문제이다.

Part II

17 – 23번   주제 파악하기

지문의 요지, 제목, 주제 등을 찾는, 대의를 파악하는 문제이다. 저자의 태도, 지문의 논조, 다음에 이어질 내용 등을 확인하는 문제이다.

24 – 37번   세부사항 파악하기 및 추론하기

세부 특정 정보를 묻는 문제, 본문 내용과 (불)일치하는 내용을 찾는 문제, 추론하는 문제, 선택지를 찾는 문제로 나눌 수 있다. 추론하는 문제는 지문 전체 내용의 파악 뿐만 아니라 세부사항까지 파악하고 있어야 정확한 답을 고를 수 있으므로, 가장 난이도가 높다고 할 수 있다.

Part III

38 – 40번   글 흐름에 어울리지 않는 문장 찾기

첫 문장이 나오고 그 뒤에 4개 문장 (a), (b), (c), (d)가 제시된다.
전체적인 내용의 흐름과 어울리지 않는 문장을 고르는 문제이다.

II Understanding the Structures in TEPS Reading

Unit **01**   분사 구문

Unit **02**   비교 구문

Unit **03**   병렬 구문

Unit **04**   도치 구문

Unit **05**   강조 구문

Unit **06**   가정 구문

Unit **07**   원인, 결과, 목적을 나타내는 구문

Unit **08**   수동태 구문

Unit 01   분사 구문〔Reduced Structure〕

독해를 어렵게 만드는 구문 중에 대표적인 것이 바로 생략절에 속하는 분사구문이다. 특히 초급자에게 어렵게 느껴지기도 하지만, 매 시험마다 빠지지 않고 나올 뿐 아니라, 거의 모든 유형의 시험에서 빠지지 않고 출제되는 문제이니만큼 정확하게 이해해둘 필요가 있다.

● 분사 구문 만드는 순서

1. 접속사 확인!

a. 일반적으로 접속사를 생략한다.

b. 강조하고 싶으면 쓴다.

While I was walking down the street, I happened to meet an old friend.

→While walking down the street, I happened to meet an old friend.

→Walking down the street, I happened to meet an old friend.

> **Tips**
>
> • 접속사를 강조하고 싶으면 남겨둔다.
> • 생략된 접속사가 무엇인지 찾아내는 것은 독해에 큰 도움이 된다.
>
> **이유**: as, because, since
> She doesn't eat meat because she is a vegetarian.
> She doesn't eat meat, being a vegetarian.
>
> **시간**: when, while,
> When he was lying on the bed, he remembered to call his boss.
> →Lying on the bed, he remembered to call his boss.
>
> **양보**: though
> Though he was tired, he continued to work.
> →Tired, he continued to work.

2. 주어 확인!

a. 주절과 주어가 같으면 생략한다.

b. 주절과 주어가 다르면 그대로 둔다.

While I was reading a book, the phone rang.

→While I reading a book, the phone rang. (correct)

→While reading a book, the phone rang. (Incorrect)

종속절의 주어는 I, 주절의 주어는 the phone으로 주어가 서로 다르기 때문에 분사구문에 주어를 밝혀야 한다.

As it was very cold, I didn't go out.
→ It being very cold, I didn't go out. (correct)
→ Being very cold, I didn't go out. (incorrect)

종속절의 주어는 it, 주절의 주어는 I로 주어가 서로 다르기 때문에 분사구문에 주어를 써야 한다. 특히 날씨를 나타내는 비인칭 주어 it는 특별히 따로 해석이 되지 않아 틀리기 쉬우니 유념한다.

3. 동사시제 확인!

a. 주절과 같은 시제이면 『동사원형 + ing』
b. 주절과 다른 시제이면 『Having + p.p.』

After he finished his homework, he watched TV.
→ Finishing his homework, he watched TV.

As he had finished his homework, he watched TV.
→ Having finished his homework, he watched TV.

> **Tips**
>
> 분사구문의 being은 자주 생략된다.
>
> Because he was unable to afford a brand new car, he bought a second hand car.
> → (Being) unable to afford a brand new car, he bought a second hand car.
>
> When she was left alone, she started sobbing.
> → (Being) left alone, she started sobbing.

A Read and match.

1. _____ Having eaten Chinese food for lunch, I don't want to eat it again.
2. _____ Having eaten Chinese food for lunch, I didn't want to eat it again.
3. _____ Satisfied with the result, they had a big party.
4. _____ The weather being fine, we had lunch in the garden.
5. _____ While he was trying to sleep last night, a mosquito kept buzzing in his ear.

a. As they were satisfied with the result, they had a big party.
b. As the weather was fine, we had lunch in the garden.
c. While he was trying to sleep last night, a mosquito kept buzzing in his ear.
d. Because I ate Chinese food for lunch, I don't want to eat it again.
e. Because I had eaten Chinese food for lunch, I didn't want to eat it again.

B Fill in the blanks. Use the word given in the parenthesis.

1. (realize) _____ that I had made a mistake, I apologized to him.
2. (not, know) _____ what to do next, I asked for his advice.
3. (spend) _____ all his paycheck, he does not have any money to live on.
4. (watch) _____ the movie before, I do not want to see it again.
5. (ask) _____ to give a speech, I suddenly felt nervous.

C Change the following into reduced sentences and translate into Korean.

1. Since he got a new job, he has been working very hard.

   _____

2. While she was driving to the office, Joan had an accident.

   _____

3. Before he left for work, he had a big breakfast.

   _____

4. Because he had never flown in an airplane, he felt a little nervous.

   _____

5. As I didn't know what to do, I asked him for some advice.

   _____

Unit 02 비교 구문(Comparative Structure)

비교할 때 정도(degree)에 따라 원급, 비교급, 최상급의 3가지 형태를 사용한다.

	길이가 짧은 형용사/부사	2음절 이상의 긴 형용사/부사
원급	**as ~ as** as old as	**as ~ as** as intelligent as
비교급	**-er than** older than	**more ~ / less ~ than** more intelligent than
최상급	**the -est** the oldest	**the most / least ~** the most intelligent

ex

Sue is 10 years old. Ann is 15 years old. Bill is 15 years old. John is 17 years old.

Ann is **as** old **as** Bill.
Sue is young**er than** Ann.
Sue is **the** young**est** of all.
John is two years old**er than** Bill.
John is **the** old**est** of all.

A 원급(Equative)

형용사, 부사의 원급형태와 함께 as ~ as 구문으로 만들어 사용한다.

This house is big.
That building is big.
This house is **as** big **as** that building.

B 비교급(Comparative)

2개의 대상을 비교할 때 사용한다.
비교를 할 때는 비교의 대상이 같아야 한다는 것에 유의한다.

California is small**er than** Texas, but it has **more** people **than** Texas.
=Texas is larg**er than** California, but it has few**er** people **than** California does.

The population of California is larg**er than** Texas. (incorrect)

→The population of California is larg**er than** that of Texas. (correct)

C   최상급(superlative)

최상급을 사용할 때는 누구 또는 어떤 것과 비교해서 최상급인지를 나타내야 한다. 따라서 최상급은 그 다음에 주로 in / of 또는 that절이 따라온다.

최상급

This house is the biggest **in** this area.

This is the biggest **of** all the houses in my neighborhood.

This house is the biggest **that** I have ever seen.

불규칙 형태

원급	비교급	최상급
good	better	best
bad	worse	worst
much / many	more	most
little	less	least
far	farther	farthest
	further	furthest

최상급 구문 : 최상급, 비교급, 원급 등을 사용하여 최상급을 만드는 방법을 확인해두자.

에베레스트 산이 이 세상에서 가장 높다는 표현은;

Mt. Everest is the highest mountain in the world.
Mt. Everest is higher than any other mountain in the world.
No other mountain in the world is higher than Mt. Everest.
No other mountain in the world is as high as Mt. Everest.

Oops!

These shoes are very good, but those are very better. (incorrect)
These shoes are very good. but those are much better. (correct)

much even still + 비교급 (by) far a lot	*ex.* It's much better.
very + 원급	*ex.* It's very good.

A Complete the sentences with the correct forms of the words in parentheses.

1. The Amazon is one of _____ rivers in the world. (long)
2. The Yangze River is _____ the Mississippi River. (long)
3. Ms. White is _____ person I have ever met. (patient)
4. Janet is as _____ as her sister. (thoughtful)
5. Frank is _____ than his colleagues. (intelligent)

B Correct the errors.

1. This cake is sweeter I have ever eaten.
2. Mike is the taller person in his family.
3. Bill's understanding of computers is better than me.
4. Winter in Alaska is cold than it is in Pittsburgh; winter there is the coldest in the States.
5. Her car is as fast mine.
6. Asia is largest continent in the world.
7. The blue whale is the bigger animal in the world.
8. Cats are more independent as dogs, but dogs are loyal than cats.
9. This is very good. But that is very better.
10. The most important part of the exam was given at the end when most people were the most exhausted.

C Put the words in order and translate into Korean.

1. than her / his dog better / he likes

   _____

2. the most prestigious club / in Korea / this is

   _____

3. of the two / the taller / he's

   _____

4. much more comfortable / this chair is / than that one.

   _____

5. doesn't know / everything / the wisest man

   _____

Unit 03 병렬 구문 (Parallel Structure)

영어는 한 문장 내에서 일정 구조의 균형을 맞추기 위해 병렬구조(Parallel Structure)를 사용한다. 등위 접속사(Coordinate Conjunctions)와 상관접속사(Paired Conjunctions)의 올바른 활용에 유의해야 병렬구조를 잘 이해할 수 있다.

A 등위 접속사의 병렬구조

등위 접속사에는 and, but, or가 있다. 등위 접속사를 사용할 때 명사, 동사, 형용사, 부사, 구, 절을 같은 구조로 연결해야 한다.

I admire him for his intelligence **and** passion.
He is short **but** fast.
You can go there by bus **or** by train.

등위 접속사를 중심으로 같은 형태를 사용한다.

B 상관 접속사의 병렬 구조

상관 접속사에는 not only A but also B / both A and B / either A or B / neither A nor B 등이 있다. 상관 접속사 사이에 들어가는 형태도 병렬 구조를 사용해야 한다.

Not only you **but also** she was at the party.
This book is **both** interesting **and** informative.
The meeting will be held **either** on Monday **or** on Wednesday.
Neither his parents **nor** he knows her.

1. 상관접속사에서 not only는 but also와, both는 and와 함께 쓰여야 하는 것처럼 상관접속사는 각각의 짝을 갖고 있다. 이렇게 각각의 짝을 맞추어 올바른 형태의 상관 접속사를 사용하도록 주의해야 한다.
2. 상관접속사를 사용할 때도 명사, 동사, 형용사, 부사, 구, 절을 같은 구조로 연결하는 병렬 구조를 사용해야 한다.

Oops!

1. 다음 예문은 병렬 구조를 사용하고 있지 않아서 틀린 문장이다.

I want either to play soccer or basketball. (incorrect)

either와 or 사이에 to play soccer와 basketball이 병렬 구조를 갖고 있지 않기 때문에 틀린 문장이다.

이 문장의 올바른 형태는 다음과 같다.

I want either to play soccer or to play basketball.

I want to play either soccer or basketball.

2. 다음 예문은 상관 접속사를 잘못 사용하여서 틀린 문장이다.

Neither he or his brother works for this company. (incorrect)

I know not only him as well as her. (incorrect)

이 문장의 올바른 형태는 다음과 같다.

Neither he nor his brother works for this company.

I know not only him but also her.

Practice Test

정답 및 해설 p.7

A Complete the sentences with the correct forms of the words in parentheses.

1. Amy (make)_____ her bed and (clean)_____ up her room every morning.
2. Yesterday I (be)_____ sick and (stay)_____ home.
3. Ms. Benson is cooking dinner and (talk)_____ on the phone.
4. Laura will stay home and (read)_____ her favorite magazine tonight.
5. My new neighbor, Mr. Gray is both (kindness)_____ and (friend)_____.
6. _____ Bill or his friends know her new address.
7. Sue enjoys (swim)_____ and (play)_____ tennis.
8. My cousin, Bill is (intelligence)_____ and (humor)_____.
9. The pasta in this restaurant is (expensively)_____ but (deliciously)_____.
10. My brother usually (ride)_____ his bike to school in the morning, but it (rain)_____ when he left the house this morning, so he (take)_____ the bus.

B Correct the errors.

1. She will either visit nor call you this afternoon.
2. The novel is both interesting as well as instructive.
3. The moon has neither air or water.
4. Dining in a restaurant is more fun than to eat at home alone.
5. This country's music is quite different from my country.

C Put the words in order and translate into English.

1. than mine / is a lot more useful / her research for the thesis

_____

2. nor in his pocket / the keys are / neither on the table

_____

3. in what he says / I'm not interested /or what he does

_____

4. and because he wants to help you / because it's his job / he is helping you

_____

5. he called not only the police department / but also the fire department / when the accident happened,

_____

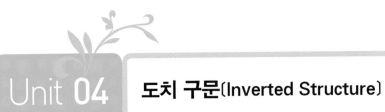

Unit 04 도치 구문 (Inverted Structure)

영어는 기본적으로 주어 + 동사의 어순을 갖는다.

영어 문장 기본 5형식 모두 주어 + 동사의 어순을 취한다.

1형식: 주어 + 동사

    I   went there.

2형식: 주어 + 동사 + 보어

    I   am happy.

3형식: 주어 + 동사 + 목적어

    I love my family.

4형식: 주어 + 동사 + 간접목적어 + 직접목적어

    I bought him   a present.

5형식: 주어 + 동사 + 목적어 + 목적격 보어

    It makes me   happy.

하지만 다음의 경우에는 동사 + 주어의 어순으로 도치된다.

A   의문문의 경우

Was he late?

Why **was he** late?

> **Tips**
>
> 간접 의문문에서는 의문사 + 주어 + 동사의 어순으로 된다는 것에 유의!
>
> I don't + know if he was late.
>   의문사+주어+동사
>
> I don't know why he was late.
>   의문사+주어+동사

B (장소)부사구가 문장 앞에 올 경우

Down came the rain.

Here comes the waiter.

On the table were the keys that I thought I had lost.

> **Tips**
>
> Here he comes.
> Here you are.
>
> 주어가 대명사일 때는 (장소)부사구가 문두에 있더라도 도치되지 않는다.

C 부정어가 문장 앞에 올 경우

Never did I dream that he would fail.

Only once has he met her before.

He will not attend the meeting, nor will his boss.

부정어휘

no	not	never	neither	nor
hardly	scarcely	barely	seldom	only

> **Tips**
>
> Only가 문두에 오면 '~할 때만 그렇고 나머지는 안 그렇다'는 의미가 되기 때문에 부정어처럼 그 다음에 도치 구문이 온다.

D if가 생략된 경우

Were it not for your help, he couldn't succeed.

(=If it were not for your help, he couldn't succeed.)

Had he tried harder, he could have passed the exam.

(=If he had tried harder, he could have passed the exam.)

if가 생략되면 동사 + 주어로 도치되어야 한다!

Practice Test

1. The lawyer asked the client when did he first meet her. (   )
2. Do you know where he lives? (   )
3. In the top drawer are the socks that you are looking for. (   )
4. Around the corner is the store you are trying to find. (   )
5. Hardly his assistant has made such a mistake. (   )
6. Little did I dream that he would lie to me. (   )
7. On no occasion did their parents yell at him. (   )
8. Should you ever visit my place again, I would be happy to show you around. (   )
9. If had he taken your advice, he would have passed the exam. (   )
10. Were he in a position to help, he would help you. (   )

1. Seldom he has tried hard to do his best.
2. Out the sun came after the rain.
3. Who did help the poor man?
4. I don't know how long will it take to get this done.
5. If were I in your shoes, I wouldn't take the offer.

1. I'm not certain where he stays now.

   _____

2. No sooner had he left than she arrived.

   _____

3. Had he known, he would have told you.

   _____

4. There is a lot of traffic on the street now.

   _____

5. At that Mexican restaurant the food was too spicy for his taste.

   _____

Unit 05 강조 구문〔Emphasized Structure〕

A It ~ that 강조 구문

강조하고 싶은 부분을 It ~ that 사이에 넣는다.

I met her here yesterday.
① ② ③ ④

① It was **I**　　　　 that • met her here yesterday.
② It was **her**　　　 that I met • here yesterday.
③ It was **here**　　 that I met her • yesterday.
④ It was **yesterday** that I met her here • .

B 일반 동사 강조

일반 동사를 강조할 때 do / does / did를 사용한다.
I did understand it.
He does love his family.

> **Tips**
>
> 조동사 do / does / did 다음에는 동사원형이 온다.

C 도치 강조

〈부사(구) + 동사 + 주어〉의 형식으로 도치하여 강조한다.
Nowhere was he so happy as he was in Florida.
Only then did I understand what he was trying to tell me.
In front of his house were several tall trees.

Practice Test

A Underline the emphasized part.

1. Never has he traveled abroad; he doesn't enjoy exotic food that much.
2. I did recognize her face, but I had forgotten her name.
3. It was how you said it, not what you said that made her upset.
4. It was he that knew the secret.
5. At the end of the hall were many students waiting for their teacher.

B Emphasize the underlined part.

1. I <u>understand</u> what you mean.
2. We do not know the importance of our health <u>until we lose it</u>.
3. I have met her <u>only once</u>.
4. The rain came <u>down</u>.
5. I saw her <u>at the park</u> this afternoon.

C Translate the following into Korean.

1. It was during the meal that they started to argue.

   _____

2. It was her, not her husband, that I met this morning.

   _____

3. It is passion that helps you to be a professional.

   _____

4. It is this coming Thursday that we will have the next meeting.

   _____

5. Rarely does he praise his staff.

   _____

Unit 06   가정 구문 (Conditionals)

가정법의 기본 규칙 및 그 다양한 주요 활용법을 이해해야 한다. 가정법을 이해하고 사용하기 위해서는, 특히 동사의 시제에 유의한다. If절에 사용하는 동사시제와, 주절의 동사시제를 잘 이해하고 기억하도록 한다.

A   가정법 기본 형태

사용되는 경우	If절	주절	예문
현재, 미래를 가정	현재시제	will + 동사원형	If I have time tonight, I'll visit you.
현재사실에 반대	과거시제	would + 동사원형	If I had time now, I would visit you.
과거사실에 반대	과거완료 시제	would + have p.p.	If I had had time, I would have visited you yesterday.

B   가정법 현재, 미래

현재나 미래 시제에 사실을 단순 가정할 때는 if절 동사는 현재 시제를 사용한다.

ex

If it is hot tomorrow, I will go swimming.
If anyone calls, please take a message for me.
If he knows the answer, he will tell you.

다음 두 문장을 비교해서 이해해보자.

If it rains tomorrow, I will stay at home.
비가 올지 안 올지 모르는 상황으로 단순 가정이다.
비가 올 수도 있고, 안 올 수도 있는 상황이다.

If it should rain tomorrow, I will stay at home.
If절에 should가 있는 경우는 불확실한 내용을 가정할 때 사용한다.
예를 들면, (밤 하늘에 별이 총총한 것을 보니, 내일 비가 올 것 같지는 않지만, 그래도) 혹시 비가 온다면, 집에 있겠다는 내용이다.

C   가정법 과거

현재 시제의 반대 사실을 가정한다. if절의 동사 시제는 과거시제이다. 특히 be동사는 단수, 복수 상관없이 항상 were를 사용한다. 격식을 덜 갖춘 informal speech에서는 was가 단수에 사용되기도 한다.

가정법 과거와 직설법의 비교

If I were with you now, I would be happy.
=As I am not with you now, I am not happy.
=I wish I were with you now.
=I am sorry I am not with you now.

'내가 당신과 지금 함께 있다면, 행복할텐데.'라는 가정은 '내가 지금 당신과 함께 있지 않아서, 행복하지 않다.'는 의미이다. 따라서 현재 사실의 반대를 가정하는 가정법 과거는 직설법 현재 시제로 고쳐야 맞다.

ex

If I were you, I would marry her.
If he were here now, she would be happy.
If we had no air, no one could live.
If he knew the answer, he would tell you.

> **Tips**
>
> **가정법 과거 공식**
>
> If + 주어 + 동사 과거시제, 주어 + 조동사 과거 + 동사원형
> be 동사의 경우 가정법 과거에서는 was를 사용하지 않고 were를 쓴다.

D   가정법 과거완료

과거사실의 반대 사실을 가정한다.
if절의 동사시제는 had + p.p.로 과거완료 형태를 사용한다.

가정법 과거완료와 직설법의 비교

If he had told me about the problem, I could have helped him.
=As he didn't tell me about the problem, I couldn't help him.
=I wish he had told me about the problem.
=I am sorry he didn't tell me about the problem.

'그가 내게 그 문제에 대해 이야기 했다면, 내가 그를 도와줄 수 있었을텐데.'라는 가정은 '그가 내게 그 문제에 대해 이야기를 하지 않았기 때문에, 내가 그를 도와줄 수 없었다.'라는 의미이다. 따라서 과거 사실의 반대를 의미하는 가정법 과거완료는 직설법 과거 시제로 고칠 수 있다.

ex

If he had known the answer, he would have told you.

If they had studied harder, they would have succeeded.

If the weather had been nice yesterday, I would have taken a walk in the park.

> **Tips**
>
> **가정법 과거완료 공식**
>
> If + 주어 + had + p.p., 주어 + 조동사 과거 + have p.p.

E 혼합 가정

TEPS 독해에서 자주 볼 수 있는 또 하나의 가정법 구문은 혼합 가정의 형태이다. 아래 예문에서 보듯이, 직설법 시제 자체가 주절과 종속절에 차이가 있는 경우이다.

직설법: It rained last night, so the road is very muddy now.

가정법: If it had not rained last night, the road wouldn't be so muddy now.

직설법: He is not a hard worker, therefore, he didn't do his best on his presentation yesterday.

가정법: If he were a hard worker, he would have done his best on his presentation yesterday.

F If 생략 구문

도치 구문에서 이미 다룬 것처럼 If가 생략된 경우가 TEPS에 자주 등장하는데, 이 때 주어와 동사의 도치가 이뤄진다.

ex

Should it rain tomorrow, I will stay at home.

=If it should rain tomorrow, I will stay at home.

Did he know the answer, he would tell you.

(=If he knew the answer, he would tell you.)

Had he known the answer, he would have told you.
(=If he had known the answer, he would have told you.)

G   if를 사용하지 않은 가정 구문

I wish you had come.
=If you had come, I would have been happy.

I **would** have been with you, but I had to finish the report.
=If I hadn't had to finish the report, I would have been with you.

I hurried; **otherwise**, I would have missed the train.
=If I had not hurried, I would have missed the train.

Without your advice, I wouldn't have made it.
=If I had not had your advice, I wouldn't have made it.

One more mistake and she would have failed the exam.
=If she had made one more mistake, she would have failed the exam.

To hear him talk, you would take him for an American.
=If you heard him talk, you would take him for an American.

He treats me **as if** I were a child.
=I am not a child.

• 정답 및 해설 p.12

A   Read and match.

1. _____ He would have gotten the job,
2. _____ If there should be a global nuclear war,
3. _____ If I were you,
4. _____ If you leave right now,
5. _____ If he had had dinner,

a. I would tell him the truth.
b. you will catch the bus.
c. if he had been better prepared.
d. he wouldn't be hungry now.
e. the world would end forever.

B   Correct the errors.

1. If he were at home last night, I would have visited him.
2. If I had realized its importance at that time, I would work out regularly.
3. If he put the leftovers in the refrigerator yesterday, the food would be fresh now.
4. Unless he were not sick, he would join us.
5. I wish I will help you.

C   Put the words in order and translate into Korean.

1. the present for you / if she had had enough money / she would have bought

   _____

2. the present for you / if she had enough money / she would buy

   _____

3. I had / extra time / I wish

   _____

4. extra money / I had had / I wish

   _____

5. will fail / or you / work harder

   _____

Unit 07 원인, 결과, 목적을 나타내는 구문 (Cause / Effect / Purpose)

문맥의 흐름과 문장과 문장의 연계성을 중요시하는 TEPS에서 자주 사용되는 구문이다. 생긴 모습이 비슷하여 자주 혼동되는 so ~ that ~ may 구문과, so that ~ may 구문과 더불어서, 원인, 결과를 나타내는 다양한 구문과 목적을 나타내는 대표 구문들을 정리해두자.

A 원인, 결과를 나타내는 구문(Expressing Cause-Effect Relations)

1. so ~ that

The weather was **so** hot **that** you could fry an egg on the sidewalk.

> **Tips**
>
> so + 형용사 / 부사 + that can[may] ~
> 너무 ~(형용사 / 부사)해서 ~할 수 있다

2. such ~ that

It was **such** a hot day **that** we couldn't play outside after lunch.

> **Tips**
>
> such + (a/an) 형용사 + 명사 + that절
> 의미는 so... that 구문과 같으나, such ... that 사이에 명사가 온다는 것이 차이점이다.

3. too ~ to

It's **too** good **to** be true.
=It is so good that it can't be true.

> **Tips**
>
> too ~ to 용법에서는 따로 부정어 not를 쓰지 않는다.

4. enough ~ to

He has **enough** money **to** buy a new house.
=He has so much money that he can buy a new house.

He is rich **enough to** buy a new house.
=He is so rich that he can buy a new house.

enough 구문은 어순에 유의한다.
- enough + 명사
- 형용사 / 부사 + enough

5. therefore

He studied very hard, **therefore**, he passed the exam.

접속 부사 therefore는 문장의 여러 곳에 위치할 수 있다.
It rained heavily. Therefore, I stayed at home.
It rained heavily. I, therefore, stayed at home.
It rained heavily. I stayed at home, therefore.

6. so

She didn't study hard, **so** she failed the exam.

7. because

Because he wanted to pass the exam, he tried hard.

because는 접속사이므로 그 다음에 '주어 + 동사'를 가진 절(clause)이 와야 한다.
because of는 전치사구이므로 그 다음에 명사 상당 어구가 와야 한다.

Because of the heavy rain, I stayed at home.
Because it rained heavily, I stayed at home.

8. due to

Due to the foggy weather, the flight to Ulsan has been canceled.

B 목적을 나타내는 구문(Expressing Purposes)

1. so that may~

He saved what he earned **so that** he **might** travel around the world.

> **Tips**
>
> 목적을 나타내는 so that may ~와 결과의 so ~ that may를 혼동하지 않도록 유의한다.

2. so as to / in order to

He is taking the summer course **so as to** get his degree ASAP.

Practice Test

A Read and match.

1. _____ Lucy was such a funny person
2. _____ Ms. Benson doesn't feel well,
3. _____ Since Sarah has poor eyesight,
4. _____ I had so little money
5. _____ The waitress kept forgetting the orders,

a. so she's going to see a doctor.
b. that I couldn't afford to buy a new car.
c. that she was very popular.
d. therefore, she was fired.
e. she has to sit in the front row.

B Choose the correct one.

1. I am happy (because / because of) you came back safely.
2. I was exhausted (because / because of) the hard work.
3. The soup is (too / very) hot to eat.
4. I felt (such / so) embarrassed that I couldn't speak in front of the audience.
5. It was (such / so) a fresh orange that he wanted to have another.

C Translate the following into Korean.

1. The weather was so cold that I wore a coat and gloves.

   _____

2. The final exam was so difficult that few students got high scores.

   _____

3. It was such an easy test that most of them passed it.

   _____

4. He works really hard so that his family may live in comfort.

   _____

5. He works so hard lest he should fail the test.

   _____

Unit 08 수동태 구문(Passive Structure)

● **수동태 구문 만드는 순서**

1. 능동 구문의 목적어를 수동 구문의 주어로!
2. 능동 구문의 동사를 수동 구문에서 be + p.p.로!
3. 능동 구문의 주어를 수동 구문에서 by + 목적격으로!

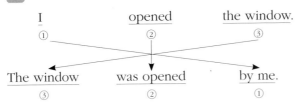

A 3형식 문장

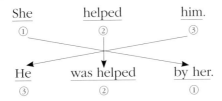

B 4형식 문장

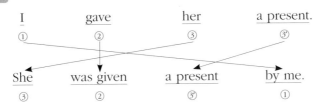

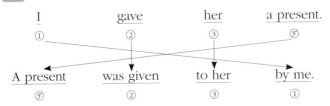

4형식 문형을 수동태로 바꾸었을 때 유의해야 할 사항:

직접 목적어가 수동태 구문의 주어로 앞으로 나가면, 간접 목적어 앞에 to, for 또는 of를 써야한다.

I bought her a present.
I bought a present for her.

• to를 사용하는 동사:
send, buy, give, tell 등

• for를 사용하는 동사:
make, buy, get, cook, sing 등

• of를 사용하는 동사:
ask

C   5형식 문장

ex

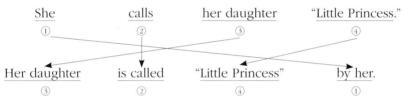

Tips

5형식 문형을 수동태로 바꾸었을 때 유의해야 할 사항:

사역동사(make, have, let)나 지각동사(hear, see)의 경우 to부정사를 써야 한다.

He made her do the job.
→She was made to do the job by him.

He saw her dance.
→She was seen to dance by him.

D　일반 주어인 문장

일반인이 주어인 문장을 수동태 구문으로 전환하면, 수동태 구문에서는 by 이하를 주로 생략한다.

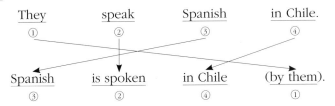

> **Tips**
>
> **수동태를 사용할 수 없는 동사!!**
>
> An accident happened. (correct)
> An accident was happended. (incorrect)
>
> 자동사(intransitive verb)는 수동태 구문을 만들 수 없다.
> 즉, 목적어가 없는 다음과 같은 동사는 수동태 구문을 만들 수 없다.
>
> | | | | | |
> |---|---|---|---|---|
> | appear | arrive | come | die | go |
> | happen | laugh | live | occur | rise |
> | sleep | stand | walk | | |

A Fill in the blanks.

1. He writes a letter to his mom every day. → A letter _____ by him to his mom every day.
2. He wrote a letter. → A letter _____ by him.
3. He has written a letter. → A letter _____ by him.
4. He is writing a letter. → A letter _____ by him.
5. He was writing a letter. → A letter _____ by him.
6. He will write a letter. → A letter _____ by him.
7. Did he write a letter? → _____ a letter _____ by him?
8. Is he writing a letter? → _____ a letter _____ by him?

B Read and match.

1. _____ She made her children some cookies.
2. _____ I saw her entering the room.
3. _____ Shakespeare wrote a lot of plays.
4. _____ The mice ate the cheese.
5. _____ Everybody knows Bill Gates.

a. The cheese was eaten by the mice.
b. She was seen entering the room.
c. Some cookies were made by her for her children.
d. A lot of plays were written by Shakespeare.
e. Bill Gates is known to everybody.

C Put them in order and translate into Korean.

1. in Brazil / grown /coffee / is

   _____

2. both English / in Canada / they speak / and French

   _____

3. is / by his company / a man / known

   _____

4. by Marie and Pierre Curie / was discovered / radium

   _____

5. in 1987 / was built / that building

   _____

III Building Up Vocabulary for TEPS Reading

Unit 01   관련 있는 내용끼리 묶어서 익히기

Unit 02   주제별 어휘 익히기

Unit 03   연어 익히기

Unit 04   어휘 형성 규칙 이해하기

Unit 05   문맥 속에서 품사 이해하기

Unit 06   합성어 익히기

Unit 07   동사구 익히기

Unit 08   혼동하기 쉬운 어휘

■ 다른 사람이 글로 쓰거나 말로 하는 어휘를 이해하는 것은 수동적인 어휘 습득 단계에
머물러 있다고 할 수 있다. 그렇다면 내가 원하는 표현을, 필요한 시기에 적절히 사용
할 수 있는 능동적인 어휘 습득 단계에 이르려면 어떻게 해야 할까?

■ 능동적인 어휘 습득 단계에 이르는 것은 시간이 걸리는 과정이다. 그렇다면 어떻게 하
면 좀 더 빠른 시간에, 더 많은 어휘를 효과적으로 습득하고, 일단 습득한 어휘를 영구
히 내 것으로 만들 수 있을까? 다음 장에서 몇 가지 효과적인 어휘 습득 방법을 제시한다.

Unit 01 관련 있는 내용끼리 묶어서 익히기
(Categorizing Related Words)

단어 하나하나를 우리말 뜻과 대응해서 외우는 것은 모래알로 집을 지으려는 것에 비유할 수 있다. '아! 이 단어 뜻이 뭐더라?', '이 단어 본 적이 있는데.', '아이 참! 이 단어 지난주에 공부했던 것인데.' 등은 학생들이 자주 하는 말이다. 그렇다. 외운다고 능사는 아니다. 외워서 나의 어휘 창고에 잘 정리를 해두어야 한다. 그래야 나중에 필요할 때 다시 꺼내서 사용할 수 있을테니까.

보다 효율적인 단어 습득 방법으로는 주제별(topic-based)로 하거나, 특정 상황과 연계된 경우, 그 상황이 전개되는 것을 따라가면서 각각의 단계에서 필요한 단어를 확인하는 것이 좋은 어휘 습득 방법이라 할 수 있다. 예를 들어 재판(trial=case)에 관련된 단어들이 좋은 본보기가 될 수 있다. 오래 전이기는 하지만 예를 들어 유명했던 O. J. Simpson 살인 사건(O.J. Simpson Murder Case=O.J. Simpson Trial)과 관련된 기사, 보고 등을 신문, 잡지, 라디오, TV 등에서 쉽게 자주 접할 수 있었다. 재판과 관련하여 사용될 수 있는 단어들을 정리해본다. 재판과 관련된 어휘들을 익힐 때는 일의 순서를 생각하면서 익히면 나중에 다시 사용해야할 때 훨씬 기억하기 편리하다.

고소하다 ⇒ 기소하다 ⇒ ~에게 유죄를 선고하다 ⇒ 판결하다
 accuse   indict   convict   sentence

● 재판 과정(trial procedures)

1. **accuse** 고발(고소)하다, ~에게 죄를 추궁하다

If you **accuse** someone of doing something wrong or dishonest, you say or tell them that you believe that they did it.

2. **indict** 기소(고발)하다

If someone is **indicted** for a crime, they are officially charged with it.

3. **convict** ~에게 유죄를 입증(선고)하다

If someone is **convicted** of a crime, they are found guilty of that crime in a law court.

4. **sentence** 선고하다, 판결하다, ~형에 처하다

In a law court, a **sentence** is the punishment that a person receives.

5. **death penalty** 사형
capital punishment 사형
lethal injection; 치사 주사《사형 집행 방법으로서》

6. **life imprisonment** 종신형
life without parole: 가석방 없는 종신형

7. **judge** 재판관, 법관, 판사
The trial **judge** specified the number of years to be spent in prison.

8. **plaintiff** 원고, 고소인
The amount of damages awarded to the **plaintiff** will be decided by the judge, not the jury.

9. **prosecutor** 원고 측 검사, 검찰관
A **prosecutor** is a lawyer or official who brings charges against someone or tries to prove in a trial that the person is guilty.

10. **defendant** 피고
We found the defendant not guilty.

11. **attorney** 피고 측 변호인 *cf.* lawyer 변호사

12. **jury** 배심원

주제별 어휘 익히기(Topic-Based Vocabulary)

1지문 1문항의 원칙이기 때문에 다루는 주제가 다른 어떤 시험보다도 다양하다. 따라서 어휘를 암기할 때 처음부터 주제별(topic-based)로 빈출 어휘들을 정리해두면 용이하다. 특히 Practice Test에서 하는 것처럼 한글을 써 놓고 영어로 정확한 철자를 쓸 수 있어야 제대로 익혔다 할 수 있겠다.

주제별로 어휘를 정리할 때는 vocabulary tree를 만들어 보는 것도 좋은 방법이다. 주제를 정하여 그곳에 열매가 달린 것처럼 단어를 정리해보거나, idea web처럼 다양한 형태를 갖고 자신의 어휘 창고를 쌓아가기를 권한다.

경제(Economy)

gross 총계의	infrastructure 산업 기반	consumer 소비자
lavish 낭비하는	frugal 절약하는	expenditure 경비, 지출
retail 소매의	wholesale 도매의	auction 경매
bid 입찰하다	revenue 세입	budget 예산, 운영비
creditor 채권자	debtor 채무자	expire 계약 만기되다
deficit 적자	surplus 잉여 자금	default 계약을 이행하지 않다.
fiscal 회계의	brisk 경기가 활기를 띤	sluggish 경기가 부진한
recession 경기 후퇴, 불경기	stable 경기가 안정된	plummet 물가가 폭락하다
soar (물가 등이) 급등하다	fluctuate 변동하다	stagnation (경기) 침체

금융(Finance)

fake 위조품	endorse 수표에 이서하다	bounce 수표가 부도나서 되돌아오다
deposit 예금하다	withdraw 인출하다	balance 잔고
stockholder 주주	dividend 배당금	delinquent 체납되어 있는
benefit 수당, 혜택	beneficiary 수령인	pension 연금
bond 채권	securities 유가 증권	coverage 보험의 보상범위

비즈니스(Business)

subsidiary 자회사	board 이사회	executive 임원, 간부
corporation 법인	incorporated 법인의	entrepreneur 기업가
revenues (회사) 총수입	asset 자산	capital 자본금
bankruptcy 파산	audit 회계 감사	liquidate (빚을) 청산하다

법률(Law)

amend 법률 등을 개정하다	breach 법률 등의 위반	infringement 위반, 침해

enact 법률을 제정하다
culprit 범죄자
conspiracy 음모
file (고소 등을) 제기하다
plea 탄원
probation 집행유예
regulate 규제하다
verdict (배심원) 평결
legislature 입법부

outlaw 불법화하다
fraud 사기(꾼)
embezzle 횡령하다
indict 기소하다
forfeit 권리를 상실하다
parole 가석방
reform 개혁하다
conservative 보수적인
judiciary 사법부

felon 중죄인
homicide 살인(죄)
custody 구금
sue 고소하다
bail 보석금
libel 명예 훼손
evidence 증거
constitution 헌법
administration 행정부

건강(Health)

sanitary 위생상의
nourish 영양분을 공급하다
contagious 전염성의
chronic 만성의
diabetes 당뇨병
heal 치료하다
malnutrition 영양실조
prescription 처방전
dose 복용량

respiratory 호흡기의
symptom 증상
epidemic 전염병의
acute 급성의
tumor 종양
remedy 치료하다
cholesterol 콜레스테롤
transplant 이식하다
over-the-counter drug 처방전 없이 구입할 수 있는 약

fracture 골절
infection 감염
immune 면역성의
ailment 질병
pneumonia 폐렴
therapy 치료(법)
nutrition 영양
pain-reliever 진통제

과학(Science)

molecule 분자
solid 고체(의)
element 요소
artificial 인공의
experiment 실험
phenomenon 현상
biology 생물학
geology 지질학
clone 복제하다

atom 원자
metal 금속
substance 물질
observe 관찰하다
hypothesis 가설
chemistry 화학
botany 식물학
gene 유전자
embryo 배아

liquid 액체(의)
synthetic 합성의
compound 화합물
analyze 분석하다
theory 이론
physics 물리학
zoology 동물학
stem cell 줄기 세포
inheritance 유전

환경(Environment)

habitat 서식지
species 종(種)
deplete 고갈시키다
contaminate 오염시키다

conserve 보존하다
atmosphere 대기
overuse 과용하다
emit 방출하다

preserve 보존하다
ozone-layer 오존층
dispose of ~을 처분하다
deforest 삼림을 벌채하다

• 정답 및 해설 p.15

A Translate the following into English.

경제(Economy)

1. 총계의	2. 소비자
3. 낭비하는	4. 절약하는
5. 입찰하다	6. 예산, 운영비
7. 계약 만기되다	8. 적자
9. 회계의	10. 불경기
11. (물가 등이) 급등하다	12. 세입
13. 변동하다	14. 경기 침체
15. 경기가 안정된	16. 물가가 폭락하다
17. 잉여자금	18. 경기가 부진한

금융(Finance)

1. 예금하다	2. 인출하다
3. 주주	4. 배당금
5. 수령인	6. 연금
7. 채권	8. 유가증권
9. 체납되이 있는	10. 보험의 보산범위

비즈니스(Business)

1. 자회사	2. 이사회
3. 법인의	4. (회사) 총수입
5. 자산	6. 자본금
7. 파산	8. (빚을) 청산하다

B Translate the following into English.

법률(Law)

1. 법률 등을 개정하다	2. 법률 등의 위반 b
3. 위반, 침해 i	4. 법률 등을 제정하다
5. 불법화하다	6. 음모
7. 횡령하다	8. 명예 훼손 l

9. (고소 등을) 제기하다	f		10. 기소하다	i	
11. 고소하다	s		12. 탄원		
13. 권리를 상실하다			14. 규제하다		
15. 개혁하다			16. 증거		
17. 보수적인			18. 헌법		
19. 입법부			20. 사법부		

건강(Health)

1. 위생상의			2. 호흡기의		
3. 증상			4. 감염		
5. 전염성의	c		6. 전염병의	e	
7. 면역성의			8. 급성의		
9. 질병	a		10. 종양		
11. 치료하다	r		12. 치료하다	h	
13. 처방전			14. 이식하다		
15. 복용량			16. 영양		

과학(Science)

1. 분자			2. 원자		
3. 합성의			4. 물질	s	
5. 화합물	c		6. 인공의		
7. 분석하다			8. 가설		
9. 현상			10. 식물학		
11. 동물학			12. 유전자		
13. 줄기 세포			14. 복제하다		
15. 배아			16. 유전		

환경(Environment)

1. 서식지			2. 종(種)		
3. 고갈시키다			4. 오존층		
5. 과용하다			6. ~을 처분하다		
7. 오염시키다			8. 방출하다	e	

Unit 03 연어 익히기 (Collocations)

사람만 궁합이 잘 맞는 짝이 있는 것이 아니다. 예를 들어 file이라는 단어와 함께 자주 사용되는 동사들을 살펴보자.

create a file	파일을 만들다
save a file	파일을 저장하다
attach a file	파일을 첨부하다
send a file	파일을 보내다
receive a file	파일을 받다
open a file	파일을 열다
delete a file	파일을 삭제하다

이처럼 한 단어를 중심으로 일어날 수 있는 상황을 생각하면서, 특히 자주 사용되는 common expressions 중심으로 익혀나가는 것이 도움이 된다. collocation의 대표적인 경우를 소개한다.

동사	+	명사	make a mistake 실수하다
형용사	+	명사	acute disease 급성질환
부사	+	동사	study hard 열심히 공부하다
부사	+	형용사	badly hurt 심하게 다친

● Example Collocations

heavy traffic 극심한 교통량

heavy burden 과중한 부담

heavy rain 폭우

a wide range of 광범위의

wide shoulders (책임을 지는) 어깨

strong coffee 진한 커피

strong accent 강한 억양

a soft voice 감미로운 목소리

a soft drink 청량음료

make a mistake 실수하다

make a promise 약속하다

make up one's mind 결심하다

do the dishes 설거지하다

do one's best 최선을 다하다

take a shower 샤워하다

take a nap 낮잠자다

take turns 번갈아 하다

catch a cold 감기에 걸리다

catch one's breath 헐떡이다, 한숨쉬다

catch the bus 버스를 잡아타다

miss the bus 버스를 놓치다

miss a call 전화소리를 못듣다

miss a class 수업에 빠지다

tell a joke 농담하다

tell a story 이야기하다

tell the truth 진실을 말하다

tell the difference 차이점을 분간하다

Example Sentences

I usually do the dishes at home. 나는 대개 집에서 설거지를 한다.

I'll give you a lift to airport. 공항까지 태워줄게요.

I have made an effort to gain weight. 나는 체중을 늘리려고 노력해왔다.

Harry is the only son of the family. 해리는 그 집안의 외아들이다.

I need a cup of water badly. 물 한잔을 꼭 마시고 싶어요.

Unit 04   어휘 형성 규칙 이해하기(Word Formation)

단어가 어떻게 형성이 되는지를 어원과 함께 접두어, 접미어를 이용하여 품사를 다양하게 익히는 것도 어휘를 손쉽게 익힐 수 있도록 도와준다.

A   접두어(Prefixes)

'부정'의 의미를 갖는 접두어: im-, in-, un-, ir-, il-, dis-

possible	**im**possible	polite	**im**polite	patient	**im**patient
convenient	**in**convenient	correct	**in**correct	visible	**in**visible
happy	**un**happy	stable	**un**stable	employed	**un**employed
regular	**ir**regular	responsible	**ir**responsible		
legal	**il**legal	legible	**il**legible		
agree	**dis**agree	honest	**dis**honest		

'지나침'을 의미하는 접두어: over-

He went to bed late and **over**slept this morning.
I think the cashier **over**charged me.

'다시'를 의미하는 접두어: re-

This is not right. I'm afraid you'll have to **re**do it.
He failed the exam, but he can **re**take it next month.

B   명사 접미어(Noun Suffixes)

-ation	inform**ation**	organiz**ation**	hesit**ation**	
-ment	develop**ment**	manage**ment**	arrange**ment**	employ**ment**
-ion	discuss**ion**	elect**ion**	act**ion**	
-ness	weak**ness**	happi**ness**		
-ity	creativ**ity**	curios**ity**	original**ity**	similar**ity**	punctual**ity**
-al	tri**al**	arriv**al**	deni**al**	approv**al**

C 형용사 접미어(Adjective Suffixes)

-able	washable	reliable	comfortable	
-ible	flexible	sensible	comprehensible	
-ful	painful	thoughtful	helpful	useful
-less	painless	mindless	useless	homeless
-ous	dangerous	glorious	famous	
-cal	musical	biological	historical	

Practice Test

A   Write the antonyms.

1.   employed _____   2. stable _____
3.   honest _____   4. regular _____
5.   agree _____   6. visible _____
7.   convenient _____   8. correct _____
9.   possible _____   10. patient _____

B   Change the words into their noun forms.

1.   elect _____   2. arrive _____
3.   employ _____   4. develop _____
5.   original _____   6. arrange _____
7.   deny _____   8. inform _____
9.   punctual _____   10. discuss _____

C   Change the words into their adjective forms.

1.   pain _____   2. thought _____
3.   home _____   4. danger _____
5.   biology _____   6. flex _____
7.   sense _____   8. comfort _____
9.   fame _____   10. comprehend _____

Unit 05 문맥 속에서 품사 이해하기 (Vocabulary in Context)

단어의 품사를 이해하는 것이 독해에 왜 중요한가?

주어진 시간 내에 빨리 내용을 이해하기 위해서 여러 가지 연습을 하는데, 그 중에서도 각 문장에서 동사를 찾아서 표시하는 것이 독해에 상당한 도움을 준다. 주절의 동사와 종속절의 동사를 구별하여 문장의 깊이를 파악하고, 동사를 제대로 찾아내면, 주어를 찾는 일이 한결 수월해지기 때문에, 동사를 찾는 활동은 독해를 향상시키는 기본 활동 중 하나로 자주 사용된다. 이와 같은 활동을 하기 위해서 각 단어의 품사를 이해하는 것이 중요하다. 동사와 명사 형태가 다를 경우(*ex.* appoint / appointment)는 크게 문제가 되지 않지만, 동사와 명사가 같은 형태일 경우(*ex.* n. promise / v. promise) 이를 구별하는 것을 어려워하는 경우가 종종 있다.

같은 형태의 단어가 문맥 속에서 다른 품사로 사용될 때가 자주 있다. 아래에 대표적인 것들을 소개한다.

● **Same Form: Noun or verb?**

I gave the **answer**.
나는 답을 했다.

Please **answer** the phone.
전화를 받아줘요.

I took a short **rest**.
난 잠시 쉬었다.

I **rested** for a while.
나는 잠시 동안 쉬었다.

I'll give him a **call** later.
나중에 그에게 전화할 것이다.

I'll **call** you later.
나중에 전화할게.

I had **dream** about her.
난 그녀 꿈을 꾸었다.

I **dreamed** about her.
난 그녀 꿈을 꾸었다.

You have a beautiful **smile**.
당신은 미소가 아름답네요.

He **smiled** at me.
그는 나를 보고 미소를 지었다.

This has a sweet **taste**.
이것은 단맛이 난다.

This **tastes** sweet.
이것은 단맛이 난다.

I read the **book**.
난 그 책을 읽었다.

I've **booked** a flight.
난 비행기표를 예약했다.

He gave a **rose** to her.
그는 그녀에게 장미를 주었다.

The sun **rose** at 6:00 this morning.
태양이 오늘 아침 6시에 떠올랐다.

Unit 06 합성어 익히기(Compound Words)

독립적인 두 단어가 합해서 하나의 새로운 단어를 형성하는 경우 합성어(compound words)라고 한다. 일상생활에서 쉽게 접할 수 있는 합성어를 정리해두면 편리하다.

A   두 단어로 쓰는 경우

mother tongue 모국어

stop sign 정지 표지판

personal computer 개인용 컴퓨터

post office 우체국

traffic jam 교통체증

coffee break 커피 브레이크, 휴식시간

dining room 식당

running shoes 운동화

movie star 영화배우

alarm clock 자명종

parking meter 주차 시간 자동 표시기

coffee shop 커피숍

credit card 신용카드

B   한 단어로 쓰는 경우

haircut 이발

toothpaste 치약

hairbrush 머리빗

raincoat 비옷

earring 귀걸이

bookshelf 책꽂이

bookstore 책방

sunglasses 선글라스

C   hyphen을 사용하는 경우

a five-star hotel 특급호텔

a ten-dollar bill 10달러짜리 지폐

a second-hand car 중고차

a good-looking boy 인물이 좋은 소년

mother-in-law 장모, 시어머니

well-made 잘 만들어진

left-handed 왼손잡이의 cf. right-handed 오른손잡이의

first-class 1등석의

part-time 파트타임, 단시간 근무제

Practice Test

• 정답 및 해설 p.16

A Fill in the blanks. Use the words given in the box.

| alarm clock | coffee shop | parking meter | credit card | movie star |

1. I parked the car next to the _____ , and inserted the correct change.
2. His _____ didn't go off this morning so he missed the train.
3. Let's meet at the _____ around the corner. They have great espresso.
4. Who is your favorite _____ ?
5. This _____ has expired.

B Fill in the blanks. Use the words given in the box.

| dining room | mother-in-law | running shoes | sunglasses | haircut |

1. I got a _____ yesterday.
2. These _____ are really comfortable. I always wear them when jogging.
3. Her _____ celebrated her 60th birthday.
4. They renovated the _____ . It looks great now.
5. He dropped his _____ and broke them.

C Fill in the blanks. Use the words given in the box.

| well-made | second-hand | left-handed | first-class | part-time |

1. I've got a _____ job; I work four hours a day on the weekends.
2. There are much more right-handed people than _____ .
3. He bought a _____ car, not a brand new one.
4. Look at those _____ shoes. They look gorgeous.
5. He purchased a _____ ticket to Rome.

Unit 07 동사구 익히기(Phrasal Verbs)

동사에 부사나 전치사 등이 결합한 형태를 동사구라고 한다. 독해에서 여러 단어와 함께 문장 속에서 섞여 있을 때, 정확하게 알고 있지 못하면, 전체 의미를 파악하는 것이 어려울 수 있기 때문에 빈출 동사구(frequently-used phrasal verbs)는 평소에 차분히 정리해서 익혀두는 것이 독해에 큰 도움이 된다.

자주 활용되는 동사구들

agree with ~와 동의하다

break down 고장 나다

call off 취소하다

cross out 삭제하다

drop out (학교)를 그만두다

fill out (서류)를 작성하다

give up 포기하다

hand in 제출하다

look forward to ~을 기대하다

participate in 참가하다

put on 옷을 입다

sign up (for) 등록하다

take advantage of 이용하다

think over 신중하게 생각하다

turn over 전복시키다

blow out (불을) 끄다

break up 헤어지다

call up 전화하다

drop in (on) (~에게) 잠시 들리다

figure out 이해하다

get over 회복하다

get through (with) (~을) 끝마치다

look into 조사하다

look over 자세히 살펴보다

pick up (차로) 데리러 가다, 들어올리다

run into 우연히 만나다

subscribe to ~을 구독하다

take off 옷을 벗다

turn down 기각 시키다

work out 일을 해결하다, 운동하다

Unit 08 혼동하기 쉬운 어휘(Confusing Words)

철자가 비슷해서 혼동이 되는 경우와, 뜻이 비슷해서 혼동이 되는 경우로 크게 나눌 수 있다. 어휘의 뜻에 따라 문장의 뜻이 크게 달라지므로 핵심 혼동 어휘를 숙지할 필요가 있다.

1. accept / except

accept: to take something that is offered
He **accepted** her apology.
그는 그녀의 사과를 받아들였다.
I **accepted** a lovely gift from my roommate.
나는 나의 룸메이트가 준 사랑스런 선물을 받았다.

except: to exclude someone or something
I like all kinds of fruit **except** kiwis.
난 키위를 제외한 모든 과일을 좋아한다.
The school rules apply to everyone **except** Principal Johnson.
학교 규율은 교장 존슨을 제외하고는 모두에게 적용된다.

2. access / excess

access: the way by which you can enter a building or reach a place
the right to see an official document, especially secret documents
Access to the papers is restricted to a few personnel.
그 서류에 접근할 수 있는 사람은 일부 인사부 사람들로 제한된다.

excess: additional and not wanted or needed because there's already enough of something
Cut any **excess** fat from the meat.
불필요한 지방을 고기에서 베어내라.

3. adapt / adopt

adapt: to change and to modify to fit in
to adjust to new conditions
He **adapts** quickly to a new environment.
그는 빨리 새로운 환경에 적응한다.

adopt: to become the parent of a child through legal proceedings
Mr. and Mrs. Smith decided to **adopt** another child.
스미스씨 부부는 아이 한 명을 더 입양하기로 결정했다.

4. advice / advise

advice: recommendations or suggestions provided to help someone
In times of trouble, I ask my mom for **advice**.
어려울 때면, 나는 어머님께 조언을 구한다.

advise: to give someone a particular kind of advice
He **advised** against hasty decisions.
그는 성급한 결정을 하지 말라고 조언했다.

5. affect / effect

affect: to influence someone or something
How did his decision **affect** his family?
그의 결정이 그의 가족에게 어떻게 영향을 미쳤는가?

effect: a result
The new medicine had an **effect** on his digestion.
새 약이 그의 소화능력에 영향을 미쳤다.

6. contend / content

contend: to argue or state that something is true
The researcher **contends** that they may reduce expenditures to make a profit.
그 연구원은 이익을 남기기 위해 비용을 절감해야할 거라고 주장한다.

content: happy and satisfied
I was **content** with the final product.
나는 결과물에 만족했다.

7. cost / price / fee

cost: is like price, but is used less for objects, and more for services or activities
The **cost** of living in the metropolitan cities is high.
대도시에서 생활비가 매우 많이 든다.

price: the amount of money for which something is bought, sold, or offered
Experts say that **prices** will rise gradually.
전문가들에 따르면 가격 상승이 점진적으로 이뤄질 것이라고 한다.

fee: the charge for professional services
Some lawyers charge exorbitant **fees**.
어떤 변호사들은 터무니없이 높은 수임료를 요구한다.

8. economic / economical

economic: connected with trade, industry, and the management of money
We are faced with an **economic** crisis.
우리는 경제 위기를 맞고 있다.

economical: using money, time, or goods carefully and without wasting anything
It is more **economical** to buy a packet of detergent that is twice the usual size.
보통 크기의 2배로 포장된 세제를 사는 것이 더 경제적이다.

9. expand / expend

expand: to become larger in size, number or amount
The population of the newly developing county **expanded** rapidly.
새로 개발되는 지역 인구가 빠르게 증가했다.

expend: to use time in order to do something
A great deal of time has been **expended** on creating the mind of recycling.
재활용 정신이 자리 잡는데, 많은 시간이 소비되었다.

10. hard / hardly

hard: not soft
The bread is very **hard**.
빵이 몹시 딱딱하다.

hard: unwillingly
Old habits die **hard**.
오랜 습관은 없애기 힘들다.

hardly: not easy

Because of his sore throat, he could **hardly** speak.

목이 너무 부어서, 그는 말을 거의 할 수 없었다.

11. high / highly

high: far above the ground, a peak

The books were on the **high** shelf, so he couldn't reach them.

책이 선반 위에 있어서, 그것들에 닿을 수 없었다.

The stock market reached a new **high** today.

주가가 오늘 최고치에 도달했다.

high: to or at a place that is far up

The bird flew **high**.

그 새는 높이 날았다.

highly: very, extremely

The play was **highly** entertaining.

그 연극은 매우 재미있었다.

12. imply / employ

imply: to suggest something,
    to indicate something without actually saying it

His smile **implied** something positive.

그의 미소는 긍정적인 의미를 내포했다.

employ: to hire someone to do work for pay,
    to use something for a particular purpose

He **employed** all the resources available to him.

그는 자신이 사용할 수 있는 모든 자원을 다 사용했다.

13. loose / lose

loose: not tight

Those pants are **loose** now. You must have lost some weight.

그 바지가 지금 헐렁하다. 당신은 체중이 줄었음에 틀림없다.

lose: to fail to keep someone or something in one's possession

Unless he tries harder, he will **lose** what he has now.

그가 더 열심히 노력하지 않으면, 그는 지금 갖고 있는 것들을 잃게 될 것이다.

14. promise / appointment

promise: a pledge to do something

I made a **promise** to take her to the mall.

(쇼핑)몰에 그녀를 데리고 가겠다고 약속을 했다.

appointment: an arranged meeting

choosing someone to fill a position or to take a job

I have an **appointment** with my client at 3:00.

오늘 3시에 고객과 약속이 있다.

The **appointment** of a good replacement is very important.

훌륭한 후임자를 임명하는 것은 매우 중요하다.

15. raise / rise

raise: to lift something

Raise your hand when you have a question.

질문이 있으면, 손을 들어라.

raise: an increase in one's salary

I asked my boss for a **raise**.

월급을 인상해달라고 사장님에게 요청했다.

rise: to become stronger, or to move upward

If the temperature is **rising**, you should take this medicine.

체온이 올라가면, 이 약을 먹어야 한다.

16. rent / borrow / lend / loan

rent: to pay money for the use of something for a short period of time

He doesn't earn enough to pay the **rent**.

그는 집세를 낼 돈도 못 벌고 있다.

borrow: to use something that belongs to someone else that you must give back to them later

May I **borrow** your pen?

펜 좀 빌려주시겠어요?

lend: to let someone borrow money from you or use something that you own, which they will give back to you later

Can you **lend** me $50 till Wednesday?

수요일까지 50달러 빌려줄 수 있어?

loan: an amount of money that you borrow from a bank, etc.

We're applying for a **loan**.

우리는 지금 대출을 신청하고 있다.

17. say / tell / speak / talk

say: in general, you say words to someone
cannot have a person as its object

I **said** hello to them.

나는 그들에게 인사했다.

I **said** that it was too much.

그것이 너무 과하다고 나는 말했다.

tell: can be followed by to infinitive.

She **told** him to do it.

그녀는 그에게 그것을 하라고 말했다.

speak: a little formal and often gives the idea that one person is saying more than any others in a conversation.

Could you **speak** a little louder, please?

좀 더 크게 말씀해주시겠어요?

I **spoke** to her this morning.

난 오늘 아침에 그녀와 이야기를 나누었다.

I don't **speak** a word of Chinese.

난 중국어는 한 마디도 못한다.

talk: is over twice as frequent in spoken English and usually suggests that two or more people are having a conversation.

They stayed up all night **talking**.

그들은 밤새워 이야기를 나누었다.

We're **talking** business.

우리는 사업이야기를 나누고 있다.

18. then / than

then: at that time
I don't remember what he was doing **then**.
나는 그가 그 때 무엇을 하고 있었는지 기억하지 못한다.

than: as compared with someone or something
My cousin, Bill, is younger **than** me.
내 사촌 빌은 나보다 어리다.

19. though / in spite of / despite

though: in spite of something
Though it rained heavily, he went out.
=**In spite of** the heavy rain, he went out.
=**Despite** the heavy rain, he went out.
though는 접속사이기 때문에 그 다음에 문장 형태의 절(clause)이 와야 한다.
in spite of / despite는 전치사이기 때문에 그 다음에 명사 상당어구(phrase)가 와야 한다.

20. while / during

while: during that time
While he was staying in Milan, he visited many beautiful places.
=**During** his stay in Milan, he visited many beautiful places.
while은 접속사이기 때문에 그 다음에 문장 형태의 절(clause)이 와야 한다.
during은 전치사이기 때문에 그 다음에 명사 상당어구(phrase)가 와야 한다.

IV Skills for TEPS Reading

Unit 01 대의 찾기

Unit 02 주요 내용을 패러프레이즈하기

Unit 03 세부 내용 파악하기

Unit 04 예측하기 & 추론하기

Unit 05 시각적 묘사

TEPS 뿐만 아니라 모든 공인시험의 독해 파트에서 고득점을 얻기 위해서는 각 시험의 유형을 잘 파악하고 그에 필요한 기술을 중점적으로 익히는 것도 중요하지만, 무엇보다도 독해의 기본을 익혀야 한다.

■ 독해를 잘하지 못하는 사람들의 특징은?
 지문의 목적을 잘 파악하지 못한다.
 독해를 하면서 지문의 구조를 잘 파악하지 못한다.
 독해를 하면서 지문을 구체적으로 시각화하거나 일목요연하게 잘 정리하지 못한다.
 독해를 하면서 예측하기, 추론하기를 잘하지 못한다.
 독해를 하면서 다른 생각을 잘하지 못한다.

■ 독해를 잘하는 사람의 특징은?
 독해를 하면서 주제에 대한 생각을 정리한다.
 독해를 하면서 주어진 실마리를 이용해서 다음에 어떤 내용이 이어질지 예측을 잘한다.
 독해를 하면서 사건과 내용의 순서를 파악한다.
 독해를 하면서 혼란스러운 부분을 명확하게 파악한다.

Unit 01 — 대의 찾기(Identifying the Main Ideas)

A 주요 개념, 주제, 핵심 어휘를 눈에 잘 띄도록 표시하라. (Mark the text while reading.)

1. 핵심어(key words)나 주제문(topic sentence)과 같이 중요한 부분을 표시한다. 밑줄을 긋거나, 동그라미를 치는 등 다양한 표시를 하는 습관을 기른다.

2. 노트 테이킹을 하면서 이미 알고 있는 내용과 새로운 자료를 연결하는 습관을 기른다.

Sample Question

The period of history known as the renaissance began in Italy around 1300 and lasted for about 300 years. The renaissance, which means rebirth, refers to a revival in art, culture, and education. During that time, the educated classes sought to bring back to life the classical cultures of Greece and Rome. Yet even though they looked towards the past, the leaders of the renaissance really set in motion the events of the future.

Q What is the main idea of the above paragraph?

(a) The renaissance lasted until around 1600.

(b) The word renaissance means rebirth.

(c) The renaissance was a revival of classical learning.

(d) The renaissance led to the world we live in today.

지문을 읽으면서, 계속 질문하라.(Question while reading.)

active reader가 되는 방법을 찾도록 한다. 주어진 지문을 우리말로 해석만 하는 passive reader 는 독해 실력을 높이는데 한계가 있다. 독해를 하면서 접하게 되는 생소한 어휘나 내용에 대해 질문 하는 습관을 갖도록 한다. 독해 중 떠오르는 질문들을 response notes에 적으면서 본문의 내용에 집중하도록 한다.

■ Sample Question

There are many reasons _____. For example, we must compare Country A's rate of inflation to the rate of its trading partner Country B. If Country A's inflation rate is higher than Country B's, then A's currency will "depreciate," or lose value. Interest rates are important as well. If Country A's interest rates are higher than other countries', currency depreciation is a real danger.

(a) a trading partner might get angry

(b) a country can easily control interest rates

(c) foreign currency is more valuable

(d) a country's currency can depreciate

Response Notes

'무역 상대국…'
'무역적자' '무역흑자'는 영어로 뭐라고 하지?
'화폐'와 '통화'는 정확하게 어떻게 차이가 있지?
interest rate 이자율
the rate of inflation /inflation rate 인플레이션율
depreciate 평가절하하다
'평가절상하다'는 영어로 뭐라고 하지?

C 전체 내용을 묻는 질문의 경우 정답을 고를 때 다음을 기억하라.

1. 지문에 언급되지 않은 것(Not Mentioned in the Passage)

모든 답은 지문 속에 있다. 독해에서 배경 지식이 중요하기는 하지만 TEPS나 다른 모든 공인시험에서 독해시험은 배경 지식이 없다고 답을 고르지 못하는 문제는 하나도 없다. 지문을 충실히 이해하도록 한다. 지문에서 언급되지 않은 내용은 오답일 확률이 높다.

2. 너무 지엽적인 것(Too Small)

선택지 내용이 본문에 충실하다고 하더라도, 질문이 전체 내용 파악을 확인하는 문제에서는 너무 지엽적인 것은 오답으로 처리한다.

3. 너무 광범위한 것(Too Big)

본문에서 다루고 있는 것보다 너무 확대해석을 한 선택지는 오답일 확률이 높다.

4. 너무 극단적인 것(Too Extreme)

너무 강하게 부정하거나, 강하게 긍정적인 내용을 강조하는 경우는 오답일 확률이 높다. 특히 all, never, every, always 등이 포함된 경우가 그렇다.

5. 상식에 어긋나는 것(Against Common Sense)

선택지 자체의 내용이 상식적으로 맞지 않을 때는 절대로 정답이 아니므로 가장 먼저 제거한다.

Unit 02

주요 내용을 패러프레이즈하기 (Paraphrase the Main Ideas)

A Paraphrase의 정의

독해에 관심을 갖고 공부를 해본 사람에게 paraphrase는 매우 익숙하고, 많이 들어본 표현일 것이다. 그 정의부터 확인해보자.

A **paraphrase** (from the Greek *paraphrasis*) is a statement or remark explained in other words or another way, so as to simplify or clarify its meaning. It can be used as a replacement for a direct quotation when the original text is unavailable or under copyright restriction. (http://en.wikipedia.org/wiki/Paraphrase)

그렇다. Paraphrase란 '글 속의 어구를 다른 말로 바꾸어서 알기 쉽게 풀이하는 것'을 의미한다. 독해에서 특히 학습자가 글을 읽고 이해를 했는지 확인하기에는 매우 좋은 방법이다. 학습자의 주어진 지문에 대한 이해도뿐 아니라, 학습자의 어휘 실력도 함께 파악할 수 있어 독해는 물론 청해 문제에서도 자주 인용되는 기법이다. 영어실력을 향상하기에 좋은 방법이니 시간과 노력이 걸리더라도 차분히, 꾸준히 연습하기를 강력히 권한다.

B Paraphrase의 특징

Paraphrase는 원문의 요약(summary)이 아니다. Paraphrase는 원문보다 독자에게 더 명확하게 전달되어 더 쉽게 이해되어질 수 있다. Paraphrase는 원문의 어휘나 표현을 그대로 사용하지 않고, 같은 의미의 다른 언어로 표현하는 경우가 많다. Paraphrase는 원문의 취지를 그대로 전달해야 한다.

ex

Immanuel Kant, one of the most influential philosophers of modern Europe, maintained the view that "existence" is obviously not a predicate.
근대 유럽의 가장 영향력 있는 철학자들 중 한 명인 임마누엘 칸트는 '현존재'는 명확하게 술어가 아니라고 주장했다.

위 문장을 다음과 같이 paraphrase 할 수 있다.

→One prominent scholar believed that "existence" is not a predicate.
한 저명한 학자는 '현존재'는 술어가 아니라고 믿었다.

C 동의어(Synonyms)

Paraphrase를 하기 위해 기본적으로 동의어를 많이 알고 있어야 다양하게 표현을 할 수 있다. 자주 인용되는 동의어를 소개한다.

accurate: precise 정확한

accelerate: speed up ~을 가속하다

adhere: stick 들러붙다

amoral: unethical 도덕성이 없는

arid: dry 마른, 습기가 없는

artificial: fake 인위적인

authority: expert 대가, 권위자

authentic: genuine 진정한, 진짜의

Bachelor's degree: college degree 학사

bliss: ecstasy 환희, 더 없는 행복

candor: honesty 솔직, 정직

choose: select ~을 고르다, 선택하다

coddle: baby 아기 같은 사람, 응석받이

collide: crash 충돌하다

complimentary: free 무료의

concise: brief, short 간결한

condone: excuse (죄)를 용서하다, 눈감아 주다

assess: evaluate ~을 평가하다

curriculum vitae: resume 이력서

dampen: moisten ~을 축축하게 하다, 축축해지다

lack: shortage 결핍, 부족

deceive: trick ~을 속이다

delicate: fragile 부서지기 쉬운, 가냘픈

deport: banish 추방하다

dignity: pride 자존감

air: broadcast 방송하다

dismal: bleak 황량한

decrease: decline 감소하다

docile: tame 다루기 쉬운, 유순한

donate: contribute 기부하다

duplicate: copy 복사

dwindle: shrink 줄다

enigmatic: mysterious 불가해한, 수수께끼 같은

examine: investigate ~을 조사[검토]하다

exhibit: display ~을 진열하다, 전시하다

fast: rapid 빠른

ferocity: fierceness 사나움

freight: cargo 화물

frequent: common 흔히 있는

hollow: empty 속이 텅 빈

hardy: strong 튼튼한

headstrong: stubborn 완고한, 고집불통의

herbivorous: plant-eating 초식의

homage: respect 존경, 경의

imminent: impending 임박한

imperious: arrogant 오만한, 거만한

improve: enhance 개선하다, 증진하다

increase: rise (수, 양 따위가) 증가하다

indecent: improper 그릇된, 음탕한

industry: diligence 근면, 부지런함

jubilee: festival 축제

keen: sharp 날카로운, 예리한

lament: grieve ~을 슬퍼하다

lodgings: accommodations 숙박설비

liberate: release ~을 자유롭게 하다, 해방하다

lethal: fatal 치명적인

main: major, principal 주된

massive: huge 거대한

mentor: counselor 조언자

metamorphosis: change 변형, 변화

murky: dark 캄캄한, 어두운

obscure: dubious 애매한

rebel: revolt 반란

ostentatious: flashy 과시하는, 허세부리는

paradox: contradiction 역설, 모순

particularly: especially 특히

peddle: sell 팔다, 장사하다

uneasiness: anxiety 불안, 걱정

piety: faith 신앙심, 경건

pompous: pretentious 젠체하는, 겉치레뿐인

proclaim: announce 공포하다, ~을 알리다

rational: logical 이성적인

recluse: hermit 은둔자

refreshments: food and drink (가벼운) 음식물, 다과

scarce: rare 희귀한, 드문

significant: crucial, vital 중요한

specific: detailed 명확한

spurn: reject ~을 받아들이지 않다

sympathy: understanding 공감

tenacious: determined 강인한, 결연한

terminate: end ~을 끝내다

tranquil: calm 조용한

transform: change 변형하다

violent: brutal 폭력적인

tumult: disorder 소란

synopsis: summary 개요, 개관

verify: confirm 확인하다

wanton: lustful 호색의

waive: give up ~을 포기하다

D   Paraphrase 연습하기

Paraphrasing – A restatement of a text or passage giving the meaning in another form for clearness; rewording.
패러프레이징이란 명확성을 위해 다른 형태나 어휘로 그 의미를 전달하는 것을 의미한다.

1. Factual Passage

Sometimes change falls out of our pockets while at home — pennies, nickels and quarters. You need to pay careful attention to what falls out of your pocket, especially pennies, if you are a pet owner. After 1982, pennies were minted with a copper coating and made with higher levels of zinc in the core compared to older ones. If your pet eats even one, its stomach acid will quickly dissolve the copper coating and levels of zinc will enter the animal's system. Eating a penny is enough to give a pet kidney failure.

가끔 집에 있을 때 주머니에서 동전 — 1센트짜리 페니, 5센트짜리 니켈, 25센트짜리 쿼터 등 — 이 떨어져 나올 때가 있다. 특히 페니가 떨어졌을 때, 집에 애완동물이 있다면, 조심할 필요가 있다. 1982년 이후, 페니는 구리로 코팅되어 주조되었고, 그 이전에 주조된 것들보다 속에는 아연이 더 많

이 들어있다. 만약 당신의 애완동물이 페니를 하나라고 삼키면, 위산이 빨리 구리 코팅을 녹이고, 아연이 몸에 흡수되게 될 것이다. 페니 하나만으로도 동물의 신장에 문제를 야기시킬 수 있다.

Paraphrase

→ Pet owners need to keep pennies away from their pets, especially those minted after 1982. These pennies contain zinc, which can be poisonous to your pet if eaten. 애완동물을 키우는 사람들은 동물들이 페니를, 특히 1982년 이후에 주조된 페니를 가까이 하지 못하게 해야 한다. 이 페니들에는 아연이 포함되어 있고, 이것이 몸에 들어가면 동물에게 독이 될 수 있다.

2. Factual Passage & a Cited Source

Of the more than 1000 bicycling deaths each year, three-fourths are caused by head injuries. Half of those killed are school-age children. One study concluded that wearing a bike helmet can reduce the risk of head injury by 85 percent. In an accident, a bike helmet absorbs the shock and cushions the head. From "Bike Helmets: Unused Lifesavers," Consumer Reports(May 1990)
해마다 1000명 이상이 자전거를 타다가 사고를 당하는데, 이들 중 3/4이 머리 부상에 의한 것이다. 사망자 중의 절반이 학생들이다. 어떤 연구 결과에 따르면, 자전거 헬멧을 착용하면 머리 부상의 위험을 85%나 감소시킬 수 있다. 사고가 나면, 자전거 헬멧은 충격을 흡수하고, 머리를 보호한다. "자전거 헬멧: 사용하지 않는 생명보호 장비" 소비자 보고서(1990년 5월)

Paraphrase

→ Most bicycle deaths are caused by head injuries, which may be prevented by wearing a helmet. Wearing a bicycle helmet can reduce the risk of head injuries by 85% as the helmet cushions the head from the impact.
자전거사고로 인한 사망 중 대부분은 머리 부상 때문이다. 하지만 이것은 헬멧을 착용함으로서 예방할 수 있다. 자전거 헬멧의 착용은 머리 부상의 위험을 85%나 줄여줄 수 있는데, 헬멧이 충격으로부터 우리 머리를 보호해주기 때문이다.

• 정답 및 해설 p.18

A Read and match.

1. _____ He will get the project done sometime.
2. _____ The lecturer made a short statement.
3. _____ The problems are not insurmountable.
4. _____ I am happy you have the opportunity to attend the conference.
5. _____ The results of the competition were entirely unexpected.
6. _____ My boss seems to welcome lively debate.

a. They can be resolved.
b. She appreciates animated discussions.
c. The competitors were shocked by the outcome.
d. He will finish the project eventually.
e. His remarks were quite brief.
f. It pleases me that you have been given such a chance.

B Match each word with its synonym.

1. adhere •	• a. investigate
2. deceive •	• b. respect
3. examine •	• c. counselor
4. freight •	• d. faith
5. homage •	• e. stick
6. lament •	• f. greive
7. mentor •	• g. change
8. piety •	• h. logical
9. rational •	• i. cargo
10. transform •	• j. trick

Unit 03
세부 내용 파악하기
(Locate Details in the Text)

독해에서 세부사항을 파악하는 문제가 차지하는 비율이 높다. 특히 독해를 시간을 갖고 실력을 향상하고자 하는 학습자는 정확하게 지문의 내용을 이해하고 확인하는 것이 매우 중요하다. 점수를 잘 받기 위해서는 선택지를 먼저 읽고 지문을 읽는다. 그렇게 하면, 지문을 읽고, 선택지를 읽은 다음 다시 지문을 읽으면서 정답을 찾을 경우보다 시간을 절약할 수 있어 효과적이다.

세부내용 파악하기를 더 잘하기 위해서 기억해야 할 전략은 아래와 같다.

1. 문제지 읽는 순서

a. 문제와 선택지를 먼저 읽는다.
b. 지문을 읽는다.
c. 지문을 읽으면서 오답과 정답을 골라낸다.

▬▬ Sample Question

Archaeologists recently found the buried remains of what might have been homes at one time near Stonehenge. The homes, located at Durrington Walls, are believed to have been organized in a way to mimic and mirror the shape of Stonehenge. Archaeological experts recently discovered homes as a monument to the dead ancestors. Researchers think that the people who made Stonehenge were sun worshippers who designed the community and Stonehenge to view the sunrise and sunset.

Q **Which of the following is correct according to the passage?**

(a) The builders of Stonehenge designed the pattern of their homes differently.

(b) Durrington Walls was built by the same people who built the Stonehenge.

(c) The inhabitants of Stonehenge wanted to watch the patterns of the sun.

(d) Durrington Walls and Stonehenge were both vibrant communities.

2. 읽으면서 질문하기

Active Reader가 되기 위한 전략을 사용한다. 읽으면서 스스로 질문하라. What / Who / When / Where / Why / How를 염두에 두고 읽는다. 세부 내용을 파악하는 문제가 Who / What / When / Where / Why / How에 대한 답을 찾아야 되는 경우는 관련이 없는 부분이 나오면 빨리 읽어내려 가고, 질문과 관련이 있는 부분은 좀 더 신경을 써서 읽는 것이 좋다.

The artistic concept of formalism has its roots in the philosophy of Plato. The theory suggests that art's value is in the way it was made - its visual aspects and mediums. Formalists believe that the subject and context of a piece of artwork is not important. Rather, only the colors, the arrangement, and the medium itself are important to the viewer. Formalism contends that regardless of the subject, it is the actual work that influences people.

Q What do formalist artists generally believe?

(a) That the theme of the painting is very important in formalism

(b) That context is of primary importance in art

(c) That the work itself greatly influences viewers of artwork

(d) That people inspire the overall subject and medium of a piece of art

3. Note-taking 하는 습관과 Marking하는 습관 기르기

필요한 정보와 중요한 정보를 자신의 것으로 정리하는 습관은 짧은 시간에 이뤄지는 것이 아니다. 주어진 다양한 내용 중에서 더 중요한 것, 또 답을 찾는데 도움이 되는 부분을 보다 잘 선별하기 위해서는 핵심 어휘(key word)와 주제 구문(topic sentence)을 Note-taking 하도록 한다. 또한 읽으면서 자신이 아는 것을 정리하는 습관도 중요하지만, 정확한 의미를 모르는 어휘나, 표현 또 확실하게 이해가 되지 않는 부분을 marking 하는 습관도 중요하다. Note-taking과 Marking은 독해를 보다 빠르고(speedy), 효과적(efficient)으로 하도록 도와준다.

Many people associate computer games with negative habits, such as violent behavior and failing to exercise the brain. But now many companies are trying to change that. They are designing computer games that they hope will emphasize positive attitudes and help children and teens _____. Researchers are currently conducting tests to determine how effective the new games are. The company hopes these games will help fight the negative reputation that computer games are beginning to get.

(a) develop healthier self-images

(b) become much more skilled

(c) maintain good health

(d) learn constructive habits

Unit 04 예측하기 & 추론하기
(Making Predictions & Inferences)

A   예측하기(Making predictions)

예측하기는 독해에서 가장 중요한 기술(skill) 중에 하나이다. 지문을 좀 더 적극적으로 이해하기 위해서, 앞서가는 독자는 끊임없이 다음에 이어질 내용을 예측한다. 예측을 잘 하기 위해서는 여러 가지가 필요하지만, 가장 근본이 되는 것은 모든 것의 기반에 해당되는 주어진 지문이며, 그 속에 제시된 실마리로부터 시작하는 것이다. Graphic organizer를 잘 사용하는 방법을 익히면, 여러 가지 면에서 도움이 된다. 예를 들면, 예측하기뿐 아니라, 대의 찾기, 익숙한 어휘, 내용과 익숙하지 못한 것 구분하기, 기존 정보에 새로운 정보 추가하기 등에 유용하다.

Graphic Organizer 예시

1.

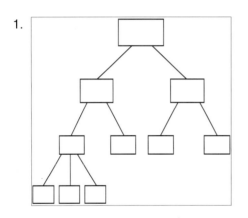

주요 개념과 그 하위 사항을 정리할 때 유용하다. 내용에 우선 순위(hierarchical information)가 있는 경우에 적합하다.

2.

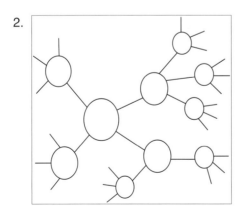

개념이나 이야기의 브레인스토밍(brainstorming)에 적합하다. 가운데 주제를 적고, 세부 사항들을 작은 원 안에 적는다.

3.

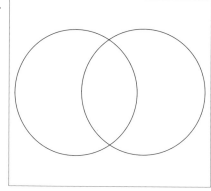

비교(comparing)와 대조(contrasting)를 할 때 유용하다.

4.

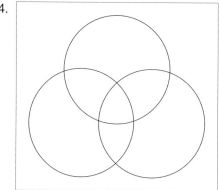

분류(classification)에 적합한 형태이다. 사물, 사고, 주제 등과 관련하여 공통된 특성과 차이점을 찾아내고, 정리하는데 유용하다.

5.

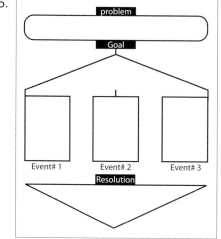

문제(problem)를 파악하여 정리하고, 그 해결책(solution)을 찾아 정리하는데 유용한 형태이다.

6.

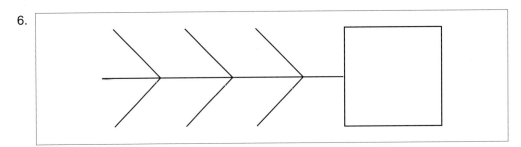

원인(cause)과 결과(effect)의 관계를 나타내는데 유용하다. '독해를 할 때 무슨 일이 발생했나? 왜 그 일이 발생했나?'를 정리하는데 도움이 되는 형태이다.

7.

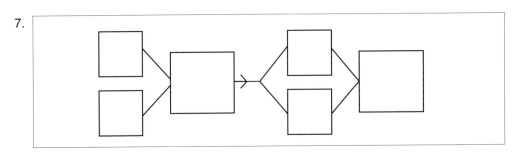

Time Line과 함께 일이 발생한 순서를 정리하는데 유용하다. 또한 원인 결과를 나타내는데도 사용할 수도 있다.

8.

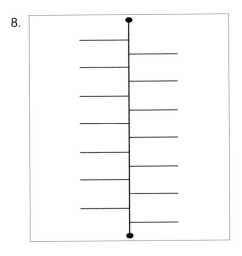

일이 발생한 순서를 정리하는데 도움이 되는 형태이다. 시간 순서(Time Line)대로 정리하는 것도 독해에 도움이 될 때가 많다.

일의 순서가 정해져 있는 경우(sequencing)에 유용한 형태이다.

1.
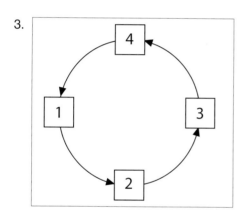

2.
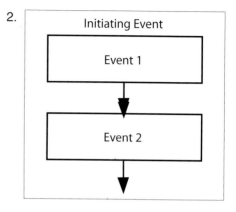

3.

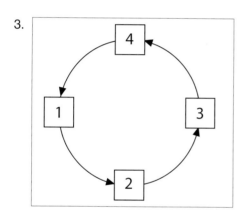

Graphic Organizer의 장점

글로 쓸 경우는 본문의 내용을 부분, 부분 그대로 인용하거나, 베껴서 사용하기 쉽다. 하지만 Graphic Organizer의 경우는 그 개념을 정리하고, 관계를 이해하는데 도움이 된다. 단순한 해석에 그치는 것이 아니라 근본 내용을 이해하고, 서로의 관계를 이해하도록 도와주며, 전체적인 흐름을 보다 잘 이해할 수 있어 좋다.

B   추론하기

추론을 잘 하기 위해서는 주어진 지문에 구체적으로 언급된 내용과 구체적으로 언급되지 않았지만 함축적으로 의미하고 있는 내용을 구별하는 습관을 길러야 한다. 함축된 의미를 확인하고 분석하는 추론 능력을 향상시키기 위해서는 지문을 읽으면서 다음과 같이 연습하도록 한다.

1. **명확하게 제시되지는 않았지만, 필자가 전달하려고 하는 내용을 파악하는 실마리(clue) 찾기**

숨겨진 보물을 찾듯이 겉으로 드러나지는 않으면서(something not directly stated) 작가가 던져준 단서(clue)를 발견하면, 그 부분의 글자가 더 커 보이거나, 색이 변하는 것 같은 착각이 들면서 기쁨을 전해준다. 해석만 하지 말고, 이처럼 뒤에 가려진 의미를 전달하는 어휘, 표현을 적극적으로 찾는 습관을 갖는 것이 추론의 첫 걸음이다.

2. **필자의 신념(belief), 태도(attitude), 관점(perspective)을 생각하기**

지문에 주어진 단서를 찾아낸 후, 그 단서들을 기본으로 필자가 어떤 생각을 갖고 있는지 예측하는 습관을 기른다.

3. **필자가 다음에 쓰려고 하는 내용을 추론해보기**

앞에서 찾아내고, 이해한 필자의 신념, 태도, 관점을 기반으로 다음에 이어질 내용을 추론하는 연습을 평소에 독해하면서 익혀둔다.

> **Tips**
>
> 함축된 의미를 파악하고 이해하기 위해 다음과 같은 질문을 스스로 하는 습관을 갖는다.
> 1. 필자가 다음에 말하려고 하는 것이 무엇일까?
> 2. 명백하게 드러나지는 않았지만, 단서가 되는 부분이 무엇일까?
> 3. 필자의 신념, 태도, 관점은 무엇일까?

Unit 05 시각적 묘사(Visualize the Text)

시각적 묘사는 기억을 상기시키고 유지시키는데 도움을 주고, 독해를 수동적 과정이 아니라, 능동적 과정으로 만드는 것을 도와준다. 이것을 위해서는 시각적이고, 감각적인 세부 묘사가 풍부한 도서를 선택하여 연습하자. 지문을 읽는 과정 중에, 의미가 정리되는 곳에서 잠시 멈추고, 방금 읽은 부분의 구체적인 내용을 시각화하는 것을 연습하자.

Sample Question

① Camels are known as the "ships of the desert" for their extraordinary ability to travel across vast expanses of barren sands while transporting heavy loads. ② They have wide, cushioned feet, which spread out as they walk and thus help them to maneuver easily across the soft sand, as well as ③ two rows of eyelashes and closeable nostrils that protect them from sandstorms. ④ In order to survive in a desert landscape, often void of water and food, camels have developed the ability to store great amounts of nutrients for long periods of time. When food and water is plentiful, they consume as much as possible, storing reserve fat in their humps and water in stomach sacs that can hold up to twenty-five gallons.

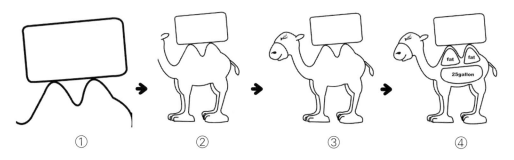

이 예시문에서 알 수 있듯이 지문이 짧지 않음에도 불구하고, 시각화(visualizing)를 일단 하고 나면, 다양한 정보도 오래 잘 기억할 수 있는 장점이 있다. 본인이 스스로 그림을 그리는 것이 익숙하지 않고, 잘 못한다고 하더라도, 시각화를 시도해볼 것을 권한다. 우리가 화가가 되고자 하는 것이 아니라 이해와 기억을 좀 더 잘 하기 위해서 다양한 시도를 할 필요가 있고, 시각화는 연습(practice)에 의해 향상될 수 있다. 시각화를 잘 하기 위해서 구체적인 질문 형태를 자신에게 던지는 것이 좋다. 효과적인 질문들로는 "What do I see?", "What do I hear?", "What do I smell?" 등이 있다.

Ⅴ Categorizing TEPS Reading Based Upon Topics

Unit **01**   정치

Unit **02**   경제

Unit **03**   사회

Unit **04**   문화

Unit **05**   예술

Unit **06**   환경

Unit **07**   과학

정치 (Politics)

1 Read the passage. Then choose the option that best completes the passage.

"A choice between the lesser of two evils" is how many French voters saw their presidential election in 2002. Jacques Chirac, who was running for his 2nd consecutive term, won in an incredible landslide with a stunning 82% of the popular vote. Although Chirac had been heavily criticized for his policies, his opponent, Jean-Marie Le Pen, _____ .

(a) managed to secure victory

(b) proved to be the more popular

(c) was happy to concede defeat

(d) was disliked even more

2 Read the passage and the question. Then choose the option that best answers the question.

One of the tensest moments in recent American history was the Cuban Missile Crisis. During the Cold War between the United States and the USSR, both governments found their enemies were building missile bases within firing range of their countries. Cuba, recently declared a socialist republic, obtained missiles from the USSR, and the world stood still on the brink of nuclear war.

Q **What can be inferred from the passage?**

   (a) The USA helped build a missile base in Cuba.

   (b) Cubans obtained missiles from the USA.

   (c) The USSR had recently launched a nuclear war.

   (d) The USSR helped build a missile base in Cuba.

Unit 02 경제(Economy)

1 Read the passage. Then choose the option that best completes the passage.

The Canadian dollar made history last week, when it approached parity with the US dollar for the first time in nearly 30 years. This comes as good news for many, _____. The dollar's increased value is good for importers, but exporters may suffer.

(a) especially during the winter months

(b) but not for all

(c) all over the country

(d) most of all, exporters

2 Read the passage. Then identify the option that does NOT belong.

Dear Professor McCrone,

As a third-year student and economics major, I have taken a lot of classes on the subject. I mean no disrespect, but must inform you that I do not understand how your lectures consistently overlook the importance of environmental economics in industry. Even in your study of coal mining, no mention was made of the costs of pollution.

Sincerely,
Scott Laing

Q What can be inferred from the passage?

(a) The student finds the professor's lectures boring.

(b) The student has studied environmental economics for three years.

(c) The student thinks the professor overlooks the importance of industry.

(d) The student thinks environmental economics have been overlooked.

1 Read the passage. Then choose the option that best completes the passage.

Apocalypto, the 2006 film by Mel Gibson, portrayed Mayan civilization as primitive and bloodthirsty. However, many anthropologists have pointed out severe inaccuracies in the film's "historical" narrative. For example, the film shows a lot of violence, _____.

(a) and typical features of Mayan culture

(b) but overlooks scientific accomplishments

(c) of which Gibson is a fan

(d) all of which are true

2 Read the passage and the question. Then choose the option that best answers the question.

A woman who had been lost for more than twenty-five years due to an inability to communicate recently made her way home. The woman took a seat on the wrong bus, and was not able to talk to anyone in her native dialect of Yawi, a rather isolated Islamic Thai language. She ended up in a hostel in a town near Thailand's border. Recently, however, new staff members of the hostel who spoke Yawi were able to determine her origin, and contacted her son. The woman is now safely back home.

Q **What is the main idea of the passage?**

(a) The lost woman rode the wrong bus because she spoke Yawi.

(b) Some Thai villages are extremely remote and hard to find.

(c) The inability to communicate can eventually be overcome.

(d) Communication problems can have far reaching effects.

3 Read the passage. Then identify the option that does NOT belong.

The term "Tent City" can be applied to any large collection of people living in non-permanent housing. (a) Recently several cities have seen such developments spring up. (b) Drug and alcohol use is often rampant. (c) Large Tent Cities have been built in Toronto, Seattle, and Saint Petersburg, Florida. (d) In nearly every case, the residents have been evicted by local authorities.

1 Read the passage. Then choose the option that best completes the passage.

If there is one truly global pop culture, it's likely B-Boy and B-Girl style. _____ has gained popularity all over the world, from Sydney to Seoul, from Rome to Rio de Janeiro. No matter where on Earth one travels, one will find examples of the American-grown style that has taken the world by storm.

(a) What began in Australia

(b) This traditional Korean style

(c) What started in ancient Spain

(d) What started in 1970s America

2 Read the passage and the question. Then choose the option that best answers the question.

REGINA — Thousands of quilters have come to the city to take part in Quilt Expo 3000. With Regina's rich quilting history, it is the perfect choice to launch quilting into the future! Exhibits include the latest in quilting technology and designs, as well as your chance to try virtual quilting in a 3-D environment! Quilt Expo runs to September 28.

Q **What can be inferred about the city of Regina from the passage?**

(a) It was named after Queen Regina.

(b) People have been quilting there for a long time.

(c) September is the best month for quilting.

(d) Thousands of quilters live there.

3 Read the passage. Then identify the option that does NOT belong.

In the early 1960s, pop music had become stagnant. (a) But suddenly, in 1963, a revolutionary sound came to the rescue of the music industry and its fans. (b) The arrival of the Beatles is celebrated as the beginning of the "British Invasion" in pop music. (c) The Beatles introduced new rhythms, harmonies and poetry to pop music. Dozens of British pop groups began to emulate this approach. Soon, musicians around the world adopted the style. (d) However, the Beatles started to copy others' works as many ridicule them.

예술(Art)

1 Read the passage. Then choose the option that best completes the passage.

Caricature artwork that pokes fun at political leaders is commonplace today. But historically, the implications of producing such opinionated artwork were harsh. _____, Honore Daumier, who made fun of the French King Louis-Philippe in a caricature, was ordered to pay one hundred francs and serve six months in jail. For insulting the king, Daumier's publisher and printer received the same sentence as well.

(a) As a rule

(b) As a result

(c) For example

(d) On the contrary

2 Read the passage and the question. Then choose the option that best answers the question.

Prior to the 1850s, most artwork was influenced by the beautiful, the romantic, and the imagined. But in the mid-nineteenth century, artists began to focus more on ordinary people and events, in a trend known as realism. Realism profoundly influenced the artistic world because it encouraged the advancement of art techniques that would portray a more realistic scene. Also among the achievements of realism is the development of photography as an art form.

Q **Which of the following is correct about realism?**

(a) It tended to portray subjects beautifully and romantically.

(b) It attempted to show the world in an honest light.

(c) It profoundly affected the Romantic movement.

(d) It was strongly impacted by photographic art.

3 Read the passage. Then identify the option that does NOT belong.

The Renaissance is one of the most important periods in art. (a) Renaissance artists were the first to use perspective in their artwork. (b) Light and shadow were also examined and used in different ways. (c) It was a time when artists created new works, the likes of which had never been seen before. (d) It was also a time for great religious changes, particularly in the Catholic faith.

1 Read the passage. Then choose the option that best completes the passage.

I recently went on a trip to northern Canada. We went on a trip to see polar bears. They were so beautiful and majestic, I almost cried! However, I also learned that global warming means that the bears' habitat is disappearing. I was glad I got to see them now, because in a few years, _____.

(a) they might be gone.

(b) I won't be going back to Canada.

(c) they won't be so majestic.

(d) their habitat won't be disappearing.

2 Read the passage and the question. Then choose the option that best answers the question.

Some governments are examining the idea of imposing a carbon pollution tax. Industries that release carbon pollutants into the air would be required to pay a fee for each ton of pollution emitted. The Australian Prime Minister has already mentioned such a move, and the European Renewable Energy Council has also suggested that governments should impose a financial consequence on businesses for their pollution. Advocates say that this tax would reinforce the motivation for adopting environmentally-friendly manufacturing practices.

Q **What can be inferred about carbon pollution?**

(a) Many governments oppose the idea of a carbon pollution tax.

(b) Australia is the nation that is most concerned about carbon pollution.

(c) A financial consequence could motivate the reduction of carbon pollution.

(d) Environmental groups came up with the concept of a carbon pollution tax.

3 Read the passage. Then identify the option that does NOT belong.

Aluminum, the Earth's most plentiful metallic element, is known for its durability, versatility and recyclability. (a) Aluminum cans are so commonly recycled that they create less than 1% of total material waste. (b) In fact, there is no limit to the amount of times aluminum can be recycled. (c) This means that aluminum thrown in the garbage today will still be intact taking up room in a landfill 500 years from now. (d) Therefore, glass is more environmentally-friendly.

Unit 07 과학(Science)

1 Read the passage. Then choose the option that best completes the passage.

You can't see it from looking at the sky, but Earth's atmosphere is full of garbage. _____ thousands of bits of junk floating in outer space. Usually left over from old satellites and space shuttles, this space junk is actually very dangerous to things like space stations. Just a tiny piece of metal could cause serious damage.

(a) Scientists think there used to be

(b) Scientists think there are

(c) Although not dangerous, there are

(d) Space stations are damaging

2 Read the passage and the question. Then choose the option that best answers the question.

Think of somewhere, anywhere on Earth. Chances are it is covered in microbes! These tiny creatures, including bacteria and viruses, have been found inside volcanoes, deep in the ocean, even in permanently-frozen Antarctica. Stick out your tongue you can't see them, but there are millions of them on it!

Q **What is the best title for this passage?**

(a) Innumerable Microbes

(b) Microbes Found In Volcanoes

(c) Tiny Creatures in the Ocean, Microbes

(d) Microbes in Strange Places

Increasingly, athletes are turning to medical science for help. (a) National sports teams hire as many doctors as they can to study their athletes. (b) They use technology to look for very specific weaknesses in muscles or technique, and tell the athletes what to work on. (c) The latest technology in shoes and clothing certainly helps, as well. (d) Doctors are now as important to athletes as traditional coaches.

VI Actual Test

Actual Test 1

Actual Test 2

Actual Test 3

Actual Test 4

Actual Test 5

Actual Test 1

TEPS

Part I Questions 1~16

Read the passage. Then choose the option that best completes the passage.

1. Exercise is typically considered to be something that a person can't really do too much of. Yet overtraining, or exercising excessively, can harm the body. Doctors have noted that exercise regimens that are too strenuous can have _____ on the joints and muscles, and can also cause insomnia, a decrease in appetite, or fatigue. In addition to these consequences of overtraining, doctors have also noticed that the immune system, particularly in attempting to ward off infection, is also weakened.

   (a) future advantages
   (b) increased benefits
   (c) adverse effects
   (d) widespread complications

2. The dodo, now long extinct, still attracts worldwide fascination and study. Dodos were native to the Indian Ocean island of Mauritius. They were so large that they could not fly. Mauritius was first visited by Europeans in the sixteenth century, and in less than 100 years, the dodo was completely gone. Yet today, the great popularity of the dodo _____ in the island's economy.

   (a) is becoming an issue
   (b) has caused job losses
   (c) neither helps nor hurts
   (d) has contributed to growth

3.

Dear Mr. Thomas,

We recently received a complaint from a customer about your conduct toward a fellow employee last month. As a result of the complaint, we will be reviewing your store as well as your management before April 30. We hope that your behavior last month was an _____, and that we can depend upon you to act more appropriately in the future.

Sincerely,
Kristin Phelps
Director of Employee Affairs
Darla's Department Stores, Inc.

(a) achieved outcome
(b) issued warning
(c) advisable action
(d) isolated incident

4. Some scholars are debating whether Shakespeare's famous tragedies could have been written by another English author, Christopher Marlowe. He is considered by many to have written the best Elizabethan tragedies prior to Shakespeare. Marlowe is generally thought to have died after being stabbed. Yet rumors of his survival abound, and many believe that he _____.

(a) continued writing under the name of William Shakespeare
(b) later plotted to kill the famous William Shakespeare
(c) penned these excellent tragedies using his own name
(d) was named as the finest author in the world by Shakespeare

5. My chemistry teacher once asked me to go to the shop classroom and borrow the lumber stretcher. I had never heard of such a thing, but pretending to know, I set off to find it. I went and asked the shop teacher if I could borrow it, and he answered with a big laugh. Then he gently told me that there was no such thing as a lumber stretcher. I returned to the chemistry classroom blushing, and _____. How could I have been so gullible?

    (a) was greeted with roaring laughter
    (b) found that the class was empty
    (c) looked up the odd phrase in a dictionary
    (d) asked more questions about the experiment

6. For spring and summer, our brand-new Foggy Island Flip-Flops are available for both men and women. Choose from the fantastic selection of carefree colors and bright prints that will make your friends, your family, and your feet smile. Leather and nylon mesh straps provide comfort and security. Select either heavy rubber and leather outsoles, or the light weight soles. All sizes and colors are in stock now, so _____ for the whole family.

    (a) remember to clean the house
    (b) take a moment to order our flip flops
    (c) start to create a new wardrobe
    (d) try to make an independent decision

7. Fire destroyed a two-story building early this morning. Fire fighters were called to the scene at 2:35 a.m. by a security guard who heard a very loud explosion and then noticed flames through a window. _____ according to investigators, who say that the blaze started when an overheated electrical circuit sparked. No one was injured, and the surrounding buildings were not threatened.

    (a) The building may be salvageable,
    (b) Arson is not suspected,
    (c) The victims should recover
    (d) The culprit hasn't yet been captured

8. Pre-K education, teaching very young children before they begin formal schooling, is an idea that is gaining increased attention. Research has shown that a quality preschool experience will improve a child's chances of success — in the classroom and throughout life. But there is substantial public and governmental debate about funding for Pre-K schools. Many argue that today's society simply cannot afford publicly financed Pre-K programs. Others claim that this money must be found to increase the chances that today's children _____.

    (a) can one day master these scientific concepts
    (b) can ultimately learn to use these resources wisely
    (c) will eventually have happy and successful lives
    (d) will be enrolled in more diverse school settings

9. A university recently placed a year of tuition up for bid on an online auction forum. Also included with the tuition were room and board, and both prospective and current students were bidding on the tuition. The university _____, hoping to draw attention.

    (a) offered the highest bid
    (b) invented the idea as a promotion
    (c) is lowering tuition for all such students
    (d) is thus altering its admissions policy

10. Wine connoisseurs and buyers say there is a global overproduction of grapes, and that wine prices are reflecting this. Prices are at all-time lows in nearly every region, with many suppliers unloading even some of their most distinguished vintages at unheard-of low prices. For would-be collectors interested in beginning a wine cellar, there _____.

    (a) is no reason to purchase wine now
    (b) may never be a better time to get started
    (c) are several rules to follow when choosing wines
    (d) may be a need to wait until the prices fall

11. The United States' entry into World War II was not favored by a majority of Americans, nor by Congress. Most citizens and their elected officials _____ _____. This prevailed into the early years of the Second World War. It was the Japanese air attack on Pearl Harbor that pushed the U.S. into war — now with overwhelming support from both congress and the general public.

    (a) thought the Europeans were responsible
    (b) considered war to be unjust
    (c) believed they should stay out of other countries' affairs
    (d) felt the war might be in the United States' interest

12. Often in literature, there is a single character who seems to represent the "typical" person in his or her profession, location, or social standing. This is known as a presentative character, or stereotype. For example, the detective in a given job would have all the characteristics one might imagine a detective to have: a trench coat, a magnifying glass, a sharp and suspicious mind. Thus, rather than having any real personality of his own, the character _____.

    (a) represents to readers a combination of impressions
    (b) shows originality through such individual traits
    (c) suggests to readers a dark, menacing personality
    (d) takes on the personalities of many of the book's characters

13. The artist Christo is famous for _____ throughout the world. He first began to experiment with unusual materials and techniques. For example, Christo wrapped a paint can in brightly painted canvas and adorned it with glue, sand and car paint. As Christo's work evolved, he created art that covered, crossed, or transformed great swaths of earth and sea. Perhaps his best-known work involved eleven islands, which he surrounded with more than 600,000 square meters of pink polypropylene.

    (a) his unusual use of color to create exciting landscapes
    (b) the large-scale environmental art that he has created
    (c) his impact on the fields of ecology and art
    (d) the way he transformed the art scene in Florida

14. One new trend in stylish hotels is _____. Two brand-new hotels, one located in Manhattan and the other in London, are offering travelers small, futuristically-designed rooms for only 89 dollars a night. These so-called pods aren't much bigger than the size of a large walk-in closet but still offer a comfortably-sized bed, a bathroom with shower, and a flat screen TV. The rooms' steel-grey and white decor closely resembles that which is frequently seen in science fiction movies. The pods at the London hotel can be rented for only four hours at a time, so business travelers can stop in for power naps and quick showers without paying for a full night's rate.

    (a) to quit taking reservations
    (b) to offer less for less
    (c) to change check-in times
    (d) to offer expensive gifts

15. Scientists have discovered another key factor in their ongoing research about obesity. Certain types of bacteria that break down food in the digestive system can cause some people to gain more weight than others. Due to genetics, these bacteria are more prone to keep calories than others. _____, this could explain why some people gain weight more easily than others.

    (a) Consequently
    (b) However
    (c) Fortunately
    (d) Coincidentally

16. The city of Idaho Springs boasts some of the finest recreation facilities in the West. Recently, vandals have damaged several of the city's sports facilities. _____, they have sprayed graffiti on the new First Street tennis courts. As the city's daily newspaper, we believe that all Idaho Springs citizens who value these priceless facilities should be on the lookout for these vandals. For information, call the newspaper at 555-2805.

    (a) Nevertheless
    (b) Consequently
    (c) Yet
    (d) For example

Part II **Questions 17~37**

Read the passage and the question. Then choose the option that best answers the question.

---

17. Caffeine is quite often used by athletes hoping to get a little boost to improve their performance in long-distance activities or events, but using caffeine to improve short-term workout performance won't help. In fact, it may hurt your performance during shorter, high-intensity workouts. Researchers studied two groups while exercising through several short cycling tests. Those who were given caffeine before the tests took longer to reach peak performance levels than those who performed the tests caffeine-free.

    Q: Which of the following is correct according to the passage?

      (a) Athletes use caffeine to improve physical performance.
      (b) Caffeine has been proven to help in cycling performance.
      (c) The effects of caffeine only last through short workouts.
      (d) Peak performance was only achieved by those given caffeine.

18. The annual conference and exhibition of the Southwest Council of Culinary Professionals(SCCP) is coming to Midland this spring. The convention will be held at the Marriott Midland North from March 23rd through March 25th. The conference's opening session will feature keynote speaker Matthew Lafitte. The public is invited to visit the exhibit hall from 5 p.m. to 8 p.m. each evening, where professionals and vendors will present cooking demonstrations. For more information, call the SCCP office at 555-3813.

    Q: What is the best title for the news article?

      (a) Chef to Highlight Cooking Show
      (b) Special March Event of Area Chefs
      (c) Kitchen of the Future
      (d) Spring Cooking Demonstrations

19. The world would not be what it is today without the work of Albert Einstein. His achievements transformed the fundamentals of physics and the foundations for technology and by doing so greatly impacted culture, society and history. His theory of light alone created the study of quantum mechanics. Not bad for a young man who left school at 15, and did his most revolutionary work at the age of 26.

Q: What is the best title of the passage?
   (a) Einstein's Most Revolutionary Work
   (b) The Influence of Einstein's Achievements
   (c) The Extraordinary Youth of Albert Einstein
   (d) Einstein's Fundamentals of Physics

20. For millions of people, antidepressant medications have brought relief from depression. Yet recent studies show there may be risks for young people. In a 2004 study, the Federal Drug Administration(FDA) analyzed 4,582 adolescents in 24 drug trials. They found that thoughts of suicide were twice as likely to occur in subjects taking antidepressants than in those taking placebo doses. Other studies are less conclusive, and the debate continues.

Q: What is the best title of the passage?
   (a) A Setback for the Treatment of Depression
   (b) Antidepressants Carrying Suicide Risk for Adolescents
   (c) Statistics Hurting Antidepressant Sales
   (d) FDA Bans Antidepressants for Children

21.

FROM: coachellison@yourmail.net
TO: jjackson@studenttalk.com
SUBJECT: Spring Season
DATE: Mon Jan 05; 15:32:12

Dear Jonathan,
I have not seen you on the roster for this spring's baseball team. Your excellent pitching was vital to us in winning the championship last season. Besides, your jokes kept us all laughing through even the toughest times. As your coach and your friend, I hope you will be with us when we begin practicing later this month.

Sincerely,
Coach Ellison

Q: What might be attached to this email?
   (a) A picture of last season's team
   (b) Jonathan's pitching record
   (c) A practice schedule
   (d) A team roster

22. One ongoing trend in American high school education is that, statistically speaking, female students earn higher grades than male students in math. But this doesn't seem to relate directly to university entrance exam tests scores, in which male students on the average score higher. This difference is largely due to the fact that female students are less likely than male students to take more advanced high school math courses.

Q: According to the passage, why do males score higher on university entrance exams?
   (a) Male students don't get as anxious while taking tests.
   (b) Female students don't take as many high-level math classes.
   (c) Female students don't work as hard to achieve better math grades.
   (d) Male students don't perform well in advanced math classes.

23. More and more surveillance cameras are being installed every day. But now, new technology is making these cameras capable of more than just recording activity. For instance, new microphones will let these cameras alert the police if a gun is shot in the area. The same will happen if the cameras' motion detectors spot someone walking in circles or leaving behind a suspicious package.

Q: How might surveillance cameras benefit business owners?

(a) It could replace more secure technology.
(b) Better cameras could notify police of suspicious activity.
(c) Microphones could record conversations in the area.
(d) New cameras could screen package contents.

24. Manon Rheaume was the first woman to ever play in a professional men's hockey game. As a little girl growing up in Canada, Rheaume begged her dad to let her play hockey. Obviously, she got her wish. During her career, Rheaume played on many amateur and professional women's hockey teams and even helped her Canadian team to win two Olympic gold medals. But what she will go down in the record books for is her one period as goalie in a men's professional game in 1992.

Q: Which of the following is correct about Manon Rheaume?

(a) She broke many records as a goalie in women's hockey.
(b) Her father was a professional Canadian hockey player.
(c) She won two gold medals on the men's Olympic team.
(d) She made history playing professionally on a men's team.

25. Don't miss Ira Levin's stage thriller *Deathtrap*, which premieres December 7th at The Community Playhouse. *Deathtrap* is the tale of an aging playwright who offers to help a former student with his manuscript, and invites the student to his house for a weekend. But soon, the young man finds himself in serious trouble. Shows are performed throughout December on Wednesday and Thursday evenings at 8 p.m., with only a matinee performance on Sundays at 2 p.m. Admission is $10, and $5 for senior citizens.

Q: Which of the following is correct about the advertised play?

(a) Deathtrap is recommended for children and adults.
(b) There will be one performance on the weekend.
(c) Deathtrap won numerous awards on Broadway.
(d) There are no women in the cast of Deathtrap.

26. Here are a few simple tips for successful dating. If you ask for the date, you should pay for it. On a first date, never discuss religious or political beliefs. Always be respectful of your date's time and schedule when planning an event. Pay close attention to personal grooming. When you have called someone new, do not attempt to reach him or her if you do not hear back.

Q: Which of the following is correct about successful dating?

(a) The rules will help you find a spouse.
(b) If your date doesn't return your call, keep trying.
(c) Discussing religion might bring you closer to a new date.
(d) Whoever asks for a date should pay for it.

27. Nearly ten tons of sugar are consumed daily in the U.S. Fixed prices are guaranteed for domestic sugar by the government, which also sets high tariffs and strict quotas on foreign sugar. This keeps sugar prices in the U.S. more than twice as high as the average world price. Because of this, a substantial number of U.S. candy makers have moved their operations overseas, eliminating thousands of American jobs while increasing their profits.

Q: Which of the following is correct about the sugar industry?

(a) American candy makers no longer support U.S. policies.
(b) Laws allow sugar manufacturers to increase their revenues.
(c) American employment has increased due to sugar industry profitability.
(d) U.S. sugar prices are half that of the world's average.

28. From its beginning, the motion picture industry has used screenwriters to adapt novels, plays, and short stories for the screen. Many film classics — *Gone With the Wind, The Wizard of Oz, The Lord of the Rings*, for instance — were based upon novels. But in recent decades, the tables have turned somewhat. Novelizations, wherein a movie is rewritten as a novel, are now in great demand.

Q: Which of the following is correct about the film industry?

(a) A movie is usually better than the book on which it is based.
(b) *The Wizard of Oz* was an original screenplay.
(c) The novel's popularity is seen as a threat by moviemakers.
(d) Writers create adaptations both for and from motion pictures.

29. In addition to the over 2,700 languages of the world, there are over 7,000 "dialects" the way a language is spoken in a specific area. This means that although people are speaking the same language, pronunciations, meanings or vocabulary can differ from region to region. Interestingly, recent studies have shown that even cows have different dialects in the way they moo. This is also based on their region and the dialect the farmer uses.

Q: Which of the following is correct according to the passage?
(a) There are more languages in the world than dialects.
(b) Cows may learn their owner's language.
(c) Words' meanings are always the same.
(d) Dialects are the ways a language is spoken in different regions.

30. Sociologists have found that students — both male and female — who do household chores with their dads, not only get along better with their classmates, but also have more friends in general. The children are also less likely to cause trouble at school. Kids learn both cooperation and democratic values when they do housework with their fathers, according to research. Furthermore, the children then carry these values on to school.

Q: Which of the following is correct about the study?
(a) Uncertain parental roles can cause depression in children.
(b) Men's new household roles reduce their effectiveness.
(c) Children are likely to share housework with their fathers.
(d) Kids who do housework with their fathers cause fewer problems at school.

31. It's Jones Pet Supplies' tenth anniversary in May. If you've shopped with us since the store's opening, you'll get a 30% discount on all of your May purchases. And for newer customers, you'll earn a 3 percent off discount for every year. If you've never shopped at Jones, please come in and accept a free gift. Take advantage of this extraordinary offer in May at Jones Pet Supplies. We hope to see you soon!

Q: Which of the following is correct according to the advertisement?
(a) Jones Pet Supplies opened for business ten years ago.
(b) Those who have shopped at Jones for five years will receive a 12% discount.
(c) The promotions apply to repeat customers.
(d) Only those customers with an open account will receive benefits.

32. Hyenas are animals that are programmed to fight literally from birth. Hyena cubs are born with wide-open eyes and a complete set of sharp teeth. It is not uncommon for the first cubs of a litter to fight one another while the mother is still giving birth to other cubs. In fact, sibling fighting kills one out of every four hyena cubs born. Sister cubs, that may one day compete to rule the pack, often engage in extremely fierce fighting against each other.

Q: Which of the following is correct about hyena cubs?
(a) All hyena cubs have sharp teeth but poor vision at birth.
(b) Female cubs usually have sharper teeth than males.
(c) Female cubs are typically more aggressive than male cubs.
(d) Mother hyenas kill one out of four cubs in each of their litters.

33. Companies sometimes go to great lengths to sell their products in other countries where a true need, based on cultural ideals, may not even exist. For example, a large company that manufactures razors tried to create consumer markets in South America, Africa and Indonesia by trying to convince men that they should start shaving. The company sent portable theaters into villages where the local people were invited to watch razor commercials. These advertisements showed men who shaved as being more accepted by other clean-shaven men. These commercials also represented clean-shaven men as more attractive and having better odds of attracting beautiful women.

Q: What can be inferred from the passage?
(a) Most men in the countries mentioned have beards.
(b) Women in the countries mentioned prefer clean-shaven men.
(c) Creating need for a product is part of successful marketing.
(d) Shaving helps people be accepted by others in the community.

34. A recent study performed by the Los Angeles Department of Public Health determined that ice dispensers in many of the city's fast food restaurants harbored a variety of bacteria. The Department of Health discovered the Escherichia coli(E. coli) bacterium in three ice dispensers. E. coli bacteria comes from the feces of mammals and can cause serious intestinal and kidney problems. In some cases, it has even been known to cause death.

Q: What can be inferred from the passage?
(a) Some of the restaurant's patrons died from E. coli.
(b) Most of L.A.'s restaurants don't have E. coli in their ice dispensers.
(c) The Department of Health closed down many restaurants.
(d) The E. coli bacterium is the deadliest of all bacteria.

35. Business experts and consultants have identified several factors common in successful managers. For example, good bosses encourage openness in communication. They realize that trust is critical for good working relationships. They give timely and honest feedback to employees. Successful managers also create supportive environments which help to motivate their workers.

Q: What does the writer suggest?

(a) Most contemporary managers do a poor job.
(b) Employees can expect a good boss to tell them the truth.
(c) Employees often do not recognize good managers.
(d) Good managers should dismiss struggling employees.

36. Harold saw a beautiful suit in a clothing store. To his surprise, the salesperson told him the suit was only $25. Harold was thrilled. But, he found that it didn't fit him at all. The tailor then suggested that Harold lift his left arm a bit. Then he told him to flex one of his knees just a bit. Now the suit fits him perfectly! Paying the salesperson, Harold shuffled awkwardly to the sidewalk, making sure to keep the suit's perfect fit. Across the street, two elderly women noticed Harold. The first sympathized with the poor crippled man across the street. Her friend agreed. "Yes," she said, "But doesn't he have the most beautiful suit?"

Q: What can be inferred from the passage?

(a) Only one of the women pitied Harold.
(b) Harold later became wealthy.
(c) The salesperson was dishonest.
(d) Harold will take the suit to a tailor for repair.

37. The French National Space Agency has launched a space satellite technologically capable of several firsts. The small 30 centimeter telescope on the satellite will be able to look inside stars to help distinguish their different physical make-ups. Plus, the telescope will also be able to detect rocky planets located outside of our solar system. These planets are expected to be much larger than Earth. Besides the telescope on board the satellite, the payload also includes two cameras, and on-board computer processors.

Q: What is the best title of the passage?
(a) New Computer Processors of the French Satellite
(b) Big Things Expected from New Satellite and its Telescope
(c) Advanced Telescope Locating New Rocky Planet
(d) New Star Composition Discovered by Satellite Telescope

38. With carbon dioxide emissions at dangerous levels, ethanol is a fuel many believe will substantially reduce dependence on fossil fuels. (a) It is made from corn, a cleaner, renewable energy source. (b) Corn farmers prefer to produce food rather than fuel. (c) Increased use of this fuel will diminish our reliance on oil from politically unstable regions. (d) A substantial increase in the use of ethanol could slow global warming and reduce international conflict.

39. Toward the end of the 15th century, European sailors and explorers began to venture out on unknown seas in search of treasure, glory, and fame. (a) The Spanish made the first major discovery when they landed on the shores of what is now America. (b) At first it was mistakenly believed that the ships had landed in the West Indies. (c) After realizing their mistake, the disheartened explorers returned to Spain and were punished. (d) British, French, Dutch and Portuguese explorers would soon follow the Spanish example, and each nation claimed dominion over parts of this vast new land.

40. After World War I, the democracies of the world focused on manufacturing civilian goods. (a) American car manufacturers came up with an entirely new marketing plan. (b) They realized that if they changed an automobile's design every year, they could sell more cars. (c) Their aim was to make existing models seem out of date by making obvious changes to their outward designs every year. (d) An example of this is the Ford Model T, which remained virtually unchanged for twenty years.

Actual Test 2

TEPS

Part I Questions 1~16

Read the passage. Then choose the option that best completes the passage.

1. Besides a thick layer of fat, walruses have another way to survive Arctic temperatures that drop to 40 degrees below zero. When walruses dive for food, they can stay under water for up to ten minutes. So to prevent its body from shutting down, the walrus's blood will concentrate so deep inside the body that the animal will _____. Only after warming up will the natural brown coloring return.

   (a) become very hungry
   (b) turn completely white
   (c) become extremely cold
   (d) temporarily fall asleep

2. Being stung by a bee can be a dangerous, even fatal event for some. Nonetheless, bee stings have been used by the Chinese to help treat illnesses for 3,000 years. Many doctors believe that the venom from bee stings repairs damaged cells, and by doing so can even cure serious diseases. However, these same doctors admit they still don't understand exactly _____.

   (a) why so many people are afraid of bees
   (b) how to treat such allergies to bee stings
   (c) why this mysterious healing occurs
   (d) how the bees produce venom at all

3.

Dear Ms. Kimura,

Thank you for your most recent online order(#987YUO). Unfortunately, we are temporarily out of stock on discounted item #324(discontinued white terry cloth robe). We do have the item on backorder and are hoping to have that shipped to you by the 24th. Should you need any further information, please visit our customer service website at www.bestbargains.com. We apologize for any inconvenience and again thank you for your valued business and _____.

Sincerely,
Jaqueline Lopez, Distribution Center Representative

    (a) continued patronage
    (b) lively correspondence
    (c) consistent communication
    (d) dedicated service

4. Mark Twain, the American author best-known for the classics *Tom Sawyer* and *Huckleberry Finn* lived a life of great success and failure. Although his early novels were financial successes, Twain lost most of his fortune due to poor investing. Later in life, Twain found himself with little money and plenty of debt. To fix this, he traveled to Europe for a lengthy schedule of performances. The sole purpose of _____ _____, which took quite some time. This extended stay in Europe lasted an entire decade.

    (a) scheduling European shows was to find a new audience
    (b) writing more novels was to make more money
    (c) taking work abroad was to pay off his debts
    (d) moving to Europe was to become an actor

5. I was ten years old when my father took me on my first deep-sea fishing trip. As our boat sailed out into the Gulf of Mexico, the excitement of catching an enormous fish was more than I could stand. Almost as soon as I dropped my line into the water I felt an enormous tug and the fight for the biggest fish of my life began. Actually, this was no trophy fish at all. My line had become tangled underneath the boat with another man's who was fishing off the other side. Sadly, we both thought _____ _____.

(a) that the fishing trip would be a memorable one
(b) we had become each other's catch of a lifetime
(c) that the fish was much larger than it actually was
(d) the other person was to blame for losing the fish

6. Want the security of a watchdog without having to own a dog? Then you need the Jake-2000, our amazing electronic watchdog. There's no need to feed or clean up after this guy. Jake is a compact unit with sensors and a speaker that plugs into any home outlet. Jake's sensors can reliably detect when someone is approaching your home. When strangers are near, Jake barks a realistic German Shepherd bark that increases in volume and intensity as strangers get closer to your home. Jake is the most affordable 24-hour security system you'll ever find. To order your Jake-2000, call 1-800-435-JAKE and _____.

(a) start experiencing affordable security system today
(b) enjoy the peace of mind only a real watchdog can offer
(c) ask for information about our other security products
(d) find how inexpensive being a pet owner can be

7. SYDNEY - Thanks to a protective vest and presence of mind, a diver _____ _____ of a great white shark and lived to tell about it. Matthew Brimby, 45, was diving for shellfish with his son, when the 10-foot-long shark attacked him, taking Brimby's head and shoulders into its mouth. Brimby said the lead-lined vest he was wearing saved him from being cut in half.

   (a) videotaped the daily eating habits
   (b) studied and learned more about the teeth
   (c) managed to avoid the terrifying jaws
   (d) escaped the frightening and deadly jaws

8. Boxing was once taught in British schools. In fact, the sport was a standard in the physical education curriculum until 1962 when it was banned. But now some schools in Bromley, London believe boxing _____. Experts who support boxing in P.E. classes say it offers mental and physical skills that apply to all types of learning. Still, medical experts concerned about student safety are asking the schools to rethink the decision.

   (a) should be reintroduced to students
   (b) could create Olympic athletes
   (c) might help students work out frustrations
   (d) ought to be banned again

9. Several different militaries are each developing their own pocket-sized robots. These tiny technological soldiers will quietly hop or crawl like insects and _____ _____ than humans can. One specific use, a robotics expert explained, is that these small robots could disable many types of vehicles. By squirting a special chemical on the tires, the rubber would immediately be destroyed.

(a) attack the enemy more violently
(b) drive military vehicles with more precision
(c) approach targets in less obvious ways
(d) cause more enemy casualties

10. If you think that some taxes are always increasing, you may be right. A "pigovian tax" is a special tax for products that are seen as harmful. For example, a company that pollutes the sky or air will have to pay higher tax to help clean up their mess. Governments put extra tax on tobacco and alcohol, as these products cause expensive medical damage. Until the harmful effects disappear, pigovian taxes on products and industries _____ .

(a) will cause more damage
(b) should stay the same
(c) will keep increasing
(d) might decrease dramatically

11. Very few people realize that on the day Abraham Lincoln gave his famous Gettysburg Address, another speaker addressed the crowd as well. Edward Everett was a famous orator and also the governor of Massachusetts. His speech went on for two hours, while Lincoln's was over in two minutes. Afterwards, Everett told Lincoln that he would be flattered if he could even hope that his two-hour speech came close to the central ideas that _____ in only two minutes.

    (a) he wrote down and practiced
    (b) Lincoln so eloquently covered
    (c) the President forgot to mention
    (d) the crowd couldn't comprehend

12. *The Tale of Kieu*, written by Nguyen Du in 1813, is commonly thought of as a literary masterpiece. But very few works of literature _____ as closely as Kieu's story has. This epic poem, which goes against traditional Confucian ideals, is the tragic tale of a young woman's personal sacrifice. All Vietnamese know this famous story and often refer to its passages in daily conversation. They also closely connect life events to events in the poem. And at the beginning of each New Year, this story is often used to try to predict the future.

    (a) have ever been embraced by their audience
    (b) have been so enthusiastically followed
    (c) have ever been translated into English
    (d) have followed society's rules

13. Andy Warhol's first pop works were painted by hand, but in 1962 he
_____. In assembly-line fashion, Warhol started using a photo-silk
screen process and a large staff of artists to create his art. It was at this same time that
Warhol began to use odd objects in his art, such as still photographs of movie stars, car
accidents and newspaper photographs. In his New York Studio, which he named
"The Factory," as many as 80 paintings could be created in one day.

    (a) changed his ways
    (b) quit painting
    (c) became a photographer
    (d) achieved fame

14. Architects and landscape designers are starting _____ that
should be used for city parks in an entirely different way. In Europe and the United
States, city park planning and design is heading in an interesting new direction.
Architects and landscape designers in the most populated cities are taking huge garbage
dumps, abandoned industrial sites and old railroad yards, and transforming them into
futuristic-looking public parks.

    (a) to plan fun and exciting playground equipment
    (b) to learn the techniques of ancient masters
    (c) to know the best building materials
    (d) to think about the type of land

15. If the world truly cared about Africa, there would no longer be a malaria epidemic across the continent. In my opinion, the solution is very simple. Working individuals who make high incomes in proportion to the average global wage should commit to paying only three dollars a year. _____, three billion dollars could be used annually to prevent malaria. Africa cannot devote these types of funds to pubic health, but the world of excess beyond its borders can.

    (a) Accordingly
    (b) Finally
    (c) Meanwhile
    (d) Similarly

16. There are many benefits of breastfeeding. In breast-fed newborns, the incidence of diarrhea and influenza is much lower than in those who are fed with artificial formulas. Other research shows protection from allergies and increased resistance to chronic diseases as benefits. Besides, studies link enhanced cognitive development to breastfeeding. _____ these researches, doctors are telling their patients that they must breast-feed their newborns through infancy and beyond.

    (a) As a result of
    (b) In spite of
    (c) In contrast to
    (d) To demonstrate

Part II **Questions 17~37**

Read the passage and the question. Then choose the option that best answers the question.

17. Fire broke out at Wow Shopping Mall just after midnight. After smelling smoke for five minutes, a security guard who was patrolling the outside grounds called and reported a possible fire. Luckily, fire fighters were able to find and put out a small blaze that originated in one of the mall's food court restaurants. Mall manager Rachel Martinez says if the security guard hadn't alerted emergency crews so quickly, the results could have been disastrous.

Q: What is the passage mainly about?
   (a) A disastrous fire at the Middleton Mall
   (b) A security guard's heroic efforts to save shoppers
   (c) The quick response to a minor fire at a local mall
   (d) A fire in the ventilation system of a mall restaurant

18. Currently, many countries are trying to help students complete their education and go on to become motivated members of their communities. For example, Cuba has changed its education format so that students can stay with the same teacher for the first three years of high school. In Scotland, the focus has become offering courses that work on improving the attitudes of detached youth. Both changes are meant to provide a more meaningful school experience.

Q: What is the best title of the passage?
   (a) New Educational Approach of Different Countries
   (b) Students More Detached From Their Communities
   (c) Motivated Adults Making a Difference in Students' Lives
   (d) Meaningful School Experience Influencing Students' Futures

19. In the early 1900s, the US experienced a major shift when the African-American population of the South began to move northward and become more urbanized. Unfortunately, many African-Americans could only find homes in the poorest areas of northern cities. These "ghettos," as they were called, were full of dilapidated apartment buildings. Rent was high for these small, dirty accommodations. Frequently, tenants were taken advantage of by greedy landlords. Sadly, children living in these buildings sometimes died from diseases caused by the unsanitary living conditions.

Q: What is the main topic of the passage?
  (a) The causes of death among African-American children in the early 1900s
  (b) Living conditions for African-Americans after migration north
  (c) The poor economic condition in northern cities after the turn of the century
  (d) Tactics landlords used to take advantage of African-Americans

20. Recent research has shown that children are less likely to use sunscreen as they grow older. However, just talking about the chances of developing skin cancer doesn't seem to encourage teens to use sunscreen. So health officials are taking a different approach to educate kids about skin cancer prevention. Appealing to teenagers' awareness about their self-images seems to be more effective. For example, stressing an increased chance of preventing premature wrinkles seems to make more teens willing to wear sunscreen.

Q: What is the main topic of the passage?
  (a) How teenagers can suntan safely.
  (b) How to survive skin cancer at an early age.
  (c) How to get teenagers to wear sunscreen.
  (d) How to prevent premature wrinkles in teens.

21. When my own mother comes upon a child with good manners, she enjoys the moment like a rare and special treat. When a young person holds the door for her or remembers to say "please" or "thank you," she thanks the child for his or her good manners, but she always thanks the nearby parent too. My mother says parents today work hard to meet all their children's emotional needs. However, she feels many seem to often forget the basics.

Q: What does the writer's mother think about today's parenting?
(a) It hasn't changed enough since her parents raised her.
(b) It tends to make the children too emotionally dependant.
(c) It places too much emphasis on teaching proper manners.
(d) It does not put enough focus on teaching basic social skills.

22.

Dear Editor,

As a regular subscriber, I usually enjoy your health magazine very much. But I was sorry to see a negative article about yoga instruction in last month's issue. I'm assuming the author may have had a bad experience. However, all the instructors I've worked with have been knowledgeable and professional. The author is entitled to her opinion, but a more balanced view of the topic is always appreciated by readers like me.

Q: What is the purpose of this letter?
(a) To suggest a feature article about yoga instructors.
(b) To request that a fair perspective be presented in the future.
(c) To cancel the subscription and ask for a full refund.
(d) To complain about the lack of instructional yoga articles.

23. Research shows that constant multi-tasking forces the brain to work overtime. While we may think we're accomplishing more, the opposite is often true. The brain has different memory systems. When performing two tasks at once, these systems have to compete with one another. This is why many of us suffer from constantly losing things like our keys, or forgetting important dates and information.

Q: What does the writer say about multitasking?

(a) It can boost one's ability to remember trivial information.
(b) It can lead to harmony between the various memory systems.
(c) It may result in a decrease in one's ability to recall things.
(d) It may cause permanent damage to the brain's memory systems.

24. The national tour of the unforgettable Broadway musical *Nowhere But New York* is coming to Fairway Hall. This award-winning musical tells the story of two life-long Manhattan neighbors in a uniquely touching way. Performances are November 2 through 4 at Caldwell University's newly renovated Fairway Hall. Tickets go on sale the 15th of October and start at $35.00. There's no other Broadway show quite like *Nowhere But New York*. Don't miss it!

Q: Which of the following is correct according to the advertisement?

(a) The musical can only be seen on Broadway.
(b) The show is about friends in New York City.
(c) Performances are scheduled for a three-day engagement.
(d) Tickets are on sale now.

25. When it comes to success, those who are *determined* may become more successful than those who are talented. New studies from the University of Pennsylvania's Psychology Department show that those who are willing to stick to their plans — regardless of failures — are more likely to experience success in school and at work. The researchers concluded that the ability to suffer through setbacks is most critical to becoming successful.

> Q: According to the passage which of the following is true regarding failure?
> (a) Determined people encounter the least amount of failure.
> (b) High achievers typically experience the most failure.
> (c) True success has little to do with either talent or failure.
> (d) Handling failure positively is necessary for achievement.

26. While trying to test its new security program, FINDER, the web's most popular search engine, accidentally revealed users' private information. Although very few users were affected, the private passwords and login information of twelve people wound up appearing on the company's public website. FINDER quickly addressed the problem, but such mistakes reveal how far away the company is from protecting its users from fraudulent web activity.

> Q: Which of the following is correct according to the passage?
> (a) Twelve people participated in a fraudulent Internet scheme.
> (b) The company did not handle a problem in an efficient way.
> (c) FINDER's security program is not ready for use.
> (d) The problem was not significant because how few were affected.

27. The natural rate of unemployment is always influenced by changes in the labor force. For instance, young workers have a tendency to quit jobs and find others several times before settling into one position. This means the unemployment rate will always increase when the number of young workers in the labor force increases. This happened in the 60s and 70s when a huge number of youth became old enough to enter the workforce. The result pushed the unemployment rate up from 5% to 7%.

Q: Which of the following is correct according to the passage?

    (a) Young workers affect the unemployment rate because they cannot find jobs.

    (b) The unemployment rate is affected by the make-up of the current population.

    (c) Unemployment rates drop when young workers enter the labor force.

    (d) Several influences change the composition of the work force.

28. Spider plants, named for their round shapes and long wiry stems and leaves, are popular houseplants. If watered regularly, these hearty, disease-resistant plants are hard to harm and often grow to be 5 meters wide and 6 meters long. Spider plants create long shoots that produce smaller spider plants at the ends. These smaller plants hang down below the original large plant thus inspiring a different name for the plant in Guatemala. The spider plant is known as 'bad mother' in Guatemala because the mother plant appears to be throwing her babies out of their home, which in this case is the pot.

Q: Which of the following is true according to the passage?

    (a) Common houseplants are most often disease-resistant.

    (b) The spider plant is commonly named for its shape.

    (c) The spider plant is one of the largest known houseplants.

    (d) Guatemalan people do not keep these plants at home.

29. "Action Painting" means an artist chooses to forego the traditional paintbrush. Instead, they drip, drop, splash and splatter the paint across the canvas. Jackson Pollock was one of the first to shock the art world with this revolutionary method in the 1950s. He believed that paint wasn't passive, but actually full of energy, and that it only needed him to release its energy.

Q: Which of the following is correct about "Action Painting"?
(a) This conventional method was popular in the 1950s.
(b) Pollock felt all paint needed to be controlled in this way.
(c) This technique was introduced to the world by Pollock.
(d) Artists use paintbrushes to drip and splatter paint.

30. In the early 1500s, the Portuguese became the first Europeans to create an overseas empire, but their impressive control of trade routes to Asia and Africa was only temporary. Portugal simply did not have enough well-trained sailors to run their trading empire. The high death rate on ships created a constant need for new sailors, but not enough experienced sailors could be found to fill these positions. Therefore, the ships operated by crews of poorly trained sailors were quite often lost at sea.

Q: Which of the following is correct about the Portuguese trading empire?
(a) Asia and Africa took control of it in the early 1500s.
(b) It was successful until a shortage of qualified sailors occurred.
(c) Well-trained sailors were often not adequate enough to handle the ships.
(d) Experienced sailors could not protect the Portuguese ships from attack.

31. An aging population and a declining birth rate are forcing Japanese toy makers to make changes. In this shrinking market, toy companies are now looking to sell toys to young adult males. One large toy manufacturer is hoping this target group of young men will find its 165 mm walking, dancing robot, the I-BOT, appealing enough to take home for the price of $260.

> Q: Which of the following is correct about Japanese toy makers?
>
> > (a) They are starting to invent toys for older men and women.
> > (b) They are experiencing decreased sales due to a smaller market.
> > (c) They are making changes to create better toys for children.
> > (d) They are focusing on more technologically-advanced toys.

32. Had it not been for the death of his teacher Socrates, Plato may have never established his own school of philosophy and science. Plato was interested in pursuing a political career until his teacher was killed by hemlock poisoning in 399 BC. Deeply affected by Socrates' death, Plato left his political plans behind in Athens. For the next several years, he traveled throughout Egypt and Italy furthering his education in math and science.

> Q: Which of the following is correct about Plato?
>
> > (a) He was Socrates' most well-educated student.
> > (b) He visited Egypt and Italy to further his political plans.
> > (c) He was killed by poisoning in 399 BC.
> > (d) He founded his own school after his teacher's death.

33. Now that summer will soon be here, The National Association for Safe Boating would like to remind all boat owners to practice responsible boating by taking the proper measures to protect yourself and your passengers. Always insist all passengers, children and adults alike, to wear life jackets. Remember that you or any other driver of the boat should always use the seat belt, and make sure you and any other person you allow to drive your boat have successfully passed a certified safe boating course.

Q: Which of the following is correct according to the announcement?
(a) Every passenger regardless of age should be made to wear life vests.
(b) Children should never be permitted to drive a boat.
(c) All passengers must successfully pass a special safe boating course.
(d) All passengers should use the safety belts on the boat.

34. Youth learn about their culture through socialization. Family, friends and the media are all important agents of socialization. Without these influences, children would have no way of understanding their culture and its expectations. Interestingly, children are often responsible for socializing their parents as well. This process is called reverse socialization, and it occurs when the children become the socializers, teaching their parents about the latest cultural trends in music, fashion and technology.

Q: Which of the following is correct according to the passage?
(a) Reverse socialization occurs when parents start new trends.
(b) Roles can be switched in that children socialize their parents.
(c) Family, friends and media affect how parents socialize kids.
(d) All expectations become reversed in the parent/child relationship.

35. Bamboo is a giant grass that grows naturally in warm regions. Some bamboo can reach heights of up to 37 meters high, while the hollow, wood-like stem can grow to 30 cm in diameter. Botanists consider bamboo the most primitive of all grasses. This prolific plant spreads quickly, but hardly ever blossoms; however some plants do blossom, but only once every 30 years. If a bamboo plant does bloom, then all the bamboo plants in the nearby area will subsequently bloom. But after a bamboo blossoms, it typically dies.

Q: What can be inferred from the passage?

(a) Bamboo has a complex structure.
(b) A primitive make-up would keep bamboo plants from dying.
(c) If one bamboo plant blossoms, all others around it will die.
(d) It takes many years for bamboo to spread.

36. Very few sources can correctly explain why the sky is blue. Sources that can adequately answer this question do so by addressing in detail three important things: what sunlight is, how it travels to Earth, and how the human eye works as well. The only way to understand why the sky is blue is to clearly understand these three factors. However, usually only college textbooks about astronomy, physics or optics teach these three components accurately.

Q: What can be inferred from the passage?

(a) The right websites can offer adequate explanations.
(b) High schools use college-level textbooks for science classes.
(c) Very few people understand why the sky is the color it is.
(d) The human eye is capable of seeing many colors in sunlight.

37. The best managers are often the best communicators. Experts estimate that managers may spend as much as 85% of their time communicating. In meetings, on the phone, through email, or by having person-to-person interactions, managers spend the majority of their time talking. This is why the most effective managers are often lifelong students of the art of effective communication. And truly great managers pass on this knowledge to their staff as well.

Q: What does the writer suggest?

(a) Successful managers know how to communicate clearly.
(b) Reading communication books isn't enough to be a good manager.
(c) Very few workers or managers are effective communicators.
(d) Eighty-five percent of all managers need better communication skills.

Part III **Questions 38~40**

Read the passage. Then identify the option that does NOT belong.

38. On Saturday, Greenpeace will once again set sail off the coast of New zealand, officially beginning their next anti-whaling campaign. (a) By confronting whalers out on the open ocean, they hope to save more whales this season than ever before. (b) Other environmental groups also use this method of confrontation to protect endangered species. (c) To protect whales, Greenpeace members place their small inflatable boats in harm's way between the whale at risk and the fishermen. (d) By their own count, 82 whales were saved this way during last year's campaign.

39. English has long been a continually-evolving language. (a) Of course, this is still true today. (b) With increasing global communication, hundreds of new words appear in the English language every year. Some of these words are borrowed from other languages like Spanish, German, French, or Arabic. (c) Additionally, new science and technology terms also contribute heavily to the always expanding English vocabulary. (d) The Internet has affected language communication in lasting ways.

40. A strange study in the Southern US has looked at why some church members handle venomous snakes in their religious ceremonies. (a) For twenty minutes out of each four-hour church service, members pick up, throw down and dance with the snake. (b) During the study, twelve members in the church received bites and were hospitalized. (c) This ceremony is meant to prove that snake handlers are truly holy. (d) The handlers believe that risking their lives for their beliefs makes them deserving of a saintly status.

Actual Test 3

TEPS

Part I **Questions 1~16**

Read the passage. Then choose the option that best completes the passage.

1. For many years, doctors have been concerned about teens drinking too much soda. But a ten-year study has shown that as teenage females grow older they may be drinking even more soda. During the study, the young women's _____ decreased by 25%, but their soda intake tripled.

   (a) intake of healthier drinks
   (b) ability to buy other drinks
   (c) preference for sugary drinks
   (d) consumption of diet soda

2. An African slave named Estevanico was one of the _____ of Mexico and the southwestern United States. Estevanico's Spanish owner liked him. So he brought him along to explore these new territories. But this was not a fun trip. Violent encounters with native residents and horrible conditions killed nearly all the men. Estevanico was only one of four who survived.

   (a) native residents
   (b) brave soldiers
   (c) first explorers
   (d) early rulers

3. Most people think bears_____, but actually they don't. Bears like Grizzly and Black bears are not true hibernators. A true hibernating animal experiences a large drop in body temperature and heart rate before falling into a deep sleep for the winter. But a bear's system only slows down a little bit below its normal rate. And bears never go into a deep sleep. Many slow down their activity during the colder months, but others stay active all winter long.

(a) sleep during the winter months
(b) die from natural causes due to old age
(c) prefer to eat vegetation more than meat
(d) have higher body temperatures than other animals

4.

Dear Mr. Han,

Please accept my sincere thanks for your support with our recent annual fund drive. Your contribution of $500 to our facility will go a long way to help with the never-ending expenses here at our community recreation center. Because of your donation, we can now buy new sports equipment and art supplies as well for our after-school program. Thanks to kind people like you, we once again have the operating budget to _____ for the neighborhood kids we serve.

Thank you for your continued support of our facility.

Sincerely,
Ms. Stacy Schwartz

(a) provide many enjoyable activities
(b) buy food and clothing
(c) purchase books and private tutoring
(d) build a new art museum

5. In 1930, 75 percent of all New Yorkers were part of immigrant families. Most of these families had come from Europe to New York by ship traveling in "steerage class." This meant that passengers who could not _____ on board could travel in the lower decks among the steering equipment. The cost of a steerage ticket at this time was fifteen dollars.

    (a) pay for safe transportation
    (b) afford better accommodations
    (c) bring expensive luggage
    (d) be hired as workers

6. Waves Waterbed Warehouse is having the sale of the century. This weekend only Waves will be offering ridiculous markdowns on all our durable, Sea-Motion mattresses. Come in and experience the sensational support of the king-sized Sea-Motion Midnight model. You'd never dream a waterbed mattress could be so supportive, yet so comfortable. Waves _____ all weekend, so come early or shop late. But don't wait to get a great deal on a brand-new waterbed from Waves.

    (a) might run low on inventory
    (b) can advertise these prices
    (c) will be closing early
    (d) will be extending our regular hours

7. The construction is finally complete. The City of Morgantown's brand-new Museum of Natural History opens for business on Monday. To celebrate, the staff is inviting the public to a pre-opening day party from 9 a.m. to 3 p.m. tomorrow. Museum Director, Sonja Pederson says that the event will be a great way for _____. Plus, the public can learn about museum memberships and the traveling exhibits that will be stopping at the museum this year.

    (a) museum staff to train volunteers
    (b) residents to preview the museum
    (c) kids to learn about famous art
    (d) the public to protest the opening

8. When I was six years old, I wished on a star that I would one day become a famous celebrity. If I had only known then what I know now, I _____. It seems that when we're very little, we want things we don't completely understand. But as we become teenagers, we begin to look at life in deeper ways, ways that often define who we are. Now I'm old enough to know that being famous comes at a very high price. And I'm also old enough to be wiser with my wishes.

    (a) wouldn't have believed in wishes
    (b) could have saved myself a lot of tears
    (c) would have never wasted that wish
    (d) might have taken acting lessons

9. Britain's school curriculum for secondary students is being updated. Education experts say more current courses are needed to help students be successful in a "changing society." The modernized curriculum is also intended to give students more "cultural and social flexibility." Mandarin, Arabic, global warming and healthy cooking are all new subjects that many hope will _____ and keep them enthusiastic about learning too.

   (a) benefit students in the real world
   (b) teach pupils how to work at home
   (c) inform teens about current global events
   (d) increase students' math and science skills

10. The world's oldest newspaper is no longer news actually printed on paper. Sweden's most famous newspaper, founded by a Swedish queen in 1645, has replaced its paper edition with an online edition. With only 1,000 subscribers to the paper edition, this wasn't Sweden's most popular newspaper. However, many in Sweden think the decision to _____ is a cultural tragedy.

   (a) hire a new, younger newspaper staff
   (b) no longer write about Sweden's history
   (c) quit producing the online newspaper
   (d) print this historic paper only in cyberspace

11. A recent report on New York City's economic future said immigrants are largely responsible for the city's strong economic growth. The 18-month study found that immigrants are starting more small businesses and creating more jobs than native residents. The report also said that _____. By bringing economic activity to previously struggling areas, many neighborhoods have been transformed.

    (a) certain areas are suffering from depressed economies
    (b) immigrant business owners are improving neighborhoods
    (c) little can be done to help small business employees
    (d) immigrants in small neighborhoods cannot find jobs

12. Indeed, it is responsible reporting to cover the recent vow by 60 countries _____ in their military conflicts. It brings hope to know that South American, African and Asian nations that have previously used children as fighters are all in support of this new international agreement. However, strict enforcement is the only thing that will protect children from such tragic fates.

    (a) to reach an international agreement
    (b) to better inform citizens about developments
    (c) to no longer use children as soldiers
    (d) to offer civilians weapons for protection

13. Eye jewelry is a new way to accessorize one's eyeballs. Eye surgeons in the Netherlands have developed a procedure in which a small jewel can be implanted on the white part of the eyeball by inserting it under the thin, clean membrane of the eye. The most common eye jewelry looks like small hearts, stars or half moons. And although _____, many doctors warn there are complications like serious eye infections that can possibly result from the procedure.

    (a) the trend is gaining popularity
    (b) no one is likely to want this accessory
    (c) the jewel options are limited at this point
    (d) the eye membrane is moist

14. Cancer researchers are creating a new cancer-fighting drug using something extraordinary — _____ a sea creature. This poison, used for defense by the small, transparent Dianzoa angulata, effectively killed cancer cells in cultures. This exciting development caused researchers to rush to create an artificial substitute. So far, the human-made version is reducing human tumors implanted in mice with no negative side effects.

    (a) the toxin released by
    (b) an exotic food made from
    (c) a poison antidote created by
    (d) the tumor tissue found inside

15. University marine biology departments and ocean life organizations are forming a collective ocean tracking network to better understand climate change effects on sea animals and advance endangered ocean wildlife management. Scientists in eleven different countries will work to electronically tag one million sea animals from turtles to whales. Five thousand sensors will be placed at important locations throughout the world's oceans. These sensors will collect valuable data from the tagged animal that swims by, but more than single animals' data will be collected. Each electronic tag is capable of storing other tagged animals' data too. _____, this will reveal to scientists what animals are encountering each other, and where, throughout the oceans of the world.

   (a) As a rule
   (b) Therefore
   (c) Nevertheless
   (d) Likewise

16. Upton Sinclair's *The Jungle* facilitated change in the meat-packing industry of the early 1900s. Sinclair's distressing novel about the repulsive conditions of America's meat processing plants angered the public, and meat sales plummeted. _____, legislation was passed to help the plant owners reassure the public that all meat would be inspected and safe for consumption.

   (a) As a result
   (b) Ordinarily
   (c) Similarly
   (d) In contrast

Part II **Questions 17~37**

Read the passage and the question. Then choose the option that best answers the question.

---

17. Being a 21st century student means becoming a global citizen. Part of this process is learning the skills needed to work in the global market. For example, students should work hard to learn different languages, and become knowledgeable and sensitive about foreign cultures. Also, they should focus on becoming creative, innovative thinkers because these are employee traits that will always be valued no matter how much the global market changes.

   Q: What is the main topic of the passage?

   (a) Global citizens uniting to improve education
   (b) The process of how to learn a new language
   (c) The ways students should prepare for future jobs
   (d) The effects of recent student innovations

18. The world's highest ski resort at 5300 meters will not be a ski resort much longer. Due to global warming, Bolivia's only ski area, Chacaltaya, will soon be a dry brown mountain year-round. Glaciers in the Andes have been consistently receding, leading to a dramatic change at Chacaltaya. What was once a popular 40-foot deep ski run is now just a trail of rocks. Local skiers say the environmental impact is tragic since this is the only ski area in the world where one could ski through the clouds at an airplane-like altitude.

   Q: What is the main idea of the passage?

   (a) Weather changes threaten to close down Bolivia's ski resort.
   (b) The world's highest ski slope offers rare high-altitude skiing.
   (c) Glaciers are receding throughout the Andes Mountain chain.
   (d) Global warming is affecting skiers in most countries.

19. Nutritionists have discovered that an intake of healthy fruits and vegetables decreases as kids become teenagers. The diets of 2,000 kids were assessed in separate surveys five years apart. The latter survey revealed that most of the teens were eating significantly fewer fruits and vegetables than they had been consuming five years earlier. Experts say this is worrisome because of teens' high nutritional needs and the habits they are setting up for adulthood.

Q: What is the best title of the passage?

(a) Teens Enjoying More Fruits and Vegetables
(b) Children Disliking Vegetables
(c) Teenagers Learning about Healthy Eating
(d) Nutritionists' Worry about Adolescent Diet

20. *Fetal psychology* studies babies' patterns of behavior in the womb. For instance, researchers now know that when a mother laughs, her upside down baby bounces up and down on his or her head. The harder she laughs, the harder and faster the baby bounces. Since the baby doesn't seem to mind one bit, some experts are led to wonder if this is why humans love amusement park rides such as roller coasters.

Q: What is the passage mainly about?

(a) Why people of all ages enjoy roller coasters
(b) How laughter influences a newborn's development
(c) The types of technology used to monitor fetuses
(d) Explaining how fetal psychology can be used

21. Because of the Indian Removal Act in 1830, 17,000 Native Americans were removed from their homes in Georgia. Contrary to many beliefs, this group of Native Americans was not violent. Still, they were forced by the US military to leave their homes and walk 1,000 miles to relocate in Oklahoma. Four thousand people died during this long journey later known as the "The Trail of Tears."

Q: What is the passage mainly about?

(a) Native Americans in Georgia lived in a nonviolent manner.

(b) "The Trail of Tears" was a 4,000-mile journey to Oklahoma.

(c) Native Americans were removed from 17,000 homes.

(d) The Indian Removal Act led to a tragic event in US History.

22.

Dear Mr. Moreau,

I am honored that your organization has invited me to speak at your annual conference. I am familiar with your agency's work and the admirable contributions it has made to the field of speech pathology. Unfortunately, I will not be able to speak on the proposed date. Due to prior commitments, I will be out of the country at that time. If you would be interested in scheduling me to speak at next year's conference, I will be free those dates and would be happy to attend.

Sincerely,

Janet Marquez

Q: What is the purpose of this letter?

(a) To make Mr. Moreau aware of Ms. Marquez's availability

(b) To suggest another appropriate speaker for the conference

(c) To thank Mr. Moreau for his organization's work

(d) To express interest in speaking at this year's conference

23. Can you stick to your schedule? Experts recommend making a weekly schedule every Sunday night. Not only should this include commitments for the week, it should also specifically list the amount of school work to be accomplished during the week. In addition, an index card with the next day's schedule should be made every night and used as a reminder throughout the day to get all necessary things done.

Q: According to the passage, what isn't recommended for improving time organization?

(a) Write down school work that must be done.
(b) Include weekly commitments on your schedule.
(c) Make all schedules on the weekend.
(d) Use separate cards for daily schedules.

24. Economic well-being is not automatically affected by inflation. People often think that inflation means that an increase in prices will lower their standard of living. But usually during a period of inflation, prices, housing costs, and income all seem to go up together. Only if wages are rising slower than living expenses will economic well-being begin to suffer.

Q: What do people generally think about inflation?

(a) Leave as is that costs and income rise together during times of inflation.
(b) Leave as is that price increases make it harder to live comfortably.
(c) Leave as is that economic well-being increases slightly because of inflation.
(d) Leave as is that economic well-being is not greatly affected by inflation.

25. Why does moon dust smell like gunpowder? Well, almost half of it is made up of silicon dioxide glass that has been created by meteoroids slamming into the moon over billions of years. Chemically, moon dust is nothing like gun powder. Why the similar smell? No one knows for sure, but one theory suggests the dust could burn when it reacts to the oxygen inside spacecraft.

Q: How is silicon dioxide glass made?

(a) Through the process of oxidation in an enclosed space
(b) By breaking down the chemicals in moon dust
(c) Through meteoroid contact with the moon's surface
(d) By burning the silicon found in gun powder

26. The philosopher Descartes believed that if one was skeptical about everything, then the truths that remained after surviving extreme tests of skepticism would be incredibly strong indeed. Descartes developed a meditation that taught the doubting method by incorporating three different levels of doubt: perceptual illusion, dreams, and a "deceiving God."

Q: What did Descartes generally believe about all perceptions?

(a) They cannot survive true tests of skepticism.
(b) The cynical mind can prove them all to be false.
(c) They should all be mistrusted until proven to be real.
(d) They are only illusions derived from dreams.

27. Ellen Ochoa, the middle of five children, was raised by a single mother who was a strong mentor. Her positive support helped her daughter make education a priority. However, gaining advanced degrees in physics, engineering and inventing new computer technology wasn't enough for Ochoa. Among her pursuits like working, classical flute playing, volleyball and cycling, Ochoa still found time to apply to NASA to become an astronaut. She wasn't chosen on her first application. But things worked out better the next time. In 1993, Ochoa became the first Hispanic female in space.

Q: Which of the following is correct about Ellen Ochoa?

(a) She became an astronaut after reaching many other goals.
(b) She is most famous for her computer technology inventions.
(c) Her success was due to focusing all her time and energy on her work.
(d) It took several attempts for her to be chosen for the NASA program.

28. Hurricane-like winds tore through parts of Germany on Sunday, leaving several residents injured, travelers stranded, and homes without electricity. More than one hundred people were injured by blowing or falling debris. Several homes were damaged by the high winds. All flights were cancelled at the Frankfurt Airport, and the Berlin Central Railway Station was closed after the extreme winds ripped a steel support from the front of the building.

Q: Which of the following is correct about the storm?

(a) All German airports were forced to cancel flights.
(b) The winds tore apart steel sections of the railway.
(c) Homes were damaged from electrical problems.
(d) It created dangerous conditions that caused injuries.

29. The Electrifying Irish Shamrock Dance Company is coming to Kennsington Auditorium on Thursday, April 11th at 3 p.m. for one performance only. Their energetic style combines traditional Irish dance with ballet, tap, and modern dance. Choreographed to live traditional Celtic music, the performance will enliven your spirit and touch your heart. Get your tickets at the Kennsington box office. Call 900-899-1234 today.

Q: Which of the following is correct about the advertisement?
   (a) The dance troupe on tour was recently formed.
   (b) Tickets will be available beginning April 11th.
   (c) The performance showcases Irish music.
   (d) The choreography blends many styles of dance.

30. India's government provides free education to all children up to the age of 14. Despite this promise, there are still tens of millions of Indian children not going to school. The biggest problem seems to be in India's rural areas. Although education is supposed to be free, many agricultural workers can't afford to send their children to school. Small fees for books, uniforms and other expenses can add up to a month's worth of wages for these parents. Also, many parents don't want their children to attend classes in rural schools that are in extremely poor conditions.

Q: Which of the following is correct according to the passage?
   (a) Free education is not provided to Indian children in rural areas.
   (b) Only expensive private schooling is offered in rural India.
   (c) Parents worry about sending their children to city schools.
   (d) Many rural schools in India are in very bad shape.

31. One company has developed a product for office workers who are tired of annoying employees hanging around their desk. The forty dollar USB Missile Launcher connects to and is controlled by the employee's office computer. Three soft foam missiles can be fired within a range of fifteen feet. The launcher can move from side to side 180 degrees, or tilt up to 45 degrees. Missile sound effects can be played through the computer's speakers.

Q: Which of the following is correct according to the passage?

(a) The software is annoying to other employees.
(b) The employee must have a computer to use the product.
(c) The silent launcher catches unwanted visitors by surprise.
(d) The launcher can shoot targets up to forty feet away.

32. Many artists use asymmetrical composition to illustrate imbalance in their work. For example, large forms look visually heavier in weight than smaller ones. The same is true for dark forms as opposed to lighter ones. Textured objects look heavier than smoother ones. However, two or more little forms next to a larger one look well-balanced, as does a smaller, dark form next to a bigger, light one.

Q: Which of the following is correct about visual balance?

(a) Large forms and small forms look well-balanced on canvas.
(b) Two small forms look balanced compared to two larger ones.
(c) Smooth forms look lighter than objects that have a texture.
(d) Dark forms appear to weigh less than lighter, colored forms.

33. Because teenagers enjoy spending money, marketers are always searching for ways to get the attention of the teenage market, but it is tough to reach them through magazines. Teens spend much more time with their computers, televisions, and radios than they do reading magazines. However more specialty magazines, like ones about skateboarding, snowboarding, or celebrities are building large readerships and gaining attention from marketers.

Q: Which of the following is correct according to the passage?

(a) Teenagers spend more time on the Internet than they do watching TV.
(b) Celebrities are building large readerships.
(c) Reaching the teenage market is very difficult for magazines.
(d) Advertisers feel magazines cannot effectively reach teenagers.

34. Sociologists have recognized among various cultures a set of standards known as mores. Mores are the traditional concepts a given culture has about certain qualities. Different than folkways, or the accepted traditions and customs a culture has, mores are considered to be on a larger scale. For example, while someone who does not greet another person may be considered rude because he or she violated a folkway, a person who kills someone is considered evil because he or she violated social mores. The degree of disapproval is vastly different.

Q: What can be inferred from the passage?

(a) Courtesy is the main aspect of mores.
(b) Folkways are more important to any given culture.
(c) Folkways carry a higher degree of disapproval if violated.
(d) Mores are often reflected in a country's laws.

35. In 1862 the United States Government passed the Homestead Act, which was intended to help populate much of the newly acquired land west of the Mississippi River. The law basically allowed military veterans, heads of households, and anyone over the age of twenty-one to acquire up to 160 acres of federal land for a nominal fee. There were only two requirements: that the individual live on and farm the land for five years. It then became the property of the person who had homesteaded it.

Q: Which of the following is correct about the Homestead Act?
(a) It was meant to make money for the government.
(b) It permitted land to be given as payment to soldiers.
(c) It required that the land be cultivated for several years.
(d) It gave away land in Mississippi to be farmed.

36. One of linguist Noam Chomsky's theories suggested that grammar has universal features. But the language of the Piraha people of the Amazonas does not support this theory. Research has shown that these intelligent people have a highly complex language that includes language features never before heard and an absence of features assumed to be used in all languages. The Piraha have no color, counting or number words and no grammatical way of putting one phrase inside another.

Q: What does the writer suggest?
(a) The language lacks features that were previously considered normal for all languages.
(b) Chomsky's theory of universal features was incorrectly applied to this language.
(c) The absence of color words and numbers makes this language one of the most simplistic.
(d) Only short sentences that include one phrase are used by the Piraha people.

37. A new memory circuit is storming the computer world. It is smaller and denser than a typical circuit, and the demonstration model stores up to 160,000 bits of memory. Its inventors are hoping that the new circuit will allow for increased memory in the future, although it has already exceeded previous sixty-four bit demonstration memory circuits. Researchers say that production is unlikely to occur for at least ten years.

Q: Which of the following is correct according to the passage?

    (a) The new memory circuit is larger and stores more information.
    (b) The circuit is already in production for the next decade.
    (c) The new circuit won't be available to the public for several years.
    (d) The memory circuit has not yet been demonstrated to the public.

Part III **Questions 38~40**

Read the passage. Then identify the option that does NOT belong.

38. There are many steps an individual can take in order to decrease his or her stress levels. (a) One of these steps is proper exercise; running, aerobics or playing a sport can vastly improve an individual's mood. (b) Another thing a person can do to relieve stress is to meditate or pray, since meditation has been shown to cause relaxation and rids the body of tenseness. (c) A third part of decreasing stress is diet, because ensuring that the body is getting proper nutrition gives the body extra energy, important in combating stress. (d) Without the proper nutrients it needs, the body is unable to fight off disease.

39. Archer County has gotten more than ten inches of snow in the last few days, and the temperature has been averaging nearly twenty below. So here are some good tips for staying warm. (a) First, bundle up with multiple thin layers instead of one thick layer. (b) Bring pets in from outside so that they don't freeze. (c) Also, drink plenty of water, since water helps the body produce heat. (d) Make sure heating units are working properly, since these temperatures can cause hypothermia.

40. Using a global positioning system and special geological markers drilled into the Earth, geologists have begun to see how continents are deformed. (a) Data reveal that most of the surface of Asia is extremely strong, but when it breaks, it breaks like a ceramic dish. (b) As a result, Asia has experienced some of the world's largest earthquakes. (c) This type of fracture is similar to what is seen in typical plate tectonics. (d) This more detailed understanding is critical to understanding earthquakes.

Actual Test 4

TEPS

Part I Questions 1~16

Read the passage. Then choose the option that best completes the passage.

1. The Midtown Art Museum's new 5,000-square-foot addition is literally making some visitors sick. The multi-story exhibit features granite walls that are slanted at unusual angles. Many patrons have complained of dizziness and nausea after visiting the new museum. The museum has issued a statement explaining that the walls, which tilt toward and away from visitors, have _____ of some people.

   (a) compromised the safety
   (b) destroyed the health
   (c) affected the balance
   (d) hurt the vision

2. Students today need to learn skills in order to quickly process large amounts of information available at their fingertips via the Internet. A _____ and a careful choosing are necessary. But students must also learn to recognize good sources from less trustworthy ones. Education experts say this is often hard for students to do.

   (a) quick understanding
   (b) further study
   (c) large database
   (d) reliable website

3. It has recently been proven that a diet of fruits, vegetables, fish, whole grains and olive oil can delay and maybe even prevent the start of Alzheimer's disease. In one study, those who occasionally followed this diet decreased their _____ of developing the disease by 53%. Those who strictly followed the diet lowered their chances of getting the disease by 68%.

    (a) fear
    (b) risk
    (c) method
    (d) habit

4. Many famous retail stores, the ones often thought of by younger shoppers as uncool or out-of-date, are reinventing their images. By partnering with famous designers, these stores now offer the younger crowd stylish merchandise at low prices. Such partnerships team discount stores with some of the biggest names in the fashion industry. Young consumers love the fact that being cool and trendy

_____.

    (a) doesn't have to cost a lot
    (b) isn't necessary to be popular
    (c) means that you know fashion
    (d) depends largely on the designer

5. Your magazine's travel review on our city did not give a balanced view of all that our city has to offer. The writer talked about the overcrowding, traffic problems and high prices tourists often face, but he failed to mention the customer service and warm hospitality of our hotels, restaurants and shops. I would encourage your readers to visit our town and form their own opinion before believing the writer's _____.

    (a) unusually accurate depictions
    (b) highly exaggerated praise
    (c) incredibly slanted views
    (d) overly positive assertions

6. Wildlife researchers have recently found a refuge in Cambodia for endangered animals. The area is in _____ the Mekong River. One of the animals the group found was an entire colony of slender-billed vultures, which are becoming scarce in Southeast Asia and are extinct in several countries. In addition to them, researchers found a red-headed vulture, a white-rumped vulture, a leaf monkey and a giant ibis; all of which are also endangered.

    (a) an extraordinary mountaintop forest far from
    (b) an extremely isolated portion of the jungle near
    (c) a heavily populated section of a city next to
    (d) a good cultivated field

7. Chocolate … _____? A new study suggests that it might be.
    A specially-formulated drink made out of cocoa rich in flavonols, which promote the
    production of a chemical that is good for circulatory health, seemed to improve blood
    vessel function. The study examined the effects of the cocoa on people of all age
    groups, but found that the elderly experienced the most benefit; the functioning of the
    blood vessels increased significantly. Interestingly, the individuals experienced this
    improvement after only six days.

    (a) influential in brain health
    (b) detrimental to the heart
    (c) good for the blood vessels
    (d) harmful for the elderly

8. I once met a polite elderly gentleman on an airplane. During the flight, I listened to
    stories about his childhood in Europe before World War II. As we landed and prepared
    to say goodbye, I thanked him for sharing his memories and told him I hoped he would
    have a nice day. In response, he told me he hoped I would have a nice life, saying that
    a wish for a nice day only lasts as long as the day itself, but a wish for a nice life lasts
    forever. Since we never know if or when we might see someone again, he told me I
    _____. He was right. He would know. He had survived Auschwitz.

    (a) should wish this for everyone I meet
    (b) could talk with anyone I wanted
    (c) might try to be kinder to strangers
    (d) would benefit from taking another trip

9. Studies have shown that our outlook on life is directly linked to our overall state of well-being. Studies have proven that people with positive outlooks enjoy longer, healthier lives than their negative counterparts. Interestingly, happy people share quite a few characteristics that keep their stress levels low and their moods up. First, they're well-connected with others, and they're by nature very generous. In addition, they tend to focus on the big picture. Put another way, such people are not typically _____.

    (a) upset by minor annoyances
    (b) concerned about major health issues
    (c) interested in the welfare of others
    (d) optimistic about their futures

10.

Dear Ms. Chan,

I was truly excited to hear about the _____ you proposed at the meeting earlier today. I wanted to let you know that I would like to be included on your team and would be willing to provide all the background research you mentioned would be needed. I hope through our past work together you know you can rely on me to be thorough, accurate and enthusiastic. Please call me early next week to talk when the planning phase of the project gets underway.

Sincerely,
Mike Saigal

    (a) revised schedule
    (b) new project
    (c) policy changes
    (d) event location

11. One of the most creative eras in the history of Western society was the High Middle Ages. Some of humankind's most incredible _____ during this time. Medieval churches are one example. In France alone, eighty Gothic cathedrals and tens of thousands of smaller village churches were built within a ninety-year span. It took more stone to build these churches in Medieval France than it did to build the pyramids of Egypt.

    (a) religions were born
    (b) architecture was created
    (c) inventions were developed
    (d) early settlements were discovered

12. Personal economic planning is very hard to do when income, employment and price levels always seem to be changing. Even the best-planned investments _____ _____. One of the most extreme cases of economic instability was the Great Depression of the 1930s. People were left begging for food and many investors took their own lives as a result.

    (a) have not been successful due to unemployment
    (b) can fail because of this type of instability
    (c) fall short of providing necessary income
    (d) are not good enough to stabilize the economy

13. In many of American painter Mary Cassatt's works she chose to show images of children with their mothers or nurses. She had a special interest in trying to convey through her art both the tension and pleasure between adults and children who are bonded in a strong, emotional way. Her artwork _____ of the many complex feelings that take place in adult-child relationships.

    (a) shows an awareness
    (b) displays a lack of knowledge
    (c) illustrates a separation
    (d) overlooks the importance

14. Usually we think of our friends as people with whom we easily bond. Because we like the same types of activities as other people, it is easy to find things to talk about. But recent studies have shown that it is not what friends like, but what they dislike that unites them. In fact, in many friendships it is common _____ about certain things or other people that establishes the friendship and then serves to keep the friends bonded.

    (a) to change a belief
    (b) to feel a common approval
    (c) to produce a positive emotion
    (d) to share a negative attitude

15. Hearty Oat Boats Cereal now has an exclusive offer available! We at Four Square Grains, Inc. know that you eat Hearty Oat Boats as a part of a healthy lifestyle. So now, for a limited time, if you take three proofs of purchase into any Silver's Gym, you can save 15% off of any membership package. Hurry into any Silver's Gym today! _____, if you bring in four proofs of purchase, you will also receive a free Hearty Oat Boats and Silver's Gym and Aerobics gym bag! But hurry — this offer won't be around forever!

    (a) Nevertheless
    (b) As a result
    (c) However
    (d) In addition

16. American Emily Dickinson's poetry is famous for its originality. Sharp contrasts in moods are a characteristic of her poems. She used many hyphens in her poems, and her work could at times be very incongruent. _____ this, Dickinson presented clear images of her own feelings in straightforward ways as they occurred, rather than planning out her work as other authors often do. Because her poetry was so personal, she didn't want to share it with other people, so most of it was published after her death in 1886.

    (a) Because of
    (b) Compared to
    (c) Despite
    (d) Instead of

Part II Questions 17~37

Read the passage and the question. Then choose the option that best answers the question.

17. In the Hungarian language the word for house is "haz." This is very similar to the German and Dutch words for house, "haus" and "huis" and the English word "house" as well. Many often think Hungarians took their word for house from the Germans, but this isn't true. It actually came from the Finnish word "koti." No connection to the Germanic language can be discovered.

    Q: What is the main topic of the passage?

    (a) The origin of the Hungarian word for house
    (b) The history of the word house
    (c) The Finnish connection to other languages
    (d) German influence on other European languages

18. A new study shows that gender impacts how well students can learn from a teacher. It showed that female students learn more effectively from female teachers, just as male students learn more effectively from male teachers. The study reviewed test scores of male and female students which showed a relationship between higher test scores and the student having a teacher of the same sex. The study also found that gender gaps in education are narrower if the number of male and female teachers is nearly equal.

    Q: What is the main idea of the passage?

    (a) Students do equally well, regardless of the teacher's gender.
    (b) Test scores of male and female students are nearly equal.
    (c) The gender of the teacher may affect how well the student learns.
    (d) Public schools should consider establishing single-sex classes.

19. Japanese scientists have developed a new way to detect explosives that could be hidden almost anywhere. A small device called SQUID uses a sensor to detect nitrogen, which is found in many explosives. SQUID is so sensitive it can easily tell the difference between many white powders like sugar, salt, flour and TNT. Scientists hope the device will one day be used for standard airport security.

Q: What is the best title of the passage?
(a) Explosive Technology Improve by Japanese Scientists
(b) New Airport Security Technology to be Installed
(c) New Technology Invented to Detect Explosives
(d) New Device to Detect Explosives at Local Airport

20. Anxiety and stress are often talked about together as if they both mean the same thing. But actually they're very different. Anxiety means feeling mentally uneasy, while stress means experiencing negative physical effects due to an overload of pressure and demands. When dealing with either or both, the most important thing to understand is the cause. Directly addressing the cause is the only effective way to eliminate anxiety and stress.

Q: What is the best title of the passage?
(a) Health Problems Caused by Physical Overload
(b) How to Deal with Pressures and Demands
(c) The Most Common Causes of Anxiety and Stress
(d) Dealing Directly with Anxiety and Stress

21. Scientists recently uncovered the two entwined skeletons of a couple who died embracing each other. The site is near Verona, Italy (interestingly, the locale for Shakespeare's Romeo and Juliet). Archaeologists believe the couple was quite young due to the condition of their teeth, but have not yet discovered why they died. This sort of burial was extremely uncommon, and no other skeletons have ever been found in such an embrace. The team is working to preserve the positions of the skeletons by keeping intact the entire chunk of rock their bones are embedded in.

Q: What is the best title for the passage?
(a) Romeo and Juliet Buried While Hugging
(b) Uncommon Burial for Skeleton Couple
(c) Skeletons of Romeo and Juliet Found
(d) Skeleton Couple Found in Embrace

22. Scientists have noticed that many more polar bears have drowned in recent years. The polar ice, where they mainly live, has retreated by 160 miles over the last 25 years. U.S. government scientists refuse to link global warming to man's increasing use of carbon-based fuels. Many other scientists and environmentalists, however, believe that increased carbon emissions are directly responsible for the melting of the ice, which threatens the existence of polar bears across the Arctic region.

Q: How is global warming supposedly affecting polar bears?
(a) It is contributing to the spread of Arctic pollution.
(b) It is linked to a loss of polar ice habitats.
(c) It is creating toxic Alaskan coastal waters.
(d) It is causing polar bears to retreat to unsafe areas.

23. It's election time, and the Colfax Voting League wants you to vote. In order to be eligible to vote, you must be a citizen of at least eighteen years of age and register with the county. You may vote in person or, if approved, you can vote with an absentee ballot. A list of voting locations will be printed in Sunday's paper. Remember, it is your responsibility to research the candidates and decide which one would best represent you. November 2 is election day: mark that date on your calendar, so you don't forget to vote!

Q: What does the announcement say about voting?

(a) That voters must have an absentee ballot to vote.
(b) That voters first enroll with the government.
(c) That voters should be listed in the newspaper.
(d) That voters must register at the voting location.

24. In the past, managers for a well-known motor company were instructed to pay attention to whether managerial candidates put salt or pepper on their food before they had tasted it. If the candidate did, they believed that he would probably make decisions before knowing all the facts. But now many business people wouldn't view this as bad. In fact, many believe the best managers are quick decision-makers who don't need to know every single fact before making good decisions.

Q: What were the motor company managers instructed to notice about candidates?

(a) The way in which the candidates seasoned the food
(b) The comments candidates made about the food
(c) The candidates' confidence level while speaking
(d) The amount of food the candidates consumed

25. When it comes to economic progress, innovators are often more important than new inventions. It is creative minds that are always necessary to adopt and practically apply new inventions in effective ways. Henry Ford was this type of innovator. It wasn't the invention of the automobile alone that made an enormous economic impact on society. It was Ford's use of mass-production technology that so greatly affected the economy.

Q: Which of the following is correct about economic progress?

(a) Economic progress relies on mass-production technology.
(b) Henry Ford's most important contribution was the automobile.
(c) Innovators are essential when it comes to economic progress.
(d) Economic progress depends solely on creative inventions.

26. One of the favorite painting mediums of medieval artists was egg tempera. This paint, made with egg yolks, was commonly used until oil paints were introduced. Oddly, the yellow color of the yolks never ruined the other colors the artists mixed into the yolks. And surprisingly, over time, egg tempera paintings retained their color and yellowed less than oil paintings. In fact, tempera paintings that are hundreds of years old still display their original vibrant colors today.

Q: Which is correct according to the passage?

(a) Paints made with egg retain their color longer than oils.
(b) Medieval artists preferred egg tempera paints to oils.
(c) Oil paints retain their colors and yellow less than temperas.
(d) Oil paintings age less over time than egg tempera paintings.

27. Galileo Galilei's desire to analyze the natural world in new and different ways led to fascinating new theories and new technologies, too. While working at a university near Venice, Galileo heard of an instrument being built elsewhere that could be used to view distant objects. Without any other information, he went to work and built the first telescope. This telescope could clearly see ships fifty miles away. For this invention, the university leaders immediately doubled his salary.

Q: Which of the following is correct according to the passage?

(a) Galileo was a respected science professor at an Italian university.
(b) The first telescope was used by Galileo to create his advanced model.
(c) Galileo's curiosity resulted in many new ideas and inventions.
(d) Telescopes invented by Galileo were used on all Italian ships.

28. In the early 1800s, the Industrial Revolution was changing Western Europe in many ways. However, there were no such changes in Russia, which remained an agricultural country. This was unfortunate for the 80 percent of the population who were permanently trapped working for rich landowners. These workers, called "serfs," were treated like slaves. It was Alexander II who freed the serfs in 1861. But even then these free but very poor people lived in a state of oppression and inequality.

Q: Which of the following is correct according to the passage?

(a) The life of a serf was difficult both prior to and after 1861.
(b) Life for the serfs improved after Alexander II's decision.
(c) Treatment of serfs differed depending on the landowner.
(d) The Industrial Revolution created changes in Russia.

29. The Aubrey Little Theatre presents *The Bridgeport Boys*! Come see the award-winning musical about the experiments of the boys of the small town of Bridgeport. Robert Caubley raves, "*The Bridgeport Boy*s is the kind of rare production that can truly move you through song and laughter..." Tickets are on sale for $28 until October 16 at the Aubrey Little Theatre, with performances every Thursday, Friday and Saturday night at 8 p.m. So come and see *The Bridgeport Boys*!

Q: Which of the following is correct according to the advertisement?

(a) The show is sponsored by Robert Caubley.
(b) The performance will only be held on the weekend.
(c) The show features both music and comedy.
(d) Tickets have not yet been released for sale.

30. Alexander Hamilton and Aaron Burr are famous early American politicians. They are also famous for something else: a duel. Burr ran for governor of New York and lost, and Alexander Hamilton said that he believed Burr shouldn't have won. As a result, Burr challenged Hamilton to a gun duel, which was then considered a fair way to settle a disagreement. On the morning of July 11, 1804, Aaron Burr killed Alexander Hamilton, who had intentionally missed Burr. Interestingly, Hamilton's son had been killed in a similar duel at that exact location two years earlier.

Q: Which of the following is correct about gun duels in early US history?

(a) They were commonly used to settle family disputes.
(b) They were used only to solve political differences.
(c) They were an appropriate way to handle an argument.
(d) They were never meant to result in murder.

31. The entertainment industry has capitalized on recent trepidation caused by the possibility of an asteroid hitting the Earth and ultimately destroying all human life, but the chances of this happening outside of a Hollywood screenplay are extremely miniscule. Experts say a kilometer-sized asteroid, the type that would be capable of total devastation, could only be expected to impact the Earth maybe once every several million years. The closest recent asteroid encounter Earth has experienced came in 2002 when an asteroid as large as a soccer field came within 75,000 miles of the Earth as it passed by in outer space.

Q: Which of the following is true according to the passage?
(a) The odds of a large asteroid hitting the Earth are very small.
(b) Earth was recently impacted by a small asteroid in 2002.
(c) Large asteroids are not capable of the destruction represented in movies.
(d) Asteroids are expected to impact the Earth once every one million years.

32. Researchers are currently testing three different vaccines that may help prevent weight gain in humans. The vaccines make the body produce antibodies that prevent certain chemicals from working properly. These targeted chemicals are the ones which cause people to feel hungry and gain weight. So far, two out of the three vaccines have been successful in studies using rats.

Q: Which of the following is correct according to the passage?
(a) Three vaccines are currently being used to prevent human weight gain.
(b) Scientists are testing vaccines that could help people lose weight.
(c) Vaccines are being developed to keep people from gaining weight.
(d) Researchers have discovered antibodies cause people to weigh too much.

33. Existing resources of iron, copper, lead and zinc are dwindling in China. However, Chinese government geologists are surveying a Tibetan plateau that is presumed to have reserves full of billions of tons of these minerals. Geological surveyors are still working to accurately locate all the many reserves, but this is an extremely difficult task since geologists must work in harsh weather conditions at an average altitude of 4,300 meters.

Q: What can be inferred from the passage?

(a) China has run out of needed minerals.
(b) The plateau will be mined in the future.
(c) All the reserves will never be located.
(d) Plateaus are the best locations for mines.

34. Frozen foods were not found in stores and homes before 1930. Improvements in refrigeration technology changed this. Clarence Birdseye launched sales of frozen foods in Springfield, Massachusetts. By the 1940s, thousands of frozen food products were available to Americans. Before mid-century, production of frozen foods had reached 2.5 billion pounds. Over the next 50 years, advances in transportation, packaging, and cooking technology combined to make frozen foods a vital part of the American diet.

Q: What does the writer suggest?

(a) Several technologies have contributed to the growth of frozen foods.
(b) Frozen foods are generally less expensive than fresh foods.
(c) Microwave ovens have increased the popularity of frozen foods.
(d) Frozen foods will revolutionize kitchens of the future.

35. The Association for Animal Safety has been providing the public with helpful pet safety information for over forty years. But still some pet owners fail to understand just how important it is to responsibly care for their animals. Each year thousands of pets die from exposure to extreme temperatures. The Association for Animal Safety would like all pet owners to better understand the dangers animals face when left inside cars during the summer or locked outdoors in the wintertime.

Q: What would the following passage most likely be about?

(a) How temperatures indirectly affect an animal's health.
(b) The examples of pet owners not caring for their pets well.
(c) How to report irresponsible pet owners.
(d) The way to check a pet for heat exposure.

36. Each giant saguaro cactus starts out as a tiny black seed that can eventually grow up to fifty feet tall and weigh six tons depending on the life span of the plant. Saguaros can live to be 200 years old. However, they are vulnerable to lightning, freezing temperatures and severe droughts all of their lives. If they can survive these occurrences, saguaros generally die of old age sometime after turning 150 years old.

Q: What can be inferred from the passage?

(a) Saguaro cactus generally live to be 200 years old.
(b) The average height of a saguaro cactus is 50 feet tall.
(c) The majority of saguaros die from old age.
(d) Many saguaros die prematurely from severe weather conditions.

37. Thomas Hobbes was one of the earliest Materialists. When it came to human nature, Hobbes viewed humans as sophisticated physical objects. Much like machines, Hobbes said that all human functions and activities could be explained in entirely mechanistic terms. Even thoughts, which most would argue distinguish humankind from machines, were said by Hobbes to be physical operations produced by mechanical operations of the nervous system.

Q: What did Hobbes generally think about the human body?

(a) It is unlike any other physical object known to humankind.
(b) All systems of the human body function in a machine-like way.
(c) It works much the same as a machine except for the thought process.
(d) It is a simple material object much like a simple machine.

Read the passage. Then identify the option that does NOT belong.

38. Yoga is widely seen as important for improving physical and mental health. (a) So it's no surprise that a majority of those who practice yoga do so for health reasons. (b) Yoga can reduce stress, relieve pain, and strengthen muscles. (c) It is important to meditate while practicing yoga. (d) Medical practitioners increasingly recommend yoga to their patients.

39. By the year 2000, online teenagers had developed a new form of the English language. (a) Users of email and instant messaging began using a combination of letters, symbols, and numbers to simplify their communications. (b) Within a few years, adults began to catch on, and many today use this new language. (c) Providers of Internet software and cell phones now offer pictures, symbols, and emoticons that promote increased use of the form. (d) Laws restricting the use of this popular trend have been proposed in a number of states and countries.

40. Linguists know better than anyone that the way people talk mirrors their upbringing, their personal view of the world and their culture's history. (a) This is why, from one language to the other, there are many "untranslatable" terms. (b) For example the word "sisu" used by Finnish people has no known equal counterpart in the English language. (c) "Sisu" is an efficient one-word term that describes an individual's excessively-determined nature and unfailing belief to never give up even when the odds are stacked against him. (d) Finnish dialect continues to influence the regional dialects of the northeastern part of the United States.

Actual Test 5

TEPS

Part I **Questions 1~16**

Read the passage. Then choose the option that best completes the passage.

1. A new poll in Great Britain has found that most high school dropouts later wish they hadn't quit school. Currently, although the British government encourages them to remain in school through age eighteen, students can legally leave school at age sixteen. As a result, many stop attending school and instead find jobs, hoping to increase their workplace experience. However, the new study found that more than fifty-one percent of students who permanently dropped out later _____.

   (a) experienced pain
   (b) expressed regret
   (c) seemed happy
   (d) suggested otherwise

2. Quadratura was a style of artwork on ceilings which represented architecture. Most commonly used during the Baroque period, quadratura artists matched the style and architecture of a building. By painting images with depth on a flat or a rounded ceiling, they could make it appear deeper and more impressive. Thus, quadratura _____. It was meant to be viewed from below and was often used in churches and palaces.

   (a) enhanced the buildings' grand Baroque exteriors
   (b) employed the subtle use of color variation
   (c) removed the ceiling altogether in many cases
   (d) used illusion to create a sense of perspective

3.

> Dear Sir,
>
> Trust Bank has a new service for its loyal customers. Our Dollar Invest Plan is a zero-maintenance stock investment program at no cost to you. This service is provided as a _____ to customers that have been with us for more than 10 years. Simply complete a form specifying the monthly amount you would like invested and return it to us. We will then send you all the information you need to understand how your money can make you money. If you have any further questions, simply call us at 1-800-368-9256. Thank you again for your loyalty to Trust Bank.
>
> Cecil Graham
> Manager
> Trust Bank

    (a) symbol of investment
    (b) reaction of customers
    (c) gesture of appreciation
    (d) reminder of loyalty

4. There's a new trend in the mobile phone business: social networking. Motivated by the success of online social networking sites, which allow users to interact with people around the world via the Internet, mobile phone companies are now letting users log in, regardless of location. Cell phone companies _____ to tap into the profits that this huge phenomenon is spawning.

    (a) offer pager services once again
    (b) use these new services
    (c) add online TV shows and movies
    (d) create attractive phone designs

5.

Dear Sir or Madam,

I am writing to _____ at one of your Paco's Tacos restaurants. My husband and I went to one last Friday, and were not seated for a long time. Once we were finally seated, we found that the glasses were filthy. Following this, the wrong order was brought out to us, our dessert was rotten, and to make matters worse, we were overcharged. We will not be returning to Paco's Tacos.

Sincerely,
Marie Evans

    (a) tell you about a lovely evening I enjoyed
    (b) commend you on your selection of waiters
    (c) inform you about a horrible experience I had
    (d) complain about the dirty facilities I encountered

6. Scientists have begun to look at weather patterns in an attempt to predict outbreaks of diseases. They believe that _____ within a particular region, they can better anticipate the conditions that breed disease. Recently, in Africa, scientists noticed warmer weather and higher rainfall. They realized that this would create ideal breeding conditions for disease-carrying mosquitoes and sent anti-malaria drugs in advance. By analyzing weather patterns, they helped avert a disaster.

    (a) by monitoring the amounts of rainfall and the temperatures
    (b) by taking a census of the sick and diseased population
    (c) by recording the outbreaks of major diseases
    (d) by predicting long-term climatic change

7. The new Roebling bicycles are on sale now at the Bike Stop. We're offering a ten-speed Roebling Series A35 bicycle for $300, and if you don't have time to get out the toolbox, we'll even _____! We also have a fifteen-speed Mountain Professional Series Roebling with a five-year warranty for only $425. For the little ones in the family, we have a Roebling tricycle available in all of their favorite colors. This sale ends Monday, so roll on in to the Bike Stop today!

   (a) give free bicycle advice
   (b) put it together for you
   (c) give you easy instructions
   (d) make it more convenient

8. Once, when I was about ten years old, I made a batch of chocolate chip cookies. I carefully measured out each ingredient and mixed them together. I was just about to bake the dough when it occurred to me that I _____. So I stuck a large amount of cookie dough into my mouth. What a nasty surprise! I had somehow mistaken salt for sugar, and instead of a sweet little treat, I got a mouthful of salt.

   (a) should test my work
   (b) would enjoy the dough
   (c) could burn the cookies
   (d) should read the recipe

9.　A new study suggests that damage to the brain's hippocampus, which controls memory, may impair the ability to imagine the future. Patients who had experienced trauma to the hippocampus were asked to describe possible scenarios for an upcoming event or conversation. Generally, _____ such a situation.

    (a) those with such experience had better memories in
    (b) people with amnesia have little trouble remembering
    (c) most people have few problems talking about
    (d) these individuals had difficulty imagining and describing

10. Parents Digest's article on the increasing pressure parents are putting on their children to win in sports was very insightful. Instead of supporting their children regardless of the game's outcome, parents are becoming overly goal-oriented and critical. Children are no longer allowed to enjoy the sport for what it is — a game. These parents don't realize how harmful this is for their children. I would _____.

    (a) like to see such children try even harder to win
    (b) encourage more parents to relax and let their kids be kids
    (c) prefer that children talk about academic problems with their parents
    (d) suggest that parents teach their kids to be more goal-oriented

11. Just what is the cost of education? A new study found that half of university students aren't attending their first-choice school. They instead decided to go to their second- or third-choice school, many factoring tuition costs into their decisions. Also, lower-ranked schools are beginning to offer more incentives for students, such as _____ based upon merit, which further affect affordability.

    (a) inexpensive meal plans
    (b) upscale housing
    (c) convenient transportation
    (d) financial assistance

12. "Human capital" refers to the resources a nation has in its people. The intelligence, education and skills an individual acquires and contributes to a company impact the overall ability of the company to be productive. Similarly, a relationship between a country's human capital and its production level has been established. The higher the human capital — that is, the more capable the work force — the more the country produces. Different people possess varying levels of human capital, _____ _____.

    (a) determined by their knowledge and experience
    (b) related to the overall quality of their education
    (c) expressed in the ways they are employed
    (d) symbolized by their position within the company

13. NEW YORK CITY — The New York Police Department and Fire Department sell popular T-shirts and baseball caps with their logos on the front. Now, there's a new city department joining the craze: the Sanitation Department. City officials are beginning to market distressed brown ball caps with the blue logo on them, and they're popular. The trend is growing, and New York City officials have plans to _____. They hope to include other logos as well, including Transportation and Parks, for example.

(a) change the departments' logos
(b) discover the fake brands
(c) limit the production
(d) expand the popular line

14. French doctors have successfully completed their third partial face transplant. Two other patients have previously received partial face transplants, a French woman and a Chinese man. Doctors faced many challenges in completing such surgery. Perhaps the greatest risk they have is the possibility of the patient's body rejecting the transplant. Despite this danger, British and American doctors are now moving forward with plans _____.

(a) to determine the advantages of a transplant
(b) to finalize the partial face transplant procedure
(c) to complete a full face transplant
(d) to progress in transplant treatments

15. Groovy Tunes is now having its biggest sale of the year. We have cut prices dramatically. You'll even get an extra fifteen percent off of already marked clearance items if you come in this weekend. _____, we have hard-to-find records from artists like The When, Cherry and Son, and even Elvin. But you had better hurry — this far-out offer won't last long.

    (a) However
    (b) On the other hand
    (c) In addition
    (d) In contrast

16. Perhaps one of the most often-used tools of literature is personification. Personification is the characterization of an animal, inanimate object or an idea as if it had human qualities. _____, the darkness might be described as evil. Yet the darkness has no real ill will or personality; it is described this way simply because it is how the author or the author's character perceives it. A classic example of personification is a talking animal. The author is simply using the animal as another character, usually to accomplish a specific purpose in the plot.

    (a) In a similar way
    (b) For example
    (c) Regardless of this
    (d) In brief

Read the passage and the question. Then choose the option that best answers the question.

17. Recent research indicates that subliminal advertising is actually ineffective. In one study, volunteers listened to self-help tapes in which subliminal messages were supposed to be present. However, part of the group was given tapes that did not have any subliminal messages in them. All volunteers thought that they had benefited from the tapes — even those volunteers who had not had any subliminal messages on their tapes.

　　Q: What is the main topic of the passage?

　　　(a) The effectiveness of self-help tapes
　　　(b) The usefulness of test groups
　　　(c) The effectiveness of subliminal advertising
　　　(d) The usefulness of positive thinking

18. Researchers recently explored the relationship between children who like school and their socio-economic status. The new study surveyed parents to determine family variables, race and income, and compared them to how well the children of those families enjoyed school. The study found that children who liked school best were often Asian females of well-educated, married parents. The parents of these students also had moderate to high income levels and lived in the suburbs.

　　Q: What is the main idea of the passage?

　　　(a) Income levels have the largest role in whether a child likes school.
　　　(b) New data shows that gender has little effect on enjoyment of school.
　　　(c) Specific traits may indicate how much a child enjoys school.
　　　(d) The study attempted to relate high grades to socio-economic status.

19. Scientists are discovering significantly more about space and the universe. They recently found a group of galaxies even smaller than typical dwarf galaxies. Within this group is the smallest galaxy discovered to date, Leo T. It is far enough from the Milky Way, which normally traps nearby galaxies in its gravitational field, that it is unaffected and independent from any of the normal pull. Scientists believe that Leo T is the tiniest galaxy still able to produce new stars.

Q: What is the best title for the passage?
   (a) Smaller Universe Discovered
   (b) The Gravitational Pull of the Milky Way
   (c) Dwarf Galaxy Located
   (d) The Smallest Galaxy Scientists Have Ever Found

20. Franz Kafka's book Metamorphosis, originally published in 1915, is the sad story of a shy man, Gregor, who begins to slowly change into an insect. Interestingly, this change occurs not only in the character's physical shape, but also in his mental state. One of the main themes of the book is Gregor's isolation; he is constantly alone, even before he has fully changed into the bug. By the end of the story, Gregor's humanity has completely disappeared.

Q: What is the passage mainly about?
   (a) The revolutionary writing style of Franz Kafka
   (b) The depression present in Metamorphosis
   (c) The key aspects of Kafka's Metamorphosis
   (d) The importance of physical form to Franz Kafka

21. It is estimated that there are more than 6,000 languages spoken on Earth. Yet many languages are being spoken so little in modern times that they are in danger of being forever forgotten. Experts have documented nearly 750 languages that are already extinct or may become so in the near future. These languages represent every continent on the face of the planet, with the exception of Antarctica. Among nations with the most numerous extinct languages are Australia, the United States, and Brazil.

Q: What is the best title for the passage?

(a) Endangered Australia
(b) Lost Languages
(c) Antarctica's Extinction
(d) Forgotten Speakers

22. Many people associate beauty products with modern times. However, the ancient Egyptians actually had numerous cosmetics that they used on a daily or regular basis. The blackish eyeliner made famous in recent years as the "Cleopatra" look was used in order to prevent the sun's glare from causing vision problems. Egyptians also had lipstick, and there is evidence that some dyed their fingernails, much like nail polish is used today. In addition, creams used to treat baldness and gray hairs have also been found in the ruins of ancient Egyptian cities. Egyptians even used scented oils in their hair and on their skin as a moisturizer to protect them from the harsh desert sun.

Q: Which of the following is a reason Egyptians used eyeliner?

(a) To moisturize their eyelids
(b) To avoid the sun's reflecting light
(c) To dye the area around the eyes
(d) To protect eyelashes from the sunlight

23.

Dear Sir,

The First City Bank and Trust would like to inform you that you have overdrawn on your checking account. Our records indicate that a purchase on July 2 of this year exceeded the funds available. As a result, a hold has been placed on your account and an overdraft fee of forty-three dollars was billed to your secondary account. You are advised that you will not be able to make any purchases by debit card and all checks will be returned. Please make arrangements immediately to pay the balance so that your account can be reinstated.

Sincerely,
John Rulley
Vice President of Accounts
First City Bank and Trust

Q: What could be enclosed with this letter?

(a) a credit card application
(b) a bank statement
(c) a new debit card
(d) a check for forty-three dollars

24. Employers are facing a new problem in attempting to fill vacant job positions with recent graduates. While the number of job openings for graduates is increasing, the number of applicants that employers deem qualified is decreasing. Companies contend that many of the graduates they are interviewing don't possess proper business skills such as deductive reasoning, the ability to work well with a group, or the ability to communicate well with coworkers, supervisors, or clients. As a result, employers face a widening margin of unfilled positions despite an increase in the overall number of graduates.

Q: Which of the following is correct about employers?

(a) They are having difficulty finding applicants for open positions.
(b) They are unable to work well with groups of employees.
(c) They have a quick turnaround in job positions that are available.
(d) They have fewer applicants with the proper skills to succeed.

25. Emma Faust Tillman died recently in Hartford, Connecticut, only four days after becoming the world's oldest person. Tillman was born in 1892 to parents who were former slaves. She had twenty-three siblings, including four who also lived at least a century. During the course of her life, she saw twenty-one American presidents take the oath of office, including presidents as far back as Benjamin Harrison. Tillman was the oldest living person for the shortest period of time ever.

Q: Which of the following is correct according to the passage?

(a) Emma Tillman was the daughter of an American president.
(b) Tillman was the world's oldest person ever.
(c) Emma Tillman had four siblings that also lived to one hundred.
(d) Tillman was the world's oldest person for twenty-one days.

26. The corpse lily, one of the largest flowers in the world, is not a typical flower. Native to Sumatra, it uses its scent, which smells like rotting flesh — to attract pollinating insects. Another of the plant's unusual features is that it is able to generate its own heat, possibly to help the smell travel further. The corpse lily only blooms once every three to four years, and the bloom can be up to nine feet tall and last for up to four days.

Q: Which of the following is correct about the corpse lily?

(a) Its bloom is the largest in the world.
(b) Its smell lasts much longer than the smell of any other flower.
(c) It generates heat to help the bloom stay alive longer.
(d) It relies on its odor to attract beneficial insects.

27. The Garbage Dump, now in its seventh year, is a show for the whole family. You are transported to an imaginative world where everything is made out of garbage. The Garbage Dump also features performances by the jazz group Two-Man Band. Now showing every weeknight and twice on Saturdays at the Jazz Heritage Concert Hall. Reservations are limited, so call 863-4511 right now.

Q: Which of the following is true according to the advertisement?
   (a) The show has many tickets still available.
   (b) It runs twice every night of the week.
   (c) It has live music on stage.
   (d) The show has run for seventeen years.

28. Deforestation is typically thought of as a modern problem caused by humankind's appetite for lumber and other products made from wood. However, deforestation was actually a severe problem in medieval times as well. Wood was the main raw material people used during that time; it was used to heat structures, as well as to build them in the first place. Woodcutters looked to the forests of Europe to meet this high demand. As a result, many forests were also severely depleted and some in fact were eliminated entirely.

Q: Which of the following is correct according to the passage?
   (a) Deforestation is a complex issue that has surfaced very recently.
   (b) Wood is used far less in the modern era than it was in medieval times.
   (c) People in medieval times replenished forests by planting new trees.
   (d) Wood was the primary construction material in medieval times.

29. The League of Women Voters, Rio Grande Chapter, offers monthly seminars on topics relating to the American electoral system. Previous topics included voter registration, political inclusiveness, and community organizing strategies. The sessions meet at 7 p.m. on the first and third Wednesday of each month at the University of Pittsburgh Continuing Education Building, Room 324. The public is invited. Donations are encouraged.

Q: Which of the following is correct according to the announcement?

    (a) The seminars last approximately 90 minutes.
    (b) Attendees may introduce topics of their own choosing.
    (c) Men are not allowed to attend the meetings.
    (d) Two seminars are held on a monthly basis.

30. In the mid-eighteenth century, satire became popular in European arts. It was during this time that William Hogarth, one of its masters, was working to complete his best-known work, The Marriage Contract in oil on canvas. It features the busy negotiations involved in marrying the daughter of a merchant to the son of a noble person. The satire is clear: the couple is sitting side-by-side, and yet both are clearly being joined only for social standing and monetary purposes.

Q: Which of the following is correct according to the passage?

    (a) Hogarth made fun of the institution of marriage among the wealthy.
    (b) William Hogarth finished The Marriage Contract around the 1850s.
    (c) A well-known merchant negotiated to purchase The Marriage Contract.
    (d) William Hogarth was famous for his satiric and ironic paintings.

31. Come to the new FUNky Clowns Circus! We have three shows a night and plenty of booths to entertain kids and adults alike. Learn how to face-paint, juggle, and even work with circus animals. This Wednesday through Saturday night at seven, experience the wonder of acrobats, elephants and most of all, clowns. Everyone is invited, and kids twelve and under get in for only five dollars. This week only at the Family Fairgrounds! The FUNky Clowns Circus!

Q: Which of the following is correct according to the advertisement?

(a) The circus will feature a three-elephant show.
(b) General admission will cost only five dollars.
(c) The face-painting exhibit will be free to all children.
(d) The circus will present three shows per day.

32. In the midst of America's Great Depression, President Franklin D. Roosevelt created a program known as the Civilian Conservation Corps (CCC). This program was founded as a part of the economic relief policy known as the New Deal. It employed men in conservation work, which included conserving national parks. The goal of the CCC was to give the men work and prevent civil unrest due to a shortage of jobs.

Q: Which of the following is correct about the Civilian Conservation Corps?

(a) It employed men to work for civilian environmental groups.
(b) It recruited men to help enforce the New Deal in times of civil unrest.
(c) It was established due to a lack of employment during the Depression.
(d) It was declared by President Roosevelt to be mandatory for the unemployed.

33. The philosophical concept of causal determinism proposes that every event and action in history has been determined by another that occurred before it. It suggests that humans cannot make spontaneous decisions, and that nothing truly happens by accident. Interestingly, this theory is in direct opposition to the idea of free will.

Q: Which of the following is true of causal determinism, according to the passage?
  (a) Spontaneity determines the action that immediately follows it.
  (b) The application of free will determines the outcome of an occurrence.
  (c) Nothing can ultimately determine a situation's outcome.
  (d) It suggests that all human action is dependent upon a previous action.

34. Annabelle could not recall the directions to the company. She had a job interview there in a half an hour, and she had quickly written down the directions, but then lost the paper! Eventually she saw an old gas station with a phone book and stopped there, finally finding the address in the Yellow Pages. She got back in her car and drove straight to the interview right next door to the gas station.

Q: What can be inferred about Annabelle from the passage?
  (a) She really didn't want to attend the interview.
  (b) She actually wanted to work at the gas station.
  (c) She had written the note so quickly that it was nearly illegible.
  (d) She remembered the company's name but didn't know how to get there.

35. Aristotle, despite his fame today, once proposed a geocentric model of the universe, which suggested that the sun and the other planets orbited the Earth. It was Aristarchus, who is much less well-known, who said that Aristotle was incorrect. Aristarchus contended that the solar system was heliocentric, meaning that the Earth and other planets actually orbited the sun. Unfortunately, although it was true, Aristarchus's theory was discounted and ridiculed.

Q: What can be inferred from the passage?

(a) Aristotle is not remembered primarily for his geocentric model.
(b) Aristarchus was the superior philosopher.
(c) The geocentric model has been forgotten.
(d) The heliocentric model has not yet been proven.

36. The word "black market" typically suggests lethal weapons or illicit drugs. Yet officials say that the wildlife black market has experienced marked growth in the last few years. Experts believe the industry has grown to more than ten billion dollars, with most products being sold to China and the U.S. This alarming figure ranks the wildlife black market third in criminal income in the world. The strong demand in countries around the world for products made from rare and endangered species seems to ensure that the wildlife black market will not disappear in the near future.

Q: Which of the following is correct about the wildlife black market?

(a) China is its third largest supplier.
(b) The number of its consumers has increased.
(c) The United States is one of its largest consumers.
(d) It is the tenth largest criminal operation in the world.

37. Mahatma Gandhi was one of the individuals who most profoundly affected India and the world. He was born in 1869 and was later educated in England to become a lawyer. He visited South Africa and experienced his first taste of discrimination. As a result, he became very politically and socially active. His principle of ahimsa, or nonviolent disobedience, changed the way that people protested against oppression, and he later led India to independence. He was also influential in the South African civil rights movement. Gandhi was assassinated in 1948 by an extremist who opposed his political involvements.

Q: Which of the following can be inferred about Gandhi according to the passage?
   (a) He had probably been a victim of discrimination since his childhood.
   (b) Activists in the South African civil rights movement considered him important.
   (c) He was assassinated by someone in the South African government.
   (d) People did not like him in England because he was Indian.

Part III   Questions 38~40

Read the passage. Then identify the option that does NOT belong.

38. For safe driving in winter conditions, a number of precautionary measures are recommended by professionals. (a) Decrease your speed and allow plenty of room to stop. (b) Don't hitchhike along the side of a snowy or icy road. (c) Use the brakes gently to avoid skids and wheels locking up. (d) Drive in higher gears for improved traction and vehicle control.

39. The number of employed citizens is essential to the Gross National Product — the amount a given country produces. (a) Okun's law estimates a two and a half percent decrease in GNP for every one percentage point unemployment increases. (b) For example, if unemployment was at only three percent, but increases to six percent, there would be an overall decrease of 7.5 percent in the GNP. (c) Thus, governments are always mindful of unemployment rates. (d) Part-time jobs are also less productive than full-time jobs.

40. It has been argued by some that the most difficult language in the world to learn is the Basque language, spoken in portions of Spain as well as in regions of France. (a) Basque has no known linguistic relatives, making it what is known as a language isolate. (b) As a result, the history of the language is generally unknown. (c) Despite that, linguists have been able to determine that the language has been influenced to some degree by the Romans; the written form of the Basque language uses Roman characters. (d) Also, there are six primary dialects of Basque as well as a few more that are less well known.

[TEPS] Test of English Proficiency Seoul National University

독해 Reading Comprehension

Actual Test 1

#	a	b	c	d		#	a	b	c	d
1	ⓐ	ⓑ	ⓒ	ⓓ		26	ⓐ	ⓑ	ⓒ	ⓓ
2	ⓐ	ⓑ	ⓒ	ⓓ		27	ⓐ	ⓑ	ⓒ	ⓓ
3	ⓐ	ⓑ	ⓒ	ⓓ		28	ⓐ	ⓑ	ⓒ	ⓓ
4	ⓐ	ⓑ	ⓒ	ⓓ		29	ⓐ	ⓑ	ⓒ	ⓓ
5	ⓐ	ⓑ	ⓒ	ⓓ		30	ⓐ	ⓑ	ⓒ	ⓓ
6	ⓐ	ⓑ	ⓒ	ⓓ		31	ⓐ	ⓑ	ⓒ	ⓓ
7	ⓐ	ⓑ	ⓒ	ⓓ		32	ⓐ	ⓑ	ⓒ	ⓓ
8	ⓐ	ⓑ	ⓒ	ⓓ		33	ⓐ	ⓑ	ⓒ	ⓓ
9	ⓐ	ⓑ	ⓒ	ⓓ		34	ⓐ	ⓑ	ⓒ	ⓓ
10	ⓐ	ⓑ	ⓒ	ⓓ		35	ⓐ	ⓑ	ⓒ	ⓓ
11	ⓐ	ⓑ	ⓒ	ⓓ		36	ⓐ	ⓑ	ⓒ	ⓓ
12	ⓐ	ⓑ	ⓒ	ⓓ		37	ⓐ	ⓑ	ⓒ	ⓓ
13	ⓐ	ⓑ	ⓒ	ⓓ		38	ⓐ	ⓑ	ⓒ	ⓓ
14	ⓐ	ⓑ	ⓒ	ⓓ		39	ⓐ	ⓑ	ⓒ	ⓓ
15	ⓐ	ⓑ	ⓒ	ⓓ		40	ⓐ	ⓑ	ⓒ	ⓓ
16	ⓐ	ⓑ	ⓒ	ⓓ						
17	ⓐ	ⓑ	ⓒ	ⓓ						
18	ⓐ	ⓑ	ⓒ	ⓓ						
19	ⓐ	ⓑ	ⓒ	ⓓ						
20	ⓐ	ⓑ	ⓒ	ⓓ						
21	ⓐ	ⓑ	ⓒ	ⓓ						
22	ⓐ	ⓑ	ⓒ	ⓓ						
23	ⓐ	ⓑ	ⓒ	ⓓ						
24	ⓐ	ⓑ	ⓒ	ⓓ						
25	ⓐ	ⓑ	ⓒ	ⓓ						

Actual Test 2

#	a	b	c	d		#	a	b	c	d
1	ⓐ	ⓑ	ⓒ	ⓓ		26	ⓐ	ⓑ	ⓒ	ⓓ
2	ⓐ	ⓑ	ⓒ	ⓓ		27	ⓐ	ⓑ	ⓒ	ⓓ
3	ⓐ	ⓑ	ⓒ	ⓓ		28	ⓐ	ⓑ	ⓒ	ⓓ
4	ⓐ	ⓑ	ⓒ	ⓓ		29	ⓐ	ⓑ	ⓒ	ⓓ
5	ⓐ	ⓑ	ⓒ	ⓓ		30	ⓐ	ⓑ	ⓒ	ⓓ
6	ⓐ	ⓑ	ⓒ	ⓓ		31	ⓐ	ⓑ	ⓒ	ⓓ
7	ⓐ	ⓑ	ⓒ	ⓓ		32	ⓐ	ⓑ	ⓒ	ⓓ
8	ⓐ	ⓑ	ⓒ	ⓓ		33	ⓐ	ⓑ	ⓒ	ⓓ
9	ⓐ	ⓑ	ⓒ	ⓓ		34	ⓐ	ⓑ	ⓒ	ⓓ
10	ⓐ	ⓑ	ⓒ	ⓓ		35	ⓐ	ⓑ	ⓒ	ⓓ
11	ⓐ	ⓑ	ⓒ	ⓓ		36	ⓐ	ⓑ	ⓒ	ⓓ
12	ⓐ	ⓑ	ⓒ	ⓓ		37	ⓐ	ⓑ	ⓒ	ⓓ
13	ⓐ	ⓑ	ⓒ	ⓓ		38	ⓐ	ⓑ	ⓒ	ⓓ
14	ⓐ	ⓑ	ⓒ	ⓓ		39	ⓐ	ⓑ	ⓒ	ⓓ
15	ⓐ	ⓑ	ⓒ	ⓓ		40	ⓐ	ⓑ	ⓒ	ⓓ
16	ⓐ	ⓑ	ⓒ	ⓓ						
17	ⓐ	ⓑ	ⓒ	ⓓ						
18	ⓐ	ⓑ	ⓒ	ⓓ						
19	ⓐ	ⓑ	ⓒ	ⓓ						
20	ⓐ	ⓑ	ⓒ	ⓓ						
21	ⓐ	ⓑ	ⓒ	ⓓ						
22	ⓐ	ⓑ	ⓒ	ⓓ						
23	ⓐ	ⓑ	ⓒ	ⓓ						
24	ⓐ	ⓑ	ⓒ	ⓓ						
25	ⓐ	ⓑ	ⓒ	ⓓ						

Actual Test 3

#	a	b	c	d		#	a	b	c	d
1	ⓐ	ⓑ	ⓒ	ⓓ		26	ⓐ	ⓑ	ⓒ	ⓓ
2	ⓐ	ⓑ	ⓒ	ⓓ		27	ⓐ	ⓑ	ⓒ	ⓓ
3	ⓐ	ⓑ	ⓒ	ⓓ		28	ⓐ	ⓑ	ⓒ	ⓓ
4	ⓐ	ⓑ	ⓒ	ⓓ		29	ⓐ	ⓑ	ⓒ	ⓓ
5	ⓐ	ⓑ	ⓒ	ⓓ		30	ⓐ	ⓑ	ⓒ	ⓓ
6	ⓐ	ⓑ	ⓒ	ⓓ		31	ⓐ	ⓑ	ⓒ	ⓓ
7	ⓐ	ⓑ	ⓒ	ⓓ		32	ⓐ	ⓑ	ⓒ	ⓓ
8	ⓐ	ⓑ	ⓒ	ⓓ		33	ⓐ	ⓑ	ⓒ	ⓓ
9	ⓐ	ⓑ	ⓒ	ⓓ		34	ⓐ	ⓑ	ⓒ	ⓓ
10	ⓐ	ⓑ	ⓒ	ⓓ		35	ⓐ	ⓑ	ⓒ	ⓓ
11	ⓐ	ⓑ	ⓒ	ⓓ		36	ⓐ	ⓑ	ⓒ	ⓓ
12	ⓐ	ⓑ	ⓒ	ⓓ		37	ⓐ	ⓑ	ⓒ	ⓓ
13	ⓐ	ⓑ	ⓒ	ⓓ		38	ⓐ	ⓑ	ⓒ	ⓓ
14	ⓐ	ⓑ	ⓒ	ⓓ		39	ⓐ	ⓑ	ⓒ	ⓓ
15	ⓐ	ⓑ	ⓒ	ⓓ		40	ⓐ	ⓑ	ⓒ	ⓓ
16	ⓐ	ⓑ	ⓒ	ⓓ						
17	ⓐ	ⓑ	ⓒ	ⓓ						
18	ⓐ	ⓑ	ⓒ	ⓓ						
19	ⓐ	ⓑ	ⓒ	ⓓ						
20	ⓐ	ⓑ	ⓒ	ⓓ						
21	ⓐ	ⓑ	ⓒ	ⓓ						
22	ⓐ	ⓑ	ⓒ	ⓓ						
23	ⓐ	ⓑ	ⓒ	ⓓ						
24	ⓐ	ⓑ	ⓒ	ⓓ						
25	ⓐ	ⓑ	ⓒ	ⓓ						

Actual Test 4

#	a	b	c	d		#	a	b	c	d
1	ⓐ	ⓑ	ⓒ	ⓓ		26	ⓐ	ⓑ	ⓒ	ⓓ
2	ⓐ	ⓑ	ⓒ	ⓓ		27	ⓐ	ⓑ	ⓒ	ⓓ
3	ⓐ	ⓑ	ⓒ	ⓓ		28	ⓐ	ⓑ	ⓒ	ⓓ
4	ⓐ	ⓑ	ⓒ	ⓓ		29	ⓐ	ⓑ	ⓒ	ⓓ
5	ⓐ	ⓑ	ⓒ	ⓓ		30	ⓐ	ⓑ	ⓒ	ⓓ
6	ⓐ	ⓑ	ⓒ	ⓓ		31	ⓐ	ⓑ	ⓒ	ⓓ
7	ⓐ	ⓑ	ⓒ	ⓓ		32	ⓐ	ⓑ	ⓒ	ⓓ
8	ⓐ	ⓑ	ⓒ	ⓓ		33	ⓐ	ⓑ	ⓒ	ⓓ
9	ⓐ	ⓑ	ⓒ	ⓓ		34	ⓐ	ⓑ	ⓒ	ⓓ
10	ⓐ	ⓑ	ⓒ	ⓓ		35	ⓐ	ⓑ	ⓒ	ⓓ
11	ⓐ	ⓑ	ⓒ	ⓓ		36	ⓐ	ⓑ	ⓒ	ⓓ
12	ⓐ	ⓑ	ⓒ	ⓓ		37	ⓐ	ⓑ	ⓒ	ⓓ
13	ⓐ	ⓑ	ⓒ	ⓓ		38	ⓐ	ⓑ	ⓒ	ⓓ
14	ⓐ	ⓑ	ⓒ	ⓓ		39	ⓐ	ⓑ	ⓒ	ⓓ
15	ⓐ	ⓑ	ⓒ	ⓓ		40	ⓐ	ⓑ	ⓒ	ⓓ
16	ⓐ	ⓑ	ⓒ	ⓓ						
17	ⓐ	ⓑ	ⓒ	ⓓ						
18	ⓐ	ⓑ	ⓒ	ⓓ						
19	ⓐ	ⓑ	ⓒ	ⓓ						
20	ⓐ	ⓑ	ⓒ	ⓓ						
21	ⓐ	ⓑ	ⓒ	ⓓ						
22	ⓐ	ⓑ	ⓒ	ⓓ						
23	ⓐ	ⓑ	ⓒ	ⓓ						
24	ⓐ	ⓑ	ⓒ	ⓓ						
25	ⓐ	ⓑ	ⓒ	ⓓ						

Actual Test 5

#	a	b	c	d		#	a	b	c	d
1	ⓐ	ⓑ	ⓒ	ⓓ		26	ⓐ	ⓑ	ⓒ	ⓓ
2	ⓐ	ⓑ	ⓒ	ⓓ		27	ⓐ	ⓑ	ⓒ	ⓓ
3	ⓐ	ⓑ	ⓒ	ⓓ		28	ⓐ	ⓑ	ⓒ	ⓓ
4	ⓐ	ⓑ	ⓒ	ⓓ		29	ⓐ	ⓑ	ⓒ	ⓓ
5	ⓐ	ⓑ	ⓒ	ⓓ		30	ⓐ	ⓑ	ⓒ	ⓓ
6	ⓐ	ⓑ	ⓒ	ⓓ		31	ⓐ	ⓑ	ⓒ	ⓓ
7	ⓐ	ⓑ	ⓒ	ⓓ		32	ⓐ	ⓑ	ⓒ	ⓓ
8	ⓐ	ⓑ	ⓒ	ⓓ		33	ⓐ	ⓑ	ⓒ	ⓓ
9	ⓐ	ⓑ	ⓒ	ⓓ		34	ⓐ	ⓑ	ⓒ	ⓓ
10	ⓐ	ⓑ	ⓒ	ⓓ		35	ⓐ	ⓑ	ⓒ	ⓓ
11	ⓐ	ⓑ	ⓒ	ⓓ		36	ⓐ	ⓑ	ⓒ	ⓓ
12	ⓐ	ⓑ	ⓒ	ⓓ		37	ⓐ	ⓑ	ⓒ	ⓓ
13	ⓐ	ⓑ	ⓒ	ⓓ		38	ⓐ	ⓑ	ⓒ	ⓓ
14	ⓐ	ⓑ	ⓒ	ⓓ		39	ⓐ	ⓑ	ⓒ	ⓓ
15	ⓐ	ⓑ	ⓒ	ⓓ		40	ⓐ	ⓑ	ⓒ	ⓓ
16	ⓐ	ⓑ	ⓒ	ⓓ						
17	ⓐ	ⓑ	ⓒ	ⓓ						
18	ⓐ	ⓑ	ⓒ	ⓓ						
19	ⓐ	ⓑ	ⓒ	ⓓ						
20	ⓐ	ⓑ	ⓒ	ⓓ						
21	ⓐ	ⓑ	ⓒ	ⓓ						
22	ⓐ	ⓑ	ⓒ	ⓓ						
23	ⓐ	ⓑ	ⓒ	ⓓ						
24	ⓐ	ⓑ	ⓒ	ⓓ						
25	ⓐ	ⓑ	ⓒ	ⓓ						

Actually...
He is so friendly

When you do TEPS!
진짜 실력을 만나다, 텝스!

민간자격국가공인 영어능력검정 (제2013-10호.1+급,1급,2+급,2급에 해당)

넥서스 수준별 TEPS 맞춤 학습 프로그램

기출·독해

서울대 기출문제

서울대 텝스 관리위원회 텝스 최신기출 1200제 문제집 3 | 서울대학교 TEPS관리위원회 문제 제공 | 352쪽 | 19,500원
서울대 텝스 관리위원회 텝스 최신기출 1200제 해설집 3 | 서울대학교 TEPS관리위원회 문제 제공 · 넥서스 TEPS연구소 해설 | 480쪽 | 25,000원
서울대 텝스 관리위원회 텝스 최신기출 1200제 문제집 2 | 서울대학교 TEPS관리위원회 문제 제공 | 352쪽 | 19,500원
서울대 텝스 관리위원회 텝스 최신기출 1200제 해설집 2 | 서울대학교 TEPS관리위원회 문제 제공 · 넥서스 TEPS연구소 해설 | 480쪽 | 25,000원
서울대 텝스 관리위원회 텝스 최신기출 1200제 문제집 1 | 서울대학교 TEPS관리위원회 문제 제공 | 352쪽 | 19,500원
서울대 텝스 관리위원회 텝스 최신기출 1200제 해설집 1 | 서울대학교 TEPS관리위원회 문제 제공 · 넥서스 TEPS연구소 해설 | 480쪽 | 25,000원
서울대 텝스 관리위원회 공식기출 1000 Listening/ Grammar/ Reading | 서울대학교 TEPS관리위원회 문제 제공 | 19,000원/ 12,000원/ 16,000원
서울대 텝스 관리위원회 최신기출 1000 | 서울대학교 TEPS관리위원회 문제 제공 · 양준희 해설 | 628쪽 | 28,000원
서울대 텝스 관리위원회 최신기출 1200/SEASON 2~3 문제집 | 서울대학교 TEPS관리위원회 문제 제공 | 352쪽 | 19,500원
서울대 텝스 관리위원회 최신기출 1200/SEASON 2~3 해설집 | 서울대학교 TEPS관리위원회 문제 제공 · 넥서스 TEPS연구소 해설 | 472쪽 | 25,000원

실전·어휘

실전 모의고사

How to TEPS 영역별 끝내기 청해 | 테리 홍 지음 | 424쪽 | 19,800원
How to TEPS 영역별 끝내기 문법 | 장보금 · 써니 박 지음 | 260쪽 | 13,500원
How to TEPS 영역별 끝내기 어휘 | 양준희 지음 | 240쪽 | 13,500원
How to TEPS 영역별 끝내기 독해 | 김무룡 · 넥서스 TEPS연구소 지음 | 504쪽 | 25,000원

텝스 청해 기출 분석 실전 8회 | 넥서스 TEPS연구소 지음 | 296쪽 | 19,500원
텝스 문법 기출 분석 실전 10회 | 장보금 · 써니 박 지음 | 248쪽 | 14,000원
텝스 어휘 기출 분석 실전 10회 | 양준희 지음 | 252쪽 | 14,000원
텝스 독해 기출 분석 실전 12회 | 넥서스 TEPS연구소 지음 | 504쪽 | 25,000

영역별

초급 (400~500점)

How to TEPS intro 청해편 | 강소영 · Jane Kim 지음 | 444쪽 | 22,000원
How to TEPS intro 문법편 | 넥서스 TEPS연구소 지음 | 424쪽 | 19,000원
How to TEPS intro 어휘편 | 에릭 김 지음 | 368쪽 | 15,000원
How to TEPS intro 독해편 | 한정림 지음 | 392쪽 | 19,500원

중급 (600~700점)

How to TEPS 실전 600 어휘편 · 청해편 · 문법편 · 독해편 | 서울대학교
관리위원회 문제 제공(어휘), 이기헌(청해), 장보금 · 써니 박(문법), 황수경 · 넥서스
구소(독해) 지음 | 어휘: 15,000원, 청해: 19,800원, 문법: 17,500원, 독해: 19,0
How to TEPS 실전 700 청해편 · 문법편 · 독해편 | 강소영 · 넥서스 TEF
구소(청해), 이신영 · 넥서스 TEPS연구소(문법), 오정우 · 넥서스 TEPS연
(독해) 지음 | 청해: 16,000원, 문법: 15,000원, 독해: 19,000원

종합서

한 권으로 끝내는 텝스 스타터 | 넥서스 TEPS연구소 지음 | 584쪽 | 22,000원
How to 텝스 초급용 모의고사 10회 | 넥서스 TEPS연구소 지음 | 296쪽 | 15,000원
How to 텝스 베이직 리스닝 | 고명희 · 넥서스 TEPS연구소 지음 | 320쪽 | 18,500원
How to 텝스 베이직 리딩 | 박미영 · 넥서스 TEPS연구소 지음 | 368쪽 | 19,500원

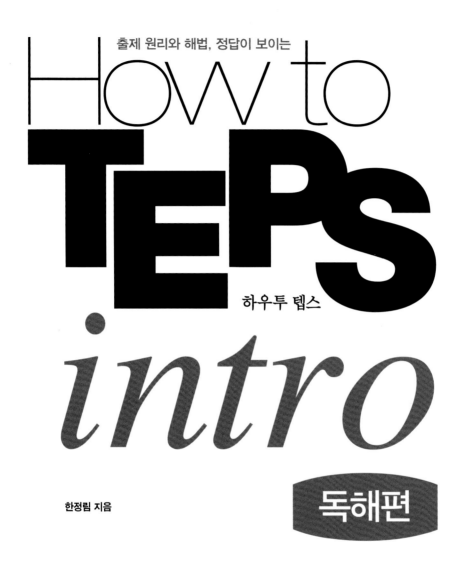

출제 원리와 해법, 정답이 보이는

How to TEPS intro

하우투 텝스

독해편

한정림 지음

정답 및 해설

넥서스

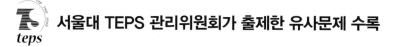

서울대 TEPS 관리위원회가 출제한 유사문제 수록

출제 원리와 해법, 정답이 보이는

How to TEPS intro

하우투 텝스

독해편

한정림 지음

정답 및 해설

넥서스

I. Introduction to TEPS Reading

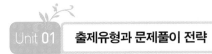

Unit 01 출제유형과 문제풀이 전략

Part I-1 빈 칸 채우기(일반유형)

Sample Question

Doctors say they are seeing more sports injuries in younger children simply due to too much physical strain. More injuries such as stress fractures and tendon problems are now treated in athletes as young as four years old. Doctors say that year-round, high-impact sports overuse developing bones. Doctors also place blame on parents and coaches who put too much pressure on physical performance and often don't allow children _____.

(a) the chance to physically prove themselves
(b) adequate time to recover from injuries
(c) enough opportunities to participate in sports
(d) rewards for their improved performance

해석 의사들에 의하면, 어린이들이 점점 더 운동 중 부상을 겪는데, 이는 심한 육체적 긴장 때문이다. 피로 골절, 힘줄의 문제들과 같은 부상치료를 받는 운동선수들 중에는 어리게는 4살 어린이까지 있다. 의사들에 따르면, 연중 계속되는 강도 높은 운동은 자라나는 뼈를 혹사시키고 있다. 의사들은 또한 부모와 코치들을 비난하는데, 부모와 코치들은 육체적 성과에 너무 많은 압력을 가하고, 종종 어린이들이 부상으로부터 회복할 수 있는 충분한 시간을 주지 않는다고 한다.

(a) 육체적으로 자신들의 능력을 증명할 기회
(b) 부상으로부터 회복할 수 있는 충분한 시간
(c) 운동에 참여할 수 있는 충분한 기회들
(d) 그들의 나아진 실력에 대한 보상

해설 어린 아동의 지나친 육체적 긴장으로 인한 피해를 지적하는 글이다. 피로골절과 힘줄의 문제와 같은 부상이 4세 정도의 어린 아동에게 발생하고 있다고 글의 전반부에서 경고하고 있다(More injuries such as stress fractures and tendon ~ four years old). 따라서 글의 후반부에서는 의사들이 이런 심각한 상태를 어떻게 회복할 수 있을 지에 대한 대안이나 이를 해결하지 않는 부모에 대한 지적이 있을 것이라 예상할 수 있다. stress fractures, tendon problems, overuse bones 등의 표현들과 가장 잘 조화를 이루는 빈칸 내용은 부상과 관련된 내용인 (b)이다. (a) physically, (c) sports, (d) performance 등은 본문 지문에서 언급한 어휘를 사용해서 오답 매력도를 높이고 있다는 것에 유의하자.

어휘 due to ~때문에
strain 긴장
fracture 골절
tendon 힘줄
athlete 운동선수
year-round 연중 계속되는
high-impact 고강도의

overuse 혹사시키다
place blame on ~을 비난하다, 나무라다
pressure 압력, 압박
adequate 충분한, 알맞은

정답 (b)

Part I-2 빈 칸 채우기(연결어)

Sample Question

Researchers are examining whether a new computer game can help adolescents fight cancer. The game features a character that wages war on cancer and teaches facts about the disease and how to fight it. One study on the results of the game suggests that it encourages those with cancer to tackle the challenges of fighting off the disease more hopefully. _____, they noticed an increase in the desire to take medication in an effort to recover.

(a) Similarly
(b) Additionally
(c) Unfortunately
(d) Ideally

해석 연구자들은 새 컴퓨터 게임은 청소년들이 암과 싸우게 도울 수 있는지를 연구하고 있다. 게임의 특징은 한 등장인물이 암과 싸우고 그 암에 대한 사실들과 싸우는 방법을 가르쳐준다. 게임의 결과에 관한 한 연구에서는 그 게임이 암 환자들로 하여금 암을 퇴치하고자 하는 당면과제를 좀더 희망적으로 다룰 수 있도록 격려해준다는 것을 시사한다. 더구나 그들은 회복하려는 노력의 일환으로 약을 복용하고자 하는 욕구가 증가되었음을 발견했다.

(a) 유사하게
(b) 추가적으로
(c) 불행하게도
(d) 이상적으로

해설 새로운 게임이 암을 퇴치하는 데 얼마나 도움을 줄 수 있는가에 관한 글이다. 한 연구는 이 게임은 환자들에게 질병과 싸우고자 하는 어려움에 맞설 수 있도록 희망을 준다(suggests that it encourages those with cancer to tackle the challenges of fighting off the disease more hopefully)고 주장한다. 바로 뒷부분은 환자들에게 희망을 준다는 내용을 추가적으로 설명해 주는 문장이 오고 있다. 따라서 빈 칸에 들어갈 정답은 (b)다.

어휘 adolescent 청소년
cancer 암
wage war on ~과 싸우다
disease 질병, 질환
tackle (문제 등) 다루다, ~에 달려들다
challenge 어려움, 도전과제
fight off 격퇴하다
effort 노력
recover 회복하다

정답 (b)

Part II-1 주제 파악

Sample Question

Characters in novels can generally be categorized as one of two different kinds. A dynamic character is someone that adapts and changes. It is important to note, however, that a dynamic character does not always make positive changes; backward movement can also occur. A static character, on the other hand, is a person in a novel that remains consistent and experiences little or no change in perception, morals, or personality.

Q What is the passage mainly about?

(a) The two different types of fiction
(b) The changes of dynamics in a novel
(c) The static categories of characters in a novel
(d) The kinds of characters in a novel

해석 소설의 인물들은 일반적으로 두 가지 종류 중 하나로 분류될 수 있다. 동적 인물은 환경에 적응하고 변화하는 사람이다. 그러나 동적 인물이 항상 긍정적인 변화만을 일으키는 것은 아니라는 것에 주의해야 한다. 역행하는 변화도 발생할 수 있다. 반면에 정적인 인물은 소설에서 일관적이고 인식이나 도덕관 혹은 성격에 있어 변화를 거의 겪지 않는 사람이다.

    Q 위 글의 요지로 알맞은 것을 고르시오.
    (a) 소설의 두 가지 종류
    (b) 소설의 역동성 변화
    (c) 소설 속 인물들의 정적 범주
    (d) 소설의 인물들의 종류

해설 본문에서 다루고 있는 내용은 소설의 등장인물들(characters in novels)에 관한 것이다. 간단히 요약을 하면, 등장인물의 종류가 두 가지 있는데, 역동적인 인물(a dynamic character)과 정적인 인물(a static character)이 있고, 각 각의 특성과 역할을 언급하고 있다. 따라서 정답은 (d)다.

어휘 **categorize** 분류하다
dynamic 동적인
adapt 적응하다
positive 긍정적인
static 정적인, 정지된
consistent 일관된
perception 인지력
moral 도덕관
personality 성격

정답 (d)

Part II-2 세부사항 파악하기

Sample Question

The toys and games of children reflect the experience and values of the times. When I was a young boy, my friends and I played soldier games. Our fathers' experiences in fighting a world war were reenacted in our play. My sisters and other little girls played with dolls and cooking toys, mimicking the real-life activities of their mothers. But now, as a father myself, I see that the times have changed.

Q What is the next paragraph likely to be about?

(a) The effects of playing with guns or dolls
(b) The toys and games of the author's children
(c) Similarities between past and present toys
(d) Internet-based games of the future

해석 어린이들의 장난감과 게임들은 시대의 경험과 가치관을 반영한다. 내가 소년이었을 때 내 친구들과 나는 병정놀이를 하고 놀았다. 세계 대전에 참전했던 우리 아버지들의 경험이 우리들의 놀이에서 재현된 것이었다. 내 여동생들과 다른 여자 아이들은 인형들과 장난감 소꿉 놀이를 하며 그들의 어머니들의 실제 활동들을 흉내 냈다. 그러나 오늘날 아버지가 된 나는 시대가 변화했다는 것을 알게 된다.

    Q 다음 문단에 나올 내용으로 알맞은 것을 고르시오.
    (a) 총이나 인형을 가지고 노는 것의 영향
    (b) 글쓴이의 아이들의 장난감들과 게임들
    (c) 과거와 현재 장난감들의 유사점들
    (d) 미래의 인터넷 게임들

해설 첫 문장이 주제문이라고 할 수 있다. 시대에 따라서 아이들이 갖고 노는 장난감도 변한다는 내용을 먼저 밝히고, 구체적인 예로, 필자가 어린 시절에는 남자는 병정놀이를, 여자는 인형과 소꿉놀이를 했다는 내용을 들고, 마지막 문장에서는 문장을 But now~로 시작하면서, 아버지가 된 현재는 예전의 이런 현상이 바뀌었음을 알게 된다고 하였다. 따라서 이어질 내용은 (b) 필자의 자녀들의 장난감과 게임에 대한 내용이 오는 것이 자연스럽다.

어휘 **reflect** 반영하다
value 가치
reenact 재현하다
mimic 모방하다

정답 (b)

Part II - 3 추론문제

Sample Question

The U.S. Census Bureau published a profile of the United States population at the close of the 20th Century. The report noted that 30% of the nation's foreign-born population lived in the state of California in 1999, for example. Much of the information revealed how Americans lived. Among other things, the study showed that nearly three-fifths of American men age 18-24 lived with their parents or in a college dormitory. Yet more than half of the women of that age lived independently.

Q What can be inferred from the passage?

(a) Less than 1/2 of 18-to-24-year-old women lived with their parents.
(b) More young men than women attended colleges in America.

(c) The U.S. Census Bureau published a book titled At the Close of the 20th Century.

(d) The percentage of foreigners living in California is increasing.

해석   미국 인구 통계국은 20세기를 마감하며 미국 인구 분석표를 출판했다. 보고서는 예를 들어, 1999년 미국 국민 중 외국에서 출생한 사람들의 30%가 캘리포니아 주에 살고 있었다는 사실을 보여주었다. 많은 정보가 미국인들의 생활 방식을 보여 주었다. 연구에 의하면 18세에서 24세의 미국 남성의 거의 5분의 3이 부모와 함께 살거나 대학 기숙사에 산다고 한다. 그러나 같은 나이 대비 여성 인구의 절반은 독립하여 살고 있는 것으로 나타났다.

Q 위 글의 내용에서 추론될 수 있는 것을 고르시오.

(a) 18세에서 24세의 여성의 절반 이하가 부모와 함께 산다.

(b) 미국에서는 여성보다 더 많은 젊은 남성들이 대학에 다닌다.

(c) 미국 인구 통계국이 〈20세기를 마감하며〉라는 제목의 책을 출판했다.

(d) 캘리포니아에 거주하는 외국인 비율이 증가하고 있다.

해설   (a) '18세에서 24세 사이의 여성의 반 이상이 독립해서 산다(Yet more than half of ~ independently)'고 했으므로 '이 연령대의 여성의 절반도 안 되는 사람들이 부모와 함께 산다'는 내용은 옳다. 따라서 (a)가 정답이다. (b) 미국 내 젊은 남성과 여성의 대학생 비율을 비교한 내용은 언급되지 않았으므로 유추할 수 없다. (c) 미국 인구 통계국이 출판한 책의 제목은 이 글에서는 알 수 없으므로 답이 아니다. (d) 캘리포니아에 사는 외국인의 비율이 증가하고 있다는 추세에 대한 보고가 아니라, 1999년 당시 외국인이 얼마나 그곳에 살고 있었는지를 밝히고 있으므로 답이 아니다.

어휘   publish 출판하다
profile 분석표, 개요
reveal 알리다, 드러내다, 폭로하다
dormitory 기숙사
independently 독립하여, 자주적으로

정답   (a)

Part III 내용의 일관성 파악

Sample Question

There are things that can be done to "cure" the problem of being messy. The first step is recognizing the problem. (a) Another lesson is that cleanliness makes life much easier. (b) Following this, messy individuals must refrain from adding to the clutter. (c) However, this will not eliminate the problem, only control it. (d) The final thing that must be done is to sort through the piles of needless junk and to maintain the organization.

해석   깔끔하지 못한 문제를 해결하기 위해 할 수 있는 것들이 있다. 첫 번째 단계는 물론 문제를 인정하는 것이다. (a) 또 다른 배울 것은 깔끔함이 인생을 훨씬 안락하게 만든다는 것이다. (b) 이것에 이어 깔끔하지 못한 사람들은 지저분함을 더 이상 추가하지 말아야 한다. (c) 그러나 이것이 문제를 사라지게 하지는 않

는다. 단지 조절만 할 뿐이다. (d) 마지막으로 해야 될 일은 필요 없는 물건들을 가려내고 그 정돈 상태를 유지하는 것이다.

해설   글의 주제는 깔끔하지 못한 문제를 해결하는 방법이다. (b), (c), (d)는 이러한 방법들이 제시되어 있는 반면, (a)는 깔끔함의 장점을 나타내고 있어 글의 전체 흐름과 어울리지 않는다. 따라서 정답은 (a)다.

어휘   cure (문제를) 해결하다
messy 난잡한, 지저분한
recognize 인정하다
individual 개인
refrain from ~을 삼가다
clutter 지저분함
eliminate 삭제하다, 제거하다
sort 가려내다, 분류하다
pile 더미
organization 구성, 편성

정답   (a)

II. Understanding the Structures in TEPS Reading

Unit 01   분사 구문 (Reduced Structure)

Practice Test

A.   **Read and match.**

  1. d   **2.** e   **3.** a   **4.** b   **5.** c

1. Having eaten Chinese food for lunch, I don't want to eat it again.

해석   점심에 중국음식을 먹어서 또 먹고 싶지 않다.

해설   분사구문이 '이유'로 쓰였으며 Having + p.p.를 보고 주절과 종속절의 시제가 다름을 알 수 있다.

정답   d. Because I ate Chinese food for lunch, I don't want to eat it again.

2. Having eaten Chinese food for lunch, I didn't want to eat it again.

해석   점심에 중국음식을 먹었었기에 또 먹고 싶지 않았다.

해설   분사구문이 '이유'로 쓰였으며 Having + p.p.가 있으므로 주어와 종속절의 시제가 다름을 알 수 있다. 주절은 과거, 종속절은 대과거로 쓰였다.

정답   e. Because I had eaten Chinese food for lunch, I didn't want to eat it again.

3. Satisfied with the result, they had a big party.

4

해석 만족스런 결과가 나와서 그들은 크게 파티를 열었다.

해설 분사구문이 '이유'로 쓰였으며 Satisfied 앞에 being이 생략되었다. 동사원형 + ing이므로 주절과 종속절의 시제가 같음을 알 수 있다.

정답 a. As they were satisfied with the result, they had a big party.

4. The weather being fine, we had lunch in the garden.

해석 날씨가 좋아서 정원에서 점심을 먹었다.

해설 분사구문이 '이유'로 쓰였으며 주절과 종속절의 주어가 달라서 종속절의 The weather를 생략하지 못했다.

정답 b. As the weather was fine, we had lunch in the garden.

5. While he was trying to sleep last night, a mosquito kept buzzing in his ear.

해석 그가 어제 잠을 자려고 할 때 모기 한 마리가 계속 귓가에서 윙윙거렸다.

해설 분사구문이 '시간'으로 쓰였으며 주절과 종속절의 주어가 달라서 종속절에 he가 살아있다. 의미 강조를 위해 분사구문에 때로는 접속사를 그대로 두기도 한다.

어휘 mosquito 모기
buzz 윙윙 소리를 내다

정답 c. While he was trying to sleep last night, a mosquito kept buzzing in his ear.

B. Fill in the blanks. Use the word given in the parenthesis.

1. (realize)_____ that I had made a mistake, I apologized to him.

해석 내가 실수했다는 것을 깨닫고 나서 그에게 사과를 했다.

해설 주절과 종속절의 시제와 주어가 같기에 realizing이 쓰였다.

어휘 apologize 사과하다

정답 Realizing

2. (not, know)_____ what to do next, I asked for his advice.

해석 더 이상 무엇을 해야 할지 몰라서 그에게 자문을 구하였다.

해설 주절과 종속절의 시제가 같고 주어가 같기에 Not knowing이 쓰였다.

어휘 ask for 요구하다, 구하다

정답 Not knowing

3. (spend)_____ all his paycheck, he does not have any money to live on.

해석 급여를 다 써버린 그는 더 이상 생활비가 없다.

해설 '이유'를 나타내는 분사구문이다. 봉급을 다 써버린 것이 이전 과거이므로 Having + p.p.를 써야 한다.

어휘 paycheck 봉급

정답 Having spent

4. (watch)_____ the movie before, I do not want to see it again.

해석 그 영화는 전에 보았던 영화라서 다시 보고 싶지 않다.

해설 '이유'를 나타내는 분사구문이다. 주절의 시제보다 종속절의 시제가 앞서기에 Having + p.p.를 써야 한다.

정답 Having watched

5. (ask)_____ to give a speech, I suddenly felt nervous.

해석 연설을 해달라는 부탁을 받았을 때 갑자기 긴장이 되었다.

해설 '시간'을 나타내는 분사구문이다.

어휘 nervous 초조한, 긴장한

정답 Asked

C. Change the following into reduced sentences and translate into Korean.

1. Since he got a new job, he has been working very hard.

해석 새로운 직장을 얻은 이후로 그는 열심히 일을 하고 있다.

해설 주절과 종속절의 주어가 같고 시제가 같으므로 getting이 되었다.

어휘 get a job 직업을 얻다

정답 Getting a new job, he has been working very hard.

2. While she was driving to the office, Joan had an accident.

해석 조안은 사무실로 가는 길에 사고를 당했다.

해설 주절과 종속절의 주어와 시제가 같아서 driving으로 쓰였다.

어휘 accident 사고

정답 Driving to the office, Joan had an accident.

3. Before he left for work, he had a big breakfast.

해석 출근하기 전에 그는 아침을 든든히 먹었다.

해설 주절과 종속절의 시제 및 주어가 같아서 주어가 생략되고 동사원형 leave + ing가 되었다.

어휘 leave for work 출근하다

정답 Leaving for work, he had a big breakfast.

4. Because he had never flown in an airplane, he felt a little nervous.

해석 그는 비행기를 한 번도 타보지 않아서 약간 긴장이 되었다.

해설 종속절의 시제가 주절보다 이전 과거이므로 having + p.p.가 쓰였다.

어휘 nervous 초조한, 신경질적인

정답 Having never flown in an airplane, he felt a little nervous.

5. As I didn't know what to do, I asked him for some advice.

해석 난 무엇을 해야 할지 몰라서 그에게 자문을 구했다.

해설 주절과 종속절의 시제와 주어가 같아서 knowing이 되었다.

어휘 advice 조언, 충고

정답 Not knowing what to do, I asked him for some advice.

Unit 02 비교 구문
(Comparative Structure)

Practice Test

A. **Complete the sentences with the correct forms of the words in parentheses.**

1. The Amazon is one of _____ rivers in the world. (long)

해석 아마존 강은 세계에서 가장 긴 강 중의 하나이다.

해설 the + -est + (한정)을 사용한 최상급 구문이다.

정답 the longest

2. The Yangze River is _____ the Mississippi River. (long)

해석 양자강은 미시시피 강보다 길다.

해설 2개의 대상을 비교하고 있으므로 비교급 + than의 형태를 취한다.

정답 longer than

3. Ms. White is _____ person I have ever met. (patient)

해석 화이트 양은 내가 만났던 사람 중에 가장 참을성이 많은 사람이다.

해설 내가 만났던 사람들 중 가장 참을성이 많았던 사람이라는 최상급 표현이다.

어휘 patient 참을성 있는

정답 the most patient

4. Janet is as _____ as her sister. (thoughtful)

해석 쟈넷은 자기 언니(혹은 여동생)만큼 사려 깊다.

해설 as ~ as를 사용한 원급 구문이다.

어휘 thoughtful 사려 깊은, 골똘히 생각하는

정답 thoughtful

5. Frank is _____ than his colleagues. (intelligent)

해설 프랭크는 그의 동료들보다 똑똑하다.

해설 프랭크와 그의 동료를 비교하고 있으므로 비교급 + than의 형태를 취한다.

어휘 colleague 동료

정답 more intelligent

B. **Correct the errors.**

1. This cake is sweeter I have ever eaten.

해석 이 케이크는 내가 먹어본 것 중에서 제일 달다.

해설 내가 먹어본 것들 중에 가장 달았다는 뜻이기에 최상급 표현이 적당하다.

어휘 ever 이제까지

정답 sweeter → the sweetest

2. Mike is the taller person in his family.

해석 마이크는 그의 가족 중 키가 제일 크다.

해설 가족이라는 무리 중에 제일 크다는 것이므로 최상급 표현이 적당하다.

어휘 tall 키가 큰

정답 taller → tallest

3. Bill's understanding of computers is better than me.

해석 빌이 나보다 컴퓨터에 대한 이해력이 높다.

해설 빌의 이해력과 나의 이해력을 비교하고 있으므로 me를 mine으로 고쳐야 한다.

어휘 understanding 이해력

정답 me → mine

4. Winter in Alaska is cold than it is in Pittsburgh; winter there is the coldest in the States.

해석 알래스카에서 겨울은 피츠버그보다 더 춥다; 미국에서 그곳의 겨울이 제일 춥다.

해설 알래스카와 피츠버그를 비교하고 있으므로 비교급 + than의 형태를 취해야 한다.

어휘 state 국가

정답 cold than → colder than

5. Her car is as fast mine.

해석 그녀의 차는 내 차만큼 빠르다.

해설 as ~ as를 사용한 원급 구문이다.

어휘 fast 빠른

정답 as fast → as fast as

6. Asia is largest continent in the world.

해석 아시아는 세계에서 가장 큰 대륙이다.

해설 the + -est + (한정)을 사용한 최상급 구문이다.

어휘 continent 대륙

정답 largest → the largest

7. The blue whale is the bigger animal in the world.

해석 흰 긴 수염 고래(혹은 푸른 고래)는 세계에서 가장 큰 동물이다.

해설 the + -est + (한정)을 사용한 최상급 구문이다. 뒤에 in the world로 한정하고 있다.

어휘 whale 고래

정답 bigger → biggest

8. Cats are more independent as dogs, but dogs are loyal than cats.

해석 독립심은 고양이가 개보다 많지만, 충성심은 개가 고양이보다 많다.

해설 개와 고양이를 비교하는 비교급 구문이다. 비교급 + than의 형태를 취한다.

어휘 independent 독립한, 독립적인
loyal 충성스러운

정답 as → than, loyal → more loyal

9. This is very good. But that is very better.

해석 이것은 정말 좋아. 하지만 저것이 훨씬 좋아.

해설 비교급 수식은 much, even, still, far, a lot 등이 한다.

어휘 better 더 좋은

정답 very → much

10. The most important part of the exam was given at the end when most people were the most exhausted.

해석 사람들이 가장 지쳐 있는 마지막 시간에 제일 중요한 시험 부분이 나왔다.

해설 최상급 형용사가 보어로 사용될 경우와 부사의 최상급에는 the를 붙이지 않는다.

어휘 exhaust 지치다, 기진맥진하다

정답 the most exhausted → most exhausted

C. Put the words in order and translate into Korean.

1. than her / his dog better / he likes

해석 그는 그녀보다 그의 개를 더 좋아한다.

정답 He likes his dog better than her.

2. the most prestigious club / in Korea / this is

해석 이 클럽은 한국에서 제일 유명한 클럽이다.

어휘 prestigious 유명한

정답 This is the most prestigious club in Korea.

3. of the two / the taller / he's

해석 둘 중에 그가 더 크다.

정답 He's the taller of the two.

4. much more comfortable / this chair is / than that one

해석 이 의자는 저 의자보다 훨씬 편하다.

어휘 comfortable 편안한

정답 This chair is much more comfortable than that one.

5. doesn't know / everything / the wisest man

해석 가장 현명한 사람도 모든 것을 알지 못한다.

어휘 wise 현명한

정답 The wisest man doesn't know everything.

Unit 03   병렬 구문 (Parallel Structure)

Practice Test

A. Complete the sentences with the correct forms of the words in parentheses.

1. Amy (make)_____ her bed and (clean) _____ up her room every morning.

해석 에이미는 아침마다 침대를 정리하고 방을 치운다.

해설 3인칭 단수(Amy)가 주어이므로 동사는 makes가 되어야 하고 동사 clean이 makes와 병렬 구조를 이루고 있어 makes and _____이므로 cleans가 되어야 한다.

어휘 make a bed 침대를 정리하다

정답 makes, cleans

2. Yesterday I (be)_____ sick and (stay)_____ home.

해석 어제는 아파서 집에 있었다.

해설 명백한 과거의 단서(Yesterday)가 있고 주어는 I이므로 be동사의 형태는 was이고 동사 stay가 was와 병렬구조를 이루고 있어 was and _____이므로 stayed가 되어야 한다.

어휘 stay 머물다

정답 was, stayed

3. Ms. Benson is cooking dinner and (talk) _____ on the phone.

해석 벤슨양은 저녁을 지으면서 통화 중이다.

해설 A and B에서 A와 B의 형태는 같아야 한다. cooking and _____이므로 talk의 ~ing형인 talking이 와야 한다.

어휘 talk on the phone 통화하다

정답 talking

4. Laura will stay home and (read)_____ her favorite magazine tonight.

로라는 오늘밤 집에 있으면서 그녀가 가장 좋아하는 잡지를 읽을 것이다.

해설 stay and _____의 구조이므로 read의 형태는 read가 되어야 한다.

어휘 magazine 잡지

정답 read

5. My new neighbor, Mr. Gray is both (kindness) _____ and (friend)_____ _____.

해석 새로운 이웃인 그레이씨는 친절하고 다정하다.

해설 both A and B에서 A와 B의 형태는 같아야 한다. is 다음에는 kindness의 형용사 kind가 와야 보어가 될 수 있다. both kind and _____의 형태가 되어 friend의 형용사 friendly가 와야 한다.

어휘 kindness 친절

정답 kind, friendly

6. _____ Bill or his friends know her new address.

해석 빌이나 그의 친구 중 하나가 그녀의 새 주소를 안다.

해설 either A or B는 'A와 B 둘 중에 하나'의 의미로 병렬구조를 이룬다.

어휘 either 어느 한쪽의

정답 Either

7. Sue enjoys (swim)_____ and (play)_____ tennis.

해석 수는 수영을 하거나 테니스 치는 것을 즐긴다.

해설 enjoy는 동명사를 목적어로 취한다. swim의 형태는 swimming이 되어야 하고 swimming and _____이므로 play 또한 playing이 되어야 한다.

어휘 enjoy 즐기다

정답 swimming, playing

8. My cousin, Bill is (intelligence)_____ and (humor)_____.

해석 내 사촌 빌은 똑똑하고 유머러스하다.

해설 동사 is의 보어가 되어야 하므로 형용사 intelligent가 되어야 하고 intelligent and _____이므로 humorous가 되어야 한다.

어휘 intelligence 총명, 지혜

정답 intelligent, humorous

9. The pasta in this restaurant is (expensively)_____ but (deliciously)_____.

해석 이 식당의 파스타는 비싸지만 맛있다.

해설 동사 is의 보어가 되어야 하므로 형용사 expensive가 되어야 하고 expensive but _____의 병렬구조이므로 delicious가 되어야 한다.

어휘 expensive 비싼

정답 expensive, delicious

10. My brother usually (ride)_____ his bike to school in the morning, but it (rain)_____ when he left the house this morning, so he (take)_____ the bus.

해석 우리 형(혹은 내 남동생)은 아침마다 주로 자전거를 타고 학교에 가는데, 오늘 아침 등교 할 때는 비가 내려서 버스를 타고 갔다.

해설 일상적인 습관을 나타낼 때는 현재 시제를 쓴다. 따라서 ride는 rides가 된다. 비가 오는 것은 아침에 집을 떠날 때의 순간적인 일이므로 진행형을 쓰는 것이 적절하다. 시제는 과거이므로 과거 진행형을 써서 was raining이다. 또한 버스를 탄 것은 과거의 사실이므로 과거 동사 took를 써야 한다.

어휘 take a bus 버스를 타다

정답 rides, was raining, took

B. Correct the errors.

1. She will either visit nor call you this afternoon.

해석 그녀는 오후에 너의 집으로 가지도 전화하지도 않을 것이다. (either → neither의 경우)
그녀는 오후에 너희 집에 전화하거나, 방문 할 것이다. (nor → or의 경우)

해설 either A or B나 neither A nor B의 형태가 올바르다.

정답 either → neither 혹은 nor → or

2. The novel is both interesting as well as instructive.

해석 그 소설은 흥미롭고 유익하다.

해설 both A and B나 A as well as B의 형태가 되어야 한다.

어휘 novel 소설
instructive 유익한

정답 as well as → and 혹은 both 삭제

3. The moon has neither air or water.

해석 달에는 공기도 물도 없다.

해설 부정문에서는 or 대신 nor를 써야 한다.

정답 or → nor

4. Dining in a restaurant is more fun than to eat at home alone.

해석 음식점에서 먹는 게 집에서 혼자 먹는 것 보다 낫다.

해설 비교의 대상도 병렬구조를 이룬다. Dining is more fun than의 형태이므로 to eat이 eating이 되어야 한다.

어휘 dining 식사

정답 to eat → eating

5. This country's music is quite different from my country.

해석 이 나라의 음악은 우리나라 음악과 다르다.

해설 비교의 대상도 같은 병렬 구조가 되어야 한다. 비교의 대상은 music이므로 country를 country's (music)로 바꿔야한다.

어휘 quite 꽤, 완전히

정답 country → country's

C. Put the words in order and translate into English.

1. than mine / is a lot more useful / her research for the thesis

해석 논문에 대한 그녀의 연구가 내 것보다 훨씬 유용하다.

어휘 thesis 논문

정답 Her research for the thesis is a lot more useful than mine.

2. nor in his pocket / the keys are / neither on the table

해석 열쇠는 테이블에도 그의 주머니에도 없다.

어휘 neither A nor B A도 B도 아니다

정답 The keys are neither on the table nor in his pocket.

3. in what he says / I'm not interested / or what he does

해석 나는 그가 뭐라 말하던 뭘 하던 관심 없다.

어휘 be interested in ~에 관심[흥미]이 있다.

정답 I'm not interested in what he says or what he does.

4. and because he wants to help you / because it's his job / he is helping you

해석 그가 너를 돕는 이유는 그게 그의 일이기 때문이며 스스로도 도와주길 원하기 때문이다.

정답 He is helping you because it's his job and because he wants to help you.

5. he called not only the police department / but also the fire department / when the accident happened,

해석 사고가 일어났을 때 그는 경찰서뿐만 아니라 소방서에도 전화를 했다.

어휘 not only A but also B A뿐만 아니라 B도

정답 When the accident happened, he called not only the police department but also the fire department.

Unit 04 도치 구문 (Inverted Structure)

Practice Test

A. Write C for correct or I for incorrect.

1. The lawyer asked the client when did he first meet her.

해석 변호사는 의뢰인에게 그가 그녀를 처음 만났을 때가 언제인지 물었다.

해설 틀린 문장. 간접의문문이므로 〈동사 + 주어〉의 어순이 〈주어 + 동사〉가 되어야 한다. when did he first meet her를 when he first met her로 바꿔야 한다.

어휘 lawyer 변호사
client 고객, 의뢰인

정답 I

2. Do you know where he lives?

해석 그가 어디 사는지 아니?

해설 간접의문문이므로 〈주어 + 동사〉의 어순이 올바르다. 틀린 곳이 없다.

정답 C

3. In the top drawer are the socks that you are looking for.

해석 맨 위 서랍에 네가 찾는 양말이 있어.

해설 〈장소의 부사구 + 자동사 + 주어〉의 어순이다. 틀린 곳이 없다. 주어가 동사 뒤에 있으므로 어순에 주의하자.

어휘 drawer 서랍
look for 찾다

정답 C

4. Around the corner is the store you are trying to find.

해석 골목 주변에 네가 찾는 가게가 있어.

해설 〈장소의 부사구 + 자동사 + 주어〉의 어순이다. 틀린 곳이 없다. 주어가 동사 뒤에 있으므로 어순에 주의하자.

어휘 around ~주변에

정답 C

5. Hardly his assistant has made such a mistake.

해석 그의 조수는 거의 실수하지 않았다.

해설 틀린 문장. 〈부정의 부사(구) + 조동사(do동사) + 주어 ~〉의 어순이 올바르다. Hardly has his assistant made ~가 되어야 한다.

어휘 assistant 보조, 조수

정답 I

6. Little did I dream that he would lie to me.

해석 그가 나에게 거짓말을 할 것이라고 상상도 안 했었다.

해설 〈부정의 부사(구) + 조동사(do동사) + 주어 ~〉의 어순이 올바르다. 따라서 틀린 곳이 없다. 일반 동사의 경우 조동사 대신 do동사를 쓴다는 점을 알아두자.

정답 C

7. On no occasion did their parents yell at him.

해석 무슨 일에도 그의 부모는 그에게 호통치지 않았다.

해설 〈부정의 부사(구) + 조동사(do동사) + 주어 ~〉의 어순이 올바르다. 따라서 틀린 곳이 없다. 일반 동사의 경우 조동사 대신 do동사를 쓴다는 점을 알아두자.

어휘 yell at ~에게 호통치다

정답 C

8. Should you ever visit my place again, I would be happy to show you around.

해석 우리 집에 다시 온다면, 집 구경을 꼭 시켜줄게.

해설 If 가정법에서 If가 생략되는 경우, 〈주어 + 동사〉의 어순이 〈동사 + 주어〉가 된다. If you should ever ~에서 If가 생략되어 Should you ever ~가 되었으므로 옳은 문장이다.

정답 C

9. If had he taken your advice, he would have passed the exam.

해석 만약 그가 네 충고를 받아들였다면, 그 시험에 합격할 수 있었을 것이다.

해설 If가 있으므로 어순이 바뀌면 안 된다. if he had ~로 바꿔야 한다.

정답 I

10. Were he in a position to help, he would help you.

해석 도와줄 처지이면 그가 너를 도울 것이다.

해설 If가 생략되었으므로 〈동사 + 주어〉의 어순이 된다. If he were ~에서 If가 생략되어 Were he ~가 되었다.

어휘 position 입장, 태도, 처지

정답 C

B. Correct the errors.

1. Seldom he has tried hard to do his best.

해석 그는 좀처럼 최선을 다하지 않았다.

해설 〈부정의 부사(구) + 조동사(do동사) + 주어 ~〉의 어순이다. he has를 has he로 바꿔야 한다.

어휘 seldom 좀처럼 ~ 않다
do one's best 최선을 다하다

정답 he has → has he

2. Out the sun came after the rain.

해석 비가 내린 후 태양이 나왔다.

해설 〈부사(구) + 자동사 + 주어〉의 어순이다. 주어와 동사의 어순이 바뀌어야 한다.

어휘 come after ~의 뒤를 잇다

정답 Out the sun came → Out came the sun

3. Who did help the poor man?

해석 누가 그 불쌍한 사람을 도와줬지?

해설 의문사가 주어이므로 조동사 did를 쓸 이유가 없다.

정답 did help → helped

4. I don't know how long will it take to get this done.

해석 이 일을 마치는데 얼마나 걸릴지 모르겠다.

해설 간접의문문이므로 〈주어 + 동사〉의 어순이 되어야 한다. will it take를 it will take로 바꿔야 한다.

정답 will it → it will

5. If were I in your shoes, I wouldn't take the offer.

해석 내가 네 입장이라면, 그 제안을 거절할 것이다.

해설 If가 생략되지 않은 형태이므로 〈주어 + 동사〉의 어순이 되어야 한다.

어휘 offer 제안

정답 were I → I were

C. Translate the following into Korean.

1. I'm not certain where he stays now.

어휘 certain 확신하는

정답 그가 어디에서 지내는지 잘 모르겠다.

2. No sooner had he left than she arrived.

어휘 no sooner A than B A하자마자 B하다

정답 그가 떠나자마자 그녀가 도착했다.

3. Had he known, he would have told you.

어휘 know 알다

정답 만약 그가 알았다면 너에게 말을 했을 것이다.

4. There is a lot of traffic on the street now.

어휘 traffic 교통, 차량

정답 지금 길은 교통체증이 심하다.

5. At that Mexican restaurant the food was too spicy for his taste.

어휘 taste 미각

정답 저 멕시코 식당 요리는 그의 입맛에는 너무 매웠다.

Practice Test

A. Underline the emphasized part.

1. Never has he traveled abroad; he doesn't enjoy exotic food that much.

   해석 그는 외국음식을 별로 좋아하지 않아 절대 외국으로 여행을 가지 않는다.

   해설 강조하기 위해 부정부사 never가 문두로 나가 있는 형태이다.

   어휘 abroad 해외로
   exotic 이국적인

   정답 Never

2. I did recognize her face, but I had forgotten her name.

   해석 난 그녀의 얼굴은 알아보았지만 이름을 잊어버렸다.

   해설 do동사는 주로 일반 동사의 의문문과 부정문에 쓰지만 평서문에 쓸 경우 강조하기 위해 쓰인다.

   어휘 recognize 알아보다

   정답 did recognize

3. It was how you said it, not what you said, that made her upset.

   해석 그녀를 화나게 한 건 네가 한말이 아니라 네가 말한 방식이다.

   해설 〈It + be동사 + 강조대상 + that ~〉에서 강조의 대상은 be동사와 that절 사이에 있는 어구이다.

   어휘 upset 화내다

   정답 how you said it, not what you said

4. It was he that knew the secret.

   해석 그 비밀을 알았던 사람은 그였다.

   해설 〈It + be동사 + 강조대상 + that ~〉에서 강조의 대상은 be동사와 that절 사이에 있는 어구이다.

   정답 he

5. At the end of the hall were many students waiting for their teacher.

   해석 복도 끝에서 많은 학생들이 선생님을 기다리고 있었다.

   해설 강조하고자 장소의 부사구가 문장 앞으로 와 있는 구조이다.

   어휘 hall 복도(=hallway)

   정답 At the end of the hall

B. Emphasize the underlined part.

1. I <u>understand</u> what you mean.

   해석 무슨 소린지 이해해.

   해설 평서문이며 일반 동사를 사용하고 있으므로 동사 앞에 do동사를 넣어 강조한다.

   정답 I <u>do understand</u> what you mean.

2. We do not know the importance of our health <u>until we lose it.</u>

   해석 건강을 잃기 전까지는 건강의 중요성을 모른다.

   해설 not과 until을 합하여 Not until을 문두로 가져간다. 이때 주의 할 점은 not을 이미 사용하였으므로 동사 다음에 not을 또 다시 사용하면 안 된다.

   어휘 importance 중요성

   정답 <u>Not until we lose it</u> do we know the importance of our health.

3. I have met her <u>only once.</u>

   해석 그녀를 만난건 딱 한 번뿐이다.

   해설 부정의 부사구 only once를 문장 처음에 써 준다.

   어휘 once 한 번

   정답 <u>Only once</u> have I met her.

4. The rain came <u>down.</u>

   해석 비가 내렸다.

   해설 부사 down을 문장 앞으로 보낸다.

   어휘 come down 내리다

   정답 <u>Down</u> came the rain.

5. I saw her <u>at the park</u> this afternoon.

   해석 오늘 오후 공원에서 그녀를 보았다.

   해설 〈주어 + 동사 + 목적어〉의 구조이므로 〈(장소) 부사구 + 자동사 + 주어〉로 바꿀 수는 없다. 〈It + be동사 + 강조대상 + that ~〉의 형태로 강조하는 것이 적절하다.

   어휘 park 공원

   정답 It was <u>at the park</u> that I saw her this afternoon.

C. Translate the following into Korean.

1. It was during the meal that they started to argue.

   어휘 argue 싸우다, 논쟁하다

   정답 그들이 논쟁을 시작한건 바로 식사 도중이었다.

2. It was her, not her husband, that I met this morning.

   어휘 husband 남편

   정답 내가 오늘 아침에 만난 사람은 그녀의 남편이 아니고 그녀였다.

3. It is passion that helps you to be a professional.

   어휘 passion 열정
   professional 전문가

   정답 여러분을 전문가가 되게 돕는 것은 바로 열정이다.

4. It is this coming Thursday that we will have the next meeting.

정답 돌아오는 목요일에 다음 회의를 할 것이다.

5. Rarely does he praise his staff.
어휘 praise 칭찬하다
정답 극히 드물게 그는 직원들을 칭찬한다.

Unit 06 가정 구문 (Conditionals)

Practice Test
A. Read and match.

1. c **2.** e **3.** a **4.** b **5.** d

1. He would have gotten the job,
해석 그가 좀 더 잘 준비했더라면 그 직업을 얻었을 것이다.
해설 과거사실에 반대를 나타내기에 if절에 과거완료, 주절에 would + have p.p.가 쓰였다.
정답 c. if he had been better prepared.

2. If there should be a global nuclear war,
해석 세계 핵전쟁이 일어난다면 세상은 멸망할 것이다.
해설 불확실한 내용을 가정할 때 if절에 should를 쓴다.
어휘 nuclear war 핵 전쟁
정답 e. the world would end forever.

3. If I were you,
해석 내가 너라면 그에게 사실을 말할 텐데.
해설 가정법 과거는 현재 시제의 반대 사실을 가정하며, be동사는 항상 were를 쓴다.
정답 a. I would tell him the truth.

4. If you leave right now,
해석 지금 바로 떠나면 버스를 탈 수 있을 것이다.
해설 단순 가정의 경우 if절에는 현재시제를, 주절에는 will + 동사원형을 쓴다.
어휘 leave 떠나다
정답 b. you will catch the bus.

5. If he had had dinner,
해석 그가 저녁을 먹었더라면 지금 배고프지 않을 것이다.
해설 if절은 과거 사실의 반대를 나타내며, 주절은 현재 사실의 반대를 나타내므로 if절엔 과거완료, 주절엔 조동사 과거+동사원형을 써야 한다.
정답 d. he wouldn't be hungry now.

B. Correct the errors.

1. If he were at home last night, I would have visited him.
해석 어제 그가 집에 있었더라면, 그를 방문했을 것이다.
해설 If절에 last night이 있으므로 과거의 사실을 가정하고 있다. were를 had been으로 바꿔야 한다.
정답 were → had been

2. If I had realized its importance at that time, I would work out regularly.
해석 그 중요성을 그 때 알았더라면 정기적으로 운동했을 것이다.
해설 If절이 가정법 과거완료이므로 주절도 〈조동사 과거형 + have + p.p.〉로 바꿔야 한다.
어휘 realize 깨닫다
    regularly 정규적으로, 규칙적으로
정답 work → have worked

3. If he put the leftovers in the refrigerator yesterday, the food would be fresh now.
해석 남은 음식을 어제 냉장고에 넣었더라면 지금 음식이 싱싱할 것이다.
해설 혼합가정법이다. If절이 과거 사실에 대한 반대내용이므로 가정법 과거완료가 되어야 한다.
어휘 leftover 남은 음식
    refrigerator 냉장고
정답 put → had put

4. Unless he were not sick, he would join us.
해석 그가 아프지 않다면 우리와 함께할 텐데.
해설 Unless 자체에 이미 부정의 의미가 포함되어 있으므로, Unless를 If로 바꿔야 한다.
어휘 join 합류하다
정답 Unless → If

5. I wish I will help you.
해석 너를 도울 수 있었으면 좋을 텐데.
해설 I wish 가정법(과거)이므로 will help를 could help로 바꾼다.
어휘 help 돕다
정답 will help → could help

C. Put the words in order and translate into Korean.

1. the present for you / if she had had enough money / she would have bought
해석 그녀에게 돈이 충분히 있었다면 너에게 선물을 사주었을 것이다.
어휘 enough 충분한

12

present 선물

정답 If she had had enough money, she would have bought the present for you.

2. the present for you / if she had enough money / she would buy

해석 그녀에게 돈이 충분히 있다면, 너에게 선물을 사줄 것이다.

정답 If she had enough money, she would buy the present for you.

3. I had / extra time / I wish

해석 시간이 좀 더 있었으면 한다.

어휘 extra 여분의

정답 I wish I had extra time.

4. extra money / I had had / I wish

해석 돈이 좀 더 있었으면 했다.

정답 I wish I had had extra money.

5. will fail / or you / work harder

해석 열심히 하지 않으면 실패할 것이다.

어휘 fail 실패하다

정답 Work harder, or you will fail.

Unit 07 원인, 결과, 목적을 나타내는 구문 (Cause / Effect / Purpose)

Practice Test

A. Read and match.

1. c   2. a   3. e   4. b   5. d

1. Lucy was such a funny person

해석 루시는 재미있는 사람이라 인기가 많았다.

해설 원인과 결과를 나타내는 such + a + 형 + 명 + that 구문으로 '너무 ~해서 …하다'는 의미이다.

어휘 popular 인기 있는

정답 c. that she was very popular.

2. Ms. Benson doesn't feel well,

해석 벤슨 양은 몸이 좋지 않아 의사를 보러 갈 예정이다.

해설 원인과 결과를 나타내는 so ~ that 구문으로 '너무 ~해서 …하다'는 의미이다.

어휘 see a doctor 의사의 진찰을 받다

정답 a. so she's going to see a doctor.

3. Since Sarah has poor eyesight,

해석 세라는 눈이 나쁘기 때문에 맨 앞줄에 앉아야 한다.

해설 원인과 결과를 나타내는 구문으로 since가 '~ 때문에'라는 원인을 나타내는 접속사로 쓰였다.

어휘 eyesight 시력
row 줄

정답 e. she has to sit in the front row.

4. I had so little money

해석 가진 돈이 너무 적어서 새 차를 살 여유가 없었다.

해설 원인과 결과를 나타내는 so ~ that 구문으로 '너무 ~해서 …하다'라는 의미이다.

어휘 afford ~할 여유가 있다

정답 b. that I couldn't afford to buy a new car.

5. The waitress kept forgetting the orders,

해석 웨이트리스는 자꾸 주문을 잊어버려서 결국 해고를 당했다.

해설 원인과 결과를 나타내는 구문으로 therefore가 쓰였다. ~했다. 그래서 …'라는 의미이다.

어휘 order 주문
fire 해고하다

정답 d. therefore, she was fired.

B. Choose the correct one.

1. I am happy (because / because of) you came back safely.

해석 네가 무사히 돌아와서 행복해.

해설 because 다음에는 문장이 오고, because of 다음에는 구 또는 단어가 온다.

어휘 safely 안전하게, 무사히

정답 because

2. I was exhausted (because / because of) the hard work.

해석 힘든 일 때문에 너무 지쳤어.

해설 명사구가 왔으므로 because of가 적절하다.

어휘 exhausted 지칠대로 지친

정답 because of

3. The soup is (too / very) hot to eat.

해석 그 스프는 너무 뜨거워서 먹을 수가 없어.

해설 〈too ~ to …〉 구문은 '너무도 ~해서 …할 수 없다'는 뜻으로 형태에 유의한다.

정답 too

4. I felt (such / so) embarrassed that I couldn't speak in front of the audience.

해석 너무 부끄러워서 관중들 앞에서 아무 말도 못하였다.

해설 〈so + 형용사, 부사 + that ~〉이다. 과거분사형의 형용사 (embarrassed)가 있으므로 so를 넣어야 한다.

어휘 embarrass 당황시키다
audience 관객

정답 so

5. It was (such / so) a fresh orange that he wanted to have another.

해석 너무 신선한 오렌지라 그는 한 개 더 원했다.

해설 〈such + a + 명사 + that ~〉이다. 명사(a fresh orange)가 있으므로 such를 넣는다.

어휘 fresh 신선한

정답 such

C. Translate the following into Korean.

1. The weather was so cold that I wore a coat and gloves.

어휘 weather 날씨
wear 입다

정답 날씨가 너무 추워서 코트를 입고 장갑을 꼈다.

2. The final exam was so difficult that few students got high scores.

어휘 final exam 기말시험
score 점수, 성적

정답 기말시험이 너무 어려워서 고득점을 획득한 학생들이 거의 없었다.

3. It was such an easy test that most of them passed it.

어휘 pass 통과하다, 합격하다

정답 너무 쉬운 시험이라 대부분이 합격하였다.

4. He works really hard so that his family may live in comfort.

어휘 comfort 편안함

정답 그는 가족들이 편하게 살 수 있도록 굉장히 열심히 일한다.

5. He works so hard lest he should fail the test.

어휘 lest+주어+(should)+V (주어가) ~하지 않도록

정답 그는 시험에 떨어지지 않도록 열심히 공부한다.

Unit 08 수동태 구문 (Passive Structure)

Practice Test

A. Fill in the blanks.

1. He writes a letter to his mom everyday. → A letter _____ by him to his mom everyday.

해석 그는 그의 엄마에게 매일 편지를 쓴다.

정답 A letter is written by him to his mom everyday.
편지는 매일 그의 엄마에게 그에 의해 작성된다.

2. He wrote a letter. → A letter _____ by him.

해석 그는 편지를 썼다.

정답 A letter was written by him.
편지가 그에 의해 작성 되었다.

3. He has written a letter. → A letter _____ by him.

해석 그는 편지를 썼었다.

정답 A letter has been written by him.
편지가 그에 의해 작성 되었었다.

4. He is writing a letter. → A letter _____ by him.

해석 그는 편지를 쓰고 있다.

정답 A letter is being written by him.
편지가 그에 의해 작성되고 있다.

5. He was writing a letter. → A letter _____ by him.

해석 그는 편지를 쓰고 있었다.

정답 A letter was being written by him.
편지가 그에 의해 작성되고 있었다.

6. He will write a letter. → A letter _____ by him.

해석 그는 편지를 쓸 것이다.

정답 A letter will be written by him.
편지는 그에 의해 작성될 것이다.

7. Did he write a letter? → _____ a letter by him?

해석 그가 편지를 썼어?

정답 Was a letter written by him?
편지가 그에 의해 작성 되었니?

8. Is he writing a letter? → _____ a letter by him?

해석 그가 편지를 쓰고 있니?

정답 Is a letter being written by him?
편지가 그에 의해 작성되고 있니?

B. Read and match.

1. c **2.** b **3.** d **4.** a **5.** e

1. She made her children some cookies.

해석 그녀는 아이들에게 쿠키를 만들어 주었다.

정답 c. Some cookies were made by her for her children.
쿠키는 그녀의 아이들을 위해 만들어 졌다.

2. I saw her entering the room.

해석 난 그녀가 방에 들어오는 것을 보았다.

어휘 enter ~에 들어가다

정답 b. She was seen entering the room.
그녀는 방에 들어가는 것이 목격 되었다.

3. Shakespeare wrote a lot of plays.

해석 셰익스피어는 많은 연극을 썼다

어휘 play 연극

정답 d. A lot of plays were written by Shakespeare.
많은 연극이 셰익스피어에 의해 쓰여졌다.

4. The mice ate the cheese.

해석 쥐들이 치즈를 먹었다

어휘 mice 쥐들(mouse의 복수형)

정답 a. The cheese was eaten by the mice.
치즈는 쥐들에 의해 먹혀졌다.

5. Everybody knows Bill Gates.

해석 모든 사람이 빌 게이츠를 안다.

정답 e. Bill Gates is known to everybody.
빌 게이츠는 모든 사람에게 알려져 있다.

C. Put the words in order and translate into Korean.

1. in Brazil / grown / coffee / is

해석 커피는 브라질에서 재배된다.

정답 Coffee is grown in Brazil.

2. both English / in Canada / they speak / and French

해석 캐나다에서는 영어와 불어가 둘 다 쓰인다.

어휘 both A and B A와 B 둘 다

정답 They speak both English and French in Canada.

3. is / by his company / a man / known

해석 사귀는 친구를 보면 그 사람을 알 수 있다.

어휘 company 친구, 동료

정답 A man is known by his company.

4. by Marie and Pierre Curie / was discovered / radium

해석 라듐은 메리와 피에르 퀴리에 의해 발견되었다.

어휘 discover 발견하다

정답 Radium was discovered by Marie and Pierre Curie.

5. in 1897 / was built / that building

해석 저 건물은 1987년에 지어졌다.

어휘 build 짓다, 만들다

정답 That building was built in 1987.

III. Building Up Vocabulary for TEPS Reading

Unit 02 **주제별 어휘 익히기
(Topic-Based Vocabulary)**

Practice

A. Translate the following into English.

경제 (Economy)

1 gross	2 consumer	3 lavish
4 frugal	5 bid	6 budget
7 expire	8 deficit	9 fiscal
10 recession	11 soar	12 revenue
13 fluctuate	14 stagnation	15 stable
16 plummet	17 surplus	18 sluggish

금융 (Finance)

1 deposit	2 withdraw	3 stockholder
4 dividend	5 beneficiary	6 pension
7 bond	8 securities	9 delinquent
10 coverage		

비즈니스 (Business)

1 subsidiary	2 board	3 incorporated
4 revenues	5 asset	6 capital
7 bankruptcy	8 liquidate	

B. Translate the following into English.

법률 (Law)

1 amend	2 breach	3 infringement
4 enact	5 outlaw	6 conspiracy
7 embezzle	8 libel	9 file
10 indict	11 sue	12 plea
13 forfeit	14 regulate	15 reform
16 evidence	17 conservative	18 constitution
19 legislature	20 judiciary	

건강 (Health)

1 sanitary	2 respiratory	3 symptom
4 infection	5 contagious	6 epidemic
7 immune	8 acute	9 ailment
10 tumor	11 remedy	12 heal
13 prescription	14 transplant	15 dose
16 nutrition		

과학 (Science)

1 molecule	2 atom	3 synthetic
4 substance	5 compound	6 artificial
7 analyze	8 hypothesis	9 phenomenon
10 botany	11 zoology	12 gene
13 stem cell	14 clone	15 embryo
16 inheritance		

환경(Environment)

1 habitat	2 species	3 deplete
4 ozone-layer	5 overuse	6 dispose of
7 contaminate	8 emit	

Unit 04 어휘 형성 규칙 이해하기 (Word Formation)

Practice Test

A. Write the antonyms.

1 unemployed	2 unstable	3 dishonest
4 irregular	5 disagree	6 invisible
7 inconvenient	8 incorrect	9 impossible
10 impatient		

B. Change the words into their noun forms.

1 election	2 arrival	3 employment
4 development	5 originality	6 arrangement
7 denial	8 information	9 punctuality
10 discussion		

C. Change the words into their adjective forms.

1 painful	2 thoughtful	3 homeless
4 dangerous	5 biological	6 flexible
7 sensible	8 comfortable	9 famous
10 comprehensible		

Unit 06 합성어 익히기 (Be Aware of Compound Words)

Practice Test

A. Fill in the blanks. Use the words given in the box.

1. I parked the car next to the _____, and inserted the correct change.

해석 난 주차요금 징수기 옆에 차를 주차했고, 정확히 잔돈을 넣었다.

어휘 **insert** 끼워 넣다
change 거스름돈, 잔돈

정답 **parking meter**

2. His _____ didn't go off this morning, so he missed the train.

해석 그의 알람시계가 오늘 아침에 울리지 않아서 기차를 놓쳤다.

어휘 **go off** 울리다

정답 **alarm clock**

3. Let's meet at the _____ around the corner. They have great espresso.

해석 모퉁이 주변에 있는 커피숍에서 만나자. 거기에 좋은 에스프레소 커피가 있어.

어휘 **around** ~ 주변에

정답 **coffee shop**

4. Who is your favorite _____?

해석 네가 가장 좋아하는 영화배우가 누구니?

어휘 **favorite** 매우 좋아하는

정답 movie star

5. This _____ has expired.

해석 이 신용카드는 만기가 되었다.

어휘 expire 만료하다, 만기가 되다

정답 credit card

B. **Fill in the blanks. Use the words given in the box.**

1. I got a _____ yesterday.

해석 나는 어제 머리를 잘랐다.

어휘 haircut 이발

정답 haircut

2. These _____ are really comfortable. I always wear them when jogging.

해석 이 운동화는 정말 편안하다. 난 항상 조깅할 때 이 운동화를 신는다.

어휘 comfortable 편안한
wear 신다

정답 running shoes

3. Her_____ celebrated her 60th birthday.

해석 그녀의 시어머니께서 60세 생신을 맞이하셨다.

어휘 mother-in-law 장모님, 시어머님

정답 mother-in-law

4. They renovated the _____. It looks great now.

해석 그들은 식당을 수리해서 지금은 더 멋있어졌다.

어휘 renovate 수리[수선]하다
dining room 식당

정답 dining room

5. He dropped his _____ and broke them.

해석 그는 선글라스를 떨어뜨려서 깨뜨렸다.

어휘 drop 떨어뜨리다(=let fall)

정답 sunglasses

C. **Fill in the blanks. Use the words given in the box.**

1. I've got a _____ job; I work four hours a day on the weekends.

해석 난 시간제 일을 구했다. 주말에 하루 4시간 일한다.

어휘 part-time job 시간제 일

정답 part-time

2. There are much more right-handed people than

_____.

해석 왼손잡이보다 오른손잡이가 훨씬 더 많다.

어휘 right-handed 오른손잡이의

정답 left-handed

3. He bought a _____ car, not a brand new one.

해석 그는 새 것이 아닌 중고차를 샀다.

어휘 second-hand 중고의
brand-new 신품의

정답 second-hand

4. Look at those _____ shoes. They look gorgeous.

해석 저 잘 만들어진 신발을 봐. 근사해 보인다.

어휘 well-made 잘 만들어진
gorgeous 화려한, 멋진

정답 well-made

5. He purchased a _____ ticket to Rome.

해석 그는 로마행 1등석 표를 구입했다.

어휘 first-class 최고급의, 1등의, 1등석의
purchase 구입[구매]하다

정답 first-class

IV. Skills for TEPS Reading

Unit 01 **대의 찾기**
(Identifying the Main Ideas)

Sample Question

The period of history known as the Renaissance began in Italy around 1300 and lasted for about 300 years. The Renaissance, which means rebirth, refers to a revival in art, culture, and education. During that time, the educated classes sought to bring back to life the classical cultures of Greece and Rome. Yet even though they looked towards the past, the leaders of the Renaissance really set in motion the events of the future.

Q What is the main idea of the above paragraph?

(a) The Renaissance lasted until around 1600.

(b) The word Renaissance means rebirth.

(c) The Renaissance was a revival of classical learning.

(d) The Renaissance led to the world we live in today.

해석 르네상스라고 알려진 역사적 시기는 이탈리아에서 시작되었고, 1300년경부터 약 300년간 지속되었다. 르네상스는 부활을 의미하는데, 예술, 문화, 교육에서의 부활을 의미한다. 르네상스

시대 동안에 교육받은 계층 사람들이 추구했던 것은 고대 그리스, 로마의 고전 문화를 부활시키는 것이었다. 르네상스 시대 사람들이 과거를 돌이켜보기는 했지만, 르네상스 지도자들은 실로 미래에 일어날 일을 시작했다.

Q 윗 글의 요지는 무엇인가?

(a) 르네상스가 1600년경까지 지속되었다.
(b) 르네상스라는 어휘는 부활을 의미한다.
(c) 르네상스는 고전 학문의 부활이다.
(d) 르네상스는 오늘날 우리가 살고 있는 시대로의 길을 열었다.

해설 (a) 르네상스 시대에 대한 언급으로는 맞지만, 주제 또는 대의에 관한 문제의 답이 되기에는 너무 지엽적이다. Too small! (b) 르네상스라는 어휘의 뜻으로 '부활(rebirth)'은 맞지만, 역시 한 글의 주제문이나 대표구문으로 되기에는 너무 지엽적이므로 답으로 적합하지 않다. Too small! (c) 르네상스가 고전주의 학문의 부활이라는 것은 너무 잘 알려졌고, 사실이지만, 역시 이 글에서 강조하는 것은 지난 역사의 사실(fact)만 나열하는 것이 아니라 마지막 문장에서 르네상스가 왜 중요한 가치와 의미를 갖는지 현재와 연계하는 부분이다. 정답을 찾기 위해서 Yet even though 이후 부분을 잘 이해하도록 한다. 미괄식 형태를 갖춰, 맨 마지막 문장에 중요 구문이 들어 있다. 따라서 (d)가 정답이다.

어휘 known as ~라고 알려진
the Renaissance 르네상스
last 지속하다
refer to ~를 언급하다
revival 부활, 재생
seek to ~을 추구하다
bring ~ back to life ~에 삶을 불어넣다
set ~ in motion ~을 추진하다, 움직이다

정답 (d)

B. Question while reading.

Sample Question

There are many reasons _____.
For example, we must compare Country A's rate of inflation to the rate of its trading partner Country B. If Country A's inflation rate is higher than Country B's, then A's currency will "depreciate," or lose value. Interest rates are important as well. If Country A's interest rates are higher than other countries', currency depreciation is a real danger.

(a) a trading partner might get angry
(b) a country can easily control interest rates
(c) foreign currency is more valuable
(d) a country's currency can depreciate

해석 한 국가의 통화가 평가절하 될 수 있는 이유에는 여러 가지가 있다. 예를 들어, A라는 국가의 인플레이션율과 그 나라의 무역교역국인 B라는 국가의 인플레이션율을 비교해야 한다. 만약 A국가의 인플레이션율이 B국가의 인플레이션율보다 높으면, A국가의 통화는 '평가 절하' 된다. 즉 가치를 잃게 된다. 이자율도 매우 중요하다. A국가의 이자율이 다른 국가들의 이자율보다 높으면, 통화의 평가절하는 매우 위험하다.

(a) 무역교역국이 화를 내는
(b) 한 국가가 쉽게 이자율을 통제할 수 있는
(c) 외국 통화가 더 가치있는
(d) 한 국가의 통화가 평가절하 될 수 있는

해설 For example 이하를 보면 그 앞에 있는 빈 칸에 어떤 내용이 와야 하는지 쉽게 추측할 수 있다. There are many reasons(이유가 여러 가지 있다). → 무엇에 대한 이유일까? → We must compare(비교를 해야한다). → 무엇과 무엇을 비교해야 할까? → Interest rates are important as well.(이자율도 왜 중요할까?) → 이자율이 다른 나라보다 높은 상태에서 화폐를 평가절하 한다면 좋을까? 아니면 나쁠까? 이처럼 지문을 읽어내려가면서 단순 번역만 하지 말고, active reader로서 스스로 질문을 하면서, 질문에 대한 답을 찾으면 그 내용을 좀 더 확실하게 이해할 수 있다. 맨 처음 문장에 빈 칸은 바로 다음에 오는 내용들이 예제(for example)를 들어 설명을 하는 내용인데, 모두 depreciation과 관련이 있는 것이므로 (d)가 정답이다.

어휘 compare A to B A를 B에 비교하다
inflation rate 인플레이션율
trading partner 무역 교역국
depreciate 평가절하하다
currency 통화
control 통제하다
foreign currency 외환

정답 (d)

Unit 02   주요 내용을 패러프레이즈하기 (Paraphrase the Main Ideas)

Practice Test

1. d   **2.** e   **3.** a   **4.** f   **5.** c   **6.** b

A. Read and match.

1. He will get the project done sometime.

해석 그는 언젠가 그 프로젝트를 끝낼 것이다.

어휘 sometime 언젠가
eventually 결국

정답 d. He will finish the project eventually.
그는 결국 그 프로젝트를 끝낼 것이다.

2. The lecturer made a short statement.

해석 그 강사는 짧은 성명서를 발표했다.

어휘 lecturer 강사
remark 비평

정답 e. His remarks were quite brief.
그의 언급은 아주 간결했다.

3. The problems are not insurmountable.

해석 그 문제들은 극복할 수 없는 것이 아니다.

어휘 **insurmountable** 이겨낼[극복할] 수 없는

정답 **a. They can be resolved.**
그것들은 해결될 수 있다.

4. I am happy you have the opportunity to attend the conference.

해석 난 네가 회의에 참석할 기회를 갖게되어 기쁘다.

어휘 **conference** 회의
opportunity 기회

정답 **f. It pleases me that you have been given such a chance.**
너에게 그러한 기회가 주어져서 난 기쁘다.

5. The results of the competition were entirely unexpected.

해석 그 시합의 결과는 전혀 예상하지 못했다.

어휘 **unexpected** 예기치 않은

정답 **c. The competitors were shocked by the outcome.**
경쟁자들은 그 결과에 놀랐다.

6. My boss seems to welcome lively debate.

해석 나의 사장님은 활발한 토론을 환영한다.

어휘 **debate** 토론, 논쟁

정답 **b. She appreciates animated discussions.**
그녀는 활발한 토론을 좋게 생각한다.

B. Match each word with its synonym.

1. adhere - e. stick
2. deceive - j. trick
3. examine - a. investigate
4. freight - i. cargo
5. homage - b. respect
6. lament - f. grieve
7. mentor - c. counselor
8. piety - d. faith
9. rational - h. logical
10. transform - g. change

Unit 03 **세부 내용 파악하기**
(Locate Details in the Text)

1. 문제지 읽는 순서

Sample Question
Archaeologists recently found the buried remains

of what might have been homes at one time near Stonehenge. The homes, located at Durrington Walls, are believed to have been organized in a way to mimic and mirror the shape of Stonehenge. Archaeological experts recently discovered homes as a monument to the dead ancestors. Researchers think that the people who made Stonehenge were sun worshippers who designed the community and Stonehenge to view the sunrise and sunset.

Q Which of the following is correct according to the passage?

(a) The builders of Stonehenge designed the pattern of their homes differently.
(b) Durrington Walls was built by the same people who built the Stonehenge.
(c) The inhabitants of Stonehenge wanted to watch the patterns of the sun.
(d) Durrington Walls and Stonehenge were both vibrant communities.

해석 고고학자들은 최근에 스톤헨지 부근에서 한 때 주거지였던 것으로 보이는 묻힌 잔해들을 발견했다. 이 주거지들은 더링턴 월즈에 위치하고 있는데 스톤헨지의 모양을 흉내내거나 반영한 것으로 믿어진다. 고고학 전문가들은 최근에 죽은 조상들에 대한 기념비로서의 주거지들을 발견했다. 연구자들은 스톤헨지를 만든 사람들이 태양을 숭배하는 사람들이었고 일출과 일몰을 보기 위해 마을과 스톤헨지를 디자인했다고 생각한다.

Q 위 글의 내용으로 올바른 것을 고르시오.
(a) 스톤헨지를 만든 사람들은 자신의 집을 다른 구조로 디자인했다.
(b) 더링턴 월즈는 스톤헨지를 만든 사람들에 의해 만들어졌다.
(c) 스톤헨지의 주민들은 태양의 패턴을 관찰하고자 했다.
(d) 더링턴 월즈와 스톤헨지는 모두 활기찬 공동체였다.

해설 세부사항을 파악하는 문제에서는 많은 오답들이 부분적으로는 맞지만, 부분적으로 틀린 내용 또는 확인할 수 없는 내용을 담고 있는 경우가 많다는 것을 기억해야 한다. (a) 발견된 주거지가 스톤헨지 근처이기는 하지만, 이 집이 다른 집들과 유형이 다르다는 내용은 이 글에는 나와 있지 않다. (b) 이 글만으로는 알 수 없는 내용이다. (c) 이 거주지를 지은 사람들이 일출과 일몰을 보기 위해 집과 스톤헨지를 건립했다고 되어 있으니 정답이다.

어휘 **archaeologist** 고고학자
recently 최근에
remains 잔해
locate 위치하다
mimic 흉내 내다
mirror 반영하다
expert 전문가
monument 기념비
ancestor 조상
worshipper 숭배자
inhabitant 거주자, 주민
vibrant 진동하는, 활기 찬

정답 (c)

2. 읽으면서 질문하기

Sample Question

The artistic concept of formalism has its roots in the philosophy of Plato. The theory suggests that art's value is in the way it was made - its visual aspects and mediums. Formalists believe that the subject and context of a piece of artwork is not important. Rather, only the colors, the arrangement, and the medium itself are important to the viewer. Formalism contends that regardless of the subject, it is the actual work that influences people.

Q What do formalist artists generally believe?

(a) That the theme of the painting is very important in formalism
(b) That context is of primary importance in art
(c) That the work itself greatly influences viewers of artwork
(d) That people inspire the overall subject and medium of a piece of art

해석 형식주의의 예술적 개념은 플라톤의 철학에 그 근원을 두고 있다. 이 이론은 예술의 가치가 그것이 만들어진 방식, 즉 시각적인 겉모습과 매개물에 달려있다고 암시한다. 형식주의자들은 예술 작품의 주제와 내용은 중요하지 않다고 믿는다. 오히려 색상, 배열과 매개물 자체가 보는 사람들에게 중요하다. 형식주의는 주제에 관계없이 사람들에게 영향을 끼치는 것은 바로 실제 작품이라고 주장한다.

Q 형식주의 작가들이 일반적으로 믿는 것은?
(a) 그림의 주제는 형식주의에서 매우 중요하다
(b) 배경이 예술에서는 가장 중요하다
(c) 작품 자체가 보는 사람에게 크게 영향을 끼친다.
(d) 사람들이 예술작품의 전체적인 주제와 매개물에 영감을 준다.

해설 세부 사항을 묻는 문제에서는 selective reading을 할 수 있으면, 많은 시간을 단축할 수 있다. 문제가 'What do formalist artists generally believe?'이니까, 세 번째 문장이 Formalists believe ...로 시작되고 있으니 답의 실마리를 주는 부분이다. 그런데 이 문장에서 not important한 것이 언급되고, 다음에 이어지는 문장에서 rather .... are important to the viewer라는 내용이 나오니까, 사실상 정답은 바로 Rather로 시작하는 네 번째 문장이후에 있다. 따라서 정답은 (c)다.

어휘 artistic 예술적인, 기교가 뛰어난
formalism 형식주의
theory 이론
visual 시각적인
medium 매개물, 매체
formalist 형식주의자
context 배경
arrangement 배열, 정리
contend 주장하다
regardless of ~에 관계없이
influence 영향을 미치다

inspire 영감을 주다

정답 (c)

3. Note-taking하는 습관과 Marking하는 습관 기르기

Sample Question

Many people associate computer games with negative habits, such as violent behavior and failing to exercise the brain. But now many companies are trying to change that. They are designing computer games that they hope will emphasize positive attitudes and help children and teens _____. Researchers are currently conducting tests to determine how effective the new games are. The company hopes these games will help fight the negative reputation that computer games are beginning to get.

(a) develop healthier self-images
(b) become much more skilled
(c) maintain good health
(d) learn constructive habits

해석 많은 사람들이 컴퓨터 게임과 폭력적인 행동, 두뇌 사용 부족 등과 같은 부정적인 습관들을 관련지어 생각한다. 그러나 현재 많은 회사들이 그것을 바꾸려고 노력하고 있다. 그들은 긍정적인 태도를 강조하고 어린이들과 십대들이 좀 더 건강한 자아상을 갖도록 도울 컴퓨터 게임들을 디자인하고 있다. 연구자들이 현재 실험들을 진행하고 있는데, 이 새로운 게임들이 얼마나 효율적인가를 알아보기 위해서이다. 회사가 바라는 바는 이러한 게임들이 컴퓨터 게임들이 얻기 시작한 나쁜 평판을 물리치는 것이다.

(a) 좀 더 건강한 자아상을 갖도록
(b) 훨씬 더 노력해지도록
(c) 좋은 건강을 유지하도록
(d) 건설적인 습관을 배우도록

해설 컴퓨터 게임에 대해 사람들이 갖고 있는 인식과 이를 바꾸려는 새로운 노력에 관한 글이다. "~ associate computer games with negative habits, such as violent behavior and failing to exercise the brain."에서 일반적으로 컴퓨터 게임에 대해 폭력적인 행동, 두뇌 사용 부족 등과 같은 부정적인 습관들과 관련지어 생각한다. 'but'에 주목하라! 현재 많은 회사에서 이런 부정적 이미지를 바꾸고 긍정적 반응에 초점을 맞추고 사람들을 지도하려는 계획을 준비 중이다(~ they hope will emphasize positive attitudes.). 따라서 빈 칸에 들어갈 내용은 아동이나 십대가 보다 긍정적 이미지를 갖도록 설계하려는 것이기 때문에 정답은 (a)다.

TIPS 주의를 요하는 연결어구들에 주의하자. 이 글은 컴퓨터 게임을 하면 사람들이 부정적인 면(negative)을 연상하지만, 게임을 만드는 회사들은 게임이 그것을 사용하는 학생들에게 긍정적인 면(positive)을 갖도록 노력한다는 내용이다. 이처럼 서로 다른 내용이 연결될 때 꼭 사용되는 연결어구들을 다시 한 번 주의해서 정리해두도록 한다. But을 표시하면 그 다음에 오는 내용이 앞의 내용과 많이 다른 내용이 온다는 것을 쉽게 알 수 있

어 편리하다. 주요한 어휘, 구문에 표시(Marking)하는 습관을
기르도록 한다.

어휘 associate A with B A와 B를 연관짓다
attitude 태도, 마음가짐
researcher 연구자, 조사자

정답 (a)

Unit 05 시각적 묘사 (Visualize the Text)

Sample Question

① Camels are known as the "ships of the desert" for their extraordinary ability to travel across vast expanses of barren sands while transporting heavy loads. ② They have wide, cushioned feet, which spread out as they walk and thus help them to maneuver easily across the soft sand, as well as ③ two rows of eyelashes and closeable nostrils that protect them from sandstorms. ④ In order to survive in a desert landscape, often void of water and food, camels have developed the ability to store great amounts of nutrients for long periods of time. When food and water is plentiful, they consume as much as possible, storing reserve fat in their humps and water in stomach sacs that can hold up to twenty-five gallons.

해석 ① 낙타는 무거운 짐을 수송하며 광범위한 불모지의 사막을 횡단하는 특별한 능력 때문에 '사막의 배'라고 알려져 있다. ② 이들이 걸을 때 넓으면서도 펼쳐질 수 있어서 부드러운 모래에서 쉽게 이동할 수 있도록 돕는 쿠션 같은 발을 가졌다. ③ 이들은 모래바람으로부터 그들을 보호할 수 있는 두 겹의 속눈썹과 닫을 수 있는 콧구멍뿐만 아니라, ④ 물과 음식이 종종 떨어지는 사막의 환경에서 살아남기 위해 낙타들은 오랜 기간 동안 막대한 양의 영양분을 저장할 수 있는 능력을 발달시켰다. 그들은 음식과 물이 많을 때 가능한 많이 섭취하는데 그들의 혹에는 예비의 지방을 저장하고 25갤런까지 채울 수 있는 위에는 수분을 저장한다.

해설 ① 짐을 나르는 낙타의 모습 ② 발이 쑥쑥 빠지는 사막에서 균형을 잡기 위해서, 발이 쿠션처럼 큰 모습 ③ 모래 폭풍으로부터 보호하기 위해 눈썹이 두 겹, 닫을 수 있는 콧구멍의 모습 ④ 영양분을 저장할 수 있는 혹, 수분을 저장할 수 있는 커다란 위의 모습 이러한 특징을 시각화해서 더 쉽게 이해하고, 오래 기억할 수 있다.

어휘 ships of the desert 사막의 배
extraordinary 특별한
vast 광범위한
barren 불모지의
transport 운송하다
spread out 널리 퍼지다

maneuver 움직이다, 이동시키다
row 줄, 열
nostril 콧구멍
protect 보호하다
void of ~이 결여된
nutrient 영양분
reserve 예비의; 비축
hump 혹

V. Categorizing TEPS Reading Based Upon Topics

Unit 01 정치 (Politics)

1. "A choice between the lesser of two evils" is how many French voters saw their presidential election in 2002. Jacques Chirac, who was running for his 2nd consecutive term, won in an incredible landslide with a stunning 82% of the popular vote. Although Chirac had been heavily criticized for his policies, his opponent, Jean-Marie Le Pen, _____.

(a) managed to secure victory
(b) proved to be the more popular
(c) was happy to concede defeat
(d) was disliked even more

해석 '나쁜 두 개 중에서 덜 나쁜 것 고르기'라는 표현이 많은 프랑스 유권자들이 2002년 대통령 선거를 어떻게 생각했는지 설명해 준다. 자크 시라크는 재임하기 위해 대통령에 출마했었다. 그는 믿기 어려울 정도로 압승을 거두었는데, 당시 82%라는 놀라운 지지를 얻었다. 비록 그가 이전에 정책 때문에 많이 비판을 받았었지만, 그의 경쟁자인 장-마리 르 펜을 <u>사람들은 훨씬 더 싫어했다.</u>

(a) 승리를 확실하게 할 수 있었다
(b) 더 인기가 있는 것으로 판명되었다.
(c) 패배를 인정해서 기뻤다.
(d) 훨씬 더 싫어했다.

해설 A choice between the lesser of two evils처럼 관용적으로 자주 사용되는 표현에 익숙해지는 것이 내용 파악에 도움이 된다. 물론 이 관용 구문을 모르더라도, 직역을 하면 '두 악마 중에서 덜 악마인 것 고르기'라는 의미를 갖게 되므로, '나쁜 것 중에 덜 나쁜 것 고르기'라는 뜻에 가깝게 갈 수 있다. (a)와 (b)는 장-마리 르 펜이 승리한 내용이므로 정답이 될 수 없다. 이 문제에서 결정적인 단서는 an incredible landslide이다. 이에 맞는 답은 (d)다. 일단 답을 고르고 난 다음 맞는지 다시 확인을 해야 하는 습관을 길러야 하는데, 이 지문에서는 A choice between the lesser of two evils와 마지막 문장에 was disliked even more를 비교하면 답이 (d)라는 것이 더욱 확실해진다.

비교급이지만 그 앞에 **the**를 갖고 오는 경우: 두 개를 비교하면서 '더 ~하다'고 할 때 사용한다.

ex. He's the taller of the two. 그가 둘 중에 더 키가 크다.
He's the more popular of the two. 그가 둘 중에 더 인기가 있다.

어휘 lesser (little의 비교급) 덜
see 보다; 생각하다, 여기다
presidential election 대통령선거
run for 출마하다
consecutive 연속의, 연달아
incredible 믿기 어려운
landslide 압승
stunning 놀라운
criticize 비판하다
opponent 상대방, 적수

정답 (d)

2. One of the tensest moments in recent American history was the Cuban Missile Crisis. During the Cold War between the United States and the USSR, both governments found their enemies were building missile bases within firing range of their countries. Cuba, recently declared a socialist republic, obtained missiles from the USSR, and the world stood still on the brink of nuclear war.

Q What can be inferred from the passage?

(a) The USA helped build a missile base in Cuba.
(b) Cubans obtained missiles from the USA.
(c) The USSR had recently launched a nuclear war.
(d) The USSR helped build a missile base in Cuba.

해석 최근 미국 역사 중 가장 긴장된 순간 중에 하나가 쿠바 미사일 위기였다. 미국과 소련 양국의 냉전 시대에, 양국은 자국이 사정권 안에 드는 미사일 기지를 적이 구축하고 있다는 것을 알게 되었다. 쿠바는 최근에 사회주의 공화국임을 선포하고, 미사일을 소련에서 얻었다. 세계는 핵전쟁 직전 상태까지 갔다.

Q 본문을 통해 추론할 수 있는 내용은 무엇인가?
(a) 미국이 미사일 기지를 쿠바에 건립하는 것을 도왔다.
(b) 쿠바인들이 미국으로부터 미사일을 얻었다.
(c) 소련은 최근 핵전쟁을 시작했다.
(d) 소련은 미사일 기지를 쿠바에 건립하는 것을 도왔다.

해설 추론 문제는 문제 유형 중 가장 난이도가 높은 형태에 속한다. 그 이유는 전체적인 지문의 요지를 파악해야 하고, 선택지 하나하나가 맞는지 확실하게 알아야 하기 때문이다. (a) 첫 문장에서 미국 역사상 가장 긴장된, 즉 어려운 시기 중에 하나가 쿠바 미사일 위기였다고 했으니 미국이 쿠바 미사일 기지 건립을 도와주었다는 것은 오답이다. (b) 이 보기처럼 문장의 일부가 맞거나, 본문에서 인용을 하여서, 언뜻 보기에는 정답처럼 보이지만, 선택지의 일부가 틀린 경우가 많다. 쿠바가 미사일을 구입한 것은 미국이 아니라 구소련(the USSR)에서였으니, 이것도 오답이다. (c) the USSR recently, nuclear war 등 본문에 나온 단어를 사용하여 오답을 매력적으로 보이게 하는 기법에 유의하자. (d) '쿠바가 소련에서 미사일을 구입했다'는 문장은 '소련이 쿠바에 미사일 기지 설립을 도왔다'는 것으로 볼

수 있으니 이것이 정답이다.

어휘 tensest '긴장한(tense)'의 최상급
missile base 미사일 기지
firing range 사정거리
declare 선포하다
socialist republic 사회주의 공화국
obtain 얻다, 취득하다
stand still 가만히 있다, 멈춘 상태를 유지하다
on the brink of 막 ~하기 직전에

정답 (d)

Unit 02 경제 (Economy)

1. The Canadian dollar made history last week, when it approached parity with the US dollar for the first time in nearly 30 years. This comes as good news for many, _____. The dollar's increased value is good for importers, but exporters may suffer.

(a) especially during the winter months
(b) but not for all
(c) all over the country
(d) most of all, exporters

해석 캐나다 달러는 지난주에 기록을 경신했다. 캐나다 달러가 미국 달러와 동가를 기록했는데, 이는 30년 만에 처음으로 있는 일이다. 이는 많은 사람들에게 좋은 소식이다. 하지만 모두에게 다 좋은 것은 아니다. 캐나다 달러가 강세를 보이는 것은 수입업자에게는 좋지만, 수출업자들에게는 고통스러운 일이다.

(a) 특히 겨울 기간 동안에
(b) 하지만 모두에게 다 좋은 것은 아니다
(c) 전국에 걸쳐서
(d) 무엇보다도, 수출업자들에게

해설 빈 칸이 있는 문장의 내용을 그 다음에 이어진 문장에서 부연하여 설명하고 있다. 이는 독해에서 자주 볼 수 있는 경우이다. 많은 글들이 전달하고 싶은 주요 내용을 문두에 먼저 말하고 그 다음에 자신이 주장하는 것을 여러 가지 방법으로 뒷받침한다. 그 방법으로 앞에서 나온 내용을 반복하기도 하고, 구체적인 예시를 들기도 한다. 지문에서는 이런 캐나다 달러 강세가 많은 사람들에게 희소식이지만, 안 좋은 사람들도 있다(but not for all)고 말한 뒤, 그 내용을 부연 설명하면서, 수입업자에게는 좋지만, 수출업자에게는 좋지 않다는 내용으로 연결된다.

어휘 make history 역사에 남을만한 일을 하다
approach (~에) 다다르다, 도착하다
parity 같은 가격, 같은 액수
importer 수입업자
exporter 수출업자
suffer 고통 받다
most of all 무엇보다도

정답 (b)

2. Dear Professor McCrone,

As a third-year student and economics major, I have taken a lot of classes in the subject. I mean no disrespect, but must inform you that I do not understand how your lectures consistently overlook the importance of environmental economics in industry. Even in your study of coal mining, no mention was made of the costs of pollution.
Sincerely,
Scott Laing

Q What can be inferred from the passage?

(a) The student finds the professor's lectures boring.
(b) The student has studied environmental economics for three years.
(c) The student thinks the professor overlooks the importance of industry.
(d) The student thinks environmental economics have been overlooked.

해석 맥크론 교수님께
　　3학년 경제학 전공생으로서, 이 과목에 대해 많은 수업을 들어왔습니다. 제가 불손한 의도가 있어서가 아닙니다. 하지만 교수님께 꼭 드리고 싶은 말씀은 제가 이해가 안 되는 부분이 있다는 것입니다. 어떻게 교수님 강의에서 계속 산업에서 환경경제학의 중요성이 간과되어지는지 모르겠습니다. 교수님께서 연구하신 석탄 채굴에서 조차도, 오염 비용에 대해 어떤 언급도 없으셨습니다.
　　스캇 래잉 드림

　　Q 이 서신을 통해 추론할 수 있는 내용은 무엇인가?
　　(a) 학생은 이 교수의 강의가 지루하다고 생각한다.
　　(b) 학생은 3년 동안 환경 경제학을 연구해오고 있다.
　　(c) 학생은 교수가 산업의 중요성을 간과하고 있다고 본다.
　　(d) 학생은 환경경제학이 간과되어지고 있다고 생각한다.

해설 서신을 읽을 때는 서신의 목적이 무엇인지 파악하는 것이 중요하다. 목적을 알아내기 위해서는 누가 누구에게 무슨 일로 편지를 쓰는 것인지 답을 할 수 있어야 한다. 예를 들어, 친구, 친지에게 안부를 묻는 경우, 구직 신청을 하는 경우, 면접 후 합격, 불합격을 알리는 경우, 주문하거나 주문 받은 내용을 확인하는 경우, 불평하는 경우, 지연을 알리거나, 도착을 알리는 경우 등 다양하게 있는데, 지문은 학생이 교수에게 강의 내용에 대해 문의하는 내용이다. 학생이 강조하는 것은 환경 경제학이 중요한데 수업 내용에 다뤄지지 않는 것에 대한 불만을 전달하는 것이므로 (d)가 정답이다.

어휘 economics 경제학
　　major 전공
　　take class 수강하다
　　disrespect 불공손함
　　consistently 계속해서
　　overlook 간과하다
　　environmental 환경의
　　coal mining 석탄 채굴
　　cost 비용
　　pollution 오염
정답 (d)

Unit 03 **사회 (Social Studies)**

1. Apocalypto, the 2006 film by Mel Gibson, portrayed Mayan civilization as primitive and bloodthirsty. However, many anthropologists have pointed out severe inaccuracies in the film's "historical" narrative. For example, the film shows a lot of violence, _____.

(a) and typical features of Mayan culture
(b) but overlooks scientific accomplishments
(c) of which Gibson is a fan
(d) all of which are true

해석 아포칼립토는 2006년도 멜 깁슨이 제작한 영화인데, 마야 문명을 원시적이고 피에 굶주린 것으로 그리고 있다. 하지만, 많은 인류학자들의 지적에 따르면 이 영화의 '역사적'인 설명이 매우 부정확하다는 것이다. 예를 들어, 이 영화는 많은 폭력적인 장면을 보여주지만, (마야 문명의) 과학적 업적은 간과하고 있다.
　　(a) 그리고 마야 문화의 전형적인 특징들을
　　(b) 그러나 과학적인 업적들은 간과하고 있다
　　(c) 깁슨이 좋아하는 것이다
　　(d) 이 모든 것이 진실된 것이다

해설 정답을 찾을 때 오답을 제거하는 방법을 사용하는 것도 도움이 된다. 지문에서 심각한 부정확성(severe inaccuracies)이라는 부분은 이 영화가 실제로 역사적인 관점에서 볼 때 오류가 있다는 것을 알 수 있다. 따라서 (d) '모든 것이 사실이다'는 답이 될 수 없다. Eliminate the incorrect one! (a)도 severe inaccuracies에서 힌트를 얻어야 한다. Mayan civilization이 본문에 나오지만, 전형적인 마야 문명을 그린 것이 아니라, 영화에서는 그릇되게 그리고 있다고 하니 '전형적인(typical)'이라는 표현과는 맞지 않는다. 그리고 남은 보기 (b), (c) 중에서 고를 때는 지문 전체의 내용에 맞는 것을 골라야 하므로 마야문명의 긍정적인 면에 대한 내용이 나오는 것이 논리적으로 맞다. 따라서 답은 (b)다.

어휘 portray 그리다, 묘사하다
　　civilization 문명
　　primitive 원시적인
　　anthropologist 인류학자
　　point out 지적하다
　　severe 심각한
　　inaccuracy 부정확함
　　violence 폭력
　　accomplishment 성취, 업적
정답 (b)

2. A woman who had been lost for more than twenty-five years due to an inability to communicate recently made her way home. The woman took a seat on the wrong bus, and was not able to talk to anyone in her native dialect of Yawi, a rather isolated Islamic Thai language. She ended up in a hostel in a town near Thailand's border. Recently, however, new staff members of the hostel who spoke Yawi were able to determine her origin, and contacted her son. The

woman is now safely back home.

Q What is the main idea of the passage?

(a) The lost woman rode the wrong bus because she spoke Yawi.

(b) Some Thai villages are extremely remote and hard to find.

(c) The inability to communicate can eventually be overcome.

(d) Communication problems can have far reaching effects.

해석 의사소통을 하지 못해 25년이 넘게 실종되었던 여인이 최근 고향으로 돌아왔다. 이 여인은 버스를 잘못 탔는데, 그녀의 고유 방언인 야위어를 알아듣는 사람이 없었다. 야위어는 소수의 사람들만이 사용하는 이슬람계 태국어이다. 이 여인은 결국에는 태국 국경 근처에 있는 한 호스텔에 도착하게 되었다. 하지만 최근에 호스텔의 새 직원이 들어왔는데, 그는 야위어를 할 줄 알았고, 그래서 그녀가 온 곳을 알게 되고 그녀의 아들에게 연락을 했다. 그녀는 이제 안전하게 집으로 돌아왔다.

Q 위 글의 요지로 알맞은 것을 고르시오.

(a) 길을 잃은 여인은 야위어를 사용했기 때문에 버스를 잘못 탔다.

(b) 일부 태국의 마을들은 매우 고립되어 찾기 힘들다.

(c) 의사소통 장애는 결국에는 극복될 수 있다.

(d) 의사소통의 문제는 상당히 큰 영향을 미칠 수도 있다.

해설 (a) 다른 사람들이 못 알아듣는 야위어를 했기 때문에 길을 잃은 여인이 버스를 잘못 탔다는 것은 사실이다. 하지만 이 글의 요지가 되지는 못한다. 기억하라. Too small! can't be the answer. (b) 본문에 나온 어휘와 유사한 어휘들(town-village, remote-isolated) 등을 사용하여 오답 매력을 높이고 있다. 하지만, 야위어가 일반적이지 않다는 이야기였지, 마을 자체가 멀리 떨어져서 찾을 수 없다는 내용은 아니다. (c) 여인이 의사소통 할 수 있었던 것은 여인의 모국어를 할 수 있는 사람이 도와주었기 때문이다. 따라서 의사소통 장애가 언젠가는 극복될 수 있다는 것은 옳지 않다. (d) 의사소통이 제대로 되지 못할 때 얼마나 큰 불편을 겪을 수 있는지 예시를 제시한 내용이므로, 의사소통이 초래할 수 있는 상당히 심각한 문제가 주제이다.

Tips 주제나 글의 목적과 같이 전체적인 내용을 묻는 문제의 답으로는 아무리 본문에 근거하여 맞는 내용이더라도, 지엽적인 사항만 언급되었을 경우는 답이 될 수 없다.

어휘 **be lost** 길을 잃다
due to ~ 때문에
inability 무능, 무력
communicate 의사소통하다
native 출생지의, 토착의
dialect 방언, 지방 사투리
isolated 격리된
border 경계, 국경
end up 끝나다, (구어) 마침내 ~으로 되다
border 국경, 경계
origin 기원, 출신, 혈통
contact 연락하다, 접촉하다

far reaching 중요한, 멀리까지 미치는

정답 (d)

3. The term "Tent City" can be applied to any large collection of people living in non-permanent housing. (a) Recently several cities have seen such developments spring up. (b) Drug and alcohol use is often rampant. (c) Large Tent Cities have been built in Toronto, Seattle, and Saint Petersburg, Florida. (d) In nearly every case, the residents have been evicted by local authorities.

해석 '텐트 도시'라는 용어는 비영구적인 주택에서 많은 사람들이 살면 어느 곳에서나 사용할 수 있다. (a) 최근에 일부 도시에서 그런 현상(텐트도시 현상)이 생겼다. (b) 마약과 알코올 사용이 빈번하다 (c) 대형 텐트 도시가 토론토, 씨애틀, 그리고 플로리다의 세인트피터스버그 등에 있다. (d) 거의 모든 경우에 있어서, 그곳의 거주자들은 지방 당국에 의해 축출당하고 있다.

Tips Saint Petersburg 다음에 주명 Florida를 덧붙인 이유는 소련의 페테스부르그(Saint Petersburg)와 구별하기 위해서이다.

해설 Social Studies라는 주제는 앞의 문제처럼 신문의 기사 뿐 아니라, 잡지, 책 등의 기사 형태로 나오는 경우가 많다. 그리고 워낙 광범위한 주제이기 때문에 평소에 신문, 잡지 등의 기사 읽는 것을 생활화하여 이 주제와 형태에 익숙하게 하는 것이 도움이 된다. (a), (c), (d) 모두 텐트 도시에 대한 내용이 언급된 반면, (b)의 마약과 술이 종종 만연하다는 내용은 흐름상 어울리지 않는다. 가건물에서 살기 때문에 가난하고, 힘든 상황으로 마약과 술을 가까이 할 거라고 추측하는 것 역시 바람직하지 않다. 오답은 (b)다. 막연한 추측, 무리한 예측 등은 글 흐름에 어울리지 않는 문장 찾기에서 금물이다.

어휘 **apply** 사용하다, (규칙을) 적용하다, 적용되다(to)
non-permanent 임시의 cf. a non-permanent member of the Security Council 비상임 이사국
development 발전
rampant (병, 소문이) 유행하는, 마구 퍼지는, 사나운
resident 거주하는, 살고 있는, 거주자
evict (법적 수속에 의해) 퇴거 시키다. (일반적으로) 축출하다
local authorities 지방 당국

정답 (b)

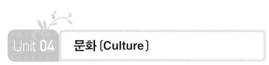

Unit 04 문화 (Culture)

1. If there is one truly global pop culture, it's likely B-Boy and B-Girl style. _____ has gained popularity all over the world, from Sydney to Seoul, from Rome to Rio de Janeiro. No matter where on Earth one travels, one will find examples of the American-grown style that has taken the world by storm.

(a) What began in Australia
(b) This traditional Korean style
(c) What started in ancient Spain
(d) What started in 1970s America

해석 진정으로 전 세계적인 팝문화가 있다면, 그것은 B-Boy,
B-Girl 스타일일 것이다. 1970년대 미국에서 시작한 이것은
전 세계에 걸쳐서 인기를 얻고 있는데, 시드니에서 서울까지,
로마에서 리오데자네이로까지 전 세계 방방곡곡에서 인기를 얻
고 있다. 세계 어느 곳을 여행하더라도, 미국에서 생성된 스타
일이 전 세계를 휩쓸고 있는 예를 찾아 볼 수 있을 것이다.

(a) 호주에서 시작한 이것은
(b) 이 전통적인 한국 스타일은
(c) 옛 스페인에서 시작한 이것은
(d) 미국에서 1970년대 시작한 이것은

해설 빈 칸 채우기 문제에서 최근 큰 변화라고 하면, 빈 칸 앞뒤 부분
만 보아서는 답을 고르기 힘든 문제들이 출제된다는 것이다. 이
문제처럼 지문을 끝까지 읽어서 전체 내용을 이해한 다음, 빈
칸의 앞 뒤 내용과 가장 어울리는 답을 고르는 연습을 해야 한
다. 예를 들면 맨 마지막 문장에 있는 the American-grown
style을 이해하지 못했다면 (a) 호주에서 시작한, (b) 한국전통
스타일에 (c) 고대 스페인에서 시작한 ~ 등과 같은 것을 놓고
고민을 하게 될 것이다. 미국에서 생성되었다는 단서가 있으므
로 정답은 응당 (d)가 되어야 한다.

어휘 global 세계적인, 세계의, 광범위한
gain (노력해서) 얻다, 입수하다, 획득하다
popularity 인기
from A to B A부터 B까지
no matter where (양보의 의미로) 어디에 있던지 간에
take A by storm 매료시키다, (청중들을) 황홀케 하다

정답 (d)

2. REGINA — Thousands of quilters have come to
the city to take part in Quilt Expo 3000. With Regina's
rich quilting history, it is the perfect choice to launch
quilting into the future! Exhibits include the latest
in quilting technology and designs, as well as your
chance to try virtual quilting in a 3-D environment!
Quilt Expo runs to September 28.

Q What can be inferred about the city of Regina from
the passage?

(a) It was named after Queen Regina.
(b) People have been quilting there for a long time.
(c) September is the best month for quilting.
(d) Thousands of quilters live there.

해석 레지나 - 수천명의 퀼트를 하는 사람들이 레지나에 왔는데, 그
목적은 퀼트 엑스포 3000에 참여하기 위해서였다. 레지나는
퀼트 역사가 풍부하기 때문에, 앞으로 퀼트를 시작하는 것은 아
주 좋은 선택이다. 전시 내용으로는 최신 퀼트 기술과 디자인이
있으며, 또한 가상으로 퀼트를 3-D로 경험할 수도 있다. 퀼트
엑스포는 9월 28일까지 계속된다.

Q 본문에 따르면 레지나 시에 관해 추론할 수 있는 것은 무엇인가?
(a) 레지나 시는 레지나 여왕의 이름을 따서 명명되었다.

(b) 오랫동안 레지나에서 퀼트를 해오고 있다.
(c) 9월이 퀼트를 하기에 제일 좋은 달이다.
(d) 수 천명의 퀼트를 하는 사람들이 그곳에서 살고 있다.

해설 추론문제에서 가장 중요한 것은 지문 전체의 내용을 먼저 파
악하는 것이 중요하다. (a) 본 지문은 기사문의 일부이기 때
문에 기사문 앞에 어느 곳에서 벌어진 일인지 지명을 적는 것
이 보편적이다. 그래서 지명이 언급되었지만, 그 지역 이름
의 유래에 대한 설명은 나와있지 않다. 답을 고를 때는 본문에
서 밝힌 내용만으로 결정을 해야 하므로 답이 아니다. (b) rich
quilting history는 quilting there for a long time과 같은
내용이므로, 이것이 맞다. (c) 본문에 언급된 날짜는 행사가 언
제까지라는 행사 기간을 밝힌 것이다. 따라서 퀼트를 하기 좋
은 시기라는 것은 무리한 주장이므로 답이 아니다. (d) 본문에
thousands of quilters를 사용해서 오답을 만든 경우이다.

어휘 quilt (솜, 털 등을 넣어 만든) 누비 이불, 퀼트제품, 퀼트를 만
들다
take part in ~에 참여하다
choice 선택
launch 시작하다, 착수하다, (신제품을) 시장에 내다
latest 최신의 cf. last 마지막의
virtual 가상의
run (연극, 영화가) 계속되다

정답 (b)

3. In the early 1960s, pop music had become stagnant.
(a) But suddenly, in 1963, a revolutionary sound came
to the rescue of the music industry and its fans. (b)The
arrival of the Beatles is celebrated as the beginning
of the "British Invasion" in pop music. (c)The Beatles
introduced new rhythms, harmonies and poetry to
pop music. (d)However, the Beatles started to copy
others' works as many ridicule them.

해석 1960년대 초기 팝 음악은 침체되었다. (a) 하지만 갑자기
1963년에 혁명적인 사운드가 음악 산업과 팬들을 구원해주었
다. (b) 비틀즈의 등장은 팝 뮤직에 '영국의 침략'의 시작으로
찬양되었다. (c) 비틀즈는 새로운 리듬, 하모니, 시를 팝 음악
에 도입했다. (d) 하지만 비틀즈는 사람들이 조롱을 하자, 다른
그룹들의 작품을 베끼기 시작했다.

해설 글의 흐름에 어울리지 않는 문장을 고를 때는 항상 다음 질문을
선택지마다 해본다. '나머지 보기들과 비교하여 내용이 상반되
지는 않는가?', '앞뒤 문장과 논리적인 결함이 있지는 않은가?',
'전체적인 주제와 일관성이 있는가?' 등의 질문들이다. 글의 전
반적인 흐름이 비틀즈에 대한 긍정적인 내용을 다루고 있는데,
(d)만 부정적인 내용을 다루고 있다.

어휘 stagnant 침체된, 변화가 없는
revolutionary 혁명의, 혁명적인
come to the rescue of ~을 구출하다
celebrate 찬양하다
invasion 침략

정답 (d)

Unit 05 예술 (Art)

1. Caricature artwork that pokes fun at political leaders is commonplace today. But historically, the implications of producing such opinionated artwork were harsh. _____, Honore Daumier, who made fun of the French King Louis-Philippe in a caricature, was ordered to pay one hundred francs and serve six months in jail. For insulting the king, Daumier's publisher and printer received the same sentence as well.

(a) As a rule
(b) As a result
(c) For example
(d) On the contrary

해석 풍자화가 정치 지도자들을 비웃는 것은 오늘날에는 매우 흔한 일이다. 그러나 역사적으로 볼 때, 이러한 강한 주장을 나타내는 삽화 제작의 결과는 가혹한 것이었다. 예를 들어, 오노레 도미에는 프랑스 왕 루이 필립을 풍자화로 조롱한 죄로 다음과 같은 명령을 받았는데, 백 프랑의 벌금을 내고 6개월 동안 옥살이를 해야 했다. 왕을 모욕한 죄로 도미에의 출판사와 인쇄사도 똑같은 형을 받았다.

(a) 일반적으로
(b) 결과적으로
(c) 예를 들어
(d) 반면에

해설 빈 칸 채우기에서 중요한 것은 빈 칸 앞뒤를 잘 읽는 것이다. 특히 본 지문은 풍자에 대한 일반적인 내용을 먼저 다루고, 구체적인 인물(Honore Daumier)을 예로 들어서 정치와 관련된 풍자화가 현대는 흔하지만 옛날에는 수용되기 힘들었다는 핵심 문장을 뒷받침하고 있는 글이다. 빈 칸 다음에 구체적인 이름들이 거명되는 경우는 '예를 들어(for example, for instance)'의 연결어구가 많이 사용된다. 빈 칸 채우기를 할 때 빈 칸 주변만 보아서는 답을 고르기 힘든 문제들이 증가하고 있다. 평소 문맥의 흐름을 읽고 이해하는 능력이 독해에서 필수라는 것을 기억하도록 한다.

어휘 caricature 풍자화, 풍자만화
artwork 삽화
poke fun at ~을 놀리다
political 정치적인, 정치(학)의
commonplace 평범한, 흔해 빠진
historically 역사상으로, 역사적으로
implication 함축, 암시, 결과
opinionated 자기 주장을 고집하는, 독선적인
harsh 가혹한, 무자비한
jail 교도소, 감옥
insult 모욕하다
sentence 판결, 선고
as well 게다가, 마찬가지로, 또한

정답 (c)

2. Prior to the 1850s, most artwork was influenced by the beautiful, the romantic, and the imagined. But in the mid-nineteenth century, artists began to focus more on ordinary people and events, in a trend known as realism. Realism profoundly influenced the artistic world because it encouraged the advancement of art techniques that would portray a more realistic scene. Also among the achievements of realism is the development of photography as an art form.

Q Which of the following is correct about realism?

(a) It tended to portray subjects beautifully and romantically.
(b) It attempted to show the world in an honest light.
(c) It profoundly affected the Romantic movement.
(d) It was strongly impacted by photographic art.

해석 1850년대 이전에 대부분의 예술 작품들은 아름답고 낭만적이고 상상적인 것들에 영향을 받았다. 그러나 19세기 중반에 예술들은 평범한 사람들과 사건들에 더 관심을 갖기 시작했는데, 이는 사실주의라고 알려졌었다. 사실주의는 예술계에 깊은 영향을 끼쳤는데 그 이유는 좀 더 실제적인 장면을 표현하는 기술의 발전을 장려했기 때문이다. 또한 사실주의의 업적들 가운데 하나는 사진을 하나의 예술 형태로 발전시켰다는 것이다.

Q 사실주의에 대한 내용으로 올바른 것은?
(a) 대상물을 아름답고 낭만적으로 표현하는 경향이 있었다.
(b) 세상을 솔직하게 보여 주려고 시도했다.
(c) 낭만주의 운동에 깊이 영향을 끼쳤다.
(d) 사진 예술에 의해 강한 영향을 받았다.

해설 (a) '아름답고, 낭만적(beautifully and romantically)'은 1850년대 이전의 특색이므로 오답이다. (b) '좀 더 실제로 묘사하기를 장려(~ portray a more realistic scene)'한다고 했으니 in an honest light와 같은 의미라 할 수 있어 정답이다. (c) 낭만적인 것에 영향을 받았으므로 오답이다. (d) 사실주의가 사진술의 발달을 도와주었는데, 거꾸로 사진 예술에 의해 크게 영향을 받았다고 되어 있으니 오답이다.

Tips Who's Doing What? 누가 무엇을 하는지를 생각하라. 특히 세부사항을 묻는 Part II의 문제에서는 더욱 유의해야 한다. 세부 사항 문제들은 구체적인 의문사를 사용하거나, 내용 확인을 묻는 문제들이므로, 평소에 지문을 접할 때 '누가 무엇을 했는가?'라는 질문을 하면서 읽는 연습을 하는 것이 도움이 된다.

어휘 focus on ~에 집중하다
ordinary 평범한
trend 유행
profoundly 심오하게, 깊게
encourage 격려하다, 장려하다
achievement 업적
light 관점, 견해

정답 (b)

3. The Renaissance is one of the most important periods in art. (a) Renaissance artists were the first to use perspective in their artwork. (b) Light and shadow were also examined and used in different ways. (c) It was a time when artists created new works, the likes of which had never been seen before. (d) It was also

26

a time for great religious changes, particularly in the Catholic faith.

해석 르네상스는 예술에서 가장 중요한 시기 중에 하나이다. (a) 르네상스 시대의 예술가들은 최초로 원근법을 미술작품에 사용하였다. (b) 빛과 그림자도 다른 방법으로 관찰되고 사용되었다. (c) 이 때가 바로 예술가들이 전에는 보지 못한 새로운 종류의 작품을 창조한 시기였다. (d) 또한 종교적으로 커다란 변화가 있었는데 특히 캐톨릭 신앙이 그것이다.

해설 글의 흐름에 어울리지 않는 문장 찾기는 각각의 문장이 잘 알려져 있는 사실이더라도, 전체 문맥의 흐름에서 벗어나거나 나머지 문장들과 가장 연계성이 적은 문장을 골라야 한다. (a), (b), (c) 모두 예술과 관련이 있고, 또한 새로운 시도를 했다는 공통점이 있다. (a) artists ~ the first (b) in different ways, (c) created new works ~ never been seen before 등이 그 예이다. 하지만 (d)의 경우는 주제를 바꾸어 종교 이야기를 하고 있으므로, 전체 흐름상 가장 연계성이 희박하다고 볼 수 있다.

어휘 the Renaissance 르네상스 시기
perspective 원근법, 관점
shadow 그림자
examine 살펴보다
in different ways 다른 방법으로
religious 종교의, 종교적인
particularly 특히
Catholic (신교 Protestant 교회에 대해) 로마 가톨릭 교회의, 천주교(의)
faith 신념, 신앙

정답 (d)

Unit 06 환경 (Environment)

1. I recently went on a trip to northern Canada. We went on a trip to see polar bears. They were so beautiful and majestic, I almost cried! However, I also learned that global warming means that the bears' habitat is disappearing. I was glad I got to see them now, because in a few years, _____.

(a) they might be gone
(b) I won't be going back to Canada
(c) they won't be so majestic
(d) their habitat won't be disappearing

해석 나는 최근에 캐나다 북부지역으로 여행을 갔었다. 우리가 여행을 간 목적은 북극곰을 보기 위해서였다. 북극곰들은 매우 아름답고 웅장했으며, 나는 (감동해서) 거의 눈물이 나올 뻔했다! 하지만, 내가 또 한 가지 느낀 점은 지구온난화가 곰의 서식지를 없애고 있다는 것이다. 내가 북극곰을 보러 간 것이 기뻤다. 왜냐하면, 몇 년 후면, 북극곰들이 사라질 지도 모르니까.

  (a) 북극곰들이 사라질지도 모르니까
  (b) 캐나다로 돌아가지 않으니까

  (c) 북극곰들이 그다지 웅장하지 않으니까
  (d) 북극곰의 서식지가 사라지지 않으니까

해설 빈 칸 채우기 문제 중 상당부분이 이 문제처럼 뒷부분에 빈 칸이 주어지는 경우가 많다. 북극곰을 볼 수 있어서 기쁜 이유를 찾아야 한다. 지문 뒷부분에 그들의 서식지가 온난화 때문에 사라지고 있다는 내용이 있었으므로, 몇 년 후면 북극곰이 사라질 수도 있다는 추측을 나타낸 (a)가 답이다. (b) 답을 고를 때는 항상 본문에 나와 있는 내용을 기초로 골라야 한다. 화자가 Canada를 다시 방문할지 안 할지는 나와 있지 않으므로, 오답이다. (c) were majestic이라고 분명히 나와 있으므로 오답이다. (d) 시험을 볼 때 긴장을 하고, 시간에 쫓겨서 읽다보면 한 두 개의 단어를 그냥 지나치고 읽기 쉽다. 하지만, 이 보기에서 보는 것처럼, not라는 단어 하나를 추가해서 본문과 전혀 다른 내용을 만드는 경우도 있으니 유의한다.

Tips Every word in the answer choices and the passage counts! 한 단어도 버릴 것이 없고, 버릴 수 없는 것이 시험 선택지와 지문이란 것을 다시 한 번 더 상기하도록 한다.

어휘 recently 최근에
go on a trip to ~로 여행가다
polar bear 북극곰
majestic 위엄 있는, 장중한, 당당한
global warming 지구 온난화
habitat (동식물의) 서식지, 거주지
disappear 사라지다

정답 (a)

2. Some governments are examining the idea of imposing a carbon pollution tax. Industries that release carbon pollutants into the air would be required to pay a fee for each ton of pollution emitted. The Australian Prime Minister has already mentioned such a move, and the European Renewable Energy Council has also suggested that governments should impose a financial consequence on businesses for their pollution. Advocates say that this tax would reinforce the motivation for adopting environmentally-friendly manufacturing practices.

Q What can be inferred about carbon pollution?

(a) Many governments oppose the idea of a carbon pollution tax.
(b) Australia is the nation that is most concerned about carbon pollution.
(c) A financial consequence could motivate the reduction of carbon pollution.
(d) Environmental groups came up with the concept of a carbon pollution tax.

해석 일부 정부들은 이산화탄소 오염에 따른 세금을 부과하는 것을 검토하고 있다. 이산화탄소 오염 물질들을 공기 중으로 방출하고 있는 산업체들은 방출하는 오염 물질에 대해 톤 당 요금을 부과받을 수 있다. 호주 국무총리는 이미 이러한 조치에 대해 언급한 바 있고 유럽 재생 에너지 협회도 정부들이 사업체들이 일으키는 오염에 대해 금전적인 지불을 제안했다. 옹호자들에 따르면 이 세금이 환경 친화적인 생산 방법을 채택하는 동기를 강화시킬 것이라고 한다.

Q 이산화탄소 오염에 대해 추론할 수 있는 내용을 고르시오.
(a) 많은 정부들이 이산화탄소 오염 세금에 반대하고 있다.
(b) 호주는 이산화탄소 오염에 대해 가장 염려하는 나라이다.
(c) 금전적인 부과가 이산화탄소 오염의 감소를 장려할 수도 있다.
(d) 환경 단체들이 이산화탄소 오염세의 개념을 고안해 냈다.

해설　(a) 지문에는 이산화탄소 세금안에 찬성하는 예만 나와 있다. 호주(the Australian Prime Minister), 유럽 재생 에너지 협회(the European Renewable Energy Council), 그리고 옹호자들(advocates)의 예를 들고 있으니, 반대하는 정부가 많다는 주장은 이 글로 추론하기 힘들다. (b) 본문에 호주 수상이 관심을 보였다는 이야기는 언급되었지만, 호주가 이산화탄소 오염에 가장 관심이 있다고 추론할 근거가 없으므로 오답이다. 여기서 기억할 것은 일반적으로 추론할 때 most, best, worst, always, every와 같은 전체적인 내용을 확신하는 것은 답이 아닐 확률이 높다는 것이다. (c) 세금(tax)과 재정적 부과(financial consequence)를 같은 의미로 보고, 환경 친화적인 생산방법을 채택하도록 동기 유발(the motivation for adopting environmentally-friendly manufacturing practices)시키는 것을 이산화탄소 오염의 감소를 장려(motivate the reduction of carbon pollution)하는 것과 같은 의미로 사용했다는 것을 통해 (c)가 정답임을 알 수 있다. paraphrasing의 기법을 다시 한 번 상기하자. (d) 환경단체에 대한 언급이 본문에 있기는 하지만, 이산화탄소 세금 부과안을 고안했다는 것은 내용과 다르다.

Tips　Paraphrasing - 동의어(synonym)를 평소에 많이 익혀두고, 동사와 명사의 전용을 자유롭게 할 수 있도록 연습하는 것이 도움이 된다.

어휘　impose (의무, 벌, 세금 등을) 부과하다
pollution 공해 *cf.* pollutant 오염물질
release 방출하다
be required to ～하도록 요구되어지다
fee 공공요금, 보수, 사례금
financial 재정(상)의
consequence 결과, 중요성
advocate 옹호자
reinforce 강화하다
motivation 자극, 동기 부여
adopt 채택하다, 택하다
environmentally-friendly 환경 친화적인
oppose ～에 반대하다
be concerned about ～에 대해 걱정하다
come up with ～을 생각해내다

정답　(c)

3. Aluminum, the Earth's most plentiful metallic element, is known for its durability, versatility and recyclability. (a) Aluminum cans are so commonly recycled that they create less than 1% of total material waste. (b) In fact, there is no limit to the amount of times aluminum can be recycled. (c) This means that aluminum thrown in the garbage today will still be intact, taking up room in a landfill 500 years from now. (d) Therefore, glass is more environmentally-friendly.

해석　알루미늄은 지구상에서 가장 흔한 금속으로 견고성, 다용성, 재활용성으로 잘 알려져 있다. (a) 알루미늄캔은 너무 재활용이 잘 되어 있어서 전체 쓰레기 양의 1% 미만이다. (b) 사실 알루미늄의 재활용 횟수에는 제한이 없다. (c) 이것이 의미하는 바는 오늘 쓰레기 매립지에 버려진 알루미늄이 지금부터 500년 후에도 쓰레기 매립지에 자리를 차지하고 있을 거라는 뜻이다. (d) 따라서 유리가 더 환경 친화적이다.

해설　화자의 tone을 이해하는 것이 큰 도움이 된다. 화자는 알루미늄이 계속해서 몇 번이고 재활용될 수 있다는 입장을 취하고 있다. 그래서 모든 보기가 알루미늄의 재활용성을 언급하고 있는데 (d)만 다른 재료(유리)가 더 낫다는 이야기를 하고 있다. 따라서 (d)가 정답이다.

어휘　plentiful 많은, 풍부한
metallic 금속의
durability 견고성
versatility 다용성 *cf.* versatile 다목적의, 다재다능한
recyclability 재활용성
less than ～ 미만의, 더 적은
there is no limit to ～에 제한이 없다.
intact 변하지 않은, 손상되지 않은
take up room 자리를 차지하다
landfill 쓰레기 매립지

정답　(d)

Unit 07　과학 (Science)

1. You can't see it from looking at the sky, but Earth's atmosphere is full of garbage. ＿＿＿＿＿＿ thousands of bits of junk floating in outer space. Usually left over from old satellites and space shuttles, this space junk is actually very dangerous to things like space stations. Just a tiny piece of metal could cause serious damage.

(a) Scientists think there used to be
(b) Scientists think there are
(c) Although not dangerous, there are
(d) Space stations are damaging

해석　그냥 하늘을 보아서는 볼 수 없지만, 지구의 대기는 쓰레기로 가득하다. <u>과학자들이 생각하기에, 수많은 쓰레기가 대기권 밖에서 떠다니고 있다.</u> 대부분이 오래된 인공위성이나 우주왕복선에서 나온 것인데, 이 우주 쓰레기는 실제로는 매우 위험하다. 예를 들면 우주 정거장 같은 곳에서는 매우 위험하다. 아주 작은 금속 조각도 심각한 피해를 줄 수 있다.
(a) 과학자들이 생각하기에 ～이 있었다
(b) 과학자들이 생각하기에 ～이 있다
(c) 비록 위험하지 않을지라도 ～이 있다

(d) 우주 정거장이 피해를 주고 있다

해설 영어에서는 같은 의미도 다른 표현을 통해 가능한 같은 표현의 반복을 피하는 경향이 있다. be full of garbage는 thousands of bits of junk floating과 같은 내용으로 볼 수 있다. (a) used to 동사 원형은 과거에는 ~했으나 현재는 더 이상 ~하지 않는 것을 의미한다. 본 지문은 현재 우주 쓰레기 문제가 심각하다는 내용이므로 과거를 의미하는 used to의 사용은 맞지 않다. (c) '우주 쓰레기는 사실 상 매우 위험하다(this space junk is actually very dangerous)'는 내용이 있으므로 '위험하지 않지만(Although not dangerous)'은 올바르지 않다. (d) 지문에서 '~ 문제를 야기할 수도 있다(could cause serious damage)'고 가능성을 제시했지만 문제를 야기시키고 있다는 현재 사실(are damaging)로 말하는 것은 잘못된 일이다. 따라서 전체 내용상 (b)가 정답이다.

어휘 atmosphere 대기
be full of ~로 가득하다
garbage 쓰레기
junk 쓰레기
float 떠다니다
outer space 외계
satellite 인공위성
be dangerous to ~에 위험하다
tiny 아주 작은
metal 금속(의)
cause 유발시키다, 원인이 되다
serious 심각한
damage 피해

정답 (b)

2. Think of somewhere, anywhere on Earth. Chances are it is covered in microbes! These tiny creatures, including bacteria and viruses, have been found inside volcanoes, deep in the ocean, even in permanently-frozen Antarctica. Stick out your tongue. You can't see them, but there are millions of them on it!

Q What is the best title for this passage?

(a) Innumerable Microbes
(b) Microbes Found In Volcanoes
(c) Tiny Creatures in the Ocean, Microbes
(d) Microbes in Strange Places

해석 지구상에 어딘가를 생각해보라. 아무 곳이나 생각해보라. 아마 미생물로 뒤덮혀 있을 것이다. 박테리아와 바이러스를 포함하는 이 매우 작은 생물체는 화산 속에서, 대양 깊은 곳에서, 심지어는 항상 얼어있는 남극에서도 발견된다. 혀를 내밀어보라. 당신 눈으로는 보이지 않지만, 당신 혀에도 (미생물이) 수백만 마리가 있다!
Q 이 글의 제목으로 가장 알맞은 것을 고르시오.
(a) 셀 수 없이 많은 미생물
(b) 화산에서 발견된 미생물
(c) 바닷속의 작은 생물체, 미생물
(d) 낯선 곳에 있는 미생물

해설 (a) 정답을 고를 때 주어진 지문에 근거하여 답을 골라야 한다.

미생물이 화산, 대양, 남극, 혀 등 모든 곳에 존재하므로 '셀 수 없이 많다'는 표현을 한 (a)가 정답이다. (b), (c) 미생물이 화산에서도 발견되었다(have been found inside volcanoes~, deep in the ocean)는 내용이 있으니 사실이다. 그러나 제목은 전체 내용을 가장 잘 설명하거나 요약하는 것이어야 하는데, (b), (c)는 세부 사항만 언급하고 있기 때문에 답이 될 수 없다. (d) '화산 내부에, 깊은 바다 속에, 꽁꽁 얼어붙은 남극 속에' 등 생명체가 살기에 적합하지 않은 낯선 곳에 있는 미생물들을 언급하고는 있지만, 본문에서 대의는 그만큼 미생물이 엄청나게 많다는 의미이므로 (d)는 정답이 아니다.

Tips 너무 지엽적인 것을 다룬 내용은 Part II의 대의나 제목을 묻는 문제에서 답이 될 수 없다.

어휘 chances are 아마 ~일 것이다
microbe 미생물, 세균
tiny creature 아주 작은 생물체
volcano 화산
permanently-frozen 영구적으로 얼어있는
stick out 내밀다

정답 (a)

3. Increasingly, athletes are turning to medical science for help. (a) National sports teams hire as many doctors as they can to study their athletes. (b) They use technology to look for very specific weaknesses in muscles or technique, and tell the athletes what to work on. (c) The latest technology in shoes and clothing certainly helps, as well. (d) Doctors are now as important to athletes as traditional coaches.

해석 점점 더 운동선수들은 의학에 의존하고 있다. (a) 국가 대표 운동 팀은 의사들을 가능한 한 많이 고용하는데 그 목적은 그 팀의 운동선수들을 살피도록 하기 위함이다. (b) 의사들은 기술을 사용해 근육과 기술에서 선수들의 매우 구체적인 약점을 찾아내고 무엇을 개선해야 할 지 선수들에게 전달한다. (c) 최신 기술이 신발과 옷에 사용되는데, 확실히 도움이 된다. (d) 의사들은 이제 기존 코치들만큼이나 운동선수들에게 중요하다.

해설 글의 흐름에 어울리지 않는 문장 찾기에서는 특히 첫 문장이 중요하다. 첫 문장의 keyword는 medical science이다. (a), (b), (d) 모두 doctors가 들어간 문장[(b)의 경우 They는 Doctors를 의미한다]이다. (c)만 의사 또는 의학에 관한 내용이 아니고, 최신 기술(the latest technology)에 관한 내용을 다루고 있다. 따라서 (c)가 정답이다.

어휘 increasingly 점차적으로
athlete 운동선수
turn to 의지하다
medical science 의학
look for 찾다
specific 구체적인
weakness 약점
muscle 근육
technique 기술
traditional 전통의

정답 (c)

VI. Actual Test

Actual Test 1

1 (c)	**2** (d)	**3** (d)	**4** (a)	**5** (a)
6 (b)	**7** (b)	**8** (c)	**9** (b)	**10** (b)
11 (c)	**12** (a)	**13** (b)	**14** (b)	**15** (a)
16 (d)	**17** (a)	**18** (b)	**19** (b)	**20** (b)
21 (c)	**22** (b)	**23** (b)	**24** (d)	**25** (b)
26 (d)	**27** (b)	**28** (d)	**29** (d)	**30** (d)
31 (a)	**32** (c)	**33** (a)	**34** (b)	**35** (b)
36 (c)	**37** (b)	**38** (b)	**39** (c)	**40** (d)

1

Exercise is typically considered to be something that a person can't really do too much of. Yet overtraining can harm the body. Doctors have noted that exercise regimens that are too strenuous can have _____ on the joints and muscles and can also cause insomnia or fatigue. In addition to these consequences of overtraining, doctors have also noticed that the immune system is weakened.

(a) future advantages
(b) increased benefits
(c) adverse effects
(d) widespread complications

해석 운동은 보통 아무리 해도 지나치지 않은 것으로 여겨진다. 하지만 지나친 훈련은 몸에 해를 끼칠 수 있다. 의사들이 지적한 바에 따르면, 너무 심한 운동 요법은 관절과 근육에 정반대의 효과들을 가져올 수 있고 또한 불면증이나 피로를 유발할 수 있다. 과도한 운동으로 인한 이러한 결과들과 더불어, 의사들은 면역 체계가 약화된다는 것을 발견했다.

(a) 미래의 이점들
(b) 증가된 혜택들
(c) 정반대의 효과들
(d) 여러 가지 합병증

해설 글의 전체 흐름을 이해하는 것이 얼마나 중요한 것인지 잘 확인할 수 있는 문제이다. 첫 문장에서 일반적으로 사람들이 생각하는 내용, 즉 '운동은 많이 할수록 좋다.' 또는 '운동은 아무리 많이 해도 해가 되지 않는다.'는 내용을 먼저 언급한다. 그 다음 이어지는 연결 어구 Yet 이후에 여러 부정적인 어휘를 사용해서 맨 앞쪽의 내용이 틀렸다는 것을 지적하는 글이다. 구체적으로 사용하고 있는 부정적인 어휘를 보면 overtraining, harm, too strenuous, immune system is weakened 등이 있다. 빈 칸에 들어갈 내용은 원래 의도와는 '정반대의 효과'를 초래한다는 내용이 글의 흐름에 가장 적합하다. (a)에 advantages나 (b)에 benefits와 같은 긍정적인 내용은 적합하지 않으므로 답에서 먼저 제외한다. (d)의 여러 가지 합병증은 부정적인 내용이기는 하지만, 운동할 때 의도와는 (c)의 정반대의 효과가 글의 흐름에 더 적합하다.

어휘 exercise 운동
overtraining 지나친 훈련
typically 전형적으로, 보통
harm 해를 끼치다
regimen (식사, 운동 등에 의한) 요법
strenuous 과도한, 격렬한
insomnia 불면증
fatigue 피로, 피곤
consequence 결과, 결말
immune system 면역체계
complication 합병증

정답 (c)

2

The dodo, now long extinct, still attracts worldwide fascination and study. Dodos were native to the Indian Ocean island of Mauritius. They were so large that they could not fly. Mauritius was first visited by Europeans in the sixteenth century, and in less than 100 years, the dodo was completely gone. Yet today, the great popularity of the dodo _____ in the island's economy.

(a) is becoming an issue
(b) has caused job losses
(c) neither helps nor hurts
(d) has contributed to growth

해석 도도새는 오래 전에 멸종했다. 그러나 이 새는 여전히 전 세계적인 매혹과 연구의 대상이다. 도도새는 인도양의 모리셔스 섬이 원산지였다. 도도새는 너무 커서 날 수 없었다. 모리셔스 섬은 16세기에 유럽인들에 의해 처음 방문되었다. 100년도 채 지나지 않아 도도새들은 완전히 사라졌다. 그러나 오늘날, 도도새의 큰 인기는 섬의 경제적 발전에 기여했다.

(a) 문제가 되고 있다
(b) 실업을 초래했다
(c) 도움도 피해도 주지 않는다
(d) 발전에 기여했다

해설 선택지만 보고 쉽게 답을 고를 수도 있다. (a), (b), (c)는
모두 부정적인 내용인 반면에 (d)만 긍정적인 내용이다.
하나씩 확인해보자. 먼저 간략히 내용을 요약하면, 도도
새는 멸종했다. 아직도 많은 인기를 누리고 있다. 도도새
서식지에 유럽인들이 들어왔다. 짧은 시기에 멸종되었다.
하지만 이 문제에서 연결어구가 글의 흐름을 파악하는데
얼마나 중요한지 잘 알 수 있다. 멸종했으나 인기가 높아
지역 경제 성장에 영향을 주고 있다는 (d)가 정답이다.

어휘 extinct 멸종된, 절멸한
attract ~를 끌어들이다
fascination 매혹, 매료
be native to ~가 원산지이다
Mauritius 모리셔스(아프리카 동쪽의 섬나라)
completely 완전히, 완벽하게
be gone 사라지다
popularity 인기, 평판
job loss 실업
contribute to ~에 기여하다

정답 (d)

3

Dear Mr. Thomas,
We recently received a complaint from a
customer about your conduct toward a fellow
employee last month. As a result of the
complaint, we will be reviewing your store as
well as your management before April 30. We
hope that your behavior last month was an
_____, and that we can depend
upon you to act more appropriately in the
future.
Sincerely,
Kristin Phelps
Director of Employee Affairs
Darla's Department Stores, Inc.

(a) achieved outcome
(b) issued warning
(c) advisable action
(d) isolated incident

해석 토마스씨께,
우리는 최근에 고객으로부터 불만사항을 접수받았습니
다. 귀하의 동료 직원에 대한 행위에 대한 것으로 지난달
에 있었던 일입니다. 불만에 대한 조치로서 4월 30일 이
전에 귀하의 상점은 물론 귀하의 관리 방침은 조사대상이
될 것입니다. 우리는 귀하의 지난달의 행위가 <u>우연한 사
건이었기</u>를 바라며, 차후 귀하가 좀 더 적절하게 처신하
리라고 신뢰하게 되기를 바랍니다.

(a) 달성된 결과
(b) 발령된 경고
(c) 바람직한 행위
(d) 우연한 사건

해설 불만(complaint)사항이 접수된 행동에 대한 내용을 고르
는 것이니, 긍정적인 내용의 (a)와 (c)는 답에서 제외한다.
또한 주절에 We hope가 있으니까, 지난 달 있었던 사건
이 딱 한 번만 있었던 일이었기를 바란다는 내용으로 하
는 것이 가장 적합하다. 따라서 답은 (d)다. isolated는
'동 떨어진', '흔하지 않은'의 의미이니까, 우연히 그 때만
그런 일이 있었기를 바란다는 내용으로 완성하는 것이 문
맥 흐름에 가장 적합하다.

Tips 「동사 + -able」은 자주 볼 수 있는 형태이다. able
은 '~할 만한'이다. advise : advisable, desire :
desirable, respect : respectable, consider :
considerable

어휘 complaint 불평, 불만
behavior 행동, 행실, 태도
depend upon ~를 신뢰하다
appropriately 적당히, 적절히
outcome 결과, 과정, 성과
issue 내다, 발하다
advisable 바람직한
isolated 우연한, 흔하지 않은
incident 사건

정답 (d)

4

Some scholars are debating whether
Shakespeare's famous tragedies could have
been written by another English author,
Christopher Marlowe. He is considered by
many to have written the best Elizabethan
tragedies prior to Shakespeare. Marlowe is
generally thought to have died after being
stabbed. Yet rumors of his survival abound,
and many believe that he _____
_____.

(a) continued writing under the name of
William Shakespeare
(b) later plotted to kill the famous William
Shakespeare
(c) penned these excellent tragedies using
his own name
(d) was named as the finest author in the
world by Shakespeare

해석 일부 학자들이 논쟁을 벌이고 있는데 논쟁 내용은 셰익스
피어의 유명한 비극들이 영국 작가 크리스토퍼 말로에 의
해 쓰여 졌을 수도 있는가이다. 많은 사람들은 그가 셰익
스피어의 작품이 등장하기 전에 최고의 엘리자베스 시대
의 비극들을 썼다고 여긴다. 말로는, 칼에 찔려 죽었다고
여겨진다. 그러나 그가 살아남았다는 소문들도 무성해서,
많은 사람들이 그가 은둔하여 윌리엄 셰익스피어라는 이
름으로 계속해서 글을 썼다고 믿는다.

(a) 윌리엄 셰익스피어라는 이름으로 계속해서 글을 썼다

(b) 나중에 유명한 윌리엄 셰익스피어를 죽이기 위한 음모를 세웠다

(c) 자신의 이름을 사용하여 이 훌륭한 비극들을 저술했다

(d) 셰익스피어에 의해 세계에서 가장 뛰어난 작가로 명명되었다

해설 빈 칸에 들어갈 내용을 고를 때, 지금 문제처럼 첫 지문이 중요한 영향을 끼칠 때가 많다. 가정하고 있는 내용이 셰익스피어의 비극이 실제로는 다른 작가에 의해서 쓰여 졌을지도 모르는 가능성(could have been written by another author)이 있다는 것이다. 글의 흐름을 이해하는 것이 중요한데 다음과 같이 간략히 정리해볼 수 있다. 셰익스피어 비극 중 어떤 것은 다른 작가가 썼을 수도 있다. 말로는 셰익스피어 이전에 최고의 비극 작가였고 일반적으로 살해되었다고 여겨졌다. 하지만 많은 사람들은 그가 살아서 셰익스피어라는 필명을 이용해서 계속 저작 활동을 했다고 믿는다. 연결어에 특히 유의하자. 내용 흐름상 말로가 계속 글을 썼다는 것과 셰익스피어의 이름을 사용했다는 것이 나와야 함으로 (a)가 정답이다.

어휘 tragedy 비극
debate 논쟁을 벌이다
author 저자, 작가
scholar 학자
stab 찔러 죽이다
prior to ~에 앞서
abound 무성하다
under the name of ~라는 이름으로
pen 글을 쓰다, 저술하다

정답 (a)

5

My chemistry teacher once asked me to go to the shop classroom and borrow the lumber stretcher. I had never heard of such a thing, but pretending to know, I set off to find it. I went and asked the shop teacher if I could borrow it, and he answered with a big laugh. Then he gently told me that there was no such thing as a lumber stretcher. I returned to the chemistry classroom blushing, and _____. How could I have been so gullible?

(a) was greeted with roaring laughter
(b) found that the class was empty
(c) looked up the odd phrase in a dictionary
(d) asked more questions about the experiment

해석 나의 화학 선생님은 공작 교실에 가서 나무 펴는 도구를 빌려 오라고 시켰다. 나는 그런 물건에 대해 들어본 적이 없었지만, 아는 척하고 그것을 구하러 갔다. 나는 공작 선생님께 나무 펴는 도구를 빌려 주실 수 있냐고 물었고 선생님은 크게 웃었다. 그리고 선생님은 나무 펴는 도구와

같은 물건은 존재하지 않는다고 친절하게 말씀해 주셨다. 나는 화학 교실에 얼굴이 빨개져서 돌아왔고 요란한 웃음소리가 나를 맞이했다. 나는 어떻게 그렇게 잘 속아 넘어갈 수가 있었을까?

(a) 요란한 웃음소리가 나를 맞이했다
(b) 교실이 텅 빈 것을 발견했다
(c) 이 이상한 단어를 사전에서 찾아 봤다
(d) 실험에 대해 더 질문을 했다

해설 전체적인 내용파악 유무를 확인하는 문제이다. 전체 내용을 간략히 정리해보면 쉽게 빈 칸에 맞는 표현을 고를 수 있다. 주인공이 모르면서도 아는 척 해서(pretending to know) 겪는 실수담이다. 특히 물건을 빌리러 간 선생님께서 크게 웃으시면서(with a big laugh), '나무 펴는 도구'는 없다는 것을 알려준 다음에 이어지는 문장이니까, 교실에 돌아왔을 때 또한 웃음 거리가 되었다(was greeted with roaring laughter)는 내용이 적합하다. 따라서 정답은 (a)다.

어휘 chemistry 화학
borrow 빌리다
return to ~로 돌아가다
pretend to+V ~인 척하다
set off 출발하다
blush 얼굴을 붉히다
roaring 시끌벅적한, 요란한
look up 찾아보다
be greeted with ~(한) 반응을 얻다
odd phrase 이상한 단어

정답 (a)

6

For spring and summer, our brand-new Foggy Island Flip-Flops are available for both men and women. Choose from the fantastic selection of carefree colors and bright prints that will make your friends, your family, and your feet smile. Leather and nylon mesh straps provide comfort and security. Select either heavy rubber and leather outsoles, or the light weight soles. All sizes and colors are in stock now, so _____ for the whole family.

(a) remember to clean the house
(b) take a moment to order our flip-flops
(c) start to create a new wardrobe
(d) try to make an independent decision

해석 봄과 여름을 위해 저희의 새로운 포기 아일랜드 슬리퍼가 남성용과 여성용으로 선보입니다. 멋지고 다양하고 편안한 색상들과 선명한 무늬들 중에서 선택하세요. 이 색상과 무늬들은 당신의 친구, 가족, 또 당신의 발까지도 미소 짓게 해줄 겁니다. 가죽과 나일론으로 된 그물 끈은 편안함과 안전함을 제공합니다. 무거운 고무와 가죽 밑창

혹은 가벼운 밑창을 선택하세요. 모든 사이즈와 색상을 현재 갖추고 있으므로 가족 전체를 위해 지금 시간을 내어 저희 슬리퍼를 주문하세요.

(a) 집을 청소하는 것을 잊지 마세요
(b) 시간을 내어 저희 슬리퍼를 주문하세요
(c) 새로운 옷을 만들기 시작하세요
(d) 독립적인 결정을 내리도록 하세요

해설 광고문을 읽고 빈 칸에 들어갈 적절한 표현을 선택하는 문제이다. 광고하는 제품은 '포기 아일랜드 슬리퍼'로서 carefree colors and bright prints, Leather and nylon mesh straps, heavy rubber and leather, lighter weight soles와 같은 표현을 통해 제품의 색깔, 특성, 소재, 그리고 사이즈 등에 관한 정보를 알 수 있다. All sizes and colors are in stock now에서 모든 사이즈가 갖추어져 있으니 필요한 제품을 주문하라는 내용이 들어가기에 가장 적절하다. 따라서 정답은 (b)다.

어휘 **flip-flops** 고무슬리퍼
carefree 편안한
print 무늬
leather 가죽, 가죽제품
comfort 편안함, 위안
mesh strap 그물 끈
security 안전함, 무사
rubber 고무
outsole 구두창
sole 밑창
in stock 재고가 있는
wardrobe 옷, 의상
independent 독립적인

정답 (b)

7

Fire destroyed a two-story building early this morning. Fire fighters were called to the scene at 2:35 a.m. by a security guard who heard a very loud explosion and then noticed flames through a window. _____ according to investigators, who say that the blaze started when an overheated electrical circuit sparked. No one was injured, and the surrounding buildings were not threatened.

(a) The building may be salvageable,
(b) Arson is not suspected,
(c) The victims should recover
(d) The culprit hasn't yet been captured

해석 오늘 아침 일찍 화재로 이층 건물이 파괴되었다. 소방관들이 오전 2시 35분에 현장으로 호출됐으며 호출한 경비원은 매우 큰 폭발음을 듣고 나서 창문으로 불길을 보았다. 조사관들에 따르면 방화는 의심되지 않는다고 하는데, 화염은 과열된 전기 회로에 불이 붙어서 시작되었다고 한다. 부상자는 없었고 주변 건물들도 피해를 입지 않았다.

(a) 건물이 구해질 수도 있다
(b) 방화는 의심되지 않는다
(c) 부상자들은 회복할 것이다
(d) 범인은 아직 잡히지 않았다

해설 대부분의 빈 칸 채우기 문제가 뒷부분에 빈 칸이 주어지는 경우가 많지만, 이처럼 문장 중간에 나오기도 한다. 빈 칸이 있는 문장과 전후의 문장을 꼼꼼히 파악하는 습관을 기르는 것이 좋다. 특히 이번 문제에는 과열된 전기 회로(overheated electrical circuit)가 실마리를 제공하고 있다. 건물이 파괴되었으므로 (a) 건물이 구해질 수 있다(salvageable)는 것은 틀린다. (c) 부상자가 없다(no one was injured)고 했으니, 부상자의 회복을 언급한 내용은 틀린다. (d) 화재 원인이 전기 회로 과열이니까, 방화가 아니고 따라서 방화범(culprit)에 대한 것도 틀린다. 따라서 답은 (b)다.

어휘 **destroy** 파괴하다, 파기하다
security guard 경비원
explosion 폭발, 파열
investigator 수사관
blaze 불꽃, 화염
overheated 과열된
electrical circuit 전기 회로
salvageable 구해질 수 있는
arson 방화
culprit 범인, 범죄자

정답 (b)

8

Pre-K education, teaching very young children before they begin formal schooling, is an idea that is gaining increased attention. Research has shown that a quality preschool experience will improve a child's chances of success — in the classroom and throughout life. But there is substantial public and governmental debate about funding for Pre-K schools. Many argue that today's society simply cannot afford publicly financed Pre-K programs. Others claim that this money must be found to increase the chances that today's children _____.

(a) can one day master these scientific concepts
(b) can ultimately learn to use these resources wisely
(c) will eventually have happy and successful lives
(d) will be enrolled in more diverse school settings

해석 Pre-K 교육은 정규 교육을 시작하기 전의 아주 어린 아동들을 교육하는 것으로 점점 더 관심을 얻고 있는 개념이다. 연구에 따르면 질 좋은 취학 전 경험은 아이가 학교생활과 인생에서 성공할 가능성을 높인다고 한다. 그러나 국민과 정부 간에 상당한 논쟁이 벌어지고 있는데 Pre-K 학교들에 자금을 제공하는 것에 대한 논쟁이다. 많은 사람들이 주장하는 바에 의하면, 오늘날의 사회가 공적으로 Pre-K 교육을 재정 지원할 여력이 없다는 것이다. 또 다른 사람들의 주장에 따르면 어린이들이 <u>행복하고 성공적인 인생을 살게 될</u> 가능성을 높이기 위해 이 돈이 마련되어야 한다.

(a) 언젠가 이러한 과학 개념에 정통하게 될 수 있는
(b) 결국 이러한 자질들을 현명하게 사용하는 법을 배울 수 있는
(c) 결국 행복하고 성공적인 인생을 살게 될
(d) 좀 더 다양한 학교에 등록할 수 있게 될

해설 빈 칸에는 Pre-K 교육에 대한 성격이 들어가야 한다. Research ~ throughout life에서 결정적인 단서를 찾을 수 있다. (a)의 scientific concepts와 (b)의 these resources, (d)의 diverse school settings는 본문에 언급된 바 없다. 따라서 답은 (c)다.

어휘 formal schooling 정규 교육
gain attention 주목을 끌다
research 연구
quality 질 높은
preschool 유치원
substantial 상당한, 많은
governmental 정치의, 정부의
debate 논쟁
fund 자금을 제공하다
argue 주장하다
can afford 지불할 능력이 있다
finance 자금을 조달하다
claim 주장하다

정답 (c)

9

A university recently placed a year of tuition up for bid on an online auction forum. Also included with the tuition were room and board, and both prospective and current students were bidding on the tuition. The university _____, hoping to draw attention.

(a) offered the highest bid
(b) invented the idea as a promotion
(c) is lowering tuition for all such students
(d) is thus altering its admissions policy

해설 한 대학은 최근에 일 년치의 등록금을 한 온라인 경매 포럼에 입찰했다. 등록금은 하숙비도 포함하고 있으며, 예비 학생들과 현재 학생들이 모두 이 등록금을 받기 위해 응찰했다. 대학 당국은 <u>이 아이디어를 홍보 수단으로 고안했으며</u> 관심을 끌기를 바라고 있다.

(a) 최고의 응찰가를 제시했으며
(b) 이 아이디어를 홍보 수단으로 고안했으며
(c) 이 모든 학생들을 위해 등록금을 낮추고 있고
(d) 이로 인해 입학 정책을 바꾸고 있으며

해설 hoping to draw attention으로 보아 빈 칸에는 등록금을 입찰한 목적이 나와야 자연스럽다. (a)처럼 응찰가격을 제시했거나 (c)처럼 등록금을 낮추거나 (d)와 같이 입학 정책을 변경한다는 내용은 나와있지 않다. 따라서 답은 (b)다.

어휘 place A up for bid A를 입찰하다
online auction forum 온라인 경매 포럼
tuition 등록금
room and board 식사를 제공하는 하숙
prospective 예상된, 기대되는
current 지금의, 현재의
draw attention 관심을 끌다
promotion 홍보
admission policy 입학 정책

정답 (b)

10

Wine connoisseurs and buyers say there is a global overproduction of grapes, and that wine prices are reflecting this. Prices are at all-time lows in nearly every region, with many suppliers unloading even some of their most distinguished vintages at unheard-of low prices. For would-be collectors interested in beginning a wine cellar, there _____.

(a) is no reason to purchase wine now
(b) may never be a better time to get started
(c) are several rules to follow when choosing wines
(d) may be a need to wait until the prices fall

해설 와인 전문가들과 구매자들은 전 세계적으로 포도가 과잉생산되었으며 와인의 가격이 이를 반영하고 있다고 말한다. 가격은 거의 전 지역에서 최저이고 많은 와인 공급업자들은 우수한 빈티지 와인들까지도 매우 낮은 가격에 처분하고 있다. 와인 수집을 시작하는 것에 관심이 있는 장래의 사람들에게는 지금보다 더 나은 시기는 없을 것이다.

(a) 지금 와인을 구매할 충분한 이유가 없다
(b) 지금보다 더 나은 시기는 없을 것이다
(c) 와인을 고를 때는 따라야 할 몇 가지 규칙이 있다
(d) 아마도 가격이 떨어질 때까지 기다릴 필요가 있다

해설 포도 과잉생산으로 가격이 하락하고 있고, 우수한 와인들이 최저가에 처분되고 있는 상황이다. 따라서 와인 구입에 관심이 있는 장래의 수집가들(would-be collectors)은 지금 구매를 하는 것이 좋다는 (b)가 정답이다.

어휘 wine connoisseurs 와인 전문가
global 세계적인, 지구 전체의
overproduction 과잉 생산
reflect 반영하다
all-time low 최저가격
unload 처분하다
distinguished 뛰어난
vintage (특정 연도에 수확된) 양질의 포도주
unheard-of 전례가 없는, 금시초문의
would-be 장래의
cellar 저장, 수집

정답 (b)

11

The United States' entry into World War II was not favored by a majority of Americans, nor by Congress. Most citizens and their elected officials _____
____. This prevailed into the early years of the Second World War. It was the Japanese air attack on Pearl Harbor that pushed the U.S. into war — now with overwhelming support from both congress and the general public.

(a) thought the Europeans were responsible
(b) considered war to be unjust
(c) believed they should stay out of other countries' affairs
(d) felt the war might be in the United States' interest

해석 미국의 세계 2차 대전 참전에 대해 대부분의 미국인들뿐만 아니라 의회도 찬성하지 않았다. 대부분의 시민들과 그들이 선출한 관리들은 미국이 다른 나라들의 문제에 관여하지 말아야 한다고 믿었다. 이것은 2차 세계대전 초기까지 만연했다. 미국을 참전하게 만든건 바로 일본의 진주만 공습이었고, 이제 미국은 의회와 일반 대중의 압도적인 지지를 받게 되었다.

(a) 유럽인들이 그 전쟁에 책임이 있다고 생각했다
(b) 전쟁은 불공정하다고 여겼다
(c) 미국이 다른 나라들의 문제에 관여하지 말아야 한다고 믿었다
(d) 전쟁이 미국에게 이익이 될지도 모른다고 생각했다

해설 영어의 특징 중에 하나가 앞에서 언급한 내용을 다른 표현으로 다시 반복해서 할 경우가 많다. '대부분의 미국인(a majority of Americans)'을 '대부분의 시민(most citizens)'으로 '의회(Congress)'를 '선출된 공무원(elected officials)'으로 바꾸고 '참전을 찬성하지 않았다(the entry of the war was not favored)'를 '다른 나라 일에 관여하지 않아야 한다(should stay out of other countries' affairs)'로 바꾸어 표현하고 있다.

어휘 entry 참전, 참가
favor 찬성하다

majority 대부분, 대다수
prevail 만연하다, 우세하다
official 공무원, 관리
overwhelming 압도적인, 저항할 수 없는
general public 일반 대중
unjust 불공정한
interest 이익

정답 (c)

12

Often in literature, there is a single character who seems to represent the "typical" person in his or her profession, location, or social standing. This is known as a presentative character, or stereotype. For example, the detective in a given job would have all the characteristics one might imagine a detective to have: a trench coat, a magnifying glass, a sharp and suspicious mind. Thus, rather than having any real personality of his own, the character _____.

(a) represents to readers a combination of impressions
(b) shows originality through such individual traits
(c) suggests to readers a dark, menacing personality
(d) takes on the personalities of many of the book's characters

해석 문학 작품에는 종종 '전형적인' 인물이 있는데, 이 전형적인 인물은 어떤 직업, 장소, 사회적 신분을 대변하는 것처럼 보인다. 이것은 대표적 성격 혹은 상투적인 이미지로 알려져 있다. 예를 들어, 주어진 임무를 수행하는 형사는 보통 사람들이 형사는 이러이러할 것이라고 상상하는 모든 특징들을 갖고 있다. 즉 바바리코트를 입고 확대경을 든 예리하고 의심이 많은 성격을 갖추고 있을 것이다. 그래서 그러한 인물은 자신의 고유한 성격을 소유하기 보다는 독자들에게 여러가지 인상들의 조합을 의미한다.

(a) 독자들에게 여러가지 인상들의 조합을 의미한다
(b) 이러한 개인의 성격을 통해 독창성을 나타낸다
(c) 독자들에게 어둡고 위협적인 성격을 암시한다
(d) 책의 인물들 다수의 성격을 가지고 있다

해설 문학 작품에 나타나는 '전형적 인물(a typical person)'에 관한 글이다. 'This is known as a representative character, or stereotype.'라는 문장을 통해서 전형적 인물에 대한 정의를 제시하고 있다. 전형적 인물에 대한 '형사'라는 구체적 인물을 예시로 들어 독자에게 상세한 정보를 주고 있다. 어떤 작품 속에서 형사라고 하면 일반적으로 바바리코트, 확대경, 의심 많은 성격 등을 연상하게 되고 이러한 요소들이 모여 형사를 떠올리게 한다(all the characteristics one might imagine in a detective: a trench coat, a magnifying glass, a sharp and suspicious mind). 따라서 빈 칸에 들어갈 내용은 have all the characteristics를 바꿔 쓴 (a)가 적절하다.

어휘 literature 문학, 문예
profession 직업
location 장소
social standing 사회적 신분
representative character 대표적 성격
stereotype 상투적인 이미지
detective 형사, 탐정
magnifying glass 확대경
trench coat 바바리 코트(벨트가 있는 레인코트)
suspicious mind 의심이 많은 성격
combination of impressions 인상들의 조합
personality 개성, 성격
originality 독창성
individual trait 개인적 특성
menacing 위협적인
take on (특정 성질이나 모습을) 가지고 있다

정답 (a)

13

The artist Christo is famous for _____ throughout the world. He first began to experiment with unusual materials and techniques. For example, Christo wrapped a paint can in brightly painted canvas and adorned it with glue, sand and car paint. As Christo's work evolved, he created art that covered, crossed, or transformed great swaths of earth and sea. Perhaps his best-known work involved eleven islands, which he surrounded with more than 600,000 square meters of pink polypropylene.

(a) his unusual use of color to create exciting landscapes
(b) the large-scale environmental art that he has created
(c) his impact on the fields of ecology and art
(d) the way he transformed the art scene in Florida

해석 예술가 크리스토는 전 세계적으로 그가 만든 대규모 환경 예술로 유명하다. 그는 먼저 평범하지 않은 재료들과 기술들을 이용하여 실험을 시작했다. 예를 들어 크리스토는 페인트 깡통을 밝은 색의 캔버스로 싸서 그것을 풀, 모래, 자동차 페인트로 장식했다. 크리스토의 작품이 발전함에 따라 그가 창조하는 작품들은 넓은 지역의 땅과 바다를 뒤덮고 가로지르고 변형하는 것이었다. 아마도 그의 가장 잘 알려진 작품은 그가 11개의 섬을 60만㎡의 핑크색의 폴리플로필렌으로 둘러 싼 것이다.

(a) 흥미로운 경치를 표현하는 색상의 특이한 이용
(b) 그가 만든 대규모 환경 예술
(c) 생태학과 예술 분야에 끼친 그의 영향
(d) 플로리다의 예술계를 변형한 방식

해설 본문에 나온 단어를 사용한 보기들에 유의한다. (a) unusual이 본문에 사용되어 언뜻 보기에는 매력 있는 선택지로 보인다. 하지만 unusual한 것은 재료(materials)와 기술(techniques)이지 색상(color)이 아니므로 오답이다. (b) earth, sea, islands를 사용한 작품을 만들었으니 '대규모 환경예술' 작품을 창조했다는 것은 맞는 말이다. 따라서 (b)가 정답이다. (c) 본문에서 자연을 언급하고, 미술을 소재로 하고 있으니 관련이 있어 보이지만, 실제 내용과는 상관 없으므로 틀렸다. (d) 전 세계 (throughout the world)에서 활동한 사람이니 Florida로 국한한 부분이 틀렸다.

어휘 experiment 실험하다
wrap 싸다, 감싸다
adorn 꾸미다, 장식하다
evolve 서서히 발전시키다
transform 변형하다
swath 넓은 지역
surround 둘러싸다
square meter 평방미터(㎡)
best-known 가장 잘 알려진
polypropylene 폴리프로필렌(합성수지 섬유의 원료)
landscape 풍경, 경치
large-scale 대규모의
impact 영향
ecology 생태학
art scene 예술계

정답 (b)

14

One new trend in stylish hotels is _____. Two brand-new hotels, one located in Manhattan and the other in London, are offering travelers small, futuristically-designed rooms for only 89 dollars a night. These so-called pods aren't much bigger than the size of a large walk-in closet but still offer a comfortably-sized bed, a bathroom with shower, and a flat screen TV. The rooms' steel-grey and white decor closely resembles that which is frequently seen in science fiction movies. The pods at the London hotel can be rented for only four hours at a time, so business travelers can stop in for power naps and quick showers without paying for a full night's rate.

(a) to quit taking reservations
(b) to offer less for less
(c) to change check-in times
(d) to offer expensive gifts

해석 최신 유행 호텔들의 하나의 새로운 경향은 적게 받고 적게 제공하는 것이다. 맨하튼과 런던에 각각 위치한 두개의 새로운 호텔들은 여행자들에게 작고 미래 지향적으로 디자인 된 방을 하루 밤에 단돈 89달러에 제공한다. 소위 pod라고 불리는 이 호텔방들은 출입할 수 있는 큰 옷장보다 약간 큰 정도지만 편안한 크기의 침대와 샤워기가 달린 욕실과 평면 TV를 갖추고 있다. 이 방들의 철회색과 흰색 장식은 공상 과학영화에 자주 등장하는 것과 매우 유사하다. 런던 호텔의 pod는 한 번에 4시간 동안만 빌릴 수도 있기 때문에 비즈니스 여행자들이 하루 밤 요금을 전부 지불하지 않고 잠시 눈을 붙이거나 샤워를 위해 잠시 들를 수 있다.

(a) 예약을 받지 않는 것
(b) 적게 받고 적게 제공하는 것
(c) 체크 인 시간을 변경하는 것
(d) 비싼 선물을 제공하는 것

해설 최신 유행 호텔의 경향에 관한 글이다. 이런 호텔의 특징을 나타내는 표현으로 'only 89 dollars at night, ~ aren't bigger than the size of a large walk-in closet'을 들 수 있다. 여기서 유추할 수 있는 내용은 크기는 작지만 가격 면에서나 안락함 면에서 매우 만족스러운 새로운 호텔에 관한 글이다. 따라서 (a), (c) 와 (d)는 본 글의 흐름과 어울리지 않고 정답은 (b)다.

어휘 trend 추세, 경향
stylish 유행하는
quit 중단하다
take reservations 예약받다
brand-new 최신의
located in ~에 위치한
futuristically-designed 미래지향적으로 디자인 된

so-called 소위, 이른바
walk-in 출입할 수 있는
decor 장식
at a time 한번에
stop in 잠시 들르다
power nap (원기 회복을 위한) 낮잠

정답 (b)

15

Scientists have discovered another key factor in their ongoing research about obesity. Certain types of bacteria that break down food in the digestive system can cause some people to gain more weight than others. Due to genetics, these bacteria are more prone to keep calories than others. _____, this could explain why some people gain weight more easily than others.

(a) Consequently
(b) However
(c) Fortunately
(d) Coincidentally

해석 과학자들이 진행 중인 비만에 대한 연구에서 다른 주요 요인을 발견했다. 어떤 박테리아는 소화계 내에서 음식을 분해하는데 이런 박테리아는 일부 사람들이 다른 사람들보다 몸무게가 더 많이 증가하도록 할 수도 있다. 유전적 특징으로 인해 이러한 박테리아는 다른 박테리아들보다 칼로리를 더 오래 보유하는 경향이 있다. 결과적으로, 이것은 왜 일부 사람들이 다른 사람들보다 몸무게가 더 쉽게 증가하는가를 설명해 준다.

(a) 결과적으로
(b) 그러나
(c) 다행히도
(d) 동시에

해설 연결어 넣기 문제는 빈 칸 앞 뒤의 흐름을 잘 파악해야 한다. 빈 칸 앞 쪽은 과학자들이 칼로리를 오래 보유하는 박테리아를 소화기 내에서 발견했다는 내용이고 빈 칸 뒤쪽은 일부 사람들이 쉽게 체중이 느는 이유를 설명해 줄 수 있다고 했으므로 자연스럽게 결과를 나타내는 (a)를 답으로 선택할 수 있다.

어휘 obesity 비만, 비대
certain 어떤, 특정한
break down 분해하다
digestive system 소화계
genetics 유전학, 유전적 특징
be prone to ~하는 경향이 있다
gain weight 몸무게가 증가되다
consequently 결과적으로, 따라서
coincidentally 동시에

정답 (a)

16

The city of Idaho Springs boasts some of the finest recreation facilities in the West. Recently, vandals have damaged several of the city's sports facilities. _____, they have sprayed graffiti on the new First Street tennis courts. As the city's daily newspaper, we believe that all Idaho Springs citizens who value these priceless facilities should be on the lookout for these vandals. For information, call the newspaper at 555-2805.

(a) Nevertheless
(b) Consequently
(c) Yet
(d) For example

해석 아이다호 스프링스 시가 자랑하는 것은 서부 지역에서 가장 뛰어난 휴양 시설들 입니다. 최근 들어 공공 기물 파괴자들이 시의 몇몇 운동 시설에 손상을 입혔습니다. 예를 들어, 그들은 새로 지은 퍼스트 가의 테니스 코트에 스프레이 페인트로 낙서를 했습니다. 시의 일간 신문으로서, 본지가 믿는 바는 이 귀중한 시설물들을 소중히 여기는 모든 아이다호 스프링스 주민들이 이러한 기물 파괴자들을 감시해야 한다는 것입니다. 더 자세한 사항은 신문사 555-2805로 연락해 주세요.

(a) 그럼에도 불구하고
(b) 결과적으로
(c) 그러나
(d) 예를 들어

해설 연결어(connectors) 문제는 보기를 먼저 보는 것이 효과적이다. 그리고 해석도 중요하지만, 연결어의 기능(function)을 확인하는 것이 중요하다. 예를 들면 (a) 그럼에도 불구하고: 양보, (b) 결과적으로: 결과, (c) 그러나: 역접, (d) 예를 들어: 예시 등으로 확인을 하고 문장을 읽기 시작한다. 공공시설 파괴가 있었다는 내용 다음에 구체적인 내용들이 이어지고 있으므로 (d)가 정답이다.

어휘 boast 자랑하다
recreation 휴양, 기분전환
facilities 시설, 설비
vandal 공공기물 파괴자
damage 손해[피해]를 입히다
graffiti 낙서
value 귀중히 여기다
outlook 감시, 경계
priceless 매우 귀중한
nevertheless 그럼에도 불구하고
consequently 결과적으로, 따라서

정답 (d)

17

Caffeine is quite often used by athletes hoping to get a little boost to improve their performance in long-distance activities or events, but using caffeine to improve short-term workout performance won't help. In fact, it may hurt your performance during shorter, high-intensity workouts. Researchers studied two groups while exercising through several short cycling tests. Those who were given caffeine before the tests took longer to reach peak performance levels than those who performed the tests caffeine-free.

Q Which of the following is correct according to the passage?

(a) Athletes use caffeine to improve physical performance.
(b) Caffeine has been proven to help in cycling performance.
(c) The effects of caffeine only last through short workouts.
(d) Peak performance was only achieved by those given caffeine.

해석 카페인은 운동선수들이 매우 자주 사용하는데, 그 목적은 장거리 활동이나 경기에서 성적을 향상시키기 위해서이다. 하지만 카페인은 단기적 운동성과를 개선하는 데는 도움이 되지 않는 경향이 있다. 사실 단거리 고강도 운동에 있어서는 오히려 해가 될 수도 있다. 연구자들은 두 집단을 연구했는데, 몇몇 짧은 사이클 테스트를 통해 운동을 하는 동안 그들을 연구했다. 실험 이전에 카페인이 제공된 사람들은 카페인 없이 실험에 임한 사람들보다 최고 성과 수준에 도달하는데 시간이 오래 걸렸다.

Q 윗글의 내용에 따라 올바른 것을 고르시오.
(a) 운동선수들은 육체적 성과를 개선하기 위해 카페인을 사용한다.
(b) 카페인은 사이클 성적에 도움이 되는 것으로 증명됐다.
(c) 카페인의 효과는 짧은 운동 동안만 지속된다.
(d) 최고 성과 수준은 카페인이 주어진 사람들에 의해서만 성취됐다.

해설 제시된 글을 읽고 본문에 나오는 사실을 선택하는 문제이다. 이런 문제 유형에서는 글을 읽기 전에 먼저 제시된 답을 읽어 보고 각 문장이 본문의 내용과 일치하는 가를 확인하는 것이 유용한 방법이다. 좋은 성적을 내고자 하는 운동선수들이 카페인을 사용한다는 전제가 단락의 맨 앞에 나와 있기 때문에 손쉽게 (a)를 정답으로 선택할 수 있다. 이 후에는 다른 문항이 정답이 될 수 있는가를 단계적으로 확인해보면 된다.

어휘 athlete 운동선수
boost 상승, 증대
performance 성적, 성과

long-distance 장거리의
event 경기
short-term 단기간의
workout 운동
high-intensity 고강도의
peak 최고점의
physical 육체적인
last 지속되다

정답 (a)

18

The annual conference and exhibition of the Southwest Council of Culinary Professionals (SCCP) is coming to Midland this spring. The convention will be held at the Marriott Midland North from March 23rd through March 25th. The conference's opening session will feature keynote speaker Matthew Lafitte. The public is invited to visit the exhibit hall from 5 p.m. to 8 p.m. each evening, where professionals and vendors will present cooking demonstrations. For more information, call the SCCP office at 555-3813.

Q What is the best title for the news article?
(a) Chef to Highlight Cooking Show
(b) Special March Event of Area Chefs
(c) Kitchen of the Future
(d) Spring Cooking Demonstrations

해석 전문 요리가들의 남서부 협회(SCCP)의 연례 회의와 전시회가 미드랜드에서 올해 봄에 열린다. 회의는 매리어트 북 미드랜드에서 개최될 예정이고, 일정은 3월 23일부터 25일까지이다. 회의 개회식에서 기조연설은 매튜 라피트가 한다. 일반인들은 매일 저녁 5시부터 8시까지 전시장을 돌아 볼 수 있으며, 그곳에서 전문가들과 판매인들이 요리 시범을 선보일 것이다. 자세한 사항은 555-3813 SCCP로 문의하면 된다.

Q 위 뉴스 기사의 제목으로 가장 알맞은 것을 고르시오.
(a) 요리쇼를 빛낸 요리사
(b) 지역 요리사들의 3월 행사
(c) 미래의 부엌
(d) 봄 요리 시범

해설 18번 문제는 Part II에서 앞부분에 해당한다. 이 경우 대의를 묻거나, 제목을 묻는 문제가 주로 출제되기 때문에 전체적인 의미파악을 하는 것이 가장 중요하다. 본 지문은 요리사들이 하는 연례 회의의 개최를 알리는 글이다. 그 다음에 이어지는 것이 장소(the Marriott Midland North), 시간(March 23rd through March 25th), 기조 연설자(keynote speaker), 일반인 관람시간(5 p.m. to 8 p.m. each evening), 문의사항 연락처 번호 등으로 이어져 있다. 따라서 맨 처음 문장에서 제목을 찾아야

한다. 답은 (b)다.

어휘 conference 협회
exhibition 전시회
culinary 요리의
professional 전문가
be held 개최되다
keynote speaker 기조연설자
feature ~을 특징으로 하다
exhibit hall 전시장
convention 회의
vendor 판매인
cooking demonstrations 요리 시범
chef 요리사
highlight 돋보이게 하다

정답 (b)

19

The world would not be what it is today without the work of Albert Einstein. His achievements transformed the fundamentals of physics and the foundations for technology and by doing so greatly impacted culture, society and history. His theory of light alone created the study of quantum mechanics. Not bad for a young man who left school at 15, and did his most revolutionary work at the age of 26.

Q What is the best title of the passage?
(a) Einstein's Most Revolutionary Work
(b) The Influence of Einstein's Achievements
(c) The Extraordinary Youth of Albert Einstein
(d) Einstein's Fundamentals of Physics

해석 알버트 아인슈타인의 업적이 없었더라면 세상은 현재와 같지 않을 것이다. 그의 업적은 물리학의 기본 원칙들과 기술의 근본을 바꾸어 놓았고 그렇게 함으로서 문화, 사회, 역사에 지대한 영향을 끼쳤다. 그의 빛의 이론 하나만으로 양자 역학이 탄생했다. 15살에 학교를 그만 둔 젊은이 치고는 과히 나쁘지 않은 일이었고 그는 자신의 가장 혁명적인 업적을 26세에 이뤄냈다.

Q 위 글의 제목으로 가장 알맞은 것을 고르시오.
(a) 아인슈타인의 가장 혁명적인 업적
(b) 아인슈타인의 업적이 끼친 영향
(c) 알버트 아인슈타인의 비범한 젊은 시절
(d) 아인슈타인의 물리학 기본 원리들

해설 글의 제목을 찾는 문제이다. 전체적인 내용을 읽고 나서 글의 내용을 함축적으로 표현해 줄 수 있는 제목을 찾아야 한다. 다시 말해, 제목은 내용을 모두 포괄할 수 있어야 한다. 전체적인 내용이 아인슈타인의 업적이 다른 분야에 어떤 영향을 미쳤는가이므로 정답은 (b)가 된다. (a), (c)는 글 하단부에 잠시 언급된 지엽적인 내용이므로 글의

내용을 함축할 수 없는 오답이다.

어휘 work 업적, 성과
achievement 업적, 위업, 성취
fundamental 기본, 근본
physics 물리학
foundation 기초, 근거, 근원
impact 영향을 주다
quantum mechanics 양자 역학
revolutionary 혁명의, 혁명적인
extraordinary 비범한, 색다른
youth 청춘기

정답 (b)

20

For millions of people, antidepressant medications have brought relief from depression. Yet recent studies show there may be risks for young people. In a 2004 study, the Federal Drug Administration(FDA) analyzed 4,582 adolescents in 24 drug trials. They found that thoughts of suicide were twice as likely to occur in subjects taking antidepressants than in those taking placebo doses. Other studies are less conclusive, and the debate continues.

Q What is the best title of the passage?
(a) A Setback for the Treatment of Depression
(b) Antidepressants Carrying Suicide Risk for Adolescents
(c) Statistics Hurting Antidepressant Sales
(d) FDA Bans Antidepressants for Children

해석 수백만 명의 사람들에게 우울증 치료제의 복용은 우울증을 완화해주었다. 하지만 최근 연구에 따르면 젊은이들이 위험할 수도 있다. 2004년 한 연구에서 식품의약청(FDA)은 4,582명의 청소년들을 분석했는데, 이들은 24개 약품 실험에 참가했다. 그들은 플라시보를 복용한 피실험자들보다 우울증 치료제를 복용한 피실험자들이 자살의 충동을 느끼게 될 확률이 두 배가 높다는 것을 발견했다. 다른 연구들은 그다지 결정적이지 않고 논쟁은 계속되고 있다.

Q 위 글의 제목으로 가장 적절한 것을 고르시오.
(a) 우울증 치료의 실패
(b) 청소년들에게 자살 위험이 있는 우울증 치료제
(c) 우울증 치료제 판매에 피해가 된 통계
(d) FDA, 어린이용 우울증 치료제 금지

해설 간단한 단락의 글에서 주제문은 앞에 위치하는 경우가 많다. 특히 지금처럼 제목을 묻는 글이 그렇다. 이번 문제의 경우는 앞부분에 유의하는 것 이 외에도 연결어를 유의해서 봐야 하는 것의 중요성을 알 수 있는 문제이다. 특

히 Yet, But, However, Even though 등은 앞에 나온 내용과 다른 내용이 이어지기 때문에 더욱 신경을 써야 한다. 우울증 치료제가 많이 사용되지만 젊은이들에게 위험할 수도 있다(may be risks for young people)는 것이 주요 전달 내용이다. 답을 고르기 위해서는 본문에 나온 young people이 보기에서 adolescents로 바뀌어 있는 것을 주목할 필요가 있다. 답은 청소년과 우울증 치료제의 위험성이 나와 있는 (b)다.

Tips 한 번 더 유의해서 봐야 하는 표현들이 있다. Recent studies show that에서 최근 연구 결과에 의해 밝혀진 것을 소개한다면, 기존에는 몰랐거나, 새로운 내용이 소개될 확률이 높고, 또 기존에 믿어져 왔던 것을 재확인하는 경우가 많으므로 주의한다. I think that, in my opinion에서 저자의 생각을 나타내는 것은 저자의 주장이 담긴 부분이 되기 때문에 주요 내용이 올 확률이 높으므로 유의한다.

어휘 antidepressant medications 우울증 치료제
depression 의기소침, 우울
relief 경감, 구제
analyze 분석하다
adolescent 청소년
suicide 자살, 자해
be likely to+V ~일 것 같다
subject 피실험자
conclusive 결정적인
setback 실패, 좌절
statistics 통계(학)
placebo 플라시보, (유효 성분이 없는) 위약
conclusive 결정적인, 단호한
bans 금지

정답 (b)

21

FROM: coachellison@yourmail.net
TO: jjackson@studenttalk.com
SUBJECT: Spring Season
DATE: Mon Jan 05; 15:32:12

Dear Jonathan,
I have not seen you on the roster for this spring's baseball team. Your excellent pitching was vital to us in winning the championship last season. Besides, your jokes kept us all laughing through even the toughest times. As your coach and your friend, I hope you will be with us when we begin practicing later this month.
Sincerely,
Coach Ellison

Q What might be attached to this email?

(a) A picture of last season's team
(b) Jonathan's pitching record
(c) A practice schedule
(d) A team roster

해석 보낸 사람: coachellison@yourmail.net
받는 사람: jjackson@studenttalk.com
제목: 봄 시즌
날짜: Mon Jan 05; 15:32:12

조나단에게,
이번 봄 야구팀 등록부에서 너의 이름을 볼 수가 없더구나. 너의 뛰어난 투구력은 지난 시즌 우리의 우승의 원동력이었어. 게다가 네 농담이 힘든 때에도 우리들을 모두 웃게 만들어 줬어. 너의 코치이자 친구로서 우리가 이번 달 하순 훈련을 시작할 때 너를 볼 수 있기를 바란다.
엘리슨 코치로부터

Q 이 이메일에는 무엇이 첨부될 수 있을까?
(a) 지난 시즌 팀 사진
(b) 조나단의 투구 기록
(c) 연습 시간표
(d) 야구팀 등록부

해설 서신 문제는 자주 출제되는 형식 중에 하나이다. 비교적 다른 형식의 글보다 독해가 쉽기 때문에 이 문제에서 틀리면 안 된다는 각오로 접근하길 권한다. 서신은 일반적으로 다음과 같은 질문을 스스로 던지면서 읽으면 내용 파악이 수월하다. 누가(발신인) 누구(수취인)에게 보낸 편지인가? 두 사람의 관계가 무엇인가? 업무적으로 아는 사이인가? 사적으로 알고 지내는 사이인가? 서신의 목적이 무엇인가? 안부, 주문, 불평 등 어떤 내용을 다루고 있는가? 문제를 먼저 읽어서 필요한 정보의 답을 찾는 selective reading을 하는 것도 효과적이다. 본 서신의 경우 학교 코치가 학생에게 야구팀 활동을 권하는 내용이다. 그리고 질문의 내용이 첨부한 내용이 무엇일지 확인하는 것이므로, 운동연습 일정표가 있을 것이란 것을 쉽게 알 수 있으니 답은 (c)다.

어휘 roster 등록부, 명부
vital 중대한, 생기가 넘치는
valuable 소중한
besides 게다가

정답 (c)

22

One ongoing trend in American high school education is that, statistically speaking, female students earn higher grades than male students in math. But this doesn't seem to relate directly to university entrance exam tests scores, in which male students on the average score higher. This difference is largely due to the fact that female students are less likely than male students to take more advanced high school math courses.

Q According to the passage, why do males score higher on university entrance exams?

(a) Male students don't get as anxious while taking tests.
(b) Female students don't take as many high-level math classes.
(c) Female students don't work as hard to achieve better math grades.
(d) Male students don't perform well in advanced math classes. ·

해석 미국 고등학교 교육에서 계속되고 있는 한 가지의 경향은 통계적으로 여학생들이 남학생들보다 수학에서 더 높은 성적을 받는다는 것이다. 그러나 이것은 대학 입학시험 점수와는 직접적으로 연결되지 않은 것으로 보이는데, 이 시험에서는 남학생들이 더 높은 점수를 받고 있다. 이 차이는 여학생들이 남학생들보다 더 어려운 수학 수업을 듣지 않는다는 사실에서 크게 기인한다.

Q 위 글에 따르면 왜 남학생들이 대학 입학시험에서 더 높은 점수를 얻는가?
(a) 남학생들은 시험을 볼 때 그다지 긴장하지 않는다.
(b) 여학생들이 어려운 수학 수업을 많이 듣지 않는다.
(c) 여학생들은 더 나은 수학 점수를 얻으려고 열심히 공부하지 않는다.
(d) 남학생들은 높은 수준의 수학 수업에서 잘 하지 못한다.

해설 구체적인 질문에 대한 답을 구하는 질문은 먼저 문제를 읽고 이와 관련된 정보를 찾으면서 글을 읽는 것이 효과적이다. 미국 고교에서 남학생과 여학생간의 수학 성적에 관한 글이다. "~statistically speaking, female students earn higher grades than male students in math."라는 문장에서 여학생이 남학생 보다 수학에서 높은 성적을 받는 것을 알 수 있다. 그러나 실제로 대학 입학시험에서는 남학생이 좋은 결과를 보인다. 그 이유는 "~ due to the fact that female students are less likely than male students to take more advanced high school math courses."에서 설명하고 있듯이 여학생들이 어려운 수학을 듣지 않기 때문이다. 따라서 정답은 (b)다.

어휘 ongoing 진행 중의, 계속 되는
statistically 통계적으로
earn 획득하다, 받다
grade 성적
relate to ~와 연관되다
directly 곧장, 똑바로
university entrance 대학입학
on the average 평균적으로
anxious 긴장하는, 근심하는
achieve 이루다, 성취하다
perform 이행하다, 실행하다
advanced 높은 수준의, 어려운

정답 (b)

23

More and more surveillance cameras are being installed every day. But now, new technology is making these cameras capable of more than just recording activity. For instance, new microphones will let these cameras alert the police if a gun is shot in the area. The same will happen if the cameras' motion detectors spot someone walking in circles or leaving behind a suspicious package.

Q How might surveillance cameras benefit business owners?

(a) It could replace more secure technology.
(b) Better cameras could notify police of suspicious activity.
(c) Microphones could record conversations in the area.
(d) New cameras could screen package contents.

해석 매일 점점 더 많은 수의 감시 카메라가 설치되고 있다. 그러나 새로운 기술은 이 카메라들의 단지 녹화 이상의 기능들을 할 수 있도록 해 준다. 예를 들어 새로운 마이크는 만일 그 지역에서 총이 발사될 경우, 이 카메라들이 경찰에 신고를 하게 할 것이다. 카메라의 동작 탐지기는 누군가가 부근을 배회하거나 의심이 가는 물건을 남겨둘 경우에도 똑같은 기능을 할 것이다(즉, 경찰에 신고를 할 것이다).
Q 감시 카메라가 사업자들에게는 어떻게 도움이 될까?
(a) 감시 카메라가 좀 더 안전한 기술을 대체할 수 있다.
(b) 개선된 카메라가 경찰에 수상한 행위를 신고할 수 있다.
(c) 마이크가 카메라 부근의 대화들을 녹음할 수 있다.

(d) 새로운 카메라는 포장된 물건의 내용물을 가려 낼 능력이 있다.

해설 보기에 나온 어휘들을 이용하여 오답 매력도를 높인다는 것은 이미 여러 차례 언급한 바 있다. Technology, microphones, record, cameras 등이 오답 선택지에 사용된 것을 기억해야 한다. 이 글의 가장 중요한 내용은 감시 카메라의 기능이 단순 녹화가 아니라, 이상이 있을 경우 자동으로 경찰에 통보가 되는 기능으로 보안이 강화된다는 것을 구체적인 예시를 들어 설명하고 있다. 따라서 정답은 (b)다.

어휘 surveillance 감시, 감독 cf. surveillance camera 감시카메라
technology 과학 기술
capable of ~ 할 수 있는
for instance 예를 들어
microphone 마이크, 확성기
alert 신고하다, 알리다
motion detector 움직임 탐지기
spot 탐지하다, 발견하다
suspicious 의심스런
secure technology 안전한 기술
notify 신고하다
screen 가려내다, 심사하다
contents 내용, 항목

정답 (b)

24

Manon Rheaume was the first woman to ever play in a professional men's hockey game. As a little girl growing up in Canada, Rheaume begged her dad to let her play hockey. Obviously, she got her wish. During her career, Rheaume played on many amateur and professional women's hockey teams and even helped her Canadian team to win two Olympic gold medals. But what she will go down in the record books for is her one period as goalie in a men's professional game in 1992.

Q Which of the following is correct about Manon Rheaume?

(a) She broke many records as a goalie in women's hockey.
(b) Her father was a professional Canadian hockey player.
(c) She won two gold medals on the men's Olympic team.
(d) She made history playing professionally on a men's team.

해석 마농 레옴은 프로 남성 하키 경기에 참가한 최초의 여성이었다. 캐나다에서 성장했던 소녀 시절에 레옴은 하키를 하게 해달라고 아버지를 졸랐다. 당연히 그녀는 소원을 이뤘다. 그녀의 경력 동안 레옴은 많은 아마추어와 프로 여성 하키팀에서 뛰었으며 캐나다 팀이 올림픽에서 2개의 금메달을 따는 데도 일조를 했다. 그러나 그녀를 기록에 오르게 할 사건은 1992년 프로 남성 하키 경기에서 그녀가 골키퍼를 본 한 피리어드이다.

Q 마농 레옴에 대해 올바른 것을 고르시오.
(a) 여자 하키 경기에서 골키퍼로써 많은 기록을 세웠다.
(b) 그녀의 아버지는 프로 캐나다 팀 하키 선수였다.
(c) 그녀는 남성 올림픽 팀에서 두 개의 금메달을 땄다.
(d) 그녀는 남성 팀에서 프로로 뜀으로써 역사적인 기록을 세웠다.

해설 마농 레옴에 관한 글이다. 그녀와 관련된 올바른 정보를 선택하는 문제이다. 그녀에 관한 정보를 정리해보면, 1) 프로 남성 하키 경기에 참가하였고, 2) 여러 아마추어와 프로 여성 하키 팀에서 활동(on many amateur and professional women's hockey teams), 3) 캐나다 팀이 올림픽에서 금메달을 따게 했으며(helped her Canadian team to win two Olympic gold medals), 4) 1992년 프로 남성 하키 경기에서 골키퍼를 보았다(her one period as goalie in a men's professional game in 1992). 따라서 그녀에 관한 올바른 정보는 (d)다.

어휘 beg 구걸하다, 조르다
obviously 당연히, 분명히
career 경력, 이력
amateur 비전문가, 아마추어
goalie 골키퍼(=goalkeeper)
professional 직업의, 직업상의
go down 남다, 기록되다
win two gold medals 금메달을 2개 따다

정답 (d)

25

Don't miss Ira Levin's stage thriller Deathtrap, which premieres December 7th at The Community Playhouse. Deathtrap is the tale of an aging playwright who offers to help a former student with his manuscript, and invites the student to his house for a weekend. But soon, the young man finds himself in serious trouble. Shows are performed throughout December on Wednesday and Thursday evenings at 8 p.m., with only a matinee performance on Sundays at 2 p.m. Admission is $10, and $5 for senior citizens.

Q Which of the following is correct about the advertised play?
(a) Deathtrap is recommended for children and adults.
(b) There will be one performance on the weekend.
(c) Deathtrap won numerous awards on Broadway.
(d) There are no women in the cast of Deathtrap.

해석 아이라 레빈의 스릴러 〈죽음의 함정〉을 놓치지 마세요. 12월 7일 커뮤니티 플레이하우스에서 첫 공연을 합니다. 〈죽음의 함정〉은 늙은 극작가의 이야기인데, 자신의 옛 제자가 대본을 쓰는 것을 도와주기로 하고, 제자를 주말 동안 자신의 집으로 초대합니다. 그러나 곧 그 젊은이는 자신이 심각한 상황에 처했다는 것을 알게 됩니다. 공연은 12월 매 주 수요일과 목요일 저녁 8시에 있으며 낮 공연은 매 주 일요일 오후 2시에만 있습니다. 입장료는 10달러이고 고령자는 5달러입니다.

Q 광고하고 있는 연극에 대한 내용으로 바른 것을 고르시오.
(a) 〈죽음의 함정〉은 어린이들과 어른들에게 추천된다.
(b) 주말에는 한 번의 공연이 있을 것이다.
(c) 〈죽음의 함정〉은 브로드웨이에서 많은 상을 받았다.
(d) 〈죽음에 함정〉에는 여성 배우가 등장하지 않는다.

해설 세부사항을 묻는 문제는 선택지를 빨리 풀어 본 후 오답을 제외시키면서 읽어내려 가는 것이 효과적이다. (a) senior citizens에 대한 언급은 있었지만, 어린이들에게 추천한다는 내용은 없다. (b) 공연시간을 정리해보면 매 주 수요일, 목요일 저녁, 일요일 오후 2시이니까, 주말 공연이 1회 밖에 없다는 내용은 옳다. (c) 수상 경력에 대한 언급은 없으므로 쉽게 답에서 제외할 수 있다. (d) 이전의 제자(a former student)와 극작가는 남성이지만(his manuscript, the younger man)배우 중에 여성이 있는 지 없는 지는 알 수 없기 때문에 답이 아니다. 따라서 정답은 (b)다.

어휘 premiere 초연을 하다
    aging 나이 든, 늙은
    playwright 극작가
    former 전의, 이전의
    manuscript 원고, 손으로 쓴 것
    matinee performance 낮 공연
    senior citizen 고령자
    recommend 추천하다
    numerous 많은
    cast 배역

정답 (b)

26

Here are a few simple tips for successful dating. If you ask for the date, you should pay for it. On a first date, never discuss religious or political beliefs. Always be respectful of your date's time and schedule when planning an event. Pay close attention to personal grooming. When you have called someone new, do not attempt to reach him or her if you do not hear back.

Q Which of the following is correct about successful dating?

(a) The rules will help you find a spouse.
(b) If your date doesn't return your call, keep trying.
(c) Discussing religion might bring you closer to a new date.
(d) Whoever asks for a date should pay for it.

해석 성공적인 데이트를 하기 위한 몇 가지 조언이 있다. 당신이 데이트를 신청하면 당신이 비용을 지불해야 한다. 첫 데이트에서는 절대 종교나 정치적 신조에 대한 이야기를 하지 마라. 이벤트를 계획한다면 항상 상대방의 시간과 스케줄을 고려해라. 개인 단장에도 각별한 주의를 기울여라. 새로 만난 사람에게 전화를 했는데 다시 전화가 오지 않거든 연락하려고 시도하지 말아라.

Q 성공적인 데이트에 대해 올바른 것을 고르시오.
(a) 이 규칙들이 배우자를 찾는 것을 도와줄 것이다.
(b) 상대가 전화를 하지 않으면 계속 시도해라.
(c) 종교에 대한 이야기를 하는 것이 서로를 가깝게 해준다.
(d) 데이트를 신청한 사람이 돈을 내야 한다.

해설 성공적 데이트에 관한 충고(a few simple tips for successful dating)의 글이다. 데이트 비용을 먼저 지불하고, 종교적 혹은 정치적 신념(religious or political beliefs)에 대한 이야기를 하지 말 것이며, 상대방의 시간과 스케줄을 존중하고 이벤트를 준비하라(Always be respectful of your date's time and schedule when planning an event.). 개인 단장에도 유념하고

전화 응답이 없다면 다시 전화 걸지 말 것을 충고하고 있다. 따라서 성공적 데이트와 관련된 올바른 답은 (d)다.

어휘 tip 조언
    successful 성공한, 좋은 결과의
    religious 종교의, 종교에 관한
    political belief 정치적 신조
    pay attention to ~에 주의를 기울이다
    respectful 존중하는, 공손한
    date 데이트 상대
    grooming 치장, 단장
    attempt to ~하려고 시도하다
    spouse 배우자, 남편

정답 (d)

27

Nearly ten tons of sugar are consumed daily in the U.S. Fixed prices are guaranteed for domestic sugar by the government, which also sets high tariffs and strict quotas on foreign sugar. This keeps sugar prices in the U.S. more than twice as high as the average world price. Because of this, a substantial number of U.S. candy makers have moved their operations overseas, eliminating thousands of American jobs while increasing their profits.

Q Which of the following is correct about the sugar industry?

(a) American candy makers no longer support U.S. policies.
(b) Laws allow sugar manufacturers to increase their revenues.
(c) American employment has increased due to sugar industry profitability.
(d) U.S. sugar prices are half that of the world's average.

해석 미국에서는 매일 거의 10톤의 설탕이 소비된다. 정부에 의해 고정 가격이 국내 시장에서 보장되고, 정부는 높은 관세와 엄격한 쿼터를 외국 설탕에 적용한다. 이것은 미국에서의 설탕 가격이 전 세계 평균 가격보다 두 배나 높게 만든다. 이것 때문에 미국의 많은 사탕 제조업자들이 자신들의 회사를 해외로 옮겨 그들의 이익을 증가시키고 있는 반면에 수 천 개의 미국 일자리들을 없애고 있다.

Q 설탕 산업에 대해 올바른 내용을 고르시오.
(a) 미국 사탕 제조업자들은 더 이상 미국의 정책을 지지하지 않는다.
(b) 법이 설탕 제조업자들이 그들의 수입을 늘릴 수 있도록 허용한다.
(c) 미국 고용률이 설탕 산업의 수익성으로 인해 증가했다.
(d) 미국 설탕 가격은 세계 평균 가격의 절반이다.

해설 세부 사항 파악 문제는 선택지를 하나씩 확인하면서 정답을 찾는다. (a) 미국 사탕 제조업자들이 미국 정책을 더 이상 지지하지 않는다는 것은 비약이 너무 크다. 따라서 정답이 아니다. (b) 법이 설탕 제조업자들의 이익을 보장하고 있다는 내용이 두 번째 문장에서 나오고 있다. 따라서 이것이 정답이다. (c) 사탕제조 공장을 해외로 옮겨서 미국 고용이 줄었다(eliminating thousands of American jobs)라고 했으니 옳지 않다. (d) 미국 설탕 가격은 세계 시장 가격의 두 배이다. 따라서 틀렸다.

Tips 세부 사항을 묻는 문제에서 보기가 지문에서 언급된 내용보다 너무 큰 내용과 범위를 다루면 정답이 아니다.

어휘 fixed price 고정 가격
guarantee 보증하다
domestic 국내의
tariff 관세
strict 엄격한
substantial 상당한, 많은
operation 회사, 사업
overseas 해외로
manufacturer 제조업자
eliminate 없애다, 삭제하다
revenues 수입
profitability 수익성
average 평균

정답 (b)

28

From its beginning, the motion picture industry has used screenwriters to adapt novels, plays, and short stories for the screen. Many film classics — *Gone With the Wind, The Wizard of Oz, The Lord of the Rings*, for instance — were based upon novels. But in recent decades, the tables have turned somewhat. Novelizations, wherein a movie is rewritten as a novel, are now in great demand.

Q Which of the following is correct about the film industry?

(a) A movie is usually better than the book on which it is based.

(b) *The Wizard of Oz* was an original screenplay

(c) The novel's popularity is seen as a threat by moviemakers.

(d) Writers create adaptations both for and from motion pictures.

해석 초기부터 영화 산업은 영화 시나리오 작가들이 소설, 희곡, 단편들을 영화로 각색하도록 해왔다. 많은 고전 영화들 – 바람과 함께 사라지다, 오즈의 마법사, 반지의 제왕 – 은 소설을 기본으로 한 것이다. 그러나 최근 몇 십 년

동안 그 방식이 다소 변했다. 소설화, 즉 영화가 소설로 다시 쓰여지는 것이 수요가 많다.

Q 영화 산업에 대한 내용으로 올바른 것을 고르시오.
(a) 영화는 주로 그것이 기본으로 한 책보다 더 낫다.
(b) 오즈의 마법사는 원래 영화 대본이었다.
(c) 소설의 인기는 영화 제작자들에게는 위협으로 여겨진다.
(d) 작가들은 영화를 위해 혹은 영화로부터 각색을 한다.

해설 선택지 별로 True or False를 확인해본다. (a) movie, book, it is based 등의 표현이 지문에 나오기는 하지만, 어느 것이 좋고 나쁘고는 언급되지 않았으므로 답이 아니다. (b) 오즈의 마법사는 책이 먼저 쓰인 다음에 책을 기본으로 영화가 만들어진 예이므로 틀린다. (c) 소설의 인기가 영화에 위협이 된다는 내용이 없다. 혹 이 선택지를 고른 사람이 있다면 독해가 많이 부족한 것으로 보인다. 좀 더 꼼꼼히 내용 파악하는 습관을 기르도록 한다. (d) 작가들이 쓴 책이 영화로 제작되기도 하고, 영화를 소재로 책을 쓰기도 한다고 했으니 (d)가 정답이다. 전치사 for, from에 유의한다.

어휘 motion picture 영화
screen writer 시나리오 작가
adapt 각색하다
play 연극
for instance 예를 들어
be based upon ~에 근거를 두다
recent 최근의, 근래의
decade 10년간
somewhat 약간
novelization 소설화
wherein 거기서, 그곳에서
screenplay 영화대본, 시나리오
popularity 인기, 평판
movie makers 영화 제작자

정답 (d)

29

In addition to the over 2,700 languages of the world, there are over 7,000 "dialects" the way a language is spoken in a specific area. This means that although people are speaking the same language, pronunciations, meanings or vocabulary can differ from region to region. Interestingly, recent studies have shown that even cows have different dialects in the way they moo. This is also based on their region and the dialect the farmer uses.

Q Which of the following is correct according to the passage?

(a) There are more languages in the world than dialects.

(b) Cows may learn their owner's language.

(c) Words' meanings are always the same.

(d) Dialects are the ways a language is spoken in different regions.

해석 전 세계 2,700개 이상의 언어와 더불어 7,000개 이상의 방언들이 있다. 방언이란 하나의 언어가 특정한 지역에서 사용되는 방식이다. 이것은 사람들이 같은 언어를 사용함에도 불구하고 발음, 의미 혹은 어휘들이 지역에 따라 다를 수 있다는 것을 의미한다. 흥미롭게도 최근의 연구에 따르면 소들이 "음매~" 하고 우는 방식에도 다른 방언들이 있다고 한다. 이것은 그들이 살고 있는 지역과 농부가 사용하는 방언에 근거를 두고 있다.

Q 위 글의 내용에 따라 올바른 것을 고르시오.
(a) 세계에는 방언 보다 많은 수의 언어가 있다.
(b) 소들은 주인들이 하는 말을 배울 수도 있다.
(c) 단어의 의미는 항상 같다.
(d) 방언은 언어가 다른 지역에서 사용되는 방식이다.

해설 (a) 방언(dialects)이 7,000여 개, 언어(languages)가 2,700여 개이니까, 방언 숫자가 더 많다. (b) 상식에 어긋나는 것은 답이 아니다. (c) always, all, every 등 전부를 단언하는 것은 답이 아닐 확률이 높다. 단어의 뜻이 항상 똑같다는 것은 내용과 부합하지 않으므로 틀린다. 답은 (d)다.

어휘 **in addition to** ~에 더하여, ~ 외에
dialect 방언, 지방 사투리
specific area 특정한 지역
pronunciation 발음
differ from ~와 다르다, ~와 차이가 있다
interestingly 흥미롭게
moo 음매하고 울다

정답 (d)

30

Sociologists have found that students — both male and female — who do household chores with their dads, not only get along better with their classmates, but also have more friends in general. The children are also less likely to cause trouble at school. Kids learn both cooperation and democratic values when they do housework with their fathers, according to research. Furthermore, the children then carry these values on to school.

Q Which of the following is correct about the study?

(a) Uncertain parental roles can cause depression in children.

(b) Men's new household roles reduce their effectiveness.

(c) Children are likely to share housework with their fathers.

(d) Kids who do housework with their fathers cause fewer problems at school.

해석 사회학자들이 알아낸 바로는 남학생과 여학생들 모두가 아버지와 함께 집안일을 하는 경우 친구들과 사이가 더 좋을 뿐만 아니라 일반적으로 친구의 수도 많다. 이런 아이들(아버지와 함께 집안일을 하는 아이들)은 또한 학교에서 말썽을 일으킬 확률도 적다. 연구에 따르면 아이들은 아버지와 함께 집안일을 할 때 협동과 민주주의적 가치관을 배운다고 한다. 게다가 아이들은 이러한 가치관을 학교생활에 적용하게 된다.

Q 연구에 관한 내용으로 올바른 것을 고르시오.
(a) 불확실한 부모의 역할은 아이들에게 우울증을 초래한다.
(b) 남자의 새로운 집안에서의 역할은 효율성을 떨어뜨린다.
(c) 어린이들은 아버지들과 집안일을 분담하는 경우가 많다.
(d) 아버지와 집안일을 하는 아이들은 학교에서 말썽을 덜 부린다.

해설 사회학자들의 연구 결과 내용을 확인하는 문제이다. 아버지와 함께 가사를 돕는 학생들의 특징을 확인해본다. (a) 아빠(dad, father)는 나오지만 확실하지 않은 부모의 역할(uncertain parental roles)에 대한 언급은 없다. (b) household에 관련된 것이 나오기는 하지만, 답이 아니다. (c) be likely to는 '~하는 경향이 있다', '~하기 쉽다'는 의미이므로 본문과 내용이 다르다. (d) 집안일을 아버지와 함께 한 아이들은 학교에서 문제를 덜 일으키는 경향이 있다(The children ~ at school)는 내용이 있으므로 (d)가 답이다.

어휘 sociologists 사회학자
어휘 sociologists 사회학자
get along with 사이좋게 지내다
household chores 가사일
classmate 동급생, 반 친구
in general 대개, 일반적으로
cooperation 협력, 협동
democratic values 민주주의적인 가치관
according to ~에 따라, ~에 의하여
uncertain 불확실한, 모호한, 분명하지 않은
parental role 부모의 역할
depression 우울증
effectiveness 유효성, 효과

정답 (d)

31

It's Jones Pet Supplies' tenth anniversary in May. If you've shopped with us since the store's opening, you'll get a 30% discount on all of your May purchases. And for newer customers, you'll earn a 3 percent off discount for every year. If you've never shopped at Jones, please come in and accept a free gift. Take advantage of this extraordinary offer in May at Jones Pet Supplies. We hope to see you soon!

Q Which of the following is correct according to the advertisement?

(a) Jones Pet Supplies opened for business ten years ago.

(b) Those who have shopped at Jones for five years will receive a 12% discount.

(c) The promotions apply to repeat customers.

(d) Only those customers with an open account will receive benefits.

해석 존스 애완동물 용품점 10주년 개점 기념을 5월에 합니다. 저희 상점이 문을 연 이래 계속 이용해 주신 분들께는 5월에 구매하시는 모든 상품에 대해 30% 할인을 받으실 수 있습니다. 그리고 새로 오신 고객들은 매년 3%의 할인을 받으실 수 있습니다. 존스에서 구매하신 적이 없으시다면 방문하셔서 무료 선물을 받아 가세요. 존스 애완동물 용품점에서 제공하는 5월의 서비스를 이용하세요. 곧 다시 뵙기를 바랍니다.

Q 위 광고 내용에 따라 올바른 내용을 고르시오.
(a) 존스 애완동물 용품점은 10년 전에 문을 열었다.
(b) 5년 간 존스에서 구매를 한 사람들은 12%의 할인을 받게 된다.
(c) 행사는 기존 고객들에게만 적용된다.
(d) 거래 계좌가 있는 손님들만 혜택을 받을 수 있다.

해설 (a) 존스 애완동물 용품점이 10주년을 기념하니까, 10년 전에 개점을 했다는 것은 맞다. 따라서 이것이 정답

이다. (b) 5월 신규 고객은 1년에 3%씩 할인을 받을 수 있다고 했으니 5년간 거래를 해온 기존 고객이 12% 혜택을 받는다는 내용은 틀렸다. (c) 5월에 오는 고객에게 30%의 할인을 해준다는 내용이 있으니 기존 고객(repeat customers)에게만 해당되는 것은 아니므로 답이 아니다. (d) 5월에 오는 고객에게는 신규 고객, 기존 고객 상관하지 않고 해당이 되고, 또한 5월 신규 고객에게 해마다 3%의 혜택을 드린다고 하니, 기존 고객에게만 혜택이 된다는 것은 틀렸다.

어휘 supplies 용품, 공급품
anniversary 기념일, 기념제
purchase 구매, 구입
customer 고객, 단골
account 거래
free gift 무료 선물
take advantage of ~을 이용하다
extraordinary 보통이 아닌, 놀랄 만한
promotion 판매 촉진, 특별 이벤트
apply to ~에 적용되다
repeat customer 재방문 고객, 기존 고객
benefit 이익, 이득

정답 (a)

32

Hyenas are animals that are programmed to fight literally from birth. Hyena cubs are born with wide-open eyes and a complete set of sharp teeth. It is not uncommon for the first cubs of a litter to fight one another while the mother is still giving birth to other cubs. In fact, sibling fighting kills one out of every four hyena cubs born. Sister cubs, which may one day compete to rule the pack, often engage in extremely fierce fighting against each other.

Q Which of the following is correct about hyena cubs?

(a) All hyena cubs have sharp teeth but poor vision at birth.

(b) Female cubs usually have sharper teeth than males.

(c) Female cubs are typically more aggressive than male cubs.

(d) Mother hyenas kill one out of four cubs in each of their litters.

해석 하이에나는 말 그대로 태어날 때부터 싸우도록 프로그램이 되어있는 동물이다. 하이에나 새끼들은 눈을 뜬 채로 날카로운 모든 이빨을 갖춘 채 태어난다. 먼저 태어난 한 배의 새끼들끼리 어미가 아직 다른 새끼들을 낳고 있는 중에도 서로 싸우는 것은 드문 일이 아니다. 실제로 형제, 자매들 간의 싸움으로 죽는 새끼의 수는 네 마리 당 한 마리 꼴이다. 자매들끼리는 언젠가 무리를 지배하기 위해

경쟁을 하게 될지도 모르기 때문에 극단적으로 치열한 싸움을 하는 경우가 자주 있다.

Q 하이에나 새끼들에 대한 설명으로 올바른 내용을 고르시오.

(a) 모든 하이에나 새끼들은 태어날 당시 날카로운 이빨이 있지만 시력은 나쁘다.

(b) 암컷 새끼들은 수컷 새끼들 보다 더 날카로운 이빨을 가지고 있다.

(c) 암컷 새끼들이 일반적으로 수컷 새끼들 보다 더 공격적이다.

(d) 어미 하이에나들을 한 배에 난 새끼들 중 네 마리 당 한 마리를 죽인다.

해설 하이에나 새끼의 특성을 물어 보는 문제이다. It is not uncommon ~이라는 표현은 강조하는 것으로 실제로는 매우 흔한 일임을 뜻하는 것이다. 하이에나는 태어날 때부터 싸우도록 되어 있으며(~ are programmed to fight literally from birth), 먼저 태어난 새끼끼리 다른 새끼가 태어나고 있는 동안에도 싸움을 하며(~ the mother is still giving birth to other cubs), 자매끼리 언젠가 무리를 지배하기 위해(to rule the pack) 극단적으로 치열한 싸움을 벌인다. 따라서 이러한 정보를 통해 정답은 (c)다. (a) 부분적으로 맞고, 부분적으로 틀린 형태의 오답에 주의하라. 태어날 때부터 날카로운 이빨을 갖고 있는 것은 맞지만, 시력이 나쁘다는 이야기는 없으므로 답이 아니다. (b) 암컷 새끼(sister cubs)가 격렬하게 싸운다는 말은 있어도, 이가 더 날카롭다는 이야기는 없으므로 답이 아니다. (c) 맨 마지막 문장에서 나중에 무리를 이끄는 자리를 놓고 싸워야 하기 때문에 암컷 새끼들이 심하게 싸운다는 마지막 문장에 따라 답이 된다. (d) 어미가 자식을 죽이는 것이 아니라, 새끼들끼리 싸우다 죽는다고 했으니 답이 아니다.

Tips Be careful of the partially right and partially wrong answers. 일부만 맞고 일부는 틀린 선택지를 흔히 볼 수 있다. 성급하게 답을 고르지 않도록 평소에 연습한다.

어휘 literally 글자 뜻대로
cub 짐승 새끼, 어린 짐승
wide-open 완전히 열린
complete 완전한, 완벽한
uncommon 드문, 이상한
litter 한 배 새끼
give birth to ~를 낳다
sibling 형제, 자매
compete 경쟁하다
pack 떼, 무리
engage in ~에 참가[참여]하다
fierce 사나운, 격렬한
vision 시력
aggressive 공격적인

정답 (c)

---

33 Companies sometimes go to great lengths to sell their products in other countries where a true need, based on cultural ideals, may not even exist. For example, a large company that manufactures razors tried to create consumer markets in South America, Africa and Indonesia by trying to convince men that they should start shaving. The company sent portable theaters into villages where the local people were invited to watch razor commercials. These advertisements showed men who shaved as being more accepted by other clean-shaven men. These commercials also represented clean-shaven men as more attractive and having better odds of attracting beautiful women.

Q What can be inferred from the passage?

(a) Most men in the countries mentioned have beards.

(b) Women in the countries mentioned prefer clean-shaven men.

(c) Creating need for a product is part of successful marketing.

(d) Shaving helps people be accepted by others in the community.

해석 회사들은 때로는 문화적 관념에 따르면 진정으로 필요하지 않은 자회사의 상품들을 다른 나라에 판매하기 위해서 어떤 일이든 서슴지 않는다. 예를 들어 면도기를 생산하는 한 대기업이 남미, 미국, 인도네시아에서 남자들은 면도를 해야 한다고 설득함으로써 소비자 시장을 창출하려고 했다. 그 회사는 이동식 극장 시설을 마을로 보내 마을 사람들이 면도기 광고를 보도록 초청했다. 이 광고는 면도를 한 남성들이 깨끗하게 면도를 한 다른 사람들에게 더욱 인정받는 모습을 보여 주었다. 또한 광고는 깨끗이 면도를 한 사람이 더욱 매력적이며, 아름다운 여성들을 매혹시킬 수 있는 확률이 더 높은 것으로 표현했다.

Q 위 글의 내용으로 유추할 수 있는 것을 고르시오.

(a) 언급된 국가들의 대부분의 남성들은 수염을 기른다.

(b) 언급된 국가들의 여성들은 깨끗이 면도한 남성을 선호한다.

(c) 상품에 대한 필요를 창출하는 것이 성공적인 마케팅의 일부다.

(d) 면도는 사람들이 사회에서 다른 사람들에게 인정받도록 도와준다.

해설 기업이 자사의 제품을 문화적으로 익숙하지 않은 나라에 어떻게 판매하는 가에 관한 글이다. 예를 들어, 어떤 나라에서 필요하지 않은 제품을 적극적인 광고와 판매 전략을 통해 성공적으로 판매하는 전략을 소개하고 있다(Companies sometimes go to great lengths to sell their products in other countries where a true need, based on cultural ideals, may not even exist.). 따라서 이 글을 통해 유추할 수 있는 내용은 보기로 제시된 회사가 제품을 팔려고 했던 나라는 남성들이 수염을 기르는 환경이라는 것을 알 수 있기 때문에 정답은 (a)다.

어휘 go to great lengths 무슨 일이든 하다
product 제품
ideal 관념, 이상
for example 예를 들어
manufacture 생산하다
consumer market 소비자 시장
convince 설득시키다
shave 면도하다
portable 휴대용의, 이동식의
commercial 상업 광고
clean-shaven 깨끗이 면도한
represent 표현하다, 묘사하다
attractive 매혹적인
odds 확률, 가능성
beard 턱수염
prefer 선호하다
community 공동체, 사회

정답 (a)

34

A recent study performed by the Los Angeles Department of Public Health determined that ice dispensers in many of the city's fast food restaurants harbored a variety of bacteria. The Department of Health discovered the Escherichia coli(E. coli) bacterium in three ice dispensers. E. coli bacteria comes from the feces of mammals and can cause serious intestinal and kidney problems. In some cases, it has even been known to cause death.

Q What can be inferred from the passage?

(a) Some of the restaurant's patrons died from E. coli.
(b) Most of L.A.'s restaurants don't have E. coli in their ice dispensers.
(c) The Department of Health closed down many restaurants.
(d) The E. coli bacterium is the deadliest of all bacteria.

해석 로스엔젤레스 공중 보건국에 의해 행해진 최근 한 연구에 따르면 시의 대다수의 패스트푸드 음식점의 얼음 분배기가 온갖 종류의 균들의 서식처가 되고 있다고 한다. 보건국은 세 개의 얼음 기계에서 이콜라이 균을 발견했다. 이콜라이 균은 포유류의 분비물에서 나오는 것으로 장과 신

장에 심한 문제를 일으킬 수 있다. 어떤 경우에는 사망까지 이르는 경우도 있는 것으로 알려졌다.

Q 위 글에서 유추할 수 있는 내용을 고르시오.
(a) 일부 식당 손님들이 이콜라이 균으로 사망했다.
(b) LA 대부분 식당의 얼음 기계에는 이콜라이 균이 없다.
(c) 보건국은 많은 식당들을 폐쇄했다.
(d) 이콜라이 균은 모든 균들 중에서 가장 치명적이다.

해설 추론하는 문제일 경우는 전체적인 내용을 파악하고, 저자의 태도(attitude)를 이해하는 것이 중요하다. 또한 선택지를 고를 때, 상식적이거나 일반적인 내용을 선택하는 것이 아니라, 지문에 충실하여 선택을 하여야 한다. (a) E. coli 균에 대한 내용이 계속 언급되기도 하고, 마지막에 감염되면 사망할 수도 있다는 내용은 있으나, 이는 일반적인 내용이고, 이미 LA 지역 식당들에서 감염이 되어 사망자가 발생했다는 내용은 없으므로 답이 아니다. (b) 여러 균이 패스트푸드 식당 여러 곳에서 발견되었다는 내용은 있지만 E. coli 균이 발견된 곳은 세 곳이라고 했으니, 대부분의 식당에 E. coli 균이 있는 곳이 없다는 내용은 맞다. 따라서 이것이 정답이다. (c) 식당을 폐쇄시켰다는 내용은 언급된 바 없다. (d) E. coli 균이 계속 언급은 되었으나 가장 치명적이라는 내용은 없다.

어휘 dispenser 분배기
harbor 서식처가 되다, 집이 되다
a variety of 다양한
bacterium bacteria의 단수
feces 배설물
mammal 포유류
intestinal 장의
kidney 신장
patron 고객, 단골손님
close down 폐쇄하다
deadly 치명적인

정답 (b)

35

Business experts and consultants have identified several factors common in successful managers. For example, good bosses encourage openness in communication. They realize that trust is critical for good working relationships. They give timely and honest feedback to employees. Successful managers also create supportive environments which help to motivate their workers.

Q What does the writer suggest?

(a) Most contemporary managers do a poor job.

(b) Employees can expect a good boss to tell them the truth.

(c) Employees often do not recognize good managers.

(d) Good managers should dismiss struggling employees.

해석 비즈니스 전문가들과 컨설턴트들은 성공적인 경영인들에게서 공통적으로 발견되는 몇몇 요인들을 발견했다. 예를 들어, 좋은 상사는 의사소통에 있어 열린 분위기를 조성한다. 그들은 신뢰가 바람직한 업무 관계에 있어 중요하다는 것을 알고 있다. 그들은 직원들에게 시기적절하고 정직한 피드백을 준다. 성공적인 경영인들은 또한 직원들에게 동기를 부여하는 격려의 환경을 조성한다.

Q 작가가 암시하고 있는 내용을 고르시오.

(a) 대부분의 현대 경영인들이 일을 제대로 하지 못한다.

(b) 직원들은 좋은 상사가 그들에게 진실을 말해주길 기대할 수 있다.

(c) 직원들은 종종 좋은 경영인들을 알아보지 못한다.

(d) 좋은 경영인들은 노력하는 직원들을 해고해야 한다.

해설 (a) 대부분의 경영자들이 일을 제대로 하지 못한다는 내용은 한 눈에 보아도 맞지 않으므로, 답에서 쉽게 제외할 수 있다. (b) 좋은 상사는 직원들이 활발하게 자신의 의견을 표현하도록 한다고 했으니, 직원들이 상사에게 진실을 말할 수 있다는 내용은 맞다. 따라서 이것이 정답이다. (c)와 (d)는 내용과 부합하지 않으니 답이 아니다.

어휘 expert 전문가
consultant 상담역, 고문
identify 확인하다, 증명하다
factor 요소
encourage 장려하다
critical 중대한
timely 시기적절한
supportive 도움이 되는, 격려해주는
motivate ~에게 동기를 부여하다
contemporary 같은 시대의, 현대의
dismiss 해고하다, 내쫓다
struggling 노력하는, 분투하는

정답 (b)

36

Harold saw a beautiful suit in a clothing store. To his surprise, the salesperson told him the suit was only $25. Harold was thrilled. But, he found that it didn't fit him at all. The tailor then suggested that Harold lift his left arm a bit. Then he told him to flex one of his knees just a bit. Now the suit fits him perfectly! Paying the salesperson, Harold shuffled awkwardly to the sidewalk, making sure to keep the suit's perfect fit. Across the street, two elderly women noticed Harold. The first sympathized with the poor crippled man across the street. Her friend agreed. "Yes," she said, "But doesn't he have the most beautiful suit?"

Q What can be inferred from the passage?

(a) Only one of the women pitied Harold.

(b) Harold later became wealthy.

(c) The salesperson was dishonest.

(d) Harold will take the suit to a tailor for repair.

해석 헤롤드는 옷가게에서 멋진 양복 한 벌을 봤다. 놀랍게도 옷 가게 직원은 양복이 겨우 25달러라고 말했다. 헤롤드는 흥분했다. 그러나 양복은 그에게 전혀 맞지 않았다. 재단사는 헤롤드에게 왼팔을 약간 들어 보라고 제안했다. 그리고 한쪽 무릎을 약간 굽혀 보라고 했다. 그러자 양복은 완벽하게 맞았다. 직원에게 돈을 내고 난 후 양복이 완전하게 맞게 하기 위해 헤롤드는 다리를 질질 끌며 엉거주춤 인도로 나섰다. 길 건너편에서 두 명의 할머니가 헤롤드를 보았다. 한 할머니가 길 건너에 있는 다리를 저는 불쌍한 남자를 동정했다. 할머니의 친구도 동의를 했다. "맞아, 그런데 양복은 너무 멋지지 않아?"

Q 위 글의 내용에서 유추할 수 있는 것을 고르시오.

(a) 두 여인들 중 한 명이 헤롤드를 동정했다.

(b) 헤롤드는 나중에 부자가 되었다.

(c) 옷가게 직원은 정직하지 않았다.

(d) 헤롤드는 양복을 수선하러 가지고 갈 것이다.

해설 결국 Herold는 점원에게 속아서 옷을 산 것이므로 점원이 정직하지 않다고 추론할 수 있다. 옷에 맞추느라 팔과 다리를 구부정하게 걷는 모습을 상상만해도 웃음이 절로 나오는 글이다. 따라서 정답은 (c)다.

어휘 suit 양복
thrill 흥분시키다
fit (옷이) 잘 맞다
tailor 재단사
flex 구부리다
shuffle 발을 질질 끌며 걷다

awkwardly 어색하게, 서투르게
side walk 인도
comment 언급하다
elderly 나이 든, 늙은
crippled 다리를 저는
dishonest 정직하지 않은
repair 수선

정답 (c)

37

The French National Space Agency has launched a space satellite technologically capable of several firsts. The small 30 centimeter telescope on the satellite will be able to look inside stars to help distinguish their different physical make-ups. Plus, the telescope will also be able to detect rocky planets located outside of our solar system. These planets are expected to be much larger than Earth. Besides the telescope on board the satellite, the payload also includes two cameras, and on-board computer processors.

Q What is the best title of the passage?
(a) New Computer Processors of the French Satellite
(b) Big Things Expected from New Satellite and its Telescope
(c) Advanced Telescope Locating New Rocky Planet
(d) New Star Composition Discovered by Satellite Telescope

해석 프랑스 국립 우주국은 기술적으로 몇 가지 작업을 최초로 수행할 수 있는 인공위성을 발사했다. 인공위성에 장착된 작은 30센티미터의 망원경은 행성의 내부를 들여다보고 그것들이 무엇으로 만들어졌는가를 구별하는 것을 도와줄 수 있다. 또한 망원경은 우리의 태양계 밖에 존재하는 암석 행성들도 감지할 수 있을 것이다. 이러한 행성들은 지구보다 훨씬 큰 것으로 예상된다. 인공위성에 장착된 망원경 외에도 탑재 장비에는 두 대의 카메라와 우주선용 컴퓨터 프로세서가 포함되어 있다.

Q 위 글의 제목으로 가장 적절한 것을 고르시오.
(a) 프랑스 인공위성의 새로운 컴퓨터 프로세서
(b) 새로운 인공위성과 장착된 망원경으로부터 기대되는 대단한 것들
(c) 새로운 암석 행성을 찾는 진보된 현미경
(d) 인공위성 현미경에 의해 발견된 새로운 행성의 구조

해설 글의 제목을 선택하는 문제는 글의 주제를 묻는 문제와 비슷하지만, 제목의 경우에는 글의 내용을 보다 집약적으로 포함하고 내용을 전달할 수 있는 표현을 선택하는 것

이 좋은 방법이다. 위의 글은 프랑스 국립 우주국이 새로운 수행 능력을 지닌 인공위성을 발사한 것에 관한 내용을 담고 있다. 그리고 본 인공위성이 지닌 다양한 기능(30 centimeter telescope on the satellite, the payload also includes two cameras~, and on-board computer processors.)을 설명하고 있기 때문에 정답은 (b)다.

어휘 launch 발사하다
telescope 망원경
satellite 위성
capable of ~할 수 있는
distinguish 구별하다
make-up 구조, 구성
detect 감지하다
locate ~를 위치시키다
solar system 태양계
payload 탑재 장비
on-board 탑재된

정답 (b)

38

With carbon dioxide emissions at dangerous levels, ethanol is a fuel many believe will substantially reduce dependence on fossil fuels. (a) It is made from corn, a cleaner, renewable energy source. (b) Corn farmers prefer to produce food rather than fuel. (c) Increased use of this fuel will diminish our reliance on oil from politically unstable regions. (d) A substantial increase in the use of ethanol could slow global warming and reduce international conflict.

해석 위험한 수준에 이른 이산화탄소 방출로 인해 많은 사람들은 에탄올이 화석 연료에 대한 의존성을 크게 줄여 줄 것이라고 믿는다. (a) 이것은 옥수수로 만들어진 더 깨끗하고 재생이 가능한 에너지원이다. (b) 옥수수 재배 농부들은 연료보다는 식량 생산을 선호한다. (c) 이 연료의 사용 증가는 정치적으로 불안정한 지역에서 생산되는 원유에 대한 우리의 의존도를 낮추어 줄 것이다. (d) 많은 에탄올 사용의 증가는 지구 온난화의 속도와 국제 분쟁을 줄일 수 있다.

해설 환경 보호의 방편으로 에탄올 사용과 관련된 글이다. 이산화탄소 방출에 의한 환경 파괴를 피하기 위해서 에탄올이 화석 연료 대체로 사용될 수 있다는 것이 주제이다. 따라서 이후에 오는 문장도 환경과 에탄올과의 관계에 초점이 맞춰져서 이어져야 한다. (a)는 에탄올의 성분과 재생 가능한 에너지(~ is made from corn, a cleaner, renewable energy source.)임을 설명하고 있고, (c)는 정치적으로 불안정한 국가에서 생산되는 원유에 대한 의존도를 줄일 수 있고(~ diminish our reliance on oil from politically unstable regions.), (d)는 온난화의 속도와 국제 분쟁을 줄일 수 있음(~ slow global warming and reduce international conflict.)을 이야기 하고 있다. 따라서 관련이 없는 문장은 (b)다.

어휘 carbon dioxide 이산화탄소
emission 방출
substantially 상당히, 많이
dependence 의뢰, 의존
fossil fuel 화석연료
renewable 재생이 가능한
energy source 에너지원
diminish 줄이다, 감소하다
prefer 선호하다
politically 정치적으로
unstable regions 불안정한 지역들
reliance 신뢰, 신용, 의지
global warming 지구온난화
international 국제적인
conflict 분쟁

정답 (b)

른 유럽 국가들도 스페인을 본받아 신대륙 일부 지역에 대한 소유권을 주장하였다(~, and each nation claimed dominion over parts of this vast new land.). 따라서 전체적인 내용과 관련이 없는 문장은 (c)다.

어휘 explorer 탐험가
venture 위험을 무릅쓰고 가다
unknown 알려지지 않은
in search of ~을 찾아서
treasure 보물
glory 명예
fame 명성
discovery 발견
shore 물가, 해안
disheartened 낙심한, 실망한
claim 요구하다, 주장하다
vast 광대한, 거대한
dominion 지배권, 소유권

정답 (c)

39

Toward the end of the 15th century, European sailors and explorers began to venture out on unknown seas in search of treasure, glory, and fame. (a) The Spanish made the first major discovery when they landed on the shores of what is now America. (b) At first it was mistakenly believed that the ships had landed in the West Indies. (c) After realizing their mistake, the disheartened explorers returned to Spain and were punished. (d) British, French, Dutch and Portuguese explorers would soon follow the Spanish example, and each nation claimed dominion over parts of this vast new land.

해석 15세기 후반부 무렵 유럽의 선원들과 탐험가들은 보물, 명예, 명성을 찾아 알려지지 않은 바다로 모험을 시작했다. (a) 스페인 인들은 현재 아메리카 대륙에 도착함으로써 최초의 중요한 발견을 이뤘다. (b) 처음에는 선박들이 서인도 제도에 도착한 것이라고 잘못 여겨졌다. (c) 그들의 실수를 알아차린 후 낙담한 탐험가들은 스페인으로 돌아갔고 처벌을 받았다. (d) 영국, 프랑스, 네덜란드, 포르투갈 탐험가들이 곧 스페인 인들의 선례를 따랐고 각 국은 이 방대한 신대륙의 일부 지역에 대한 소유권을 주장했다.

해설 15세기 후반 무렵 유럽 선원들과 탐험가들에 의한 바다 모험에 관한 글이다. (a) 스페인 인들이 아메리카 대륙에 도착해서 중요한 발견을 하였고(~ made the first major discovery when they landed on the shores of what is now America), (b) 처음에는 이를 서인도 제도로 착각하고(~ mistakenly believed that the ships had landed in the West Indies), (d) 다

40

After World War I, the democracies of the world focused on manufacturing civilian goods. (a) American car manufacturers came up with an entirely new marketing plan. (b) They realized that if they changed an automobile's design every year, they could sell more cars. (c) Their aim was to make existing models seem out of date by making obvious changes to their outward designs every year. (d) An example of this is the Ford Model T, which remained virtually unchanged for twenty years.

해석 1차 세계 대전 후에 세계의 민주주의는 민간인 상품을 제조하는데 초점을 맞추었다. (a) 미국 자동차 제조업자들이 완전히 새로운 마케팅 계획을 고안해냈다. (b) 그들이 깨달은 것은 자동차의 디자인을 매 년 바꾼다면 더 많은 차를 팔 수 있을 거라는 것이었다. (c) 그들의 목표는 매 년 외부 디자인을 확실히 변형함으로써 현존하는 모델들이 구식처럼 보이게 만드는 것이었다. (d) 이러한 예는 포드 모델 T인데 그것은 실제로 20년 동안 변하지 않았다.

해설 문장 흐름을 파악하는 문제를 잘 푸는 요령은 두 가지가 있는데, 첫째는 문맥 전체의 흐름을 잘 이어가고 있는지 확인하는 것과 둘째는 선택지 간에 서로 연계성이 있는지 확인하는 방법이다. 이번 문제는 어느 쪽을 선택하더라도 쉽게 답을 고를 수 있다. 전체적인 내용이 미국 자동차 회사들이 매출을 늘리기 위하여, 매년 다른 디자인을 한 차들을 생산하여 바로 이전의 차들조차 구형으로 보이도록 한다는 내용이므로, 20년 동안 같은 형태를 고집하는 것은 앞의 글의 흐름이라 볼 수 없다. 따라서 답은 (d)다.

어휘 democracy 민주주의
focus on ~에 초점을 맞추다
manufacture 제조하다

civilian 민간인, 민간인의
goods 물품, 상품
come up with ~을 고안해 내다
out of date 구식의, 낡은
outward design 외부 디자인
obvious 명백한, 알기 쉬운
virtually 실제로
unchanged 변하지 않는

정답 (d)

Actual Test 2

1 (b)	**2** (c)	**3** (a)	**4** (c)	**5** (b)
6 (a)	**7** (d)	**8** (a)	**9** (c)	**10** (c)
11 (b)	**12** (a)	**13** (a)	**14** (d)	**15** (a)
16 (a)	**17** (c)	**18** (a)	**19** (b)	**20** (c)
21 (d)	**22** (b)	**23** (c)	**24** (c)	**25** (d)
26 (c)	**27** (b)	**28** (b)	**29** (c)	**30** (b)
31 (b)	**32** (d)	**33** (a)	**34** (b)	**35** (c)
36 (c)	**37** (a)	**38** (b)	**39** (d)	**40** (b)

1

Besides a thick layer of fat, walruses have another way to survive Arctic temperatures that drop to 40 degrees below zero. When walruses dive for food, they can stay under water for up to ten minutes. So to prevent its body from shutting down, the walrus's blood will concentrate so deep inside the body that the animal will _____. Only after warming up will the natural brown coloring return.

(a) become very hungry
(b) turn completely white
(c) become extremely cold
(d) temporarily fall asleep

해석 두꺼운 지방층 이외에도 해마는 북극의 기온에서 살아남기 위한 또 다른 수단을 가지고 있는데 북극은 영하 40도까지 기온이 떨어진다. 해마는 먹이를 찾아 다이빙을 할 때 물속에 10분까지 머무를 수 있다. 몸이 작동을 정지하는 것을 막기 위하여 해마의 혈액은 몸 안으로 매우 깊이 몰려서 해마는 완전히 흰색으로 변한다. 몸이 따뜻해진 후에야 원래의 갈색이 돌아오게 된다.

(a) 매우 배가 고파진다
(b) 완전히 흰색으로 변한다
(c) 극도로 추워진다
(d) 일시적으로 잠이 든다

해설 문맥에 알맞은 적절한 동사구를 찾는 문제이다. so~ that... 문장 구조에 주목하라! 해마가 북극의 기온을 견디기 위해 사용하는 수단에 관한 글이다. 해마는 다이빙할 때 물속에 10분 가량을 머물 수 있는데 몸의 작동이 정지되는 것을 방지하기 위해서 해마의 혈액이 몸 안에 집결

된다는 것이다(So to prevent its body from shutting down, the walrus's blood will concentrate so deep inside the body). 빈곳의 뒷부분에 나오는 내용이 '몸이 따뜻해 진 후에는 원래의 갈색으로 된다(will the natural brown coloring return.)'는 내용이 있다. 따라서 빈 칸에는 해마의 색깔과 관련된 내용이 들어가야 적절하다. 정답은 (b)다.

어휘 besides ~ 외에도, ~ 밖에도
walrus 해마
survive 살아남다, 보다 오래 살다
Arctic 북극의, 북극
temperature 온도, 체온
up to ~까지
prevent 막다, 방해하다, 예방하다
shut down 정지하다, 작동을 멈추다
concentrate 한 곳에 몰리다

정답 (b)

2

Being stung by a bee can be a dangerous, even fatal event for some. Nonetheless, bee stings have been used by the Chinese to help treat illnesses for 3,000 years. Many doctors believe that the venom from bee stings repairs damaged cells, and by doing so can even cure serious diseases. However, these same doctors admit they still don't understand exactly _____.

(a) why so many people are afraid of bees
(b) how to treat such allergies to bee stings
(c) why this mysterious healing occurs
(d) how the bees produce venom at all

해석 벌에게 물리는 것은 위험하고 일부 사람들에게 치명적인 사건일 수도 있다. 그럼에도 불구하고 벌침은 중국인들에 의해 질병을 치료하는 것을 돕는데 3천년 동안 사용되었다. 많은 의사들이 벌침에서 나오는 독이 손상된 세포를 회복시키고 그렇게 함으로써 심각한 질병들을 치유할 수 있다고 믿는다. 하지만 이러한 의사들도 여전히 왜 이 신비로운 치유가 발생하는지를 정확히 이해하지 못한다고 인정한다.

(a) 왜 그렇게 많은 사람들이 벌을 두려워하는지
(b) 이런 벌침에 대한 알레르기를 어떻게 치료하는지
(c) 왜 이 신비로운 치유가 발생하는지
(d) 어떻게 벌들이 독을 만들어 내는지

해설 문맥의 흐름을 연결해주는 장치를 활용하라! however에 주목하라! 중국인들이 물리면 치명적일 수도 있는 벌침을 치료에 사용하는 것과 관련된 내용이다. 'Many doctors believe that the venom from the bee stings repairs damaged cells, and by doing so can even cure serious diseases.'라는 대목에서 많은 의사들이 벌침에서 나오는 독이 세포를 회복시키고 질

병을 치유한다고 믿고 있다는 것을 알 수 있다. 그러나 however로 다음 문장이 연결되면서 이런 의사들조차 이러한 치료효과에 대해서는 정확히 파악하지 못하고 있음을 알 수 있다. 따라서 정답은 (c)다.

어휘 sting 찌르다, 쏘다, 자극하다
dangerous 위험한
fatal 치명적인, 운명의
nonetheless 그럼에도 불구하고, 그래도, 역시
venom 독액
cure 치료하다, 고치다
disease 병, 질병, 질환
admit 인정하다, 허락하다
exactly 정확하게, 엄밀하게, 꼭

정답 (c)

3

Dear Ms. Kimura,
Thank you for your most recent online order (#987YUO). Unfortunately, we are temporarily out of stock on discounted item #324 (discontinued white terry cloth robe). We do have the item on backorder and are hoping to have that shipped to you by the 24th. Should you need any further information, please visit our customer service website at www.bestbargains.com. We apologize for any inconvenience and again thank you for your valued business and _____
_____.

Sincerely,
Jaqueline Lopez, Distribution Center Representative

(a) continued patronage
(b) lively correspondence
(c) consistent communication
(d) dedicated service

해석 키무라씨께
최근에 온라인 주문(#987YUO)을 해주셔서 감사드립니다. 유감스럽게도 할인 품목 #324(생산이 중단된 흰 색 테리 천 가운)는 한정적으로 품절된 상태입니다. 제품은 재 주문된 상태이고 귀하께 24일까지 배송해 드리기를 바라고 있습니다. 더 자세한 사항을 알고 싶으시면 저희 고객서비스 웹사이트 www.bestbargains.com을 방문해 주십시오. 불편을 끼쳐 드려서 죄송하며 귀하의 소중한 거래와 계속적인 애용에 다시 한 번 감사드립니다.
유통 센터 책임자, 재클린 로페즈 드림

(a) 계속적인 애용
(b) 활기 찬 서신 왕래
(c) 지속적인 연락
(d) 헌신적인 서비스

해설 편지를 읽을 때는 보낸 이와 받는 이, 그리고 편지를 보낸 의도를 파악하는 것이 중요하다! 온라인 주문에 대답하는 비즈니스 편지이다. 편지의 의도는 주문된 제품이 품절되어 재 주문된 상황과 배송 일에 관한 정보를 주는 것이다. 빈 칸에 들어갈 적절한 표현은 '＿＿＿＿＿＿＿에 대해 감사를 드린다.'는 것이기 때문에 먼저 (b)와 (d)는 적절하지 않다. 또한 빈 칸의 앞부분에 나와 있는 '소중한 거래(We apologize for any inconvenience and again thank you for your valued business and ＿＿＿＿＿＿.)'와 내용상 연결되기 위해서는 (a)가 정답이다.

어휘 order 주문
unfortunately 불행하게도, 유감스럽게도
temporarily 일시적으로, 임시로
out of stock 매진되어, 품절되어
discounted item 할인 품목
discontinue 중단시키다
robe 길고 헐거운 겉옷
backorder 이월 주문
ship 선적하다, 운송하다
further 더 먼, 그 이상의
apologize 사과하다, 사죄하다
inconvenience 불편, 불편한 것
patronage 단골거래
correspondence 서신 왕래

정답 (a)

4

Mark Twain, the American author best-known for the classics Tom Sawyer and Huckleberry Finn lived a life of great success and failure. Although his early novels were financial successes, Twain lost most of his fortune due to poor investing. Later in life, Twain found himself with little money and plenty of debt. To fix this, he traveled to Europe for a lengthy schedule of performances. The sole purpose of ＿＿＿＿＿＿＿＿＿＿＿＿＿＿, which took quite some time. This extended stay in Europe lasted an entire decade.

(a) scheduling European shows was to find a new audience
(b) writing more novels was to make more money
(c) taking work abroad was to pay off his debts
(d) moving to Europe was to become an actor

해석 마크 트웨인은 미국 작가로 고전 작품들인 톰 소여와 허클베리 핀이 가장 잘 알려졌으며 큰 성공과 실패의 삶을 살았다. 그의 초기 소설들이 금전적인 성공을 거두긴 했지

만 트웨인은 재산의 대부분을 잃었는데, 잘못된 투자 때문이었다. 말년의 트웨인은 돈은 없었고 많은 빚을 지고 있었다. 이 문제를 해결하기 위해서 그는 유럽으로 긴 여정의 공연을 떠났다. 외국에서 일을 맡은 유일한 목적은 빚을 청산하기 위한 것이었고 그것은 꽤 오랜 시간이 걸렸다. 이 긴 유럽에서의 체류는 십 년이나 지속되었다.

(a) 유럽 공연을 계획한 (유일한 목적은) 새로운 관객을 찾기 위한 것
(b) 더 많은 소설들을 쓴 (유일한 목적은) 더 많은 돈을 벌기 위한 것
(c) 외국에서 일을 하는 (유일한 목적은) 빚을 청산하기 위한 것
(d) 유럽으로 이주한 (유일한 목적은) 배우가 되기 위한 것

해설 톰 소여와 허클베리 핀으로 유명한 미국 소설가 마크 트웨인의 일화이다. '~ a life of great success and failure. Although his early novels were financial successes, Twain lost most of his fortune due to poor investing.'에서 밝히고 있듯이 그의 삶은 소설로는 성공을 하여 많은 돈을 벌었지만 잘못된 투자로 많은 돈을 잃게 되었다. 그리고 이러한 경제적 손실을 만회하기 위해서 나이가 들었을 때는 유럽에서 긴 기간 동안의 공연을 떠나게 되었다. 빈 칸에 들어가야 할 내용은 이 여행의 목적을 묻는 것이다. (b)와 (c)가 조금 비슷하기 때문에 혼란스러울 수 있으나, 문단의 흐름에 따르면 유럽 체류의 목적을 물어 보는 것이기 때문에 정답은 (c)다.

어휘 author 저자, 작가, 저술가
classic 고전, 걸작
live a life 삶을 살다
financial 재정(상)의, 재무의, 재계의
fortune 부, 재산, 재물
due to ~ 때문에
invest 투자하다
plenty of 많은
debt 빚, 부채, 채무
lengthy 긴, 오랜, 장황한
sole 단 하나의, 단독의
extended 장기간에 걸친
pay off 청산하다, 다 갚다

정답 (c)

5

I was ten years old when my father took me on my first deep-sea fishing trip. As our boat sailed out into the Gulf of Mexico, the excitement of catching an enormous fish was more than I could stand. Almost as soon as I dropped my line into the water I felt an enormous tug and the fight for the biggest fish of my life began. Actually, this was no trophy fish at all. My line had become tangled underneath the boat with another man's who was fishing off the other side. Sadly, we both thought _____.

(a) that the fishing trip would be a memorable one
(b) we had become each other's catch of a lifetime
(c) that the fish was much larger than it actually was
(d) the other person was to blame for losing the fish

해석 내가 10살 때 아버지는 나를 심해 바다낚시에 처음으로 데리고 갔다. 우리가 탄 배가 멕시코 만으로 들어섰을 때 거대한 고기를 잡는다는 흥분은 내가 감당할 수 없을 정도였다. 물속으로 낚시 줄을 던지자마자 나는 엄청나게 당겨지는 것을 느꼈고 내 생애 가장 큰 물고기를 잡기 위한 전투가 시작되었다. 실은 이것은 전혀 월척이 아니었다. 내 낚시 줄이 반대편에서 낚시를 하고 있던 다른 사람의 낚시 줄과 배 밑에서 엉킨 것이었다. 슬프게도 우리 둘은 상대방이 일생 최대의 월척이라고 착각했었다.

(a) 낚시 여행이 기억에 남는 것이 될 거라고
(b) 상대방이 일생 최대의 월척이라고
(c) 물고기가 실제보다 훨씬 컸다고
(d) 물고기를 놓친 것이 상대방 탓이라고

해설 1인칭 화자의 입장에서 전달하는 일화를 읽고 빈 칸에 적절하게 들어갈 표현을 선택하는 문제이다. 글쓴이가 10살 때 바다낚시를 갔을 때의 이야기이다. 낚시 줄을 바다에 던지고 엄청나게 당겨지는 것을 느껴 큰 물고기를 잡았다고 착각했던 장면을 상상해보아라. actually, sadly 와 같은 문장의 흐름을 전환시켜주는 장치에 주목하라! 'Actually, this was no trophy fish at all. My line had become tangled underneath the boat with another man's who was fishing off the other side.'라는 문장을 통해서 실제로는 상대방의 낚시 줄과 엉킨 상황임을 알 수 있다. 따라서 '슬프게도'라는 장치 뒤에는 서로 간의 오해를 표현해야 하기 때문에 정답은 (b)다.

어휘 deep-sea 심해의
gulf 만 *cf.* the Gulf of Mexico 멕시코 만
excitement 흥분(상태), 동요, 자극
enormous 거대한, 막대한, 엄청난

stand 참다, 견디다
as soon as ~하자마자
tug 힘껏 당김
trophy fish 월척
not ~ at all 조금도 ~아니다
tangle 엉키게 하다, 엉키다
underneath ~의 아래에
memorable 기억할 만한
blame 나무라다, 탓하다

정답 (b)

6

Want the security of a watchdog without having to own a dog? Then you need the Jake-2000, our amazing electronic watchdog. There's no need to feed or clean up after this guy. Jake is a compact unit with sensors and a speaker that plugs into any home outlet. Jake's sensors can reliably detect when someone is approaching your home. When strangers are near, Jake barks a realistic German Shepherd bark that increases in volume and intensity as strangers get closer to your home. Jake is the most affordable 24-hour security system you'll ever find. To order your Jake-2000, call 1-800-435-JAKE and _____.

(a) start experiencing affordable security system today
(b) enjoy the peace of mind only a real watchdog can offer
(c) ask for information about our other security products
(d) find how inexpensive being a pet owner can be

해석 개를 기르지 않고도 경비견의 신변 보호를 원하십니까? 그렇다면 귀하는 저희 회사의 놀라운 전자 경비견인 제이크 2000이 필요합니다. 제이크는 먹이를 주거나 변을 치워주지 않아도 됩니다. 제이크는 센서와 함께 모든 가정의 콘센트에 꽂을 수 있는 스피커를 갖춘 소형 기기입니다. 제이크의 센서는 누군가가 당신의 집에 접근하는 것을 확실하게 감지할 수 있습니다. 낯선 사람이 가까이 오면 제이크는 진짜 독일 셰퍼드의 소리로 짖으며 낯선 사람이 가까이 다가올 수록 그 음량은 커지고 강해집니다. 제이크는 여러분이 찾아 볼 수 있는 가장 저렴한 가격의 24시간 경비 시스템입니다. 제이크 2000을 주문하시려면 1-800-435-JAKE로 전화하시고 저렴한 경비 시스템의 경험을 오늘 시작해 보세요.

(a) 저렴한 경비 시스템의 경험을 오늘 시작해 보세요
(b) 진짜 경비견만이 제공할 수 있는 안도감을 맛보세요
(c) 저희 회사의 다른 경비 제품들에 대해 문의하세요

(d) 애완동물을 기르는 것이 얼마나 저렴한지 알아보세요

해설 전자 경비견 제이크 2000을 소개하는 광고글이다. 광고문을 읽을 때는 광고하는 제품의 특성, 제품의 성능, 제품 사용방법, 그리고 구매 방법이나 연락 방법 등의 정보를 파악하는 것이 기본적인 방법이다. 본 광고가 선전하고 있는 전자 경비견 제이크 2000은 손쉽게 모든 가정의 콘센트에 꽂아 사용할 수 있는 소형 기기로 낯선 사람이 다가올수록 음량이 커지고 강해지는 특성을 갖고 있다. 가격은 저렴하며 24시간 경비시스템이다(Jake barks a realistic German Shepherd bark that increases in volume and intensity as strangers get closer to your home. Jake is the most affordable, 24-hour security system ~). 이 부분까지 제품의 성능 및 특성에 대해 자세하게 소개하고 있고 빈 칸에는 구매를 함으로써 이 제품에서 얻을 수 있는 이익이나 혜택 등이 들어가는 것이 자연스럽다. 따라서 정답은 (a)다.

어휘 security 안전, 경비
watchdog 집 지키는 개, 경비견
amazing 놀랄만한
feed 먹이를 주다
clean up (더러운 것을) 치우다
electronic 전자의, 전자 공학의
sensor 감지 장치
plug into (기구의) 플러그를 꽂다
outlet (전기의) 코드 구멍, 콘센트
reliably 믿을 수 있게, 확실하게
detect 탐지하다
intensity 세기, 강도
affordable 적당한, 가격이 알맞은
inexpensive 값 싼

정답 (a)

7

SYDNEY — Thanks to a protective vest and presence of mind, a diver _____ _____ of a great white shark and lived to tell about it. Matthew Brimby, 45, was diving for shellfish with his son, when the 10-foot-long shark attacked him, taking Brimby's head and shoulders into its mouth. Brimby said the lead-lined vest he was wearing saved him from being cut in half.

(a) videotaped the daily eating habits
(b) studied and learned more about the teeth
(c) managed to avoid the terrifying jaws
(d) escaped the frightening and deadly jaws

해석 시드니 – 보호 조끼와 침착함 덕분에 한 다이버가 거대한 백상어의 두렵고 치명적인 주둥이에서 탈출하여 그의 생존에 대해 이야기 할 수 있었다. 45세의 매튜 브림비는

아들과 함께 조개를 잡기 위해 다이빙을 하고 있었는데 10피트 길이의 상어가 브림비의 머리와 어깨를 입에 물어 공격했다. 브림비는 그가 입고 있었던 납을 댄 조끼가 그가 반 토막이 나는 것을 막아 줬다고 말했다.

(a) 일상의 식습관을 비디오에 담아서
(b) 이빨에 대해 좀 더 연구하고 배워서
(c) 가까스로 무시무시한 주둥이를 피해서
(d) 두렵고 치명적인 주둥이에서 탈출하여

해설 간단히 선택지 동사만 보고 고를 수도 있다. 본 지문은 (a) ~를 비디오로 녹화했다. (b) 치아에 대해 더 많은 것을 연구했다. (c) 무시무시한 주둥이를 피할 수 있었다. (d) 목숨을 빼앗아 갈 수 있는 주둥이에서 탈출했다. 이 중에서 (c)를 답으로 잘 못 고를 수도 있으나 이미 Brimby는 머리와 어깨를 물렸다는 내용이 있으므로 맞지 않다. 물렸다가 탈출했으니 escaped를 사용한 (d)가 정답이다.

어휘 protective vest 보호조끼
presence of mind 태연자약, 침착
shellfish 조개, 갑각류
lead-lined vest 납을 댄 조끼
in half 반으로, 2등분으로
videotape 비디오테이프에 녹화하다
manage to+V 간신히 ~하다
terrifying 무서운
threatening 위협하는
deadly 치명적인

정답 (d)

8

Boxing was once taught in British schools. In fact, the sport was a standard in the physical education curriculum until 1962 when it was banned. But now some schools in Bromley, London believe boxing _____ _____. Experts who support boxing in P.E. classes say it offers mental and physical skills that apply to all types of learning. Still, medical experts concerned about student safety are asking the schools to rethink the decision.

(a) should be reintroduced to students
(b) could create Olympic athletes
(c) might help students work out frustrations
(d) ought to be banned again

해설 권투는 한 때 영국 학교에서 가르쳐졌다. 실제로 권투는 체육 교과 과정에 기본 과목으로 금지된 때인 1962년까지 포함되어 있었다. 하지만 현재 런던 브롬리의 일부 학교들은 권투가 학생들에게 다시 소개되어야 한다고 생각한다. 체육 수업에 권투가 포함될 것을 지지하는 전문가들은 권투가 모든 종류의 학습에 적용되는 정신적, 신체적 기술들을 제공한다고 말한다. 그러나 의학 전문가들은

학생들의 안전을 염려하여 학교가 그 결정을 재검토할 것을 요구하고 있다.

(a) 학생들에게 다시 소개되어야 한다
(b) 올림픽 선수들을 만들어 낼 수 있다
(c) 학생들이 좌절감을 떨치도록 도울 수 있다
(d) 다시 금지되어야만 한다

해설 권투가 영국에서 체육 교과 과정의 기본 과목으로 사용되었던 배경에 관한 글이다. 권투가 교과과정의 일부로 포함 되어야 하는 가에 관한 찬반 논쟁을 주제로 하고 있기 때문에 찬성 주장과 반대 주장을 명확하게 파악해야 한다. 'But now some schools in Bromley, London believe boxing _____ . Experts who support boxing in P.E. classes say it offers mental and physical skills that apply to all types of learning.'의 문장은 권투가 교과과정의 일부가 되어야 한다는 주장이기 때문에, 빈 칸에 들어갈 표현은 (a)가 적절하다.

어휘 boxing 권투
standard 표준, 기준, 규격
physical education 체육
curriculum 교과과정
ban 금지하다
expert 전문가
apply to ~에 적용되다
be concerned about ~에 대해 걱정하다
rethink 재고하다, 생각을 고치다
reintroduce 다시 소개하다
work out 제거하다
frustration 좌절

정답 (a)

9

Several different militaries are each developing their own pocket-sized robots. These tiny technological soldiers will quietly hop or crawl like insects and _____ than humans can. One specific use, a robotics expert explained, is that these small robots could disable many types of vehicles. By squirting a special chemical on the tires, the rubber would immediately be destroyed.

(a) attack the enemy more violently
(b) drive military vehicles with more precision
(c) approach targets in less obvious ways
(d) cause more enemy casualties

해석 몇몇 군대에서는 주머니 크기의 소형 로봇들을 개발하고 있다. 이 소형의 테크노 병사들은 곤충들처럼 조용히 뛰어 오르거나 기어서 인간이 할 수 있는 것보다 눈에 덜 띄는 방식으로 목표물에 접근한다. 한 로봇 전문가가 설명

하기를 이러한 작은 로봇들의 한 가지 특별한 용도는 많은 종류의 차량들을 무력화 시킬 수 있다는 것이다. 특수 화학품을 바퀴에 뿌리게 되면 고무는 즉시 파괴된다.

(a) 적을 좀 더 폭력적으로 공격한다
(b) 좀 더 정확하게 군사 차량을 운전한다
(c) 눈에 덜 띄는 방식으로 목표물에 접근한다
(d) 좀 더 많은 적 사상자를 낸다

해설 군대에서 개발된 소형 로봇을 소개하는 글이다. 이 소형 로봇의 특성은 'These tiny technological soldiers will quietly hop or crawl like insects and _____ than humans can.'에서 설명하고 있기 때문에 이 문장 내에서 빈 칸에 들어갈 정보를 파악할 수 밖에 없다. quietly와 small 등의 실마리에 주목한다면, 이 소형 기술 병사는 크기가 매우 작고 조용하게 작동되는 것임을 알 수 있다. 또한 빈 칸 앞에 and는 문장의 흐름이 같은 의미로 엮어진다는 것을 암시하기 때문에 정답은 (c)다.

어휘 several 몇몇의, 몇 개의
military 군대, 군
pocket-sized 주머니 크기의
technological 과학기술의
quietly 조용히, 고요히, 침착하게
hop (깡총) 뛰다
crawl 기어가다, 기다, 포복하다
specific 명확한, 뚜렷한, 구체적인, 특정한
vehicle 탈것, 운송 수단
robotics 로봇공학
disable 무력화시키다
squirt 분출시키다, 분출하다
chemical 화학약품
immediately 곧, 즉시
violently 폭력적으로
precision 정확, 정밀
casualties 사상자, 희생자

정답 (c)

10

If you think that some taxes are always increasing, you may be right. A "pigovian tax" is a special tax for products that are seen as harmful. For example, a company that pollutes the sky or air will have to pay higher tax to help clean up their mess. Governments put extra tax on tobacco and alcohol, as these products cause expensive medical damage. Until the harmful effects disappear, pigovian taxes on products and industries _____ .

(a) will cause more damage
(b) should stay the same
(c) will keep increasing
(d) might decrease dramatically

어떤 세금은 항상 증가한다고 생각하면 그것은 맞는 말일
수도 있다. '피고비언 세금'은 유해한 것으로 간주되는 상
품에 부여되는 특별 세금이다. 예를 들어, 어떤 회사가
공기를 오염시키면 세금을 더 내야만 하는데, 그 목적은
그 회사가 오염시킨 공기를 정화시키기 위해서이다. 정부
는 담배 회사와 주류 회사에 더 많이 세금을 부과하는데,
그 이유는 이 상품들이 의학적으로 피해를 주어 많은 비
용이 들게 하기 때문이다. 유해한 영향이 사라질 때까지,
이 상품들에 피고비언 세금은 <u>계속 증가할 것이다.</u>

(a) 더 많은 해를 유발시킬 것이다.
(b) 같은 상태를 유지해야만 한다.
(c) 계속 증가할 것이다.
(d) 급격하게 줄어들 것이다.

해설 Pigovian tax가 무엇인지 설명하고, 그 예를 들어 이해
하기 좋게 설명하고 있다. 간략히 전체 내용을 정리해보
면, 일반적으로 세금이 항상 오르는 것처럼 생각된다. 피
고피언 세금이 무엇이고, 왜 부과되는지, 또 구체적인 예
로는 어떤 것이 있는지 살펴본다. 사회에 나쁜 영향을 주
는 상품을 만드는 회사는 그것을 되돌리기 위해서, 많은
좋은 일을 해야 한다. 그러기 위해서는 세금이 증가해야
한다는 것을 자연스럽게 정답으로 고를 수 있다. 따라서,
답은 (c)다.

Tips A Pigovian tax(Pigouvian tax)는 사회에 부정적인
면을 초래할 때 이를 시정할 수 있도록 세금을 부여하
는 과세를 의미한다. 오염(pollution), 술(alcohol), 담
배(cigarettes) 등에 부과되는 세금을 종종 의미하기도
한다.

어휘 tax 세금
harmful 해로운, 유해한
see A as B A를 B로 간주하다
pollute 오염시키다
clean up 정화하다
mess 엉망, 더러운 것
extra 추가의, 특별한
medical 의학적인
damage 손해, 손상
disappear 사라지다
dramatically 급격히, 극적으로

정답 (c)

11

Very few people realize that on the day
Abraham Lincoln gave his famous Gettysburg
Address, another speaker addressed
the crowd as well. Edward Everett was a
famous orator and also the governor of
Massachusetts. His speech went on for
two hours, while Lincoln's was over in two
minutes. Afterwards, Everett told Lincoln that
he would be flattered if he could even hope
that his two-hour speech came close to the
central ideas that _____ in
only two minutes.

(a) he wrote down and practiced
(b) Lincoln so eloquently covered
(c) the President forgot to mention
(d) the crowd couldn't comprehend

해석 에이브러험 링컨이 유명한 게티즈버그 연설을 했던 바로
그 날, 군중들에게 연설을 했던 사람이 또 한 명 있었다는
사실은 거의 알려지지 않았다. 에드워드 에버레트는 유명
한 연설자이자 메사추세츠의 주지사였다. 그의 연설은 두
시간 동안 계속되었다, 반면에 링컨의 연설은 겨우 2분만
에 끝났다. 이 후 에버레트는 링컨에게 말하기를 자신의
2시간짜리 연설이 단 2분 동안 링컨이 너무나도 설득력
있게 다룬 중심 사상에 근접했기를 바랄 수만 있어도 영
광으로 여길 것이라고 했다.

(a) 그가 쓰고 연습한
(b) 링컨이 너무나도 설득력 있게 다룬
(c) 대통령이 잊고 언급하지 않은
(d) 군중들이 이해할 수 없었던

해설 링컨의 게티즈버그 연설이 있던 날 연설을 했던 에드워드
에버레트와 관련된 역사적 내용이다. very few people
이라는 표현이 거의 알려지지 않은 역사적 사실임을 강
조하고 있다. 링컨의 연설은 단 2분 동안 행해졌지만 에
베레트의 연설은 2시간 동안 지속되었다(His speech
went on for two hours, while Lincoln's was over
in two minutes.). 빈 칸에 들어갈 부분은, 2시간 동안
연설을 했던 에베레트가 "_____ 된다면 영광으로
여길 것(he would be flattered if ~)"이란 말을 함으로
써 링컨의 연설에 대한 긍정적 설명이 들어가야 한다. 따
라서 정답은 (b)다.

어휘 address 연설, 연설하다
as well 게다가, 또한
orator 연설자, 웅변가
governor 통치자, 주지사
afterwards 후에, 나중에
flatter 기쁘게 하다, 즐겁게 하다
come close to ~에 가까이 가다
central 중심적인, 주요한
write down 적다, 쓰다
eloquently 설득력 있게, 웅변적으로

comprehend 이해하다

(b)

12

The Tale of Kieu, written by Nguyen Du in 1813, is commonly thought of as a literary masterpiece. But very few works of literature _____ as closely as Kieu's story has. This epic poem, which goes against traditional Confucian ideals, is the tragic tale of a young woman's personal sacrifice. All Vietnamese know this famous story and often refer to its passages in daily conversation. They also closely connect life events to events in the poem. And at the beginning of each New Year, this story is often used to try to predict the future.

(a) have ever been embraced by their audience
(b) have been so enthusiastically followed
(c) have ever been translated into English
(d) have followed society's rules

해석 〈키에우 이야기〉는 1813년 뉴엔 듀가 썼는데, 걸작으로 널리 인정받는다. 그러나 키에우의 이야기만큼 친밀하게 독자들에 의해 수용된 문학 작품은 매우 드물다. 이 서사시는 전통적인 유교 사상에 반대되는 내용으로 한 젊은 여성의 개인적 희생에 대한 비극적인 이야기다. 모든 베트남 인들은 이 유명한 이야기를 알고 있으며 종종 일상의 대화에서 글의 일부를 이용하곤 한다. 그들은 또한 인생의 사건들을 시 속의 사건들과 근접하게 연결시킨다. 그리고 매년 새해가 되면 이 이야기가 종종 사용되는데 그 목적은 미래를 예견하기 위해서이다.

(a) 독자들에 의해 수용된
(b) 열성적으로 추종된
(c) 영어로 번역된
(d) 사회의 규율을 따른

해설 〈키에우 이야기〉라는 뉴엔 듀의 작품에 관한 글이다. 빈 칸에 들어갈 정보를 찾기 전에 먼저 제시된 글에서 이 작품에 관한 정보를 모두 모아야 한다. 먼저 '~ is commonly thought of as a literary masterpiece.'라는 문장에서 이 작품이 대중적으로 명작으로 여겨진다는 것을 알 수 있다 또한, 'All Vietnamese know this famous story and often refer to passages in daily conversation. They also closely connect life events to poem events.'라는 문장을 통해서 모든 베트남 사람들이 이 유명한 이야기를 알고 있으며 이를 일상의 대화에 이용한다는 것도 알 수 있다. 따라서 빈 칸에 들어가는 내용은 이 작품이 독자들에 의해 매우 폭넓게 받아들여 진다는 (a)가 정답이다.

어휘 **commonly** 일반적으로, 보통으로, 통속적으로
literary 문학의, 문학적인, 문어의

masterpiece 걸작, 명작, 대표작
work 작품, 저술
epic poem 서사시
confucian 유교의, 공자의
tragic 비극의, 비극적인
sacrifice 희생
Vietnamese 베트남 사람
refer to 언급하다, 인용하다
passage 구절
predict 예언하다, 예보하다
embrace 수용하다
audience 독자
enthusiastically 열광적으로
translate 번역하다

정답 (a)

13

Andy Warhol's first pop works were painted by hand, but in 1962 he _____. In assembly-line fashion, Warhol started using a photo-silkscreen process and a large staff of artists to create his art. It was at this same time that Warhol began to use odd objects in his art, such as still photographs of movie stars, car accidents and newspaper photographs. In his New York Studio, which he named "The Factory," as many as 80 paintings could be created in one day.

(a) changed his ways
(b) quit painting
(c) became a photographer
(d) achieved fame

해석 앤디 워홀의 초기 팝 아트 작품들은 손으로 그려졌지만 1962년 그는 그의 방식들을 바꾸었다. 조립의 방식으로 워홀은 사진 실크 스크린 공정과 많은 수의 예술가들을 이용하기 시작했는데 그 목적은 자신의 작품을 창조하기 위해서였다. 이 시기가 바로 워홀이 특이한 물체들, 예를 들어, 영화배우들의 사진들, 자동차 사고와 신문 보도 사진 등과 같은 것들을 그의 작품에서 사용하기 시작한 때이다. 그의 뉴욕 작업실에서는, 그런데 그는 그 작업실을 공장이라고 불렀는데, 하루에 많게는 80점의 그림이 제작될 수 있었다.

(a) 그의 방식을 변형했다
(b) 그림 그리기를 그만뒀다
(c) 사진작가가 되었다
(d) 명성을 얻었다

해설 유명한 팝 아티스트 앤디 워홀의 작품 제작 방식에 관련된 글이다. 'Andy Warhol's first pop works were painted by hand, but in 1962 he _____. In assembly-line fashion'이라는 주제 문장을 통해서 초기에는 그가 손으로 작품을 그렸지만 1962년에는 어떤

변화를 갖게 되었다는 것을 유추할 수 있다. 또한 빈 칸이 있는 바로 다음 문장에서 '조립 방식'이란 표현을 사용함으로써 앤디 워홀이 초기에는 손수 손으로 작품을 만들다가 이때를 기점으로 많은 작품을 대량으로 조립하듯 제작하는 방식을 택하였음을 알 수 있다. 따라서 빈 칸에 들어가는 답은 (a)다.

어휘 work 작품, 저작, 저술
assembly-line 조립 라인
fashion 방법
process 과정, 공정
odd 이상한
such as 예컨대, 이를테면
accident 사고, 재난, 고장

정답 (a)

14

Architects and landscape designers are starting _____ that should be used for city parks in an entirely different way. In Europe and the United States, city park planning and design is heading in an interesting new direction. Architects and landscape designers in the most populated cities are taking huge garbage dumps, abandoned industrial sites and old railroad yards, and transforming them into futuristic-looking public parks.

(a) to plan fun and exciting playground equipment
(b) to learn the techniques of ancient masters
(c) to know the best building materials
(d) to think about the type of land

해석 건축가들과 조경 디자이너들은 땅의 종류에 대해 생각하기 시작하고 있는데, 이 땅들은 전적으로 다른 방식으로 도시 공원으로 이용될 수 있어야 하는 곳이다. 유럽과 미국에서 도시 공원 계획과 디자인은 흥미로운 새 방향을 택하고 있다. 인구가 매우 밀집된 도시들의 건축가들과 조경 디자이너들은 넓은 쓰레기장, 버려진 공업 단지와 오래된 철도 정거장을 택하여 그것들을 초현대적인 모습의 공원들로 변모시키고 있다.

(a) 재미있고 신나는 놀이 기구 계획하기
(b) 고대 거장들의 기술들을 배우기
(c) 최고의 건축 자재에 대해 알기
(d) 땅의 종류에 대해 생각하기

해설 유럽과 미국에서 도시 공원 계획과 디자인의 새로운 발전 방향에 관한 문제이다. 문단의 첫 번째 문장은 이 글 전체의 주제를 말하고 있다(Architects and landscape designers are starting _____ that should be used for city parks in an entirely different way.). 빈 칸에 들어갈 부분은 새로운 변화

의 방향이 무엇인가를 언급하는 부분이다. 이런 경우에는 문단의 후반부에서 주제문에 대한 증거를 제시하거나 지지하는 내용을 찾을 수 있다. '~ taking huge garbage dumps, abandoned industrial sites and old railroad yards and transforming them into futuristic-looking public parks.'에서 알 수 있듯이 땅을 어떻게 활용하고 있는지에 대한 정보가 있으므로 정답은 (d)다.

어휘 architect 건축가, 건축 기사
landscape 풍경, 경치
populate 거주시키다
garbage 음식 찌꺼기, 쓰레기, 폐물
abandon 버리다, 유기하다, 그만두다
dump 쓰레기 버리는 곳, 쓰레기 더미
site 대지, 집터, 용지, 부지
transform 변형시키다, 변모시키다
futuristic 초 현대적인, 선진적인

정답 (d)

15

If the world truly cared about Africa, there would no longer be a malaria epidemic across the continent. In my opinion, the solution is very simple. Working individuals who make high incomes in proportion to the average global wage should commit to paying only three dollars a year. _____, three billion dollars could be used annually to prevent malaria. Africa cannot devote these types of funds to pubic health, but the world of excess beyond its borders can.

(a) Accordingly
(b) Finally
(c) Meanwhile
(d) Similarly

해석 만일 인류가 진정으로 아프리카에 대해 염려를 한다면 말라리아가 더 이상 아프리카 대륙에 만연하지 않을 것이다. 내 생각에 해결책은 매우 단순하다. 전 세계 평균 임금에 비례하여 고소득인 개인들이 일 년에 3달러씩만 지출하기로 하면 된다. 그에 따라 30억 달러가 매년 말라리아 예방에 사용될 수 있다. 아프리카는 이러한 종류의 자금을 공중 보건에 쓸 형편이 되지 않지만 다른 나라의 부유한 사람들은 할 수 있다.

(a) 그에 따라
(b) 마침내
(c) 한편
(d) 마찬가지로

해설 아프리카 대륙에서 만연하고 있는 말라리아를 퇴치시키는 방안을 독자들에게 권유하는 글이다. 글쓴이는 전 세계의 평균 이상의 고소득 임금자에게 일 년에 3달러씩을 기부하면 이것이 모여서 아프리카 대륙의 말라리아 발병을

예방할 수 있다고 제안하고 있다(Working individuals who make high incomes in proportion to the average global wage should commit to paying only three dollars a year.). 빈 칸에 들어갈 부분은 이렇게 각각의 고 소득자가 기부한 3달러가 모여서 30억이 된다는 내용이기 때문에 (a)가 가장 적절하다.

어휘 malaria 말라리아, 학질
epidemic 유행병
continent 대륙, 육지, 본토
solution 해결, 해석, 설명
in proportion to ~에 비례하여
commit 약속하다, 책임지다
annually 매년, 1년에 한 번씩
prevent 막다, 방해하다, 예방하다
devote 바치다, 쏟다, 기울이다
excess 초과, 과다, 지나침, 과도
beyond ~을 넘어서, ~의 범위를 넘어서
border 가장자리, 변두리, 경계

정답 (a)

이 수유를 권한다는 내용으로 이어지고 있다. 따라서 (b) in spite of는 '~에도 불구하고'라는 뜻으로 '양보'를 의미하니까 자연스럽지 못하다. (c) in contrast to는 '~에 대조적으로'의 뜻으로 뒤에 상반되는 내용이 와야 함으로 답이 아니다. (d)는 목적을 의미하므로 역시 틀린다. 따라서 정답은 (a)다.

어휘 breast-feed 모유로 키우다
newborn 신생아
incidence 발병율
diarrhea 설사
influenza 유행성 감기
artificial 인공적인
formula 분유
resistance 저항
chronic disease 만성질환
enhanced 향상된
cognitive 인지의
infancy 유년, 유아기

정답 (a)

16

There are many benefits of breast-feeding. In breast-fed newborns, the incidence of diarrhea and influenza is much lower than in those who are fed with artificial formulas. Other research shows protection from allergies and increased resistance to chronic diseases as benefits. Besides, studies link enhanced cognitive development to breast-feeding. _____ these researches, doctors are telling their patients that they must breast-feed their newborns through infancy and beyond.

(a) As a result of
(b) In spite of
(c) In contrast to
(d) To demonstrate

해석 모유 수유에 많은 장점들이 있다. 모유를 먹은 신생아들에게서 설사나 독감의 발병율은 분유를 먹인 아이들보다 훨씬 낮다. 또 다른 연구에 의하면 알레르기 방어 능력과 만성적인 질병에 대한 저항력이 모유 수유의 혜택들이다. 게다가 연구결과는 높은 인지력 발달과 모유 수유간에 관계가 있다고 한다. 이 연구의 결과로서 의사들이 환자들에게 권하는 바는 신생아시기와 더 나중까지 모유를 먹이라는 것이다.

(a) 의 결과로서
(b) 에도 불구하고
(c) 와는 대조적으로
(d) 을 증명하기 위하여

해설 맨 처음 문장부터 빈 칸 앞까지 모두 모유를 수유했을 때의 장점을 나열하고 있다. 그리고 빈 칸 다음에는 의사들

17

Fire broke out at Wow Shopping Mall just after midnight. After smelling smoke for five minutes, a security guard who was patrolling the outside grounds called and reported a possible fire. Luckily, fire fighters were able to find and put out a small blaze that originated in one of the mall's food court restaurants. Mall manager Rachel Martinez says if the security guard hadn't alerted emergency crews so quickly, the results could have been disastrous.

Q What is the passage mainly about?

(a) A disastrous fire at the Middleton Mall
(b) A security guard's heroic efforts to save shoppers
(c) The quick response to a minor fire at a local mall
(d) A fire in the ventilation system of a mall restaurant

해석 와우 쇼핑몰에서 자정이 지난 직후 화재가 발생했다. 연기 냄새가 5분 정도 난 후 경비원이 건물 밖을 순찰하고 있었는데 화재가 발생했는지도 모른다고 신고를 했다. 다행히도 소방수들이 작은 불을 발견하고 소화시켰는데, 이 불은 몰의 식당가 식당 중에 한 곳에서 시작되었다. 몰 지배인 레이첼 마르티네즈가 말하기를 경비원이 매우 긴급하게 비상구조요원에게 알려주지 않았더라면, 심각한 결과를 초래할 수도 있었을 것이라 했다.

Q 위 글의 요지로 알맞은 것을 고르시오.
(a) 미들턴 몰에서의 끔찍한 화재

(b) 쇼핑객들을 구하려는 경비원의 영웅적인 노력

(c) 한 지역 몰에서의 작은 화재에 대한 재빠른 대응

(d) 몰 식당 통풍 시스템에 난 화재

해설 글의 요지를 묻는 문제이다. 지난밤에 발생한 화재 사건에 관한 글이기 때문에 사건 발생 장소, 시간, 원인 그리고 관련된 사람에 관한 기사를 예측할 수 있다. 'Fire broke out at WOW Shopping Mall just after midnight.'라는 문장에서 대략적 정보를 알 수 있으며, 'if the security guard hadn't alerted emergency crews so quickly ~' 부분에서 화재가 재빠른 대응으로 무사히 해결되었음을 알 수 있다. 따라서 정답은 (c)다.

어휘 **break out** (화재, 사건이) 발생하다
security guard 경비원
patrol 순찰하다
report 신고하다
put out 불을 끄다
blaze 불, 화재
originate 유래하다, 시작하다
alert 경고하다, 알려주다
emergency crew 비상구조요원
ventilation 통풍
disastrous 재난의

정답 (c)

18

Currently, many countries are trying to help students complete their education and go on to become motivated members of their communities. For example, Cuba has changed its education format so that students can stay with the same teacher for the first three years of high school. In Scotland, the focus has become offering courses that work on improving the attitudes of detached youth. Both changes are meant to provide a more meaningful school experience.

Q What is the best title of the passage?

(a) New Educational Approaches of Different Countries

(b) Students More Detached From Their Communities

(c) Motivated Adults Makeing a Difference in Students' Lives

(d) Meaningful School Experience Influencing Students' Futures

해석 현재, 많은 나라들이 학생들을 도와서 교육을 마치고 사회에 나가 의욕적인 사회의 일원이 되게 하도록 애쓰고 있다. 예를 들어, 쿠바는 교육 형태를 변형하여 학생들이 고등학교 처음 3년을 같은 교사와 공부할 수 있도록 했다.

스코틀랜드에서 주안점은 관심이 없는 젊은이들의 태도를 개선할 수업들을 제공하는 것이다. 두 변화 모두 좀 더 의미 있는 학교생활 경험을 제공하기 위해 의도된 것이다.

Q 위 글의 제목으로 가장 적절한 것을 고르시오.

(a) 여러 국가들의 새로운 교육적 접근법

(b) 사회로부터 더욱 고립되는 학생들

(c) 학생들의 인생에 중요한 역할을 하는 의욕적인 성인들

(d) 학교 경험이 학생들의 미래에 영향을 끼치는 의미있는 학교

해설 주요한 내용은 여러 국가가 앞장서서 학생들이 교육을 잘 마칠 수 있도록 다양하게 노력하고 있다는 내용이다. (b) 학생들이 지역공동체와 더욱 멀어지고 있다는 내용은 본문과 맞지 않는 내용이므로 답이 될 수 없다. (c) 의욕적인 성인들이 학생들의 삶을 바꾼다는 것은 전혀 답이 아니다. 그럼에도 불구하고, 지문에 나온 여러 단어들 (motivated, students) 때문에 오답이지만 매력적인 함정을 갖고 있다. (d)는 전반적인 내용을 의미하는 제목으로는 부족하다. 선택지가 본문의 지문에 비추어 사실이더라도, 이 문제는 지문의 전반적인 내용을 잘 나타내는 제목을 찾아야 함으로 전체 내용을 포괄하고 있는 (a)가 답이다.

어휘 **currently** 현재
complete 끝마치다
motivated 의욕적인
format 형태, 체제
detached 고립된
meaningful 의미심장한, 뜻있는,
remain 여전히 ~이다, 남다, 머무르다

정답 (a)

19

In the early 1900s, the US experienced a major shift when the African-American population of the South began to move northward and become more urbanized. Unfortunately, many African-Americans could only find homes in the poorest areas of northern cities. These 'ghettos,' as they were called, were full of dilapidated apartment buildings. Rent was high for these small, dirty accommodations. Frequently, tenants were taken advantage of by greedy landlords. Sadly, children living in these buildings sometimes died from diseases caused by the unsanitary living conditions.

Q What is the main topic of the passage?

(a) The causes of death among African-American children in the early 1900s
(b) Living conditions for African-Americans after migration north
(c) The poor economic condition in northern cities after the turn of the century
(d) Tactics landlords used to take advantage of African-Americans

해석 1900년대 초 미국은 남부의 아프리카 계 미국인들이 북쪽으로 이동하고 좀 더 도시화 되자 주요한 변동을 경험했다. 불행히도 많은 아프리카 계 미국인들이 북부 도시들의 가장 가난한 지역에 집을 구할 수밖에 없었다. '게토'라고 불린 이 지역에는 낡아빠진 아파트 건물들이 많았다. 이렇게 작고 더러운 주거지들에 대한 집세는 비쌌다. 종종 세입자들은 욕심 많은 집 주인들에게 이용을 당했다. 슬프게도 이 건물에 사는 어린이들은 때때로 비위생적인 생활환경으로 인한 질병으로 죽었다.

Q 위 글의 주제로 알맞은 것을 고르시오.
(a) 1900년대 초에 아프리카 계 미국 어린이들의 죽음의 원인들
(b) 북으로 이주한 후의 아프리카 계 미국인들의 생활 여건들
(c) 세기가 변한 후의 북부 도시에서의 궁핍한 경제 조건
(d) 아프리카 계 미국인들을 이용하기 위해 집주인들이 사용한 술책

해설 글의 주제를 선택하는 문제는 글 전체를 우선 읽어 보고 문장의 내용을 정리해보는 것이 도움이 된다. 1990년대 초 미국의 남부 아프리카 흑인들이 거주지를 옮기면서 가난한 지역에 모여 살게 되고 이런 지역을 '게토'라고 부르게 되었다. 글의 후반부에서는 이들이 또한 비싼 집세를 내며 아동들이 비위생적 생활환경에서 질병으로 죽게 되는 사례를 설명하고 있기 때문에, 글의 전체적인 초점은 이들의 생활 여건에 관한 것이다. 따라서 이런 내용을 포

괄하고 있는 것은 (b)다.

어휘 shift 변화
northward 북부 향한, 북쪽으로의
urbanize 도시화하다, 도시로의 이주를 촉진하다
dilapidated 황폐한, 헐어 빠진, 초라한
accommodations 숙박시설
tenant 세입자
take advantage of ~을 이용하다
greedy 탐욕스런
landlord 집주인
unsanitary 비위생적인
migration 이주
turn 변화
tactics 전술, 책략

정답 (b)

20

Recent research has shown that children are less likely to use sunscreen as they grow older. However, just talking about the chances of developing skin cancer doesn't seem to encourage teens to use sunscreen. So health officials are taking a different approach to educate kids about skin cancer prevention. Appealing to teenagers' awareness about their self-images seems to be more effective. For example, stressing an increased chance of preventing premature wrinkles seems to make more teens willing to wear sunscreen.

Q What is the main topic of the passage?

(a) How teenagers can suntan safely.
(b) How to survive skin cancer at an early age.
(c) How to get teenagers to wear sunscreen.
(d) How to prevent premature wrinkles in teens.

해석 최근의 연구에 따르면 아이들이 나이가 듦에 따라 자외선 차단제를 덜 사용한다. 그러나 단지 피부암에 걸릴 가능성에 대해 이야기를 하는 것만으로는 십대들이 자외선 차단제를 사용하도록 장려할 수 없을 듯하다. 그래서 보건 관계자들은 다른 접근법들을 사용하여 아이들에게 피부암 예방에 관해 교육을 시키고 있다. 십대들의 자아 이미지 자각에 호소하는 것이 더욱 효과적인 듯하다. 예를 들어 일찍 주름살이 생기는 것을 방지해 줄 수 있다는 것을 강조하는 것이 더 많은 십대들이 기꺼이 자외선 차단제를 바르도록 하는 것으로 보인다.

Q 위 글의 주제로 알맞은 것을 고르시오.
(a) 어떻게 십대들이 안전하게 선탠을 할 수 있는가
(b) 어린 나이에 어떻게 피부암에서 살아남을 것인가
(c) 어떻게 십대들이 자외선 차단제를 바르게 할 것인가

(d) 어떻게 십대들의 조기 주름을 방지할 것인가

해설 글을 읽고 알맞은 주제를 선택하는 문제이다. 전체적인 내용을 정확하게 파악하고 이를 대표할 수 있는 주제 문장을 선택하는 것이기 때문에 내용 정리가 필수적이다. 한 연구에 따르면 아동들이 나이가 들수록 자외선 차단제를 덜 사용하려고 하기 때문에 피부암 발생에 대해 경고하는 것 외에 다른 효과적인 사용 장려 방법을 강구해야 한다(So health officials are taking a different approach to educate kids about skin cancer prevention.). for example은 앞 문장에 대한 구체적인 예시를 제시하는 것이기 때문에 주목해야 한다. 이 글에서는 주름살 방지 책의 하나로 자외선 차단제를 사용할 수 있다는 것을 십대들에게 교육시켜야 한다고 제안하고 있다. 따라서 이 글의 주제는 (c)가 적절하다.

어휘 research 연구, 조사
sunscreen 자외선 차단제
skin cancer 피부암
encourage ~의 용기[기운]을 북돋우다, 장려하다
official 공무원, 관(공)리
prevention 저지, 예방
appeal 애원하다, 간청하다, 호소하다
awareness 알아채고 있음, 자각, 인식
self-image 자기 이미지, 자상, 자아상
premature 조숙한, 시기상조의
wrinkle 주름, 주름살
willing to+V 기꺼이 ~하는

정답 (c)

21

When my own mother comes upon a child with good manners, she enjoys the moment like a rare and special treat. When a young person holds the door for her or remembers to say "please" or "thank you," she thanks the child for his or her good manners, but she always thanks the nearby parent too. My mother says parents today work hard to meet all their children's emotional needs. However, she feels many seem to often forget the basics.

Q What does the writer's mother think about today's parenting?
(a) It hasn't changed enough since her parents raised her.
(b) It tends to make the children too emotionally dependant.
(c) It places too much emphasis on teaching proper manners.
(d) It does not put enough focus on teaching basic social skills.

해석 나의 어머니는 예절 바른 아이를 볼 때 그 순간이 마치 아주 드문 특별한 기쁨이라도 되는 듯 즐기신다. 어린이가 어머니를 위해 문을 잡아 주거나 '해 주시겠어요?' 혹은 '감사합니다'와 같은 말을 잊지 않고 할 때면 어머니는 아이의 공손함에 고맙다고 하지만 항상 그 곁에 있는 부모에게도 감사의 말씀을 하신다. 어머니 말씀에 따르면 오늘 날의 부모들은 자식들의 감정적 요구를 충족시키기 위해 열심히 노력한다. 하지만 많은 부모들이 기본적인 것들을 자주 망각하는 것 같다고 생각하신다.

Q 글쓴이의 어머니가 오늘날 자녀 양육법에 대해 생각하는 바를 고르시오.
(a) 그녀의 부모가 그녀를 기르던 때와 별로 크게 다르지 않다.
(b) 아이들을 너무 감정적으로 의존하도록 만드는 경향이 있다.
(c) 적절한 예절을 가르치는 데 너무 많은 강조를 한다.
(d) 기본적인 사교 기술을 충분히 강조하지 않고 있다.

해설 오늘날 자녀 양육법에 대한 글쓴이의 어머니의 견해를 물어보는 문제이다. 글쓴이의 어머니는 예절 바른 아이를 대할 때면 매우 기뻐하시는데(~ "thank you" or "please," she thanks the child for his or her good manners ~), thank you 혹은 please는 가장 기본적인 사회성을 나타낼 수 있는 표현들이다. 글쓴이의 어머니는 요즘의 부모들이 자녀들에게 기본적인 것들을 가르치지 않는다고 지적하고 있다(However, she feels many seem to often forget the basics.). 따라서 정답은 (d)다.

어휘 come upon 우연히 만나다
manners 예의범절
rare 드문, 진기한, 희한한
treat 대접, 큰 기쁨
nearby 가까운
emotional 감정적인, 감정에 호소하는
basic 기본, 기초
dependant 의존인
place emphasis on ~를 강조하다
social skill 사교 기술

정답 (d)

22

Dear Editor,

As a regular subscriber, I usually enjoy your health magazine very much. But I was sorry to see a negative article about yoga instruction in last month's issue. I'm assuming the author may have had a bad experience. However, all the instructors I've worked with have been knowledgeable and professional. The author is entitled to her opinion, but a more balanced view of the topic is always appreciated by readers like me.

Q What is the purpose of this letter?

(a) To suggest a feature article about yoga instructors.

(b) To request that a fair perspective be presented in the future.

(c) To cancel the subscription and ask for a full refund.

(d) To complain about the lack of instructional yoga articles.

해석 편집자에게,

정기 구독자로서 저는 귀사의 건강 잡지를 매우 즐겨보곤 합니다. 그러나 유감스럽게도 요가 강습에 대한 부정적인 기사를 지난 달 호에서 보았습니다. 추측하건대 글쓴이가 나쁜 경험을 한 것 같습니다. 그러나 제가 함께 일해본 모든 강사들은 박식했고 전문적이었습니다. 글쓴이는 자신의 의견을 표명할 권리가 있지만 저와 같은 독자들은 주제에 관한 좀 더 균형 잡힌 관점을 항상 소중히 여깁니다.

Q 이 편지의 목적으로 알맞은 것을 고르시오.

(a) 요가 강사에 대한 특집 기사를 제안하기 위해서

(b) 차후 공정한 관점이 제시되길 요청하기 위해서

(c) 정기 구독을 취소하고 전액 환불을 받기 위해서

(d) 요가 교육 기사의 부족에 대해 불평하기 위해서

해설 확실하게 답이 아닌 것부터 제외시킨다. (c)는 한 눈에 보아도 틀리다는 것을 쉽게 알 수 있다. 첫 문장에서 I usually enjoy your magazin이라고 했으니까, 구독을 취소하고, 환불을 요구하는 것은 아니다. 또한 이 편지는 전반적으로 불평(complaint letter)하는 서신이지만, 불평하는 내용은 기사의 내용이 좀 더 균형 있게, 공평하게 하자는 것이지, 요가를 가르치는 기사가 부족하다는 내용이 아니므로 (d)도 답이 아니다. 저자가 제안하는 내용은 맨 마지막 문장의 내용으로서 좀 더 공정하고 균형 잡힌 내용의 기사를 실어달라는 (b)가 맞다. A more balanced view가 a fair perspective로 바뀌어서 답으로 제시되었다.

어휘 subscriber 구독자, 신청자, 응모자
issue 발행물, 발행 부수, 발행
negative 부정적인, 반대의
instruction 강의, 교육

instructor 강사
knowledgeable 박식한
professional 전문적인
feature article 특집기사
perspective 관점, 견해
present 제출하다, 제시하다
assume 추측하다
be entitled to ~에 대한 권리가 있다
opinion 의견, 견해, 판단
appreciate 진가를 인정하다, 높이 평가하다, 감사하다

정답 (b)

23

Research shows that constant multitasking forces the brain to work overtime. While we may think we're accomplishing more, the opposite is often true. The brain has different memory systems. When performing two tasks at once, these systems have to compete with one another. This is why many of us suffer from constantly losing things like our keys, or forgetting important dates and information.

Q What does the writer say about multi-tasking?

(a) It can boost one's ability to remember trivial information.

(b) It can lead to harmony between the various memory systems.

(c) It may result in a decrease in one's ability to recall things.

(d) It may cause permanent damage to the brain's memory systems.

해석 연구에 따르면 지속적인 다중 처리는 뇌가 시간 외 근무를 하도록 강요한다. 그래서 우리는 좀 더 많은 일을 해내고 있다고 생각할 수도 있지만 그 반대의 경우가 더 보편적이다.(사실상 더 많은 일을 하는 것이 아닌 경우가 많다.) 뇌는 다른 기억 체계를 가지고 있다. 두 가지 일을 한꺼번에 실행할 때 이 체계들은 서로 경쟁을 할 수 밖에 없다. 이것이 우리 중 많은 사람들이 계속해서 열쇠와 같은 물건들을 잃어버리거나 중요한 날짜나 정보를 잊음으로써 고통을 받는 이유다.

Q 다중 처리에 대해 글쓴이가 말하고 있는 내용을 고르시오.

(a) 사소한 정보들을 기억하는 능력을 강화시켜 줄 수 있다.

(b) 다양한 기억 체계 간의 조화를 가져온다.

(c) 기억 능력에 감소를 초래할 수도 있다.

(d) 뇌의 기억 체계에 영구적인 피해를 끼칠 수도 있다.

해설 작가의 전반적인 태도(attitude)를 이해하면 좀 더 쉽게 답을 고를 수 있다. 지속적인 다중 처리를 할 경우 시간 외 근무를 해야 하고(working overtime), 일반적으로

생각하는 것과는 달리, 실적으로는 일을 더 많이 하는 것이 아니다(the opposite is true)라고 했으니, 기억력을 증강시킨다는 긍정적 내용의 (a)와 다양한 기억 체계의 조화를 갖게 한다는 (b)는 답이 아니다. 여러 가지 기억력이 제대로 작동하지 못하는 예가 나오기는 했지만, 뇌의 기억 체계가 영원히 손상 받는다는 (d)는 주어진 내용보다 너무 크게 확대 해석한 것이므로 답이 아니다. 그러므로 기억력 감퇴를 초래한다는 (c)가 가장 적합한 답이 될 수 있다.

Tips Too big!!! 선택지 중에서 답이 될 수 없는 것 중에 하나가 주어진 내용보다 너무 크게 확대했을 경우 그것은 답이 될 수 없다. 반대로 전체의 내용을 묻는 문제의 경우 Too small의 선택지도 답이 될 수 없다는 것을 기억하자.

어휘 constantly 지속적인
multitasking 다중 처리
force 억지로 시키다, 강요하다
work overtime 초과 근무하다
accomplish 이루다, 성취하다, 완수하다
opposite 반대의 것[일]
perform 이행하다, 실행하다
task 직무, 과제, 과업, 일
at once 동시에, 당장, 즉시
compete 경쟁하다, 겨루다, 맞서다
suffer 괴로워하다, 고생하다
boost 증대시키다
trivial 사소한
result in 초래하다

정답 (c)

24
The national tour of the unforgettable Broadway musical Nowhere But New York is coming to Fairway Hall. This award-winning musical tells the story of two life-long Manhattan neighbors in a uniquely touching way. Performances are November 2 through 4 at Caldwell University's newly renovated Fairway Hall. Tickets go on sale the 15th of October and start at $35.00. There's no other Broadway show quite like Nowhere But New York. Don't miss it!

Q Which of the following is correct according to the advertisement?
(a) The musical can only be seen on Broadway.
(b) The show is about friends in New York City.
(c) Performances are scheduled for a three-day engagement.
(d) Tickets are on sale now.

해석 기억에 남을 브로드웨이 뮤지컬 〈뉴욕이 아니면 어디에도〉의 전국 순회공연이 페어웨이 홀에 옵니다. 수상 경력이 있는 이 작품은 맨하튼의 두 명의 평생 이웃의 이야기를 독특하게 감동적으로 전합니다. 공연은 11월 2일부터 4일까지 콜드웰 대학의 새로 단장된 페어웨이 홀에서 있습니다. 표는 15일부터 판매되며 가격은 35달러부터 시작합니다. 〈뉴욕이 아니면 어디에도〉와 같은 브로드웨이 작품은 없습니다. 놓치지 마세요!

Q 위 광고의 내용과 일치하는 것을 고르시오.
(a) 뮤지컬은 브로드웨이에서만 관람할 수 있다.
(b) 공연은 뉴욕의 친구들에 관한 것이다.
(c) 공연은 삼 일 동안 할 예정이다.
(d) 표는 현재 판매 중이다.

해설 광고문을 읽고 광고에서 전달하고자 하는 내용을 파악하는 문제이다. 브로드웨이 뮤지컬 〈뉴욕이 아니면 어디에도〉의 공연 일정 소개, 티켓 가격, 수상 경력 등에 관한 내용이다. This award-winning musical tells the story of two life-long Manhattan neighbors in a uniquely touching way ~, November 2 through 4 at Caldwell University's newly renovated Fairway Hall ~, on sale the 15th and start at 35 dollars ~ 등의 정보를 통해 (c)가 정답이란 것을 알 수 있다.

어휘 unforgettable 잊을 수 없는
award-winning 상을 수상한
life-long 일생의
performance 공연
uniquely 특이하게
renovate ~을 새롭게 하다, 수선[수리]하다
go on sale 판매하다
miss 놓치다, 빠뜨리다, 피하다
engagement 약속, 예정

정답 (c)

25

When it comes to success, those who are determined may become more successful than those who are talented. New studies from the University of Pennsylvania's Psychology Department show that those who are willing to stick to their plans — regardless of failures — are more likely to experience success in school and at work. The researchers concluded that the ability to suffer through setbacks is most critical to becoming successful.

Q According to the passage which of the following is true regarding failure?

(a) Determined people encounter the least amount of failure.

(b) High achievers typically experience the most failure.

(c) True success has little to do with either talent or failure.

(d) Handling failure positively is necessary for achievement.

해석 성공에 있어서 의지가 강한 사람들이 재능이 있는 사람들보다 더욱 성공하게 될 수도 있다. 펜실베니아 대학 심리학과의 새로운 연구에 따르면, 실패에 상관하지 않고 자신들의 계획을 고수하고자 하는 사람들이 학교와 직장 생활에서 성공할 가능성이 더 많다. 연구자들은 좌절을 견딜 수 있는 능력이 성공하는 데 있어 가장 결정적이라고 결론지었다.

Q 실패에 대해 위 글에서 언급한 내용 중 옳은 것을 고르시오.

(a) 의지가 강한 사람이 가장 적은 실패와 마주친다.

(b) 성공한 사람들은 보통 가장 많은 실패를 경험한다.

(c) 진정한 성공은 재능이나 실패와는 관계가 거의 없다.

(d) 성공을 위해서는 실패를 긍정적으로 다루는 것이 필요하다.

해설 간략히 지문에서 밝혀진 성공에 대한 내용을 요약해보면 다음과 같다. 의지가 강한 사람(determined), 실패를 하더라도 계획한대로 계획을 추진하는 사람(willing to stick to their plans), 좌절을 견딜 수 있는 능력이 있는 사람(suffer through setbacks). 따라서 (d)의 실패를 긍정적으로 받아들이는 것이 성공에 필요하다는 (d)가 정답이다.

어휘 when it comes to ~에 관해서, ~에 관해 말하자면
determined 결심이 굳은
talented 재능이 있는
psychology 심리학
be willing to 기꺼이 ~하다
stick to ~을 고수하다
regardless of ~와 관계없이

conclude 결론짓다
setback 방해, 좌절
critical 중요한, 결정적인
have little to do with ~와 관계가 거의 없다

정답 (d)

26

While trying to test its new security program, FINDER, the web's most popular search engine, accidentally revealed users' private information. Although very few users were affected, the private passwords and login information of twelve people wound up appearing on the company's public website. FINDER quickly addressed the problem, but such mistakes reveal how far away the company is from protecting its users from fraudulent web activity.

Q Which of the following is correct according to the passage?

(a) Twelve people participated in a fraudulent Internet scheme.

(b) The company did not handle a problem in an efficient way.

(c) FINDER's security program is not ready for use.

(d) The problem was not significant because few were affected.

해석 새로운 보안 프로그램을 실험해 보던 중 온라인상에서 가장 인기 있는 검색 엔진인 파인더가 뜻하지 않게 사용자들의 개인 정보를 유출했다. 영향을 받은 사용자들은 거의 없었지만 12명의 개인 패스워드와 접속 정보가 회사의 공공 웹사이트에 공개되었다. 파인더는 재빨리 문제 해결에 착수했지만 이러한 실수들은 회사가 사기성 온라인 활동으로부터 사용자들을 보호하는 것과는 얼마나 거리가 먼가를 보여준다.

Q 위 글의 내용과 일치하는 것을 고르시오.

(a) 열 두 명의 사람들이 인터넷 사기에 참여했다.

(b) 회사는 문제를 효율적인 방식으로 다루지 않았다.

(c) 파인더의 보안 프로그램은 아직 사용할 준비가 되지 않았다.

(d) 영향을 받은 사람이 거의 없어서 문제는 심각하지 않았다.

해설 글의 내용과 일치하는 문장을 선택하는 문제이다. 이런 문제는 전체적으로 글을 대략적으로 읽고 난 후에 제시된 예문을 일대일로 대입하여 확인해보는 것이 좋다. 온라인의 가장 인기 있는 서치 엔진인 파인더가 새 보안 프로그램 실험 중 사용자의 개인 정보를 유출하였고(~ accidentally revealed users' private information ~), 피해를 본 사람은 많지는 않지만(~ very few users were affected ~), 12명의 정보가 유출되었다. 마지막 문장에서는 큰 피해는 없었지만 회사가 개인 사용자들을 보호하는데 얼마나 부족한지를 강조하고 있다. 따라서 마지막 문장에 함축되어 있는 내용은 아직 이 프로그램이 사용될 단계에 있지 않다는 것이다. 따라서 정답은 (c)다.

어휘 security 안전, 보안
search 검색
accidentally 우연히, 뜻하지 않게
reveal 적발하다, 밝히다
private 사적인, 사사로운, 비밀의
password 암호
wind up ~ing 결국 ~로 끝나다
address a problem 문제를 처리하다
fraudulent 사기(행위)의, 부정의
participate in ~에 참여하다
scheme 음모, 계략

정답 (c)

27

The natural rate of unemployment is always influenced by changes in the labor force. For instance, young workers have a tendency to quit jobs and find others several times before settling into one position. This means the unemployment rate will always increase when the number of young workers in the labor force increases. This happened in the 60s and 70s when a huge number of youth became old enough to enter the workforce. The result pushed the unemployment rate up from 5% to 7%.

Q Which of the following is correct according to the passage?

(a) Young workers affect the unemployment rate because they cannot find jobs.

(b) The unemployment rate is affected by the make-up of the current population.

(c) Unemployment rates drop when young workers enter the labor force.

(d) Several influences change the composition of the work force.

해석 자연적 실업률이 항상 영향을 받는 것은 노동력의 변동에 의해서이다. 예를 들어 젊은 노동자들은 한 일자리에 정착하기 전에 여러 번 일을 그만두고 새 일자리를 찾는 경향이 있다. 이것이 의미하는 바는 노동 인구 중 젊은이들의 수가 증가할 때 실업률이 항상 증가한다는 것이다. 이런 현상은 60년대와 70년대에 발생했었는데, 이 시기에는 엄청난 수의 젊은이들이 노동 인구에 포함될 나이가 되었던 때이다. 그 결과는 실업률을 5%에서 7%로 끌어 올렸다.

Q 위 글의 내용과 일치하는 것을 고르시오.

(a) 젊은 노동자들이 직장을 구하지 못해서 실업률에 영향을 끼친다.

(b) 실업률은 현재의 인구 구성에 의해 영향을 받는다.

(c) 젊은이들이 노동 인구에 포함되면 실업률은 떨어진다.

(d) 몇 가지 영향이 노동력의 구성을 변화시킨다.

해설 자연적 실업률과 노동력 변동과의 관련성에 관한 글이다. 글의 첫 부분에서 문장 전체의 주제를 전달하고 있다. 'The natural rate of unemployment is always influenced by changes in the labor force.'에서 실업률이 항상 노동력의 변화의 영향을 받는다는 것을 알 수 있다. 'This means the unemployment rate will always increase when the number of young workers in the labor force increases.'에서 다시 한 번 설명해주고 있다. 따라서 글의 내용과 일치하는 정답은 (b)다.

어휘 unemployment 실업
labor force 노동력
for instance 예를 들어
have a tendency to+V ~하는 경향이 있다
quit 그만두다, 중지하다
workforce 전 종업원, 노동력, 노동 인구
make-up 구성

정답 (b)

28

Spider plants, named for their round shapes and long wiry stems and leaves, are popular houseplants. If watered regularly, these hearty, disease-resistant plants are hard to harm and often grow to be 5 meters wide and 6 meters long. Spider plants create long shoots that produce smaller spider plants at the ends. These smaller plants hang down below the original large plant thus inspiring a different name for the plant in Guatemala. The spider plant is known as "bad mother" in Guatemala because the mother plant appears to be throwing her babies out of their home, which in this case is the pot.

Q Which of the following is true according to the passage?

(a) Common houseplants are most often disease-resistant.

(b) The spider plant is commonly named for its shape.

(c) The spider plant is one of the largest known houseplants.

(d) Guatemalan people do not keep these plants at home.

해석 둥근 모양과 기다랗고 질긴 줄기와 잎으로 인해 그 이름이 붙은 거미 식물은 인기 있는 가정용 화초이다. 정기적으로 물을 줄 경우 이 강인하고 질병에 잘 견디는 식물들은 피해가 없이 종종 너비가 5미터 길이가 6미터까지 자란다. 거미 식물은 기다란 가지 끝에 작은 거미 식물들을 만들어 내는 싹을 만든다. 이 작은 식물들은 원래의 큰 식물 아래 달려 있는데 이로 인해 과테말라에서 이 식물은 다른 이름을 가지고 있다. 거미 식물은 과테말라에서 '나쁜 엄마'라는 이름으로 알려져 있는데 모체 식물이 집, 즉 화분으로부터 아기들을 던지는 것처럼 보이기 때문이다.

Q 위 글의 내용에 따르면 사실인 것을 고르시오.
(a) 일반적인 가정용 화초들은 종종 질병에 잘 견딘다.
(b) 거미 식물은 보통 그 모양에서 그 이름을 얻었다.
(c) 거미 식물은 가장 큰 가정용 화초들 중 하나이다.
(d) 과테말라 사람들은 이 식물들을 집에서 기르지 않는다.

해설 식물에 관련된 글을 읽고 본문의 내용에 따라 사실인 것을 선택하는 문제이다. 첫 문장, 'Spider plants, named for their round shapes and long wiry stems and leaves, are popular houseplants.'에서 거미 식물이 둥근 모양과 기다랗고 질긴 줄기와 잎의 모양 때문에 그런 이름으로 불리운다는 것을 알 수 있다. 따라서 이 문장에서 정답 (b)를 찾아낼 수 있다. 다른 문장들은 본문의 내용과 일치하지 않는다.

어휘 wiry 억센, 철사 모양의
stem (초목의) 줄기, 대
houseplant 실내 화분용 화초
water 물주다
hearty 튼튼한
disease-resistant 질병에 잘 견디는
shoot 새싹
hang down 매달리다, 늘어뜨리다
inspire 고무시키다, 불어넣다
pot 화분
keep 기르다

정답 (b)

"Action Painting" means an artist chooses to forego the traditional paintbrush. Instead, they drip, drop, splash and splatter the paint across the canvas. Jackson Pollock was one of the first to shock the art world with this revolutionary method in the 1950s. He believed that paint wasn't passive, but actually full of energy, and that it only needed him to release its energy.

Q Which of the following is correct about "Action Painting"?
(a) This conventional method was popular in the 1950s.
(b) Pollock felt all paint needed to be controlled in this way.
(c) This technique was introduced to the world by Pollock.
(d) Artists use paintbrushes to drip and splatter paint.

해석 액션 페인팅은 예술가가 전통적인 붓 기법을 버린다는 것을 의미한다. (전통적인 기법) 대신에 캔버스에 물감을 흘리고 떨어뜨리고 튀긴다. 잭슨 폴락은 처음 이런 것을 시도한 예술가 중 한 사람으로서 1950년대 이 혁명적인 기법으로 미술계를 놀라게 했다. 그가 믿었던 것은 물감은 수동적이지 않고 에너지로 가득 차 있으며, 물감은 그 에너지를 분출하기 위해 그가 필요했을 뿐이었다.

Q 액션 페인팅에 관한 내용과 일치하는 것을 고르시오.
(a) 이 전통적인 기법은 1950년대에 인기가 있었다.
(b) 폴락은 모든 물감이 이런 식으로 통제되어야 한다고 생각했다.
(c) 이 기술은 폴락에 의해 세상에 소개되었다.
(d) 예술가들은 붓을 이용하여 물감을 떨어뜨리고 튀게 한다.

해설 이 기법이 1950년대 사람들을 놀라게 했다는 내용이 있었으니 50년대에는 선구자적이고, 소개하는 단계였을 거라고 추측할 수 있으므로, 대중적이고 인기가 있었다(popular)는 (a)는 답이 아니다. Pollock이 주장한 바로는 물감이 에너지로 가득 찬 존재이지 수동적이지 않다(not passive)고 했으니 be controlled는 적합하지 않다. 따라서 (b)는 틀렸다. Pollock은 이 분야의 선구자들 중에 한 사람(one of the first)이고 그가 세상을 놀라게 했다고 했으니 (c)가 맞다.

어휘 forego ~없이 지내다, 버리다
traditional 전통의, 전설의
paintbrush 화필, 그림 붓
drip 똑똑 떨어뜨리다
splash 튀기다, 더럽히다, 튀다
splatter 튀기다, 튀겨서 더럽히다
revolutionary 혁명의, 혁명적인

passive 수동적인, 소극적인
release 놓아주다, 방출하다
conventional 전통적인

정답 (c)

30

In the early 1500s, the Portuguese became the first Europeans to create an overseas empire, but their impressive control of trade routes to Asia and Africa was only temporary. Portugal simply did not have enough well-trained sailors to run their trading empire. The high death rate on ships created a constant need for new sailors, but not enough experienced sailors could be found to fill these positions. Therefore, the ships operated by crews of poorly trained sailors were quite often lost at sea.

Q Which of the following is correct about the Portuguese trading empire?

(a) Asia and Africa took control of it in the early 1500s.

(b) It was successful until a shortage of qualified sailors occurred.

(c) Well-trained sailors were often not adequate enough to handle the ships.

(d) Experienced sailors could not protect the Portuguese ships from attack.

해석 1500년 초기에 포르투갈 인들은 해외 제국을 건설한 최초의 유럽인들이 되었지만 그들의 아시아와 아프리카로 향하는 무역 항로의 인상적인 장악은 단지 일시적이었다. 포르투갈은 그들의 무역 제국을 경영할 만큼 충분히 잘 훈련된 선원들이 없었다. 선상에서의 높은 사망률은 끊임없이 새로운 선원들을 필요로 했지만 이 빈 자리들을 채울 경험 있는 선원들은 충분하지 않았다. 그래서 선박들은 제대로 훈련 받지 못한 선원들에 의해 운행되었고 종종 바다에서 길을 잃곤 했다.

Q 포르투갈 무역 제국에 관한 사실로 알맞은 것을 고르시오.

(a) 아시아와 아프리카는 1500년대 초기에 제국을 지배했다.

(b) 자격을 갖춘 선원들의 부족이 발생하기 전까지는 성공적이었다.

(c) 제대로 훈련 받은 선원들은 종종 선박을 다룰 적임자들이 아니었다.

(d) 경험 있는 선원들은 포르투갈 선박들을 공격으로부터 보호할 수 없었다.

해설 포르투갈 무역 제국에 관한 역사적 사실에 관한 문제이다. 문장을 읽고 사실 여부를 파악하는 문제는 전체 글을 읽은 후에 제시된 문장과 일대일로 비교 분석하는 것

이 가장 기본적인 방법이다. 1500년대 초에 포르투갈이 해외 제국을 건설했지만 이를 경영할 정도의 훈련된 선원이 없었고(Portugal simply did not have enough well-trained sailors to run their trading empire.), 보충할만한 충분한 선원도 없었던(but not enough experienced sailors could be found to fill these positions.) 문제가 있었다. 따라서 (a), (c), 그리고 (d)는 모두 본문의 내용과 어긋나며 (b)는 글을 읽고 충분히 유추할 수 있는 내용이다. 따라서 정답은 (b)다.

어휘 Portuguese 포르투갈 사람, 포르투갈 말
overseas empire 해외 제국
impressive 강한 인상을 주는 감동적인, 장엄한
temporary 일시적인, 잠시의, 임시의, 당장의
run 경영하다, 관리하다
constant 지속적인
fill 채우다
operate 움직이다, 작동하다
crew 승무원
take control of ~을 지배하다
shortage 부족
qualified 자격을 갖춘
adequate 알맞은

정답 (b)

31

An aging population and a declining birth rate are forcing Japanese toy makers to make changes. In this shrinking market, toy companies are now looking to sell toys to young adult males. One large toy manufacturer is hoping this target group of young men will find its 165 mm walking, dancing robot, the I-BOT, appealing enough to take home for the price of $260.

Q Which of the following is correct about Japanese toy makers?

(a) They are starting to invent toys for older men and women.

(b) They are experiencing decreased sales due to a smaller market.

(c) They are making changes to create better toys for children.

(d) They are focusing on more technologically-advanced toys.

해석 노화되는 인구와 감소하는 출생률은 일본 장난감 생산자들이 변화를 꾀하도록 강요하고 있다. 이 축소되고 있는 시장에서 장난감 회사들은 현재 젊은 성인 남자들에게 장난감을 판매하고자 한다. 한 대형 장난감 제조업체가 희망하고 있는 것은 이 젊은 남성 목표 집단이 그들이 만든 165밀리미터의 걷고 춤추는 로봇, I-BOT을 매우 좋아하게 되어 260달러를 기꺼이 지불하고 구매하는 것이다.

Q 일본 장난감 제조업체에 대한 내용으로 옳은 것을 고르시오.
(a) 나이가 든 남성들과 여성들을 위한 장난감들을 발명하고 있다.
(b) 줄어든 시장 때문에 판매 감소를 경험하고 있다.
(c) 어린이들을 위해 더 나은 장난감을 만들기 위해 변화하고 있다.
(d) 기술적으로 더 진보된 장난감들을 만드는데 집중하고 있다.

해설 인구의 노령화와 출생률 감소에 따라 장난감 제조업체들의 판매 전략 변경을 다룬 글이다. 일본 장난감 제조업자들에 관한 사항을 묻는 것이기 때문에 글을 읽기 전에 우선 문제의 핵심을 마음에 담고 이에 초점을 두고 글을 읽는 것이 좋은 전략이 될 수 있다. 'An aging population and a declining birth rate are forcing Japanese toy makers to make changes.'라는 주제 문장을 통해서 장난감 생산자들이 겪을 문제를 예상할 수 있으며, 바로 이어지는 문장에서 shrinking이란 표현을 통해 판매가 줄고 있음을 알 수 있다. 또한 이 문장에서는 이러한 문제점을 극복하기 위해서 젊은 성인 남성을 겨냥한 장난감 출시를 하고 있다는 예를 들고있다. 따라서 정답은 (b)다.

어휘 age 노화하다, 늙다
force 강요하다
decline 감소하다, 하락하다
birth rate 출생률
shrink 줄어들다
look to+V ~하기를 기대하다
manufacturer 제조업자, 제작자
target 과녁, 목표
appeal 애원하다, 간청하다, 호소하다
focus on ~에 집중하다

정답 (b)

Had it not been for the death of his teacher Socrates, Plato may have never established his own school of philosophy and science. Plato was interested in pursuing a political career until his teacher was killed by hemlock poisoning in 399 BC. Deeply affected by Socrates' death, Plato left his political plans behind in Athens. For the next several years, he traveled throughout Egypt and Italy furthering his education in math and science.

Q Which of the following is correct about Plato?
(a) He was Socrates' most well-educated student.
(b) He visited Egypt and Italy to further his political plans.
(c) He was killed by poisoning in 399 BC.
(d) He founded his own school after his teacher's death.

해석 그의 스승 소크라테스의 죽음이 아니었더라면 플라톤은 자신의 철학 과학 학파를 설립하지 않았을는지도 모른다. 플라톤은 정계에 진출하는 데 관심이 있었는데 그의 스승이 기원전 399년 헴록 독을 마시고 죽을 때까지는 그러했다. 소크라테스의 죽음에 깊이 영향을 받아 플라톤은 그의 정치적 계획들은 아테네에 남겨둔 채 떠났다. 그 후 몇 년 동안 그는 이집트와 이태리 곳곳을 여행하면서 수학과 과학에 대한 지식을 넓혔다.

Q 플라톤에 관한 내용으로 알맞은 것을 고르시오.
(a) 소크라테스의 가장 잘 교육된 제자였다.
(b) 정치적 계획을 추진하기 위해 이집트와 이태리를 방문했다.
(c) 기원전 399년에 독을 마시고 죽었다.
(d) 스승의 죽음 후에 자신의 학파를 설립했다.

해설 플라톤이 철학 과학 학파를 설립하게 된 배경을 말하는 글이다. 이 글에 따라 플라톤에 관한 정보를 정리해보면, 스승 소크라테스의 죽음 후에 철학 과학 학파를 설립했다. 첫 번째 문장은 내용 전달을 강하게 하기 위한 장치로 조건절의 if가 생략되면서 주어 동사가 생략되어, 'Had it not been for the death of his teacher Socrates, Plato may have never ~'라는 문장형식을 갖게 된 것이다. 스승의 죽음 후에 정치적 활동을 중단하고 아테네를 떠나 여행하면서 수학과 과학에 대한 지식을 쌓게 되었다(~ Italy furthering his education in math and sciences ~). 따라서 플라톤에 관한 알맞은 내용은 (d)다.

어휘 death 죽음, 사망
establish 설립하다, 개설하다
school 학파
philosophy 철학, 형이상학
pursue 추구하다

hemlock 미나리과의 독초, 그것에서 뽑은 독약
affect ~에 영향을 미치다
throughout 도처에, 온통, 두루
further 촉진시키다, 증진시키다
found 설립하다

정답 (d)

33

Now that summer will soon be here, The National Association for Safe Boating would like to remind all boat owners to practice responsible boating by taking the proper measures to protect yourself and your passengers. Always insist all passengers, children and adults alike, to wear life jackets. Remember that you or any other driver of the boat should always use the seat belt, and make sure you and any other person you allow to drive your boat have successfully passed a certified safe boating course.

Q Which of the following is correct according to the announcement?

(a) Every passenger regardless of age should be made to wear life vests.

(b) Children should never be permitted to drive a boat.

(c) All passengers must successfully pass a special safe boating course.

(d) All passengers should use the safety belts on the boat.

해석 여름이 곧 다가오고 있으므로 전국 안전 보트 운행 연합에서는 보트를 소유하신 모든 분들이 적절한 조치를 취함으로써 책임감 있게 보트를 운행할 것을 상기시켜 드리고자 합니다. 이렇게 하는 것의 목적은 여러분과 승객들을 보호하기 위함입니다. 항상 모든 승객들, 어린이와 성인 모두 구명조끼를 착용하도록 하십시오. 여러분이나 보트를 운전하는 사람은 항상 안전벨트를 매야 합니다. 여러분과 여러분의 보트를 운전하도록 허락 받은 사람은 모두 공인된 안전 보트운행 코스를 성공적으로 통과한 사람이어야 한다는 것을 명심하십시오.

Q 위 공고문의 내용과 일치하는 것을 고르시오.

(a) 모든 승객에게 나이에 상관없이 구명조끼를 입혀야 한다.

(b) 어린이들은 절대 보트를 운전하도록 허락되어서는 안 된다.

(c) 모든 승객들은 특수 안전 보트 운행 코스를 통과해야만 한다.

(d) 모든 승객들은 보트 위에서 안전벨트를 매야 한다.

해설 전국 안전 보트 운행 연합에서 보트 소유자들에게 전달하는 공고문을 읽고 일치하는 내용을 선택하는 문제이다.

보트 소유자에게 모든 승객을 보호하기 위한 조치를 취하고 책임감 있게 보트를 운행할 것을 상기시키는 글이다(~ all boat owners to practice responsible boating by taking the proper measures to protect yourself and your passengers ~). 안전 관리를 위한 첫 번째 안으로 always를 사용하여 항상 구명조끼를 착용하도록 권하고, remember라는 명령형을 사용하여 안전벨트를 착용할 것을 강조하고 있다. 또한 운전자가 될 수 있는 조건에 대해서도 언급하고 있다. 따라서 공고문과 일치하는 정답은 (a)다.

어휘 now that ~이니까
remind 생각나게 하다, 상기시키다
responsible 책임이 있는, 신뢰할 수 있는
proper 적당한, 예의 바른, 고유의
take measures 조치를 취하다
life jacket[vest] 구명조끼
insist 강요하다, 주장하다
seat belt 안전벨트
successfully 성공적으로, 운 좋게
certified 보증된, 증명된
regardless of ~와 관계없이

정답 (a)

34

Youth learn about their culture through socialization. Family, friends and the media are all important agents of socialization. Without these influences, children would have no way of understanding their culture and its expectations. Interestingly, children are often responsible for socializing their parents as well. This process is called reverse socialization, and it occurs when the children become the socializers, teaching their parents about the latest cultural trends in music, fashion and technology.

Q Which of the following is correct according to the passage?

(a) Reverse socialization occurs when parents start new trends.

(b) Roles can be switched in that children socialize their parents.

(c) Family, friends and media affect how parents socialize kids.

(d) All expectations become reversed in the parent/child relationship.

해석 어린이들이 자신들의 문화에 대해 배우는 것은 사회화를 통해서이다. 가족, 친구들, 대중 매체는 사회화에 있어 모두 중요한 매개체이다. 이러한 것들의 영향력이 없다면 어린이들은 자신들의 문화와 기대되는 것들을 절대로 이해하지 못할 것이다. 흥미롭게도 어린이들이 종종 그들의 부모를 또한 사회화시킬 책임이 있다. 이 과정은 역 사회화라고 불리며 이 역사회화는 어린이들이 사회화를 시키는 사람이 될 때이다, 즉 부모들에게 음악, 패션, 기술에서의 최근 문화적 경향에 대해 가르칠 때 발생한다.

Q 위 글의 내용과 일치하는 것을 고르시오.
(a) 역 사회화는 부모가 새로운 유행을 시작할 때 발생한다.
(b) 어린이들이 부모를 사회화 시킨다는 점에서 역할은 바뀔 수도 있다.
(c) 가족, 친구들과 미디어는 부모가 아이들을 사회화 시키는 방법에 영향을 끼친다.
(d) 모든 기대들은 부모 자식 간의 관계에서 정반대가 된다.

해설 아동이 사회화를 통해 문화를 배워가는 과정과 또한 성인이 아동을 통해 사회화될 수 있는 역 사회화 현상에 관한 글이다. 'Without these influences, children would have no way of understanding their culture and its expectations.'에서 without은 if not과 동일한 장치이다. 즉 '~이 없었다면'의 의미를 전달한다. 앞 문장에서 가족, 친구 그리고 미디어가 사회화의 중요한 요인임을 강조하고 이들의 영향 없이는 아동이 사회화되기 힘들다는 것을 강조하고 있다. 또한 interestingly라는 문맥 전환 장치를 통해 아동이 성인의 역 사회화의 주체임을 전달하고 있다. 따라서 이 글과 일치하는 것은 (b)다.

어휘 socialization 사회화
agent (변화의) 요인, 힘
expectation 기대, 예상
interestingly 흥미롭게도, 재미있게도
responsible for ~에 책임이 있는
as well 또한
reverse 거꾸로의, 반대의
occur 일어나다, 생기다, 발생하다
latest 최신의, 최근의
switch 바꾸다, 교환하다
in that ~라는 점에서

정답 (b)

35

Bamboo is a giant grass that grows naturally in warm regions. Some bamboo can reach heights of up to 37 meters high, while the hollow, wood-like stem can grow to 30 cm in diameter. Botanists consider bamboo the most primitive of all grasses. This prolific plant spreads quickly, but hardly ever blossoms; however some plants do blossom, but only once every 30 years. If a bamboo plant does bloom, then all the bamboo plants in the nearby area will subsequently bloom. But after a bamboo blossoms, it typically dies.

Q What can be inferred from the passage?
(a) Bamboo has a complex structure.
(b) A primitive make-up would keep bamboo plants from dying.
(c) If one bamboo plant blossoms, all others around it will die.
(d) It takes many years for bamboo to spread.

해석 대나무는 거대한 풀의 일종으로 따뜻한 지역에서 자연적으로 자란다. 어떤 대나무들은 높이가 37미터에 달하고 속이 빈 나무같이 생긴 줄기는 직경이 30센티미터까지 자랄 수 있다. 식물학자들의 생각으로는 대나무는 가장 원시적인 형태의 풀이다. 이 번식력이 강한 식물은 매우 빠르게 퍼지지만 꽃이 피는 경우는 드물다. 그러나 일부 대나무는 꽃이 피기도 하지만 30년마다 한 번뿐이다. 만일 한 대나무에 꽃이 피면 주변 지역에 있는 모든 대나무들에도 뒤를 이어 꽃이 핀다. 하지만 대나무는 꽃이 핀 후에 죽는 것이 일반적이다.

Q 위 글의 내용으로 유추할 수 있는 것을 고르시오.
(a) 대나무는 복잡한 구조를 가지고 있다.
(b) 원시적인 구조가 대나무가 죽는 것을 막아 준다.
(c) 한 대나무에 꽃이 피면 그 주변의 다른 대나무들 모두가 죽게 될 것이다.
(d) 대나무가 퍼지는 데는 여러 해가 걸린다.

해설 추론을 할 때는 대개 일반적으로 지문을 모두 읽고, 그 지문에서 주장하거나 전달하려는 내용을 먼저 잘 이해를 해야 정답을 고를 수 있다. 본문을 요약(summarize)해보면 다음과 같다. 대나무는 크게 자랄 수 있다. 대나무는 가장 오래된 풀이다. 번식력이 강하지만 꽃이 피는 경우는 드물다. 한 그루가 꽃이 피면 주변 대나무들도 꽃을 피운다. 꽃이 피면, 대나무는 죽는다. 따라서 한그루가 꽃이 피면, 다른 것들도 죽는다.

Tips 글을 읽고 내용을 유추하는 문제이다. 대나무의 특성에 관한 정보를 주는 글이다. 대나무의 높이와 줄기 크기를 알려주고(Some bamboo can reach heights up to 37 meters high, while the hollow, wood-like stem can grow to 30 cm in diameter.), 대나무의 번식과 관련된 정보를 제공한다. 'This prolific plant spreads quickly, but hardly ever blossoms; however some plants do blossom, but only once every 30 years.' 문장에서, 대나무가 꽃이 피는 경우가 거의 드물지만 가끔 30년에 한번 정도 피는 경우도 있음을 알 수 있다. 그러나 but에 주목하라! 한 대나무에서 꽃이 피고 나면 주변의 다른 모든 대나무에서 꽃이 피는데 일반적으로 꽃이 피고 나면 죽게 된다는 것이다. 따라서 유추할 수 있는 내용은 (c)다.

어휘 bamboo 대(나무)
height 높이, 고도, 신장
hollow 속이 빈, 오목한, 공허한
stem 줄기, 대, 잎자루
diameter 지름, 직경
botanist 식물학자
primitive 원시의, 원시적인
prolific 아이를 많이 낳는, 번식력이 강한
hardly 거의 ~않다, 조금도 ~않다
blossom 꽃 피다, 개화하다
bloom 꽃이 피다
subsequently 그 후에, 다음에
typically 전형적으로, 일반적으로
complex 복잡한
make-up 구성, 구조

정답 (c)

36

Very few sources can correctly explain why the sky is blue. Sources that can adequately answer this question do so by addressing in detail three important things: what sunlight is, how it travels to Earth, and how the human eye works as well. The only way to understand why the sky is blue is to clearly understand these three factors. However, usually only college textbooks about astronomy, physics or optics teach these three components accurately.

Q What can be inferred from the passage?
(a) The right websites can offer adequate explanations.
(b) High schools use college-level textbooks for science classes.
(c) Very few people understand why the sky is the color it is.
(d) The human eye is capable of seeing many colors in sunlight.

해석 왜 하늘이 파란지를 정확하게 설명할 수 있는 자료는 거의 없다. 이 질문에 적절하게 답할 수 있는 자료들은 세 가지 중요한 사실들을 자세히 설명하고 있는데 그것들은

햇빛이란 무엇인가, 어떻게 지구까지 햇빛이 이동하는가와 어떻게 인간의 눈이 작동하는가이다. 하늘이 왜 파란가를 이해하는 유일한 방법은 이 세 가지 요인들을 정확하게 이해하는 것이다. 그러나 일반적으로 천문학, 물리학 혹은 광학에 관한 대학 교과서들만이 이러한 세 가지 구성 요소들을 정확하게 지도하고 있다.

Q 위 글의 내용으로부터 유추할 수 있는 것을 고르시오.
(a) 올바른 웹사이트들은 적절한 설명을 제공할 수 있다.
(b) 고등학교들은 과학 수업에 대학 수준의 교과서들을 사용한다.
(c) 하늘이 왜 하늘색인지를 아는 사람은 거의 없다.
(d) 인간의 눈은 햇빛에서 많은 색깔들을 볼 수 있다.

해설 특히 추론문제에서는 주제문이 두괄식일 경우가 많다. 본 지문도 첫 문장이 주제문이라 할 수 있다. 하늘의 색이 왜 파란색인지 원인을 정확하게 설명하는 것이 힘들다는 내용이 전반적이 내용이라 할 수 있다. 특히 유의해야 할 부분은 the only ~부분과 however ~부분이다. 하늘색을 이해하는 유일한 방법이 하나 있기는 하지만, 그러나 그 방법은 너무나 전문적인 지식을 요하는 것이라고 함으로서, 대부분의 사람들이 이해하기 힘들다는 내용을 다시 한 번 더 뒷받침하고 있다. 따라서 답은 (c)다.

어휘 source 원천, 근원, 출처
adequately 알맞게, 적당하게
address 말하다, 언급하다
in detail 상세히, 세부에 걸쳐
clearly 뚜렷하게, 명료하게, 명확히
factor 요인, 요소, 원인
astronomy 천문학
physics 물리학
optics 광학
component 구성요소, 성분
accurately 정확히, 정밀하게
capable of ~할 수 있는

정답 (c)

37

The best managers are often the best communicators. Experts estimate that managers may spend as much as 85% of their time communicating. In meetings, on the phone, through email, or by having person-to-person interactions, managers spend the majority of their time talking. This is why the most effective managers are often lifelong students of the art of effective communication. And truly great managers pass on this knowledge to their staff as well.

Q What does the writer suggest?

(a) Successful managers know how to communicate clearly.

(b) Reading communication books isn't enough to be a good manager.

(c) Very few workers or managers are effective communicators.

(d) Eighty-five percent of all managers need better communication skills.

해석 최고의 경영자들은 의사소통에 뛰어난 사람들인 경우가 많다. 전문가들은 추측하건대 경영자들은 자신의 시간의 85%를 다른 사람들과 의사소통을 하면서 보낸다고 한다. 회의에서, 전화상으로, 이메일을 통해서 혹은 직접 사람을 만나 접촉함으로써 경영자는 그들 시간의 대부분을 말을 하며 보낸다. 이것이 왜 가장 효율적인 경영자들이 평생을 두고 효과적인 의사소통의 기술을 배우는 지에 대한 이유다. 진정으로 뛰어난 경영자들은 이 지식을 직원들에게도 전달한다.

Q 글쓴이가 암시하고 있는 것을 고르시오.

(a) 성공적인 경영자들은 명확하게 의사소통하는 방식을 알고 있다.

(b) 의사소통에 관한 책을 읽는 것은 좋은 경영자가 되기 위해 충분하지 않다.

(c) 직원들이나 경영자들이 효율적인 의사 전달자인 경우는 거의 없다.

(d) 모든 경영자들의 85%가 더 나은 의사소통 기술을 필요로 한다.

해설 글 전체에서 강조하는 것은 최고 경영자들과 의소 소통 기능의 관계 및 중요성에 대한 것이다. (a) successful manager는 the best managers를 know how to clearly communicate는 the best communicators를 달리 표현한 것이기 때문에 글의 요지를 대표하는 내용으로 (a)가 정답이다. (b) 추측을 할 때도 본문에 주어진 내용을 기반으로만 해야 한다. 비약은 금물이다. 독서에 대한 언급은 따로 없었으므로 답이 될 수 없다. (c) 본문에 사용된 어휘인 managers, effective, communicators 등을 사용하여 오답을 만든 예이다. (d) 역시 본문에 사용된 표현 85%, managers, better(best와 유사), communication 등이 본문과 상

당히 연관성이 있는 선택지를 보이게 하지만 본문과 내용과는 거리가 멀기 때문에 오답이다.

Tips 글이 암시하는 내용을 선택하는 문제이다. 글의 첫 부분에서 'The best managers are often the best communicators.'라고 말하여 최고 경영자들이 의사소통에 뛰어난 사람임을 강조하고 있다. 'In meetings, on the phone, through email, or by having person-to-person interactions, ~'에서 그들이 회의, 전화, 이메일 혹은 직접 사람을 만나서 대화를 하는 사례를 설명한다. 따라서 이 글에서 암시하는 내용은 최고 경영자들이 효과적으로 의사소통하는 방법을 알고 있다는 것이다.

어휘 **manager** 지배인, 경영자, 책임자
communicate 의사소통하다
estimate 추정하다
interaction 상호 작용, 상호의 영향
majority 대부분, 대다수
lifelong 일생의, 필생의
pass on A to B A를 B에게 전달하다
as well 게다가, 더욱이, 더구나

정답 (a)

38

On Saturday, Greenpeace will once again set sail off the coast of New Zealand, officially beginning their next anti-whaling campaign. (a) By confronting whalers out on the open ocean, they hope to save more whales this season than ever before. (b) Other environmental groups also use this method of confrontation to protect endangered species. (c) To protect whales, Greenpeace members place their small inflatable boats in harm's way between the whale at risk and the fishermen. (d) By their own count, 82 whales were saved this way during last year's campaign.

해석 토요일 그린피스는 다시 한 번 뉴질랜드 해안으로부터 항해를 떠남으로써 그들의 다음 고래잡이 반대 캠페인을 공식적으로 시작하게 된다. (a) 공해상에서 고래잡이들에게 맞섬으로써 그들은 이번 시기에 전례 없이 많은 고래들을 구조하고자 한다. (b) 다른 환경 단체들 또한 이 직접 대면 방법을 이용하여 멸종 위기 종들을 보호한다. (c) 고래를 보호하기 위해서 그린피스 회원들은 위험 천만하게도 그들의 작은 고무 구명보트들을 위험에 처한 고래와 고래잡이들 사이에 띄운다. (d) 그들의 계산에 따르면 82마리의 고래가 이러한 방식으로 지난 해 캠페인 기간 동안 구조됐다.

해설 문맥의 흐름에 적절하게 포함되지 않는 문장을 선택하는 문제이다. 이 글은 그린피스가 고래잡이 반대 캠페인을 시작하는 것과 관련된 내용이다. (a) 그린피스가 공해상

에서 고래잡이들과 맞서 싸워서 고래를 구조하겠다, (c) 고래 보호를 위해 그린피스 회원들이 작은 구명보트를 고래잡이 어선 사이에 띄운다, 그리고 (d) 약 82마리의 고래가 이런 방식으로 작년에 구조되었다는 것이다. 따라서 이 세 문장은 모두 그린피스의 고래 구출 작전과 관련이 있는 내용이지만 (b)는 갑자기 다른 환경 보호 단체들이 멸종 위기 종을 보호한다는 의미이므로 전체적인 맥락에 어울리지 않는다. 따라서 이것이 답이다.

어휘 officially 공식으로, 공무상
anti 반대의, 반대하는
campaign 운동, 캠페인
confront 직면하다, 맞서다, 대면시키다
whaler 포경선
environmental 환경의, 주위의
confrontation 대면, 직면, 대결
endangered 위험에 처한, 멸종될 위기에 이른
protect 보호하다, 막다, 지키다
inflatable boat (공기를 넣어 부풀리는) 고무보트

정답 (b)

39

English has long been a continually-evolving language. (a) Of course, this is still true today. (b) With increasing global communication, hundreds of new words appear in the English language every year. Some of these words are borrowed from other languages like Spanish, German, French, or Arabic. (c) Additionally, new science and technology terms also contribute heavily to the always expanding English vocabulary. (d) The Internet has affected language communication in lasting ways.

해석 영어는 오랫동안 지속적으로 진화해 온 언어다. (a) 물론 이것은 (계속 진화하는 언어라는 것은) 오늘날에도 사실이다. (b) 증가하는 국제 교류와 함께 매년 수 백 개의 새로운 영어 단어들이 생겨난다. 이 단어들 중의 일부는 스페인어, 독일어, 불어, 아랍어와 같은 다른 언어들에서 온 것이다. (c) 더구나 새로운 과학과 기술 용어들 또한 항상 증가하고 있는 영어 어휘에 크게 기여한다. (d) 인터넷은 지속적인 방식으로 언어 교류에 영향을 끼쳐 왔다.

해설 영어가 계속적으로 진화하고 있는(a continually-evolving language) 언어라는 것과 관련된 글이다. (a)는 현재도 영어가 진화하고 있고, (b)는 국제 교류가 증가하면서 새로운 영어 어휘가 생긴다, (c)는 새로운 과학과 기술 용어가 증가하면서 영어 어휘도 증가한다는 내용으로 모두 이 글의 주제와 관련이 된다. 그러나 (d)는 인터넷 사용이 언어 교류에 영향을 주었다는 것으로 이 글의 전체적인 문맥의 흐름과는 연결되지 않는다. 따라서 이것이 답이다.

어휘 continually 계속해서, 계속적으로, 줄곧

evolve 서서히 발전하다, 진화하다
global 세계적인, 지구 전체의, 전체적인
appear 나타나다, 출현하다
additionally 추가적으로
term 용어
contribute 기부하다, 기여하다
expand 넓히다, 확장하다
affect ~에 영향을 미치다

정답 (d)

40

A strange study in the Southern US has looked at why some church members handle venomous snakes in their religious ceremonies. (a) For twenty minutes out of each four-hour church service, members pick up, throw down and dance with the snake. (b) During the study, twelve members in the church received bites and were hospitalized. (c) This ceremony is meant to prove that snake handlers are truly holy. (d) The handlers believe that risking their lives for their beliefs makes them deserving of a saintly status.

해석 미국 남부 지역에서 이상한 연구가 진행되었는데, 이 연구에서 살펴본 것은 왜 소수 교회 신도들이 독사 다루기를 그들의 종교의식에 포함시켰는지에 관한 것이다. (a) 매 4시간 예배 중 20분 동안 신도들은 이 치명적인 독사들을 집어 들고 내던지고 함께 춤을 춘다. (b) 연구 기간 동안 12명의 신도들이 뱀에 물려 병원 신세를 졌다. (c) 이 의식에서 입증하려고 하는 것은 뱀을 다루는 사람은 진정으로 신앙심이 깊은 사람들이라는 것이다. (d) 뱀을 만지는 사람들이 믿고 있는 것은 믿음을 위해 목숨을 거는 것이 자신들에게 성인과 같은 지위를 얻을 자격을 준다는 것이다.

해설 글의 흐름을 이해하는 것이 매우 중요하다. 본 지문의 첫 문장에서는 종교의식 중에 뱀을 다루는 사람들이 있는데 그 이유를 알아보려고 연구가 있었고, (a)는 어떻게 예배 중에 뱀을 다루는지 설명을 하고, (c)는 왜 뱀을 다루는지에 대한 이유를 설명하며, (d)는 뱀을 다루는 사람들이 어떤 믿음을 갖고 그런 예배 의식에 참가하는지가 설명되어 있으므로 전체적인 흐름이 잘 연결이 된다. 하지만 (b)는 연구 중에 일어난 사실을 언급하고 있으므로 상대적으로 글의 흐름에 꼭 필요한 글이 아니다. 따라서 답은 (b)다.

어휘 look at 조사하다
venomous 독이 있는
religious ceremony 종교의식
service 예배
pick up 집다, 집어 올리다
throw down 내던지다, 넘어뜨리다
bite 물기, 물음
hospitalize 입원시키다, 병원 치료하다
be meant to do ~하기로 되어 있다

holy 신성한, 경건한, 독실한
risk one's life 목숨을 걸다
deserve ~할 만하다, ~할 가치가 있다
saintly 성인다운, 거룩한
status 지위, 신분

정답 (b)

Actual Test 3

1 (a)	**2** (c)	**3** (a)	**4** (a)	**5** (b)
6 (d)	**7** (b)	**8** (c)	**9** (a)	**10** (d)
11 (b)	**12** (c)	**13** (a)	**14** (a)	**15** (b)
16 (a)	**17** (c)	**18** (a)	**19** (d)	**20** (d)
21 (d)	**22** (a)	**23** (c)	**24** (b)	**25** (c)
26 (c)	**27** (a)	**28** (d)	**29** (d)	**30** (d)
31 (b)	**32** (c)	**33** (c)	**34** (d)	**35** (c)
36 (a)	**37** (c)	**38** (d)	**39** (b)	**40** (b)

1

For many years, doctors have been concerned about teens drinking too much soda. But a ten-year study has shown that as teenage females grow older they may be drinking even more soda. During the study, the young women's _____ decreased by 25%, but their soda intake tripled.

(a) intake of healthier drinks
(b) ability to buy other drinks
(c) preference for sugary drinks
(d) consumption of diet soda

해석 수년 동안 의사들이 염려해온 것은 십대들이 너무 많은 탄산음료를 마신다는 점이다. 그러나 십 년간의 한 연구가 보여준 바로는 십대 소녀들은 나이가 들면서 훨씬 더 많은 탄산음료를 마신다. 연구 기간 동안 젊은 여성들의 건강에 좋은 음료 섭취는 25% 줄어들었다. 그러나 그들의 탄산음료 섭취는 3배로 증가했다.

(a) 건강에 좋은 음료 섭취
(b) 다른 음료를 살 수 있는 능력
(c) 단 음료에 대한 선호
(d) 다이어트 탄산음료의 소비

해설 탄산음료 소비 증가와 십대 소녀 및 여성 건강과의 관계를 다룬 글이다. 여러 해 동안, 십대가 탄산음료를 과다 소비한다고 지적해왔는데, 특히 십대 소녀가 나이가 들수록 탄산음료를 더 많이 마신다는 결과가 밝혀졌다(But a ten-year study has shown that as teenage females grow older they may be drinking even more soda.). 문장의 연결 장치인 but에 주목하라. 젊은 여성의 _____가 25% 감소했지만, '그러나' 탄산음료 섭취는 3배로 증가했다는 내용이므로 빈 칸에는 탄산음료와는 반대되는 몸에 좋은 음료가 들어가야 문맥의 연결이 매끄럽다. 따라서 정답은 (a)다.

어휘 be concerned about ~에 대해 걱정[염려]하다
soda 탄산음료
teenage 십대(13~19세까지)
female 여성, (동물의) 암컷
decrease 감소하다, (서서히) 줄다
intake 섭취(량), 흡입(량)
triple 3배가 되다

정답 (a)

2

An African slave named Estevanico was one of the _____ of Mexico and the southwestern United States. Estevanico's Spanish owner liked him. So he brought him along to explore these new territories. But this was not a fun trip. Violent encounters with native residents and horrible conditions killed nearly all the men. Estevanico was only one of four who survived.

(a) native residents
(b) brave soldiers
(c) first explorers
(d) early rulers

해석 에스테바니코라는 이름의 한 아프리카 노예는 멕시코와 미국 남서부를 처음 탐사한 사람들 중 하나였다. 에스테바니코의 스페인인 주인은 그를 좋아했다. 그래서 그는 이 새 영토들을 탐험하는 데 그를 데리고 갔다. 그러나 이것은 재미있는 여행이 아니었다. 원주민들과의 폭력적인 교전들과 끔찍한 상황들로 인해 거의 모든 사람들이 죽었다. 에스테바니코는 살아 남은 4명 중의 한 명이었다.

(a) 원주민들
(b) 용감한 병사들
(c) 처음 탐사한 사람들
(d) 초기 통치자들

해설 아프리카 노예였던 에스테바니코의 생애에 관한 글이다. 글의 후반부를 읽어 보면, 그의 스페인 주인이 그를 좋아해서 새 영토 탐험하는데 그를 데리고 갔다는 것을 알 수 있다. 이 문장에서의 new territories는 앞 문장에서 언급된 멕시코와 미국 남서부 지역을 의미한다. 따라서 explore란 단어를 이용한 (c)가 정답이라는 것을 쉽게 알 수 있다.

어휘 slave 노예
Spanish 스페인 사람, 스페인어
explore 탐험[답사]하다
territory 영토, 토지, 지역
violent 폭력적인, 난폭한, 격렬한
encounter (적과의) 교전, 전투
resident 거주자
horrible 무서운, 끔찍한
survive 살아남다

정답 (c)

3

Most people think bears _____ ___, but actually they don't. Bears like Grizzly and Black bears are not true hibernators. A true hibernating animal experiences a large drop in body temperature and heart rate before falling into a deep sleep for the winter. But a bear's system only slows down a little bit below its normal rate. And bears never go into a deep sleep. Many slow down their activity during the colder months, but others stay active all winter long.

(a) sleep during the winter months
(b) die from natural causes due to old age
(c) prefer to eat vegetation more than meat
(d) have higher body temperatures than other animals

해석 대부분의 사람들은 곰이 겨울 동안에 잠을 잔다고 생각하지만 실제로 그들은 그러지 않는다. 회색 곰과 검은 곰은 진정으로 동면하는 동물들이 아니다. 진짜로 동면하는 동물은 겨울 동안 깊은 잠이 들기 전에 체온이 크게 떨어지고 심장 박동이 늦어진다. 하지만 곰은 보통 수준 이하로 약간 떨어지기만 한다. 그리고 곰은 절대 깊은 잠에 빠지지 않는다. 많은 곰들이 추운 달 동안에는 활동이 적긴 하지만 몇몇 다른 곰들은 겨울 내내 활동적이다.

(a) 겨울 동안에 잠을 잔다
(b) 늙어서 자연사한다
(c) 육류보다 채식을 선호한다
(d) 다른 동물들보다 체온이 더 높다

해설 단락의 첫 문장은 보통 글 전체의 주제를 담고 있다. 그러나 첫 문장에 빈 칸이 있기 때문에 글 전체를 정확하게 읽고 내용을 정리해야 한다. 먼저, but actually they don't에 주목하라. 빈 칸이 들어 있는 문장은 흔히 사람들이 갖고 있는 편견이며 실제로는 곰이 그렇지 않다는 것을 강조하는 것이다. 'A true hibernating animal experiences a large drop in body temperature and heart rate before falling into a deep sleep for the winter.'에서 실제로 곰이 동면하는 동물이 아님을 강조하고 있다. 또한 마지막 문장에서 '~, but others stay active all winter long.'이라고 말함으로써 곰이 겨울 동안 자는 것이 아님을 알 수 있다. 따라서 정답은 (a)다.

어휘 grizzly bear 회색곰
hibernator 동면하는 동물
drop 하락, 감소, 저하
temperature 온도, 기온
heart rate 심장 박동 수
fall into sleep 잠들다
activity 활동, 행동, 움직임

vegetation (한 지방의) 식물, 초목

정답 (a)

4

Dear Mr. Han,
Please accept my sincere thanks for your support with our recent annual fund drive. Your contribution of $500 to our facility will go a long way to help with the never-ending expenses here at our community recreation center. Because of your donation, we can now buy new sports equipment and art supplies as well for our after-school program. Thanks to kind people like you, we once again have the operating budget to _____ _____ for the neighborhood kids we serve.
Thank you for your continued support of our facility.
Sincerely,
Ms. Stacy Schwartz

(a) provide many enjoyable activities
(b) buy food and clothing
(c) purchase books and private tutoring
(d) build a new art museum

recent 최근의, 근래의
annual 연간의, 1년간의
fund drive 모금운동
contribution 기부(금), 기여, 기증(품)
facility 시설, 설비, 기관
go a long way 큰 도움이 되다
expense 비용, 경비
community 지역 사회[공동체]
donation 기증, 기부
equipment 장비, 설비
operate 운영[경영]하다
budget 예산
private tutoring 개인 교습

정답 (a)

해석 한 선생님께,
최근에 있었던 저희의 연간 자금 모금 도움을 주신 것에 대해 진심으로 감사드립니다. 저희 시설에 보내 주신 귀하의 기부금 500달러는 지역 사회 레크리에이션 센터에서 끊임 없이 드는 비용들을 충당하는 데 큰 도움이 될 것입니다. 귀하의 기부금 덕분에 저희는 방과 후 프로그램을 위한 새로운 운동 기구들과 미술 도구들을 구입할 수 있게 되었습니다. 귀하와 같은 친절한 분들 덕택에 저희는 지역의 어린이들에게 많은 즐거운 활동들을 제공할 운영예산을 다시 한 번 마련하였습니다. 저희 시설에 대한 귀하의 지속적인 도움에 감사드립니다.
진심을 담아,
스테이시 슈왈츠

(a) 많은 즐거운 활동들을 제공할
(b) 음식과 의류를 구입할
(c) 도서와 개인 교습비를 지불할
(d) 새로운 미술관을 지을

해설 편지 글을 읽는 경우에는 편지를 보낸 이, 받는 이, 편지의 의도를 기본적으로 파악해야 한다. 이 편지는 연간 자금 모금 운동에 도움을 준 사람에게 감사의 뜻을 표하는 편지이다. 또한 이 기부금의 사용 계획에 주목해야 한다. 네 번째 줄에서 알 수 있듯이 이 기부금을 주로 레크레이션 센터에서 필요로 하는 경비를 충당하는데 사용한다고 한다. 따라서 빈 칸에 들어갈 답은 (a)다.

어휘 sincere 진심의

5

In 1930, 75 percent of all New Yorkers were part of immigrant families. Most of these families had come from Europe to New York by ship traveling in "steerage class." This meant that passengers who could not _____ _____ on board could travel in the lower decks among the steering equipment. The cost of a steerage ticket at this time was fifteen dollars.

(a) pay for safe transportation
(b) afford better accommodations
(c) bring expensive luggage
(d) be hired as workers

해석 1930년 뉴욕 주민의 75%는 이민자 가족이었다. 이 가족들의 대부분은 유럽에서부터 뉴욕으로 배의 '3등 칸'을 타고 도착했다. 이것은 배에서 좀 더 나은 숙박 시설에 비용을 지불할 형편이 안 됐던 승객들이 갑판 아래쪽의 조타실 장비들 사이에서 여행을 했다는 뜻이다. 당시 3등 칸의 요금은 15달러였다.

(a) 안전한 교통수단에 지불할
(b) 좀 더 나은 숙박 시설에 비용을 지불할
(c) 비싼 수화물을 가지고 올
(d) 노동자로서 고용될

해설 유럽에서 미국으로 이민한 이민자에 관한 글이다. 뉴욕 주민의 75%는 이민자 가족이었는데 이들은 '3등 칸'을 타고 도착했다(~ from Europe to New York by ship traveling in "steerage class."). 빈 칸에는 3등 칸의 의미를 설명할 수 있는 표현이 들어가야 한다. 당시 3등 칸을 이용했다는 것은 갑판 아래쪽에 조타실 장비들 사이에서 여행을 했다(~ in the lower decks among the steering equipment ~)는 것이고 경비도 15달러로 저렴하였다. 따라서 이들이 경제적으로 풍요롭지 못했다는 것을 유추할 수 있다. 그러므로 정답은 (b)다.

어휘 immigrant 이민자, 이주민
steerage 3등 칸
passenger 승객, 선객

steering equipment 조정 장비
accommodation 숙박 시설
luggage 수하물, 소형 여행 가방

6

Waves Waterbed Warehouse is having the sale of the century. This weekend only Waves will be offering ridiculous markdowns on all our durable, Sea-Motion mattresses. Come in and experience the sensational support of the king-sized Sea-Motion Midnight model. You'd never dream a waterbed mattress could be so supportive, yet so comfortable. Waves _____ all weekend, so come early or shop late. But don't wait to get a great deal on a brand-new waterbed from Waves.

(a) might run low on inventory
(b) can advertise these prices
(c) will be closing early
(d) will be extending our regular hours

해석 웨이브 물침대 창고에서는 금세기의 전례 없는 세일을 하고 있습니다. 이번 주말에 한하여 웨이브 침대에서는 터무니없이 낮은 가격으로 모든 튼튼한 시모션 매트리스를 제공합니다. 직접 오셔서 킹 사이즈 시모션 미드나잇 모델의 놀라운 탄력을 경험해보세요. 물침대 매트리스가 이렇게 탄탄하면서도 편안할 수 있다고는 상상하지 못하실 겁니다. 웨이브 침대는 주말 내내 영업시간을 연장할 예정이므로 일찍 오시거나 늦게까지 쇼핑을 즐기세요. 하지만 웨이브 침대의 새로운 물침대를 좋은 가격에 장만하기 위해 더 이상 기다리지 마세요.
(a) 재고 수량이 모자랄 수 있으므로
(b) 이 가격들을 광고할 수 있으므로
(c) 일찍 문을 닫을 예정이므로
(d) 영업시간을 연장할 예정이므로

해설 웨이브 물침대 창고에서 하는 세일 광고이다. 광고문을 읽을 때는 광고의 대상, 제품의 특성, 구매하기 위한 연락처 혹은 구매 기간 등에 관한 정보를 파악해야 한다. 본 광고에서 홍보하는 제품은 웨이브 물침대의 시모션 매트리스이다. 이 제품의 특성은 탄탄하면서도 편한 것이다(You'd never dream a waterbed mattress could be so supportive, yet so comfortable.). 빈 칸에 들어갈 내용은 바로 뒤의 "all weekend, so come early or shop late."와 연결되어야 하기 때문에 구매가능 시간 혹은 영업시간과 관련된 정보임을 추측할 수 있다. 따라서 정답은 (d)다.

어휘 warehouse 창고
century 100년, 1세기
offer 제공하다, 권하다
ridiculous 터무니없는, 조롱 받을 만한

markdown 가격 인하(폭)
durable 튼튼한, 내구력이 있는
sensational 선풍적인, 소문이 자자한
comfortable 안정된, 편안한
run low 줄어들다, 적어지다
extend 늘리다, 연장하다

7

The construction is finally complete. The City of Morgantown's brand-new Museum of Natural History opens for business on Monday. To celebrate, the staff is inviting the public to a pre-opening day party from 9 a.m. to 3 p.m. tomorrow. Museum Director, Sonja Pederson says that the event will be a great way for _____. Plus, the public can learn about museum memberships and the traveling exhibits that will be stopping at the museum this year.

(a) museum staff to train volunteers
(b) residents to preview the museum
(c) kids to learn about famous art
(d) the public to protest the opening

해석 공사가 마침내 완공되었습니다. 모건타운 시의 새로운 자연 박물관이 월요일 개장됩니다. 개장을 축하하기 위해 전 직원들이 내일 오전 9시부터 3시까지 있을 개장전 파티에 일반인들을 초대합니다. 박물관장 소냐 피더슨은 이 행사가 주민들이 박물관을 미리 살펴 볼 수 있는 좋은 기회가 될 것이라고 말합니다. 또한 일반인들은 박물관의 회원제와 올해 박물관에서 있을 순회 전시에 대한 정보를 얻을 수 있습니다.
(a) 박물관 직원들이 자원봉사자들을 훈련시킬
(b) 주민들이 박물관을 미리 살펴 볼 수 있는
(c) 아이들이 유명 예술품들에 대해 배울 수 있는
(d) 일반인들이 개장에 항의할 수 있는

해설 모건타운 시의 새로운 자연 박물관 개장에 관한 기사이다. 월요일 개장을 앞두고 오전 9시부터 3시까지 파티에 일반인을 초대한다(To celebrate, the staff is inviting the public to a pre-opening day party from 9 a.m. to 3 p.m. tomorrow.). 이는 _____ 할 수 있는 좋은 기회가 될 것이라는 내용을 선택해야 한다. plus에 주목하라. 일반인이 박물관 회원제와 박물관 순회 전시에 대한 정보를 얻을 수 있다고 하였다. 따라서 빈 칸에는 일반적으로 박물관 파티에서 얻을 수 있는 이점을 생각해보아야 한다. 따라서 정답은 (b)가 가장 적절하다.

어휘 construction 건설, 건축
complete 완성[완료]된, 완전한
brand-new 최신의
celebrate 기념하다, 경축하다
staff 직원

traveling exhibit 순회전시회
preview 사전 검토[조사]하다, 미리 보다
protest 항의하다, 이의를 제기하다

정답 (b)

define 정의하다, 범위를 한정하다, 설명하다
at a high price 비싼 가격으로, 많은 대가를 치르고

정답 (c)

8

When I was six years old, I wished on a star that I would one day become a famous celebrity. If I had only known then what I know now, I _____. It seems that when we're very little, we want things we don't completely understand. But as we become teenagers, we begin to look at life in deeper ways, ways that often define who we are. Now I'm old enough to know that being famous comes at a very high price. And I'm also old enough to be wiser with my wishes.

(a) wouldn't have believed in wishes
(b) could have saved myself a lot of tears
(c) would have never wasted that wish
(d) might have taken acting lessons

해석 6살 때 나는 별을 보며 언젠가 유명인이 되게 해달라고 소원을 빌었다. 내가 지금 알고 있는 것을 그때도 알았더라면 나는 그 소원을 낭비하지 않았을 것이다. 아주 어릴 때 우리는 완전히 이해하지 못하는 것들을 원하는 듯하다. 하지만 우리는 십대가 되면서 인생을 좀 더 깊은 방식으로, 종종 우리가 누구인가를 정의하는 방식으로 보기 시작한다. 지금 나는 유명해지는 것이 매우 값비싼 대가를 요구한다는 것을 알 만큼 나이가 들었다. 그리고 나는 현명하게 소원을 빌 만큼 나이를 먹었다.

(a) 소원을 믿지 않았을 것이다
(b) 많은 눈물을 흘리지 않았을 것이다
(c) 그 소원을 낭비하지 않았을 것이다
(d) 연기 수업을 들었을 것이다

해설 처음 두 문장은 글쓴이의 바램과 가정법을 사용하여 그의 어릴 적 희망에 대해 이야기하고 있다. '~ that I would one day become a famous celebrity. If I had only known then what I know now, I _____.'를 통해 글쓴이가 어렸을 때, 유명인이 되기를 소원했지만 지금 그러한 꿈이 _____ 라는 것을 깨닫게 되었다는 것이다. 'Now I'm old enough to know that being famous comes at a very high price. And I'm also old enough to be wiser with my wishes.'에서 이제는 성인이 되어 헛된 꿈에 시간을 낭비하지 않을 만큼 현명해졌다는 것을 알 수 있다. 따라서 어린 나이에 현명하지 못했음을 후회하고 있으므로, 빈 칸에는 (c)가 적절하다.

어휘 celebrity 유명[저명] 인사, 명성
waste ~을 낭비하다, 허비하다
teenager 십대(의)

9

Britain's school curriculum for secondary students is being updated. Education experts say more current courses are needed to help students be successful in a "changing society." The modernized curriculum is also intended to give students more "cultural and social flexibility." Mandarin, Arabic, global warming and healthy cooking are all new subjects that many hope will _____ and keep them enthusiastic about learning too.

(a) benefit students in the real world
(b) teach pupils how to work at home
(c) inform teens about current global events
(d) increase students' math and science skills

해석 영국의 중등 교과과정이 개정되고 있다. 교육 전문가들에 따르면 좀 더 최신의 교육들이 요구되는데 그 목적은 학생들이 '변화하는 사회'에서 성공하도록 돕기 위해서이다. 현대화된 교육과정이 또한 의도하는 바는 학생들에게 좀 더 많은 '문화적, 사회적 융통성'을 제공하는 것이다. 중국어, 아랍어, 지구 온난화와 건강 요리법은 완전히 새로운 과목들로, 많은 사람들은 이러한 과목들이 학생들에게 현실 세계에서 도움이 되고 그들의 배움에 대한 열정을 유지해 주기를 바란다.

(a) 학생들에게 현실 세계에서 도움이 되고
(b) 학생들이 집에서 어떻게 공부해야 하는가를 가르치고
(c) 십대들에게 현재 세계의 사건에 대해 알리고
(d) 학생들의 수학과 과학 기술을 증가시키고

해설 영국 중등 교육과정 개정과 관련된 글이다. 변화하는 사회에 학생이 적응할 수 있도록 돕기 위한 노력이 필요하다(~ more current courses are needed to help students be successful in a "changing society."). 이러한 교육과정은 학생들에게 '문화적, 사회적 융통성(cultural and social flexibility)'을 제공하기 위해 기획된 것으로 중국어, 아랍어, 지구 온난화와 건강 요리법 등이 있다. 이러한 과목의 특성을 찾아 빈 칸을 채울 정답을 찾아야 한다. 이러한 과목은 그들의 배움에 대한 열정을 유지하고 또한 학생들에게 현실 세계에 적응할 수 있는 능력을 갖추어 준다. 따라서 정답은 (a)다.

어휘 curriculum 교과 과정, 교육 과정
secondary 중등 교육[학교]의
update 새롭게 하다, 갱신[개정]하다
education 교육, 교양
expert 전문가, 숙련가

current 지금의, 현재의, 최신의
modernize 현대화[근대화]하다
intend to ~할 작정이다, ~하려고 하다
flexibility 융통성, 유연성
enthusiastic 열정[열광]적인, 열심인
pupil 학생, 제자
inform 알려주다

정답 (a)

decision 결정, 결정사항
cultural 문화의, 문화적인, 교양의
tragedy 비극
quit ~을 그만두다

정답 (d)

10

The world's oldest newspaper is no longer news actually printed on paper. Sweden's most famous newspaper, founded by a Swedish queen in 1645, has replaced its paper edition with an online edition. With only 1,000 subscribers to the paper edition, this wasn't Sweden's most popular newspaper. However, many in Sweden think the decision to _____ is a cultural tragedy.

(a) hire a new, younger newspaper staff
(b) no longer write about Sweden's history
(c) quit producing the online newspaper
(d) print this historic paper only in cyberspace

해석 세계에서 가장 오래된 신문은 더 이상 종이 위에 인쇄된 뉴스가 아니다. 스웨덴 여왕에 의해 1645년에 창간된 스웨덴의 가장 유명한 신문은 창간 인쇄판을 온라인 판으로 대체했다. 종이 신문의 구독자들이 겨우 1,000명인 것을 감안할 때 이것은 가장 인기 있는 신문은 아니었다. 그러나 많은 스웨덴 사람들은 이 역사적인 신문을 사이버 공간에서만 출판하기로 한 결정이 문화적 비극이라고 여긴다.

(a) 새롭고 젊은 신문사 직원들을 고용하기로 한
(b) 더 이상 스웨덴의 역사에 대해 쓰지 않기로 한
(c) 온라인 신문 출판을 그만 두기로 한
(d) 이 역사적인 신문을 사이버 공간에서만 출판하기로 한

해설 1645년에 설립된 유명한 스웨덴 신문이 온라인 판으로 대체된 것과 관련된 글이다. '~ has replaced its paper edition with an online edition.'은 인쇄판 신문이 온라인 판으로 대체되었다는 표현이다. 이 종이 신문의 구독자들은 1,000명 정도에 불과하고 가장 인기 있는 신문은 아니라고 했지만 문맥을 반전시키는 however에 주목해야 한다. 스웨덴의 많은 사람들은 이 역사적 신문을 더 이상 종이로 찍어내지 않고 _____ 한 결정이 문화적 비극이라고 지적하고 있다. 빈 칸에는 인터넷에서만 출판되기로 했다는 내용이 들어가야 하므로 정답은 (d)다.

어휘 no longer 더 이상 ~가 아니다
replace ~을 대신[대체]하다
edition (간행물의) 판
subscriber 구독자, 응모자
popular 인기 있는, 평판이 좋은

11

A recent report on New York City's economic future said immigrants are largely responsible for the city's strong economic growth. The 18-month study found that immigrants are starting more small businesses and creating more jobs than native residents. The report also said that _____ _____. By bringing economic activity to previously struggling areas, many neighborhoods have been transformed.

(a) certain areas are suffering from depressed economies
(b) immigrant business owners are improving neighborhoods
(c) little can be done to help small business employees
(d) immigrants in small neighborhoods cannot find jobs

해석 미래의 뉴욕 경제에 대한 최근의 한 보고에 따르면 이민자들이 도시의 강력한 경제 발전에 크게 기여한다고 한다. 18개월간의 연구가 밝힌 바로는 이민자들이 원래 토착 주민들보다 더 많은 소규모 사업들을 시작해서 더 많은 일자리들을 창출하고 있다. 또한 보고서에 따르면 이민자 사업가들이 이웃 환경을 개선하고 있다. 이전에 어려움을 겪고 있던 지역들에 경제 활동을 일으킴으로써 그들은 많은 지역 사회들을 변화시켰다.

(a) 일부 지역들이 침체된 경제로 고생하고 있다
(b) 이민자 사업가들이 이웃 환경을 개선하고 있다
(c) 소규모 사업체의 직원들을 돕기 위해 할 일이 거의 없다
(d) 작은 동네들의 이민자들이 일자리를 구할 수 없다

해설 뉴욕 이민자들에 관한 글이다. 이민자들이 뉴욕의 경제 발전에 큰 기여를 하고 있다(~ are largely responsible for the city's strong economic growth.)는 것이 주제 문장이다. 이에 대한 구체적 설명으로 이민자들이 토착 주민들보다 소규모 사업을 더 많이 시작하고 따라서 일자리 창출도 많이 하고 있다고 했다. 빈 칸에는 유사한 내용으로 이민자들이 뉴욕의 발전을 위한 긍정적 일을 한다는 내용이 들어가야 하기 때문에 우선 (a), (d)는 제외되어야 한다. 또한 (c)의 'little can be done to ~'라는 표현은 소규모 사업체의 직원을 돕기 위해 한 일이 거의 없다는 것이기 때문에 문장의 의도와는 거리가 멀다. 따라서 정답은 (b)다.

어휘 economic 경제(상)의, 경제학(상)의
immigrant 이주민, 이민
responsible for ~에 책임이 있는

resident 거주자
previously 미리, 전에
struggling 버둥거리는, 고군분투하는, 몸부림치는
transform ~을 바꾸다, 변형시키다
depressed 불경기의, 침체된

정답 (b)

12

> Indeed, it is responsible reporting to cover the recent vow by 60 countries _____ in their military conflicts. It brings hope to know that South American, African and Asian nations that have previously used children as fighters are all in support of this new international agreement. However, strict enforcement is the only thing that will protect children from such tragic fates.
>
> (a) to reach an international agreement
> (b) to better inform citizens about developments
> (c) to no longer use children as soldiers
> (d) to offer civilians weapons for protection

해석 군사 분쟁에서 더 이상 어린이들을 병사로 이용하지 않기로 한 60개국의 최근 서약을 보도한 것은 진정으로 책임감 있는 일입니다. 이전에 어린이들을 병사로 이용했던 남미, 아프리카, 아시아의 국가들이 이 새로운 국제 협정을 지지한다는 것을 알게 되어 희망적입니다. 그러나 엄격한 시행만이 어린이들을 이러한 비극적인 운명으로부터 보호할 수 있습니다.

(a) 국제 협정에 동의하기로 한
(b) 시민들에게 사실에 대해 잘 알리기로 한
(c) 더 이상 어린이들을 병사로 이용하지 않기로 한
(d) 시민들에게 보호용 무기들을 제공하기로 한

해설 빈 칸이 앞에 있는 경우는 끝까지 다 읽고 문제를 해결하지 말고, 빈 칸이 있는 문장과 주변 문장을 집중적으로 이해 하고나서 선택지에서 답을 고르는 것이 더 효과적이다. 바로 다음에 이어지는 문장에서 어린이들을 병사로 이용한 이야기가 나오므로, 어린이를 병사로 이용하지 않겠다는 서약을 했다는 내용을 골라야 한다. 첫 문장에서 이런 서약을 기사화 한 것을 칭찬하고(responsible reporting), 또 이어지는 문장에서 희망이 보인다(brings hope)고 했으므로 정답은 (c)다.

어휘 indeed 참으로, 실로, 진정으로
military 군(대)의, 군사의
conflict 분쟁, 투쟁, 충동
fighter 싸우는 사람, 투사, 전사
agreement 약속, 협정, 협약
strict 엄격한, 엄한
enforcement 시행, 실시, 적용
fate 운명
inform ~에게 알리다, 통지하다

development 사건, 사실
civilian 시민, 일반국민

정답 (c)

13

> Eye jewelry is a new way to accessorize one's eyeballs. Eye surgeons in the Netherlands have developed a procedure in which a small jewel can be implanted on the white part of the eyeball by inserting it under the thin, clean membrane of the eye. The most common eye jewelry looks like small hearts, stars or half moons. And although _____, many doctors warn there are complications like serious eye infections that can possibly result from the procedure.
>
> (a) the trend is gaining popularity
> (b) no one is likely to want this accessory
> (c) the jewel options are limited at this point
> (d) the eye membrane is moist

해석 눈 장신구는 안구에 액세서리를 다는 새로운 방법이다. 네덜란드의 안과 의사들은 작은 보석을 눈의 얇고 맑은 막 아래에 삽입함으로써 안구의 흰자 위에 이식하는 수술을 개발했다. 가장 보편적인 눈 장신구는 작은 심장, 별 혹은 반달처럼 생겼다. 그리고 이 추세가 인기를 더해가고 있음에도 불구하고, 많은 의사들은 이러한 수술로부터 심각한 눈 염증과 같은 합병증이 초래될 수 있다고 경고한다.

(a) 이 추세가 인기를 더해가고 있다
(b) 이 장신구를 원하는 사람은 아무도 없을 것 같다
(c) 현재 장신구 선택의 폭이 좁다
(d) 눈의 막이 촉촉하다

해설 안구에 액세서리를 다는 눈 장신구에 관한 글이다. 네덜란드의 안과 의사들이 이 수술을 개발했는데 안구의 흰자 위에 장신구를 이식하는 것이다. although라는 연결사에 주목해야 한다. 빈 칸에 들어오는 내용과는 달리 '많은 의사들은 심각한 눈 염증과 같은 합병증이 수술에 의해 초래될 수 있다(~ there are complications like serious eye infections that can possibly result from the procedure.)'는 것을 경고하고 있다. 따라서 빈 칸에는 실제로 '이런 추세가 증가하고 있거나 혹은 인기를 더해가고 있다'라는 표현이 들어가야 하기 때문에 정답은 (a)다.

어휘 jewelry 보석류, 장신구
accessorize 액세서리를 달다
eye surgeon 안과 의사
procedure 순서, 절차, 방식
implant ~을 심다, 끼워넣다, 이식하다
insert 삽입하다
membrane (얇은) 막
complication 합병증
infection 감염, 전염, 염증

result from ~의 결과로 생기다
moist 습한, 축축한, (눈물로) 젖은

14

Cancer researchers are creating a new cancer-fighting drug using something extraordinary — _____ a sea creature. This poison, used for defense by the small, transparent Dianzoa angulata, effectively killed cancer cells in cultures. This exciting development caused researchers to rush to create an artificial substitute. So far, the human-made version is reducing human tumors implanted in mice with no negative side effects.

(a) the toxin released by
(b) an exotic food made from
(c) a poison antidote created by
(d) the tumor tissue found inside

해석 암 연구원들은 새로운 암 치료제를 만들고 있는데, 특이한 물질 – 바다 생물에 의해 방출되는 독 – 을 이용하고 있다. 이 독은 작고 투명한 디안조아 안굴라타에 의해 방어 수단으로 사용되는데 배양 상태에서 암 세포들을 효과적으로 제거했다. 이 흥미로운 개발은 연구자들이 서둘러 인공 대체물을 만들게 했다. 지금까지 인간이 만든 이 독은 실험용 쥐들에게 이식된 인간의 종양들을 아무런 부작용 없이 감소시키고 있다.

(a) (바다 생물)에 의해 방출되는 독
(b) (바다 생물)로부터 만들어지는 이국적인 음식
(c) (바다 생물)에 의해 만들어진 해독제
(d) (바다 생물) 내부에서 발견되는 종양 조직

해설 새롭게 개발된 암 치료제와 관련된 글이다. 빈 칸에 들어갈 내용은 암 치료제에 사용된 특이한 물질이 무엇인가를 다시 한 번 설명하는 내용이어야 한다. 따라서 빈 칸이 있는 다음 문장을 자세하게 읽어서 문맥의 흐름을 파악해야 한다. 'This poison, used for defense by the small, transparent Dianzoa angulata, effectively killed cancer cells in cultures.'에서 앞 문장에서 언급된 물질을 this poison이라고 밝힘으로써 독성 물질임을 알 수 있다. 따라서 정답은 (a)다.

어휘 cancer 암
researcher 조사원, 연구자
extraordinary 비범한, 별난, 보통이 아닌
transparent 투명한
effectively 효과적으로
culture (생물) 배양; 배양균
rush 돌진하다, 급하게 가다
artificial 인공적인, 인공의, 모조의
substitute 대체물[대체인]
reduce 줄이다, 감소시키다, 절감하다

tumor 종기, 종양
negative 부정적인, 부정의, 소극적인, 비관적인
side effect 부작용
toxin 독소
exotic 외래의, 미국풍의
antidote 해독제
tissue 조직

15

University marine biology departments and ocean life organizations are forming a collective ocean tracking network to better understand climate change effects on sea animals and advance endangered ocean wildlife management. Scientists in eleven different countries will work to electronically tag one million sea animals from turtles to whales. Five thousand sensors will be placed at important locations throughout the world's oceans. These sensors will collect valuable data from the tagged animal that swims by, but more than that, single animals' data will be collected. Each electronic tag is capable of storing other tagged animals' data too. _____, this will reveal to scientists what animals are encountering each other, and where, throughout the oceans of the world.

(a) As a rule
(b) Therefore
(c) Nevertheless
(d) Likewise

해석 대학의 해양 생물학부와 해양 생물 기관들은 바다 동물들에 대한 기후 변화의 영향을 더 잘 이해하고 멸종 위기의 바다 야생동물들을 잘 관리하기 위해 공동의 해양 추적 네트워크를 결성하고 있다. 11개국 과학자들이 거북이에서 고래까지 백만 마리의 바다 동물에게 전자 인식표를 붙이기 위한 작업을 할 것이다. 오천 개의 센서들이 전 세계 해양의 중요한 위치에 설치될 것이다. 이러한 센서들은 그 곁을 지나가는 인식표를 단 동물로부터 귀중한 자료를 수집하게 되지만 한 동물의 자료 이상의 것이 수집될 것이다. 각 전자 인식표는 인식표를 단 다른 동물들의 자료들도 저장할 수 있다. 그러므로 이것은 전 세계 해양에서 어떤 동물들이 어디에서 서로 마주치게 되는지를 과학자들에게 알려줄 것이다.

(a) 일반적으로
(b) 그러므로
(c) 그럼에도 불구하고
(d) 이와 같이

정답 및 해설 85

해설 문장의 흐름을 적절하게 이어주는 장치를 찾는 문제이다. 이런 유형의 문제는 빈 칸의 앞뒤 내용을 정확하게 파악하여 적절한 글의 흐름을 알아내야 한다. 빈 칸의 앞부분에서는 대학의 해양 생물학부와 해양 생물 기관이 바다 야생동물을 관리하기 위해 네트워크를 결성하고 전자 인식표(tag)를 도입한다는 설명을 하고 있다. 전자 인식표는 다른 동물의 정보도 알려주는데, 어떤 동물들이 어디에서 마주치는지를 알게된다고 했으므로 빈 칸 앞뒤 문장은 원인/결과의 연결관계가 되어야 한다. 따라서 정답은 (b)가 적절하다.

어휘 marine biology 해양생물학
organization 기관
climate 기후
collective 공동의, 집합적인
advance 향상시키다
endangered 멸종 위기에 처한
electronically 전자적으로
tag 인식표를 달다, 인식표
location 위치
valuable 가치가 있는, 귀중한
encounter 마주치다
as a rule 대체로, 일반적으로
likewise 마찬가지로, 똑같이

정답 (b)

해설 연결어를 찾는 문제는 보기의 연결어로써의 기능(function)을 먼저 간단히 짚어 보고 본문을 읽는 것이 시간을 절약할 수 있는 방법이다. As a result(결과적으로)는 인과관계에 있는 내용을 연결할 때 사용하고, Ordinarily(일반적으로)와 Similarly(유사하게)는 앞에 나온 문장의 내용과 유사한 내용을 이을 때 사용한다. In contrast(대조적으로)는 상반되는 내용이 이어질 때 사용한다. 본문 내용에 비추어 볼 때, 공장이 불결해서, 대중이 분노했고, 육류소비가 줄었다. (그 결과로) 법을 제정해서 소비자들을 안심시켰다는 흐름이 논리적으로 적합하므로 (a)가 정답이다.

어휘 facilitate 촉진(조장)하다, 용이하게 하다
meat-packing 정육업
industry 산업
distressing 괴롭히는, 고통을 주는
repulsive 혐오감을 일으키는, 불쾌한
processing 가공, 처리
anger 성나게 하다
plummet 급격히 줄어들다
legislation 법률 제정, 입법 행위
reassure 안심시키다, 기운 나게 하다
inspect ~을 조사하다, 점검하다

정답 (a)

16

Upton Sinclair's *The Jungle* facilitated change in the meat-packing industry of the early 1900s. Sinclair's distressing novel about the repulsive conditions of America's meat processing plants angered the public, and meat sales plummeted. _____, legislation was passed to help the plant owners reassure the public that all meat would be inspected and safe for consumption.

(a) As a result
(b) Ordinarily
(c) Similarly
(d) In contrast

해석 업톤 싱클레어의 〈정글〉은 1900년대 초반에 정육업계의 변화를 촉진시켰다. 미국의 정육 가공 공장들의 위험 요소들과 혐오감을 일으키는 위생 상태에 대한 싱클레어의 비참한 소설은 일반인들의 분노를 일으켰고 육류 판매량이 급격히 줄어들었다. 그 결과로 공장 소유주들로 하여금 모든 육류가 검열을 받고 먹기에 안전하다고 사람들을 안심시키게 할 법안이 통과되었다.

(a) 그 결과로
(b) 대개
(c) 유사하게
(d) 대조적으로

17

Being a 21st century student means becoming a global citizen. Part of this process is learning the skills needed to work in the global market. For example, students should work hard to learn different languages, and become knowledgeable and sensitive about foreign cultures. Also, they should focus on becoming creative, innovative thinkers because these are employee traits that will always be valued no matter how much the global market changes.

Q What is the main topic of the passage?

(a) Global citizens uniting to improve education
(b) The process of how to learn a new language
(c) The ways students should prepare for future jobs
(d) The effects of recent student innovations

해석 21세기 학생이 된다는 것은 세계 시민이 된다는 것을 의미한다. 이 과정의 일부는 세계 시장에서 필요로 하는 기술들을 배우는 것이다. 예를 들어, 학생들은 다른 언어들을 배우기 위해 노력해야 하고, 외국 문화에 대해 정통하고 민감해야 한다. 또한 그들은 창조적이고 진보적인 사고를 갖도록 집중해야 하는 데, 이러한 것들이 세계 시장이 아무리 변화하더라도 항상 중요하게 여겨질 인재의 특징들이기 때문이다.

Q 지문의 주제는 무엇인가?

(a) 교육을 개선하기 위해 뭉친 전 세계 시민들

(b) 새로운 언어를 배우는 과정

(c) 학생들이 미래의 직업을 준비하는 방식

(d) 최근 학생 개혁의 결과들

해설 글의 주제를 고르는 문제이다. 21세기의 학생이 된다는 것은 '세계 시민이 된다는 것(becoming a global citizen)'임을 강조하고 있다. 다음 문장에서는 for example을 사용하여 세계 시민이 된다는 것에 대한 예를 제시하고 있다. 다른 언어를 배우고 외국 문화에 정통하고 민감해지기 위해 애써야 한다. 또한 창조적이고 진보적이 되도록 해야 하는데, 이런 것이 세계 시장이 변화해도 항상 중요하게 여겨지는 '인재의 특징'이라고 언급한다. 따라서 이 글의 요점은 21세기 학생이 되기 위해서 학생들이 준비해야 하는 것에 관한 내용이다. 정답은 (c)다.

어휘 global 전 세계의, 지구상의

citizen 시민

knowledgeable 정통한, 박식한

sensitive 민감한, 예민한

focus on ~에 집중하다

innovative 혁신적인, 진보적인

employee 피고용인, 종업원

trait 특징, 특색

value ~을 중요시하다

정답 (c)

18

The world's highest ski resort at 5300 meters will not be a ski resort much longer. Due to global warming, Bolivia's only ski area, Chacaltaya, will soon be a dry brown mountain year-round. Glaciers in the Andes have been consistently receding, leading to a dramatic change at Chacaltaya. What was once a popular 40-foot deep ski run is now just a trail of rocks. Local skiers say the environmental impact is tragic since this is the only ski area in the world where one could ski through the clouds at an airplane-like altitude.

Q What is the main idea of the passage?

(a) Weather changes threaten to close down Bolivia's ski resort.

(b) The world's highest ski slope offers rare high-altitude skiing.

(c) Glaciers are receding throughout the Andes Mountain chain.

(d) Global warming is affecting skiers in most countries.

해석 5300미터 높이에 있는 세계에서 가장 높은 스키 리조트가 얼마 오래 가지 못할 것이다. 볼리비아의 유일한 스키장인 차칼타야는 지구 온난화로 인해 곧 일년내내 마른 갈색 산이 될 것이다. 안데스 산맥의 빙하가 지속적으로 감소하고 있으며 이것은 차칼타야에 극적인 변화를 일으켰다. 한때 인기 있었던 40피트 깊이의 스키 코스는 현재 바위의 흔적들뿐이다. 그 지역 스키 인들은 환경의 영향이 비극적이라고 하는데, 이곳은 비행기와 같은 고도에서 구름 사이로 스키를 탈 수 있는 전 세계에서 유일한 스키장이기 때문이다.

Q 위 글의 요지는 무엇인가?

(a) 기후 변화로 볼리비아의 스키 리조트가 폐쇄 위험에 처했다.

(b) 세계에서 가장 높은 스키장에서 보기 드문 높은 고도 스키를 제공한다.

(c) 안데스 산맥 전역에서 빙하가 감소하고 있다.

(d) 지구 온난화가 대부분의 국가의 스키 인들에게 영향을 끼치고 있다.

해설 요지를 찾는 문제이기 때문에 글의 전체적인 내용을 파악해서 핵심적 내용을 선택해야 한다. 세계에서 가장 높은 스키 리조트에 관한 글이다. 단락의 첫 문장 'The world's highest ski resort at 5300 meters will not be a ski resort much longer.'에서 이 리조트가 오래 가지 못할 것이라는 것을 말하고, 바로 뒷 문장에서 due to를 사용하여 지구 온난화에 의한 현상임을 밝히고 있다. 지구 온난화로 인하여 안데스 산맥의 빙하가 지속적으로 올라가서 이 스키장의 코스는 현재 바위 흔적만이 남았다고 했다. 결과적으로 이 스키장이 폐쇄 위기에 놓이게 되었기 때문에 정답은 (a)다.

어휘 resort 휴양지

global warming 지구 온난화

year-round 일년내내

consistently 끊임없이, 지속적으로, 일관되게

recede 감소하다

dramatic 극적인

trail 자국, 흔적

local 지역의, 장소의, 위치의

environmental 환경(상)의

impact 영향, 충격

tragic 비극적인

altitude 고도, 높이

threaten 위협하다

정답 (a)

19

Nutritionists have discovered that an intake of healthy fruits and vegetables decreases as kids become teenagers. The diets of 2,000 kids were assessed in separate surveys five years apart. The latter survey revealed that most of the teens were eating significantly fewer fruits and vegetables than they had been consuming five years earlier. Experts say this is worrisome because of teens' high nutritional needs and the habits they are setting up for adulthood.

Q What is the best title of the passage?
(a) Teens Enjoying More Fruits and Vegetables
(b) Children Disliking Vegetables
(c) Teenagers Learing about Healthy Eating
(d) Nutritionists' Worry about Adolescent Diet

해석 영양학자들이 발견한 바로는 건강에 좋은 과일과 야채의 섭취가 아이들이 십대가 되면서 감소한다. 2천명의 아이들의 식습관이 5년 간격으로 별도로 조사되어 평가되었다. 나중에 행해진 조사에 따르면 대부분의 십대들이 5년 전에 비해 훨씬 적은 과일과 야채를 먹고 있다는 것이 밝혀졌다. 전문가들은 십대들이 많은 영양을 필요로 하며 성인기의 식습관을 형성하고 있는 중이기 때문에 이것이 걱정할 만한 일이라고 말한다.

Q 위 글의 제목으로 가장 적절한 것을 고르시오.
(a) 더 많은 과일과 야채를 즐기는 십대들
(b) 야채를 싫어하는 아이들
(c) 건강에 좋은 식사에 대해 배우는 십대들
(d) 청소년들의 식습관에 대한 영양학자들의 우려

해설 글의 제목을 선택하는 문제이다. 제목은 전체 내용을 요약해서 표현해야 한다. 영양학자들은 십대가 될수록 건강에 필요한 과일과 야채 섭취가 감소한다고 지적하고 5년 간격으로 조사한 연구에서 5년 전에 비해 과일과 야채의 섭취량이 훨씬 줄었는데, 이 시기가 성인기의 식습관을 형성하는 기간이기 때문에 문제가 된다고 했다. 따라서 (a)와 (c)는 문장의 내용과 정면으로 위배되며, (b)는 제목으로서는 부적절하다. 따라서 정답은 (d)다.

어휘 nutritionist 영양학자
intake 섭취[흡입]량
discover 발견하다
decrease 감소하다
assess 평가하다
latter (양자 중) 뒤에 말한, 후자의
reveal 밝히다, 드러내다, 폭로하다
significantly 상당히
consume 소비하다, 소모하다
nutritional 영양의, 영양상의

adulthood 성인기, 성인임
adolescent 청소년기의, 청년, 십대 청소년

정답 (d)

20

Fetal psychology studies babies' patterns of behavior in the womb. For instance, researchers now know that when a mother laughs, her upside down baby bounces up and down on his or her head. The harder she laughs, the harder and faster the baby bounces. Since the baby doesn't seem to mind one bit, some experts are led to wonder if this is why humans love amusement park rides such as roller coasters.

Q What is the passage mainly about?
(a) Why people of all ages enjoy roller coasters
(b) How laughter influences a newborn's development
(c) The types of technology used to monitor fetuses
(d) Explaining how fetal psychology can be used

해석 태아 심리학이 연구하는 것은 자궁 속에서의 아기의 행동 패턴이다. 예를 들어 엄마가 웃을 때 거꾸로 위치하고 있는 아기는 위 아래로 튄다는 것을 연구원들은 이제 안다. 엄마가 심하게 웃을수록 아기는 더 세고 빠르게 튄다. 아기는 이것을 전혀 싫어하지 않는 것으로 보이기 때문에 일부 전문가들은 이것이 인간이 롤러코스터와 같은 놀이공원의 탈 것들을 즐기는 이유가 아닐까 생각하고 있다.

Q 위 글의 요지로 알맞은 것을 고르시오.
(a) 모든 연령대의 사람들이 롤러코스터를 좋아하는 이유
(b) 웃음이 신생아의 발달에 영향을 미치는 방법
(c) 태아를 관찰하기 위해 사용되는 기술의 종류들
(d) 태아 심리학이 어떻게 이용될 수 있는가에 대한 설명

해설 태아의 행동패턴을 연구해서 인간의 특성을 설명할 수도 있다는 것을 보여주는 글이다. 구체적으로 임산부가 웃으면 태아가 아래위로 튀고, 태아는 그것을 싫어하지 않는다는 것을 밝히면서, 인간이 롤러코스터와 같이 움직임이 빠르고 많은 것을 즐기는 이유를 찾고 있다. 따라서 정답은 (d)다.

어휘 fetal 태아의 cf. fetus 태아
psychology 심리학
womb 자궁
upside down 뒤집힌
bounce 튀다
up and down 위아래로
mind 꺼려하다, 싫어하다
amusement park 놀이공원

ride 탈것
newborn 신생아

21

Because of the Indian Removal Act in 1830, 17,000 Native Americans were removed from their homes in Georgia. Contrary to many beliefs, this group of Native Americans was not violent. Still, they were forced by the US military to leave their homes and walk 1,000 miles to relocate in Oklahoma. Four thousand people died during this long journey later known as the "The Trail of Tears."

Q What is the passage mainly about?

(a) Native Americans in Georgia lived in a nonviolent manner.

(b) "The Trail of Tears" was a 4,000-mile journey to Oklahoma.

(c) Native Americans were removed from 17,000 homes.

(d) The Indian Removal Act led to a tragic event in US History.

해석 1830년에 제정된 인디언 강제 이주법 때문에 17,000명의 미국 원주민들이 조지아의 자신의 집으로부터 강제로 이주 당했다. 많은 사람들의 믿음과는 달리 이 원주민들은 폭력적인 집단이 아니었다. 그러나 그들은 미국 군대에 의해 강제로 자신들의 집을 떠나 그들의 정착지로 정해진 오클라호마까지 천 마일을 걸어가도록 강요당했다. 나중에 '눈물의 여정'으로 알려진 이 길고 고통스러운 여행 중에 4,000명의 사람들이 사망했다.

Q 위 글의 요지로 알맞은 것을 고르시오.

(a) 조지아의 원주민들은 비폭력인 방식으로 생활했다.

(b) '눈물의 여정'은 오클라호마까지의 4천 마일의 여행이었다.

(c) 원주민들이 17,000가구나 이주했다.

(d) 인디언 강제 이주법은 미국 역사에서 비극적인 사건을 초래했다.

해설 (a) 본문에 나온 내용과 일치하기는 하지만, 요지로 고르기에는 너무 세부적이다. (b) The Trail of Tears는 천 마일이다. 따라서 내용이 맞지 않기도 하고, 또한 요지로 고르기에는 부적합하다. (c) 17,000명의 인디언들이 이주를 했다는 내용이 나왔지만, 그 숫자가 구체적인 가정 수를 의미하는 것은 아니다. 비폭력적인 인디언들을 강압적으로 이송하면서 많은 사상자가 났다는 내용과 잘 부합하므로 (d)가 정답이다.

어휘 **remove** 이동시키다
contrary to ~와는 대조적으로
belief 믿음, 신념
violent 폭력적인

relocate 이주시키다, 재배치하다
journey 여행, 여정
tragic 비극적인

22

Dear Mr. Moreau,
I am honored that your organization has invited me to speak at your annual conference. I am familiar with your agency's work and the admirable contributions it has made to the field of speech pathology. Unfortunately, I will not be able to speak on the proposed date. Due to prior commitments, I will be out of the country at that time. If you would be interested in scheduling me to speak at next year's conference, I will be free those dates and would be happy to attend.
Sincerely,
Janet Marquez

Q What is the purpose of this letter?

(a) To make Mr. Moreau aware of Ms. Marquez's availability

(b) To suggest another appropriate speaker for the conference

(c) To thank Mr. Moreau for his organization's work

(d) To express interest in speaking at this year's conference

해석 모로씨께
귀하의 회사가 연례 총회에서 연설을 하도록 저를 초청해 주신 것을 영광으로 생각합니다. 저는 귀사의 업적과 언어 병리학 분야에 가져 온 존경할만한 기여에 대해 잘 알고 있습니다. 유감스럽게도 저는 제안된 날짜에 연설을 할 수 없을 것 같습니다. 이미 정해진 선약 때문에 저는 그 시기에 국외에 나가 있을 예정입니다. 귀하가 내년 회의에 저를 연사로 초청하실 계획이 있으시다면 그 날짜에 시간을 내어 기꺼이 귀하의 편의를 도모할 것입니다.

진심을 담아,
자넷 마케즈

Q 이 편지의 목적으로 알맞은 것을 고르시오.

(a) 모로씨에게 자신의 일정을 알리기 위해서

(b) 회의에 다른 적절한 연사를 제안하기 위해서

(c) 모로씨에게 그의 회사의 업적에 대해 감사하기 위해서

(d) 올해 회의에서 연설하는 데 관심을 표명하기 위해서

해설 편지의 의도를 물어보는 질문이다. 자넷 마케즈씨는 모로씨 회사의 총회에서 연설을 하도록 초청되었으나 제안된 날짜에 연설을 할 수 없다는 것을 알리는 편지 (Unfortunately, I will not be able to speak on the proposed date.)이다. 불가능한 이유를 due to를 이

용하여 설명한다. 정해진 선약 때문에 그 기간 동안 해외에 나가게 되서 올해에는 연설을 할 수 없다는 것을 알리는 편지내용이다. 따라서 정답은 (a)다.

어휘 honored 명예로운, 영광인
organization 조직, 기구
annual conference 연례 총회
be familiar with ~와 친숙[친밀]하다
admirable 감탄[칭찬]할 만한, 훌륭한
contribution 기부, 기여
pathology 병리학
unfortunately 불행[불운]하게도
prior commitment 선약
be interested in ~에 흥미가 있다
availability 이용가능성

정답 (a)

23

Can you stick to your schedule? Experts recommend making a weekly schedule every Sunday night. Not only should this include commitments for the week, it should also specifically list the amount of school work to be accomplished during the week. In addition, an index card with the next day's schedule should be made every night and used as a reminder throughout the day to get all necessary things done.

Q According to the passage, what isn't recommended for improving time organization?

(a) Write down school work that must be done.
(b) Include weekly commitments on your schedule.
(c) Make all schedules on the weekend.
(d) Use separate cards for daily schedules.

해석 당신은 일정표를 준수하는가? 전문가들은 매주 일요일 밤에 한 주의 계획을 세우라고 권한다. 이것은 일주일 동안 해야 하는 일들을 포함해야 할뿐만 아니라, 그 주 동안에 마쳐야 하는 학업의 양도 정확하게 나열해야 한다. 뿐만 아니라 다음 날의 계획을 적은 카드를 매일 밤 만들어서 하루 종일 필요한 일들을 하도록 스스로에게 상기시켜야 한다.

Q 위 글에서 보다 나은 시간 이용을 위해 권장되는 것이 아닌 것을 고르시오.
(a) 마쳐야 하는 학교 공부들을 적어 둔다.
(b) 주별로 할 일들을 계획에 포함한다.
(c) 모든 일들을 주말에 계획한다.
(d) 그날 그날의 계획을 위해 따로 카드를 사용한다.

해설 구체적으로 학습량을 적으라(specifically list the

---

amount of school work)고 충고했으니 (a)는 맞고 해야 할 일을 적으라(include commitments for the week)고 했으니 (b)도 맞다. 매주 일요일 저녁에 주말 일정표를 짜고, 매일 밤 그 다음날 할 일을 카드로 정리하라고 했으니, 모든 일을 주말에 몰아서 하라는 (c)는 본문의 내용과 어긋난다. 따라서 답은 (c)다.

어휘 stick to ~를 고수하다, 끝까지 해내다
recommend 추천하다, 권하다, 장려하다
commitment 약속, 책임
specifically 명확하게, 확실하게
accomplish 성취[수행]하다, 이룩하다
reminder 생각나게 하는 것
throughout 전부, 처음부터 끝까지
necessary 필요한

정답 (c)

24

Economic well-being is not automatically affected by inflation. People often think that inflation means that an increase in prices will lower their standard of living. But usually during a period of inflation, prices, housing costs, and income all seem to go up together. Only if wages are rising slower than living expenses will economic well-being begin to suffer.

Q What do people generally think about inflation?

(a) That costs and income rise together during times of inflation.
(b) That price increases make it harder to live comfortably.
(c) That economic well-being increases slightly because of inflation.
(d) That economic well-being is not greatly affected by inflation.

해석 경제적 안녕이 항상 자동적으로 인플레이션에 의해 영향을 받는 것은 아니다. 사람들은 종종 인플레이션이 물가의 증가로 그들의 생활 수준을 떨어지게 하는 것을 의미한다고 생각한다. 하지만 일반적으로 인플레이션 기간 동안 물가, 주택 가격, 소득은 함께 오르는 것으로 보인다. 봉급이 생활비보다 느린 속도로 인상될 때만 경제적 안녕이 타격을 받게 될 것이다.

Q 사람들이 일반적으로 인플레이션에 대해 생각하는 것을 고르시오.
(a) 인플레이션 기간 동안 생활비와 소득이 함께 증가한다고 생각한다.
(b) 물가 인상이 편안하게 살기 힘들게 한다고 생각한다.
(c) 인플레이션 때문에 경제적 안녕이 약간 증가한다고 생각한다.
(d) 경제적 안녕이 인플레이션에 의해 그다지 큰 영향을

받지 않는다고 생각한다.

해설 세부사항을 파악하는 문제는 선택지를 먼저 보는 것이 효과적일 경우가 많다. 질문을 잘 이해하는 것이 매우 중요한데, 사람들이 일반적으로 인플레이션에 대해 어떻게 생각하는지는 두 번째 문장(People often think that ~)에 나와 있다. 즉 일반적으로 물가 인상이 생활수준의 저하를 갖고 온다고 믿어서 더 안락하게 사는 것을 어렵게 만든다는 (b)가 정답이다.

어휘 **well-being** 복지, 안녕, 행복
automatically 자동적으로, 무의식적으로
inflation 물가 폭등
lower 낮추다, 떨어뜨리다
standard 수준, 기준, 표준
period 기간, 시기
rise 오르다
expense 비용, 경비
suffer 괴로워하다, 고민하다, 손해를 보다
slightly 약간, 조금

정답 (b)

25

Why does moon dust smell like gunpowder? Well, almost half of it is made up of silicon dioxide glass that has been created by meteoroids slamming into the moon over billions of years. Chemically, moon dust is nothing like gun powder. Why the similar smell? No one knows for sure, but one theory suggests the dust could burn when it reacts to the oxygen inside spacecrafts.

Q How is silicon dioxide glass made?

(a) Through the process of oxidation in an enclosed space
(b) By breaking down the chemicals in moon dust
(c) Through meteoroid contact with the moon's surface
(d) By burning the silicon found in gun-powder

해석 왜 달 먼지에서 화약과 같은 냄새가 날까? 그것은 아마도 먼지의 절반이 수십억 년 전 유성이 달에 충돌했을 때 생성된 이산화규소 유리로 만들어졌기 때문일 것이다. 화학적으로 볼 때 달 먼지는 화약과 전혀 다르다. 그러면 왜 비슷한 냄새가 나는 것일까? 확실히 알 수는 없지만, 한 가지 이론에 따르면 먼지가 우주선 내의 산소와 반응했을 때 산화 과정을 거치면서 연소되었을 것이라고 한다.

Q 이산화규소 유리는 어떻게 만들어지는가?
(a) 닫힌 공간에서의 산화 과정을 통해
(b) 달 먼지의 화학 물질들을 분해함으로써
(c) 유성과 달 표면의 접촉을 통해서

(d) 화약에서 발견된 실리콘을 태움으로써

해설 세부사항 파악문제는 질문에서 묻는 내용이 지문의 어느 부분에 해당되는지 찾는 것이 매우 중요하다. 본문 중에 silicon dioxide는 두 번째 문장에 위치하고 있다. 따라서 그 문장을 중점적으로 보면 답을 고를 수 있다. 'Created by meteoroids slamming into the moon'이라고 했으니, 달과 유성이 부딪히면서 생긴 것이라는 (c)가 정답이다.

어휘 **gun-powder** 화약
be made up of ~로 구성되다
silicon dioxide 이산화규소
meteoroid 유성(체)
slam into ~에 세게 부딪히다
react 반응하다
oxygen 산소
spacecraft 우주선
oxidation 산화
enclosed 밀폐된
break down 분해하다
chemical 화학물질

정답 (c)

26

The philosopher Descartes believed that if one was skeptical about everything, then the truths that remained after surviving extreme tests of skepticism would be incredibly strong indeed. Descartes developed a meditation that taught the doubting method by incorporating three different levels of doubt: perceptual illusion, dreams, and a "deceiving God."

Q What did Descartes generally believe about all perceptions?

(a) They cannot survive true tests of skepticism.
(b) The cynical mind can prove them all to be false.
(c) They should all be mistrusted until proven to be real.
(d) They are only illusions derived from dreams.

해석 철학자 데카르트는 사람이 모든 것에 대해 회의적이라면 극단적인 회의론의 시험을 거친 후 남아있는 진실이야 말로 정말로 의심할 여지가 없는 진실이라고 믿었다. 데카르트는 세 가지 다른 단계의 의심을 결합함으로 의심하는 방법을 가르치는 명상법을 개발했는데, 지각적인 환상, 꿈, 그리고 기만적인 신이다.

Q 모든 지각 능력들에 대한 데카르트의 생각으로 올바른 것을 고르시오.

(a) 회의론의 진정한 시험을 통과할 수 없다.

(b) 냉소적인 마음가짐은 그것들이 모두 거짓이라고 증명할 수 있다.

(c) 진실인 것으로 판명될 때까지 불신되어야 한다.

(d) 그것들은 꿈에서 유래한 환상에 불과하다.

해설 데카르트가 믿었던 내용은 첫 문장에 잘 나와 있다. 모든 것을 회의적으로 생각하고(be skeptical about everything), 그렇게 되면 모든 일이 회의주의의 심판을 받게 될 것이고, 회의적으로 생각한 후에도 살아남는 것이 있으면 그것이야말로 진실 중에 진실이라는 그의 논리가 나타난 첫 문장을 잘 이해해야 한다. 따라서 답은 (c)다.

Tips 철학은 독해에서 가끔 다뤄지는 주제이다. 앞에서도 언급한 바와 같이 TEPS는 영어능력을 테스트하는 시험이지 상식이나 다른 기타 지식 능력을 측정하는 시험이 아니다. 다만 평소에 다양한 주제를 다룬 글을 접해서 익숙해지면, 짧은 시간에 많은 문제를 풀 때 큰 도움이 된다.

어휘 skeptical 회의적인
remain 남다
skepticism 의심, 회의(론)
incredibly 믿을 수 없을 정도로
meditation 명상, 숙고
incorporate 결합하다
perception 지각(력)
illusion 환상
deceiving 기만하는, 속이는
cynical 냉소적인, 비꼬는
mistrust ~을 의심하다
derive from ~에서 유래하다

정답 (c)

27

Ellen Ochoa, the middle of five children, was raised by a single mother who was a strong mentor. Her positive support helped her daughter make education a priority. However, gaining advanced degrees in physics, engineering and inventing new computer technology wasn't enough for Ochoa. Among her pursuits like working, classical flute playing, volleyball and cycling, Ochoa still found time to apply to NASA to become an astronaut. She wasn't chosen on her first application. But things worked out better the next time. In 1993, Ochoa became the first Hispanic female in space.

Q Which of the following is correct about Ellen Ochoa?

(a) She became an astronaut after reaching many other goals.

(b) She is most famous for her computer technology inventions.

(c) Her success was due to focusing all her time and energy on her work.

(d) It took several attempts for her to be chosen for the NASA program.

해석 엘렌 오초아는 다섯 남매 중 가운데로 태어나 든든한 조언자였던 홀어머니에 의해 키워졌다. 그녀의 적극적인 지원은 딸이 배움을 최선으로 여기도록 도왔다. 그러나 물리학에서 더 높은 학위를 따고 새로운 컴퓨터 기술을 설계하고 발명하는 것은 오초아에게는 충분하지 않았다. 일을 하고, 클래식 플루트를 연주하고, 배구를 하고, 자전거를 타는 등의 취미를 즐기는 중에도 오초아는 우주 비행사가 되기 위해 NASA에 지원할 시간을 마련했다. 그녀는 첫 번째 지원에서는 선택되지 않았다. 하지만 그 다음 번에는 일이 더 잘 풀렸다. 1993년 오초아는 최초의 라틴 아메리카계 여성 우주인이 되었다.

Q 엘렌 오초아에 대한 내용으로 올바른 것은?

(a) 그녀는 많은 다른 목표들을 달성한 후에 우주 비행사가 되었다.

(b) 그녀는 그녀의 컴퓨터 기술 발명으로 가장 유명하다.

(c) 그녀는 자신의 시간과 에너지를 일에 쏟았기 때문에 성공했다.

(d) NASA 프로그램에 선택되기까지 그녀는 몇 번의 시도를 했다.

해설 글을 읽고 엘렌 오초아라는 인물에 관해 맞는 내용을 선택하는 문제이다. 어머니는 든든한 조언자(a strong mentor)였으며, 그녀는 물리학에서 학위를 취득하고, 새로운 컴퓨터 기술을 설계하였다. 그러나 이 모든 것이 그녀에게는 충분하지 않았다(However, gaining advanced degrees in physics, ~ wasn't enough for Ochoa.). 따라서 그녀가 우주 비행사가 되기 전에 다양한 경력을 갖고 있었음을 알 수 있다. 그녀는 첫 번째 지원에서는 선택되지는 않았지만, 1993년 최초의 라틴 아메리카계 여성 우주인이 되어 더 일이 잘 풀렸음을 알 수 있다. 따라서 정답은 (a)다.

어휘 mentor 멘토, 조언자
single mother 홀어머니
positive support 적극적인 지원
priority 상위, 우선권
degree 학위, 등급, 단계
pursuit 일, 연구, 추구
apply to ~에 지원하다
astronaut 우주비행사
application 지원
work out (문제가) 풀리다
goal 목표
attempt 시도하다

정답 (a)

28

Hurricane-like winds tore through parts of Germany on Sunday, leaving several residents injured, travelers stranded, and homes without electricity. More than one hundred people were injured by blowing or falling debris. Several homes were damaged by the high winds. All flights were cancelled at the Frankfurt Airport, and the Berlin Central Railway Station was closed after the extreme winds ripped a steel support from the front of the building.

Q Which of the following is correct about the storm?

(a) All German airports were forced to cancel flights.

(b) The winds tore apart steel sections of the railway.

(c) Homes were damaged from electrical problems.

(d) It created dangerous conditions that caused injuries.

해석 허리케인과 같은 바람이 독일 일부 지역을 일요일에 휩쓸고 지나가며 몇몇 주민들에게 부상을 입히고, 여행자들을 고립되게 하고, 가정에 전기가 끊기도록 만들었다. 백명 이상의 사람들이 날아다니거나 떨어지는 잔해들에 의해 부상을 당했다. 여러 집이 세찬 바람에 피해를 입었다. 프랑크푸르트 공항의 모든 비행기는 취소되었고, 베를린 중앙 기차역은 강한 바람이 건물 앞부분의 강철 기둥을 뜯어 간 후에 폐쇄되었다.

Q 위 글의 폭풍에 대한 내용으로 올바른 것을 고르시오.

(a) 모든 독일 공항이 비행 편을 취소해야 했다.

(b) 바람이 철로의 강철로 된 부분을 뜯어냈다.

(c) 집들이 전기적 문제들로 피해를 입었다.

(d) 부상을 일으킨 위험한 상황을 초래했다.

해설 공항중에는 프랑크푸르트 공항만 언급되었으므로 (a)는 답이 아니고, 철 기둥(steel support)이 기차역의 앞부분에서 떨어져 나간 것이지 철로에서 떨어져 나간 것은 아니므로 (b)도 틀렸다. 정전이 되었다(homes without electricity)는 내용만 언급되었지, 전기와 관련한 문제들이 언급된 부분은 없으므로 (c)도 오답이다. 다양한 피해 소식이 언급되면서, 상황이 다급했다는 것을 나타내므로 (d)가 답이다.

Tips 보기에 all, always, every 등이 들어간 것은 답이 아닐 경우가 많다.

어휘 tear 찢다, 째다
several 몇 몇의, 몇 개의, 몇 사람의
resident 거주자
injure 상처 입히다
stranded 발이 묶인
electricity 전기
debris 잔해, 파편, 부스러기
damage 손해[손상, 부상]를 입히다
high wind 세찬[모진] 바람
cancel 취소하다, 무효로 하다
rip 찢다, 벗기다
be forced to+V ~하지 않을 수 없다

정답 (d)

29

The Electrifying Irish Shamrock Dance Company is coming to Kennsington Auditorium on Thursday, April 11th at 3 p.m. for one performance only. Their energetic style combines traditional Irish dance with ballet, tap, and modern dance. Choreographed to live traditional Celtic music, the performance will enliven your spirit and touch your heart. Get your tickets at the Kennsington box office. Call 900-899-1234 today.

Q Which of the following is correct about the advertisement?

(a) The dance troupe on tour was recently formed.

(b) Tickets will be available beginning April 11th.

(c) The performance showcases Irish music.

(d) The choreography blends many styles of dance.

해석 감동의 아이리쉬 샴록 무용단이 켄싱턴 강당에서 4월 11

일 목요일 3시 단 일회의 공연을 선보입니다. 무용단의 활기찬 스타일은 전통 아일랜드 춤과 발레, 탭 댄스, 현대 무용을 결합하고 있습니다. 전통 켈트 생음악 연주에 안무를 맞춘 이 공연은 여러분에게 생기를 불어 넣어 주고 감동을 전해 줄 것입니다. 켄싱턴 매표소에서 표를 구매하세요. 오늘 900-899-1234로 전화하세요.

Q 위 광고의 내용으로 알맞은 것을 고르시오.
(a) 순회공연을 하는 무용단은 최근에 결성되었다.
(b) 입장권은 4월 11일부터 구매 가능하다.
(c) 공연은 아일랜드 음악을 선보인다.
(d) 안무는 많은 종류의 춤을 혼합했다.

해설 무용단의 설립 시기는 언급되지 않았으므로 (a)는 답이 아니고, 공연날짜가 4월 11일이고, 예매가 가능하므로 (b)도 답이 아니다. 공연은 음악 공연이 아니라, 무용 공연이므로 (c)도 답이 아니다. 발레, 탭댄스, 현대무용 등이 어우러졌다는 내용이 있으므로 (d)가 정답이다.

어휘 **electrify** 깜짝 놀라게 하다, 감동시키다
company 회사, 집단
auditorium 강당
energetic 활동적인, 원기 왕성한
combine 결합하다, 연합하다, 병합하다
traditional 전통의, 전통적인
spirit 마음, 생기, 영혼
choreograph (음악에) 안무하다
enliven ~을 활기띠게 하다
troupe [연예인 등] 일단
blend 섞다, 혼합하다
showcase 전시하다, 소개하다

정답 (d)

30

India's government provides free education to all children up to the age of 14. Despite this promise, there are still tens of millions of Indian children not going to school. The biggest problem seems to be in India's rural areas. Although education is supposed to be free, many agricultural workers can't afford to send their children to school. Small fees for books, uniforms and other expenses can add up to a month's worth of wages for these parents. Also, many parents don't want their children to attend classes in rural schools that are in extremely poor conditions.

Q Which of the following is correct according to the passage?
(a) Free education is not provided to Indian children in rural areas.
(b) Only expensive private schooling is offered in rural India.
(c) Parents worry about sending their children to city schools.
(d) Many rural schools in India are in very bad shape.

해석 인도 정부는 모든 어린이들에게 14살까지 무상 교육을 제공한다. 이러한 약속에도 불구하고 아직도 수 천만 명의 아이들이 학교에 다니지 않는다. 가장 큰 문제는 인도의 시골 지역에 있는 듯하다. 교육이 무료임에도 불구하고 많은 농업 노동자들은 그들의 아이들을 학교에 보낼 여유가 없다. 책, 교복을 살 비용과 다른 기타 비용들이 이 부모들의 한 달 치 월급에 달하기 때문이다. 또한 많은 부모들은 매우 빈약한 조건들을 갖춘 시골 학교에 아이들을 보내고 싶어 하지 않는다.

Q 위 글의 내용과 일치하는 것을 고르시오.
(a) 무상 교육은 시골 지역 인도 어린이들에게는 제공되지 않는다.
(b) 인도의 시골지역에서는 비싼 사교육만이 제공된다.
(c) 부모들은 아이들을 도시 학교에 보내는 것을 염려한다.
(d) 인도의 많은 시골 학교들의 조건이 매우 열악하다.

해설 인도의 무상교육에 관한 글이다. 'Despite this promise ~'에 주목하라! 14세까지 무상 교육이지만 실제로는 수천만 명의 학생들이 학교에 가지 않는다. 이러한 현상의 이유는 'The biggest problem seems to be in India's rural areas. Although education is supposed to be free, many agricultural workers can't afford to send their children to school.'에 제시되어있다. 가장 큰 이유는 시골 지역에서 학교를 보내기 어렵기 때문이다. 따라서 정답은 (d)다.

어휘 **despite** ~에도 불구하고
rural 시골의, 시골에 사는

be supposed to ~하기로 되어 있다
agricultural 농업의, 농사의
can't afford to ~할 여유가 없다
add up to 합계가 ~이다
wage 임금, 급료
attend 참여하다, 참석하다
extremely 극단적으로, 극도로
private schooling 사교육
in bad shape 상태가 좋지 않은

정답 (d)

31

One company has developed a product for office workers who are tired of annoying employees hanging around their desk. The forty dollar USB Missile Launcher connects to and is controlled by the employee's office computer. Three soft foam missiles can be fired within a range of fifteen feet. The launcher can move from side to side 180 degrees, or tilt up to 45 degrees. Missile sound effects can be played through the computer's speakers.

Q Which of the following is correct according to the passage?

(a) The software is annoying to other employees.
(b) The employee must have a computer to use the product.
(c) The silent launcher catches unwanted visitors by surprise.
(d) The launcher can shoot targets up to forty feet away.

해석 자신들의 업무 공간에서 어슬렁거리는 귀찮은 동료 직원들에게 지친 사무실 직원들을 위해 한 회사가 상품을 개발했다. 이 40달러 USB 미사일 발사대는 직원의 사무실 컴퓨터에 연결되어 조종된다. 원하지 않는 방해가 되는 손님이 다가 올 경우, 세 개의 부드러운 거품 미사일이 15피트 반경 내에서 발사될 수 있다. 발사대는 좌우로 180도 움직이거나 상하 45도 각도로 움직일 수 있다. 미사일의 음향 효과는 컴퓨터의 스피커를 통해 들을 수 있다.

Q 위 글의 내용과 일치하는 것을 고르시오.
(a) 소프트웨어는 다른 직원들에게 방해가 된다.
(b) 직원이 이 상품을 이용하기 위해 컴퓨터가 있어야 한다.
(c) 조용한 발사대는 원하지 않는 손님을 깜짝 놀라게 해서 잡는다.
(d) 발사대는 40피트 떨어져 있는 목표물까지 맞출 수 있다.

해설 소프트웨어가 다른 직원들을 짜증나게 하는 것이 아니라, 짜증나게 만드는 직원들을 물리치기 위한 것이므로 (a)는

틀린 답이다. 이 상품은 컴퓨터를 이용해서 사용한다는 내용이 소개되었으므로 (b)가 답이다. 소리에 대한 언급은 있었지만, 음향 효과로 사람을 놀라게 한다는 것을 유추할 증거가 될 만한 실마리가 없으므로 (c)는 답이 아니다. forty라는 숫자는 가격을 언급할 때 나왔고, 미사일이 날아갈 수 있는 거리는 15피트이므로 (d)도 틀린다.

Tips 세부 사항을 확인하는 문제를 풀 때는 "Who Is Doing What?"을 기억하라. 누가 어떤 것을 하는지 주의 깊게 보아야 한다. 이번 문제의 경우 40이라는 숫자는 가격과 연관이 있었고, 거리를 언급할 때는 15라는 숫자를 기억해야 된다.

어휘 annoying 귀찮은, 성가신
hang around 어슬렁거리다
launcher (미사일, 로켓 등의) 발사대, 발사 장치
connect 연결하다, 결합하다
range 범위, 사거리
tilt 상하로 움직이다
fire 발사하다
degree 정도, (각도의 단위) 도
unwanted 요구되지 않은, 바라지 않은

정답 (b)

32

Many artists use asymmetrical composition to illustrate imbalance in their work. For example, large forms look visually heavier in weight than smaller ones. The same is true for dark forms as opposed to lighter ones. Textured objects look heavier than smoother ones. However, two or more little forms next to a larger one look well-balanced, as does a smaller, dark form next to a bigger, light one.

Q Which of the following is correct about visual balance?

(a) Large forms and small forms look well-balanced on canvas.
(b) Two small forms look balanced compared to two larger ones.
(c) Smooth forms look lighter than objects that have a texture.
(d) Dark forms appear to weigh less than lighter, colored forms.

해석 많은 미술가들이 그들의 작품에서 불균형을 묘사하기 위해서 비대칭구도를 사용한다. 예를 들어 큰 형체는 그보다 작은 형체보다 시각적으로 더 무거워 보인다. 밝은 형체에 비해 어두운 형체도 더 무거워 보인다. 질감이 있는 물체들은 부드러운 물체들보다 더 무거워 보인다. 그러나 하나의 큰 형체 옆에 있는 두 개 혹은 그 이상의 작은 형체들은 균형이 잡혀 보이고, 크고 밝은 형체 옆에 있는 작고 어두운 형체도 균형이 잡혀 보이게 된다.

Q 시각적 균형에 관한 내용으로 올바른 사실을 고르시오.

(a) 큰 형체들과 작은 형체들을 화폭에서 균형이 잡혀 보인다.

(b) 두 개의 작은 형체들은 두 개의 큰 형체에 비해 균형 있어 보인다.

(c) 부드러운 형체는 질감이 있는 물체보다 가벼워 보인다.

(d) 어두운 형체는 밝은 색상의 형체들보다 가벼워 보인다.

해설 형체가 크면 더 무거워 보인다고 했는데, 균형이 잘 잡혔다는 (a)의 내용은 맞지 않다. 크기가 다른 점을 이용해서 불균형(imbalance)의 예를 나타내고 있다. 어두울수록 더 무거워 보인다며 명암이 비대칭의 예로 사용되는 것으로 소개했는데, (b)에서는 균형이 잡혔다고 하니 틀린다. 질감이 있을수록 더 무거워 보인다, 즉 면이 매끄러운 것이 더 가벼워 보인다는 뜻이므로 (c)가 정답이다. 어두운 형태가 더 가벼워 보인다는 것은 본문 내용과 틀리므로 (d)는 오답이다.

어휘 asymmetrical 비대칭의, 불균형의
composition 구성, 작곡
illustrate 설명하다, 삽화하다
imbalance 불균형
visually 시각적으로
object 물건, 물체
as opposed to ~와 대조적으로
textured 질감이 있는
well-balanced 균형이 잡힌
compared to ~와 비교해서

정답 (c)

33

Because teenagers enjoy spending money, marketers are always searching for ways to get the attention of the teenage market, but it is tough to reach them through magazines. Teens spend much more time with their computers, televisions, and radios than they do reading magazines. However, more specialty magazines like ones about skateboarding, snowboarding, or celebrities are building large readerships and gaining attention from marketers.

Q Which of the following is correct according to the passage?

(a) Teenagers spend more time on the Internet than they do watching TV.

(b) Celebrities are building large readerships.

(c) Reaching the teenage market is very difficult for magazines.

(d) Advertisers feel magazines cannot effectively reach teenagers.

해석 십대들은 돈 쓰기를 좋아하기 때문에 마케팅 담당자들은 항상 십대들의 시장의 관심을 끌기 위한 방법을 찾는다. 그러나 잡지를 통해 십대에 다가가는 것은 어렵다. 십대들은 잡지를 읽기 보다는 자신들의 컴퓨터, 텔레비전, 라디오와 더 많은 시간을 보낸다. 그러나 스케이트보딩, 스노우보딩 혹은 연예인에 대한 잡지들과 같은 많은 전문 잡지들은 많은 독자들을 확보하고 있으며, 마케팅 담당자들의 관심을 끌고 있다.

Q 위 글의 내용과 일치하는 것을 고르시오.

(a) 십대들은 TV를 보는 것보다 인터넷에 더 많은 시간을 소비한다.

(b) 유명인사들은 많은 구독자들을 거느리고 있다.

(c) 잡지들이 십대 시장에 접근하는 것은 매우 힘들다.

(d) 광고주들은 잡지들이 효과적으로 십대에게 접근할 수 없다고 생각한다.

해설 세부 사항을 파악하는 문제이므로 선택지를 하나씩 살펴보면서 오답을 제거하는 방법으로 정답을 찾는 것이 좋다. 십대가 잡지를 읽는 것보다 컴퓨터와 TV를 보는데 더 많은 시간을 보낸다고 했지만 그 둘을 비교하지는 않았으니 (a)는 답이 아니다. 연예인이 아니라 연예인에 대한 잡지를 구독을 하는 사람들이 많으므로 (b)도 답이 아니다. 십대들의 독서량이 작기 때문에 잡지로 십대 마음을 움직이는 것은 어려울 것을 알 수 있으므로 (c)가 정답이다. 광고주들 중에서 십대가 특정 잡지들에 관심을 갖고 있는 경우도 있다고 했으므로 단정적으로 잡지가 효과적이지 않다고 하는 (d)는 정답이 아니다.

어휘 tough 힘든, 거친
specialty 전문
readership 독자(층)
celebrity 유명인사
advertiser 광고주

정답 (c)

34

Sociologists have recognized among various cultures a set of standards known as mores. Mores are the traditional concepts a given culture has about certain qualities. Different than folkways, or the accepted traditions and customs a culture has, mores are considered to be on a larger scale. For example, while someone who does not greet another person may be considered rude because he or she violated a folkway, a person who kills someone is considered evil because he or she violated social mores. The degree of disapproval is vastly different.

Q What can be inferred from the passage?

(a) Courtesy is the main aspect of mores.

(b) Folkways are more important to any given culture.

(c) Folkways carry a higher degree of disapproval if violated.

(d) Mores are often reflected in a country's laws.

해석 사회학자들은 다양한 문화들 간에 모레스라고 알려진 사회적 규범이 존재한다는 것을 발견했다. 모레스는 한 문화가 일정한 특성들에 대해 가지고 있는 전통적인 개념들이다. 민간 풍습 혹은 한 문화가 가지고 있는 일반적으로 받아들여지는 전통과 관습과는 달리 모레스는 좀 더 대규모로 여겨진다. 예를 들어 다른 사람에게 인사를 하지 않는 사람이 민간 풍습을 어겼기 때문에 무례한 것으로 여겨질 수 있는 반면에, 살인을 한 사람은 사회의 모레스를 어겼기 때문에 사악한 것으로 여겨진다. 용인할 수 없는 것의 정도가 크게 다르다.

Q 위 글에서 유추할 수 있는 것을 고르시오.
(a) 예의 바름이 모레스의 초점이다.
(b) 어느 문화에서든 민간 풍습이 더 중요하다.
(c) 민간 풍습이 어겨질 경우 더 심하게 용인되지 않는다.
(d) 모레스는 종종 한 국가의 법에 반영된다.

해설 글을 읽고 유추할 수 있는 내용을 선택하는 문제이다. 내용을 유추하는 것은 겉에 드러난 내용을 바탕으로 숨겨진 내용을 파악할 수 있는 능력도 있어야 한다. 다양한 문화 속에 존재하는 사회적 규범인 '모레스'에 관한 글이다. 모레스에 대한 개념 정의로 '~ the traditional concepts a given culture has about certain qualities ~'라고 설명하여 한 문화가 특정 자질에 관해 갖고 있는 전통적 개념이란 것을 강조한다. 일반적 전통은 관습과는 다르게 좀 더 대규모로 여겨진다는 차이가 있다(Different than folkways, or the accepted traditions and customs a culture has ~). 이 두 가지의 차이로, 인사를 안 하는 것은 민간 풍습을 어기는 것이지만 살인은 모레스를 위반한 것으로 용인될 수 없다. 따라서 유추할 수 있는 내용은 모레스를 어기는 경우에 처벌될 수 있다

는 것이다. 정답은 (d)다.

어휘 sociologist 사회학자
mores (사회적) 관습, 관행
traditional 전통적인
folkways 습관, 풍속
violate (약속 등을) 어기다, 위반하다
disapproval 불찬성, 불승인
vastly 엄청나게 큰, 거대한
courtesy 예의(바름), 공손
aspect 양상, 관점, 국면

정답 (d)

35

In 1862 the United States Government passed the Homestead Act, which was intended to help populate much of the newly acquired land west of the Mississippi River. The law basically allowed military veterans, heads of households, and anyone over the age of twenty-one to acquire up to 160 acres of federal land for a nominal fee. There were only two requirements: that the individual live on and farm the land for five years. It then became the property of the person who had homesteaded it.

Q Which of the following is correct about the Homestead Act?

(a) It was meant to make money for the government.

(b) It permitted land to be given as payment to soldiers.

(c) It required that the land be cultivated for several years.

(d) It gave away land in Mississippi to be farmed.

해석 1862년 미국 정부는 자영 농지법을 통과시켰는데 이 법은 미시시피 강 서부에 새로 획득한 토지들에 인구를 늘리기 위한 것이었다. 이 법은 기본적으로 군인들, 가장들, 21세가 넘은 사람은 누구나 최대 160에이커까지 연방 정부의 땅을 싼 가격에 얻을 수 있도록 하는 내용이었다. 이것에는 단지 두 가지의 자격 요건이 있었다. 개인은 5년간 그 땅에 살면서 농사를 지어야 했다. 그리고 나면 그 토지는 그곳에 살며 농사를 지은 사람의 소유지가 되었다.

Q 자영 농지법에 대한 내용으로 올바른 것을 고르시오.
(a) 정부가 돈을 벌기 위해 의도되었다.
(b) 군인들에게 보수로 땅을 주도록 한 것이다.
(c) 몇 년 동안 토지가 경작될 것을 요구했다.
(d) 미시시피의 땅을 농사를 짓도록 나누어 주었다.

해설 1862년 미국 정부에서 제시한 자영 농지법에 관한 글이다. 이 법의 궁극적 목적은 미시시피 강 근처에 생긴 토지

에 인구를 증가하는 것이다(~, which was intended to help populate much of the newly acquired land west of the Mississippi River.). 법의 기본적인 내용은 군인, 가장 혹은 21세 이상의 누구에게나 싼 가격으로 얻을 수 있게 하는 것이다(~ to acquire up to 160 acres of federal land for a nominal fee.). 여기에는 두 가지 요구 사항이 있는데, 5년간 거주하면서 농사를 지어야 하며, 그 이후는 토지 소유자가 될 수 있다고 했다. 따라서 정답은 (c)다.

어휘 Homestead Act 남북전쟁 때인 1862년에 만든 미국의 자영농지법
intend to ~할 작정이다
populate (지역에) 살다, 거주하다
acquire 얻다, 취득하다
veteran 퇴역군인
nominal fee 매우 적은 수수료
individual 개인적인
property 재산, 소유지
cultivate 경작하다, 재배하다
give away 분배하다

정답 (c)

36

One of linguist Noam Chomsky's theories suggested that grammar has universal features. But the language of the Piraha people of the Amazonas does not support this theory. Research has shown that these intelligent people have a highly complex language that includes language features never before heard and an absence of features assumed to be used in all languages. The Piraha have no color, counting or number words and no grammatical way of putting one phrase inside another.

Q What does the writer suggest?

(a) The language lacks features that were previously considered normal for all languages.
(b) Chomsky's theory of universal features was incorrectly applied to this language.
(c) The absence of color words and numbers makes this language one of the most simplistic.
(d) Only short sentences that include one phrase are used by the Piraha people.

해석 언어학자 노엄 촘스키의 이론들 중 하나는 문법이 공통의 특징들을 가지고 있다고 암시한다. 그러나 아마조나스의 피라하 사람들의 언어는 이 이론에 해당되지 않는다. 연

구에 따르면 이 지적인 사람들은 매우 복잡한 언어를 가지고 있는데, 이 언어는 전에 들어 본적이 없는 특징들을 지니고 있고, 모든 언어들이 가지고 있다고 여겨진 특징들은 가지고 있지 않다. 피라하 사람들은 색깔, 셈 혹은 숫자 단어들이 없고, 하나의 구절을 다른 구절 안에 넣는데도 아무런 문법적 규칙이 없다.

Q 글쓴이가 암시하고 있는 바를 고르시오.

(a) 그 언어는 모든 언어들에 있어 일반적이라고 여겨졌던 특징들을 갖고 있지 않다.
(b) 촘스키의 공통적 특징 이론은 이 언어에 부정확하게 응용되었다.
(c) 색깔 단어와 숫자의 부재로 인해 이 언어는 가장 단순한 언어 중의 하나다.
(d) 피라하 사람들은 한 구절로 된 짧은 문장만을 사용한다.

해설 노엄 촘스키의 모든 언어 문법은 공통적 특징을 갖고 있다는 주장이 해당되지 않는 언어에 관한 글이다. 글의 흐름을 전환시키는 but에 주목하라. 아마조나스의 피라하 사람들의 언어는 매우 복잡한 구조를 가지고 있는데, 이 언어는 새로운 특징을 지니고 있고, 모든 언어들이 가지고 있다고 여겨진 특징들은 가지고 있지 않다. 예를 들어, 색, 셈 혹은 숫자 단어가 없고, 한 구절을 다른 구절에 삽입하는 규칙도 없다고 언급했다. 따라서 정답은 (a)다.

어휘 linguist 언어학자
theory 이론, 학설
universal 일반적인, 보편적인, 우주의
feature 특징, 특색
intelligent 지능이 좋은, 총명한
highly 매우
complex 복잡한, 뒤얽힌
include ~을 포함[포괄]하다
absence 부재
assume 가정하다, 추정하다
grammatical 문법(상)의, 문법적인
previously 이전에, 미리
incorrectly 부정확하게
simplistic 간소화[단순화]한

정답 (a)

37

A new memory circuit is storming the computer world. It is smaller and denser than a typical circuit, and the demonstration model stores up to 160,000 bits of memory. Its inventors are hoping that the new circuit will allow for increased memory in the future, although it has already exceeded previous sixty-four bit demonstration memory circuits. Researchers say that production is unlikely to occur for at least ten years.

Q Which of the following is correct according to the passage?
(a) The new memory circuit is larger and stores more information.
(b) The circuit is already in production for the next decade.
(c) The new circuit won't be available to the public for several years.
(d) The memory circuit has not yet been demonstrated to the public.

해석 새로운 메모리 회로가 컴퓨터계를 급습하고 있다. 이것은 일반적인 회로보다 더 작고 촘촘하며, 시범 모델은 16만 비트까지 저장할 수 있다. 이것의 발명가들은 이 새로운 회로가 이미 이전의 64비트 시범 메모리 회로를 넘어서고 있지만 미래에 증가된 메모리를 제공해 줄 것을 기대하고 있다. 연구자들은 적어도 10년 동안은 생산이 되지 않을 것이라고 말한다.

Q 위 글의 내용과 일치하는 것을 고르시오.
(a) 새로운 메모리 회로는 더 크고 더 많은 정보를 저장한다.
(b) 그 회로는 이미 다음 10년을 대비하여 생산 중이다.
(c) 새로운 회로는 몇 년 동안 일반인에게 판매되지 않을 것이다.
(d) 메모리 회로는 아직 일반인에게 시범을 보이지 않았다.

해설 새롭게 개발된 메모리 회로에 글이다. 한 새로운 메모리 회로가 컴퓨터계를 급습하고 있다(A new memory circuit is storming the computer world.). 이 회로의 특징은 일반 회로보다 더 작고 촘촘하며 16만 비트까지 저장한다고 한다. although를 사용해서 현재의 용량과 미래의 가능 용량을 비교한다. 즉, 미래에는 더 증가된 메모리를 제공해 줄 것이라고 기대하는데(~ the new circuit will allow for increased memory in the future, although it has already exceeded ~), 실제적인 생산은 10년 정도 후가 될 것이다(~ that production is unlikely to occur for at least ten years.)라고 했으므로 정답은 (c)다.

어휘 circuit 회로
storm 습격하다, 쇄도하다
dense 촘촘한, 밀집한

typical 전형적인, 일반적인
demonstration model 시범모델
exceed 초과하다
be unlikely to ~할 것 같지 않다
at least 최소한, 적어도
decade 10년

정답 (c)

38

There are many steps an individual can take in order to decrease his or her stress levels. (a) One of these steps is proper exercise; running, aerobics or playing a sport can vastly improve an individual's mood. (b) Another thing a person can do to relieve stress is to meditate or pray, since meditation has been shown to cause relaxation and rid the body of tenseness. (c) A third part of decreasing stress is diet, because ensuring that the body is getting proper nutrition gives the body extra energy, important in combating stress. (d) Without the proper nutrients it needs, the body is unable to fight off disease.

해석 개인이 자신의 스트레스 정도를 낮추기 위해서 취할 수 있는 많은 방법들이 있다. (a) 이러한 방법들 중의 하나는 적절한 운동이고 달리기, 에어로빅, 운동 경기는 개인의 기분을 크게 향상 시킬 수 있다. (b) 개인이 스트레스를 완화하기 위해 할 수 있는 또 하나는 명상을 하거나 기도를 하는 것으로 명상은 안정을 제공하고 몸의 긴장을 제거하는 것으로 나타났다. (c) 스트레스를 감소시키는 세 번째 부분은 식단으로, 몸이 적절한 영양분을 제공받도록 보증해 주는 것이 몸에 여분의 활력을 주게 되는데, 이것은 스트레스와 싸우는데 중요한 부분이다. (d) 적절한 영양분이 없이 몸은 질병을 물리칠 수 없다.

해설 스트레스 정도를 낮추기 위해 개인이 취할 수 있는 방법을(~ steps an individual can take in order to decrease his or her stress levels ~) 설명하는 글이다. 이 중 속하지 않는 내용을 선택하는 문제이다. (a) 달리기, 에어로빅, 혹은 운동 경기를 통해, (b) 명상 혹은 기도 등으로 안정을 제공하고 긴장을 제거하기, (c) 적절한 영양분을 제공하여 몸에 여분의 활력소를 제공하기 등으로 모두 스트레스를 해소하는 방법과 일관성이 있는 내용이다. 그러나 (d)는 이러한 주제와는 전혀 관계가 없다. 따라서 답은 (d)다.

어휘 decrease 감소시키다
proper 적합한, 알맞은
relieve 완화[경감]시키다
meditation 명상
relaxation (긴장, 근육의) 풀림, 이완
rid 없애다, 제거하다
tenseness 팽팽함, 긴장감
ensure 책임지다, 확실하게 하다

nutrition 영양분 *cf.* nutrient 영양분
combat 싸우다
fight off 물리치다

정답 (d)

39

Archer County has gotten more than ten inches of snow in the last few days, and the temperature has been averaging nearly twenty below. So here are some good tips for staying warm. (a) First, bundle up with multiple thin layers instead of one thick layer. (b) Bring pets in from outside so that they don't freeze. (c) Also, drink plenty of water, since water helps the body produce heat. (d) Make sure heating units are working properly, since these temperatures can cause hypothermia.

해석 아처 카운티는 지난 며칠 동안 10인치가 넘는 눈이 내렸고, 기온도 거의 평균 영하 20도에 달하고 있습니다. 이러한 날씨 속에 따뜻하게 지낼 수 있는 몇 가지 요령들을 소개합니다. (a) 먼저 하나의 두꺼운 옷보다는 얇은 옷을 여러 겹 껴입으십시오. (b) 애완동물을 집 안에 들여 얼어 죽지 않도록 하십시오. (c) 또한 물은 몸이 열을 내는 것을 도와주므로 충분한 물을 마시십시오. (d) 이 낮은 기온은 저체온증을 일으킬 수 있으므로 난방 장치가 제대로 작동하는지를 살피십시오.

해설 아처 카운티에서 폭설이 내리고 평균 기온이 저하 되었는데(Archer County has gotten more than ten inches of snow in the last few days, and the temperature has been averaging nearly twenty below.), 이런 환경에서 따뜻하게 지낼 수 있는 방법(some good tips)에 관한 글이다. (a) 얇은 옷을 여러 겹 껴입기, (b) 애완동물을 집안에서 키우기, (c) 몸에 열이 나도록 돕기 위해 물 마시기, (d) 난방 장치가 잘 작동하는 지 확인하기 등이다. 나머지는 모두 개인이 자신의 체온 유지를 위해 할 수 있는 것이고 (b)만이 애완동물 돌보기와 관련이 되는 것이기 때문에 정답은 (b)다.

어휘 temperature 온도, 기온
nearly 거의
bundle up 따뜻하게 몸을 감싸다
multiple 다수의, 다중의
freeze 얼어 죽다
hypothermia 저체온증

정답 (b)

40

Using a global positioning system and special geological markers drilled into the Earth,. geologists have begun to see how continents are deformed. (a) Data reveal that most of the surface of Asia is extremely strong, but when it breaks, it breaks like a ceramic dish. (b) As a result, Asia has experienced some of the world's largest earthquakes. (c) This type of fracture is similar to what is seen in typical plate tectonics. (d) This more detailed understanding is critical to understanding earthquakes.

해석 위치 추적 시스템과 지구 내부에 장치된 특수 지질학적 표식들을 이용하여 지질학자들은 대륙이 변형된 방법을 찾기 시작했다. (a) 자료들에 따르면 아시아 대륙의 표면의 대부분은 매우 단단하지만, 균열이 생길 경우 마치 도자기 접시가 깨우지는 것 같은 방식으로 붕괴된다고 한다. (b) 그로 인해 아시아는 세계적으로 가장 큰 규모의 지진들을 경험한 적이 있다. (c) 이러한 균열의 방식은 판 구조론에서 전형적인 방식이다. (d) 이와 같이 좀 더 세부적인 부분을 이해하는 것은 지진을 이해하는 데 있어 중요하다.

해설 지구과학과 관련된 글이다. (a), (c), (d)는 지질학의 일반적인 내용을 다루고 있는 반면, (b)는 아시아에서 있었던 사실을 기사보도처럼 밝히는 문장이므로 나머지 다른 부분과 자연스럽게 연결되지 못한다. 글의 흐름 파악을 확인하는 문제는 전체 주제, 저자의 태도(attitude) 등과 어울리는지 확인하고, 나머지 다른 보기들과의 연계성을 확인하는 것도 좋은 방법이다. 지금처럼 나머지 3개의 선택지는 일반적인 사실을 언급하는 반면에, (b)는 factual한 내용을 전달하므로 전체 흐름을 방해한다. 따라서 답은 (b)다. 또한 (c)에 나오는 fracture가 (a)의 when it breaks ~ 부분과 자연스럽게 연결되는 것이고 (b)가 흐름을 방해하기 위해 삽입된 문장임을 알 수 있다. 따라서 답은 (b)다.

어휘 geological 지질학(상)의
geologist 지질학자
continent 대륙
deform 변형시키다, 변모시키다
earthquake 지진
ceramic 도자기
fracture 골절, 부서지기, 갈라진 틈
typical 전형적인, 대표적인
plate tectonics 판구조론
critical 중요한

정답 (b)

1 (c)	**2** (a)	**3** (b)	**4** (a)	**5** (c)
6 (b)	**7** (c)	**8** (a)	**9** (a)	**10** (b)
11 (b)	**12** (b)	**13** (a)	**14** (d)	**15** (d)
16 (c)	**17** (a)	**18** (c)	**19** (c)	**20** (d)
21 (d)	**22** (b)	**23** (b)	**24** (a)	**25** (c)
26 (a)	**27** (c)	**28** (a)	**29** (c)	**30** (c)
31 (a)	**32** (c)	**33** (b)	**34** (a)	**35** (b)
36 (d)	**37** (b)	**38** (c)	**39** (d)	**40** (d)

어지럼증과 구토를 호소하고 있는 것이다. 뒤에 이어지는 문장에서 벽이 이리저리 기울어져 있기(~ explaining that the walls, which tilt toward and away) 때문에 라는 글에 가장 부합하는 내용이 빈 칸에 들어가야 한다. 따라서 (c)가 적절하다.

어휘 addition 증축 부분, 추가물
multi-story 여러 층의, 다층의
granite 화강암
slanted 기울어진
unusual 보통이 아닌, 드문
patrons 단골손님, 고객, 방문자
complain 불평하다, 한탄하다
dizziness 어지럼증
nausea 멀미, 메스꺼움
tilt 기울다
comprise 손상시키다
vision 시력

정답 (c)

1

The Midtown Art Museum's new 5,000-square-foot addition is literally making some visitors sick. The multi-story exhibit features granite walls that are slanted at unusual angles. Many patrons have complained of dizziness and nausea after visiting the new museum. The museum has issued a statement explaining that the walls, which tilt toward and away from visitors, have _____ of some people.

(a) compromised the safety
(b) destroyed the health
(c) affected the balance
(d) hurt the vision

해석 미드 타운 예술 박물관의 새로운 5천 스퀘어 피트의 증축 건물이 사실상 일부 방문객들에게 불편을 끼치고 있다. 이 여러 층으로 된 전시 공간은 특이한 각도로 기울어져 있는 대리석 벽이 특징이다. 많은 방문객들이 이 박물관을 방문한 후 어지럼증과 구토를 호소하고 있다. 박물관 측은 성명을 발표하여 벽이 이리저리 기울어져 있어서 일부 방문객들의 균형감각에 영향을 끼쳤다고 설명했다.

(a) 안전을 해쳤다
(b) 건강을 해쳤다
(c) 균형감각에 영향을 끼쳤다
(d) 시력을 해쳤다

해설 문단의 첫 문장에서 글의 전체적인 의미를 파악할 수 있다. 미드 타운 박물관의 증축으로 인한 방문객들의 불편에 관한 글이다. 글의 내용에서 '박물관은 특이한 각도(unusual angles)라고 되어 있다'라는 부분에 주목할 필요가 있다. 이 특이한 각도로 인해 박물관의 방문객들이

2

Students today need to learn skills in order to quickly process large amounts of information available at their fingertips via the Internet. A _____ and a careful choosing are necessary. But students must also learn to recognize good sources from less trustworthy ones. Education experts say this is often hard for students to do.

(a) quick understanding
(b) further study
(c) large database
(d) reliable website

해석 오늘날의 학생들은 인터넷을 이용하여 즉시 이용할 수 있는 대량의 정보들을 빠르게 처리하기 위한 기술을 배울 필요가 있다. 빠른 이해력과 신중한 선택이 필요하다. 그러나 학생들은 또한 좋은 자료와 믿지 못할 자료를 가려내는 법을 배워야 한다. 교육 전문가들은 이것이 종종 학생들에게 있어 어려운 일이라고 말한다.

(a) 빠른 이해력
(b) 추가적인 연구
(c) 방대한 자료
(d) 믿을만한 웹사이트

해설 문단의 첫 문장에서 주제 문장을 제시하여, 인터넷 사용을 통해 방대한 양의 자료를 접할 수 있는 요즘에 학생들이 해야 할 것 중의 하나는 많은 정보를 신속하게 처리할 수 있는 기술임을 강조하고 있다. 이를 좀 더 보충하기 위해서 다음 문장의 빈 칸에서는 주제문과 연결된 구문이 들어가야 한다. 정보의 홍수 속에서 학생들이 해야 할 것은 신속하게 이해하고 선택해야 하는 것이다. 따라서 정답은 (a)가 적절하다. 문단의 후반부에서는 또한 빠른 이해를 통해 정보를 얻고 믿을만한 자료와 믿을만하지 못한 자료

를 구분해내는 것도 배워야 한다고 강조하고 있다.

어휘 in order to ~하기 위해서
process 처리하다
large amounts of 다량[많은 양]의
available 이용할 수 있는, 쓸모 있는
at one's fingertips 쉽게, 가까이에
recognize 알아보다, 인지하다
source 자료, 출처
trustworthy 신뢰 할 수 있는
experts 숙련가

정답 (a)

3

It has recently been proven that a diet of fruits, vegetables, fish, whole grains and olive oil can delay and maybe even prevent the start of Alzheimer's disease. In one study, those who occasionally followed this diet decreased their _____ of developing the disease by 53%. Those who strictly followed the diet lowered their chances of getting the disease by 68%.

(a) fear
(b) risk
(c) method
(d) habit

해석 과일, 야채, 생선, 곡물, 올리브 오일로 구성된 식단이 치매의 시작을 예방하고 지연시킬 수 있다는 것이 최근에 증명되었다. 한 연구에 따르면 이 식품들을 가끔 섭취한 사람들은 치매의 걸릴 위험이 53% 감소되었다. 그리고 이 식단을 철저하게 따른 사람들은 치매에 걸릴 가능성이 68% 낮아졌다.

(a) 두려움
(b) 위험
(c) 방법
(d) 습관

해설 음식섭취가 치매를 예방할 수 있다는 내용의 글이다. 문장의 빈 칸에 들어가야 할 것은 앞부분의 내용을 정확하게 파악해야 가능하다. 앞부분에서는 과일, 야채, 생선 등으로 구성된 식단이 치매 시작을 지연시키고 예방시킬 수 있다(It has recently been proven that a diet of fruits, vegetables, fish, whole grains and olive oil can delay and maybe even prevent the start of Alzheimer's disease.)는 내용이기 때문에 빈 칸에 들어가는 표현은 이러한 식이요법이 치매의 위험을 53% 감소시킬 수 있다는 내용이어야 한다. 따라서 답은 (b)다.

어휘 recently 요즘, 최근에
prevent (~의 발생을) 막다, 예방하다
grain 곡물
delay 늦추다, 지연시키다
occasionally 때때로, 가끔

decrease 감소시키다
strictly 엄격히, 정확히
lower 낮추다, 감소시키다

정답 (b)

4

Many famous retail stores, the ones often thought of by younger shoppers as uncool or out-of-date, are reinventing their images. By partnering with famous designers, these stores now offer the younger crowd stylish merchandise at low prices. Such partnerships team discount stores with some of the biggest names in the fashion industry. Young consumers love the fact that being cool and trendy _____.

(a) doesn't have to cost a lot
(b) isn't necessary to be popular
(c) means that you know fashion
(d) depends largely on the designer

해석 젊은 구매자들에게 세련되지 않거나 유행에 뒤떨어진 곳으로 여겨지는 많은 유명한 소매점들이 이미지를 개혁하고 있다. 유명한 디자이너들과 함께 협력함으로써 이 상점들은 현재 젊은이들에게 최신 스타일의 상품들을 낮은 가격에 제공한다. 이러한 협력 관계는 할인점과 패션계의 유명인들을 연결시킨다. 젊은 소비자들은 세련되고 유행에 따르는 것이 꼭 돈이 많이 들 필요는 없다는 사실을 좋아한다.

(a) 꼭 돈이 많이 들 필요는 없다
(b) 반드시 인기 있는 것은 아니다
(c) 패션을 안다는 것을 의미한다
(d) 디자이너에게 크게 의존한다

해설 패션계의 새로운 경향을 소개하는 글이다. 유명한 상점들이 젊은 소비자층에게 유행에 떨어지거나 세련되지 않다는 이미지를 바꾸기 위한 노력을 소개한다. 'By partnering with famous designers, these stores now offer the younger crowd stylish merchandise at low prices.'의 문장에서 'By ~ing'는 '이런 것을 함으로써'라는 표현으로 이 글에서는 유명한 디자이너와 협력해서 저렴한 가격으로 상품을 판매한다는 것이 중점적 내용이다. 따라서 빈 칸에 들어가는 표현은 젊은 소비자들이 비싼 돈을 들이지 않아도 세련된 제품을 선택할 수 있다는 것이기 때문에 정답은 (a)다.

어휘 retail store 소매점
uncool 세련되지 못한, 볼 품 없는
out-of-date 낡은, 시대에 뒤떨어진
partner 제휴하다
reinvent 재 발명하다
merchandise 상품
team 연결시키다, 결합하다
consumer 소비자

trendy 최신 유행의

5

Your magazine's travel review on our city did not give a balanced view of all that our city has to offer. The writer talked about the overcrowding, traffic problems and high prices tourists often face, but he failed to mention the customer service and warm hospitality of our hotels, restaurants and shops. I would encourage your readers to visit our town and form their own opinion before believing the writer's

_____ .

(a) unusually accurate depictions
(b) highly exaggerated praise
(c) incredibly slanted views
(d) overly positive assertions

해석 귀사 잡지의 여행 평론은 저희 도시가 제공하는 모든 것들에 대한 균형 잡힌 시각을 반영하지 못했습니다. 관광객들이 흔히 겪게 되는 혼잡함과 교통 문제와 비싼 가격들에 대해선 지적했습니다. 하지만 저희 도시의 호텔들과 식당들, 상점들에서 흔히 볼 수 있는 고객 서비스와 친절함에 대해서는 제대로 언급하지 못했습니다. 저는 귀 잡지의 독자들이 글쓴이의 <u>터무니없이 편향된 견해</u>를 믿기 전에 저희 도시를 직접 방문하여 스스로의 의견을 형성할 것을 권해드립니다.

(a) 대단히 정확한 묘사
(b) 매우 과장된 칭찬
(c) 터무니없이 편향된 견해
(d) 지나치게 긍정적인 주장

해설 글의 정확한 내용 파악을 위해서는 글쓴이의 의도를 먼저 알아야 한다. 이 글을 쓴 사람은 자신의 도시에 대한 잘못된 잡지사의 평론에 대한 불만과 함께 이 글을 읽는 독자들에게 직접 자신의 도시를 방문하여 잡지의 글이 객관적이지 못하다는 것을 깨닫기를 부탁하고 있다. 'Your magazine's travel review on our city did not give a balanced view of all that our city has to offer.' 에서 나타나 있듯이 "균형있는 견해"를 제공하지 못했다는 것이다. 이와 비슷한 맥락으로 '~ but he failed to mention the customer service and warm hospitality of our hotels, restaurants and shops.' 를 연결해서 생각할 수 있다. 따라서 빈 칸에 들어갈 표현은 (c)가 적절하다.

어휘 review 평론
overcrowding 혼잡
face 겪다, 직면하다
mention ~에 대해 쓰다, 말하다
hospitality 환대
encourage 촉진하다, 장려하다, 권하다
depiction 묘사

exaggerated 과장된
slanted 치우친, 편향된
assertion 주장, 단정

6

Wildlife researchers have recently found a refuge in Cambodia for endangered animals. The area is in _____ the Mekong River. One of the animals the group found was an entire colony of slender-billed vultures, which are becoming scarce in Southeast Asia and are extinct in several countries. In addition to them, researchers found a red-headed vulture, a white-rumped vulture, a leaf monkey and a giant ibis; all of which are also endangered.

(a) an extraordinary mountaintop forest far from
(b) an extremely isolated portion of the jungle near
(c) a heavily populated section of a city next to
(d) a good cultivated field

해석 야생동물 연구자들은 최근에 캄보디아에서 멸종 위기의 동물들을 위한 피난처를 발견했다. 그 지역은 메콩강 <u>근처 정글의 매우 고립된 부분</u>에 있다. 그 집단이 발견한 동물들 중에는 가느다란 부리 독수리의 집단 서식지가 있었다. 그것들은 동남아시아에서 수가 적어지고 있으며 몇몇 국가들에서는 멸종했다. 가느다란 부리 독수리들 이외에도 연구자들은 빨간 머리 독수리, 흰 엉덩이 독수리, 잎사귀 원숭이와 큰 따오기를 발견했는데 이 동물들은 모두 멸종 위기에 처한 동물들이다.

(a) 멀리 떨어진 특이한 산꼭대기 숲
(b) 근처 정글의 매우 고립된 부분
(c) 옆에 인구가 밀집된 지역
(d) 잘 경작된 지역

해설 캄보디아 지역에서 잘 알려지지 않은 멸종 위기 동물들의 피난처를 발견한 것과 관련된 글이다. 글의 전체적인 내용은 이러한 피난처에서 발견한 동물 중 가느다란 부리 독수리(slender billed vulture)에 관한 설명이 대부분이다. 따라서 빈 칸에 들어갈 표현에 관한 정보는 뒷부분에서는 많이 제공되어 있지 않기 때문에 제시된 네 가지 가능성을 대입해보는 방법 밖에 없다. 우선 메콩 강과 연결되는 것이기 때문에 높은 산이나 인구 밀집지역과는 관련이 없다. 따라서 (a)와 (c)는 제외된다. 정답은 문맥상 (b)가 적절하다.

어휘 wildlife 야생 동물
endangered 멸종 위기에 처한
colony 서식지
slender-billed 가느다란 부리를 한

vulture 독수리
extinct 멸종된
in addition to ~외에도, ~에 더하여
populated 인구가 많은
cultivated 경작된

정답 (b)

blood vessel 혈관
function 기능
benefit 이익, 혜택
significantly 상당히
influential 영향을 미치는
detrimental 해로운

정답 (c)

7

Chocolate ... _____?
A new study suggests that it might be. A specially-formulated drink made out of cocoa rich in flavonols, which promote the production of a chemical that is good for circulatory health, seemed to improve blood vessel function. The study examined the effects of the cocoa on people of all age groups, but found that the elderly experienced the most benefit; the functioning of the blood vessels increased significantly. Interestingly, the individuals experienced this improvement after only six days.

(a) influential in brain health
(b) detrimental to the heart
(c) good for the blood vessels
(d) harmful for the elderly

해석 초콜릿은 혈관에 좋을까? 새로운 연구에 따르면 그럴 수도 있다고 한다. 순환계 건강에 좋은 화학 물질의 생산을 돕는 플라보놀이 풍부한 코코아로 특수 제조된 음료수가 혈관 기능을 개선하는 것 같다. 연구는 모든 연령층의 사람들에게 끼치는 코코아의 영향을 조사했는데 노인들이 가장 많은 혜택을 경험했으며 그들의 혈관기능이 현저히 증가한 것을 발견했다. 흥미롭게도 사람들은 단지 6일 후에 이러한 개선을 경험했다.

(a) 두뇌 건강에 영향이 있을까
(b) 심장에 해로울까
(c) 혈관에 좋을까
(d) 노인들에게 해로울까

해설 글의 앞부분에는 대개의 경우 주제 문장이 오기 때문에 앞부분의 빈 칸을 채우기 위해서는 전체적인 글의 요점을 파악하는 것이 중요하다. 이 글의 전체적 내용은 순환계 건강과 관련이 있는 플라보놀이 풍부하게 함양되어 있는 코코아의 영향에 관한 글이다. '~ which promote the production of a chemical that is good for circulatory health, seemed to improve blood vessel function.'에서 알 수 있듯이 코코아가 혈관기능과 관련이 있다는 연구를 소개하고 있기 때문에 빈 칸에는 이와 관련된 (c)가 정답이 된다.

어휘 formulate 만들다
promote 증진시키다
chemical 화학물질
circulatory 순환계의

8

I once met a polite elderly gentleman on an airplane. During the flight, I listened to stories about his childhood in Europe before World War II. As we landed and prepared to say goodbye, I thanked him for sharing his memories and told him I hoped he would have a nice day. In response, he told me he hoped I would have a nice life, saying that a wish for a nice day only lasts as long as the day itself, but a wish for a nice life lasts forever. Since we never know if or when we might see someone again, he told me I _____. He was right. He would know. He had survived Auschwitz.

(a) should wish this for everyone I meet
(b) could talk with anyone I wanted
(c) might try to be kinder to strangers
(d) would benefit from taking another trip

해석 나는 우연히 비행기에서 공손한 노신사를 만났다. 비행기를 타고 가는 동안, 나는 2차 세계대전 이전 유럽에서 보낸 그의 어린 시절 이야기를 들었다. 비행기가 착륙하고 각자의 갈 길을 준비하면서, 나는 이야기를 들려 준 것에 대해 그에게 감사하고 즐거운 하루를 보내기를 바란다고 말했다. 대답으로 그는 내가 즐거운 인생을 살기를 바란다고 말하면서, 즐거운 하루를 기원하는 것은 하루 동안만 지속되지만 즐거운 인생을 살라는 바램은 영원히 지속된다고 설명했다. 우리는 누군가를 언제 다시 보게 될지를 전혀 알 수 없기 때문에 내가 만나는 모든 사람들에게 이것을 기원해야 한다고 말했다. 그의 말이 옳았다. 그는 잘 알고 있었다. 그는 아우슈비츠의 생존자였다.

(a) 내가 만나는 모든 사람들에게 이것을 기원해야 한다
(b) 내가 원하는 모든 사람과 이야기를 할 수 있다
(c) 낯선 사람들에게 좀 더 친절하도록 노력해야 한다
(d) 또 다른 여행을 함으로써 얻는 것이 있을 것이다

해설 비행기에서 서로 처음 만난 두 사람이 나눈 대화와 관련된 글이다. 2차 세계대전을 겪은 한 노인이 헤어지면서 글쓴이가 '좋은 하루를 보내세요(I hoped he would have a nice day.).'라고 한 것에 대해 좋은 하루를 빌어 주는 것은 하루만 지속되지만 즐거운 인생을 빌어 주는 것은 영원히 지속된다고 함으로써 빈 칸에 들어갈 수 있는 표현과 연결시켜야 한다. 따라서 글쓴이가 'Since we never know if or when we might see someone again, ~'이라는 문장을 통해 누군가를 언제 다시 볼 수 있을지를 알 수 없기 때문에 그에게 '즐거운 인생'을 기원해주어야

한다는 암시가 들어있다. 따라서 정답은 (a)다.

어휘 polite 공손한, 예의바른
land 착륙하다
prepare 준비하다
response 대답, 반응
last 지속되다

정답 (a)

9

Studies have shown that our outlook on life is directly linked to our overall state of well-being. Studies have proven that people with positive outlooks enjoy longer, healthier lives than their negative counterparts. Interestingly, happy people share quite a few characteristics that keep their stress levels low and their moods up. First, they're well-connected with others, and they're by nature very generous. In addition, they tend to focus on the big picture. Put another way, such people are not typically _____.

(a) upset by minor annoyances
(b) concerned about major health issues
(c) interested in the welfare of others
(d) optimistic about their futures

해석 연구에 따르면 우리의 삶에 대한 관점은 전반적인 행복도에 직접적으로 연관이 있다고 한다. 연구는 긍정적인 관점을 가진 사람들이 부정적인 관점을 가진 사람들보다 더 오래 건강하게 산다는 것을 증명했다. 흥미롭게도 행복한 사람들에게는 스트레스 정도를 낮추고 기분을 좋게 유지하는 꽤 많은 공통점들이 있다. 먼저, 그들은 다른 사람들과 관계가 좋으며 천성적으로 매우 관대하다. 또한 그들은 대국적으로 판단하는 경향이 있다. 다른 말로 하자면 이 사람들은 일반적으로 <u>사소한 골칫거리들에 의해 방해를 받지 않는다.</u>

(a) 사소한 골칫거리들에 의해 방해를 받지 않는다
(b) 주요한 건강 문제들에 대해 염려하지 않는다
(c) 다른 사람들의 행복에 관심이 없다
(d) 자신들의 미래에 대해 낙관적이지 않다

해설 글의 전체적인 내용을 마지막 부분에 요약하는 표현을 선택하는 문제이다. 삶에 대한 긍정적인 태도를 갖고 있는 사람이 부정적 태도를 갖고 있는 사람보다 건강한 삶을 살 수 있다는 주제문장과 함께, 이런 사람들에게 공통적으로 자신의 스트레스를 낮추고 기분을 유지하는 방법(quite a few characteristics that keep their stress levels low and their moods up)을 소개하고 있다. 이들의 특징을 설명하면서(In addition, they tend to focus on the big picture.) 이들이 사소한 것에 구애 받지 않는다는 것을 강조하고 있다. 따라서 정답은 (a)다.

어휘 outlook 시각, 관점
directly 직접적으로
link 연결하다, 잇다
overall 전부의, 총체적인
well-being 행복, 복지
counterpart 대응자[물]
quite a few 꽤 많은, 상당수의
characteristic 특징
generous 관대한
in addition 또한, 게다가
focus on ~에 집중하다, 몰두하다
big picture 전체상, 대국관
put another way 바꿔말하면
annoyance 성가심, 불쾌함
optimistic 낙천주의의, 낙관적인

정답 (a)

10

Dear Ms. Chan,
I was truly excited to hear about the _____ you proposed at the meeting earlier today. I wanted to let you know that I would like to be included on your team and would be willing to provide all the background research you mentioned would be needed. I hope through our past work together you know you can rely on me to be thorough, accurate and enthusiastic. Please call me early next week to talk when the planning phase of the project gets underway.
Sincerely,
Mike Saigal

(a) revised schedule
(b) new project
(c) policy changes
(d) event location

해석 찬 선생님께,
저는 귀하가 오늘 아침에 있었던 회의에서 제안하신 새로운 프로젝트에 대해 듣게 되어 진정으로 기쁩니다. 저는 귀하의 팀에 일원이 되어 귀하가 필요하다고 언급하신 모든 기본 조사들을 할 용의가 있다는 것을 알려 드리고자 합니다. 과거에 함께 일했던 경험을 통해 제가 철저하고, 정확하고, 열성적으로 일하리라는 것을 귀하가 확신하시기를 바랍니다. 프로젝트의 기획 단계가 진행되면 다음 주 초 제게 연락을 주십시오.
진심 어린 마음으로,
마이크 세겔

(a) 변경된 스케줄
(b) 새로운 프로젝트
(c) 정책 변경
(d) 행사 장소

해설 전체적인 편지의 분위기로 판단해볼 때 Mike Saigal은 어떤 업무에 참여하기를 원하는 것을 알 수 있다. 본문에 나오는 'I would like to be included on your team and would be ~ needed'에서 이 글을 받는 사람이 필요로 하는 기본 조사를 기꺼이 하겠다고 말하고 있기 때문에 (a), (d)는 정답에서 제외된다. 또한 맨 마지막 문장 'Please call me ~ when the planning phase of the project ~'에서 언급되고 있듯이 프로젝트의 기초단계가 진행되면 연락을 줄 것을 바라고 있기 때문에 정답은 (b)다.

어휘 background 바탕, 기본
be willing to+V 기꺼이 ~하다
mention 언급하다
thorough 철저한
accurate 정확한
enthusiastic 열성[열정]적인
phase 단계
underway 진행 중인

정답 (b)

11

One of the most creative eras in the history of Western society was the High Middle Ages. Some of humankind's most incredible _____ during this time. Medieval churches are one example. In France alone, eighty Gothic cathedrals and tens of thousands of smaller village churches were built within a ninety-year span. It took more stone to build these churches in Medieval France than it did to build the pyramids of Egypt.

(a) religions were born
(b) architecture was created
(c) inventions were developed
(d) early settlements were discovered

해석 서구 역사상 가장 창조적인 시대 중 하나는 중세 전성기였다. 인류 역사상 가장 놀라운 건축물들이 창조된 것은 이 시기이다. 중세 교회들이 그 하나의 예이다. 프랑스에서만 80개의 고딕 성당들과 수 만개의 소규모 마을 교회들이 90년이라는 기간 안에 지어졌다. 중세 프랑스에서 이러한 교회들을 짓는 데는 이집트의 피라미드를 짓는 것보다 많은 돌이 사용되었다.

(a) 종교들이 태어난 것
(b) 건축물들이 창조된 것
(c) 발명품들이 개발된 것
(d) 초기 정착지들이 발견된 것

해설 중세 전성기의 특징을 설명하는 글이다. 빈 칸에는 인류 역사상 가장 놀라운 일에 관한 내용이 들어가야 한다. 빈 칸의 뒷부분에는 'Medieval churches are one example. In France alone, eighty Gothic cathedrals and tens of thousands of smaller village churches were built within a ninety-year

span.'라는 문장을 통해 중세시기에 프랑스에서 수많은 고딕 성당과 교회가 지어졌다는 사실을 상세하게 설명하고 있다. 따라서 정답은 (b)다.

어휘 creative 창조적인, 독창적인
era 시대, 시기
humankind 인류, 인간
incredible 놀라운, (믿기 어려울 만큼) 훌륭한
medieval 중세의
Gothic cathedrals 고딕 양식의 성당
religion 종교
span (특정 길이의) 기간
architecture 건축, 건축학
settlement 정착지, 정착

정답 (b)

12

Personal economic planning is very hard to do when income, employment and price levels always seem to be changing. Even the best-planned investments _____ _____. One of the most extreme cases of economic instability was the Great Depression of the 1930s. People were left begging for food and many investors took their own lives as a result.

(a) have not been successful due to unemployment
(b) can fail because of this type of instability
(c) fall short of providing necessary income
(d) are not good enough to stabilize the economy

해석 소득, 직업, 물가 수준이 항상 변화하는 것처럼 보일 때는 개인의 재정 계획을 세우는 것이 어렵다. 매우 잘 계획된 투자도 이러한 불안정함 때문에 실패할 수도 있다. 가장 극심한 경우의 경제적 불안정의 예는 1930년대의 대공황이다. 사람들은 음식을 구걸해야 했으며 많은 투자자들이 스스로 목숨을 끊는 결과를 가져 왔다.

(a) 실업 때문에 성공하지 못하기도 했다
(b) 이러한 불안정함 때문에 실패할 수도 있다
(c) 필요한 소득을 제공하기에는 부족하다
(d) 경제를 안정시키기에는 충분하지 않다

해설 첫 번째 문장에서 글의 주제를 전달하고 있다. 'Personal economic planning is very hard to do when income, employment and price levels always seem to be changing.'라는 문장을 통해 소득, 직업, 물가 수준이 항상 변화하기 때문에 재정 계획 수립이 어렵다는 것이다. 빈 칸에 들어갈 것은 이러한 변화에 관한 내용이어야 하는데, 단락의 후반부에 'One of the most extreme cases of economic instability'라는 표현이 나오기 때문에 쉽게 해결할 수 있는 문제이다. 따라서 정답은 (b)다.

어휘 economic 경제학의, 경제의
income 수입, 소득
instability 불안정한 상태, 불안정
unemployment 실업, 실직
necessary 필요한, 없어서는 안 될
fall short 부족하다
stabilize 안정시키다, 고정시키다

정답 (b)

illustrate 설명하다, 예증하다
separation 분리, 분할
overlook 간과하다

정답 (a)

13

In many of American painter Mary Cassatt's works she chose to show images of children with their mothers or nurses. She had a special interest in trying to convey through her art both the tension and pleasure between adults and children who are bonded in a strong, emotional way. Her artwork _____ of the many complex feelings that take place in adult-child relationships.

(a) shows an awareness
(b) displays a lack of knowledge
(c) illustrates a separation
(d) overlooks the importance

해석 미국 화가 메리 커셋은 많은 작품들에서 어머니 혹은 유모와 함께 있는 어린이들의 모습을 표현했다. 그녀는 자신의 작품을 통해 강한 유대 관계로 결합된 어른과 어린이들 간의 긴장감과 즐거움을 전달하는데 특히 관심이 있었다. 그녀의 작품은 어른과 아이의 관계에서 발생하는 많은 복잡한 감정들의 자각을 표현한다.
(a) 자각을 표현한다
(b) 지식의 부족을 나타낸다
(c) 분리를 설명한다
(d) 중요성을 간과한다

해설 메리 커셋이라는 화가의 특성을 설명하는 글이다. '~ a special interest in trying to convey through her art both the tension and pleasure between adults and children ~'에 명시되어 있듯이 이 작가는 성인과 아동간의 유대관계에서 표출되는 긴장감과 즐거움을 전달하는 것에 관심을 갖고 있다. 따라서 빈 칸에 들어가야 할 것은 이러한 작가의 특성이나 이 작가의 작품의 특성을 설명하는 것이어야 한다. 결국 그녀의 작품은 성인과 아동간의 복잡한 감정의 자각을 표현하는 것이다. 따라서 정답은 (a)다.

어휘 convey 전달하다, 알리다
tension 긴장, 불안, 흥분
pleasure 즐거움, 유쾌
bond 유대관계를 맺다
emotional 감정적인, 감수성이 강한
complex 복잡한
awareness 알아채고 있음, 자각
display 전시하다, 진열하다, 나타내다

14

Usually we think of our friends as people with whom we easily bond. Because we like the same types of activities as other people, it is easy to find things to talk about. But recent studies have shown that it is not what friends like, but what they dislike that unites them. In fact, in many friendships it is common _____ about certain things or other people that establishes the friendship and then serves to keep the friends bonded.

(a) to change a belief
(b) to feel a common approval
(c) to produce a positive emotion
(d) to share a negative attitude

해석 보통 우리는 친구를 쉽게 유대감을 느낄 수 있는 사람이라고 생각한다. 우리들은 같은 종류의 활동들과 사람들을 좋아하기 때문에, 이야기할 거리들을 찾는 것이 쉽다. 그러나 최근의 연구에 따르면 공통적으로 좋아하는 것이 아니라 싫어하는 것이 친구들을 결속해준다고 한다. 실제로 많은 친구 관계에서 어떤 사물이나 혹은 사람들에 대해 부정적인 태도를 공유하는 것이 우정을 쌓게 해주고 친구로 남아있도록 해 준다.
(a) 신념을 바꾸는 것
(b) 공통적으로 인정하는 것
(c) 긍정적인 감정을 갖는 것
(d) 부정적인 태도를 공유하는 것

해설 문장 연결 장치에 주목하라! usually와 but를 이용해서 우리가 일반적으로 알고 있는 통념과 실제 연구에서 발견한 내용을 비교하는 글이다. 우리는 같은 종류의 활동이나 사람들을 좋아하기 때문에 유대감을 느끼고 친구가 되기 싫다고 생각하고 있다(Because we like the same types of activities and other people, it is easy to find things to talk about.). 그러나 실제로는 싫어하는 것을 공유하는 사람끼리 유대감을 형성할 수 있다(~ , but what they dislike that unites them.). 따라서 빈 칸에 들어갈 내용은 이러한 점을 다시 한 번 설명해주는 '부정적 태도'를 공유하는 것이라는 (d)가 적절하다.

어휘 bond 인연을 맺다, 유대감을 형성하다
recent 최근의, 근래의
unite 결속시키다
common 일반적인
certain 특정한
establish 확립하다
serve to +V ~하는데 도움이 되다, 쓸모가 있다

approval 동의, 인증
attitude 태도, 마음가짐

정답 (d)

purchase 사다, 구입하다, 획득하다
nevertheless 그럼에도 불구하고

정답 (d)

15

Hearty Oat Boats Cereal now has an exclusive offer available! We at Four Square Grains, Inc. know that you eat Hearty Oat Boats as a part of a healthy lifestyle. So now, for a limited time, if you take three proofs of purchase into any Silver's Gym, you can save 15% off of any membership package. Hurry into any Silver's Gym today! _____, if you bring in four proofs of purchase, you will also receive a free Hearty Oat Boats and Silver's Gym and Aerobics gym bag! But hurry - this offer won't be around forever!

(a) Nevertheless
(b) As a result
(c) However
(d) In addition

16

American Emily Dickinson's poetry is famous for its originality. Sharp contrasts in moods are a characteristic of her poems. She used many hyphens in her poems, and her work could at times be very incongruent. _____ this, Dickinson presented clear images of her own feelings in straightforward ways as they occurred, rather than planning out her work as other authors often do. Because her poetry was so personal, she didn't want to share it with other people, so most of it was published after her death in 1886.

(a) Because of
(b) Compared to
(c) Despite
(d) Instead of

해석 영양 만점 귀리 시리얼이 현재 특별 행사를 시행하고 있습니다! 저희 포 스퀘어 그레인 사(社)는 여러분께서 건강한 생활 습관의 일부로 영양 만점 귀리 시리얼을 드신다는 것을 잘 알고 있습니다. 그래서 한정된 기간 동안 세 건의 구매 증거를 실버헬스클럽으로 가지고 오시면 회원권 패키지를 15% 할인해 드립니다. 오늘 실버 헬스클럽으로 서둘러 오세요! 또한 네 건의 구매 증거를 가지고 오시는 분께는 무료로 영양 만점 귀리 시리얼과 실버 헬스클럽 에어로빅 가방도 드립니다! 하지만 서두르세요. 이 행사는 매일 있는 것이 아닙니다!

(a) 그럼에도 불구하고
(b) 결과적으로
(c) 그러나
(d) 또한

해설 글의 전체적인 내용을 파악하고 문맥의 흐름을 자연스럽게 연결해주는 장치를 선택하는 문제이다. Hearty Oat Boats Cereal에서 특별한 사은행사를 준비하고 있는데, 이 시리얼의 구매 증거를 세 개 가져오면 실버 헬스클럽에서 15% 할인된 가격으로 회원권 패키지를 살 수 있다. 그리고 빈 칸과 연결된 문장에서는 무료 시리얼과 함께 헬스클럽 에어로빅 가방을 선물로 제공한다는 내용이 오기 때문에 보다 추가된 구매 증거를 제시해야 할 것이다. 따라서 빈 칸에는 글의 흐름이 자연스럽게 연결되도록 (d)가 들어가야 한다.

어휘 exclusive 독점적인, 한정된, 특종의
Inc. 주식회사(=incorporated)
lifestyle 생활양식
limited 한정된, 제한을 받는
membership 회원권
proof 증명, 증거

해석 미국 작가인 에밀리 디킨슨의 시는 독창적인 것으로 잘 알려져 있다. 분위기의 날카로운 대조는 디킨슨 시의 특징이다. 그녀는 자신의 작품에서 하이픈을 많이 사용하였고 종이 위에 표현된 그녀의 생각들은 때로는 큰 부조화를 이루기도 했다. 그럼에도 불구하고, 다른 작가들이 했던 했던 것처럼 인위적으로 구상하기 구상하기 보다는 디킨슨은 아름답고 선명한 자신의 감정 상태들을 느껴지는 대로 직접적으로 표현했다. 그녀의 시는 매우 개인적이어서 자신의 작품을 공유하는 것을 꺼렸고, 그 결과 1886년 그녀가 사망한 후에야 시의 대부분이 출판되었다.

(a) ~ 때문에
(b) ~와 비교하여
(c) ~에도 불구하고
(d) ~ 대신에

해설 문장의 흐름을 자연스럽게 연결하는 표현을 선택하는 문제이다. 미국 작가 에밀리 디킨슨의 시의 특성은 하이픈을 자주 사용하였으며 종이 위에 표현된 생각이 부조화(and her work could at times be very incongruent)를 이루기도 한다는 것이다. 그러나 빈 칸 뒤에 오는 문장에서는 '~, Dickinson presented clear images of her own feelings in straightforward ways as they occurred, rather than planning out her work as other authors often do.'라고 밝힘으로써 앞에서 지적한 단점과는 다른 장점을 언급하고 있기 때문에 두 문장의 흐름을 바꾸는 (c)가 정답이다.

어휘 originality 독창성, 독창력
poetry 시, 운문
contrast 대조, 대비
characteristic 특색, 특성

incongruent 맞지 않는, 부적당한
present 나타내다, 표현하다
straightforward 솔직한, 직접적인
plan out 면밀히 계획하다

정답 (c)

Finnish 핀란드어(의)
origin 기원, 유래
influence 영향

정답 (a)

17

In the Hungarian language the word for house is "haz." This is very similar to the German and Dutch words for house, "haus" and "huis" and the English word "house" as well. Many often think Hungarians took their word for house from the Germans, but this isn't true. It actually came from the Finnish word "koti." No connection to the Germanic language can be discovered.

Q What is the main topic of the passage?

(a) The origin of the Hungarian word for house
(b) The history of the word house
(c) The Finnish connection to other languages
(d) German influence on other European languages

해석 헝가리어로 집을 가리키는 단어는 haz이다. 이것은 집을 가리키는 독일어와 네덜란드어 단어인 haus, huis와 영어 단어 house와 매우 유사하다. 많은 사람들이 헝가리인들이 집을 가리키는 단어를 독일인들로부터 빌어 왔다고 생각하지만 이것은 사실이 아니다. 이것은 사실 핀란드 단어 koti에서 온 것이다. 독일계 언어와 아무 관계도 없다는 것이 밝혀 질 수 있다.

Q 위 글의 주제로 알맞은 것을 고르시오.
(a) house를 뜻하는 헝가리어의 유래
(b) 단어 house의 역사
(c) 핀란드어의 다른 언어들과의 관계
(d) 다른 유럽 언어에 대한 독일어의 영향

해설 글의 주제를 선택하는 문제에서는 전체 글을 차분하게 읽고 내용을 요약하는 능력이 필요하다. 헝가리어에서 집을 지칭하는 has라는 단어의 유래와 관련된 내용이다. 독일어와 네덜란드어 단어가 유사하고 또한 헝가리의 '집'이란 어휘가 독일어에서 유래했다고 생각하지만 실제로는 핀란드어 koti에서 왔다는 내용이다. 따라서 이 글은 헝가리어인 haz의 유래에 관한 것이기 때문에 정답은 (a)다.

어휘 Hungarian 헝가리어(의), 헝가리 사람(의)
similar to ~와 비슷한, 유사한
German 독일어(의)
Dutch 네덜란드어(의)
actually 실제로
connection 연결, 관계
discover 발견하다

18

A new study shows that gender impacts how well students can learn from a teacher. It showed that female students learn more effectively from female teachers, just as male students learn more effectively from male teachers. The study reviewed test scores of male and female students which showed a relationship between higher test scores and the student having a teacher of the same sex. The study also found that gender gaps in education are narrower if the number of male and female teachers is nearly equal.

Q What is the main idea of the passage?

(a) Students do equally well, regardless of the teacher's gender.
(b) Test scores of male and female students are nearly equal.
(c) The gender of the teacher may affect how well the student learns.
(d) Public schools should consider establishing single-sex classes.

해석 새로운 연구는 학생들의 성별이 교사에게서 배우는 학습의 정도에 영향을 미친다는 것을 보여주고 있다. 그 연구에 따르면 여학생들은 여성 교사들로부터 더 효율적으로 배우고, 남학생들은 남성 교사들로부터 더 효율적으로 배우게 된다고 한다. 연구는 남학생들과 여학생들의 시험 성적을 살펴보고 더 높은 성적과 같은 성별의 교사를 가진 학생들 간의 관계를 성립했다. 또한 이 연구는 교육에서 성별에 따른 효과의 차이는 남성 교사들과 여성 교사들의 수가 거의 같을 때 좁아진다는 것을 발견했다.

Q 위 글의 요지로 알맞은 것을 고르시오.
(a) 학생들은 교사의 성별에 관계없이 똑같이 잘한다.
(b) 남학생들과 여학생들의 시험 성적이 거의 유사하다.
(c) 교사의 성별이 학생이 얼마나 잘 배우는가에 영향을 끼칠 수도 있다.
(d) 공립학교들은 같은 성별로만 된 학급을 만드는 것을 고려해야 한다.

해설 글의 요지를 묻는 문제이다. 첫 번째 문장에서 'A new study shows that gender impacts how well students can learn from a teacher.'라고 밝힘으로써 학습결과와 교사의 성별 간에 관련성이 있음을 밝히고 있다. 그 후에 오는 문장에서는 남학생은 남성 교사에게, 여학생은 여성교사에게 배웠을 때 더 높은 성적을 보였다는 증거를 제시하여 주제 문장을 지지하고 있다.

또한 'The study also found that gender gaps in education are narrower ~'라는 문장을 통해서 교사의 성별이 균등한 경우에 성별 때문에 생기는 교육적 효과의 차이가 줄어든다는 연구를 소개하고 있다. 따라서 이 글의 요지는 (c)다.

정답 (c)

19

Japanese scientists have developed a new way to detect explosives that could be hidden almost anywhere. A small device called SQUID uses a sensor to detect nitrogen, which is found in many explosives. SQUID is so sensitive it can easily tell the difference between many white powders like sugar, salt, flour and TNT. Scientists hope the device will one day be used for standard airport security.

Q What is the best title of the passage?

(a) Explosive Technology Improved by Japanese Scientists

(b) New Airport Security Technology to be Installed

(c) New Technology Invented to Detect Explosives

(d) New Device to Detect Explosives at Local Airport

해석 일본 과학자들은 어디든지 숨길 수 있는 폭탄을 감지할 수 있는 방법을 개발했다. 스퀴드라고 불리는 이 소형기기는 센서를 이용하여 많은 폭탄들에서 발견되는 질소를 감지한다. 스퀴드는 매우 민감하여 설탕, 소금, 밀가루와 같은 흰 가루와 TNT 간의 차이를 쉽게 감지할 수 있다. 과학자들은 이 기기가 언젠가는 공항의 표준 보안수단으로 사용되기를 바라고 있다.

Q 위 글의 제목으로 가장 알맞은 것을 고르시오.

(a) 일본 과학자들에 의해 개선된 폭탄기술

(b) 설치될 새로운 공항 보안기술

(c) 폭발물을 감지하기 위해 발명된 새기술

(d) 지역 공항에서 폭발물을 감지할 새로운 장비

해설 글의 제목을 선택하는 문제는 글의 전체적인 내용을 파악하고 이를 집약할 수 있는 표현을 선택하는 것이기 때문에 쉽게 해결할 수 있는 것은 아니다. 일본 과학자들이 스퀴드라는 소형기기를 개발하였는데 이는 매우 민감한 기기로서 설탕, 소금, 밀가루등과 같은 흰 가루와 TNT 간의 차이까지도 쉽게 감지할 수 있다(SQUID is so

sensitive it can easily tell the difference between many white powders like sugar, salt, flour and TNT.). 따라서 이 글의 제목은 이러한 새로운 기기가 탄생된 의도를 설명해야 하기 때문에 (c)가 정답이다.

정답 (c)

20

Anxiety and stress are often talked about together as if they both mean the same thing. But actually they're very different. Anxiety means feeling mentally uneasy, while stress means experiencing negative physical effects due to an overload of pressure and demands. When dealing with either or both, the most important thing to understand is the cause. Directly addressing the cause is the only effective way to eliminate anxiety and stress.

Q What is the best title of the passage?

(a) Health Problems Caused by Physical Overload

(b) How to Deal with Pressures and Demands

(c) The Most Common Causes of Anxiety and Stress

(d) Dealing Directly with Anxiety and Stress

해석 불안과 스트레스는 종종 같은 것인 것처럼 이야기된다. 하지만 실제로 이 두 가지는 매우 다르다. 불안이란 정신적으로 불안정을 느끼는 것인데 반해, 스트레스는 지나친 압력과 요구로 인해 나타나는 불쾌한 신체적 결과들이다. 이 두 가지들 중 하나 혹은 두 가지 모두를 다룰 때 가장 중요한 것은 원인을 파악하는 것이다. 직접적으로 원인에 대처하는 것이 불안과 스트레스를 감소시킬 수 있는 유일하게 효과적인 방법이다.

Q 위 글의 제목으로 가장 적절한 것을 고르시오.

(a) 신체적 과로로 인한 건강 문제들

(b) 압력과 요구들을 대처하는 방법

(c) 불안과 스트레스의 가장 보편적인 원인들

(d) 불안과 스트레스에 직접적으로 대처하기

해설 불안과 스트레스를 같은 것으로 여기는 편견을 지적하면서(But actually they're very different. Anxiety means feeling mentally uneasy, while stress means experiencing negative physical effects due to an overload of pressure and demands.), 불안과 스트레스는 별개의 것이라는 것을 설명하고 있다. 특히 이러한 현상을 다룰 때 중요한 것은 '원인 파악'을 하는 것이라는 설명을 하는데 the most important thing to understand~와 같은 강력한 표현이 나오면 이에 주목하는 것도 효과적 책략이다. 글쓴이의 의도를 강하게 전달하는 방법이기 때문이다. 저자는 두 현상의 '원인'을 파악하는 것이 중요하다고 강조하고 있기 때문에 정답은 (d)다.

어휘 anxiety 걱정, 불안
mentally 정신적으로
uneasy 불안한
negative 부정적인
physical 신체의
due to ~에 기인하는, ~ 때문에
overload 과도한 부담
pressure 압력
address 다루다, 처리하다
eliminate 제거하다, 삭제하다

정답 (d)

21
Scientists recently uncovered the two entwined skeletons of a couple who died embracing each other. The site is near Verona, Italy (interestingly, the locale for Shakespeare's Romeo and Juliet). Archaeologists believe the couple was quite young due to the condition of their teeth, but have not yet discovered why they died. This sort of burial was extremely uncommon, and no other skeletons have ever been found in such an embrace. The team is working to preserve the positions of the skeletons by keeping intact the entire chunk of rock their bones are embedded in.

Q What is the best title for the passage?
(a) Romeo and Juliet Buried While Hugging
(b) Uncommon Burial for Skeleton Couple
(c) Skeletons of Romeo and Juliet Found
(d) Skeleton Couple Found in Embrace

해석 과학자들은 최근에 서로를 포옹한 채 죽은 한 남녀의 서로 얽혀있는 해골들을 공개했다. 그 장소는 이태리의 베로나인데, 흥미롭게도 이곳은 셰익스피어의 로미오와 줄리엣의 무대로 유명하다. 고고학자들은 그들의 치아 상태로 볼 때 이 남녀가 매우 젊었다고 생각하고 있지만 왜 그들이 사망했는지를 아직 밝혀내지 못했다. 이러한 종류의 매장은 매우 드문 것이기 때문에 어떤 해골들도 이런 포

옹 상태로 발견된 적이 없었다. 발굴팀은 그들의 유골이 파묻혀있는 바위 덩어리 전체를 보존함으로써 해골들의 위치를 보존하기 위해 노력하고 있다.

Q 위 글의 제목으로 가장 적절한 것을 고르시오.
(a) 포옹한 채로 묻힌 로미오와 줄리엣
(b) 해골 남녀의 희귀한 매장
(c) 로미오와 줄리엣의 유골 발견
(d) 포옹한 채 발견된 남녀 유골

해설 Part II의 앞부분 문제는 주제, 제목 등을 묻는 문제이기 때문에 전체적인 내용 파악이 중요하다. 따라서 이번 문제의 경우처럼 선택지의 단어들이 비슷해서 의미가 비슷해 보이지만 사실상 매우 다른 선택지이다. (a), (c)에 로미오와 줄리엣이 들어있는데, 매우 친숙하기는 하지만, 제목에 들어갈 수 없다는 것은 전체적인 내용파악을 제대로 했다면 알 수 있다. (b)의 경우는 해골 남녀를 매장한 희귀한 방법이고 (d)는 포옹한 채 발견된 남녀 유골이기 때문에 (d)가 정답이다.

어휘 uncover 공개하다
entwined 엉켜있는
embrace 포옹하다
site 유적, (사건 등의) 장소
locale 장소, 배경
due to ~ 때문에
burial 매장
preserve 보존하다
intact 손상되지 않은
chunk 큰 덩어리
embed 파묻다

정답 (d)

22

Scientists have noticed that many more polar bears have drowned in recent years. The polar ice, where they mainly live, has retreated by 160 miles over the last 25 years. U.S. government scientists refuse to link global warming to man's increasing use of carbon-based fuels. Many other scientists and environmentalists, however, believe that increased carbon emissions are directly responsible for the melting of the ice, which threatens the existence of polar bears across the Arctic region.

Q How is global warming supposedly affecting polar bears?

(a) It is contributing to the spread of Arctic pollution.

(b) It is linked to a loss of polar ice habitats.

(c) It is creating toxic Alaskan coastal waters.

(d) It is causing polar bears to retreat to unsafe areas.

drown 익사하다
polar bear 북극곰
retreat 후퇴[퇴각]하다, 물러서다
emission 방출, 방사
threaten 위협하다
existence 생존, 존재
Arctic 북극(의)
contribute to ~에 기여하다
habitat 서식지
toxic 독극물

정답 (b)

해석 과학자들은 최근 몇 년간 익사하는 북극곰의 수가 증가했다는 것을 발견했다. 북극곰들의 주요 서식지인 북극의 얼음이 25년에 걸쳐 160마일 줄어들었다 한다. 미국 정부 과학자들은 이 지구 온난화를 인류의 탄소를 기반으로 한 연료 사용 증가와 연계시키지 않으려고 한다. 그러나 많은 다른 과학자들과 환경론자들은 북극 얼음 용해의 직접적인 원인이 탄소 방출의 증가라고 믿고 있다. 그리고 바로 이 얼음의 용해가 북극지역에서 북극곰들의 생존에 위협을 가하고 있다.

Q 어떻게 지구 온난화가 북극곰들에게 영향을 끼치고 있다고 짐작하고 있는가?

(a) 북극 오염이 확대되는 것에 기여하고 있다.

(b) 극지방 얼음 서식지의 손실과 관련이 있다.

(c) 알래스카 연안에 독극물을 만들어낸다.

(d) 북극곰들이 위험한 지역으로 후퇴하도록 만든다.

해설 지구 온난화가 북극곰에게 어떤 영향을 주는 가를 파악하는 문제이다. 처음에는 미국 정부 과학자들이 지구 온난화의 증거를 인류의 탄소 연료 사용 증가와 연계시키지 않으려고 하였으나 직접적인 원인이 탄소 방출의 증가라는 것을 믿기 시작했다는 것이 중요한 점이다. 마지막 문장 (~ that increased carbon emissions are directly responsible for the melting of the ice which threatens the existence of polar bears across the Arctic region.)에 언급되어 있듯이 탄소의 증가가 얼음 용해와 관련이 있으며 이것이 북극곰의 생존 위협의 원인이 되고 있는 것이다. 따라서 정답은 (b)다.

어휘 notice 알아차리다

23

It's election time, and the Colfax Voting League wants you to vote. In order to be eligible to vote, you must be a citizen of at least eighteen years of age and register with the county. You may vote in person or, if approved, you can vote with an absentee ballot. A list of voting locations will be printed in Sunday's paper. Remember, it is your responsibility to research the candidates and decide which one would best represent you. November 2 is election day: mark that date on your calendar, so you don't forget to vote!

Q What does the announcement say about voting?

(a) That voters must have an absentee ballot to vote.

(b) That voters first enroll with the government.

(c) That voters should be listed in the newspaper.

(d) That voters must register at the voting location.

해석 선거철이 다가왔으며 콜팩스 선거 연합회에서는 귀하가 투표에 참가하기를 바랍니다. 투표를 할 자격이 되기 위해서는 적어도 18세 이상인 시민으로서 지역에 등록해야 합니다. 직접 선거를 할 수도 있고 승인된 경우 부재자 선거를 할 수 있습니다. 투표 장소는 일요일 신문에 게재될 것입니다. 기억하세요, 후보자에 대해 조사를 하고 누가 당신을 대표할 적임자인지를 결정하는 것은 당신의 의무입니다. 11월 2일은 선거일입니다. 달력에 표시해 두시고, 잊지 말고 투표하세요!

Q 공고문은 투표에 대해 무엇을 말하고 있는가?

(a) 투표를 하기 위해서는 부재자 투표가 필요하다

(b) 투표자들은 먼저 정부에 등록을 해야 한다.

(c) 투표자들은 신문에 명단이 올라가야 한다.

(d) 투표자들은 투표 장소에 등록해야만 한다

해설 선거에서 투표할 자격을 얻기 위해서 해야 할 의무와 방법에 대해 고지하는 글이다. 첫째 18세 이상의 시민으로 지역에 등록해야 하며, 투표 장소는 신문에 게재될 예정이다. 또한 후보자에 대해 조사하고 뽑아 줄 후보를 결정해야 한다. 'In order to be eligible to vote'라는 표현을 통해 선거에 참여해서 투표할 자격을 얻기 위해서는 먼저 '등록(register)'해야 한다는 것을 강조하고 있다. 따라서 정답은 (b)다.

어휘 election 선거
vote 투표하다
eligible 자격이 있는
register 등록하다
absentee ballot 부재자 투표
candidate 후보자
represent ~을 대표하다
enroll 등록하다

정답 (b)

24

In the past, managers for a well-known motor company were instructed to pay attention to whether managerial candidates put salt or pepper on their food before they had tasted it. If the candidate did, they believed that he would probably make decisions before knowing all the facts. But now many business people wouldn't view this as bad. In fact, many believe the best managers are quick decision-makers who don't need to know every single fact before making good decisions.

Q What were the motor company managers instructed to notice about candidates?

(a) The way in which the candidates seasoned the food

(b) The comments candidates made about the food

(c) The candidates' confidence level while speaking

(d) The amount of food the candidates consumed

해석 과거에 한 유명한 자동차 회사의 관리자들은 관리직 후보자들이 음식을 맛보기 전에 자신의 음식에 소금이나 후추를 치는지에 주의 깊게 살펴보려는 지시를 받았다. 만일 후보자가 그런다면 그 후보자는 모든 사실들을 알기도 전에 결정을 내리는 사람이라고 믿었다. 하지만 업무 세계에서 많은 사람들은 이것을 단점으로 여기지 않는다. 실제로 많은 사람들은 훌륭한 관리인들은 재빨리 결정을 내리는 사람으로, 만족스런 결정을 내리기 전에 모든 사실들을 알 필요는 없다고 믿는다.

Q 자동차 회사의 간부들은 후보자들에 대해 무엇을 눈여겨 볼 것을 지시 받았는가?

(a) 후보자들이 음식의 간을 맞추는 방법

(b) 후보자가 음식에 대해 한 말

(c) 이야기를 하는 동안의 후보자의 자신감 정도

(d) 후보자가 먹는 음식의 양

해설 어떤 구체적인 사항에 대한 정답을 요구하는 문제는 우선 질문의 요지를 파악하고 그 질문에 대한 답이 언급되어 있는 부분을 집중해서 읽는 것이 효과적이다. 자동차 회사의 간부들이 후보자들의 어떤 행동을 눈여겨 보도록 지시를 받았는가에 관한 답을 선택하는 문제이다. '~to pay attention to whether managerial candidates put salt or pepper on their food before they had tasted it.'에 나와 있는 것처럼 음식을 맛보기도 전에 소금과 후추를 넣은 행동을 하는 사람은 사실을 충분히 파악하지 않고 결정을 내리는 사람이라고 단정 지었던 데서 유래한 것이다. 따라서 정답은 (a)다.

어휘 well-known 잘 알려진
instruct 가르치다, 교육하다, 지시하다
pay attention to ~에 유의하다, 주목하다
managerial 관리의, 경영의
candidate 후보자, 지원자
probably 아마도
confidence 자신감
season 간을 맞추다

정답 (a)

25

When it comes to economic progress, innovators are often more important than new inventions. It is creative minds that are always necessary to adopt and practically apply new inventions in effective ways. Henry Ford was this type of innovator. It wasn't the invention of the automobile alone that made an enormous economic impact on society. It was Ford's use of mass-production technology that so greatly affected the economy.

Q Which of the following is correct about economic progress?

(a) Economic progress relies on mass-production technology.

(b) Henry Ford's most important contribution was the automobile.

(c) Innovators are essential when it comes to economic progress.

(d) Economic progress depends solely on creative inventions.

해석 경제 발전에 있어서 개혁자들이 새로운 발명품보다 더욱 중요한 경우가 많다. 새로운 발명품들을 채택하고 실제로 효과적인 방식으로 적용하는데 항상 필요한 것은 바로 창조적인 사고방식이다. 헨리 포드는 이러한 타입의 개혁자였다. 사회에 거대한 경제적인 영향을 끼친 것은 자동차

발명만이 아니었다. 경제에 큰 영향을 끼친 것은 포드의 대량 생산 기술의 이용이었다.

Q 경제 발전에 관해 언급된 내용으로 옳은 것은?
(a) 경제 발전은 대량 생산 기술에 의존한다.
(b) 헨리 포드의 가장 중요한 기여는 자동차였다.
(c) 개혁자들은 경제 발전에 있어 필수적이다.
(d) 경제 발전은 전적으로 창조적인 발명에 달려있다.

해설 경제 발전에 있어서의 창조적인 개혁자의 중요성에 관한 글이다. 'When it comes to economic progress, innovators are often more important than new inventions.'라는 주제가 첫 문장에 정확하게 명시되어 있다. 즉 어떤 개별적인 새로운 발명품보다는 이를 발명한 개혁자가 훨씬 중요하다는 것이다. 이를 입증하기 위해 Henry Ford의 예를 사용하였다. 즉 그가 만든 자동차 자체가 중요한 것이 아니라 Ford가 자동차 개발을 통해 미친 경제적 파급 효과가 훨씬 중요하다는 것을 강조하고 있다. 이를 표현하는 'It wasn't the invention of the automobile alone ~ It was Ford's use of mass-production technology ~'구문에 주의해라. 정답은 (c)다.

어휘 **when it comes to** ~에 관해서(라면)
economic 경제적인
progress 발전, 전진
innovator 개혁자, 혁신자
invention 발명, 발명품
adopt 채택하다
practically 실제로, 실용적으로
effective 효과적인
enormous 거대한, 엄청난
impact 영향
mass-production 대량 생산
affect ~에 영향을 미치다
rely on ~에 의존하다
solely 단지, 오로지

정답 (c)

26

One of the favorite painting mediums of medieval artists was egg tempera. This paint, made with egg yolks, was commonly used until oil paints were introduced. Oddly, the yellow color of the yolks never ruined the other colors the artists mixed into the yolks. And surprisingly, over time, egg tempera paintings retained their color and yellowed less than oil paintings. In fact, tempera paintings that are hundreds of years old still display their original vibrant colors today.

Q Which is correct according to the passage?
(a) Paints made with egg retain their color longer than oils.
(b) Medieval artists preferred egg tempera paints to oils.
(c) Oil paints retain their colors and yellow less than temperas.
(d) Oil paintings age less over time than egg tempera paintings.

해석 중세 화가들이 즐겨 사용한 회화 기법 중의 하나는 계란 템페라였다. 계란 노른자로 만들어진 이 물감은 유성 물감이 소개되기 전까지 보편적으로 이용되었다. 이상하게도 노른자의 노란색은 화가가 노른자와 섞은 다른 색깔들을 망치는 법이 없었다. 그리고 놀랍게도 시간이 지나도 계란 템페라 기법의 그림들은 유화에 비해 색상이 오래 지속되고 노랗게 변색되는 것이 덜했다. 실제로 수백 년 된 템페라 기법의 그림들은 오늘 날에도 여전히 원래의 밝은 색상을 보이고 있다.

Q 위 글의 내용과 일치하는 것을 고르시오.
(a) 계란으로 만들어진 물감이 유성 물감보다 색상이 더 오래 유지된다.
(b) 중세 화가들은 계란 템페라 물감을 유성물감보다 선호했다.
(c) 템페라보다 유성 물감의 색상이 더 오래 갔고 변색도 덜했다.
(d) 유화들은 시간이 지나도 계란 템페라 그림들보다 덜 낡게 된다.

해설 중세시대에 사용된 '계란 템페라' 기법과 관련된 글이다. 유성 물감과 비교해보았을 때 계란 노른자로 만들어진 이 물감은 여러 가지 장점이 있다. 예를 들면, 다른 물감과 섞었을 때 망치는 경우가 없으며, 색감이 유화에 비해 오래 지속되며 오랜 시간이 지나도 여전히 원래의 색을 유지한다는 것이다. oddly라는 단어를 사용함으로써 일반적인 편견을 부정하는 다양한 예를 강조하고 있다. 따라서 정답은 (a)다.

어휘 **favorite** 매우 좋아하는
medium 수단, 매체
medieval 중세의, 중세풍의

tempera 템페라 그림 물감
yolk 노른자
oddly 기묘하게, 이상하게
mix into ~와 섞다
retain 유지[보유]하다
yellow 노랗게 변하다
display 전시하다, 진열하다
original 원래의
vibrant 활발한, 활기에 넘치는, 선명한, 강력한

정답 (a)

27

Galileo Galilei's desire to analyze the natural world in new and different ways led to fascinating new theories and new technologies, too. While working at a university near Venice, Galileo heard of an instrument being built elsewhere that could be used to view distant objects. Without any other information, he went to work and built the first telescope. This telescope could clearly see ships fifty miles away. For this invention, the university leaders immediately doubled his salary.

Q Which of the following is correct according to the passage?

(a) Galileo was a respected science professor at an Italian university.
(b) The first telescope was used by Galileo to create his advanced model.
(c) Galileo's curiosity resulted in many new ideas and inventions.
(d) Telescopes invented by Galileo were used on all Italian ships.

해석 갈릴레오 갈릴레이는 자연계를 새롭고 다른 방식들로 분석하고자 했으며 그것은 매혹적이고 새로운 이론들과 새로운 기술을 초래했다. 베니스 근처 한 대학에서 근무하고 있던 중 갈릴레오는 다른 곳에서 제작되고 있었던 멀리 있는 물체를 볼 수 있는 기구에 대해 듣게 된다. 다른 아무런 정보도 없이 그는 출근을 해서 최초의 망원경을 제작했다. 이 망원경을 이용하여 오십 마일 밖에 있는 선박들을 똑똑히 볼 수 있었다. 이 발명으로 대학 관계자들은 즉시 그의 봉급을 두 배로 올려 주었다.

Q 위 글의 내용과 일치하는 것을 고르시오.
(a) 갈릴레오는 한 이태리 대학의 존경 받는 과학 교수였다.
(b) 갈릴레오는 진보된 모델을 제작하기 위해 최초의 망원경을 사용했다.
(c) 갈릴레오의 호기심은 많은 새로운 사고들과 발명품을 가져왔다.
(d) 갈릴레오가 발명한 망원경들은 모든 이태리 선박에서 사용되었다.

해설 갈릴레오 갈릴레이의 망원경 개발과 관련된 내용의 글이다. 그는 자연계를 새롭고 다른 방식으로 분석하고자 했으며 이러한 성향이 매혹적이며 새로운 이론과 새 기술을 초래했다(Galileo Galilei's desire to analyze the natural world in new and different ways led to fascinating new theories and new technologies, too.). 그는 다른 곳에서 제작되는 멀리 있는 물체를 보는 기구에 대한 이야기만을 듣고 어떤 정보도 없이 최초의 망원경을 제작하게 되었다. 따라서 그의 호기심과 새로운 사고가 발명품 제작으로 이어졌다는 (c)가 정답이다.

어휘 analyze 분석[분해]하다
lead to ~을 초래하다
theory 이론
fascinating 매혹적인, 황홀한
instrument 기계, 도구
distant 거리가 먼, 원격의
telescope 망원경
invention 발명
immediately 즉시, 곧
double 두 배로 올리다
respected 존경받는
result in ~을 초래하다

정답 (c)

28

In the early 1800s, the Industrial Revolution was changing Western Europe in many ways. However, there were no such changes in Russia, which remained an agricultural country. This was unfortunate for the 80 percent of the population who were permanently trapped working for rich landowners. These workers, called "serfs," were treated like slaves. It was Alexander II who freed the serfs in 1861. But even then these free but very poor people lived in a state of oppression and inequality.

Q Which of the following is correct according to the passage?

(a) The life of a serf was difficult both prior to and after 1861.
(b) Life for the serfs improved after Alexander II's decision.
(c) Treatment of serfs differed depending on the landowner.
(d) The Industrial Revolution created changes in Russia.

해석 1800년대 초에 산업 혁명은 서구 유럽을 많은 방식으로 변모시켰다. 그러나 러시아에서는 그러한 변화가 일어나지 않았고 러시아는 농업국가로 남아있었다. 이것은 부유한 지주들을 위해 영원히 일할 수 밖에 없었던 인구의 80%에게 있어서는 매우 불행한 일이었다. '농노'라고 불

린 이 노동자들은 노예와 같은 대우를 받았다. 알렉산더 2세가 농노들을 해방시킨 것은 1861년이었다. 그러나 심지어 그 후에도 이 자유롭지만 매우 가난한 사람들은 억압과 불평등의 상태에 살았다.

Q 위 글의 내용과 일치하는 내용을 고르시오.
(a) 농노의 삶은 1861년 이전과 이후에도 고단했다.
(b) 농노들의 삶은 알렉산더 2세의 결정 이후 개선되었다.
(c) 농노들이 받은 대우는 지주에 따라 다양했다.
(d) 산업 혁명은 러시아에 변화를 가져 왔다.

해설 서구 유럽에서 시작된 산업혁명과 관련된 글이다. 특히 이러한 산업혁명이 러시아에서는 발생하지 않아서 러시아가 여전히 농업국가로 남게 되면서 농노들이 겪었던 억압과 불평등에 관한 글이다. 글의 내용과 일치되는 세부사항을 물어보는 문제이기 때문에 글 전체를 자세하게 읽어보아야 하며 특히 역사적 내용이기 때문에 등장인물이나 연도 등에도 주의를 기울여야 한다. 러시아 인구의 80%를 차지하는 농노가 1861년, 알렉산더 2세의 해방 운동 이후에도 자유는 얻었으나 여전히 가난과 억압, 불평등 속에 고통 받았다는 것을 강조하고 있다(But even then these free but very poor people lived in a state of oppression and inequality.). 따라서 정답은 (a)다.

어휘 Industrial Revolution 산업 혁명
remain 남아있다, 여전히 (~의 상태로) 있다
agricultural country 농업 국가
unfortunate 불행한
population 인구
permanently 영구히
trap 가두다
landowner 토지 소유자, 지주
serf 농노
slave 노예
free 해방시키다
oppression 압박, 억압
inequality 불평등
prior to ~ 이전에
depending on ~에 따라

정답 (a)

29

The Aubrey Little Theatre presents The Bridgeport Boys! Come see the award-winning musical about the experiments of the boys of the small town of Bridgeport. Robert Caubley raves, "The Bridgeport Boys is the kind of rare production that can truly move you through song and laughter." Tickets are on sale for $28 until October 16 at the Aubrey Little Theatre, with performances every Thursday, Friday and Saturday night at 8 p.m. So come and see The Bridgeport Boys!

Q Which of the following is correct according to the advertisement?
(a) The show is sponsored by Robert Caubley.
(b) The performance will only be held on the weekend.
(c) The show features both music and comedy.
(d) Tickets have not yet been released for sale.

해석 오브리 리틀 극장이 브리지포트 보이즈를 소개합니다. 작은 마을 브리지포트의 소년들의 실험에 관한 수상경력이 있는 뮤지컬을 보러 오세요. 로버트 코블리는 "브리지포트 보이즈는 노래와 유쾌함을 통해 진정한 감동을 전해 줄 수 있는 드문 작품"이라고 격찬합니다. 표는 오브리 리틀 극장에서 $28에 10월 16일까지 판매되며 공연은 매주 목요일, 금요일, 토요일 밤 8시입니다. 오셔서 브리지포트 보이즈를 만나 보세요!

Q 위 광고의 내용과 일치하는 것을 고르시오.
(a) 로버트 코블리가 쇼를 후원한다.
(b) 공연은 주말에만 있을 것이다.
(c) 음악과 코미디가 공연의 특징이다.
(d) 표는 아직 판매가 시작되지 않았다.

해설 오브리 리틀 극장에서 선보이는 '브리지포트 보이즈' 공연에 관한 안내문이다. 공연의 특성, 공연 일정, 공연 장소, 티켓 구매 방법 등에 관한 상세한 정보를 알려주고 있다. 따라서 이 광고의 내용과 일치하는 문장을 선택하기 위해서는 제시된 4개의 가능한 답을 글을 읽어 가면서 확인해가는 과정이 필요하다. 우선 본 극장이 이 쇼를 후원하는 것이 아니기 때문에 (a)는 정답이 될 수 없으며, 공연은 매주 목요일, 금요일, 그리고 토요일에 열리기 때문에 (b)도 정답이 아니다. 또한 티켓은 10월 16일까지 구매가능하기 때문에(Tickets are on sale for $28 until October 16 at the Aubrey Little Theatre ~), 정답은 (c)가 된다.

어휘 award-winning 수상경력이 있는
experiment 실험, 시도

rave 격찬하다
rare 드문, 귀한
performance 공연, 연주, 상연
sponsor 후원하다
feature ~을 특징으로 하다
release 발매하다

정답 (c)

30

Alexander Hamilton and Aaron Burr are famous early American politicians. They are also famous for something else: a duel. Burr ran for governor of New York and lost, and Alexander Hamilton said that he believed Burr shouldn't have won. As a result, Burr challenged Hamilton to a gun duel, which was then considered a fair way to settle a disagreement. On the morning of July 11, 1804, Aaron Burr killed Alexander Hamilton, who had intentionally missed Burr. Interestingly, Hamilton's son had been killed in a similar duel at that exact location two years earlier.

Q Which of the following is correct about gun duels in early US history?

(a) They were commonly used to settle family disputes.

(b) They were used only to solve political differences.

(c) They were an appropriate way to handle an argument.

(d) They were never meant to result in murder.

해석 알렉산더 해밀턴과 애론 버는 유명한 미국의 초기 정치인들이다. 해밀턴과 버는 또한 다른 것으로 유명한데 그것은 결투이다. 버는 뉴욕 지사로 선거에 나섰지만 패배했고 알렉산더 해밀턴은 공공연히 버가 적절한 후보자가 아니었다고 떠들고 다녔다. 그 결과로 버는 해밀턴에게 권총 결투를 신청하게 되는데 당시에 결투는 분쟁을 해결하는 적절한 수단으로 여겨졌다. 1804년 7월 11일 아침 버는 의도적으로 자신을 명중시키지 않았던 해밀턴을 죽이게 되었다. 흥미롭게도 2년 전 같은 장소에서 해밀턴의 아들도 유사한 결투 중에 사망했다.

Q 초기 미국 역사에서 권총 결투에 대한 내용으로 올바른 것을 고르시오.

(a) 가족 간의 분쟁을 해결하는데 보편적으로 이용됐다.

(b) 정치적 의견 차이를 해결하는 데만 사용됐다.

(c) 분쟁을 다루는 적절한 방법이었다.

(d) 절대 살인으로 끝나도록 의도되지는 않았다.

해설 초기 미국 역사 중 합법적으로 허용되었던 권총 결투에 관한 내용을 묻는 글이다. 알렉산더 해밀턴과 애론 버는 정치인들로 서로 간의 분쟁을 해결하기 위해 결투를 벌였으며, 그 당시에 이것은 합법적으로 허용되었다는 설명이 제시되어 있다(Burr challenged Hamilton to a gun duel, which was then considered a fair way to settle a disagreement.). 또한 해밀턴의 아들도 2년 전에 비슷한 장소에서 권총 결투로 인해서 사망했다는 사실을 보면 그 당시 권총 결투가 많이 있었음을 추론할 수 있다. 따라서 정답은 (c)다.

어휘 politician 정치가
governor 주지사, (조직 등의) 관리자
duel 결투
run for ~로 출마하다
as a result 결과적으로
challenge 도전하다, (시합 등을) 걸다
disagreement 논쟁, 의견 차이
intentionally 의도적으로, 고의로
miss 빗맞히다
location 장소, 위치
settle 해결하다
dispute 분쟁
be meant to+V ~하도록 의도되다

정답 (c)

31

The entertainment industry has capitalized on recent trepidation caused by the possibility of an asteroid hitting the Earth and ultimately destroying all human life, but the chances of this happening outside of a Hollywood screenplay are extremely miniscule. Experts say a kilometer-sized asteroid, the type that would be capable of total devastation, could only be expected to impact the Earth maybe once every several million years. The closest recent asteroid encounter Earth has experienced came in 2002 when an asteroid as large as a soccer field came within 75,000 miles of the Earth as it passed by in outer space.

Q Which of the following is true according to the passage?

(a) The odds of a large asteroid hitting the Earth are very small.

(b) Earth was recently impacted by a small asteroid in 2002.

(c) Large asteroids are not capable of the destruction represented in movies.

(d) Asteroids are expected to impact the Earth once every one million years.

해석 연예계는 행성이 지구와 충돌하여 결국 모든 인류를 파괴할 수 있는 가능성을 활용한 공포를 이용했지만, 이것이 할리우드 영화 밖에서 일어나게 될 확률은 매우 적다. 전문가들은 (지구를) 완전히 파괴할 수 있는 1km 크기의 행성은 아마도 몇 백만 년의 한 번 정도 지구에 영향을 줄 것이라고 말한다. 지구와 행성과의 가장 가까운 근접은 축구장만한 행성이 우주에서 지구로부터 75,000마일 반경 이내를 통과했던 2002년에 발생했다.

Q 위 글의 내용과 일치하는 것을 고르시오.
(a) 거대 소행성이 지구와 충돌할 확률은 매우 작다.
(b) 지구는 최근 2002년 작은 소행성에 의해 영향을 받았다.
(c) 거대 소행성들은 영화에 나오는 것과 같은 파괴를 일으킬 수 없다.
(d) 소행성들은 백만 년에 한 번씩 지구에 영향을 끼치는 것으로 예상된다.

해설 본문의 내용과 일치하는 문장을 선택하는 내용이다. 이런 경우에는 예시된 문장을 본문과 대비시켜 함께 읽어가는 것이 효과적이다. 할리우드 영화에서 종종 행성이 지구와 충돌하여 인류를 파괴할 수 있다는 소재를 영화화하여 성공하고 있지만 실제로 이런 일이 발생할 경우는 희박하다는 것이 주제이다(but the chances of this happening outside of a Hollywood screenplay are extremely miniscule.). 특히 but에 주의를 기울여라. 따라서 정답은 (a)다.

어휘 entertainment industry 연예계
capitalize on ~를 이용하다
trepidation 공포, 당황
asteroid 소행성
ultimately 결국은, 긍정적으로
miniscule 대단히 작은, 하찮은
be capable of ~의 능력이 있다
devastation 황폐, 폐허
encounter 만남, 근접
odds 확률

정답 (a)

32

Researchers are currently testing three different vaccines that may help prevent weight gain in humans. The vaccines make the body produce antibodies that prevent certain chemicals from working properly. These targeted chemicals are the ones which cause people to feel hungry and gain weight. So far, two out of the three vaccines have been successful in studies using rats.

Q Which of the following is correct according to the passage?
(a) Three vaccines are currently being used to prevent human weight gain.
(b) Scientists are testing vaccines that could help people lose weight.
(c) Vaccines are being developed to keep people from gaining weight.
(d) Researchers have discovered antibodies cause people to weigh too much.

해석 연구자들은 현재 인간의 체중 증가 억제를 도울 수 있는 세 가지 다른 종류의 백신을 연구하고 있다. 백신들은 신체가 항체를 형성하여 특정한 화학 물질이 제대로 작동하지 못하도록 한다. 이러한 목표가 되고 있는 화학 물질들은 사람들이 배고픔을 느끼고 몸무게가 늘도록 하는 물질들이다. 현재까지 세 가지 백신들 중에서 두 가지 백신이 쥐를 이용한 실험에서 성공했다.

Q 위 글의 내용과 일치하는 것을 고르시오.
(a) 세 가지 백신이 현재 인간의 체중 증가 방지에 사용되고 있다.
(b) 과학자들은 체중을 줄일 수 있는 백신들을 실험 중이다.
(c) 백신들이 사람들의 체중 증가를 막기 위해 개발되고 있다.
(d) 연구자들은 항체가 체중을 너무 많이 증가시킨다는 것을 발견했다.

해설 인간의 체중 증가 방지를 도와주는 세 가지 다른 종류의 백신의 연구에 관한 글이다. 이 백신들은 신체가 항체를 형성하여 화학 물질이 작동하지 못하도록 하는 것이다. 'These targeted chemicals are the ones which cause people to feel hungry and gain weight.'에서 언급된 바처럼 연구의 대상이 되고 있는 화학물질은 사람들이 배고픔을 느끼고 몸무게가 늘도록 하는 물질이다. 이미 두 개의 백신은 실험에 성공을 하였다는 내용이다. 따라서 (a)와 (b)는 글의 내용과 명백히 어긋나며, 이 글의 내용과 일치하는 것은 (c)다.

어휘 researcher 연구원, 조사원
prevent ~을 막다, 방해하다, 예방하다
antibody 항체
certain 특정한, 어떤
properly 적당히, 적절히, 알맞게, 올바르게

target 목표로 삼다
chemical 화학물질
gain weight 체중이 늘다
rat 쥐
lose weight 체중이 줄다
weigh 무게가 ~ 나가다

정답 (c)

33

Existing resources of iron, copper, lead and zinc are dwindling in China. However, Chinese government geologists are surveying a Tibetan plateau that is presumed to have reserves full of billions of tons of these minerals. Geological surveyors are still working to accurately locate all the many reserves, but this is an extremely difficult task since geologists must work in harsh weather conditions at an average altitude of 4,300 meters.

Q What can be inferred from the passage?
(a) China has run out of needed minerals.
(b) The plateau will be mined in the future.
(c) All the reserves will never be located.
(d) Plateaus are the best locations for mines.

해석 철, 구리, 납, 아연 같은 현존하는 자원들이 중국에서 점차 줄어들고 있다. 그러나 중국 정부 지질학자들은 이러한 자원 수십억 톤이 저장되어 있는 것으로 추정되고 있는 티벳 고원을 조사 중이다. 저장 장소들을 정확히 파악하기 위한 조사가 여전히 진행 중이다. 하지만 지질학자들은 평균 고도 4300미터의 거친 기후 조건에서 작업을 해야 하기 때문에 이것은 매우 어려운 작업이다.

Q 위 글에서 추론할 수 있는 내용을 고르시오.
(a) 중국은 필요한 광물들이 고갈되었다.
(b) 티벳 고원은 앞으로 채굴될 것이다.
(c) 모든 저장지들은 절대 발견되지 않을 것이다.
(d) 고원들은 광산으로써는 최적지이다.

해설 글의 내용을 읽고 추론하는 문제이다. 글의 내용을 추론하기 위해서는 우선 글을 정확하게 이해하고 이를 바탕으로 저자가 전달하고자 하는 의도를 파악해야 한다. 최근 중국에서는 자원이 감소하고 있는데, 이러한 문제를 해결하기 위해서 중국 정부의 지질학자들이 티벳 고원을 조사 중이다(Chinese government geologists are surveying a Tibetan plateau that is presumed to have reserves full of billions of tons of these minerals.)라는 내용이 있기 때문에 앞으로 티벳 고원이 채굴될 것임을 추론할 수 있다. 정답은 (b)다.

어휘 resources 자원
dwindle 줄다, 감소되다
plateau 고원, 대지

presume 추정하다, 여기다
reserve 매장량, 저장지
accurately 정확히
locate 위치를 찾다
harsh 가혹한, 거친
altitude 고도, 해발
run out of ~이 고갈되다
mine 채굴하다, 광산

정답 (b)

34

Frozen foods were not found in stores and homes before 1930. Improvements in refrigeration technology changed this. Clarence Birdseye launched sales of frozen foods in Springfield, Massachusetts. By the 1940s, thousands of frozen food products were available to Americans. Before mid-century, production of frozen foods had reached 2.5 billion pounds. Over the next 50 years, advances in transportation, packaging, and cooking technology combined to make frozen foods a vital part of the American diet.

Q What does the writer suggest?
(a) Several technologies have contributed to the growth of frozen foods.
(b) Frozen foods are generally less expensive than fresh foods.
(c) Microwave ovens have increased the popularity of frozen foods.
(d) Frozen foods will revolutionize kitchens of the future.

해석 상점과 가정에서 냉동식품은 1930년 이전에는 찾아 볼 수 없었다. 냉동 기술의 발달이 이것을 바꾸어 놓았다. 클레런스 버즈아이가 매사추세츠 스프링필드에서 냉동식품의 판매를 시작했다. 1940년대가 되었을 때쯤 미국인들은 수 천 개의 냉동식품들을 구매할 수 있었다. 1950년대 이전에 냉동식품의 생산은 25억 파운드에 이르렀다. 그 후 50년 동안 수송 수단, 포장, 조리 기술의 발달이 결합되어 냉동식품은 미국 식생활의 주요 부분이 되었다.

Q 윗글에서 글쓴이가 암시하고 있는 것을 고르시오.
(a) 몇몇 기술들이 냉동식품의 성장에 기여했다.
(b) 냉동식품은 일반적으로 자연식품[비냉동식품]보다 싸다.
(c) 전자레인지가 냉동식품의 인기를 높였다.
(d) 냉동식품은 미래의 주방에 혁명을 일으킬 것이다.

해설 냉동식품의 발달 과정에 관련된 글이다. 1930년 전에는 냉동식품을 전혀 사용하지 않았지만, 냉동 기술의 발달로 인해 1940년대 무렵에는 수천 개의 냉동식품이 등장하게 되었으며(By the 1940s, thousands of frozen food products were available to Americans.), 그 후 50년 간 수송 수단의 발달, 포장, 조리 기술 등의 발전으로 냉동식품이 미국 식생활의 중요한 부분이 되었다 (~ advances in transportation, packaging, and cooking technology ~)는 것이 글의 핵심적 내용이다. 따라서 글쓴이가 암시하고자 하는 것은 (a)다.

어휘 **frozen food** 냉동식품
improvement 개선, 발달
refrigeration technology 냉동 기술
launch 착수하다, (신제품, 상품 따위를) 시장에 내다
advance 전진, 진보
transportation 수송, 운송
packaging 짐 꾸러기, 포장
vital 극히 중대한, 절대 필요한, 생명의
contribute to ~에 기여하다
microwave oven 전자레인지
revolutionize 혁명을 일으키다

정답 (a)

35

The Association for Animal Safety has been providing the public with helpful pet safety information for over forty years. But still some pet owners fail to understand just how important it is to responsibly care for their animals. Each year thousands of pets die from exposure to extreme temperatures. The Association for Animal Safety would like all pet owners to better understand the dangers animals face when left inside cars during the summer or locked outdoors in the wintertime.

Q What would the following passage most likely be about?

(a) How temperatures indirectly affect an animal's health.
(b) The examples of pet owners not caring for their pets well.
(c) How to report irresponsible pet owners.
(d) The way to check a pet for heat exposure.

해석 동물 안전 협회에서는 일반인들에게 도움이 되는 애완동물 안전 정보를 사십 년 이상 제공해 오고 있습니다. 그러나 아직도 일부 애완동물 주인들이 자신들의 동물을 책임 있게 보살피는 것이 얼마나 중요한가를 이해하지 못하고 있습니다. 매 년 수천 마리의 애완동물들이 극한의 온도에 노출되어 사망합니다. 동물 안전 협회는 모든 애완동물 주인들이 동물들을 여름에 차 안에 내버려 두거나, 겨울에 실외에 두는 것이 위험하다는 것을 더 잘 깨닫기를 바랍니다.

Q 다음에 이어질 글은 무엇에 관한 내용일지 고르시오.
(a) 애완동물 주인들이 그들의 애완동물을 잘못 돌보는 예들

(b) 애완동물 주인들이 그들의 애완동물을 잘못 돌보는 예들
(c) 무책임한 애완동물 주인들을 어떻게 신고할 것인가
(d) 애완동물이 열에 노출되었는가를 알아보는 법

해설 이 글을 읽고 뒤에 이어질 내용을 추측하는 문제이다. 이런 유형의 질문에서는 우선 본 글에서 전달하고자 하는 내용을 정확하게 파악하고 뒤에 이어질 내용을 추론해야 한다. 동물 안전 협회에 따르면 애완동물 안전 정보를 40년 이상 제공해오고 있지만 아직도 동물 주인의 무책임한 보살핌 때문에 피해동물이 생기고 있다. 이러한 피해 사례를 설명하기 위해서 여름에는 동물을 차 안에 두고 잠그는 경우와 겨울에 실외에 두는 경우를 들어, 매년 극심한 날씨에 의한 사망(Each year thousands of pets die from exposure to extreme temperatures.)을 강조하고 있기 때문에 이후에 이어질 내용으로는 (b)가 적절하다.

어휘 **provide** 제공하다
helpful 도움이 되는, 유익한
responsibly 책임감 있게
exposure 노출
extreme 극도의, 극심한
temperature 온도
would like+목+to+V ~가 …하기를 바라다
face 직면하다
report 신고하다

정답 (b)

36

Each giant saguaro cactus starts out as a tiny black seed that can eventually grow up to fifty feet tall and weigh six tons depending on the lifespan of the plant. Saguaros can live to be 200 years old. However, they are vulnerable to lightning, freezing temperatures and severe droughts all of their lives. If they can survive these occurrences, saguaros generally die of old age sometime after turning 150 years old.

Q What can be inferred from the passage?

(a) Saguaro cactus generally live to be 200 years old.
(b) The average height of a saguaro cactus is 50 feet tall.
(c) The majority of saguaros die from old age.
(d) Many saguaros die prematurely from severe weather conditions.

해석 거대한 사구아로 선인장은 작은 까만색 씨에서 시작되어, 수명에 따라 키가 50 피트, 무게가 6톤이 되도록 자랄 수 있다. 사구아로 선인장은 200살까지 살기도 한다. 그러

나 이 선인장들은 평생 빛, 영하의 기온들과 심한 가뭄에 취약하다. 만일 이런 어려움들을 극복할 수 있다면, 사구아로 선인장은 150살까지 산 후 죽는다.

Q 위 글의 내용에서 추론할 수 있는 내용을 고르시오.
(a) 사구아로 선인장은 보통 200살까지 산다.
(b) 사구아로 선인장의 평균 키는 50피트다.
(c) 이 선인장들의 대부분은 늙어서 죽는다.
(d) 많은 선인장들이 심한 기후 조건 때문에 일찍 죽는다.

해설 글을 읽고 내용을 추론하는 유형이기 때문에 본문의 내용을 단순하게 파악해서 대답하는 것보다 훨씬 어려울 수 있다. 거대한 사구아로 선인장의 크기, 수명, 그리고 무게 등에 관한 글이다. 그러나 전체적인 내용은 키가 50피트도 되고 무게가 6톤이 되도록 자랄 수도 있고, 200년을 살기도 하지만, 'However, they are vulnerable to lightning, freezing temperatures and severe droughts all of their lives.'라는 문장에 이 선인장들은 실제로는 심한 기후 조건에 취약하다고 했기 때문에 유추할 수 있는 내용은 (d)다.

어휘 cactus 선인장
eventually 결국, 드디어, 마침내
depending on ~에 따라
lifespan 수명
vulnerable 상처 입기 쉬운, 약한
severe 극심한
occurrence 사건, 일어난 일
generally 일반적으로
prematurely 조기에, 일찍

정답 (d)

해석 토마스 홉스는 초기 유물론자 중의 한 사람이다. 인간의 본성에 관하여 홉스는 인간을 정교한 물리적 대상으로 보았다. 홉스는 마치 기계와 같이 모든 인간의 기능과 활동들이 완전히 기계적인 용어들로 설명될 수 있다고 말했다. 인간과 기계와의 차별점이라고 많은 사람들이 주장하는 사고력조차도 홉스는 신경계의 기계적 작동에 의해 만들어지는 물리적 작용이라고 말했다.

Q 인체에 대한 홉스의 생각으로 알맞은 것을 고르시오.
(a) 인간에게 알려진 모든 물리적 대상과 다르다.
(b) 인체의 모든 체계들은 기계와 같은 방식으로 작동한다.
(c) 사고 체계를 제외하고는 기계와 같은 방식으로 작용한다.
(d) 단순한 기계와 같은 단순한 물질적 대상이다.

해설 인체에 대한 홉스의 견해를 묻는 질문이다. 홉스는 인간을 물리적 대상으로 보고, 마치 기계처럼 인간의 기능과 활동을 기계적 용어로 설명할 수 있다고 하였다 (All human functions and activities could be explained in entirely mechanistic terms.). 그리고 even에 주목하라. 홉스는 심지어 인간의 사고력조차 신경계의 기계적 작동에 의해 만들어지는 물리적 작용이라고 설명한다. 따라서 정답은 (b)다.

어휘 materialist 유물론자
nature 본성
sophisticated 세련된, 정교한
function 기능
entirely 완전히, 전부
mechanistic 기계적인
distinguish A from B A와 B를 구별하다
operation 작용
nervous system 신경계

정답 (b)

37

Thomas Hobbes was one of the earliest Materialists. When it came to human nature, Hobbes viewed humans as sophisticated physical objects. Much like machines, Hobbes said that all human functions and activities could be explained in entirely mechanistic terms. Even thoughts, which most would argue distinguish humankind from machines, were said by Hobbes to be physical operations produced by mechanical operations of the nervous system.

Q What did Hobbes generally think about the human body?
(a) It is unlike any other physical object known to humankind.
(b) All systems of the human body function in a machine-like way.
(c) It works much the same as a machine except for the thought process.
(d) It is a simple material object much like a simple machine.

38

Yoga is widely seen as important for improving physical and mental health. (a) So it's no surprise that a majority of those who practice yoga do so for health reasons. (b) Yoga can reduce stress, relieve pain, and strengthen muscles. (c) It is important to meditate while practicing yoga. (d) Medical practitioners increasingly recommend yoga to their patients.

해석 요가는 보편적으로 신체적, 정신적 건강을 개선시키는 데 중요한 것으로 여겨진다. (a) 그래서 대부분의 사람들이 건강상의 이유로 요가를 한다는 것은 놀라운 사실이 아니다. (b) 요가는 스트레스를 감소시키고 통증을 완화시키고 근육을 강화시킨다. (c) 요가를 하는 동안 명상을 하는 것은 중요하다. (d) 점점 더 많은 의사들이 환자들에게 요가를 권유한다.

해설 문맥에 어울리지 않는 문장을 찾아내는 문제이다. 이런 질문에서는 단락의 주제 문장을 찾아 그 주제와 연관이 없는 문장을 선택하면 쉽게 해결할 수 있다. 'Yoga is widely seen as important for improving physical and mental health.'라는 첫 문장을 통해서 요가와 신체적 정신적 건강 개선과 밀접한 관련이 있음을 알 수 있다. 따라서 (a), (b), (d)는 모두 요가의 건강에 미치는 효과가 좋으며 의사들이 권하는 치료법임을 알 수 있다. 따라서 정답은 (c)다.

어휘 widely 일반적으로, 널리
improve 증진시키다, 개선시키다
physical 육체의, 신체의
mental 마음의, 정신의
reduce 감소시키다
relieve 경감하다
strengthen 강하게 하다, 튼튼하게 하다
meditate 명상하다, 묵상하다, 숙고하다
medical practitioner 의사 *cf.* legal practitioner 변호사
recommend 추천하다, 권하다, 충고하다

정답 (c)

39

By the year 2000, online teenagers had developed a new form of the English language. (a) Users of email and instant messaging began using a combination of letters, symbols, and numbers to simplify their communications. (b) Within a few years, adults began to catch on, and many today use this new language. (c) Providers of Internet software and cell phones now offer pictures, symbols, and emoticons that promote increased use of the form. (d) Laws restricting the use of this popular trend have been proposed in a number of states and countries.

해석 2000년경 온라인을 사용하는 십대들은 새로운 형태의 영어를 만들어 냈다. (a) 이메일과 인스턴트 메시지를 사용하는 이들은 자신들의 의사전달을 단순화하기 위해 문자, 상징, 숫자들의 조합을 이용하기 시작했다. (b) 몇 년 내에 어른들도 배우기 시작했고, 오늘날 많은 사람들이 이러한 새로운 언어를 사용한다. (c) 인터넷 소프트웨어와 이동 통신 회사들은 현재 이러한 형태의 언어 사용을 장려하는 사진, 상징, 이모티콘을 제공하고 있다. (d) 이러한 유행의 이용을 제한하는 법률이 많은 주와 국가들에서 제안되었다.

해설 온라인을 적극적으로 사용하는 십대들에 의한 새로운 영어 언어 형태(a new form of the English language)에 관한 글이다. 그렇다면 이러한 주제 문장 다음에는 이러한 새로운 언어 형태의 예, 혹은 사회적 확산등과 관련된 내용이 오는 것이 자연스러울 것이다. (a)는 이메일과 인스턴트 메시지 사용을 통해 간단하게 의사 표현을 할 수 있는 문자, 상징, 숫자 등의 이용에 관한 내용이며, (b)는

이것이 성인에게 까지 확산되고 (c)는 인터넷 소프트웨어 회사와 이동 통신 회사에서 제공하고 있는 다양한 사진, 상징, 이모티콘에 관한 내용이다. 따라서 이 글의 문맥과는 어울리지 않는 것은 (d)다.

어휘 instant 즉각의, 인스턴트의
combination 결합, 배합
simplify 단순화하다, 간단하게 하다
communication 의사소통
catch on 배우다
emoticon 〈emotion+icon〉 그림문자
promote 증진시키다, 장려하다
restrict 제한하다, 한정하다

정답 (d)

40

Linguists know better than anyone that the way people talk mirrors their upbringing, their personal view of the world and their culture's history. (a) This is why, from one language to the other, there are many "untranslatable" terms. (b) For example the word "sisu" used by Finnish people has no known equal counterpart in the English language. (c) "Sisu" is an efficient one-word term that describes an individual's excessively-determined nature and unfailing belief to never give up even when the odds are stacked against him. (d) Finnish dialect continues to influence the regional dialects of the northeastern part of the United States.

해석 언어학자들은 사람들이 말하는 방식이 그들의 가정교육, 개인의 세계관, 문화적 역사를 반영한다는 것을 누구보다도 잘 알고 있다. (a) 이 때문에 한 언어에서 다른 언어로 '번역될 수 없는' 용어들이 많이 존재한다. (b) 예를 들어 핀란드 사람들이 사용하는 '시수'라는 단어는 영어로는 동일한 의미를 나타내는 단어가 알려지지 않았다. (c) '시수'는 개인의 극도로 단호한 성격과 어떠한 어려운 상황에서도 절대 포기하지 않는 변함없는 신념을 한 단어로 효율적으로 표현한 용어다. (d) 핀란드 방언은 미국 북동부 지역의 방언에 계속해서 영향을 끼치고 있다.

해설 글을 전체적으로 읽어 가면서 적절하게 연결되지 않은 문장을 선택하는 문제이다. 먼저 주제문에 주의를 기울여라! 사람들이 말하는 방식이 가정교육, 개인의 세계관, 문화적 역사를 반영하고, 또한 이 때문에 언어 간에 번역될 수 없는 용어들이 존재한다는 것이 글의 주제이다. 이후에 제시되는 문장에서는 이와 관련된 예를 제공하게 된다.(a), (b), (c)는 한 언어가 다른 언어로 번역될 수 없다는 것과 그것에 대한 예가 제시되어 있지만 (d)는 이것과 관련 없는 내용이므로 (d)가 정답이다.

어휘 mirror 반영하다
upbringing 가정교육

untranslatable 번역될 수 없는
counterpart 대응물, 상응하는 것
describe 묘사하다
excessively 과도하게, 지나치게
the odds are stacked against ~에게 성공할
확률이 낮다
influence 영향을 미치다
dialect 방언, 사투리

정답 (d)

Actual Test 5

1 (b)	**2** (d)	**3** (c)	**4** (b)	**5** (c)
6 (a)	**7** (b)	**8** (a)	**9** (d)	**10** (b)
11 (d)	**12** (a)	**13** (d)	**14** (c)	**15** (c)
16 (b)	**17** (c)	**18** (c)	**19** (d)	**20** (c)
21 (b)	**22** (b)	**23** (b)	**24** (d)	**25** (c)
26 (d)	**27** (c)	**28** (d)	**29** (d)	**30** (a)
31 (d)	**32** (c)	**33** (d)	**34** (d)	**35** (a)
36 (c)	**37** (b)	**38** (b)	**39** (d)	**40** (d)

1

A new poll in Great Britain has found that most high school dropouts later wish they hadn't quit school. Currently, although the British government encourages them to remain in school through age eighteen, students can legally leave school at age sixteen. As a result, many stop attending school and instead find jobs, hoping to increase their workplace experience. However, the new study found that more than fifty-one percent of students who permanently dropped out later _____.

(a) experienced pain
(b) expressed regret
(c) seemed happy
(d) suggested otherwise

해석 영국의 한 여론조사에 따르면 대부분의 고등학교 중퇴자들이 나중에 바라는 것은 자신들이 학교를 그만두지 말았어야 했다는 것이다. 현재 영국 정부가 학생들이 18세까지 학교에 다니기를 장려하고 있지만 학생들은 법적으로 16세에 학교를 그만둘 수 있다. 결과적으로 많은 학생들이 학교를 그만두고 일자리를 찾아 직장 경험을 늘리고자 한다. 하지만 새로운 연구는 학교를 중퇴한 학생들 중의 51%가 나중에 후회한다는 것을 보여 주었다.

(a) 고통을 경험한다는 것을
(b) 후회한다는 것을
(c) 행복해 보인다는 것을
(d) 그렇지 않다는 것을 암시함을

해설 영국에서의 고교 중퇴자들과 관련된 글이다. 첫 문장에서 '~ most high school dropouts later wish they hadn't quit school.'이라고 말함으로써 고교 중퇴자들이 나중에 후회한다는 것을 밝히고 있다. 학생들은 16세가 되면 법적으로 학교를 그만둘 수 있기 때문에 정부에서 학교를 다니라고 장려를 해도 그만두는 사례가 늘고 있다. as a result라는 장치를 이용하여 이러한 결과로 학생들이 학교를 그만두고 직장 경험을 늘리고자 한다는 것을 강조하고 있다. however는 앞 뒤 문장의 흐름이 전환되는 장치이기 때문에, 실제로 학교를 중도에 포기한 학생들이 나중에는 후회한다는 내용이 와야 한다. 따라서 정답은 (b)다.

어휘 poll 여론조사
dropout 탈락자; 중퇴자
currently 현재
encourage 장려하다
legally 법률적[합법적]으로
permanently 영구히
regret 후회

정답 (b)

2

Quadratura was a style of artwork on ceilings which represented architecture. Most commonly used during the Baroque period, quadratura artists matched the style and architecture of a building. By painting images with depth on a flat or a rounded ceiling, they could make it appear deeper and more impressive. Thus, quadratura _____. It was meant to be viewed from below and was often used in churches and palaces.

(a) enhanced the buildings' grand Baroque exteriors
(b) employed the subtle use of color variation
(c) removed the ceiling altogether in many cases
(d) used illusion to create a sense of perspective

해석 쾨드라투라는 건축 양식을 대표하는 천장에 그려지는 미술 양식이다. 이것이 가장 많이 사용된 때는 바로크 시대였다. 쾨드라투라 예술가들은 건물 건축에 이 양식을 맞추었다. 예술가들은 평평하거나 둥근 천장에 깊이를 나타내도록 그림을 그려서 좀 더 원근감 있고 인상적이게 할 수 있었다. 그러므로 쾨드라투라는 원근감을 조성하기 위해 착시를 이용했다. 이 그림은 아래에서 보도록 되어있었고 종종 교회나 궁전에 사용되었다.

(a) 건물의 웅장한 바로크 풍의 외관을 강화했다
(b) 미묘한 색상 변화를 사용했다
(c) 많은 경우에 천장을 아예 없앴다
(d) 원근감을 조성하기 위해 착시를 이용했다

해설 빈 칸이 있는 문장이 Thus로 시작이 되기 때문에, 앞 문장이 원인을 나타내는 내용이 들어 있다는 것을 쉽게 짐작할 수 있다. 따라서 빈 칸 바로 앞 문장을 집중적으로 이해하는 것이 중요하다. 앞 문장의 주요 내용은 '평평하거나 둥근 평면에 깊이를 나타내도록(with depth) 그림을 그려서 더욱 원근감(deeper)을 주었다. 그 다음에 이어질 내용으로는 원근감(a sense of perspective)이 있는 (d)가 정답이다.

어휘 ceiling 천장
represent 대표하다
architecture 건축
the Baroque period 바로크 시대
match ~을 맞추다, ~을 어울리게 하다
depth 깊이(deep의 명사형)
flat 평평한
impressive 인상적인
be meant to ~하기로 되어 있다
view 보다
enhance 강화하다
exterior 외부, 외관
subtle 미묘한
variation 변화
remove 제거하다; 없애다
illusion 환상
a sense of perspective 원근감

정답 (d)

3

Dear Sir:
Trust Bank has a new service for its loyal customers. Our Dollar Invest Plan is a zero-maintenance stock investment program at no cost to you. This service is provided as a _____ to customers that have been with us for more than 10 years. Simply complete a form specifying the monthly amount you would like invested and return it to us. We will then send you all the information you need to understand how your money can make you money. If you have any further questions, simply call us at 1-800-368-9256. Thank you again for your loyalty to Trust Bank.
Cecil Graham
Manager
Trust Bank

(a) symbol of investment
(b) reaction of customers
(c) gesture of appreciation
(d) reminder of loyalty

해석 귀하께,

트러스트 은행은 우수 고객들에게 새로운 서비스를 제공하고 있습니다. 저희의 달러 투자 플랜은 관리가 필요 없는 주식 투자 프로그램으로 귀하의 비용 부담 없이 제공합니다. 이 서비스는 10년 이상을 거래해 오신 고객들에게 감사의 표시로 제공됩니다. 귀하께서 이 프로그램에 등록하고 싶으시다면 매달 투자하기를 원하시는 금액을 기입한 양식을 작성해서 보내 주십시오. 그러면 어떻게 귀하의 자산이 증대되는지 이해하실 수 있도록 모든 필요한 정보를 보내 드릴 것입니다. 만일 질문이 있으시면 저희 투자 서비스 부서 1-800-368-9256으로 전화하십시오. 트러스트 은행을 신뢰해주신 것에 다시 한 번 감사드립니다.

세실 그래험
과장
트러스트 은행

(a) 투자의 상징
(b) 고객들의 반응
(c) 감사의 표시
(d) 충성을 상기시키는 것

해설 트러스트 은행에서 우수 고객들에게 새로운 서비스(Trust Bank has a new service to its loyal customers.)를 제공한다는 것을 홍보하는 편지를 보낸 것이다. 이 주식 투자 프로그램의 특성은 a zero-maintenance stock investment program at no cost to you에서 설명하고 있듯이 소비자가 관리할 필요가 없는 무료 서비스이다. 특히 이 서비스는 10년 이상을 거래해온 고객들에게 _____ 로 제공되는 것이다. 따라서 빈 칸에 들어갈 내용은 고객들에 대한 감사 혹은 보답의 의미가 들어가야 한다. 따라서 정답은 (c)가 적절하다.

어휘 loyal customer 우수 고객 *cf.* loyalty 충절, 충성
zero-maintenance 관리가 필요 없는
at no cost 전혀 비용이 들지 않는
specify ~에 기입하다
complete a form 양식을 작성하다
as a gesture of appreciation 감사의 표시로
reminder 상기시키는 것, 생각나게 하는 것

정답 (c)

4

There's a new trend in the mobile phone business: social networking. Motivated by the success of online social networking sites, which allow users to interact with people around the world via the Internet, mobile phone companies are now letting users log in, regardless of location. Cell phone companies _____ to tap into the profits that this huge phenomenon is spawning.

(a) offer pager services once again
(b) use these new services
(c) add online TV shows and movies
(d) create attractive phone designs

해석 새로운 경향이 이동 전화 업계에 등장했는데 그것은 친목을 도모하는 네트워킹이다. 이동 전화 회사들이 온라인 친목 네트워킹 사이트들의 성공에 영향을 받았는데, 이런 싸이트들은 인터넷을 통해 사용자들이 서로 교류하도록 해준다. 이동 전화 회사들은 위치에 상관없이 회원들이 이동 전화를 통해 이 사이트에 접속할 수 있도록 해주고 있다. 이동 전화 회사들은 이러한 새로운 서비스를 이용하는데 그 목적은 이 거대한 현상이 만들어내고 있는 이익을 얻기 위해서이다.

(a) 호출기 서비스를 다시 제공하는데
(b) 이러한 새 서비스를 이용하는데
(c) 온라인 TV쇼와 영화를 추가하는데
(d) 매력적인 전화기 디자인을 만드는데

해설 이동 전화 회사(mobile phone business, cell phone companies)가 _____ 을 하는데 그 목적이 이런 큰 현상이 만들어내고 있는 이익에 동참하려는 것이라는 마지막 문장을 완성해야 한다. 첫 문장에 이동 전화 사업에 a new trend가 있다고 했으니 신규 서비스를 사용해서, 거대한 시장 변화에서 생기는 이익을 얻으려고 한다는 것이 논리적으로 적합한 내용이다. 따라서 (b)가 정답이다.

어휘 trend 추세, 경향
social networking 친목 도모
motivate 동기를 부여하다, 자극하다
interact with ~와 교류하다
via ~을 통해서
log in 접속하다
regardless of ~에 상관없이
tap into ~을 얻어내다
profit 이익
phenomenon 현상
spawn ~을 생기게 하다, 일으키다
pager 호출기
attractive 매력적인

정답 (b)

5

Dear Sir or Madam:
I am writing to _____ at one of your Paco's Tacos restaurants. My husband and I went to one last Friday, and were not seated for a long time. Once we were finally seated, we found that the glasses were filthy. Following this, the wrong order was brought out to us, our dessert was rotten, and to make matters worse, we were overcharged. We will not be returning to Paco's Tacos.
Sincerely,
Marie Evans

(a) tell you about a lovely evening I enjoyed
(b) commend you on your selection of waiters
(c) inform you about a horrible experience I had
(d) complain about the dirty facilities I encountered

해석 담당자께,
저는 귀하의 파코스 타코 식당에서의 끔찍한 경험에 대해 알리려고 편지를 씁니다. 제 남편과 저는 지난 금요일 식당에 갔었고 오랜 시간 동안 좌석을 안내 받지 못했습니다. 마침내 자리에 앉았는데 컵이 더러운 것을 발견했습니다. 이어서 주문한 것과 다른 음식이 나왔고 우리 후식은 상했고 설상가상으로 계산서에는 부당한 가격이 청구됐습니다. 우리는 다시는 파코스 타코에 가지 않을 것입니다.
마리 에반스

(a) 즐거운 시간을 보낸 저녁 식사에 대해 말씀 드리려고
(b) 귀하의 웨이터 선택에 찬사를 보내고자
(c) 끔찍한 경험에 대해 알리려고
(d) 제가 경험한 더러운 시설에 대해 불평을 하고자

해설 전체적으로 불만을 호소하는 서신(complaint letter)이다. 오랫동안 기다렸던 것, 컵이 깨끗하지 못했던 것, 주문하지 않은 음식이 나왔던 것, 후식이 신선하지 못했던 것, 그리고 부당하게 가격을 청구한 것 등 여러 가지 부당하게 대접을 받았던 것을 불평하는 서신이므로 긍정적인 내용인 (a), (b)는 답이 아니다. 또한 다룬 내용이 청결에만 국한된 것이 아니므로 답은 (c)다.

어휘 be seated 앉다
filthy 더러운, 불결한
rotten 상한
to make matters worse 설상가상으로
commend 칭찬하다
facilities 시설
encounter 마주치다, 만나다

정답 (c)

6

Scientists have begun to look at weather patterns in an attempt to predict outbreaks of diseases. They believe that _____ within a particular region, they can better anticipate the conditions that breed disease. Recently, in Africa, scientists noticed warmer weather and higher rainfall. They realized that this would create ideal breeding conditions for disease-carrying mosquitoes and sent anti-malaria drugs in advance. By analyzing weather patterns, they helped avert a disaster.

(a) by monitoring the amounts of rainfall and the temperatures
(b) by taking a census of the sick and diseased population
(c) by recording the outbreaks of major diseases
(d) by predicting long-term climatic change

해석 과학자들은 날씨의 패턴을 살피기 시작했는데 그 목적은 질병들의 발생을 예측하기 위해서이다. 과학자들은 특정 지역에서 강수량과 기온을 모니터함으로써 질병을 초래하는 조건들을 더 잘 예상할 수 있다고 믿는다. 최근에 과학자들은 아프리카 날씨가 더 따뜻해지고 강수량이 더 많아졌음을 알아냈다. 과학자들은 이것이 질병을 옮기는 모기들에게 이상적인 증식 조건이 된다는 것을 깨닫고 말라리아 약을 사전에 보냈다. 날씨 패턴을 적절하게 분석할 수 있었기 때문에 재앙을 피할 수 있었다.

(a) 강수량과 기온을 모니터함으로써
(b) 아프고 병든 사람들의 수를 조사함으로써
(c) 주요 질병들의 발생을 기록함으로써
(d) 장기간의 기후 변화를 예측함으로써

해설 날씨(weather patterns)와 관련하여 연관이 있을만한 것은 (a)와 (d)다. (a)에 rainfall, temperatures와 (d)에 climatic change가 가장 답이 될 확률이 높은 선택지이다. 그 다음에 이어지는 내용이 빈 칸을 뒷받침해주는 예문이기 때문에 warmer weather and higher rainfall이라는 내용으로 보아서 강수량과 기온을 언급하고 있는 (a)가 답이다.

어휘 in an attempt to ~하려는 시도로
predict 예견하다, 예측하다
outbreak 발발, 발생
region 지역
anticipate 예견하다, 예상하다
breed disease 병을 초래하다
in advance 미리, 사전에
analyze 분석하다 *cf.* analysis 분석
avert ~을 피하다, 막다
monitor 모니터하다; 감시[탐지]하다
take a census 인구조사하다

climatic change 기후변화

정답 (a)

7

The new Roebling bicycles are on sale now at the Bike Stop. We're offering a ten-speed Roebling Series A35 bicycle for $300, and if you don't have time to get out the toolbox, we'll even _____ ! We also have a fifteen-speed Mountain Professional Series Roebling with a five-year warranty for only $425. For the little ones in the family, we have a Roebling tricycle available in all of their favorite colors. This sale ends Monday, so roll on in to the Bike Stop today!

(a) give free bicycle advice
(b) put it together for you
(c) give you easy instructions
(d) make it more convenient

해석 새로운 로블링 자전거가 현재 바이크 스탑에서 세일을 하고 있습니다. 저희는 10단 변속의 로블링 시리즈 A35 자전거를 300달러에 판매하고 있으며 만일 여러분이 연장통을 꺼낼 시간이 없으시다면 조립까지 해드립니다! 저희는 또한 15단 변속의 마운틴 프로페셔널 시리즈 로블링을 5년간의 보증 기관과 함께 425달러에 판매합니다. 어린이들을 위하여 우리는 어린이들이 좋아할 만한 다양한 색깔의 로블링 세발자전거를 구비하고 있습니다. 이 세일은 월요일에 끝나므로 오늘 바이크 스탑으로 서둘러 오세요!

(a) 자전거에 대한 무료 조언을 드립니다
(b) 여러분을 위해 조립을 해드립니다
(c) 쉬운 설명서를 드립니다
(d) 그것을 좀 더 편리하게 해드립니다

해설 로블링 자전거 판매에 관한 광고문이다. 광고문에서는 선전하고자 하는 제품, 제품의 특성, 가격, 구매처, 혹은 사용 방법 등에 관한 정보를 제시한다. 이 제품은 바이크 스탑에서 살 수 있다. 로블링 시리즈 A35 자전거의 가격은 300불이며 빈 칸에 들어갈 표현은 'if you don't have time to get out the toolbox, ~'와 이어지는 것이어야 한다. 연장을 꺼내야 한다는 것은 이 자전거가 조립식이란 것을 함축한다. 따라서 (a)와 (d)는 우선적으로 답에서 제외되고 (c)보다는 (b)가 문맥에 가장 적합하다.

어휘 toolbox 연장통
ten-speed 10단 변속의
put together 조립하다
a five-year warranty 5년 보증기간
tricycle 세발자전거
roll on 서두르다
convenient 편리한

정답 (b)

8

Once, when I was about ten years old, I made a batch of chocolate chip cookies. I carefully measured out each ingredient and mixed them together. I was just about to bake the dough when it occurred to me that I _____ . So I stuck a large amount of cookie dough into my mouth. What a nasty surprise! I had somehow mistaken salt for sugar, and instead of a sweet little treat, I got a mouthful of salt.

(a) should test my work
(b) would enjoy the dough
(c) could burn the cookies
(d) should read the recipe

해석 한 번은 내가 열 살쯤 되었을 때 나는 초콜릿 칩 쿠키를 한 판 구웠다. 나는 조심스럽게 각각의 재료를 계량했고 함께 섞었다. 내가 반죽을 구우려고 할 때 내 작품을 테스트 해봐야겠다는 생각이 들었다. 그래서 나는 큰 쿠키 반죽 덩어리를 입 안에 넣었다. 끔찍한 맛이었다. 나는 어찌해서인지 소금을.설탕으로 알았고 나는 기대했던 달콤한 간식이 아닌 입 안 가득 소금 덩어리를 맛보았다.

(a) 내 작품을 테스트해봐야겠다는
(b) 반죽을 좋아하게 될 거라는
(c) 쿠키를 태울 수도 있다는
(d) 요리법을 읽어 봐야 겠다는

해설 빈 칸 다음에 오는 내용이 입안에 쿠기 반죽을 넣는 내용 (stuck a large amount of cookie dough into my mouth)이 나오니까, 맛을 보는 내용의 (a)가 가장 적합하다. be about to는 '막 ~하려고 하다'니까, 빈 칸이 있는 문장 앞부분에 I was about to bake the dough 를 통해 아직 반죽을 오븐에 넣지 않았다는 것을 알 수 있으므로 (c)를 가장 먼저 선택지에서 제외한다. 따라서 정답은 (a)다.

어휘 a batch of 한 판의
measure out 측정하여 나누다[덜다]
ingredient 재료
be about to+V 막 ~하려고 하다
occur to ~에게 (생각이) 떠오르다
stick something into one's mouth ~의 입에 …을 넣다
nasty 메스꺼운, 끔찍한, 역겨운
mistake A for B A를 B로 착각하다
treat 대접, 만족을 주는 것[사람]

정답 (a)

9

A new study suggests that damage to the brain's hippocampus, which controls memory, may impair the ability to imagine the future. Patients who had experienced trauma to the hippocampus were asked to describe possible scenarios for an upcoming event or conversation. Generally, _____ _____ such a situation.

(a) those with such experience had better memories in

(b) people with amnesia have little trouble remembering

(c) most people have few problems talking about

(d) these individuals had difficulty imagining and describing

해석 새로운 연구가 시사하는 바로는 기억력을 조절하는 뇌의 해마상 융기의 손상이 미래를 상상하는 능력을 손상시킬 수 있다. 뇌의 해마상 융기에의 충격을 경험한 환자들은 다가오는 행사나 대화에 대한 가능한 시나리오를 묘사해 보라는 지시를 받았다. 일반적으로 이 사람들은 (이러한 상황을) 상상하고 묘사하는데 어려움이 있었다.

(a) 이러한 경험을 가진 사람들은 (이러한 상황에서) 더 기억력이 좋았다

(b) 기억상실증이 있는 사람들은 (이러한 상황을) 기억하는데 문제가 거의 없다

(c) 대부분의 사람들이 (이러한 상황에 대해) 이야기하는데 거의 문제가 없다

(d) 이들이 (이러한 상황을) 상상하고 묘사하는데 어려움이 있었다

해설 a new study 또는 a recent study 다음에 오는 내용을 주시할 필요가 있다. 새로운 사실이 밝혀졌다거나, 기존에 알고 있던 것과는 다른 내용이 오는 경우가 많기 때문이다. 본 지문에서 첫 문장이 주제문이고, 그 다음에 이어진 문장(Patients ~ conversation.)에는 주제문을 확실하게 하는 예시가 들어있다. 따라서 해마상 융기에 손상이 있는 사람들이 상상력과 묘사부분을 잘 하지 못하고 어려워 한다는 (d)가 가장 설득력이 있다.

어휘 damage 손상, 피해
brain 뇌
hippocampus (뇌의) 해마상 융기
impair 손상시키다
trauma 충격
describe 묘사하다
upcoming 다가오는
event 사건
amnesia 기억상실증

정답 (d)

10

Parents Digest's article on the increasing pressure parents are putting on their children to win in sports was very insightful. Instead of supporting their children regardless of the game's outcome, parents are becoming overly goal-oriented and critical. Children are no longer allowed to enjoy the sport for what it is — a game. These parents don't realize how harmful this is for their children. I would _____ _____.

(a) like to see such children try even harder to win

(b) encourage more parents to relax and let their kids be kids

(c) prefer that children talk about academic problems with their parents

(d) suggest that parents teach their kids to be more goal-oriented

해석 부모들이 아이들에게 스포츠에서 이기라고 점점 많은 압력을 가한다는 것에 대한 다이제스트의 기사는 매우 통찰력이 있었다. 경기의 결과에 상관없이 아이들을 격려하는 대신 부모들은 지나치게 득점에 연연하고 비판적이게 된다. 아이들은 더 이상 운동을 경기 그 자체로 즐기도록 허락되지 않는다. 이러한 부모들은 이것이 아이들에게 얼마나 해로운지를 깨닫지 못하고 있다. 나는 더 많은 부모들이 느긋하게 아이들을 아이들답게 내버려 둘 것을 장려한다.

(a) 그러한 아이들이 이기기 위해 좀 더 노력하는 모습을 보고 싶다

(b) 더 많은 부모들이 느긋하게 아이들을 아이들답게 내버려 둘 것을 장려한다

(c) 아이들이 학업 문제들에 대해 그들의 부모들과 이야기할 것을 선호한다

(d) 부모들이 아이들을 좀 더 득점에 연연하도록 가르칠 것을 제안한다

해설 (a) 글 전반적으로 부모가 자녀에게 부담을 주는 것을 강하게 비판하고 있으므로 (a)는 절대로 답이 될 수 없다. (b) 부모들이 좀 더 여유를 갖고 아이들을 아이들답게 키울 것을 장려한다는 것은 문맥상 아주 자유롭게 이어진다. (c) 학습적인 부분은 본 지문 어느 곳에서도 나와 있지 않으므로 선택지에서 제외한다. (d) 운동을 운동 그 자체로 이해하고 즐겨야 하는데, 현실이 그렇지 못함을 안타까워하고, 득점 지향(goal-oriented)적인 것을 비난하는 입장이므로 답이 될 수 없다. 따라서 정답은 (b)다.

어휘 article 기사
pressure 압력, 부담
insightful 통찰력이 있는
support 지지하다, 격려하다
regardless of ~에 상관없이
outcome 결과

overly 지나치게
goal-oriented 득점 지향적인
critical 비판적인
harmful 유해한, 나쁜
academic 학구적인, 학업의

11

Just what is the cost of education? A new study found that half of university students aren't attending their first-choice school. They instead decided to go to their second- or third-choice school, many factoring tuition costs into their decisions. Also, lower-ranked schools are beginning to offer more incentives for students, such as _____ based upon merit, which further affect affordability.

(a) inexpensive meal plans
(b) upscale housing
(c) convenient transportation
(d) financial assistance

해석 교육의 비용이라는 것이 무엇일까? 새로운 연구에 따르면 학생들의 절반이 자신이 처음 선택한 학교에 다니지 않는다. 대신 그들은 두 번째 혹은 세 번째로 택한 학교에 가기로 결정했는데, 다수가 등록금을 고려하여 그 결정을 했다. 또한 하위권의 대학들이 학생들에게 실력에 따른 재정적인 지원과 같이 더 많은 인센티브를 제공하고 있는데, 이것은 교육비 감당 여부에 더 큰 영향을 끼친다고 한다.

(a) 저렴한 식단
(b) 고급 주택
(c) 편리한 교통수단
(d) 재정적 지원

해설 이 글에서 전체적으로 흐르는 내용은 교육과 돈에 관한 것이다. 예를 들어, cost of education ~, factoring tuition costs into their decisions가 그 예라 할 수 있다. 따라서 우선순위가 밀리는 조금 안 좋은 학교들이 학생들에게 인센티브를 제안하기 시작했다면, 그 인센티브는 금전적인 것과 연관된 것이어야 한다. 따라서 정답은 (d)다.

어휘 cost 비용
attend ~에 다니다, 출석하다
instead 대신에
factor 요인으로 고려하다, 계산에 넣다
tuition 수업료
lower-ranked 인기가 덜 있는, 덜 선호하는
incentive 장려금, 보상책
based upon ~을 기초로
merit 장점, 자질
affordability 지불 능력
upscale 고급의, 상류의

정답 (d)

12

"Human capital" is the resources a nation has in its people. The intelligence, education and skills an individual acquires and contributes to a company impact the overall ability of the company to be productive. Similarly, a relationship between a country's human capital and its production level has been established. The higher the human capital — that is, the more capable the work force — the more the country produces. Different people possess varying levels of human capital, _____.

(a) determined by their knowledge and experience
(b) related to the overall quality of their education
(c) expressed in the ways they are employed
(d) symbolized by their position within the company

해석 인적 자원은 한 나라의 국민들이 가지고 있는 자원이다. 개인이 습득하고 한 회사에 기여하는 지식, 교육과 기술들은 그 회사의 전반적인 생산 능력에 영향을 미친다. 마찬가지로, 한 국가의 인적자원과 생산력 사이에도 이러한 관계가 성립된다. 인적 자원이 높을수록, 즉 노동력이 더욱 역량이 있을수록 국가는 더 많이 생산한다. 다양한 사람들이 그들의 지식과 경험에 의해 결정된 다양한 수준의 인적 자원을 소유하고 있다.

(a) 그들의 지식과 경험에 의해 결정된
(b) 교육의 전반적인 질에 관련하여
(c) 그들이 채용된 방식에서 표현된
(d) 회사 내에서 그들의 지위에 의해 상징된

해설 인적자원(human capital)과 경쟁력과의 관계를 설명하는 글이다. 먼저 인적자원이 무엇인지 정의 내리고 (the resources a nation has in its people), 개인 (individual)과 회사(company)와의 관계를 먼저 설명한 후 국민(people)과 국가(country)와의 관계를 설명하는 방식을 취하고 있다. 다양한 인적자원의 수준이란 다름아닌 국민의 지식과 경험에 의한 것이라는 것을 쉽게 알 수 있으므로 답은 (a)다.

어휘 capital 자본, 자산
resources 자원
intelligence 지식, 지능
acquire 습득하다
contribute to ~에 공헌하다, 기여하다
impact 영향을 미치다
overall 전반적인
productive 생산적인
varying 다양한, 가지각색의
determine ~을 결정하다

정답 (a)

13

NEW YORK CITY — The New York Police Department and Fire Department sell popular T-shirts and baseball caps with their logos on the front. Now, there's a new city department joining the craze: the Sanitation Department. City officials are beginning to market distressed brown ball caps with the blue logo on them, and they're popular. The trend is growing, and New York City officials have plans to _____. They hope to include other logos as well, including Transportation and Parks, for example.

(a) change the departments' logos
(b) discover the fake brands
(c) limit the production
(d) expand the popular line

해석 뉴욕시 – 뉴욕 경찰국과 소방국이 파는 것은 인기 있는 티셔츠나 야구 모자들인데, 이들은 앞에 로고가 있다. 현재 시의 새로운 부서가 이 유행에 동참하고 있는데 바로 위생국이다. 시 관계자들은 푸른색 로고가 새겨진 오래된 것처럼 꾸민 갈색 야구 모자를 판촉하기 시작했는데, 이 것들은 인기가 있다. 이 유행은 점점 더 커지고 있다. 뉴욕 시 관계자들은 이 인기 있는 상품을 확장할 계획이다. 그들은 예를 들어, 교통부, 공원부 등과 같은 다른 부서들의 로고들도 포함하기를 바란다.

(a) 부서의 로고들을 바꿀
(b) 가짜 상표를 찾을
(c) 생산을 제한할
(d) 이 인기 있는 상품을 확장할

해설 공공기관의 로고가 있는 상품들이 하나의 유행을 이루어 상품화되어 팔리고 있으며, 이런 유행을 좀 더 확산시키고자 하는 정부 당국의 바램을 다루는 글이다. 이 글은 두괄식이 아니라, 처음에 구체적인 예시를 제시하고 있다. NYPD나 NYFD의 로고가 새겨진 티셔츠, 모자가 잘 팔리고 있고, 또 다른 예시로 위생국의 경우도 소개하고 있다. 그런 다음 이처럼 로고가 찍힌 상품이 인기 있는 이런 유행이 점점 확산되고 있고, 그래서 뉴욕시는 (어떤) 계획을 세웠다. 이 때 '어떤'에 해당하는 빈 칸에 맞는 내용은 '이 인기 있는 상품을 확장할 것'이라는 내용이 맞다. 따라서 답은 (d)다.

어휘 department 부서
join 함께 하다, 동참하다
craze 유행
sanitation 위생
market 판촉하다, 팔기 위해 내놓다
distressed 오래된 것처럼 꾸민
fake 가짜의
brand 브랜드
limit 제한하다
expand 확장하다

정답 (d)

14

French doctors have successfully completed their third partial face transplant. Two other patients have previously received partial face transplants, a French woman and a Chinese man. Doctors faced many challenges in completing such surgery. Perhaps the greatest risk they have is the possibility of the patient's body rejecting the transplant. Despite this danger, British and American doctors are now moving forward with plans _____.

(a) to determine the advantages of a transplant
(b) to finalize the partial face transplant procedure
(c) to complete a full face transplant
(d) to progress in transplant treatments

해석 프랑스 의사들은 세 번째 부분 안면 이식에 성공했다. 이전에 부분 안면 이식을 받은 두 명의 다른 환자들은 프랑스 여성과 중국인 남성이었다. 의사들은 이 수술을 마치는데 많은 어려움에 직면했다. 아마도 그들이 가진 가장 큰 위험성은 환자의 몸이 이식에 거부 반응을 보일 수 있는 가능성일 것이다. 이러한 위험에도 불구하고 영국과 미국의 의사들은 현재 전체 안면 이식을 수행하고자 하는 계획을 추진하고 있다.

(a) 이식의 장점들을 결정하고자 하는
(b) 부분 안면 이식 절차를 마무리하는
(c) 전체 안면 이식을 수행하고자 하는
(d) 이식 치료에서 진보하고자 하는

해설 지문을 간단히 요약하면 다음과 같다. 안면 이식 수술이 성공했다. 안면 이식 수술은 이식 거부반응 때문에 매우 어렵다. (하지만) 영국과 미국 의사들은 (어떠한) 계획을 예정대로 진행하고 있다. 여기서 빈 칸에 해당하는 부분의 답을 찾는데 despite this danger가 중요한 역할을 한다. 연결어(connector)의 역할은 문맥의 흐름을 결정하는데, 빈 칸 앞 문장에서는 수술 성공사례와 함께, 이런 수술의 위험성에 대한 언급을 한 후, 그럼에도 불구하고 수술을 예정대로 하겠다는 것이 자연스러운 흐름이라 할 수 있다. 따라서 답은 (c)다.

어휘 complete 마치다, 완료하다
partial 부분의
transplant 이식
previously 이전에
face challenges 도전에 직면하다, 어려움을 겪다
move forward 진행하다, 전진하다
progress 진보하다

정답 (c)

15

Groovy Tunes is now having its biggest sale of the year. We have cut prices dramatically. You'll even get an extra fifteen percent off of already marked clearance items if you come in this weekend. _____, we have hard-to-find records from artists like The When, Cherry and Son, and even Elvin. But you had better hurry — this far-out offer won't last long.

(a) However
(b) On the other hand
(c) In addition
(d) In contrast

해석 구루비 튠이 현재 연중 최대 세일을 하고 있습니다. 우리는 파격적으로 가격을 낮췄습니다. 이번 주에 오시면 이미 할인된 재고 제품에서 15%를 추가로 할인해 드립니다. 게다가 저희는 더 웬, 체리앤 선, 엘빈과 같은 아티스트들의 구하기 힘든 레코드도 보유하고 있습니다. 하지만 서두르세요. 이 파격적인 세일은 오래 지속되지 않습니다.

(a) 그러나
(b) 반면에
(c) 게다가
(d) 대조적으로

해설 연결어구 관련 문제를 풀 때는 선택지를 먼저 보고, 각각의 function을 생각하는 것이 효과적인 풀이 방법이다. (a) However(그러나)는 앞의 내용과 다른 내용이 이어질 때 쓴다. (b) On the other hand(반면에)는 앞의 내용과 상반된 내용이 이어질 때 쓴다. (c) In addition(게다가)은 앞의 내용에 새로운 내용이 추가될 때 쓴다. (d) In contrast(대조적으로)는 앞의 내용과 상반되는 내용이 이어질 때 쓴다. 이렇게 정리해보면 아주 간단하게 답이 (c)라는 것을 쉽게 알 수 있다. (a), (b), (d)는 모두 앞에 나온 내용과는 다른 내용이 이어지는 반면에 (c)는 추가하는 내용이기 때문이다. 가격이 아주 저렴할 뿐 아니라 구하기 힘든 상품들도 마련되어 있다는 내용이므로 답은 (c)다.

어휘 cut prices 가격을 낮추다
dramatically 파격적으로, 매우 많이
extra 추가의
clearance items 재고 제품
hard-to-find 구하기 힘든
far-out 파격적인
last 지속하다

정답 (c)

16

Perhaps one of the most often-used tools of literature is personification. Personification is the characterization of an animal, inanimate object or an idea as if it has human qualities. _____, the darkness might be described as evil. Yet the darkness has no real ill will or personality; it is described this way simply because it is how the author or the author's character perceives it. A classic example of personification is a talking animal. The author is simply using the animal as another character, usually to accomplish a specific purpose in the plot.

(a) In a similar way
(b) For example
(c) Regardless of this
(d) In brief

해석 아마도 문학에서 가장 자주 사용되는 도구들 중의 하나는 의인화일 것이다. 의인화는 동물, 무생물체나 개념이 마치 인간적인 자질들이 있는 것처럼 묘사하는 것이다. 예를 들어, 어둠은 사악한 것으로 묘사될 수 있다. 그러나 어둠은 실제 나쁜 의도나 성격을 가지고 있지 않다. 이것은 단지 작가나 등장인물이 그것을 인식하는 방식 때문에 그렇게 묘사된다. 의인화의 고전적인 예시는 말하는 동물이다. 작가는 보통 줄거리에서 특정한 목적을 이루고자 단순히 동물을 다른 하나의 등장인물로 이용한다.

(a) 유사한 방식으로
(b) 예를 들어
(c) 이와 관계없이
(d) 간단히 말해서

해설 문학작품에서 자주 사용되는 '의인화(personification)'에 관한 글이다. 의인화는 작가가 글의 깊이를 더하기 위해 사용하는 것으로 '동물, 무생물체, 혹은 개념이 인간과 같은 자질을 갖고 있는 것처럼 표현하는 것 (Personification is the characterization of an animal, inanimate object or an idea as if it has human qualities.)'이라는 정의를 제시하여 의인화에 대한 간결한 설명을 문단의 앞부분에서 제시하고 있다. 빈칸 다음에 오는 문장의 내용은 어둠을 사악한 것으로 묘사하는 경우를 설명하고 있다. 따라서 이 문장은 의인화에 대한 구체적인 예시를 제시하는 것이기 때문에 빈 칸에는 (b)가 들어가는 것이 적절하다.

어휘 perhaps 아마도
personification 의인화
characterization 성격묘사, 특징부여
inanimate 생명이 없는
human qualities 인간적인 자질들
ill will 나쁜 의도, 악의
personality 성격
perceive 인식하다
classic 고전적인

character 등장인물
specific 구체적인
plot 줄거리
in brief 간략하게 말해서

정답 (b)

17

Recent research indicates that subliminal advertising is actually ineffective. In one study, volunteers listened to self-help tapes in which subliminal messages were supposed to be present. However, part of the group was given tapes that did not have any subliminal messages in them. All volunteers thought that they had benefited from the tapes — even those volunteers who had not had any subliminal messages on their tapes.

Q What is the main topic of the passage?
(a) The effectiveness of self-help tapes
(b) The usefulness of test groups
(c) The effectiveness of subliminal advertising
(d) The usefulness of positive thinking

해석 최근의 연구에 따르면 잠재의식에 작용하는 광고가 실제로 효과가 없다고 한다. 과학자들은 한 연구에서 지원자들에게 잠재의식에 작용하는 메시지가 있다고 알려진 자기계발 테이프들을 듣게 했다. 그러나 집단의 일부에게 주어진 테이프에는 이러한 메시지가 전혀 없었다. 이 연구의 결과에 따르면 테이프에 잠재의식에 작용하는 메시지가 없었던 지원자들까지도 모두 그 테이프로부터 이익을 얻었다고 생각했다.

Q 위 글의 주제로 알맞은 것을 고르시오.
(a) 자기 계발 테이프의 효율성
(b) 실험 집단의 유용성
(c) 잠재광고의 효율성
(d) 긍정적 사고의 유용성

해설 선택지 모두에 the effectiveness 또는 the usefulness 가 있다. 그렇다면, 이 글이 어떤 것의 효용성을 논의하고 있는 것인가를 생각해봐야 한다. (a) self-help tapes 는 구체적인 예를 들기 위한 실험에 사용된 것이기 때문에 답이 될 수 없다. 맨 앞 문장에서 연구 결과를 밝힐 때 잠재의식에 작용하는 광고의 비효율성에 대한 것이므로 (c)가 정답이다.

어휘 subliminal 잠재의식의
ineffective 무효의, 효과가 없는, 비효율적인
volunteer 지원자
be supposed to ~하도록 되어 있다
benefit from ~에서 이익을 얻다
test group 실험 집단
positive 긍정적인

정답 (c)

18

Researchers recently explored the relationship between children who like school and their socio-economic status. The new study surveyed parents to determine family variables, race and income, and compared it to how well the children of those families enjoyed school. The study found that children who liked school best were often Asian females of well-educated, married parents. The parents of these students also had moderate to high income levels and lived in the suburbs.

Q What is the main idea of the passage?
(a) Income levels have the largest role in whether a child likes school.
(b) New data shows that gender has little effect on enjoyment of school.
(c) Specific traits may indicate how much a child enjoys school.
(d) The study attempted to relate how high grades were to socio-economic status.

해석 연구자들은 최근에 학교를 좋아하는 아이들과 그들의 사회 경제적 지위 간의 관계를 연구했다. 이 새로운 연구에서 부모들에게 질문을 했는데, 그 목적은 가족의 유동성, 인종, 소득 수준을 결정하기 위해서였고 또한 그 결과를 이 가정의 아이들이 얼마나 학교생활을 좋아하는가와 비교했다. 연구에 따르면 학교생활을 가장 즐기는 아이들은 교육 수준이 높고 결혼한 상태의 부모를 가진 아시아계 여학생들이었다. 이 학생들의 부모들은 또한 중간 혹은 고소득층이며 교외에 살고 있었다.

Q 위 글의 요지로 알맞은 것을 고르시오.
(a) 소득 수준은 아이가 학교를 좋아하는지 여부에 가장 큰 역할을 한다.
(b) 새로운 자료에 따르면 성별이 학교생활을 즐기는 것에 거의 영향을 미치지 않는다.
(c) 구체적인 특징들이 아이가 학교를 얼마나 좋아하는지를 보여 줄 수 있다.
(d) 연구는 성적이 얼마나 높은가를 사회 경제적 지위와 관련짓고자 했다.

해설 글의 요지를 파악하는 문제이다. 학교를 좋아하는 아이들과 그들의 사회 경제적 지위 간의 관계를 보고한 연구에 관한 글이다. 연구에 따르면 가족 변수, 인종, 소득 수준을 결정하기 위해 부모들을 조사하고 이 가정의 아이들이 학교를 좋아하는 가(~ surveyed parents to determine family variables, race and income, and compared it to how well the children of those families enjoyed school ~)를 조사하였다. 결과적으로 교육 수준이 높고 결혼한 상태의 부모를 가진 아시아계 여학생들이 학교생활을 가장 즐기는 것으로 나타났다. (a)가 답인 것처럼 여길 수 있으나 소득 수준이 가

장 중요한 요인은 아니며, (d)가 말하는 성적은 연구에서 고려하지 않은 요소이다. 따라서 정답은 (c)가 된다.

어휘 explore 탐험하다, 조사하다
socio-economic status 사회 경제적 지위
survey 조사하다, 연구하다
variables 유동성
race 인종
female 여성의 *cf.* male 남성의
well-educated 교육 수준이 높은
married parents 결혼한 부모
moderate 보통의, 중간 정도의
income 수입, 소득
suburb 교외, 시외
specific 구체적인
trait 특성

정답 (c)

19

Scientists are discovering significantly more about space and the universe. They recently found a group of galaxies even smaller than typical dwarf galaxies. Within this group is the smallest galaxy discovered to date, Leo T. It is far enough from the Milky Way, which normally traps nearby galaxies in its gravitational field, that it is unaffected and independent from any of the normal pull. Scientists believe that Leo T is the tiniest galaxy still able to produce new stars.

Q What is the best title for the passage?
(a) Smaller Universe Discovered
(b) The Gravitational Pull of the Milky Way
(c) Dwarf Galaxy Located
(d) The Smallest Galaxy Scientists Have Ever Found

해석 과학자들은 우주 공간과 우주에 대해 상당히 많은 것들을 발견하고 있다. 그들은 최근에 한 집단의 은하를 발견했는데 이것들은 전형적인 소규모 은하들보다도 훨씬 작았다. 이러한 집단 내부에서 지금까지 발견된 가장 작은 은하계는 레오 티이다. 이것은 일반적으로 부근의 은하들을 그 중력장에 포함하고 있는 은하계에서 매우 멀리 떨어져 있기 때문에 일반적인 중력에 영향을 받지 않고 독립적이다. 과학자들은 레오 티가 여전히 새로운 별들을 만들어낼 수 있는 최소의 은하라고 믿는다.

Q 위 글의 제목으로 가장 적절한 것을 고르시오.
(a) 더 작은 우주의 발견
(b) 은하수의 중력
(c) 위치가 파악된 소은하
(d) 과학자들이 발견한 최소 은하

해설 글의 제목을 선택하는 문제이다. 최근에 과학자들이 일

반적인 소규모 은하보다 작은 은하를 발견하였는데, 가장 작은 은하는 레오 티이다(Within this group is the smallest galaxy discovered to date, Leo T.). 이 문장 이후로는 이 가장 작은 은하에 대한 설명으로 이어진다. 특이한 사항 중 하나는 인근의 다른 은하들은 중력장에 갇혀 있는데 레오 티는 은하계수에서 멀리 떨어져 있기 때문에 일반적인 중력에 영향을 받지 않고 독립적(~ it is unaffected and independent from any of the normal pull.)이란 점이다. 마지막 부분에 다시 한 번 주제 문장이 나와서 레오 티가 새로운 별을 만들어낼 수 있는 최소 은하(the tiniest galaxy still able to produce new stars)임을 강조하고 있다. 따라서 글의 제목으로는 (d)가 적절하다.

어휘 significantly 상당히, 매우
typical 전형적인
galaxy 은하
dwarf 소형의, 작은
to date 지금까지
the Milky Way 은하계[수]
trap 가두다
gravitational field 중력장
unaffected 영향을 받지 않는
tiny 작은, 조그마한

정답 (d)

20

Franz Kafka's book Metamorphosis, originally published in 1915, is the sad story of a shy man, Gregor, who begins to slowly change into an insect. Interestingly, this change occurs not only in the character's physical shape, but also in his mental state. One of the main themes of the book is Gregor's isolation; he is constantly alone, even before he has fully changed into the bug. By the end of the story, Gregor's humanity has completely disappeared.

Q What is the passage mainly about?
(a) The revolutionary writing style of Franz Kafka
(b) The depression present in Metamorphosis
(c) The key aspects of Kafka's Metamorphosis
(d) The importance of physical form to Franz Kafka

해석 원래 1915년에 출간된 프란츠 카프카의 〈변신〉은 서서히 곤충으로 변화하는 수줍음이 많은 남자 그레고의 슬픈 이야기다. 흥미롭게도 이 변화는 인물의 신체적 외형에만 발생한 것이 아니라 그의 정신 상태에도 발생한다. 책의 주요 주제들 중의 하나는 그레고의 고립인데, 그는 벌레

로 완전히 변하기 이전에도 계속 혼자이다. 이야기의 말미에, 그레고의 인간성은 완전히 사라졌다.

Q 위 글은 무엇에 관한 글인가?
(a) 프란츠 카프카의 개혁적인 집필 스타일
(b) 〈변신〉에 내재하는 우울증
(c) 카프카의 〈변신〉의 주요 양상들
(d) 프란츠 카프카에게 있어 외형의 중요성

해설 본 지문은 〈변신〉이라는 책에 관한 주요 내용을 다루고 있다. 누가 저자이며(Franz Kafka), 언제 출판되었고 (originally published in 1915), 주인공이 누구이고 (a shy man, Gregor), 어떤 내용인지(a sad story of a man who begins to slowly change into an insect) 등이다. 또한, 그레고가 육체적 변신 뿐만 아니라 정신적 변신도 했다는 점, 〈변신〉의 주요 주제 중 하나인 고립을 다룬 점 모두 카프카의 〈변신〉의 주요 양상들이라고 할 수 있다. 따라서 답은 (c)다.

어휘 metamorphosis 변형, 변태
originally 원래
change into ~로 변하다
physical 육체적인
mental 정신적인
main 주요한
isolation 고립(감)
bug 벌레
humanity 인간성
revolutionary 개혁적인, 혁명적인
depression 우울증

정답 (c)

21

It is estimated that there are more than 6,000 languages spoken on Earth. Yet many languages are being spoken so little in modern times that they are in danger of being forever forgotten. Experts have documented nearly 750 languages that are already extinct or may become so in the near future. These languages represent every continent on the face of the planet, with the exception of Antarctica. Among nations with the most numerous extinct languages are Australia, the United States, and Brazil.

Q What is the best title for the passage?

(a) Endangered Australia
(b) Lost Languages
(c) Antarctica's Extinction
(d) Forgotten Speakers

해석 추정되는 바로는 지구상에 6천 개 이상의 언어가 말해지고 있다. 그러나 많은 언어들이 현대에 거의 사용되지 않기 때문에 영원히 잊혀 질 위기에 처해있다. 전문가들은

이미 거의 750개의 언어들이 이미 사라졌거나 가까운 미래에 그렇게 될 것이라는 증거를 확보했다. 이러한 언어들은 남극을 제외한 지구상의 모든 대륙을 대표한다. 가장 많은 수의 소멸된 언어를 가진 나라들 중에는 호주, 미국, 브라질이 있다.

Q 위 글에 가장 알맞은 제목을 고르시오.
(a) 위험에 처한 호주
(b) 사라진 언어들
(c) 남극의 소멸
(d) 잊혀 진 언어 사용자들

해설 지구상에 존재하는 언어의 소실에 관한 글이다. 문두에 이 글의 주제를 밝히고 있으며 그 뒤는 그에 대한 세부설명들이다. (a)와 (c)는 언어 얘기가 아닌 대륙 자체의 위험을 나타내므로 답이 될 수 없으며 (d)는 이 글이 언어 사용자가 아니라 언어가 잊혀 진다는 것이므로 답이 될 수 없다. 따라서 답은 (b)다.

어휘 estimate 추정하다
be in danger 위험에 처하다
forever 영원히
document 문서로 정리하다, 증거를 확보하다
extinct 멸종된 *cf.* extinction 멸종
represent 대표하다
with the exception of ~을 제외하고
Antarctica 남극 대륙
numerous 수많은
endangered 위험[위기]에 처한

정답 (b)

22

Many people associate beauty products with modern times. However, the ancient Egyptians actually had numerous cosmetics that they used on a daily or regular basis. The blackish eyeliner made famous in recent years as the "Cleopatra" look was used in order to prevent the sun's glare from causing vision problems. Egyptians also had lipstick, and there is evidence that some dyed their fingernails, much like nail polish is used today. In addition, creams used to treat baldness and gray hairs have also been found in the ruins of ancient Egyptian cities. Egyptians even used scented oils in their hair and on their skin as a moisturizer to protect them from the harsh desert sun.

Q Which of the following is a reason Egyptians used eyeliner?

(a) To moisturize their eyelids
(b) To avoid the sun's reflecting light
(c) To dye the area around the eyes
(d) To protect eyelashes from the sunlight

해석 많은 사람들이 미용 재료들을 현대와 연관시킨다. 그러나 고대 이집트인들은 실제로 수많은 화장품들을 매일 혹은 정기적으로 사용했다. 최근에 클레오파트라 화장법으로 알려진 검은 아이라이너는 시야를 흐리는 태양의 눈부심을 피하기 위해 사용되었다. 이집트인들은 또한 립스틱을 사용했고 일부 사람들은 오늘날 사용되는 매니큐어처럼 손톱에 물을 들였다는 증거가 있다. 더구나 대머리와 새치를 다루는데 사용된 크림이 고대 이집트 도시들의 유적지에서 발견되었다. 이집트인들은 또한 향기 나는 오일들을 수분 공급제로 머리와 피부에 사용하여 견디기 힘든 사막의 태양으로부터 머리카락과 피부를 보호했다.

Q 이집트인들이 아이라이너를 사용한 이유는 무엇인가?
(a) 눈꺼풀에 수분을 제공하기 위해서
(b) 태양에 반사되는 빛을 피하기 위해서
(c) 눈 부위를 염색하기 위해서
(d) 햇빛으로부터 속눈썹을 보호하기 위해서

해설 구체적인 정보를 묻는 질문이다. 이런 유형의 질문은 우선 문제를 먼저 읽고 문제에 대한 세부적인 정보를 찾아 읽는 것이 효과적이다! 고대 이집트에서 수많은 화장품이 사용되었다. 구체적인 예로, 검은 아이라이너는 태양의 눈부심을 피하기 위해서(~ was used in order to prevent the sun's glare from causing vision problems.)라고 본문에서 확인할 수 있으며 립스틱과 매니큐어를 사용했다는 점(~ had lipstick, and there is evidence that some dyed their fingernails, ~)과 대머리와 새치에 사용한 크림, 향기나는 오일을 이용한 수분 공급제 등이 있다. 따라서 본 질문에 대한 정답은 (b)다.

어휘 associate A with B A와 B를 연관짓다
cosmetics 화장품
blackish 거무스름한, 검은
glare 번쩍이는 빛, 눈부심
vision 시야
polish 광택, 윤
scented oil 향기나는 오일
moisturizer 피부에 습기를 주는 화장품, 수분 공급제
cf. moisturize (피부에) 습기를 주다
harsh 가혹한, 견디기 힘든
eyelid 눈꺼풀
eyelashes 속눈썹

정답 (b)

23

Dear Sir,
The First City Bank and Trust would like to inform you that you have overdrawn on your checking account. Our records indicate that a purchase on July 2 of this year exceeded the funds available. As a result, a hold has been placed on your account and an overdraft fee of forty-three dollars was billed to your secondary account. You are advised that you will not be able to make any purchases by debit card and all checks will be returned. Please make arrangements immediately to pay the balance so that your account can be reinstated.
Sincerely,
John Rulley
Vice President of Accounts
First City Bank and Trust

Q What could be enclosed with this letter?
(a) a credit card application
(b) a bank statement
(c) a new debit card
(d) a check for forty-three dollars

해석 귀하께,
퍼스트 시티 금융 신탁에서 알려드리고자 하는 것은 귀하의 당좌예금 계좌에서 초과 인출이 발생했다는 것입니다. 저희 기록에 따르면 올해 7월 2일의 구매가 지출 가능한 금액을 초과했습니다. 그 결과로 귀하의 계좌는 일시 거래 정지가 된 상태이고 초과 인출 요금 43달러가 귀하의 두 번째 계좌에 청구되었습니다. 귀하는 직불 카드를 이용하여 구매를 할 수 없으며 모든 발행 수표는 반송될 것이라는 것을 통보합니다. 신속히 초과 금액을 지불하셔서 귀하의 계좌가 다시 복구될 수 있도록 하시기 바랍니다.
진심어린 마음으로
존 룰리
계좌 담당 부사장
퍼스트 시티 금융 신탁

Q 이 편지에 무엇이 동봉되어 있을까?
(a) 신용카드 발행 신청서
(b) 은행 잔고 증명서
(c) 새로운 직불 카드
(d) 43달러 수표

해설 은행에서 고객에게 보낸 편지이다. 편지는 보낸 이와 받는 이의 관계는 무엇인가, 형식적인 편지인가 친근한 편지인가, 편지의 의도는 무엇인가 등을 기본적으로 파악해야 한다! 이 편지는 수취인의 계좌에서 초과 인출이 발생(~ you have overdrawn on your checking account.)하였음을 통보하는 것이 목적이다. 초과 인출이 발생하였기 때문에 현재 계좌는 일시 정지된 상태(As a result, a hold has been placed on your account ~)이며 초과 인출 요금 43달러가 두 번째 계좌에서 청구되었다. 이 문제에서는 편지에 무엇이 동봉되었는가를 물어 보고 있는데, 현재 이러한 상황을 알려줄 은행 잔고 증명서가 동봉되는 것이 보통의 경우이다. 따라서 정답은 (b)다.

어휘 checking account 당좌 예금 계좌
overdraw 초과 인출하다
exceed (~의) 한도를 넘다, 초과하다
overdraft fee 초과 인출 요금
bill 청구하다
debit card 직불 카드
make arrangements ~을 준비[마련]하다
pay the balance 차액을 지불하다
reinstate 원상태로 하다
enclose 동봉하다

정답 (b)

24

Employers are facing a new problem in attempting to fill vacant job positions with recent graduates. While the number of job openings for graduates is increasing, the number of applicants that employers deem qualified is decreasing. Companies contend that many of the graduates they are interviewing don't possess proper business skills such as deductive reasoning, the ability to work well with a group, or the ability to communicate well with coworkers, supervisors, or clients. As a result, employers face a widening margin of unfilled positions despite an increase in the overall number of graduates.

Q Which of the following is correct about employers?
(a) They are having difficulty finding applicants for open positions.
(b) They are unable to work well with groups of employees.
(c) They have a quick turnaround in job positions that are available.
(d) They have fewer applicants with the proper skills to succeed.

해석 고용주들은 최근 졸업생들을 고용하여 빈 일자리를 채우려고 노력하는 과정에서 어려움을 겪고 있다. 졸업생들을 위한 일자리의 수는 증가하고 있지만 고용주들이 자격을 갖추었다고 여기는 지원자들의 수는 감소하고 있다. 회사들은 면접하고 있는 많은 졸업생들이 추론적 사고, 집단과 함께 일하는 능력, 혹은 동료들, 상사들, 고객들과 의사소통을 원활히 할 수 있는 능력과 같은 적절한 비즈니스

기술들을 갖추지 못했다고 주장한다. 그 결과로서 고용주들은 전체적으로 증가한 졸업생들의 수에도 불구하고 채워지지 않은 빈 일자리들에 직면하고 있다.

Q 고용주들에 대한 내용으로 알맞은 것을 고르시오.
(a) 일자리에 지원할 사람들을 찾는데 어려움이 있다.
(b) 여러 직원들과 함께 일을 잘하지 못하고 있다.
(c) 빈 일자리들에서 변동이 잦다.
(d) 성공하는데 필요한 기술들을 갖춘 지원자들이 적다.

해설 고용주의 입장을 묻는 질문이다. 문단의 첫 문장이 글 전체의 핵심적 내용을 담고 있다. 'Employers are facing a new problem in attempting to fill vacant job positions with recent graduates.'에서 지적하고 있듯이 고용주들은 빈 일자리를 채우는데 어려움을 겪고 있다. 문장과 문장을 이어주는 while에 주목하라! 즉, 졸업생을 위한 일자리 수는 증가하고 있지만, 실제로 자격을 갖춘 지원자의 수는 감소하고 있으며(~ the number of applicants that employers deem qualified is decreasing.) 이런 지원자들은 추론적 사고, 집단에서 일하는 능력, 의사소통 능력 등과 같이 비즈니스 기술이 부족하다(~ proper business skills such as deductive reasoning, the ability to work well with a group, or the ability ~). 따라서 정답은 (d)다.

어휘 vacant 빈, 공석의
graduate 졸업생
job opening (직장의) 빈 자리
applicant 지원자
deem 생각하다, 여기다
qualified 자격을 갖춘
contend ~을 주장하다
deductive 추론적인
turnaround 전향, 전환

정답 (d)

25

Emma Faust Tillman died recently in Hartford, Connecticut, only four days after becoming the world's oldest person. Tillman was born in 1892 to parents who were former slaves. She had twenty-three siblings, including four who also lived at least a century. During the course of her life, she saw twenty-one American presidents take the oath of office, including presidents as far back as Benjamin Harrison. Tillman was the oldest living person for the shortest period of time ever.

Q Which of the following is correct according to the passage?

(a) Emma Tillman was the daughter of an American president.

(b) Tillman was the world's oldest person ever.

(c) Emma Tillman had four siblings that also lived to one hundred.

(d) Tillman was the world's oldest person for twenty-one days.

해석 엠마 파우스트 틸맨이 세계에서 최고령자가 된지 겨우 나흘 뒤에 최근 코네티컷 주 하트포드에서 사망했다. 틸맨은 1892년에 노예 출신이었던 부모 밑에 태어났다. 그녀는 23명의 형제, 자매들이 있었는데 그 중 4명이 최소 100살까지 살았다. 그녀의 일생 동안 그녀는 21명의 미국 대통령이 취임하는 것을 보았는데 벤자민 해리슨 대통령까지 거슬러 올라간다. 틸맨은 가장 짧은 기간 동안 세계 최고령자였던 사람이었다.

Q 위 글의 내용으로 알맞은 것을 고르시오.
(a) 엠마 틸맨은 미국 대통령의 딸이었다.
(b) 틸맨은 지금껏 세계에서 가장 나이가 많은 사람이었다.
(c) 엠마 틸맨은 100살까지 살았던 4명의 형제와 자매가 있었다.
(d) 틸맨은 21일 동안 세계에서 가장 나이가 많은 사람이었다.

해설 짧은 기간 동안 세계에서 최고령자였던 엠마 파우스트 틸맨에 관한 뉴스기사이다. 그는 세계에서 가장 고령자가 된 지 겨우 나흘 뒤에 최근 코네티컷 주 하트포드에서 사망했다(Emma Faust Tillman died recently in Hartford, Connecticut, only four days after becoming the world's oldest person.). 문제는 지문의 내용과 맞는 것을 고르는 것이기 때문에 자세하게 내용을 정리해야 한다. 그녀의 가족은 23명의 형제, 자매가 있는데 그 중 4명이 100살까지 산 장수 집안이다. 'During the course of her life, ~ twenty-one American presidents take the oath of office, including presidents as far back as Benjamin Harrison.'에서 말하듯이 그녀는 21명의 대통령 취임을

보았다. 따라서 글의 내용과 일치하는 것은 (c)다.

어휘 siblings 형제, 자매
take the oath of office 취임 선서하다

정답 (c)

26

The corpse lily, one of the largest flowers in the world, is not a typical flower. Native to Sumatra, it uses its scent which smells like rotting flesh — to attract pollinating insects. Another of the plant's unusual features is that it is able to generate its own heat, possibly to help the smell travel further. The corpse lily only blooms once every three to four years, and the bloom can be up to nine feet tall and last for up to four days.

Q Which of the following is correct about the corpse lily?

(a) Its bloom is the largest in the world.

(b) Its smell lasts much longer than the smell of any other flower.

(c) It generates heat to help the bloom stay alive longer.

(d) It relies on its odor to attract beneficial insects.

해석 송장 백합은 세계에서 가장 큰 꽃 중의 하나인데, 전형적인 꽃이 아니다. 원산지가 수마트라인데, 이 꽃은 고기 썩은 냄새가 나는 것 같은 그것의 향을 이용하여 가루받이를 하는 곤충들을 유인한다. 이 식물의 또 다른 특징들 중 하나는 이것이 열을 발생할 수 있다는 것인데, 아마 이것이 냄새가 멀리까지 퍼지도록 해주는 것 같다. 송장 백합은 3, 4년 만에 한 번씩 꽃을 피우고 꽃은 9피트까지 자랄 수 있으며 나흘 동안 지속된다.

Q 송장 백합에 관한 내용으로 올바른 것을 고르시오.
(a) 그 꽃은 세계에서 가장 크다.
(b) 지구상의 어떤 꽃보다 냄새가 오래 간다.
(c) 꽃이 오래 살아있도록 열을 발생한다.
(d) 냄새로 도움이 되는 곤충들을 모은다.

해설 (a) one of the largest flowers라고 했지, the largest flower라고 하지 않았으므로 답이 아니다. (b) 냄새가 멀리 퍼져 나가기는 하지만, 냄새가 다른 꽃들보다 오래 간다는 내용은 없다. (c) 열을 스스로 발산하기는 하지만, 이 열은 냄새를 멀리 퍼지게 한다고만 되어 있지, 꽃의 수명을 연장한다는 이야기는 없으므로 답이 아니다. (d) 냄새를 퍼뜨려서 가루받이 하는 곤충을 유인하니까 이것이 정답이다.

Tips 부분적으로 맞고 부분적으로 틀린 선택지를 유의한다. 예를 들어, (c)에서 'It generates heat to help.'까지는 맞는데, 그 다음에 이어지는 내용이 틀렸다. 또한 (a)의 the largest flower와 one of the largest flowers는

비슷해 보이지만, 같은 것이 아니므로 혼동하기 쉽다. 유의하도록 한다.

27

The Garbage Dump, now in its seventh year, is a show for the whole family. You can be transported to an imaginative world where everything is made out of garbage. The Garbage Dump also features performances by the jazz group Two-Man Band. Now showing every week night and twice on Saturdays at the Jazz Heritage Concert Hall. Reservations are limited, so call 863-4511 right now.

Q Which of the following is true according to the advertisement?

(a) The show has many tickets still available.
(b) It runs twice every night of the week.
(c) It has live music on stage.
(d) The show has run for seventeen years.

해석 〈쓰레기 처리장〉은 현재 7년째 공연되고 있는 온 가족을 위한 쇼입니다! 모든 것이 쓰레기로부터 만들어지는 상상의 세계로 이동해보세요. 〈쓰레기 처리장〉에는 또한 재즈 그룹 투맨 밴드가 출연합니다. 현재 평일 밤과 토요일 2회 재즈 헤리티지 콘서트홀에서 공연합니다. 예약석이 제한되어 있으므로 지금 863-4511로 전화하세요.

Q 광고에 따르면 사실인 내용을 고르시오.
(a) 쇼는 표가 아직 많이 남아 있다.
(b) 매일 밤에 2회 공연이 있다.
(c) 라이브 음악이 연주된다.
(d) 쇼는 17년간 공연되고 있다.

해석 (a) Reservations are limited라고 했으니, 좌석이 많이 남아있다는 내용은 틀린다. (b) 토요일만 2회 공연이 있으므로 매일밤 2회 공연은 옳지 않다. (c) 재즈 그룹 공연이 주요 특징 중에 하나이므로 맞다. (d) 7년 장기 공연이라고 했으므로 17년은 틀린다. 따라서 정답은 (c)다.

28

Deforestation is typically thought of as a modern problem caused by humankind's appetite for lumber and other products made from wood. However, deforestation was actually a severe problem in medieval times as well. Wood was the main raw material people used during that time; it was used to heat structures, as well as to build them in the first place. Woodcutters looked to the forests of Europe to meet this high demand. As a result, many forests were also severely depleted and some in fact were eliminated entirely.

Q Which of the following is correct according to the passage?

(a) Deforestation is a complex issue that has surfaced very recently.
(b) Wood is used far less in the modern era than it was in medieval times.
(c) People in medieval times replenished forests by planting new trees.
(d) Wood was the primary construction material in medieval times.

해석 삼림 파괴는 일반적으로 인간의 목재와 다른 나무로 만든 제품들에 대한 욕구로 인한 현대의 문제로 생각된다. 그러나 삼림 파괴는 실제로 중세 시대에도 심각한 문제였다. 나무는 그 당시 사람들이 이용했던 주요 원자재였다. 그것은 건물을 짓는데 사용되었을 뿐만 아니라 난방에도 이용되었다. 벌목꾼들은 이러한 높은 수요를 충족시키고자 유럽의 삼림으로 눈을 돌렸다. 그 결과로 많은 삼림들이 심각하게 고갈되었으며 실제로 완전히 없어졌다.

Q 위 글의 내용으로 올바른 것을 고르시오.
(a) 삼림 파괴는 바로 최근에 등장한 복잡한 문제이다.
(b) 나무는 중세 시대보다 현대에 훨씬 덜 사용된다.
(c) 중세의 사람들은 새 나무들을 심음으로써 삼림을 보충했다.
(d) 나무는 중세 시대에 주요 건축 자재였다.

해석 중세와 현대의 삼림 파괴 문제에 관한 글이다. 'Deforestation is typically thought of as a modern problem caused by humankind's appetite for lumber and other products made from wood.'에

서 삼림 파괴 문제가 현대 문제로 인식되고 있다고 여겨지지만 however를 사용하여 실제로 중세에도 심각한 문제였음을 지적하고 있다. 본문의 내용에 따르면 중세 시대에는 건물 짓는 것, 난방 등에도 사용되어서 삼림이 고갈되었기 때문에 완전히 없어졌으며(~ it was used to heat structures, as well as to build them in the first place.) 이것으로 중세 시대에 나무가 주요 건축자재임을 알 수 있다. 따라서 정답은 (d)다.

어휘 deforestation 삼림 벌채, 삼림 파괴
humankind 인류, 인간
appetite 욕망, 욕구
lumber 목재
severe 심한, 심각한
medieval 중세의
raw material 원자재, 원료
woodcutter 나무꾼, 벌목꾼
deplete 고갈시키다
eliminate 제거하다, 없애다
surface (문제가) 나타나다, 등장하다
replenish 보충[보급]하다

정답 (d)

29

The League of Women Voters, Rio Grande Chapter, offers monthly seminars on topics relating to the American electoral system. Previous topics included voter registration, political inclusiveness, and community organizing strategies. The sessions meet at 7 p.m. on the first and third Wednesday of each month at the University of Pittsburgh Continuing Education Building, Room 324. The public is invited. Donations are encouraged.

Q Which of the following is correct according to the announcement?

(a) The seminars last approximately 90 minutes.
(b) Attendees may introduce topics of their own choosing.
(c) Men are not allowed to attend the meetings.
(d) Two seminars are held on a monthly basis.

해석 여성 투표자 연맹 리오그란데 챕터가 미국 선거 체계에 관련된 주제들에 대해 월간 세미나를 개최합니다. 이전의 주제들은 선거자 등록, 정치적 참여, 지역 사회 편성 전략이었습니다. 회의는 매달 첫 번째와 세 번째 수요일 7시에 피츠버그 대학 평생 교육 건물 324호에서 열립니다. 일반인 환영입니다. 기부금도 환영합니다.
 Q 위 글의 내용과 일치하는 것을 고르시오.

(a) 세미나는 약 90분간 계속된다.
(b) 참석자들은 직접 고른 주제들을 소개할 수도 있다.
(c) 남자들은 회의에 참석할 수 없다.
(d) 월별로 두 세미나가 개최된다.

해설 (a) 세미나가 7시에 시작한다는 말은 있으나, 언제까지 한다는 것은 밝혀있지 않으므로, 정확하게 얼마 동안 지속되는지 알 수 없으므로 답이 아니다. (b) 세미나 주제는 참가자들이 선택할 수 있다는 근거를 본문에는 알 수 없다. 오히려 주최 측이 정하여 공지하는 것으로 볼 수 있으므로 답이 아니다. (c) The public is invited.라고 했으니 남자가 참석할 수 없다는 말은 없다. 세미나를 주체하는 기구의 이름이 The League of Women Voters라서 혼동할 수도 있으나 유의하자. (d) on the first and third Wednesday of each month이니까 한 달에 두 번 열리는 것이 맞다. 따라서 (d)가 정답이다.

어휘 relate to ~와 관련되다
electoral system 선거제도
registration 등록
inclusiveness 참여
strategy 전략
session 회합
meet 열리다
donation 기증, 기부
approximately 거의
attendee 참가자

정답 (d)

30

In the mid-eighteenth century, satire became popular in European arts. It was during this time that William Hogarth, one of its masters, was working to complete his best-known work, The Marriage Contract in oil on canvas. It features the busy negotiations involved in marrying the daughter of a merchant to the son of a noble person. The satire is clear: the couple is sitting side-by-side, and yet both are clearly being joined only for social standing and monetary purposes.

Q Which of the following is correct according to the passage?

(a) Hogarth made fun of the institution of marriage among the wealthy.
(b) William Hogarth finished The Marriage Contract around the 1850s.
(c) A well-known merchant negotiated to purchase The Marriage Contract.
(d) William Hogarth was famous for his satiric and ironic paintings.

해석 18세기 중반 풍자는 유럽 예술에서 인기가 있었다. 바로 이 시기에 풍자의 대가인 윌리엄 호가스는 그의 유명한 유화 작품인 〈결혼 계약〉을 마무리하고 있었다. 이 작품은 상인의 딸을 귀족의 아들과 결혼시키기 위해 바쁘게 협상하는 것을 표현하고 있다. 풍자가 분명하게 나타나는데, 이 그림에서 남녀가 나란히 앉아 있지만 둘 다 서로에게는 관심이 없고 단지 사회적인 지위와 금전적인 목적을 위해서만 결합되고 있음을 표현하고 있다.

Q 위 글의 내용으로 올바른 것을 고르시오.
(a) 호가스는 부자들의 결혼 제도를 풍자했다.
(b) 윌리엄 호가스는 1850년대 경에 〈결혼 계약〉을 완성했다.
(c) 유명한 상인이 〈결혼 계약〉을 구매하기 위해서 협상했다.
(d) 윌리엄 호가스는 그의 풍자적이고 반어적인 그림으로 유명했다.

해설 (a) 풍자가 한창 인기 있을 때 작품 활동을 하던 호가스의 작품을 예시로 들고 있는 내용이다. 따라서 부유층 사이에서 사랑이 없는 결혼을 제도화하는 것을 조롱하는 그림을 그렸다는 내용이 있으니 이것이 정답이다. (b) 호가스가 활동한 시기는 18세기 중반이라고 했는데, 18세기는 1701년부터 1800년 사이를 의미하니까, 1750년대 경이어야 한다. 따라서 (b)는 답이 될 수 없다. (c) 본문에 나온 단어들 또는 유사 의미의 단어들(well-known, merchant, negotiated, The Marriage Contract)을 이용하여 오답을 매력적으로 보이게 하고 있다. (d) 호가스 작품이 반어적이라는 내용이 언급된 바 없으므로 답으로 고르면 안 된다. 따라서 정답은 (a)다.

어휘 satire 풍자 cf. satiric 풍자적인
master 대가
negotiation 협상
merchant 상인
side-by-side 나란히
social standing 사회적 지위
monetary 금전의, 금전적인
ironic 반어적인
make fun of ~을 조롱하다
institution 제도

정답 (a)

31

Come to the new FUNky Clowns Circus! We have three shows a night and plenty of booths to entertain kids and adults alike. Learn how to face-paint, juggle, and even work with circus animals. This Wednesday through Saturday night at seven, experience the wonder of acrobats, elephants and most of all, clowns. Everyone is invited, and kids twelve and under get in for only five dollars. This week only at the Family Fairgrounds! The FUNky Clowns Circus!

Q Which of the following is correct according to the advertisement?
(a) The circus will feature a three-elephant show.
(b) General admission will cost only five dollars.
(c) The face-painting exhibit will be free to all children.
(d) The circus will present three shows per day.

해석 새로운 펑키 어릿광대 서커스에 오세요! 저희는 하루 3회의 공연을 하며 아이들과 어른들을 모두 즐겁게 해 줄 코너들이 많습니다. 페이스페인팅, 저글링, 서커스 동물들과 함께 일을 하는 법을 배워 보세요. 이번 수요일부터 토요일 밤 7시까지 놀라운 곡예와 코끼리들, 무엇보다도 어릿광대들을 만나 보세요. 모든 분들을 환영하고 12세 이하 어린이들은 단돈 5달러에 입장할 수 있습니다. 이번 주에 한해 패밀리 박람회장에서 펑키 어릿광대 서커스를 만나 보세요!

Q 위 광고의 내용으로 올바른 것을 고르시오.
(a) 서커스는 세 마리 코끼리 쇼를 한다.
(b) 일반 입장권은 겨우 5달러다.
(c) 페이스페인팅 전시는 모든 어린이들에게 무료다.
(d) 서커스는 하루 세 번의 쇼를 한다.

해설 (a) 본문에 사용된 어휘를 이용하여 오답을 만든 대표적인 예이다. circus, three, elephant, show 등은 언급이 되었지만, 코끼리 세 마리가 벌이는 쇼에 대한 것은 구체적으로 언급되고 있지 않으므로 답이 아니다. (b) 입장료는 5세 이하일 때 5달러라고만 나와 있지, 일반인 입장료에 대한 언급은 없다. (c) 역시 본문 어휘를 사용한 오답이다. (d) 처음 문장에서 three shows a night라고 되어 있으니 이것이 정답이다.

어휘 clown 광대
plenty of 풍부한, 많은
entertain 즐겁게 하다
wonder 놀라운 일
acrobat 곡예사
invite 초대하다
feature ~을 특징으로 하다

admission 입장료
exhibit 전시

32

In the midst of America's Great Depression, President Franklin D. Roosevelt created a program known as the Civilian Conservation Corps (CCC). This program was founded as a part of the economic relief policy known as the New Deal. It employed men in conservation work, which included conserving national parks. The goal of the CCC was to give the men work and prevent civil unrest due to a shortage of jobs.

Q Which of the following is correct about the Civilian Conservation Corps?

(a) It employed men to work for civilian environmental groups.

(b) It recruited men to help enforce the New Deal in times of civil unrest.

(c) It was established due to a lack of employment during the Depression.

(d) It was declared by President Roosevelt to be mandatory for the unemployed.

해석 미국 대공황 중반부에 프랭클린 루즈벨트 대통령은 프로그램을 창설했는데, 이 프로그램은 민간 자원 보존단(CCC)으로 알려져 있다. 이 프로그램은 뉴딜 정책으로 알려진 경제 구제책의 일부로 설립되었는데 국립공원 보호와 같은 자연 보존 작업에 사람들을 고용했다. CCC의 목표는 사람들에게 일자리를 제공하고 일자리 부족으로 인한 국가의 불안을 막는 것이었다.

Q 민간 자원 보존단에 대한 설명으로 바른 것을 고르시오.

(a) 시민 환경 단체들을 위해 사람들을 고용했다.

(b) 국가가 불안한 시기에 뉴딜 정책 강화를 돕기 위해 사람들을 선발했다.

(c) 대공황 시기 동안의 일자리 부족 때문에 설립되었다.

(d) 실업자들에게 의무 사항으로 루즈벨트 대통령에 의하여 선포되었다.

해설 (a) 시민환경단체를 위해 사람들을 고용한 것이 아니라. 자연 보호 작업을 하기 위해 고용을 했으니까 (a)는 답이 아니다. (b) 뉴딜정책을 강화하기 위해 사람들을 고용한 것이 아니라, CCC는 뉴딜 정책의 일부이다. (c) 공황 중에 일자리가 부족한 상황에서 일자리 부족으로 인해 생기는 사회 불안감을 잠식시키기 위해서 생긴 프로그램이므로 이것이 맞는 내용이다. (d) 루즈벨트 대통령이 만든 것은 맞지만, 실업자들의 의무 사항(mandatory)이라는 말은 없으므로 답이 아니다. 따라서 정답은 (c)다.

어휘 **Great Depression** 대공황
known as ~로 알려진

relief 구제
conserve 보호하다, 보존하다
unrest 불안
shortage 부족
recruit 모집하다, 선발하다
declare 선포하다, 선언하다
mandatory 의무적인

33

The philosophical concept of causal determinism proposes that every event and action in history has been determined by another that occurred before it. It suggests that humans cannot make spontaneous decisions, and that nothing truly happens by accident. Interestingly, this theory is in direct opposition to the idea of free will.

Q Which of the following is true of causal determinism, according to the passage?

(a) Spontaneity determines the action that immediately follows it.

(b) The application of free will determines the outcome of an occurrence.

(c) Nothing can ultimately determine a situation's outcome.

(d) It suggests that all human action is dependent upon a previous action.

해석 인과 결정론의 철학적 개념이 주장하는 바는 역사상의 모든 사건과 행동이 그 이전에 발생한 사건이나 행동에 의해 결정된다는 것이다. 이것이 암시하는 바는 인간이 자발적인 결정을 내릴 수 없으며 우연히 일어나는 일은 하나도 없다는 것이다. 흥미롭게도 이 이론은 자유 의지의 개념과는 정반대이다.

Q 인과 결정론에 관한 내용으로 올바른 것을 고르시오.

(a) 자발성은 즉각적으로 따라 오는 행동을 결정한다.

(b) 자유 의지의 적용이 사건의 결과를 결정한다.

(c) 아무 것도 궁극적으로 어떤 상황의 결과를 결정할 수 없다.

(d) 모든 인간 행동이 이전 행동에 달려 있다고 암시한다.

해설 (a) 인간이 자발적인 결정을 내릴 수 없다(~ humans cannot make spontaneous decisions)고 했으므로 (a)는 답이 될 수 없다. (b) 자유 의지와는 정반대 개념 (this theory is in direct opposition to the idea of free will)이라고 했으니 (b)도 답이 될 수 없다. (c) 모든 사건이 그 전에 일어났던 것에 의해 결정이 난다(every event and action ~ determined by another that occurred before it)고 했으니, 어떤 것도 결과를 결정할 수 없다는 것은 본 지문의 내용에 어긋난다. (d) 모든 인간의 행동이 그 이전의 행동에 달려있다는 내용은 본 지문의 내용과 부합되므로 이것이 정답이다.

어휘 philosophical 철학적인
concept 개념
casual determinism 인과 결정론
propose 제안하다, 주장하다
event 사건
spontaneous 자발적인 cf. spontaneity 자발성
opposition 반대
free will 자유 의지
outcome 결과물
occurrence 사건
ultimately 궁극적으로
be dependent on[upon] ~에 달려있다

정답 (d)

34

Annabelle could not recall the directions to the company. She had a job interview there in a half an hour, and she had quickly written down the directions, but then lost the paper! Eventually she saw an old gas station with a phone book and stopped there, finally finding the address in the Yellow Pages. She got back in her car and drove straight to the interview right next door to the gas station.

Q What can be inferred about Annabelle from the passage?

(a) She really didn't want to attend the interview.
(b) She actually wanted to work at the gas station.
(c) She had written the note so quickly that it was nearly illegible.
(d) She remembered the company's name but didn't know how to get there.

해석 애나벨은 회사로 가는 방향을 기억할 수 없었다. 그녀는 30분 후에 그곳에서 면접 약속이 있었고 작은 노란 종이 쪽지에 가는 길을 적어 두었지만, 그 메모지를 잃어버렸다. 그녀는 전화번호부가 있는 낡은 주유소를 발견하고 그곳에 멈춰 마침내 전화번호부에서 주소를 찾았다. 그녀는 다시 차에 타서 면접 장소로 직행했는데 그곳은 주유소 바로 옆이었다.

Q 위 글의 내용으로 애나벨에 대해 추론할 수 있는 것을 고르시오.
(a) 면접에 가고 싶은 마음이 없었다.
(b) 실제로는 주유소에서 일하길 원했다.
(c) 너무 서둘러 메모를 해서 읽을 수가 없을 지경이었다.
(d) 회사 이름을 기억했지만 그곳에 어떻게 가는지는 몰랐다.

해설 (a) 면접에 가고 싶어 했기 때문에 메모지가 없어진 다음에도 그 회사 전화번호를 전화번호부에서 찾았으니 (a)는 맞지 않다. (b) 주유소(gas station)가 두 번이나 나

오지만, 그곳이 일을 하고 싶어 하는 곳은 아니므로 답이 될 수 없다. (c) quickly written down the direction 이라고 했지만, 너무 빨리 써서 글씨를 알아보지 못한다는 내용과는 전혀 상관이 없다. 혹 이것을 답으로 고른 사람인 경우 Partly right! 부분적으로만 맞았다. Partly wrong을 기억하자. 오답은 일부분은 맞지만, 맞지 않는 부분이 섞여 있는 경우가 많다. (d) 길을 기억은 못했지만, 전화번호부에서 그곳의 주소를 알아냈다는 것은 회사명을 기억했다는 의미이기 때문에 이것이 정답이다.

어휘 recall 회상하다, 기억하다
job interview 취업 면접
directions 방향, 찾아가는 길
write down 적다, 기록하다
eventually 마침내, 궁극적으로
the Yellow Pages 전화번호부(표지가 노란색이어서 붙여진 이름으로, 이 속에는 각종 다양한 지역 정보가 실려 있다.)
straight 곧장
illegible (문자를) 읽기 어려운

정답 (d)

35

Aristotle, despite his fame today, once proposed a geocentric model of the universe, which suggested that the sun and the other planets orbited the Earth. It was Aristarchus, who is much less well-known, who said that Aristotle was incorrect. Aristarchus contended that the solar system was heliocentric, meaning that the Earth and other planets actually orbited the sun. Unfortunately, although it was true, Aristarchus's theory was discounted and ridiculed.

Q What can be inferred from the passage?

(a) Aristotle is not remembered primarily for his geocentric model.
(b) Aristarchus was the superior philosopher.
(c) The geocentric model has been forgotten.
(d) The heliocentric model has not yet been proven.

해석 아리스토텔레스는 오늘날 그의 명성에도 불구하고, 그가 제안한 우주의 천동설 모델은 태양과 다른 행성들이 지구를 중심으로 공전한다는 것이다. 아리스타코스는 훨씬 덜 알려진 사람인데, 그는 아리스토텔레스가 틀렸다고 주장했다. 아리스타르코스가 주장하기를 태양계가 태양 중심, 즉 지구와 다른 행성들이 태양 주변을 공전한다고 했다. 안타깝게도 이것이 사실임에도 불구하고, 아리스타르코스의 이론은 받아들여지지 않았고 조롱당했다.

Q 위 글에서 추론할 수 있는 내용을 고르시오.
(a) 아리스토텔레스는 그의 천동설 모델로 주로 기억되지는 않는다.
(b) 아리스타르코스는 더 뛰어난 철학자였다.
(c) 천동설 모델은 잊혀졌다.
(d) 지동설 모델은 아직 증명되지 않았다.

해설 (a) 오늘날에 아리스토텔레스가 유명한 것은 사실이다 (despite his fame today). 하지만 그의 잘못된 이론인 천동설(geocentric model) 때문에 그를 기억하는 것은 아니니까, 그를 다른 것 때문에 기억한다는 (a)가 맞다. (b) 아리스타코스가 훨씬 덜 알려져 있다(much less well-know)는 내용으로 보아서, 아리스토텔레스보다 더 우수하다고 보기는 무리가 있다. (c) 천동설이 잊혀 졌다는 것이 아니라, 천동설은 기억하되, 옳지 않은 것으로 기억되고 있으므로 틀린다. (d) 지동설(the heliocentric model)은 현재 사실로 받아 들여진 내용이므로, 이 보기는 틀린다. 따라서 정답은 (a)다.

어휘 despite ~에도 불구하고
fame 명성
geocentric 지구를 중심으로 보는 *cf.* geocentricism 천동설, 지구 중심설
orbit 공전하다
contend 주장하다
heliocentric 태양을 중심으로 보는
cf. the heliocentric theory (코페르니쿠스의) 지동설, 태양중심설
discount 무시하다, 도외시하다
ridicule 조롱하다
superior 더 우수한

정답 (a)

36

The word "black market" typically suggests lethal weapons or illicit drugs. Yet officials say that the wildlife black market has experienced marked growth in the last few years. Experts believe the industry has grown to more than ten billion dollars, with most products being sold to China and the U.S. This alarming figure ranks the wildlife black market third in criminal income in the world. The strong demand in countries around the world for products made from rare and endangered species seems to ensure that the wildlife black market will not disappear in the near future.

Q Which of the following is correct about the wildlife black market?
(a) China is its third largest supplier.
(b) The number of its consumers has increased.
(c) The United States is one of its largest consumers.
(d) It is the tenth largest criminal operation in the world.

해석 암시장이라는 단어가 일반적으로 암시하는 것은 치명적인 무기나 불법 마약을 의미한다. 그러나 정부 관리들에 따르면 야생 생물 암시장이 지난 몇 년 동안 두드러진 성장을 보였다. 전문가들이 믿는 바로는 이 산업이 100억 달러 규모로 성장했으며 대부분의 상품들이 중국과 미국으로 팔리고 있다. 이 놀라운 수치로 야생 생물 암시장은 전 세계에서 범죄로 인한 소득 3위를 차지한다. 희귀하고 멸종 위기에 처한 생물들로 만들어진 제품들에 대한 전 세계적인 높은 수요로 볼 때 야생 생물 암시장이 가까운 미래에 사라지지는 않을 것 같다.

Q 야생 생물 암시장에 대한 내용으로 올바른 것을 고르시오.
(a) 중국은 야생 생물 암시장의 세 번째로 큰 공급국가이다.
(b) 야생 생물 암시장의 소비자가 증가하고 있다.
(c) 미국은 야생 생물 암시장의 큰 소비자들 중 하나이다.
(d) 야생 생물 암시장은 전 세계에서 10번째로 큰 범죄 사업이다.

해설 (a)에서 China는 야생 생물들이 팔리는 국가이지, 야생 생물 공급국가가 아니다. (b)에서 야생 생물 암시장이 지난 몇 년 동안 성장했다는 사실이 있지만 그것으로 현재까지 소비자가 계속 증가하고 있는지는 확인할 수 없다. (c) 본문에서 암시장의 대부분의 상품들이 중국과 미국으로 팔리고 있다고 했으므로 정답이다. (d) 야생 생물 암시장은 전 세계에서 범죄로 인한 소득이 3위라고 했지 전 세계에서 10번째로 큰 범죄 사업은 아니다. 따라서 정답은 (c)다.

어휘 lethal 치명적인
illicit 불법[부정]의
wildlife 야생 생물, 야생 동물
criminal 범죄의
supplier 공급하는 사람[것], 공급지[공급국가]
operation 사업

정답 (c)

37

Mahatma Gandhi was one of the individuals who most profoundly affected India and the world. He was born in 1869 and was later educated in England to become a lawyer. He visited South Africa and experienced his first taste of discrimination. As a result, he became very politically and socially active. His principle of ahimsa, or nonviolent disobedience, changed the way that people protested against oppression, and he later led India to independence. He was also influential in the South African civil rights movement. Gandhi was assassinated in 1948 by an extremist who opposed his political involvements.

Q Which of the following can be inferred about Gandhi according to the passage?

(a) He had probably been a victim of discrimination since his childhood.

(b) Activists in the South African civil rights movement considered him important.

(c) He was assassinated by someone in the South African government.

(d) People did not like him in England because he was Indian.

해석 마하트마 간디는 인도와 전 세계에 가장 깊이 영향을 끼친 사람들 중의 하나다. 그는 1869년에 태어났고 이후 영국에서 변호사가 되기 위한 교육을 받았다. 그는 남아프리카 공화국을 방문하였을 때 처음으로 차별을 경험했다. 그 결과 그는 정치적 사회적으로 매우 활동적이 되었다. 그의 무살생, 즉 비폭력 불복종의 원칙은 사람들이 억압에 저항하는 방식을 변화시켰고 그는 나중에 인도의 독립을 이끌었다. 그는 남아프리카의 시민 인권 운동에도 영향을 끼쳤다. 간디는 1948년 그의 정치 참여에 반대하는 한 급진주의자에 의해 암살당했다.

Q 간디에 대해 추론될 수 있는 내용으로 알맞은 것을 고르시오.

(a) 그는 어린 시절부터 차별의 희생자였을 것이다

(b) 남아프리카 공화국 시민 인권 운동가들은 그를 중요하게 여겼다

(c) 그는 남아프리카 공화국 정부 일원에 의해 암살되었다.

(d) 영국에서 사람들은 그가 인도인이라서 좋아하지 않았다.

해설 (a) 언뜻 생각하면 간디가 인종차별을 어릴 때부터 겪어 와서 인종차별에 대한 의식을 갖은 것처럼 볼 수 있으나, 그가 남아프리카 공화국에서 처음으로 인종차별을 겪은 것이 어느 때인지 정확하게 나와 있지 않기 때문에 답이 될 수 없다. (b) 끝에서 두 번째 문장 'He was also influential in....'을 통해 그가 남아프리카 공화국의 인권운동에 영향을 미쳤다는 것을 알 수 있고 따라서 그 나라 운동가들이 간디를 중요시한다는 것은 쉽게 알 수 있다. (c) 남아프리카 공화국 사람에 의해 암살당한 것이 아니므로 오답이다. (d) 그가 인도인이라서 차별을 받은 것은 영국에서가 아니라 남아프리카 공화국에서였으므로, 답이 아니다. 따라서 답은 (b)다.

어휘 profoundly 깊이
discrimination 차별
principle 원칙, 원리
ahimsa 불살생, 비폭력주의
disobedience 불복종
nonviolent 비폭력적인
protest 저항하다, 항의하다
oppression 압박, 억압
independence 독립
influential 영향력 있는
assassinate 암살하다
extremist 극단주의자
oppose 반대(반항)하다
involvement 개입, 연루

정답 (b)

38

For safe driving in winter conditions, a number of precautionary measures are recommended by professionals. (a) Decrease your speed and allow plenty of room to stop. (b) Don't hitchhike along the side of a snowy or icy road. (c) Use the brakes gently to avoid skids and wheels locking up. (d) Drive in higher gears for improved traction and vehicle control.

해석 겨울에 안전한 운전을 하기 위해서 많은 예방책들이 전문가들에 의해 추천된다. (a) 속도를 줄이고 정차할 공간을 충분히 확보하라. (b) 눈이 덮였거나 얼은 길가에서 차를 얻어 타지 말아라. (c) 미끄러짐과 바퀴가 멈추는 것을 방지하기 위해 브레이크를 부드럽게 사용하라. (d) 마찰력을 증가시키고 차량을 제어하기 위해 고속 기어로 운전을 해라.

해설 글의 흐름을 파악할 때는 보기끼리 비교하는 것도 정답을 고르는 방법이 될 수 있다. 세 개의 보기들, 즉 (a), (c), (d)는 운전자의 입장에서 하는 말인데, (b)는 차를 얻어 타는 이야기를 하고 있으므로 보기만 보고도 (b)가 다른 보기들과 연계성이 없음을 알 수 있다. 이처럼 많은 경우 문법적인 면에서 뿐만 아니라 내용면에서 상식적으로 답

을 골라낼 수 있다. 따라서 답은 (b)다.

어휘 safe 안전한
a number of 많은
precautionary measure 예방책
recommend 추천하다
decrease 서서히 줄이다, 감소시키다
allow 허락하다
avoid 피하다
skid 미끄러짐
lock up 잠그다, 회전을 멈추다
improve 향상시키다, 개선시키다
traction 마찰력

정답 (b)

39

The number of employed citizens is essential to the Gross National Product — the amount a given country produces. (a) Okun's law estimates a two and a half percent decrease in GNP for every one percentage point unemployment increases. (b) For example, if unemployment was at only three percent, but increases to six percent, there would be an overall decrease of 7.5 percent in the GNP. (c) Thus, governments are always mindful of unemployment rates. (d) Part-time jobs are also less productive than full-time jobs.

해석 일을 하고 있는 국민들의 수는 해당 국가가 생산하는 국민총생산에 중요하다. (a) 오컨의 법칙은 실업률이 1퍼센트 증가할 때마다 생산이 2.5퍼센트 감소한다고 추정한다. (b) 예를 들어, 만일 실업률이 단지 3퍼센트에서 6퍼센트로 증가한다면 국민총생산에는 총 7.5퍼센트의 감소가 발생한다. (c) 따라서 정부는 항상 실업률을 염두에 둔다. (d) 비정규직 일자리들은 정규직 일자리보다 훨씬 덜 생산적이다.

해설 실업률과 국민총생산과의 관계를 나타내는 글이다. (a), (b), (c)는 모두 국민총생산(GNP)과 실업률이 어떻게 연관성을 갖는지 구체적인 예를 들고 있지만 (d)는 비정규직과 정규직에 대한 것으로 다른 보기들과는 연계성이 없다. 따라서 답은 (d)다.

어휘 essential to ～에 필수적인
Gross National Product 국민총생산
estimate 추정하다, 어림잡다
unemployment 실업
increase 증가하다
overall 전반적인
decrease 감소하다
mindful of ～을 주의하는, 잊지 않는
part-time job 시간제 일
productive 생산적인
full-time job 정규직 일

정답 (d)

40

It has been argued by some that the most difficult language in the world to learn is the Basque language, spoken in portions of Spain as well as in regions of France. (a) Basque has no known linguistic relatives, making it what is known as a language isolate. (b) As a result, the history of the language is generally unknown. (c) Despite that, linguists have been able to determine that the language has been influenced to some degree by the Romans; the written form of the Basque language uses Roman characters. (d) Also, there are six primary dialects of Basque as well as a few more that are less well known.

해석 일부 사람들은 세계에서 가장 배우기 어려운 언어가 스페인과 프랑스의 일부 지역에서 사용되는 바스크라고 주장한다. (a) 바스크는 그와 유사한 언어가 알려진 바 없는 고립어이다. (b) 결과적으로 그 언어의 역사는 일반적으로 알려지지 않았다. (c) 그것에 불구하고 언어학자들은 바스크어가 어느 정도 로마어에 영향을 받아 왔다고 결론을 내릴 수 있었는데 바스크어의 문자화 된 형태가 로마글자를 이용하고 있기 때문이다. (d) 또한 바스크에는 여섯 개의 방언들 뿐 만 아니라 잘 알려지지 않은 몇 개의 방언들이 더 있다.

해설 바스크어가 왜 세계에서 가장 배우기 어려운 언어 인가를 설명하는 내용이 되어야 한다. (a) 유사한 언어가 알려지지 않은 고립어라는 점, (b) 언어의 역사가 알려지지 않은 점 (c) 문자화된 형태가 로마글자를 이용하고 있는 점은 바스크어가 왜 어려운 언어인가를 뒷받침 해 주고 있다. 그러나 (d) 바스크어의 방언에 대한 설명은 바스크어의 난이도와는 상관없기 때문에 답은 (d)다.

어휘 argue 주장하다, 논쟁하다
difficult 어려운
portion 일부, 부분
region 지역
linguistic 언어의, 언어학의
generally 일반적으로, 대게
despite ～에도 불구하고
primary 주요한, 최초의
dialect 방언

정답 (d)

[TEPS] Test of English Proficiency Seoul National University

독해 Reading Comprehension

Actual Test 1

#	a	b	c	d		#	a	b	c	d
1	ⓐ	ⓑ	ⓒ	ⓓ		26	ⓐ	ⓑ	ⓒ	ⓓ
2	ⓐ	ⓑ	ⓒ	ⓓ		27	ⓐ	ⓑ	ⓒ	ⓓ
3	ⓐ	ⓑ	ⓒ	ⓓ		28	ⓐ	ⓑ	ⓒ	ⓓ
4	ⓐ	ⓑ	ⓒ	ⓓ		29	ⓐ	ⓑ	ⓒ	ⓓ
5	ⓐ	ⓑ	ⓒ	ⓓ		30	ⓐ	ⓑ	ⓒ	ⓓ
6	ⓐ	ⓑ	ⓒ	ⓓ		31	ⓐ	ⓑ	ⓒ	ⓓ
7	ⓐ	ⓑ	ⓒ	ⓓ		32	ⓐ	ⓑ	ⓒ	ⓓ
8	ⓐ	ⓑ	ⓒ	ⓓ		33	ⓐ	ⓑ	ⓒ	ⓓ
9	ⓐ	ⓑ	ⓒ	ⓓ		34	ⓐ	ⓑ	ⓒ	ⓓ
10	ⓐ	ⓑ	ⓒ	ⓓ		35	ⓐ	ⓑ	ⓒ	ⓓ
11	ⓐ	ⓑ	ⓒ	ⓓ		36	ⓐ	ⓑ	ⓒ	ⓓ
12	ⓐ	ⓑ	ⓒ	ⓓ		37	ⓐ	ⓑ	ⓒ	ⓓ
13	ⓐ	ⓑ	ⓒ	ⓓ		38	ⓐ	ⓑ	ⓒ	ⓓ
14	ⓐ	ⓑ	ⓒ	ⓓ		39	ⓐ	ⓑ	ⓒ	ⓓ
15	ⓐ	ⓑ	ⓒ	ⓓ		40	ⓐ	ⓑ	ⓒ	ⓓ
16	ⓐ	ⓑ	ⓒ	ⓓ						
17	ⓐ	ⓑ	ⓒ	ⓓ						
18	ⓐ	ⓑ	ⓒ	ⓓ						
19	ⓐ	ⓑ	ⓒ	ⓓ						
20	ⓐ	ⓑ	ⓒ	ⓓ						
21	ⓐ	ⓑ	ⓒ	ⓓ						
22	ⓐ	ⓑ	ⓒ	ⓓ						
23	ⓐ	ⓑ	ⓒ	ⓓ						
24	ⓐ	ⓑ	ⓒ	ⓓ						
25	ⓐ	ⓑ	ⓒ	ⓓ						

Actual Test 2

#	a	b	c	d		#	a	b	c	d
1	ⓐ	ⓑ	ⓒ	ⓓ		26	ⓐ	ⓑ	ⓒ	ⓓ
2	ⓐ	ⓑ	ⓒ	ⓓ		27	ⓐ	ⓑ	ⓒ	ⓓ
3	ⓐ	ⓑ	ⓒ	ⓓ		28	ⓐ	ⓑ	ⓒ	ⓓ
4	ⓐ	ⓑ	ⓒ	ⓓ		29	ⓐ	ⓑ	ⓒ	ⓓ
5	ⓐ	ⓑ	ⓒ	ⓓ		30	ⓐ	ⓑ	ⓒ	ⓓ
6	ⓐ	ⓑ	ⓒ	ⓓ		31	ⓐ	ⓑ	ⓒ	ⓓ
7	ⓐ	ⓑ	ⓒ	ⓓ		32	ⓐ	ⓑ	ⓒ	ⓓ
8	ⓐ	ⓑ	ⓒ	ⓓ		33	ⓐ	ⓑ	ⓒ	ⓓ
9	ⓐ	ⓑ	ⓒ	ⓓ		34	ⓐ	ⓑ	ⓒ	ⓓ
10	ⓐ	ⓑ	ⓒ	ⓓ		35	ⓐ	ⓑ	ⓒ	ⓓ
11	ⓐ	ⓑ	ⓒ	ⓓ		36	ⓐ	ⓑ	ⓒ	ⓓ
12	ⓐ	ⓑ	ⓒ	ⓓ		37	ⓐ	ⓑ	ⓒ	ⓓ
13	ⓐ	ⓑ	ⓒ	ⓓ		38	ⓐ	ⓑ	ⓒ	ⓓ
14	ⓐ	ⓑ	ⓒ	ⓓ		39	ⓐ	ⓑ	ⓒ	ⓓ
15	ⓐ	ⓑ	ⓒ	ⓓ		40	ⓐ	ⓑ	ⓒ	ⓓ
16	ⓐ	ⓑ	ⓒ	ⓓ						
17	ⓐ	ⓑ	ⓒ	ⓓ						
18	ⓐ	ⓑ	ⓒ	ⓓ						
19	ⓐ	ⓑ	ⓒ	ⓓ						
20	ⓐ	ⓑ	ⓒ	ⓓ						
21	ⓐ	ⓑ	ⓒ	ⓓ						
22	ⓐ	ⓑ	ⓒ	ⓓ						
23	ⓐ	ⓑ	ⓒ	ⓓ						
24	ⓐ	ⓑ	ⓒ	ⓓ						
25	ⓐ	ⓑ	ⓒ	ⓓ						

Actual Test 3

#	a	b	c	d		#	a	b	c	d
1	ⓐ	ⓑ	ⓒ	ⓓ		26	ⓐ	ⓑ	ⓒ	ⓓ
2	ⓐ	ⓑ	ⓒ	ⓓ		27	ⓐ	ⓑ	ⓒ	ⓓ
3	ⓐ	ⓑ	ⓒ	ⓓ		28	ⓐ	ⓑ	ⓒ	ⓓ
4	ⓐ	ⓑ	ⓒ	ⓓ		29	ⓐ	ⓑ	ⓒ	ⓓ
5	ⓐ	ⓑ	ⓒ	ⓓ		30	ⓐ	ⓑ	ⓒ	ⓓ
6	ⓐ	ⓑ	ⓒ	ⓓ		31	ⓐ	ⓑ	ⓒ	ⓓ
7	ⓐ	ⓑ	ⓒ	ⓓ		32	ⓐ	ⓑ	ⓒ	ⓓ
8	ⓐ	ⓑ	ⓒ	ⓓ		33	ⓐ	ⓑ	ⓒ	ⓓ
9	ⓐ	ⓑ	ⓒ	ⓓ		34	ⓐ	ⓑ	ⓒ	ⓓ
10	ⓐ	ⓑ	ⓒ	ⓓ		35	ⓐ	ⓑ	ⓒ	ⓓ
11	ⓐ	ⓑ	ⓒ	ⓓ		36	ⓐ	ⓑ	ⓒ	ⓓ
12	ⓐ	ⓑ	ⓒ	ⓓ		37	ⓐ	ⓑ	ⓒ	ⓓ
13	ⓐ	ⓑ	ⓒ	ⓓ		38	ⓐ	ⓑ	ⓒ	ⓓ
14	ⓐ	ⓑ	ⓒ	ⓓ		39	ⓐ	ⓑ	ⓒ	ⓓ
15	ⓐ	ⓑ	ⓒ	ⓓ		40	ⓐ	ⓑ	ⓒ	ⓓ
16	ⓐ	ⓑ	ⓒ	ⓓ						
17	ⓐ	ⓑ	ⓒ	ⓓ						
18	ⓐ	ⓑ	ⓒ	ⓓ						
19	ⓐ	ⓑ	ⓒ	ⓓ						
20	ⓐ	ⓑ	ⓒ	ⓓ						
21	ⓐ	ⓑ	ⓒ	ⓓ						
22	ⓐ	ⓑ	ⓒ	ⓓ						
23	ⓐ	ⓑ	ⓒ	ⓓ						
24	ⓐ	ⓑ	ⓒ	ⓓ						
25	ⓐ	ⓑ	ⓒ	ⓓ						

Actual Test 4

#	a	b	c	d		#	a	b	c	d
1	ⓐ	ⓑ	ⓒ	ⓓ		26	ⓐ	ⓑ	ⓒ	ⓓ
2	ⓐ	ⓑ	ⓒ	ⓓ		27	ⓐ	ⓑ	ⓒ	ⓓ
3	ⓐ	ⓑ	ⓒ	ⓓ		28	ⓐ	ⓑ	ⓒ	ⓓ
4	ⓐ	ⓑ	ⓒ	ⓓ		29	ⓐ	ⓑ	ⓒ	ⓓ
5	ⓐ	ⓑ	ⓒ	ⓓ		30	ⓐ	ⓑ	ⓒ	ⓓ
6	ⓐ	ⓑ	ⓒ	ⓓ		31	ⓐ	ⓑ	ⓒ	ⓓ
7	ⓐ	ⓑ	ⓒ	ⓓ		32	ⓐ	ⓑ	ⓒ	ⓓ
8	ⓐ	ⓑ	ⓒ	ⓓ		33	ⓐ	ⓑ	ⓒ	ⓓ
9	ⓐ	ⓑ	ⓒ	ⓓ		34	ⓐ	ⓑ	ⓒ	ⓓ
10	ⓐ	ⓑ	ⓒ	ⓓ		35	ⓐ	ⓑ	ⓒ	ⓓ
11	ⓐ	ⓑ	ⓒ	ⓓ		36	ⓐ	ⓑ	ⓒ	ⓓ
12	ⓐ	ⓑ	ⓒ	ⓓ		37	ⓐ	ⓑ	ⓒ	ⓓ
13	ⓐ	ⓑ	ⓒ	ⓓ		38	ⓐ	ⓑ	ⓒ	ⓓ
14	ⓐ	ⓑ	ⓒ	ⓓ		39	ⓐ	ⓑ	ⓒ	ⓓ
15	ⓐ	ⓑ	ⓒ	ⓓ		40	ⓐ	ⓑ	ⓒ	ⓓ
16	ⓐ	ⓑ	ⓒ	ⓓ						
17	ⓐ	ⓑ	ⓒ	ⓓ						
18	ⓐ	ⓑ	ⓒ	ⓓ						
19	ⓐ	ⓑ	ⓒ	ⓓ						
20	ⓐ	ⓑ	ⓒ	ⓓ						
21	ⓐ	ⓑ	ⓒ	ⓓ						
22	ⓐ	ⓑ	ⓒ	ⓓ						
23	ⓐ	ⓑ	ⓒ	ⓓ						
24	ⓐ	ⓑ	ⓒ	ⓓ						
25	ⓐ	ⓑ	ⓒ	ⓓ						

Actual Test 5

#	a	b	c	d		#	a	b	c	d
1	ⓐ	ⓑ	ⓒ	ⓓ		26	ⓐ	ⓑ	ⓒ	ⓓ
2	ⓐ	ⓑ	ⓒ	ⓓ		27	ⓐ	ⓑ	ⓒ	ⓓ
3	ⓐ	ⓑ	ⓒ	ⓓ		28	ⓐ	ⓑ	ⓒ	ⓓ
4	ⓐ	ⓑ	ⓒ	ⓓ		29	ⓐ	ⓑ	ⓒ	ⓓ
5	ⓐ	ⓑ	ⓒ	ⓓ		30	ⓐ	ⓑ	ⓒ	ⓓ
6	ⓐ	ⓑ	ⓒ	ⓓ		31	ⓐ	ⓑ	ⓒ	ⓓ
7	ⓐ	ⓑ	ⓒ	ⓓ		32	ⓐ	ⓑ	ⓒ	ⓓ
8	ⓐ	ⓑ	ⓒ	ⓓ		33	ⓐ	ⓑ	ⓒ	ⓓ
9	ⓐ	ⓑ	ⓒ	ⓓ		34	ⓐ	ⓑ	ⓒ	ⓓ
10	ⓐ	ⓑ	ⓒ	ⓓ		35	ⓐ	ⓑ	ⓒ	ⓓ
11	ⓐ	ⓑ	ⓒ	ⓓ		36	ⓐ	ⓑ	ⓒ	ⓓ
12	ⓐ	ⓑ	ⓒ	ⓓ		37	ⓐ	ⓑ	ⓒ	ⓓ
13	ⓐ	ⓑ	ⓒ	ⓓ		38	ⓐ	ⓑ	ⓒ	ⓓ
14	ⓐ	ⓑ	ⓒ	ⓓ		39	ⓐ	ⓑ	ⓒ	ⓓ
15	ⓐ	ⓑ	ⓒ	ⓓ		40	ⓐ	ⓑ	ⓒ	ⓓ
16	ⓐ	ⓑ	ⓒ	ⓓ						
17	ⓐ	ⓑ	ⓒ	ⓓ						
18	ⓐ	ⓑ	ⓒ	ⓓ						
19	ⓐ	ⓑ	ⓒ	ⓓ						
20	ⓐ	ⓑ	ⓒ	ⓓ						
21	ⓐ	ⓑ	ⓒ	ⓓ						
22	ⓐ	ⓑ	ⓒ	ⓓ						
23	ⓐ	ⓑ	ⓒ	ⓓ						
24	ⓐ	ⓑ	ⓒ	ⓓ						
25	ⓐ	ⓑ	ⓒ	ⓓ						